ANNUAL EDITIONS

Western Civilization Volume 2

11th Edition

Early Modern through the Twentieth Century

EDITOR

Robert L. Lembright
James Madison University

Robert L. Lembright teaches World Civilization, Ancient Near East, Byzantine, Islamic, and Greek/Roman history at James Madison University. He received his B.A. from Miami University and his M.A. and Ph.D. from The Ohio State University. Dr. Lembright has been a participant in many National Endowment for the Humanities Summer Seminars and Institutes on Egyptology, the Ancient Near East, Byzantine History, and the Ottoman Empire. He has written several articles in the four editions of *The Global Experience*, as well as articles in the *James Madison Journal* and *Western Views of China and the Far East*. His research has concentrated on the French Renaissance of the sixteenth century, and he has published reports in the *Bulletins et Memoires, Societe Archaeologique et Historique de la Charente*. In addition, Dr. Lembright has written many book reviews on the ancient world and Byzantine and Islamic history for *History: Reviews of New Books*.

McGraw-Hill/Dushkin
530 Old Whitfield Street, Guilford, Connecticut 06437

Visit us on the Internet
http://www.dushkin.com

Credits

1. The Age of Power
Unit photo—© 2000 by PhotoDisc, Inc. 21, 22—Weidenfeld Archives. 24, 25, 26—*History Today* Archives. 35—*History Today* map by Colin Barker.

2. Rationalism, Enlightenment, and Revolution
Unit photo—National Gallery of Art

3. Industry, Ideology, Nationalism, and Imperialism: The Nineteenth Century
Unit photo—National Archives. 97, 102, 104—Mancell Collection. 99—*Punch,* November 1858. 100—*Punch,* October 1958. 112—The Mary Evans Picture Library. 120, 123 (bottom), 124 (top)—Courtesy Lawrence James. 122, 124 (bottom)—Mansell Collection. 123 (top)—*History Today* Archives.

4. Modernism, Statism, and Total War: The Twentieth Century
Unit photo—Courtesy of the Library of Congress. 136—*History Today* Archives. 140—Bettmann Archives. 141, 142—Illustrated London News Picture Library. 143—UPI/Bettmann. 144—Map by Bowring Cartographic. 157—Courtesy of the Rand Corporation.

5. Conclusion: The New Millennium and the Human Prospective
Unit photo—United Nations photo by Y. Nagata.

Cataloging in Publication Data
Main entry under title: Annual Editions: Western Civilization, Vol. II: Early Modern through the Twentieth Century. 11/E.
    1. Civilization—Periodicals. 2. World history—Periodicals. I. Lembright, Robert L. *comp.* II. Title: Western civilization, vol. II: Modern through the twentieth century.
901.9'05   82–645823   ISBN 0–07–242580–6   ISSN 0735-0392

© 2001 by McGraw-Hill/Dushkin, Guilford, CT 06437, A Division of The McGraw-Hill Companies.

Eleventh Edition

Cover image © 2001 by PhotoDisc, Inc.

Printed in the United States of America   1234567890BAHBAH54321   Printed on Recycled Paper

In publishing ANNUAL EDITIONS we recognize the enormous role played by the magazines, newspapers, and journals of the public press in providing current, first-rate educational information in a broad spectrum of interest areas. Many of these articles are appropriate for students, researchers, and professionals seeking accurate, current material to help bridge the gap between principles and theories and the real world. These articles, however, become more useful for study when those of lasting value are carefully collected, organized, indexed, and reproduced in a low-cost format, which provides easy and permanent access when the material is needed. That is the role played by ANNUAL EDITIONS.

New to ANNUAL EDITIONS is the inclusion of related World Wide Web sites. These sites have been selected by our editorial staff to represent some of the best resources found on the World Wide Web today. Through our carefully developed topic guide, we have linked these Web resources to the articles covered in this ANNUAL EDITIONS reader. We think that you will find this volume useful, and we hope that you will take a moment to visit us on the Web at **http://www.dushkin.com** to tell us what you think.

What does it mean to say that we are attempting to study the history of Western civilization?

A traditional course in Western civilization was often a chronological survey in the development of European institutions and ideas, with a slight reference to the Near East and the Americas and other places where Westernization has occurred. Typically it moved from the Greeks to the Romans and on to the medieval period, and finally to the modern era, explaining the distinctive characteristics of each stage, as well as each period's relation to the preceding and succeeding events. Of course, in a survey so broad (from Adam to the atomic age in two semesters), a certain superficiality was inevitable. Main characters and events galloped by; often there was little opportunity to absorb and digest the complex ideas that have shaped Western culture.

It is tempting to excuse these shortcomings as unavoidable. However, to present a course in Western civilization that leaves students with only a scrambled series of events, names, dates, and places is to miss a great opportunity. For the promise of such a broad course of study is that it enables students to explore great turning points or shifts in the development of Western culture. Close analysis of these moments enables students to understand the dynamics of continuity and change over time. At best, the course can give a coherent view of the Western tradition and its interplay with non-Western cultures. It can offer opportunities for students to compare various historical forms of authority, religion, and economic organization, to assess the great struggles over the meaning of truth and reality that have sometimes divided Western culture, and even to reflect on the price of progress.

Yet, to focus exclusively on Western civilization can lead us to ignore non-Western peoples and cultures or else to perceive them in ways that some label as "Eurocentric." But contemporary courses in Western history are rarely, if ever, mere exercises in European tribalism. Indeed, they offer an opportunity to subject the Western tradition to critical scrutiny, to assess its accomplishments and its shortfalls. Few of us who teach these courses would argue that Western history is the only history that contemporary students should know. Yet it should be an essential part of what they learn, for it is impossible to understand the modern world without some specific knowledge of the basic tenets of the Western tradition.

When students have learned the distinctive traits of the West, they can develop a sense of the dynamism of history. They can begin to understand how ideas relate to social structures and social forces. They will come to appreciate the nature and significance of innovation and recognize how values often influence events. More specifically, they can trace the evolution of Western ideas about such essential matters as nature, humans, authority, the gods, even history itself; that is, they learn how the West developed its distinctive character. And, as historian Reed Dasenbrock has observed, in an age that seeks multicultural understanding there is much to be learned from "the fundamental multiculturalism of Western culture, the fact that it has been constructed out of a fusion of disparate and often conflicting cultural traditions." Of course, the articles collected in this volume cannot deal with all these matters, but by providing an alternative to the summaries of most textbooks, they can help students better understand the diverse traditions and processes that we call Western civilization.

This volume of *Annual Editions: Western Civilization, Volume II,* contains *World Wide Web* sites that can be used to further explore topics that are addressed in the essays. These sites are cross-referenced by number in the *topic guide* and can be hot-linked through the *Annual Editions* home page: *http://www.dushkin.com/annualeditions.*

This book is like our history—unfinished, always in process. It will be revised on a regular basis. Comments and criticisms are welcome from all who use this book. To that end a post-paid *article rating form* is included at the end of the book. Please feel free to recommend articles that might improve the next edition. With your assistance, this anthology will continue to improve.

Robert L. Lembright

Robert L. Lembright
Editor

Contents

UNIT 1

The Age of Power

Six selections trace the evolution of political power in early modern times. Topics include the European state system, the emergence of British power, and the introduction of new cultures in developing areas.

The concepts in bold italics are developed in the article. For further expansion please refer to the Topic Guide and the Index.

UNIT 2

Rationalism, Enlightenment, and Revolution

Nine articles discuss the impact of science, politics, changing social attitudes, and the rights of women in the Age of Enlightenment.

The concepts in bold italics are developed in the article. For further expansion please refer to the Topic Guide and the Index.

UNIT 3

Industry, Ideology, Nationalism, and Imperialism: The Nineteenth Century

Seven articles focus on the nineteenth century in the Western world. Topics include the Industrial Revolution, role models, social issues, and the expansion of Europe.

The concepts in bold italics are developed in the article. For further expansion please refer to the Topic Guide and the Index.

UNIT 4

Modernism, Statism, and Total War: The Twentieth Century

Nine selections discuss the evolution of the modern Western world, the world wars, the Nazi state, and the status of U.S. economic and political dominance in world affairs.

The concepts in bold italics are developed in the article. For further expansion please refer to the Topic Guide and the Index.

The concepts in bold italics are developed in the article. For further expansion please refer to the Topic Guide and the Index.

UNIT 5

Conclusion: The New Millennium and the Human Prospective

Ten articles examine how politics, war, economics, and culture affect the prospects of humankind.

The concepts in bold italics are developed in the article. For further expansion please refer to the Topic Guide and the Index.

The concepts in bold italics are developed in the article. For further expansion please refer to the Topic Guide and the Index.

Topic Guide

This topic guide suggests how the selections and World Wide Web sites found in the next section of this book relate to topics of traditional concern to Western civilization students and professionals. It is useful for locating interrelated articles and Web sites for reading and research. The guide is arranged alphabetically according to topic.

The relevant Web sites, which are numbered and annotated on pages 4 and 5, are easily identified by the Web icon (●) under the topic articles. By linking the articles and the Web sites by topic, this ANNUAL EDITIONS reader becomes a powerful learning and research tool.

TOPIC AREA	TREATED IN	TOPIC AREA	TREATED IN
Art/ Archaeology	15. Napoleon in Egypt 24. When Cubism Met the Decorative Arts in France ● **1, 13**		41. Whither Western Civilization? ● **6, 8, 17, 19**
Business	4. Taste of Empire, 1600–1800 16. Arkwright: Cotton King or Spin Doctor? 17. Samuel Smiles: The Gospel of Self-Help ● **10, 11, 12, 18, 28, 29, 31**	**Economics**	16. Arkwright: Cotton King or Spin Doctor? 38. Poor and the Rich ● **8, 18, 29**
Cities	2. London and the Modern Monarchy 3. Golden Age: Innovation in Dutch Cities, 1648–1720 11. Blacks in the Gordon Riots ● **9, 10, 13, 14, 19, 28, 31**	**Enlightenment**	9. Declaring an Open Season on the Wisdom of the Ages 12. Passion of Antoine Lavoisier 13. First Feminist ● **7, 8, 9, 13, 14, 15**
Cold War	29. Future That Never Came 30. Face-Off 41. Whither Western Civilization? ● **20, 21, 22, 24**	**Ethnic Issues**	6. Brazil's African Legacy 11. Blacks in the Gordon Riots 18. Giuseppe Garibaldi 22. 'White Man's Burden'? 27. Nazism in the Classroom 36. Belonging in the West 37. Folly & Failure in the Balkans ● **1, 10, 12, 17, 25, 27, 28, 29, 31, 33**
Colonialism	6. Brazil's African Legacy 22. 'White Man's Burden'? ● **10, 12**	**Facism**	27. Nazism in the Classroom ● **19, 24**
Culture	6. Brazil's African Legacy 9. Declaring an Open Season on the Wisdom of the Ages 10. Witchcraft: The Spell That Didn't Break 15. Napoleon in Egypt 20. Age of Philanthropy 21. Women Murderers in Victorian Britain 27. Nazism in the Classroom 31. Mutable Destiny: The End of the American Century? 32. Exhibiting the Nation 33. Way the World Ends 36. Belonging in the West 37. Folly & Failure in the Balkans 41. Whither Western Civilization? ● **10, 12, 19**	**Ideology**	7. Descartes the Dreamer 13. First Feminist 17. Samuel Smiles: The Gospel of Self-Help 19. Conversations with Malthus 20. Age of Philanthropy ● **12, 15, 17, 19, 24, 31**
		Imperialism	4. Taste of Empire, 1600–1800 22. 'White Man's Burden'? ● **10**
		Industrial Revolution	16. Arkwright: Cotton King or Spin Doctor?
		Labor	20. Brazil's African Legacy ● **10, 12, 26, 28, 31**
Democracy	36. Belonging in the West 40. Falling Tide: Global Trends and U.S. Civil Society	**Liberalism**	20. Age of Philanthropy 40. Falling Tide: Global Trends and U.S. Civil Society

◉ AE: Western Civilization, Volume II

The following World Wide Web sites have been carefully researched and selected to support the articles found in this reader. If you are interested in learning more about specific topics found in this book, these Web sites are a good place to start. The sites are cross-referenced by number and appear in the topic guide on the previous two pages. Also, you can link to these Web sites through our DUSHKIN ONLINE support site at *http://www.dushkin.com/online/*.

The following sites were available at the time of publication. Visit our Web site—we update DUSHKIN ONLINE regularly to reflect any changes.

General Sources

1. Archaeological Institute of America (AIA)
http://www.archaeological.org
Review this site of the AIA for information about various eras in Western civilization.

2. Archive of Texts and Documents
http://history.hanover.edu/texts.html
This Hanover College historical texts project is very creative. Sources are available on Europe and East Asia.

3. Discover's Web
http://www.win.tue.nl/~engels/discovery/index.html
Data on historical voyages of discovery and exploration from ancient to modern times are available from this Web site.

4. Facets of Religion/Caspar Voogt
http://bounty.bcca.org/~cvoogt/Religion/mainpage.html
Caspar Voogt offers this virtual library of links to information on major world religions, including Islam, Judaism, Zoroastrianism, Baha'ism, and Christianity.

5. The History of Costumes
http://www.siue.edu/COSTUMES/history.html
This distinctive site illustrates garments worn by people in various historical eras. Clothing of common people is presented along with that worn by nobility.

6. Library of Congress
http://www.loc.gov
Examine this Web site to learn about the extensive resource tools, library services/resources, exhibitions, and databases available through the Library of Congress in many different subfields of historical studies.

7. Michigan Electronic Library
http://mel.lib.mi.us/humanities/history/
Browse through this enormous history site for an array of resources on the study of Western civilization, which are broken down by historical era, geographical area, and more.

8. Smithsonian Institution
http://www.si.edu
This site provides access to the enormous resources of the Smithsonian, which holds some 140 million artifacts and specimens in its trust. Here you can learn about social, cultural, economic, and political history of the United States.

The Age of Power

9. EuroDocs: Primary Historical Documents from Western Europe
http://www.lib.byu.edu/~rdh/eurodocs/
This excellent collection from the Brigham Young University Library is a high-quality set of historical documents from Western Europe. Facsimiles, translations, and even selected transcriptions are included. Click on the links to materials related to "Europe as a Supernational Region" and individual countries.

10. 1492: An Ongoing Voyage/Library of Congress
http://lcweb.loc.gov/exhibits/1492/
Displays examining the causes and effects of Columbus's voyages to the Americas are provided on this site. "An Ongoing Voyage" explores the rich mixture of societies coexisting in five areas of the Western Hemisphere before European arrival. It also surveys the polyglot Mediterranean world at a dynamic turning point in its development.

11. Medieval Maps/University of Kansas
http://www.ukans.edu/kansas/medieval/graphics/maps/
Check out this unusual site for access to interesting, full-color maps of Europe. Each map is keyed to a specific date, and some pertain to the Age of Power.

12. World Wide Web Virtual Library/Latin American Studies
http://lanic.utexas.edu/las.html
This is the site of first resort for the exploration of a topic dealing with Latin America. It lists resources available on the Web for historical topics and related cultural subjects.

Rationalism, Enlightenment, and Revolution

13. Eighteenth-Century Resources/Jack Lynch
http://andromeda.rutgers.edu/~jlynch/18th/
Open this page to find links in eighteenth-century studies, including History, Literature, Religion and Theology, Science and Mathematics, and Art. Click on History, for example, for a number of resources for study of topics from Napoleon, to piracy and gambling, to a discussion of Catalonia.

14. Western European Specialists Section/Association of College and Research Libraries
http://www.lib.virginia.edu/wess/
WESS provides links in regional and historical resources in European studies, as well as materials on contemporary Europe. Visit this site for texts and text collections, guides to library resources, book reviews, and WESS publications.

15. Women and Philosophy Website
http://www.nd.edu/~colldev/subjects/wss.html
Explore the many materials available through this site. It provides Internet collections of resources, ethics updates, bibliographies, information on organizations, and access to newsletters and journals.

Industry, Ideology, Nationalism, and Imperialism: The Nineteenth Century

16. Anthony S. Wohl/Vassar College
http://www.stg.brown.edu/projects/hypertext/landow/victorian/race/rcov.html
For information on Victorian England, start from this page, a "Race and Class Overview" of Victorian England, to find interesting data on the Victorian era.

17. Historical U.S. Census Data Browser
http://fisher.lib.virginia.edu/census/
At this site, the interuniversity Consortium for Political and Social Research offers materials in various categories of histori-

cal social, economic, and demographic data. Access here a statistical overview of the United States, beginning in the late eighteenth century.

18. Society for Economic Anthropology Homepage
http://sea.agnesscott.edu
This is the home page of the Society for Economic Anthropology, an association that strives to understand diversity and change in the economic systems of the world, and, hence, in the organization of society and culture.

Modernism, Statism, and Total War: The Twentieth Century

19. History Net
http://www.thehistorynet.com/THNarchives/AmericanHistory/
This National Historical Society site provides information on a wide range of topics, with emphasis on American history, book reviews, and special interviews.

20. Inter-American Dialogue (IAD)
http://www.iadialog.org
This is the Web site for IAD, a premier U.S. center for policy analysis, communication, and exchange in Western Hemisphere affairs. The organization has helped to shape the agenda of issues and choices in hemispheric relations.

21. ISN International Relations and Security Network
http://www.isn.ethz.ch
This site, maintained by the Center for Security Studies and Conflict Research, is a clearinghouse for extensive information on international relations and security policy. The many topics are listed by category (Traditional Dimensions of Security, New Dimensions of Security) and by major world regions.

22. Russian and East European Network Information Center/University of Texas at Austin
http://reenic.utexas.edu/reenic.html
This is *the* Web site for exhaustive information on Russia and other republics of the former Soviet Union and Central/Eastern Europe on a large range of topics.

23. Terrorism Research Center
http://www.terrorism.com
The Terrorism Research Center features original research on terrorism, counterterrorism documents, a comprehensive list of Web links, and monthly profiles of terrorist and counterterrorist groups.

24. World History Review/Scott Danford and Jon Larr
http://members.aol.com/sniper43/index.html
Associated with a college course, this site will lead you to information and links on a number of major topics of interest when studying Western civilization in the twentieth century: Imperialism, the Russian Revolution, World War I, World War II, the cold war, the Korean War, and Vietnam.

Conclusion: The New Millennium and the Human Prospective

25. Center for Middle Eastern Students/University of Texas/
http://menic.utexas.edu/menic/religion.html
This site provides links to Web sites on Islam and the Islamic world. Information on Judaism and Christianity is also available through this Middle East Network Information Center.

26. Europa: European Union
http://europa.eu.int
This site leads you to the history of the European Union (and its predecessors such as the European Community and European Common Market); descriptions of the increasingly powerful regional organization's policies, institutions, and goals; and documentation of treaties and other materials.

27. InterAction
http://www.interaction.pair.com/advocacy/
InterAction encourages grassroots action and engages government bodies and policymakers on various advocacy issues. Its Advocacy Committee provides this site to inform people on its initiatives to expand international humanitarian relief, refugee, and development-assistance programs.

28. The North-South Institute
http://www.nsi-ins.ca/ensi/index.html
Searching this site of the North-South Institute—which works to strengthen international development cooperation and enhance gender and social equity—will help you find information and debates on a variety of global issues.

29. Organization for Economic Co-operation and Development/FDI Statistics
http://www.oecd.org/daf/statistics.htm
Explore world trade and investment trends and statistics on this site that provides links to related topics and addresses global economic issues on a country-by-country basis.

30. U.S. Agency for International Development
http://www.info.usaid.gov
This Web site covers such issues as democracy, population and health, economic growth, and development. It provides specific information about different regions and countries.

31. Virtual Seminar in Global Political Economy/Global Cities & Social Movements
http://csf.colorado.edu/gpe/gpe95b/resources.html
This site of Internet resources is rich in links to subjects of interest in assessing the human condition today and in the future, covering topics such as sustainable cities, megacities, and urban planning.

32. World Bank
http://www.worldbank.org
Review this site and its links for information on immigration and development now and in the future. News (press releases, summaries of new projects, speeches), publications, and coverage of numerous topics regarding development, countries, and regions are provided here.

33. World Wide Web Virtual Library: International Affairs Resources
http://www.etown.edu/vl/
Surf this site and its extensive links to learn about specific countries and regions, to research various think tanks and international organizations, and to study such vital topics as international law, human rights, and peacekeeping.

We highly recommend that you review our Web site for expanded information and our other product lines. We are continually updating and adding links to our Web site in order to offer you the most usable and useful information that will support and expand the value of your Annual Editions. You can reach us at: http://www.dushkin.com/annualeditions/.

www.dushkin.com/online/

Unit Selections

1. **The Emergence of the Great Powers,** Gordon A. Craig and Alexander L. George
2. **London and the Modern Monarchy,** Penelope Corfield
3. **A Golden Age: Innovation in Dutch Cities, 1648–1720,** Jonathan Israel
4. **A Taste of Empire, 1600–1800,** James Walvin
5. **"Thus in the Beginning All the World Was America,"** Edward Cline
6. **Brazil's African Legacy,** John Geipel

Key Points to Consider

❖ How did the modern international order evolve?

❖ What was the relationship between the people of London and the crown after 1660?

❖ Why were the Dutch used as the model for urban reconstruction by other countries?

❖ In what way did Europe's imports of tropical exotica from the New World change Europe, America, and Africa?

❖ How did John Locke influence constitutional government?

❖ Using Brazil as a test case, what African influences can be identified in the emerging Atlantic phase of Western civilization?

 **Links**   **www.dushkin.com/online/**

9. **EuroDocs: Primary Historical Documents from Western Europe**
   http://www.lib.byu.edu/~rdh/eurodocs/
10. **1492: An Ongoing Voyage/Library of Congress**
    http://lcweb.loc.gov/exhibits/1492/
11. **Medieval Maps/University of Kansas**
    http://www.ukans.edu/kansas/medieval/graphics/maps/
12. **World Wide Web Virtual Library/Latin American Studies**
    http://lanic.utexas.edu/las.html

These sites are annotated on pages 4 and 5.

The early modern period (c. 1450–c.1700) was a time of profound change for Western civilization. During this epoch the medieval frame of reference gave way to a recognizably modern orientation. The old order had been simply, but rigidly, structured. There was little social or geographical mobility. Europe was relatively backward and isolated from much of the world. The economy was dominated by self-sufficient agriculture. Trade and cities did not flourish. There were few rewards for technological innovation. A person's life seemed more attuned to revelation than to reason and science. The Church both inspired and limited intellectual and artistic expression. Most people were prepared to suppress their concerns to a higher order—whether religious or social.

This narrow world gradually gave way to the modern world. There is no absolute date that marks the separation, but elements of modernity were evident throughout Western civilization by the eighteenth century. In this context the late Medieval, Renaissance, and Reformation periods were transitional. They linked the medieval to the modern. But what were the facets of this emerging modernity? Beginning with the economic foundation, an economy based on money and commerce overlaid the old agrarian system, thus creating a new and important middle class in society. Urban life became increasingly important, allowing greater scope for personal expression. Modernity involved a state of mind as well. Europeans of the early modern period were conscious that their way of life was different from that of their ancestors. In addition, these moderns developed a different sense of time—for urban people, clock time superseded the natural rhythms of the changing seasons and the familiar cycles of planting and harvesting. As for the intellect, humanism, rationalism, and science began to take precedence over tradition—though not without a struggle. Protestantism presented yet another challenge to orthodoxy. And, as economic and political institutions evolved, new attitudes about power and authority emerged.

The early modern period is often called the Age of Power, because the modern state, with its power to tax, conscript, subsidize, and coerce, was taking shape. Its growth was facilitated by the changing economic order, which made it possible for governments to acquire money in unprecedented amounts—to hire civil servants, raise armies, protect

and encourage national enterprise, and expand their power to the national boundaries and beyond.

Power, in various early modern manifestations, is the subject of the articles assembled in this unit. The first essay, "The Emergence of the Great Powers," surveys the shifting international balance of power during the seventeenth and eighteenth centuries. "London and the Modern Monarchy" explores the relationship of the English monarchs to their capital city. "A Golden Age: Innovation in Dutch Cities, 1648–1720" shows how the economic power of the Dutch was translated into cultural influence. "A Taste of Empire, 1600–1800" describes the influence of imperial conquest upon Old World tastes and social customs. And, the article by Edward Cline deals with John Locke and his influence on constitutional power in England and America as seen in " 'Thus in the Beginning All the World Was America.' " The last article deals with the European demand for American commodities, especially sugar, which drove the corresponding New World demand for African slave labor and thus transformed Western civilization into an Atlantic culture that combined European, American, and African elements, as we see in "Brazil's African Legacy."

The Age of Power

The Emergence of the Great Powers

Gordon A. Craig and Alexander L. George

I

Although the term *great power* was used in a treaty for the first time only in 1815, it had been part of the general political vocabulary since the middle of the eighteenth century and was generally understood to mean Great Britain, France, Austria, Prussia, and Russia. This would not have been true in the year 1600, when the term itself would have meant nothing and a ranking of the European states in terms of political weight and influence would not have included three of the countries just mentioned. In 1600, Russia, for instance, was a remote and ineffectual land, separated from Europe by the large territory that was called Poland-Lithuania with whose rulers it waged periodic territorial conflicts, as it did with the Ottoman Turks to the south; Prussia did not exist in its later sense but, as the Electorate of Brandenburg, lived a purely German existence, like Bavaria or Wurttemberg, with no European significance; and Great Britain, a country of some commercial importance, was not accorded primary political significance, although it had, in 1588, demonstrated its will and its capacity for self-defense in repelling the Spanish Armada. In 1600, it is fair to say that, politically, the strongest center in Europe was the old Holy Roman Empire, with its capital in Vienna and its alliances with Spain (one of the most formidable military powers in Europe) and the Catholic states of southern Germany—an empire inspired by a militant

Catholicism that dreamed of restoring Charles V's claims of universal dominion. In comparison with Austria and Spain, France seemed destined to play a minor role in European politics, because of the state of internal anarchy and religious strife that followed the murder of Henri IV in 1610.

Why did this situation not persist? Or, to put it another way, why was the European system transformed so radically that the empire became an insignificant political force and the continent came in the eighteenth century to be dominated by Great Britain, France, Austria, Prussia, and Russia? The answer, of course, is war, or, rather more precisely, wars—a long series of religious and dynastic conflicts which raged intermittently from 1618 until 1721 and changed the rank order of European states by exhausting some and exalting others. As if bent upon supplying materials for the nineteenth-century Darwinians, the states mentioned above proved themselves in the grinding struggle of the seventeenth century to be the fittest, the ones best organized to meet the demands of protracted international competition.

The process of transformation began with the Thirty Years War, which stretched from 1618 to 1648. It is sometimes called the last of the religious wars, a description that is justified by the fact that it was motivated originally by the desire of the House of Habsburg and its Jesuit advisers to restore the Protestant parts of the empire to the true faith and because, in thirty years of fighting, the religious motive gave way

to political considerations and, in the spreading of the conflict from its German center to embrace all of Europe, some governments, notably France, waged war against their own coreligionists for material reasons. For the states that initiated this wasting conflict, which before it was over had reduced the population of central Europe by at least a third, the war was an unmitigated disaster. The House of Habsburg was so debilitated by it that it lost the control it had formerly possessed over the German states, which meant that they became sovereign in their own right and that the empire now became a mere adjunct of the Austrian crown lands. Austria was, moreover, so weakened by the exertions and losses of that war that in the period after 1648 it had the greatest difficulty in protecting its eastern possessions from the depredations of the Turks and in 1683 was threatened with capture of Vienna by a Turkish army. Until this threat was contained, Austria ceased to be a potent factor in European affairs. At the same time, its strongest ally, Spain, had thrown away an infantry once judged to be the best in Europe in battles like that at Nordlingen in 1634, one of those victories that bleed a nation white. Spain's decline began not with the failure of the Armada, but with the terrible losses suffered in Germany and the Netherlands during the Thirty Years War.

In contrast, the states that profited from the war were the Netherlands, which completed the winning of its independence from Spain in the course of the war and became a commercial and

From *Force and Statecraft: Diplomatic Problems of Our Time, Third Edition* by Gordon A. Craig and Alexander L. George, pp. 3-16. © 1983 by Oxford University Press. Inc. Third Edition available © 1995. Used by permission of Oxford University Press, Inc.

financial center of major importance; the kingdom of Sweden, which under the leadership of Gustavus Adolphus, the Lion of the North, plunged into the conflict in 1630 and emerged as the strongest power in the Baltic region; and France, which entered the war formally in 1635 and came out of it as the most powerful state in western Europe.

It is perhaps no accident that these particular states were so successful, for they were excellent examples of the process that historians have described as the emergence of the modern state, the three principal characteristics of which were effective armed forces, an able bureaucracy, and a theory of state that restrained dynastic exuberance and defined political interest in practical terms. The seventeenth century saw the emergence of what came to be called *raison d'état* or *ragione di stato*—the idea that the state was more than its ruler and more than the expression of his wishes; that it transcended crown and land, prince and people; that it had its particular set of interests and a particular set of necessities based upon them; and that the art of government lay in recognizing those interests and necessities and acting in accordance with them, even if this might violate ordinary religious or ethical standards. The effective state must have the kind of servants who would interpret *raison d'état* wisely and the kind of material and physical resources necessary to implement it. In the first part of the seventeenth century, the Dutch, under leaders like Maurice of Nassau and Jan de Witt, the Swedes, under Gustavus Adolphus and Oxenstierna, and the French, under the inspired ministry of Richelieu, developed the administration and the forces and theoretical skills that exemplify this ideal of modern statehood. That they survived the rigors of the Thirty Years War was not an accident, but rather the result of the fact that they never lost sight of their objectives and never sought objectives that were in excess of their capabilities. Gustavus Adolphus doubtless brought his country into the Thirty Years War to save the cause of Protestantism when it was at a low ebb, but he never for a moment forgot the imperatives of national interest that impelled him to see the war also as a means of winning Swedish supremacy along the shore of the Baltic Sea. Cardinal Richelieu has been called the greatest public servant France ever had,

but that title, as Sir George Clark has drily remarked, "was not achieved without many acts little fitting the character of a churchman." It was his clear recognition of France's needs and his absolute unconditionality in pursuing them that made him the most respected statesman of his age.

The Thirty Years War, then, brought a sensible change in the balance of forces in Europe, gravely weakening Austria, starting the irreversible decline of Spain, and bringing to the fore the most modern, best organized, and, if you will, most rationally motivated states: the Netherlands, Sweden, and France. This, however, was a somewhat misleading result, and the Netherlands was soon to yield its commercial and naval primacy to Great Britain (which had been paralyzed by civil conflict during the Thirty Years War), while Sweden, under a less rational ruler, was to throw its great gains away.

The gains made by France were more substantial, so much so that in the second half of the century, in the heyday of Louis XIV, they became oppressive. For that ruler was intoxicated by the power that Richelieu and his successor Mazarin had brought to France, and he wished to enhance it. As he wrote in his memoirs:

> The love of glory assuredly takes precedence over all other [passions] in my soul. . . . The hot blood of my youth and the violent desire I had to heighten my reputation instilled in me a strong passion for action. . . . *La Gloire,* when all is said and done, is not a mistress that one can ever neglect; nor can one be ever worthy of her slightest favors if one does not constantly long for fresh ones.

No one can say that Louis XIV was a man of small ambition. He dreamed in universal terms and sought to realize those dreams by a combination of diplomatic and military means. He maintained alliances with the Swedes in the north and the Turks in the south and thus prevented Russian interference while he placed his own candidate, Jan Sobieski, on the throne of Poland. His Turkish connection he used also to harry the eastern frontiers of Austria, and if he did not incite Kara Mustafa's expedition against Vienna in 1683, he knew of it. Austria's distractions enabled him to dabble freely in German politics. Bavaria and the Palatinate were bound

to the French court by marriage, and almost all of the other German princes accepted subsidies at one time or another from France. It did not seem unlikely on one occasion that Louis would put himself or his son forward as candidate for Holy Roman emperor. The same method of infiltration was practiced in Italy, Portugal, and Spain, where the young king married a French princess and French ambassadors exerted so much influence in internal affairs that they succeeded in discrediting the strongest antagonist to French influence, Don Juan of Austria, the victor over the Turks at the battle of Lepanto. In addition to all of this, Louis sought to undermine the independence of the Netherlands and gave the English king Charles II a pension in order to reduce the possibility of British interference as he did so.

French influence was so great in Europe in the second half of the seventeenth century that it threatened the independent development of other nations. This was particularly true, the German historian Leopold von Ranke was to write in the nineteenth century, because it

> was supported by a preeminence in literature. Italian literature had already run its course, English literature had not yet risen to general significance, and German literature did not exist at that time. French literature, light, brilliant and animated, in strictly regulated but charming form, intelligible to everyone and yet of individual, national character was beginning to dominate Europe. . . .[It] completely corresponded to the state and helped the latter to attain its supremacy[.] Paris was the capital of Europe. She wielded a dominion as did no other city, over language, over custom, and particularly over the world of fashion and the ruling classes. Here was the center of the community of Europe.

The effect upon the cultural independence of other parts of Europe—and one cannot separate cultural independence from political will—was devastating. In Germany, the dependence upon French example was almost abject, and the writer Moscherosch commented bitterly about "our little Germans who trot to the French and have no heart of their own, no speech of their own; but French opinion is their opinion, French speech, food, drink, morals and deportment their speech, food, drink, morals and deportment whether they are good or bad."

But this kind of dominance was bound to invite resistance on the part of others, and out of that resistance combinations and alliances were bound to take place. And this indeed happened. In Ranke's words, "The concept of the European balance of power was developed in order that the union of many other states might resist the pretensions of the 'exorbitant' court, as it was called." This is a statement worth noting. The principle of the balance of power had been practiced in Machiavelli's time in the intermittent warfare between the city states of the Italian peninsula. Now it was being deliberately invoked as a principle of European statecraft, as a safeguard against universal domination. We shall have occasion to note the evolution and elaboration of this term in the eighteenth century and in the nineteenth, when it became one of the basic principles of the European system.

Opposition to France's universal pretensions centered first upon the Dutch, who were threatened most directly in a territorial sense by the French, and their gifted ruler, William III. But for their opposition to be successful, the Dutch needed strong allies, and they did not get them until the English had severed the connection that had existed between England and France under the later Stuarts and until Austria had modernized its administration and armed forces, contained the threat from the east, and regained the ability to play a role in the politics of central and western Europe. The Glorious Revolution of 1688 and the assumption of the English throne by the Dutch king moved England solidly into the anti-French camp. The repulse of the Turks at the gates of Vienna in 1683 marked the turning point in Austrian fortunes, and the brilliant campaigns of Eugene of Savoy in the subsequent period, which culminated in the smashing victory over the Turks at Zenta and the suppression of the Rakoczi revolt in Hungary, freed Austrian energies for collaboration in the containment of France. The last years of Louis XIV, therefore, were the years of the brilliant partnership of Henry Churchill, Duke of Marlborough, and Eugene of Savoy, a team that defeated a supposedly invulnerable French army at Blenheim in 1704, Ramillies in 1706, Oudenarde in 1708, and the bloody confrontation of Malplaquet in 1709.

These battles laid the basis for the Peace of Utrecht of 1713–1715, by which France was forced to recognize the results of the revolution in England, renounce the idea of a union of the French and Spanish thrones, surrender the Spanish Netherlands to Austria, raze the fortifications at Dunkirk, and hand important territories in America over to Great Britain. The broader significance of the settlement was that it restored an equilibrium of forces to western Europe and marked the return of Austria and the emergence of Britain as its supports. Indeed, the Peace of Utrecht was the first European treaty that specifically mentioned the balance of power. In the letters patent that accompanied Article VI of the treaty between Queen Anne and King Louis XIV, the French ruler noted that the Spanish renunciation of all rights to the throne of France was actuated by the hope of "obtaining a general Peace and securing the Tranquillity of *Europe* by a Ballance of Power," and the king of Spain acknowledged the importance of "the Maxim of securing for ever the universal Good and Quiet of Europe, by an equal Weight of Power, so that many being united in one, the Ballance of the Equality desired, might not turn to the Advantage of one, and the Danger and Hazard of the rest."

Meanwhile, in northern Europe, France's ally Sweden was forced to yield its primacy to the rising powers of Russia and Prussia. This was due in part to the drain on Swedish resources caused by its participation in France's wars against the Dutch; but essentially the decline was caused, in the first instance, by the fact that Sweden had too many rivals for the position of supremacy in the Baltic area and, in the second, by the lack of perspective and restraint that characterized the policy of Gustavus Adolphus's most gifted successor, Charles XII. Sweden's most formidable rivals were Denmark, Poland, which in 1699 acquired an ambitious and unscrupulous new king in the person of Augustus the Strong of Saxony, and Russia, ruled since 1683 by a young and vigorous leader who was to gain the name Peter the Great. In 1700, Peter and Augustus made a pact to attack and despoil Sweden and persuaded Frederick of Denmark to join them in this enterprise. The Danes and the Saxons immediately invaded Sweden and to their considerable dismay were routed and driven from the country by armies led by the eighteen-

year-old ruler, Charles XII. The Danes capitulated at once, and Charles without pause threw his army across the Baltic, fell upon Russian forces that were advancing on Narva, and, although his own forces were outnumbered five to one, dispersed, captured, or killed an army of forty thousand Russians. But brilliant victories are often the foundation of greater defeats. Charles now resolved to punish Augustus and plunged into the morass of Polish politics. It was his undoing. While he strove to control an intractable situation, an undertaking that occupied him for seven years, Peter was carrying through the reforms that were to bring Russia from its oriental past into the modern world. When his army was reorganized, he began a systematic conquest of the Swedish Baltic possessions. Charles responded, not with an attempt to retake those areas, but with an invasion of Russia—and this, like other later invasions, was defeated by winter and famine and ultimately by a lost battle, that of Pultawa in 1709, which broke the power of Sweden and marked the emergence of Russia as its successor.

Sweden had another rival which was also gathering its forces in these years. This was Prussia. At the beginning of the seventeenth century, it had, as the Electorate of Brandenburg, been a mere collection of territories, mostly centered upon Berlin, but with bits and pieces on the Rhine and in East Prussia, and was rich neither in population nor resources. Its rulers, the Hohenzollerns, found it difficult to administer these lands or, in time of trouble, defend them; and during the Thirty Years War, Brandenburg was overrun with foreign armies and its population and substance depleted by famine and pestilence. Things did not begin to change until 1640, when Frederick William, the so-called Great Elector, assumed the throne. An uncompromising realist, he saw that if he was to have security in a dangerous world, he would have to create what he considered to be the sinews of independence: a centralized state with an efficient bureaucracy and a strong army. The last was the key to the whole. As he wrote in his political testament, "A ruler is treated with no consideration if he does not have troops of his own. It is these, thank God! that have made me *considerable* since the time I began to have them"—and in the course of his reign, after purging his force of unruly and incompetent elements, Frederick William rapidly built an efficient force of thirty thousand men, so efficient indeed that in 1675, during the Franco-Swedish war against the Dutch, it came to the aid of the Dutch by defeating the Swedes at Fehrbellin and subsequently driving them out of Pomerania. It was to administer this army that Frederick William laid the foundations of the soon famous Prussian bureaucracy; it was to support it that he encouraged the growth of a native textile industry; it was with its aid that he smashed the recalcitrant provincial diets and centralized the state. And finally it was this army that, by its participation after the Great Elector's death in the wars against Louis XIV and its steadiness under fire at Ramillies and Malplaquet, induced the European powers to recognize his successor Frederick I as king of Prussia.

Under Frederick, an extravagant and thoughtless man, the new kingdom threatened to outrun its resources. But the ruler who assumed the throne in 1715, Frederick William I, resumed the work begun by the Great Elector, restored Prussia's financial stability, and completed the centralization and modernization of the state apparatus by elaborating a body of law and statute that clarified rights and responsibilities for all subjects. He nationalized the officer corps of the army, improved its dress and weapons, wrote its first handbook of field regulations, prescribing manual exercises and tactical evolutions, and rapidly increased its size. When Frederick William took the throne after the lax rule of his predecessor, there were rumors of an impending coup by his neighbors, like that attempted against Sweden in 1700. That kind of talk soon died away as the king's work proceeded, and it is easy to see why. In the course of his reign, he increased the size of his military establishment to eighty-three thousand men, a figure that made Prussia's army the fourth largest in Europe, although the state ranked only tenth from the standpoint of territory and thirteenth in population.

Before the eighteenth century was far advanced, then, the threat of French universal dominance had been defeated, a balance of power existed in western Europe, and two new powers had emerged as partners of the older established ones. It was generally recognized that in terms of power and influence, the leading states in Europe were Britain, France, Austria, Russia, and probably Prussia. The doubts on the last score were soon to be removed; and these five powers were to be the ones that dominated European and world politics until 1914.

II

Something should be said at this point about diplomacy, for it was in the seventeenth and eighteenth centuries that it assumed its modern form. The use of envoys and emissaries to convey messages from one ruler to another probably goes back to the beginning of history; there are heralds in the *Iliad* and, in the second letter to the Church of Corinth, the Apostle Paul describes himself as an ambassador. But modern diplomacy as we know it had its origins in the Italian city states of the Renaissance period, and particularly in the republic of Venice and the states of Milan and Tuscany. In the fourteenth and fifteenth centuries, Venice was a great commercial power whose prosperity depended upon shrewd calculation of risks, accurate reports upon conditions in foreign markets, and effective negotiation. Because it did so, Venice developed the first systemized diplomatic service known to history, a network of agents who pursued the interests of the republic with fidelity, with a realistic appraisal of risks, with freedom from sentimentality and illusion.

From Venice the new practice of systematic diplomacy was passed on to the states of central Italy which, because they were situated in a political arena that was characterized by incessant rivalry and coalition warfare, were always vulnerable to external threats and consequently put an even greater premium than the Venetians upon accurate information and skillful negotiation. The mainland cities soon considered diplomacy so useful that they began to establish permanent embassies abroad, a practice instituted by Milan and Mantua in the fifteenth century, while their political thinkers (like the Florentine Machiavelli) reflected upon the principles best calculated to make diplomacy effective and tried to codify rules of procedure and diplomatic immunity. This last development facilitated the transmission of the shared experience of the Italian cities to the rising nation states of the west that soon dwarfed Florence and Venice in magnitude and strength. Thus, when the great powers emerged in the seventeenth century, they already possessed a highly developed system of diplomacy based upon long experience. The employment of occasional missions to foreign courts had given way to the practice of maintaining permanent missions. While the ambassadors abroad represented their princes and communicated with them directly, their reports were studied in, and they received their instructions from, permanent, organized bureaus which were the first foreign offices. France led the way in this and was followed by most other states, and the establishment of a foreign Ministry on the French model was one of Peter the Great's important reforms. The emergence of a single individual who was charged with the coordination of all foreign business and who represented his sovereign in the conduct of foreign affairs came a bit later, but by the beginning of the eighteenth century, the major powers all had such officials, who came to be known as foreign ministers or secretaries of state for foreign affairs.

From earliest times, an aura of intrigue, conspiracy, and disingenuousness surrounded the person of the diplomat, and we have all heard the famous quip of Sir Henry Wotton, ambassador of James I to the court of Venice, who said that an ambassador was "an honest man sent to lie abroad for the good of his country." Moralists were always worried by this unsavory reputation, which they feared was deserved, and they sought to reform it by exhortation. In the fifteenth century, Bernard du Rosier, provost and later archbishop of Toulouse, wrote a treatise in which he argued that the business of an ambassador is peace, that ambassadors must labor for the common good, and that they should never be sent to stir up wars or internal dissensions; and in the nineteenth century, Sir Robert Peel the younger was to define diplomacy in general as "the great engine used by civilized society for the purpose of maintaining peace."

The realists always opposed this ethical emphasis. In the fifteenth century, in one of the first treatises on ambassadorial functions, Ermalao Barbaro wrote: "The first duty of an ambassador is exactly the same as that of any other servant of government: that is, to do, say, advise and think whatever may best serve the preservation and aggrandizement of his own state."

Seventeenth-century theorists were inclined to Barbaro's view. This was certainly the position of Abram de Wicquefort, who coined the definition of the diplomat as "an honorable spy," and who, in his own career, demonstrated that he did not take the adjectival qualification very seriously. A subject of Holland by birth, Wicquefort at various times in his checkered career performed diplomatic services for the courts of Brandenburg, Luneburg, and France as well as for his own country, and he had no scruples about serving as a double agent, a practice that eventually led to his imprisonment in a Dutch jail. It was here that he wrote his treatise *L'Ambassadeur et ses fonctions,* a work that was both an amusing commentary on the political morals of the baroque age and an incisive analysis of the art and practice of diplomacy.

Wicquefort was not abashed by the peccadilloes of his colleagues, which varied from financial peculation and sins of the flesh to crimes of violence. He took the line that in a corrupt age, one could not expect that embassies would be oases of virtue. Morality was, in any case, an irrelevant consideration in diplomacy; a country could afford to be served by bad men, but not by incompetent ones. Competence began with a clear understanding on the diplomat's part of the nature of his job and a willingness to accept the fact that it had nothing to do with personal gratification or self-aggrandizement. The ambassador's principal function, Wicquefort wrote, "consisted in maintaining effective communication between the two princes, in delivering letters that his master writes to the Prince as whose court he resides, in soliciting answers to them, . . . in protecting his Master's subjects and conserving his interests." He must have the charm and cultivation that would enable him to ingratiate himself at the court to which he was accredited and the adroitness needed to ferret out information that would reveal threats to his master's interests or opportunities for advancing them. He must possess the ability to gauge the temperament and intelligence of those with whom he had to deal and to use this knowledge profitably in negotiation. "Ministers are but men and as such have their weaknesses, that is to say, their passions and interests, which the ambassador ought to know if he wishes to do honor to himself and his Master."

In pursuing this intelligence, the qualities he should cultivate most as-siduously were *prudence* and *modération.* The former Wicquefort equated with caution and reflection, and also with the gifts of silence and indirection, the art of "making it appear that one is not interested in the things one desires the most." The diplomat who possessed prudence did not have to resort to mendacity or deceit or to *tromperies* or *artifices,* which were usually, in any case, counterproductive. *Modération* was the ability to curb one's temper and remain cool and phlegmatic in moments of tension. "Those spirits who are compounded of sulphur and saltpeter, whom the slightest spark can set afire, are easily capable of compromising affairs by their excitability, because it is so easy to put them in a rage or drive them to a fury, so that they don't know what they are doing." Diplomacy is a cold and rational business, in short, not to be practiced by the moralist, or the enthusiast, or the man with a low boiling point.

The same point was made in the most famous of the eighteenth-century essays on diplomacy, Francois de Callières's *On the Manner of Negotiating with Princes* (1716), in which persons interested in the career of diplomacy were advised to consider whether they were born with "the qualities necessary for success." These, the author wrote, included an observant mind, a spirit of application which refused to be distracted by pleasures or frivolous amusements, a sound judgment which takes the measure of things, as they are, and which goes straight to its goal by the shortest and most neutral paths without wandering into useless refinements and subtleties which as a rule only succeed in repelling those with whom one is dealing.

Important also were the kind of penetration that is useful in discovering the thoughts of men, a fertility in expedients when difficulties arise, an equable humor and a patient temperament, and easy and agreeable manners. Above, all, Callières observed, in a probably not unconscious echo of Wicquefort's insistence upon moderation, the diplomat must

have sufficient control over himself to resist the longing to speak before he has really thought what he shall say. He should not endeavour to gain the reputation of being able to reply immediately and without premeditation to every proposition which is made, and he should take a special care not to fall into the error of one famous foreign ambassador of our time who so loved an argument that each time he warmed up in controversy he revealed important secrets in order to support his opinion.

In his treatment of the art of negotiation, Callières drew from a wealth of experience to which Wicquefort could not pretend, for he was one of Louis XIV's most gifted diplomats and ended his career as head of the French delegation during the negotiations at Ryswick in 1697. It is interesting, in light of the heavy reliance upon lawyers in contemporary United States diplomacy (one thinks of President Eisenhower's secretary of state and President Reagan's national security adviser) and of the modern practice of negotiating in large gatherings, that Callières had no confidence in either of these preferences. The legal mind, he felt, was at once too narrow, too intent upon hair-splitting, and too contentious to be useful in a field where success, in the last analysis, was best assured by agreements that provided mutuality of advantage. As for large conferences—"vast concourses of ambassadors and envoys"—his view was that they were generally too clumsy to achieve anything very useful. Most successful conferences were the result of careful preliminary work by small groups of negotiators who hammered out the essential bases of agreement and secured approval for them from their governments before handing them over, for formal purposes, to the *omnium-gatherums* that were later celebrated in the history books.

Perhaps the most distinctive feature of Callières's treatise was the passion with which he argued that a nation's foreign relations should be conducted by persons trained for the task.

Diplomacy is a profession by itself which deserves the same preparation and assiduity of attention that men give to other recognized professions . . . . The diplomatic genius is born, not made. But there are many qualities which may be developed with practice, and the greatest part of the necessary knowledge can only be acquired, by constant application to the subject. In this sense, diplomacy is certainly a profession itself capable of occupying a man's whole career, and those who think to embark upon a diplomatic mission as a pleasant diversion from their common task only prepare disappointment for themselves and disaster for the cause which they serve.

These words represented not only a personal view but an acknowledgment of the requirements of the age. The states that emerged as recognizedly great powers in the course of the seventeenth and eighteenth centuries were the states that had modernized their governmental structure, mobilized their economic and other resources in a rational manner, built up effective and disciplined military establishments, and elaborated a professional civil service that administered state business in accordance with the principles of *raison d'état*. An indispensable part of that civil service was the Foreign Office and the diplomatic corps, which had the important task of formulating the foreign policy that protected and advanced the state's vital interests and of seeing that it was carried out.

BIBLIOGRAPHICAL ESSAY

For the general state of international relations before the eighteenth century, the following are useful: Marvin R. O'Connell, *The Counter-Reformation, 1559–1610* (New York, 1974); Carl J. Friedrich, *The Age of the Baroque, 1610–1660* (New York, 1952), a brilliant volume; C. V. Wedgwood, The *Thirty Years War* (London, 1938, and later editions); Frederick L. Nussbaum, *The Triumph of Science and Reason, 1660–1685* (New York, 1953); and John B. Wolf, *The Emergence of the Great Powers, 1685–1715* (New York, 1951). On Austrian policy in the seventeenth century, see especially Max Braubach, *Prinz Eugen von Savoyen,* 5 vols. (Vienna, 1963–1965); on Prussian, Otto Hintze, *Die Hohenzollern und ihr Werk* (Berlin, 1915) and, brief but useful, Sidney B. Fay, *The Rise of Brandenburg-Prussia* (New York, 1937). A classical essay on great-power politics in the early modern period is Leopold von Ranke, *Die grossen Mächte,* which can be found in English translation in the appendix of Theodore von Laue, *Leopold Ranke: The Formative Years* (Princeton, 1950). The standard work on *raison d'état* is Friedrick Meinecke, *Die Idee der Staatsräsan,* 3rd ed. (Munich, 1963), translated by Douglas Scoff as *Machiavellianism* (New Haven, 1957).

On the origins and development of diplomacy, see D. P. Heatley, *Diplomacy and the Study of International Relations* (Oxford, 1919); Leon van der Essen, *La Diplomatie: Ses origines et son organisation* (Brussels, 1953); Ragnar Numelin, *Les origines de la diplomatie,* trans. from the Swedish by Jean-Louis Perret (Paris, 1943); and especially Heinrich Wildner, *Die Technik der Diplomatie: L'Art de négocier* (Vienna, 1959). Highly readable is Harold Nicolson, *Diplomacy,* 2nd ed. (London, 1950). An interesting comparative study is Adda B. Bozeman, *Politics and Culture in International History* (Princeton, 1960).

There is no modern edition of *L'amhassadeur et ses fonctions par Monsieur de Wicquefort* (College, 1690); but Callières's classic of 1776 can be found: Francois de Callières, *On the Manner of Negotiating with Princes,* trans. A. F. Whyte (London, 1919, and later editions).

London and the Modern Monarchy

Penelope Corfield
explores the interdependent relationship between crown and capital from the 17th century onwards that the monarchy ignored at its peril.

E T Archive

George III entering by the garden entrance.

WHEN CHARLES I stepped from the first floor of the Banqueting House in Whitehall to his execution in January 1649, it was an epoch-making moment. The powers of anointed kingship were challenged in the most explicit way. This was no secret murder but the public removal of a king who was adjudged a traitor to his own people. Nor did the event happen hastily on a battlefield. The execution took place at Whitehall, the political nerve-centre of the rebellious capital city, praised by the republican Milton as the very 'mansion-house of Liberty'. More pointedly, the King was executed before the very Banqueting House that his father had first commissioned in 1619, to beautify the royal palace of Whitehall. Kingship was felled amid its own splendour, before the gaze of the London crowds.

Restoration, when it came in 1660, was designed to restore the old ways. The status of monarchy was, however, irrevocably changed, as was confirmed at the Glorious Revolution of 1688–89. Thereafter kingship had to function in an evolving political environment, without either the trappings or the reality of absolute power. A suitable responsiveness to public opinion was thus required.

This point was highlighted by the Whig opposition leader Charles James Fox in an eloquent parliamentary oration of January 1795:

> Our constitution was a republic, in the just sense of the word; it was a monarchy founded on the good of the people. . . .

Of course, Britain had not literally followed America's example. Hereditary monarchy survived, complete with considerable prerogative powers; and the institution remained a focus for patriotic loyalty, as historians such as Linda Colley have argued.

Yet there were also some implicit boundaries to the authority of the crown, created by what may be termed an unwritten contract between crown and people. Public opinion could not be ignored for too long. And its force was graphically embodied by the millions of Londoners who lived close to the heart of government. They included among their ranks the political opinion formers, the media, the monied men, the middle classes, and the masses: collectively, a formidable force. It was not that Britain's capital city was constantly seething with republican sentiment, though a covert republican tradition continued to survive, but the individual monarchs were undoubtedly expected to live up to their symbolic role: neither negligent of their duties on the one hand, nor too flamboyantly costly in their performance on the other. As the prime audience for the royal show, the London populace was often loyal, sometimes critical, but ever-present.

The underlying tensions between the crown and the capital can be analysed in various ways: in the comparative modesty of the royal palaces in London—yet also in the court's continuing role as a fashionable venue for smart society; in the relative unimportance of court life to the multifarious London economy—contrasted with the overriding need for the monarchy to maintain a presence close to the urban heart of its empire, whatever personal inclination individual royals harboured for the tranquillity of country life.

Already by the seventeenth century, the old medieval system of a peripatetic court, moving around the country in stately progression, had ended—an outward sign of the changing status of monarchy. Elizabeth I was the last monarch to live like that. Her immediate successors adopted as their chief permanent residence in London the sprawling old Whitehall Palace. This stately habitation was not particularly beautiful or well arranged, but was located at the very heart of government.

It is true that Charles II, flushed with his political success in the years 1682–85, decided to commission a new palace from Sir Christopher Wren. The construction was sited in historic Winchester, to inaugurate a new capital city far from turbulent London. But the edifice was never inhabited by the King or his successors. Instead, Winchester Palace became an army barracks, before finally burning down in 1894.

Monarchical ostentation was politically damaging. Instead, a de facto process of rationalisation of state palaces occurred in the later seventeenth and early eighteenth centuries. The Tower of London, where Charles II lived for a short time on his return to England, was redeployed as an arsenal and barracks. The Palace of Westminster was dedicated entirely to its constitutional role as the Houses of Parliament. Downstream on the River Thames, the magnificent buildings of Greenwich Palace, enlarged under Charles II, were further extended in the 1690s for their new function to house the Royal Hospital for Seamen and (until 1998) the Royal Naval College. Upstream, the Tudor palace of Hampton Court, purloined from Cardinal Wolsey by Henry VIII and beautified by William III, was relegated from the mid-eighteenth century onwards to providing 'grace and favour' housing for retired courtiers.

Most striking was the unwillingness of either King or Parliament to build a new state residence in central London. When the Palace of Whitehall burnt down in 1698, after a fire in the servants' quarters, the site was quietly vacated, leaving only the Banqueting Hall

---

Most striking was the unwillingness of either King or Parliament to build a new state residence in London.

---

and a few other remnants now encased by government buildings. In contrast, Parliament agreed a grant in 1705, to celebrate the Duke of Marlborough's success in battle against France. As a result, the magnificent Blenheim Palace was constructed not for Queen Anne but for her victorious general.

Meanwhile, the royal headquarters were simply removed across St James's Park (affably opened to the public by Charles II) to the nearby Court of St James. This was a low-rise, brick-built Tudor palace of modest proportions. It contained some grand state rooms but did not impress outwardly. A foreign visitor found it little better than 'a stables', although he thought that was suitable for the horse-loving English. In 1766, the architectural writer John Gwynn commented that St James's was 'universally condemned'. The contrast with the opulent splendour enjoyed by the French kings at Versailles or the Austrian emperors at Schönbrunn was dramatic. Foreign ambassadors who were accredited to the Court of St James (as they still are today) were surprised at its simplicity. Daniel Defoe, in 1724, agreed:

The king's palace [at St James's], tho' the receptacle of all the pomp and glory of Great Britain, is really mean, in comparison of the rich furniture within, I mean the living furniture, the glorious Court of the King of Great Britain. . . .

Despite the plain surroundings in which the early Hanoverians were accommodated, smart society still liked to bask in 'such divinity doth hedge a king'. The court therefore remained a perennial magnet. It was not only a meeting-place for fashionable society but also a key arena for the leading politicians of the day. Moreover, courtly behaviour was taken to represent the ideal of good manners. Thus Castiglione's Courtier (1528), first translated into English in 1588, was still being reprinted in the eighteenth century as a standard 'courtesy' manual.

At the same time, however, there was also a tradition of criticism. If the monarchical entourage seemed corrupt and unworthy, then it quickly became a target of public abuse. 'Say to the Court it glows/And shines like rotten wood', as Sir Walter Raleigh had versified contemptuously in 1614. When kings were dull and virtuous, then the criticisms abated, as they did also in times of acute national peril, when people rallied behind the crown. If, on the other hand, the court was both scandalous and costly, then the satirists did not restrain themselves. In the later eighteenth century, even the bluff George III who 'gloried in the name of Briton' had periods of unpopularity. His eldest son, the Prince Regent (1810–20), later George IV (1820–30), was one of the most satirised and unpopular kings in British history. An active impresario in promoting improvements to the capital city, this did little to help palliate his failings in the eyes of his subjects. It was not George IV but his rejected wife Queen Caroline who became the heroine of the London crowds.

As a social magnet, the court undoubtedly contributed to the process of metropolitan growth. Senior aristocrats had positions in attendance upon the king, which brought them and their families regularly up to town. The diary of Robert Greville, a young nobleman appointed in 1781 as equerry in charge of the royal stables, recorded that his first weeks in the post were 'the happiest Month of My Life . . .'. Permanent courtiers were, however, fairly few in number. In Britain, the social elite visited rather than resided at court. Moreover, over time, there was a marked reduction in the number of salaried courtiers. In the 1630s, there were some 1,450 royal servants, who carried out a wide range of duties. By the 1720s—less than a century later—there were no more than 950. Since then, the number of salaried staff in royal service has remained around that figure into modern times. Hence the direct contribution of the court to employment within the metropolis has been minimal, in notable contrast with the mammoth state civil service.

Indirectly, however, the monarchy did have considerable impact. Many great landed families came to London each year, during the long winter 'season', which ran from October to May. Their motives for this migration were varied, but part of the attraction was the presence of royalty. The Hanoverians held regular court receptions when in London: with early evening 'drawing rooms' three times a week, frequented by both men and women; and morning 'levées', for men only, where business (such as the presentation of petitions) was mingled with sociability. Attendance there was a mark of social success.

The appeal of the court varied considerably over time, however. Some monarchs were more fashionable and accessible, while others were not happy with the requirement to be on show. Queen Victoria had a notoriously prolonged period of seclusion after the death of Prince Albert in 1861. Not all those thronging to court enjoyed the royal lifestyle. Some found it intensely boring. As already noted, Robert Greville enjoyed being courtier to George III, revelling in the male camaraderie and the frequent riding expeditions. In the same years, however, the middle-class novelist Fanny Burney had a quite different experience. From 1786 to 1791 she was second Keeper of the Robes to George III's Queen Charlotte. Burney's ambitious father was delighted, although friends cautioned that the move would harm her literary career. They proved to be right. Fanny Burney found herself closely supervised, bored by her fellow courtiers, and physically exhausted by the convention that forbade subjects to sit before royalty: 'I was lost to all private comfort;.. and fatigued with laborious watchfulness and attendance', she

confessed. A letter she wrote in 1789 added mournfully:

> We all go on here [at Windsor], day by day, night by night, so precisely the same, that monotony cannot be more perfect.

Eventually, her health broke down and she retired with a pension.

Court life was ordered by routine and ritual that changed only gradually. For example, it was only after Queen Anne's death in 1714 that the custom that required servants to kneel when handing dishes to the monarch at dinner was discarded. But, while the British monarchy has shown a long-term capacity for successful survival, it has also faced the need for intermittent periods of modernisation. As David Cannadine has argued, much twentieth-century royal ritual was

---

As a social magnet, the court undoubtedly contributed to the process of metropolitan growth.

---

invented in its current form only in the later nineteenth century. Once established, the pageantry quickly acquired a historic patina. Each time, the ritual has ossified anew. This is particularly apparent in the late 1990s, when new pressures for reform are being forced upon the royal family, following criticisms of their stilted public response to the death of Diana, Princess of Wales.

London as a metropolis, meanwhile, always had a momentum and social diversity of its own. The fact that it housed the court and government was undoubtedly a factor in its predominance. There was no British version of a separately planned capital city like Versailles or Canberra. As a result, London had an immensely variegated economy. While the royal court stood at the epicentre of one network that brought people to town, there were many others.

And, even in terms of polite society, there were important alternative venues for elite socialising. Both Disraeli and Trollope, for example, wrote about the glitter of the great aristocratic households rather than the stifled grandeur of the court. The most famous of London's smart town residences was Apsley House, near Hyde Park, built in the early 1770s and extended in 1828–29. When it was the home of the Duke of Wellington, the house was known, tellingly, as 'Number 1, London'. Its splendours included the huge Waterloo Chamber. Here Wellington held an annual public dinner to celebrate his famous military victory against Napoleon. That indicated the Duke's quasi-regal status. Indeed, this magnificent room vied with the royal Waterloo Chamber at Windsor Castle, where another notable Waterloo dinner was also hosted in commemoration of the British victory.

Collectively, the aristocracy and London's business elite were far greater investors in the constant building and rebuilding of London than was the monarchy. This was because the monarch was not one of the great landowners holding large estates within the metropolitan area. Furthermore, few British kings or queens were interested in town planning or urban architecture. The only one with a sustained involvement was the controversial George IV, who faced levels of popular republicanism not seen in England since the 1640s. His lavish patronage of architects won no plaudits from his subjects, even though it has been subsequently admired by architectural historians. As a result, George IV's association with John Nash (1752–1835), who built the grand terracing of Regent Street and who laid out Regent's Park, remains a significant and singular episode in London history. Yet it did not bring political dividends. Instead, the King's extravagance became another grievance. While George III had been satirised for his parsimony (he was nicknamed 'Candle Ends'), George IV was attacked for the reverse failing. Indeed, Nash's ambitious remodelling of central London was never completed, due to his patron's financial problems.

Eventually, the metropolis did acquire some of the accoutrements of an imperial capital. But the process was haphazard and gradual. When Victoria was made Empress of India in 1876, she did not also become Empress of Britain, and London was not redesigned as an imperial city. There was no English Hausmann to create a grid of ceremonial boulevards, although the building of Admiralty Arch in 1901 did at last provide a road link from Trafalgar Square to the Mall. Visually, it was 'governmental London' in Whitehall rather than 'monarchical London' that best represented the late nineteenth-century empire. Thus the resplendent Foreign and India Office building (1867–68) was the outward symbol of Britain's dominance overseas. But, as modern tourists discover, the institutional glories of London are scattered rather than interlinked: it remains an accidental, rather than an ordered city; a diverse metropolis, rather than a specialist capital.

Furthermore, London's complex evolution has occurred without reference to monarchical preferences. None of the rulers who succeeded George IV sought to intervene in the planning of the city. Prince Albert did take the initiative in proposing the Great Exhibition of 1851, which led to the construction of Paxton's inspirational iron and glass Crystal Palace in Hyde Park, but the project was cast as a national celebration rather than a monarchical triumph. Only recently, since the 1980s, has Prince Charles revived a controversial royal interest in architecture. His critique of urban modernism, however, is neither changing the face of London's development, nor gaining him much popularity for his pains.

From the monarchical viewpoint, the surrounding city crowds were both necessary and potentially intrusive. They provided the mass audiences for royal pageantry on major state occasions. Important funerals, weddings and commemorations needed the accolade of mass attention. Famous examples included Victoria's Golden Jubilee in 1887 and Diamond Jubilee in 1897, when the Queen resolutely sported her widow's bonnet instead of a crown. Yet the popular mood was not invariably sympathetic to royal pomp. In bad times, crowds could shout or jeer, as in the case of the angry protesters who threw stones, hissed, and cried 'Bread, bread' as George III drove to Parliament's state opening in October 1795. Such events did not happen often. But mass emotion could send pointed messages across the barriers of formal rank, as in the recent case of the spontaneously improvised public mourning for Princess Diana, which implicitly rebuked the inadequacies of royal protocol. In other words, the crowds were not passive onlookers but were major protagonists in the performance. The size of the turnout and the nature of the public responses gave meaning to the event. In effect, the crowd's role signified that the monarchy, when on public show, was permanently subject to audience approval and the popular gaze. Little wonder that Victoria in her bereavement sought seclusion from London.

From the monarchy's viewpoint, the city crowds were both necessary and potentially intrusive.

To lighten the pressures, members of the royal family increasingly differentiated between state functions and their private lives. Within London, a new palace was adopted, as St James's proved too poky even for a scaled-down monarchy. Buckingham House, initially purchased by George III in 1762 as the London home for his growing family, was upgraded in the 1820s by George IV. As Buckingham Palace, replete with Regency grandeur, it became the premier state palace, the royal equivalent of 'the office'. Some discreet adaptations have followed, to encompass the gradual shift from constitutional rule to full democracy by the twentieth century. For example, in 1913, the Mall frontage of the Palace was refaced in Portland stone, with a long balcony for ceremonial waving. And, recently, the state rooms have been opened to public view.

Personal privacy, meanwhile, was provided by a discreet flight from the metropolis. This was easiest in summer, when Parliament was not in session. Successive kings and queens built or renovated their own private residences, to which they could retreat, while attending London for state business. William and Mary built Kensington Palace, while the Hanoverians in turn preferred Hampton Court, Kew, Richmond Lodge and Frogmore House. Even George IV had interests outside the capital, whether in his extraordinary oriental fantasy, Brighton Pavilion (1815–22) or in Windsor Castle, which he drastically remodelled in the 1820s as part state palace and part private apartments.

Later still, Victoria favoured family holidays on the Isle of Wight at Osborne House (built 1845–51) which subsequently became an officers' hospital. She also made regular spring and autumn visits to Balmoral Castle in Scotland (built 1852–54), while in the 1870s her eldest son the Prince of Wales, later Edward VII, commissioned Sandringham House in Norfolk.

Had any of these residences become a permanent court, then London might have been challenged. But, in practice, the equation worked the other way round. The metropolis was much too important for the crown to ignore or abandon. Hence the Hanoverians chose summer palaces in the Home Counties, a coach-ride away to the west of London, while the Victorians were able to travel further afield only thanks to the new railway system. The monarchs might have preferred the life of country aristocrats; but they had to co-exist with the metropolitan bourgeoisie and proletariat. The crowded, smoky, sweaty, sometimes rebellious city, housing at least 10 per cent of the nation's population in 1700 and a growing percentage thereafter, was too entrenched as the national headquarters to be neglected. Throughout the growth of the worldwide British empire, from the seventeenth to the twentieth centuries, the chief state residence of the British monarchy has stayed firmly in London.

Statues can be found across the metropolis, commemorating every ruler since Elizabeth I except Edward VIII. Yet, with some prominent exceptions such as the Albert Memorial, this royal iconography is little known. Few people, for example, recognise the aerial figure of George I upon the spire of St George's Church, Bloomsbury, or realise that Edward VII stands pensively outside Tooting Broadway underground station. Meanwhile, London's over 600 other public monuments celebrate a veritable horde of non-royal heroes. Most pointedly, a statue of Oliver Cromwell is positioned immediately outside Parliament, while Charles I on horseback is relegated to an undistinguished traffic island in Trafalgar Square, overshadowed by a gigantic Nelson on his column.

All this provides a realistic historical message. Kings who desert their capital cities may put themselves in jeopardy, as did Charles I in 1642. Three hundred years later, George VI's determination not to leave London during the Blitz materially assisted the long-term survival of Britain's monarchy. On a lesser scale, the initial decision of Elizabeth II to remain at Balmoral after Diana's death in August 1997 was a tactical error. When the Queen did return to London, she quickly broadcast to the nation, sitting before a backdrop of milling crowds at the Palace gates. The imagery signalled a regained sympathy with the masses.

London's huge population—its residents supplemented by visitor's on great occasions—collectively embodies and crystallises the tumultuous power of public opinion, both among the wider populace and the so-called opinion formers or 'chattering classes'. As a result, Britain's monarchy requires metropolitan approval. Modern kingship lives and dies among the city crowds.

FOR FURTHER READING

L. Colley, *Britons: Forging the Nation, 1707–1837* (Yale University Press, 1992); D. Pearce, *London's Mansions: the Palatial Houses of the Nobility* (Batsford, 1986); J.M. Robinson, *Royal Residences* (MacDonald, 1982); A. Tricomi, *Anti-Court Drama in England,* 1603–42 (University Press of Virginia, 1989); R. Williams, *The Contentious Crown: Public Discussion of the British Monarchy in the Reign of Queen Victoria* (Ashgate, 1997); Simon Thurley, *The Lost Palace of Whitehall* (RIBA, 1998).

Penelope Corfield is Professor of History at Royal Holloway, University of London. She is co-author, with C. Harvey and E. Green, of *The Westminster Historical Database: Voters, Social Structure and Electoral Behaviour,* 1998.

A Golden Age: Innovation in Dutch Cities, 1648–1720

Jonathan Israel *describes how the genius of the seventeenth-century Netherlands lay not just in painting but in blazing a trail in civic pride and technological improvements for the rest of Europe.*

Jonathan Israel is Professor of Dutch History and Institutions at University College, London and author of The Dutch Republic: Its Rise, Greatness and Fall, 1477–1806, *published by Oxford University Press (1995).*

Between April and June 1648 the most elaborate and impressive celebrations which had thus far ever been held in the northern Netherlands—parades, pageants, thanksgiving services, open-air theatrical performances, a series of bonfire and fire-work displays, sumptuous militia and regent banquets—were held in Amsterdam and most other Dutch cities. The reason for this unprecedented outlay, disruption of normal activity and quest to impress and involve the general public was the final ratification of the Peace of Münster (April 1648). This not only ended the Eighty Years' War in the Low Countries, one of the greatest struggles of Europe of early modern times, but marked the successful conclusion of decades of effort to establish and consolidate the Dutch Republic as a free and independent state on territory formerly ruled by the king of Spain.

That this was no small achievement can be seen from the fact that the United Provinces, as the Republic was officially called, was the only new state—as well as new type of state—created by means of a people's revolution against the power of monarchs in the early modern era before the 1770s, when the North Americans embarked on their great struggle (on occasion with the Dutch example in mind) against the British crown.

At the same time, these celebrations were the Dutch contribution to a wider set of festivities held all across northern and central Europe to mark the end of the unprecedentedly destructive Thirty Years' War. As such, the festivities of 1648, both in their Dutch and wider European context, were a psychological turning-point between a dreadfully bleak era of struggle and dislocation, and the deep pessimism and gloom which had resulted, and a more hopeful era; one of rebuilding and reconstruction. Many of the cities of Germany had been severely damaged by the war, as well as the slump and disease which had come in its wake; while even those which had not been, such as Hamburg and Bremen, had nevertheless shared in the general sense of fear and uncertainty and, like Copenhagen, tended to avoid all major new city extensions and build-

ing projects for the duration of the conflict, except only for large-scale improvements to city fortifications.

With the Thirty and Eighty Years' Wars simultaneously out of the way, city governments could now think about reconstructing their war-torn cities and, in the case of the Scandinavian capitals and flourishing Hamburg, embark on those ambitious projects and city extensions which it had seemed prudent to postpone whilst the fighting and disruption continued. Furthermore, since at that time the Dutch Republic was economically and culturally the most dynamic and flourishing country in Europe, it was entirely natural that many of these cities whether or not they had been devastated, especially those in the Protestant north, should look to the Dutch Republic for most of the ideas, designs, methods and technology which was to shape their general renovation and reconstruction during the second half of the seventeenth century and (particularly in the case of St Petersburg, Russia's window on the West) at the beginning of the eighteenth.

However, if we are to grasp how it was possible for such a small country as the Dutch provinces to have exerted such an immense influence over urban development in northern Europe, an influence which was, in most respects, far greater than that of Britain or France down to around 1720, it is by no means sufficient just to point to the general readiness for renovation and refurbishment, or to the special dynamism of the Dutch economy at that time. The phenomenon is more complex than that. For the Dutch cities were themselves then entering a major new phase of expansion and renewal, shaped by a dazzling array of innovations and new techniques and, more than anything else, it is this which gave them their special relevance and immense influence over such a considerable period.

If French influence in Europe in the late seventeenth century and early eighteenth century emanated, above all, from the court of Louis XIV, Dutch influence did not emanate from any arm of the Dutch state. Invariably, we find that it was not the Dutch Republic as such which appealed but specifically the Dutch cities, especially—but by no means only—Amsterdam. Over recent decades the Dutch Republic had proved remarkably effective politically, militarily and not least, in its financial operations. Yet this had been achieved without the new state intruding on the local autonomy of the cities. Somehow a remarkable balance had been struck between civic (and other local) particularism, on the one hand, and the 'Generality', as the Dutch then termed their federal institutions, on the other. Since the main cities and the provinces (each with its own local assembly) had been the backbone of the Revolt against Spain, this had indeed been a *sine que non* for the successful establishment of a Dutch state, and is what ensured that it would also be an entirely new type of state. For even in 1648 there was not yet a fully-fledged Dutch national identity. That was only to emerge more or less in its modern form at the end of the eighteenth century.

Most Dutchmen, like most Germans and Italians at the time, identified most strongly, and felt their principal political allegiance to, their city or locality rather than to the country as a whole. But they shared not just in the collective experience of the Revolt against Spain but, linked to this, an intense pride in the 'freedom' which they had won, the new political, religious and social context which they had created in which civic and local autonomy was combined with

what we would call a federal, overarching, state. Of course, they can hardly have grasped that they had forged the world's first real federal republic— Switzerland being an earlier but only partial step towards genuine federalism. They can not have known that theirs would also be the only real federal republic until the American Revolution created the United States of America, but that this would one day (since Germany adopted the federal model after the Second World War) become possibly the most important type of state in the western world. But ordinary Dutchmen and Dutch women did vaguely grasp that they had achieved something altogether exceptional and remarkable which they referred to as their 'freedom'.

By 1648, the impact of the Dutch cities on the European urban scene was already very considerable and had been growing, especially since the 1590s. The seemingly miraculous expansion of Dutch commerce and shipping which had begun to take over the 'rich trades' of the world in the 1590s, elbowing all rivals aside, had reached such a point that it had aroused intense envy and resentment in almost every part of Europe and not least in England. Moreover, by 1648 those parts of Europe—especially Scandinavia, northern Germany and the Baltic—which were particularly susceptible to Dutch cultural influences were already so steeped in Dutch methods, styles and ways of doing things that everything else had been pushed into the background. When Hamburg and Copenhagen rebuilt their city fortifications during the second decade of the century they did so using Dutch engineers and Dutch designs.

If Christian IV (1588–1648) was the greatest builder and art collector in the history of the Danish-Norwegian monarchy, it is equally evident from the architects, engineers and artists he employed (who were nearly all Dutch) and the designs and styles he adopted, that the imposing cultural framework he created was essentially an extension of the Dutch Golden Age. Yet, notwithstanding this vast impact of Dutch commerce and shipping, and of Holland's art, architecture and engineering (particularly drainage, harbours and fortifications), those aspects of Dutch culture which were to have the greatest impact on urban development, refurbishment and planning after 1648, were only just beginning to be noticed.

The chief reason why the Dutch had not yet begun even potentially to make their real impact in the sphere of urban improvements, health care, town planning and public services is that the Dutch cities too, like those of Germany and Scandinavia, had since around 1620 been systematically postponing major new investment in buildings and city extensions. Just as Amsterdam needed a new and larger city hall long before 1648 but work on the new edifice began only in that year, and Leiden put up with old and delapidated gate-houses, only replacing them with magnificent new structures after 1648, so all big projects were put off. But once the Eighty and Thirty Years' Wars were finally over, the accumulation of grandiose and ambitious schemes led to a frenetic burst of building and refurbishment throughout the length and breadth of Holland. Not only were numerous large public buildings erected in the 1650s and 1660s, far

Table: The Demographic Expansion of the Ten Largest Dutch Cities

City	1570	1600	1632	1647	1672	1700
			(estimates)			
Amsterdam	30,000	60,000	116,000	140,000	200,000	200,000
Leiden	15,000	26,000	54,000	60,000	72,000	63,000
Haarlem	15,000	30,000	42,000	45,000	50,000	40,000
Rotterdam	8,000	12,000	20,000	30,000	45,000	45,000
The Hague	5,000	10,000	16,000	1,000	30,000	30,000
Middelburg	10,000	20,000	28,000	30,000	30,000	30,000
Utrecht	26,000	-	-	30,000	-	30,000
Delft	14,000	17,500	21,000	21,000	24,000	19,000
Dordrecht	10,800	15,000	18,000	20,000	20,000	20,000
Gouda	9,000	13,000	15,000	15,000	20,000	20,000

more than in the previous three decades, but those cities which achieved an impressive measure of growth between 1648 and 1672, especially Amsterdam, Leiden, Rotterdam, The Hague and also Haarlem (see Table below) also laid out whole new urban quarters, constructed new canals and roads, and planned new housing as part of integrated urban development schemes. Delft too, though it grew much less than some others, had to be extensively rebuilt following the great gunpowder explosion of 1654 which devastated the city centre. Even Utrecht, a city quite stagnant compared with the Holland towns, seeing the ambitious projects of the others, drew up far-reaching plans, hoping by means of investing in redevelopment to attract more immigrants and activity.

However, the integrated reality of Dutch city planning and improvements after 1648 could not be emulated elsewhere in its entirety because many features of the Dutch urban scene were highly specific to Holland and Zeeland. Thus numerous foreign travellers of the period remarked that Amsterdam was much cleaner and less cluttered than London or Hamburg. But one of the main reasons for this was that the city government banned the use of horse-drawn coaches and wagons in the city, insisting that goods, supplies and furniture be moved by water and digging new

Franz Hals' 1664 painting—'Lady Governors of the Old Men's Home': social provision and public works were an important expression of Dutch civic governance.

canals and improving old ones to facilitate such traffic. This was perfectly feasible also in other Holland and Zeeland towns, but hardly practice elsewhere.

Another feature which could not be imitated elsewhere were the regular passenger services between towns by means of horse-drawn passenger barges, with departures several times daily between the main towns, working according to a published schedule, a phenomenon which

has been brilliantly researched by the American historian Jan de Vries. Furthermore, not only these but also many other Dutch urban improvements of the period could only be effectively implemented because of the almost absolute power of the city governments within their cities and jurisdictions. Although they had to pay some attention to opinion within their city, the regents who staffed the city governments could otherwise raise money through municipal taxation of one sort or another, and decide what went on in their city, largely as they saw fit. If a city government wished to implement an ambitious and costly urban plan there was no question of this being opposed by any authority or body outside. In this respect, Swiss and some German Imperial Free Cities enjoyed a comparable freedom of action but cities under monarchs, such as London, Paris, Copenhagen or Stockholm, did not. Monarchs had their own agendas and priorities and, in most cases, a considerable sway over resources.

But what other European cities, including London, could and did do, some sooner, some later, was to adopt in full, or in part, such individual urban improvements and innovations introduced by the Dutch cities as did not need specifically Dutch conditions for their implementation. A classic instance of such successful borrowing was the adoption of the Dutch system of public street lighting. Europe's first proper system of public street-lighting was planned, in con-

Making the world go round: Berckheyde's portrayal of the Amsterdam Bourse.

junction with members of the Amsterdam city government, by the artist-inventor Jan van der Heyden (1637–1712). Van der Heyden designed a street-lamp manufactured of metal and glass with shielded airholes able to let out smoke without letting in the wind. The lamps burnt through the night on a mixture of plant oils with wicks of twisted Cypriot cotton.

Besides the considerable cost, the plans to light up the whole of Amsterdam at night presented appreciable problems. But the burgomasters and regents decided to go ahead, motivated by a desire further to improve orderliness in the city, and reduce crime, as well as the incidence of drunkards falling into the canals at night and drowning. The plans were finalised and approved in 1669. By January 1670, the entire city was lit up after dark—what an amazing sight it must have been—by 1,800 public lamps (increased to 2,000 before long) affixed to posts or the walls of public buildings. The lampposts were placed 125 to 150 feet apart, Van der Heyden having calculated that maximum lighting efficiency with minimum wastage of oil and equipment was achieved with that spacing. One hundred public lamplighters were recruited who each re-filled, lit and, in the morning, extinguished, twenty of the lanterns. It took about fifteen minutes to light up the whole city. By 1681, another 600 public lamps had been added to the

original 2,000. The advantages of lighting up the city at night were so obvious that first other Dutch cities, and then cities outside the United Provinces began to follow Amsterdam's example. Dordrecht installed the new system in 1674. Having ordered the equipment from Amsterdam, both Berlin and Cologne installed hundreds of Dutch lampposts and lit up their cities in 1682.

Another urban improvement which was widely imitated in late seventeenth-century Europe was Amsterdam's remarkable new fire-fighting service. Here again the technology involved was devised by Van der Heyden. But the key to success was the ability of the city government, having seen the potential of his innovations, to back them with funds and a sophisticated civic organisation. Although Van der Heyden was not the first Dutch expert to contrive a pump able to throw up a continuous jet of water from the canals, he produced improved pumps and was the first to join them to (leather) hoses. After being put in charge of the city's fire-fighting service, in 1672, he created an organisation the key element in which was the distribution of quantities of pumps and hoses around the city and their storage in special depots; and the assigning of able-bodied guild members in each quarter to take charge of the equipment and to ensure that it was promptly rushed to the scene and used in the event of fire. The sight of the new water

pumps and hoses in action greatly impressed contemporaries, the effect being heightened by Van der Heyden's dramatic and well-publicised illustrations of fire-fighting scenes. One astonished English visitor described the hoses as being 'as big as a man's thigh which by the assistance of pumps, at which they labour continually for three or four hours, throw up water to the tops of the highest houses and force it three hundred paces over the tiling'.

Naturally, other northern cities were quick to see the value of the Dutch pumps and hoses and, albeit with a few years' time lag, proceeded to adopt similar systems based on the Dutch equipment. The revised civic fire regulations published in Hamburg in 1695, for example, are clearly based on the Amsterdam example, the central element being the storage of pumps and hoses in designated depots around the city and the assignment of responsibility, in each city quarter, for the maintenance and use of the equipment. Cologne obtained its pumps from Amsterdam; probably Hamburg did too.

One of the most crucial of the Dutch urban improvements of the mid-seventeenth century and one which was widely imitated, especially in Germany, Switzerland and Scandinavia, was the setting up in Amsterdam of a civic medical board called the *collegium medicum* consisting of three university-trained physicians and two prominent apothecaries to inspect, supervise, license and register medical practice in the city. Earlier there had been only the most rudimentary supervision over who practiced medicine, what medicines were sold in apothecaries' shops, how far the ingredients of medicines matched what was on the labels, and over how much was charged for medicines and medical supplies.

When the system of control was first introduced by the Amsterdam city government, by city edict of March 23rd, 1639, the chief concern seems to have been to curb the abuses going on in apothecaries' shops, especially the selling of impure or bogus medicines and wide discrepancies in charges. The edict laid down that the physicians of the collegium were to visit and inspect all the apothecaries' shops in the city 'two or three times per year', without prior notice, and verify what was being sold. At the same time, the city published a list of authorised prices for medicines to which apothecaries were expected to ad-

VOC warehouses and shipbuilding wharves underlining the maritime contribution to the Dutch profile in Europe after 1648.

here and it was laid down that apothecaries and their assistants would only be permitted to practice in the city if they satisfied the collegium that they had adequate knowledge and expertise. Other Dutch cities followed and, soon, so did various German and Swiss cities. The city of Bremen published a new civic health *Ordnung,* based on the Amsterdam example, as early as 1644, the two main elements of which were the setting up of a system for regular inspection of apothecaries' shops by the city physician and the drawing up of a list of authorised prices for drugs and medicines. The Baltic city of Rostock adopted the system in 1659. In Stockholm, a *collegium medicum,* modelled on the Amsterdam example, was introduced in 1663.

While the original emphasis was mainly on supervision of apothecaries, the Dutch system of regulating civic health care gradually evolved during the middle and late decades of the seventeenth century becoming more comprehensive as well as more sophisticated. Notable additions to the original conception include the Amsterdam city law of May 1668, laying down that 'no one shall be allowed to practice as a midwife in the city unless she has first been examined by the *inspecteurs* of the collegium . . . and obtained a certificate of expertise' and the by-law of 1675, stipulating as a necessary qualification for obtaining a license to practice as a midwife, from the *inspecteurs,* to have worked as an assistant to a qualified midwife for a minimum of four years.

The Dutch city governments of this period, eager as they were to attract immigrants and increase the populations of their cities, made a serious and sustained effort, and with some success, to improve living conditions and health care. At the same time, they vied with each other in erecting imposing public buildings—hospitals and orphanages, as well as town halls, gate-houses and churches—beautification and splendour being essential aspects of the urban development schemes which they so intensively devised and debated. As the English physician Walter Harris remarked, in 1699, Holland contained 'a greater number of large, populous and considerable towns, than possibly are to be found so near together in any other part of the universe' so that, together with the great ease of passenger traffic between these cities, ordinary folk as well as the more sophisticated, were constantly appraising and making comparisons between them. If, as William Bromley remarked in his *Several Years' Travels,* the new Amsterdam city hall was 'the most magnificent structure of its kind in Europe', this is precisely what the Amsterdam city fathers had intended.

With both practical and aesthetic considerations firmly in mind, nothing appealed to the Dutch city governments of this period more than opportunities to combine public utility with beautification. A development which gave them precisely such an opportunity was the arrival in the middle decades of the century of new types of very large public clocks which (especially after the 1650s) also kept time much more accurately than the clocks of the past. In their drive to embellish Leiden, the city government there developed a veritable mania for affixing such clocks to the city's public buildings, including one, manufactured at The Hague, which was installed on the octagonal tower of their handsome new church (the Marekerk) in 1648. Another was placed at the top of the imposing new White Gate (built in 1650), near where the passenger barges loaded and unloaded the travelling public so as to facilitate punctuality in barge departures.

A typical feature of the new town hall of Maastricht built in the years 1659–64 to designs by Pieter Post (1608–69), one of the leading exponents of Dutch classicist architecture, were spaces assigned both inside and outside the structure for public clocks. The clocks, which were manufactured in Amsterdam, were installed a few years later. Needless to say the fashion caught on also outside the borders of the United Provinces. Dutch-style public clocks were affixed to several of the principal church-towers of Hamburg as early as the 1660s and 1670s.

The expansion of the Dutch economy, and of the Dutch cities, ended abruptly with the Anglo-French attack on the United Provinces in 1672. In that year Louis XIV invaded the Republic and occupied its eastern provinces while the French army, combined with the English and French fleets, delivered a blow to Dutch commerce and industry from which they were never fully to recover. After 1672, it was unquestionably England which was the most dynamic and the fastest-growing commercial economy in the western world. Nevertheless, it is important to note that at that time there were in Britain no large cities other than London (albeit as large as Amsterdam and the six next largest Dutch cities combined) which was by all accounts a somewhat disorderly and chaotic place compared with the Dutch cities.

Moreover, despite their stagnation after 1672, the Dutch cities were at that time sufficiently far ahead of England in technological innovations, health care and urban planning to retain something of an edge not only down to the end of the seventeenth century but even for a decade or two into the eighteenth. It was not until after around 1720 that Britain can be said to have overtaken the Dutch Republic in terms of technological sophistication.

Consequently, despite the emergence of England as the world's most dynamic economic and colonial power after 1672, it was still the Dutch cities, rather than the British, which were the main model for urban planning and improvements in northern Europe for another half a century.

FOR FURTHER READING:

C. A. Davids, 'Technological Change and the economic Expansion of the Dutch Republic' in C. A. Davids and L. Noordegraaf (eds.) *The Dutch Economy in the Golden Age* (Amsterdam, 1993); J. I. Israel, *Dutch Primacy in World Trade, 1585–1740* (Oxford, 1989); L. S. Multhauf, 'The Light of Lamp-lanterns: Street Lighting in 17th-century Amsterdam', *Technology and Culture* 26 (1985); J. L. Price, *Holland and the Dutch Republic in the Seventeenth Century* (Oxford, 1994); C. D. Strien, *British Travellers in Holland during the Stuart Period* (Leiden, 1993); Jan de Vries, *Barges and Capitalism: Passenger Transportation in the Dutch Economy (1632–1839)* (Wageningen, 1978).

Nice cuppa: Cruickshank's caricature of 'ordinary folk' partaking of the fashionable beverage at the Bayswater Tea Garden, 1796.

A Taste of Empire, 1600–1800

James Walvin *on how tea, sugar and tobacco hooked Britons into a fondness for the fruits of imperial expansion.*

What could be more British than a sweet cup of tea? Has there ever been a more typical or ubiquitous presence in modern social life (until recently) than clouds of tobacco smoke? Wasn't the post-rationing rush for chocolate characteristically British? The consumption of luxury staples, notably sugar, tobacco, tea, coffee and chocolate—is part of the warp and weft of British life. Yet each and many more of these habits are British only by adoption. The peculiarly British customs associated with these staples developed in a relatively short period of time and involved commodities imported from the very edge of colonial settlement and trade, at a time of increasing mass consumption at home. All took root roughly in the years 1600–1800; i.e. in the period which saw the development of a powerful British imperial and global trading presence. They were in effect one consequence of Britain's emergence as an aggressive global power, but in the process they changed the nature of domestic British social life forever.

Today Western societies take for granted cheap and readily-available commodities plucked from the far edges of the world and air-freighted to our local supermarkets for our nourishment and pleasure. Yet the history of the consumption of tropical exotica helps to explain key elements of British social life that are of interest both for consumers and producers alike. Why, for example, did the British become attached to *sweet* tea (quite unlike tea-drinkers in tea's native Chinese habitat)? And why did the British come to like their chocolate heavily sweetened (in drinking form initially, later as solid eating chocolate), when the indigenous Central American consumers had mixed it with spices and chillies? Why too were those key arenas of eighteenth century male sociability—the coffee house and the tavern—shrouded in clouds of tobacco smoke?

The answer of course lies in the eighteenth-century British pre-eminence as Atlantic slave traders, and the economic importance of British slave colonies in the Caribbean and North America. Armies of Africans and their local-born descendants toiled, out of sight and generally out-of-mind, to bring forth sugar (and rum) from the luxuriant islands, and tobacco from the Chesapeake—all for the pleasure (and profit) of Europeans. Africa held the key. In the words of one mid-eighteenth-century commentator, Africa could yield slaves 'by the thousands, nay millions, and go on doing the same to the end of time'.

In all these cases—and more—the imported produce began as a costly luxury, destined only for the fashionable tables of British élites. Yet by the end of our period they had become the cheap, accessible necessity of common people across the nation. In the last years of the eighteenth-century, when Britain teetered on the brink of mass starvation, social commentators were perplexed and often irritated by the plebeian attachment to apparently luxurious imports. Sir Frederick Eden's survey of the poor in the 1790s revealed the universal attachment of labouring people to sweet tea. In Middlesex and Surrey, he found, at meal times:

> . . . in poor families, tea is not only the usual beverage in the morning and evening, but is generally drank in large quantities even at dinner.

Of course, by then, the luxuries of an earlier generation had become cheap basics in the make-up of the diet even of the poor. The British working class found it hard to imagine life without their sweetened tea. Yet the tea was imported from China, the sugar from the West Indies.

This process was one example of the 'Columbian Exchange', that post-Columbus exchange of peoples, beasts, flora, fauna and diseases which utterly transformed the physical face of the globe. British tastes for imported staples then were fashioned in the wake of that remarkable explosion in global trade, which saw commodities and produce from the very edges of the known-world shipped in growing profusion to its domestic heartlands. There was, however, more to the transformation than the mere accidental development of trade and overseas settlement. What underpinned these changes in British social life was the rapid emergence of Britain as a commercial and military power resulting in the often brutal imposition of economic and strategic interests on distant peoples and regions.

This is spectacularly true in the case of sugar. What helped create the infamous British sweet tooth was the remarkable development of the Atlantic slave system for sugar production. True, the British did not pioneer African labour in the Americas. But they did perfect it, moulding it into an efficient, expansive and profitable business, whose ramifications were deep-reaching. The British transported more Africans than any other nation and it was British ports which waxed prosperous on the Atlantic trade. Of the over 11,000 British slaving voyages in the eighteenth century, more than half originated in Liverpool. But dozens of small ports also joined in this lucrative trade—who today thinks of Lyme Regis, Lancaster or Whitehaven in this context? Few areas remained immune from the contagion of the Atlantic trades. Foodstuffs, produce and manufactured goods from throughout Britain (along with goods transported from Europe and Asia) filled the holds of these African-bound slave ships. The slaves were bought with, or bartered in exchange for, a massive range of British goods and produce. The foodstuffs from the lowlands of Scotland and Ireland, metal goods from the Black Country, cloth, clothing, shoes and hats, sails and nails, plates, pans—and hundreds of thousands of firearms—were loaded into the outbound slave ships. Their place in the holds was taken on the second leg—the Middle Passage—by African slaves. The return voyage saw the vessels filled with tropical produce bound for British markets. In the New World the planters and slaves and the communities they forged were sustained by a mercantilist system which formed an umbilical cord be-

Social smoke screen: far removed from the chain gangs, gentlemen enjoy tobacco and conversation in the civilised confines of the coffee house in this broadside of 1677.

tween British industries and dependent tropical settlement. They needed Britain, and Britain needed their produce.

The very great bulk of the 11 million-plus Africans landed in the Americas—a figure which does not include millions of casualties who died in Africa and at sea—were destined, initially at least, for sugar colonies. Plantations proliferated Brazil, then Barbados in the early seventeenth century and in Jamaica after 1655. Fruitful land, European capital and management and African labour; all came together in the rapid development of the sugar economy. And the whole was kept in place by an increasingly powerful British state, its economic and fiscal muscle flexed by the patrolling Royal Navy. Naval power kept out other Europeans and was the ultimate instrument for the physical control of the ever-resistant armies of brutalised Africans. Commercial interests, military strategy and economic well-being came together in the creation and maintenance of the slave empires.

And all for what? So the British people—and many others of course—could enjoy, cheaply, the sweet pleasures which only recently had been the costly preserve of their social betters. Sugar entered the British blood stream. The few thousand tons imported in the 1650s had grown to 23,000 tons in 1700. By 1800 it stood at 245,000 tons. The Scottish theologian, Duncan Forbes, could remember a time when tea had been expensive, recalling how, '*Sugar, the inseperable Companion of Tea,* came to be in the possession of the poorest Housewife, where formally it had been a Rarity . . .'. It sweetened bitter drinks; tea from China, chocolate from Central America and coffee from the Yemen. Each of these commodities was later transplanted to other colonial possessions for more convenient and profitable cultivation. The end result was that sugar became a basic ingredient in a host of British dishes, and was enshrined in a range of cookbooks and domestic handbooks. 'Sweeten to taste' became the watchword of the British cook.

Like other exotic items, sugar entered Britain in the seventeenth century, as one of the apothecary's ingredients. So, too, did tobacco. Chewed, mixed, ground; smoked, drunk, swallowed and snorted, tobacco offered a host of apparent cures and remedies. Time and again, tropical staples were promoted as cures or palliatives for a host of medical complaints. Pepys worried, in June 1665, about the advance of the Plague. He turned to tobacco; 'I was forced to buy some roll tobacco to smell to and to chaw—which took away the apprehension'.

Along with sweetened drinks, tobacco could be bought and consumed in the tavern and coffee house. But increasingly, it was available from those myriad shops which proliferated across the face of Britain, penetrating the remotest of communities. Adam Smith's (and Napoleon's) 'nation of shopkeepers' did much of their trade by concentrating on the sale of tropical staples to British consumers (of all sorts and conditions). The typical shop, far removed from the glamour of Oxford Street, was little more than a counter in a front room. Yet even the smallest of shops, in the most

Tea (or coffee) for two: in 1805 engraving thought to depict the Twining brothers, who had opened their tea warehouse in the Strand, London, in 1787.

isolated of places, could be relied on, by the mid-eighteenth century, to provide sugar, tea and tobacco.

These initially took root as ingredients in contemporary medicine, but each quickly established a culinary and social life of its own. Around the consumption of these and other commodities there evolved elaborate social habits which became important characteristics of British life. Smoking, for example, quickly became a masculine pursuit. Women with pipes in their hands could still be found, of course, but, by the late eighteenth century they represented a declining fashion—an image used by caricaturists as the very essence of unladylike behaviour. Men smoked—women (certainly ladies) did not. (A pattern not changed until the rise of the twentieth century cigarette industry). But how did this, and other social habits linked to tropical staples, emerge?

Tobacco became widely available through ale houses and coffee shops, later through general stores and tobac-

conists. Chesapeake tobacco production was staggering. The 65,000 lbs of the 1620s had grown to a million lbs in the 1630s—and to 20 million lbs by the 1670s. By then it was cultivated by African slaves rather than European indentured labourers. Each tropical staple was encouraged in its movement down the social scale by the dramatic fall in costs—as production in the Americas rapidly reduced the unit cost (despite heavy duties). In the process of social diffusion, the role of domestic servants was critical. Fashionable tastes were picked up by people labouring below stairs, who then took the habits back to their homes and communities, just as old shoes and damaged domestic artefacts were handed down from wealthy masters and mistresses to their servants.

Tea was central. Pepys first drank it in 1660; his wife tried it on the recommendation of an apothecary. Of the imports of the East India Company, tea in the 1670s formed a mere trickle, but by 1720 about 9 million lbs were landed—increasing to 37 million by the mid-century. And this occurred despite punitive duties (though helped by a thriving smuggling trade which supplied a substantial share of the British market for tea). Commentators were perplexed—and irritated—by the widespread popularity of tea:

The young and the old, the healthy and the infirm, and the superlatively rich, down to the vagabonds and beggars, drink this enchanting beverage when they are thirsty, and when they are not thirsty. It is the foolishness of folly.

Jonas Hanway was not alone in his annoyance that 'the labourer and mechanic will ape the lord'. And all of them seemed unhappy unless they were able to 'consume the product of the remote country of China'. The same was true at the upper end of the social spectrum. William Dutton wrote from Eton to his father:

I wish you would be so kind as to let me have Tea and Sugar here to drink in the afternoon, without which there is no such thing as keeping company with other boys of my standing.

Understandably then, the West India lobby actively encouraged the consumption of tea, because as tea consumption increased, so too did the demand for West Indian slave-grown sugar. Similarly, the massive importations of tableware, of cups and saucers, teapots and—significantly—sugar bowls, saw their diffusion throughout British society. By 1791 the East India Company had imported 215 million pieces of porcelain. British crockery manufacturers watched as the market was paved by imported goods. The East India Company secured the social high ground; the rest would follow. All hinged, once more, on the recently-cultivated taste for exotic imports. And that, in its turn, depended on colonial domination (for tropical cultivation) or strategic power over key shipping lanes. The most minute aspects of British social experience—propertied ladies at their fashionable tea-parties, labouring people saving pennies for the cheapest of adulterated tea—began to depend on the exercise of British economic and military power in distant parts of the globe.

It was a process which came full circle on board the ships, even lubricating the grim business of enslavement itself. The drink which eased the harsh existence of the common sailor was, of course, rum; and rum was produced by slaves in the West Indies. Slaves were also given rum on board, while slave ships headed for the African coast with consignments of pipes and tobacco, to pacify the Africans who would later be wedged below decks in their transatlantic misery. Tobacco was then used to fumigate the pestilential filth of the slave decks, when the slaves had been removed and sold on to their New World destinations.

British consumers, however, turned to their nearest shop for these products. The small shop-keepers were responsible, as Adam Smith noted, for 'breaking and dividing . . . rude and manufactured produce into such small parcels as suited the occasional demands of those who want them. . . .'

Among the tens of thousands of late eighteenth-century vendors purveying these fruits of Empire to an apparently insatiable British market was Ignatius Sancho. Born to an African mother on board a slave ship mid-Atlantic, Sancho passed through various jobs, enslaved and free, before finding his place as a domestic servant in London. Like so many others, he ran away, was later adopted by a wealthy patron, and encouraged in his natural intellectual interests. In 1773 he became a shopkeeper in Charles Street, Westminister, where he rubbed shoulders with the fashionable and the famous (including Charles James Fox—for whom Sancho voted in 1780). On his trade card, Sancho depicted American Indians and African slaves working to produce one of his main products—tobacco. And behind the counter, as Sancho talked to customers, his black wife, Anne, could be seen breaking down the sugar loaves and packaging sugar for customers. It was a scene rich in irony. Here were the descendants of African slaves, whose presence in Britain (like the contemporary black community itself) was entirely due to the Atlantic slave empire, making a livelihood by selling slave-grown produce to British customers.

In his free time, Sancho became an active letter-writer, mainly to the good and the great—but notably to Laurence Sterne. Sancho died in 1780 and later his letters were published, offering a powerful argument in the abolitionist attacks against the slave trade and slavery. Here was a vivid example of an African making good in ways which contemporary men of sensibility could recognise. Sancho—and a small band of other Africans living in Britain—could be held up as shining examples of African attainments in a country grown accustomed to thinking of the African as a mere beast of burden, fit onto to tap the economic potential of the Americas for the material benefits and pleasure of Europeans. The products of slave labour seemed so far removed from the horrors of slavery, that few contemporaries made the connection. Who so much as thought about the slaves, as they enjoyed their communal pipe in the local alehouse, indulged in witty repartee in a fashionable metropolitan coffee house, or haggled with a local shopkeeper in the village shop?

Gradually, even the slaves came to use, and need, the very goods they had been enslaved to produce. By the late eighteenth century, visitors to the slave colonies were curious to see social habits which were thought of as European—tea and coffee drinking, the lavish use of sugar, universal consumption of tobacco—replicating themselves among the slaves. Slaves began to acquire domestic items and social habits which helped to shape a more varied domestic environment. They became, themselves, consumers; of cotton and woollen goods, of pipes and pottery, of metalware, mosquito nets, of tools for the home and the garden. In 1788 it was even reported from St Ann in Jamaica that a clock had been stolen from a slave cabin. Whatever their use or significance, such acquisitions were made possible by the slaves' independent efforts.

Some whites began to worry, especially after the volcanic slave eruption in Haiti in the 1790s, that encouraging slaves to *acquire* material items—to become consumers—was the road to plantocratic ruin. Wherever we look on the fringes of British colonial settlement—on the slave coast of Africa, on the isolated plantations of Jamaica, or on the margins of settlement, where Europeans lived in uncomfortable proximity with North American Indians—local peoples had, by the late eighteenth century, become accustomed to acquiring and enjoying imported British goods.

Those goods were, by and large, part of that remarkably complex economic exchange which in turn sustained the British appetite for imported pleasures of their own. It is no accident that the most memorable of hostile American reactions to British fiscal policy in North America—the 'Boston Tea Party' of 1773—was an attack on imported tea. American patriots already appreciated that there was nothing more British than a cup of tea.

FOR FURTHER READING:

James Axtell, *Beyond 1492, Encounters in Colonial North America*, (Oxford University Press, 1992); Alfred W. Crosby, *The Columbian Exchange, Biological and Cultural Consequences of 1492*, (Greenwood Press, 1972); Sidney Mintz, *Sweetness and Power*, (Viking, 1985); James Walvin, *Fruits of Empire, Exotic Produce and British Taste, 1660–1800*, (London, 1996). For details of Ignatius Sancho, see exhibition (and associated book), *Ignatius Sancho: An African Man of Letters*, National Portrait Gallery, London, January 24th–May 11th 1997.

James Walvin is Professor of History at York University and author of Black Ivory: A History of British Slavery (*Fontana, 1994*).

"Thus in the beginning all the world was America"

—*John Locke, Second Treatise of Government*

by Edward Cline

THE TWO MEN most responsible for the founding of the United States never set foot in it, though their intellectual signatures are stamped on the Declaration of Independence as indelibly as any of the signers' flourishes: Aristotle and John Locke. It was the Greek philosopher who bequeathed to the West—via Thomas Acquinas—the fundamental rules of reason and logic and the means for men to determine their purpose for living on earth. It was Locke who applied reason to politics more thoroughly and convincingly than had any political thinker before him. And it was to Locke that the Founders turned for their most trenchant arguments in the conflict with Britain. As Dr. Harry Binswanger, a lecturer on Locke's importance in the history of ideas, has said, "As far as I can determine, Locke is the originator of individual rights."

Locke may even be granted indirect credit for the naming of Williamsburg—and even for its founding. It was during the reigns of Charles II and James II (the Restoration) that he wrote his most important works in response to the struggles between Parliament and the Stuarts, which culminated in 1688 with the abdication and flight of James II and with the Convention Parliament's welcome of William and Mary as regents of England, Scotland, Ireland, and France in 1689. The College of William and Mary, founded in 1693, was named in their honor. (Mary died in 1694, thus sparing the town fathers, in 1699, the task of devising what could only have been an awkward compound name for the new

capital.) Locke's *Two Treatises of Government* and *A Letter concerning Toleration,* written between 1680 and 1685, contributed at least part of the intellectual basis for that "Glorious Revolution." They were to have a more profound influence on the thinking of another generation of revolutionaries.

Almost 100 years later, Samuel Adams wrote to a friend: "Mr. Locke has often been quoted in the present dispute between Britain and her colonies, and very much to our purpose. His reasoning is so forcible, that no one has even attempted to confute it." Thomas Jefferson displayed the portraits of Isaac Newton, Francis Bacon, and Locke on the walls of his Monticello home. In a letter to Benjamin Rush, he wrote that these "were my trinity of the three greatest men the world had ever produced." Lockean phraseology and style of expression color many of the most eloquent statements in the Declaration, which Jefferson composed.

POLITICS HAS DOMINATED history books and commanded men's first concerns because it is the most immediate, tangible application of philosophical inquiry; the effect of a tax, a law, or an injustice is more obvious and personal than that of a proposition, a syllogism, or an abstract deduction in metaphysics or epistemology, even though the latter two fields can determine the ultimate efficacy or tragedy of any political system. Locke lived, thought, and wrote in the tempestuous world of 17th-century England and for-

mulated a political philosophy that would accelerate the pace of men's progress from abject deference and servility to kings and bishops to valuing life, liberty, and property as norms to be championed and defended. Locke began his thinking life as a "conservative" and ended it as a "radical," in both political theory and epistemology, thanks to his commitment to truth, which made possible his intellectual honesty. "[He] who has raised himself above the Alms-Basket, and not content to live lazily on scraps of begg'd Opinions, sets his own Thoughts on work, to find and follow Truth," he observed in "The Epistle to the Reader" of *An Essay concerning Human Understanding.*

Locke did not regard himself as a formal philosopher nor even much of an innovator in the realm of ideas. This was not false modesty but an integral part of his character. "There was an introverted, valetudinarian component in Locke's nature," writes Peter H. Nidditch, editor of one edition of the *Essay.* "He was a careful, cautious man possessed of a good sense of business and method." Carefulness and caution were Locke's bywords, inculcated in him in the often perilous times of the Civil War, Cromwell's Commonwealth and Protectorate, and the Restoration.

LOCKE WAS, if not a philosopher, then an intellectual. As Adam Smith did in the field of economics nearly a century later, he drew together all the disparate threads of thought on rights, liberty, and property

From *Colonial Williamsburg,* April/May 1999, pp. 29-35. © 1999 by the Colonial Williamsburg Foundation. Reprinted by permission.

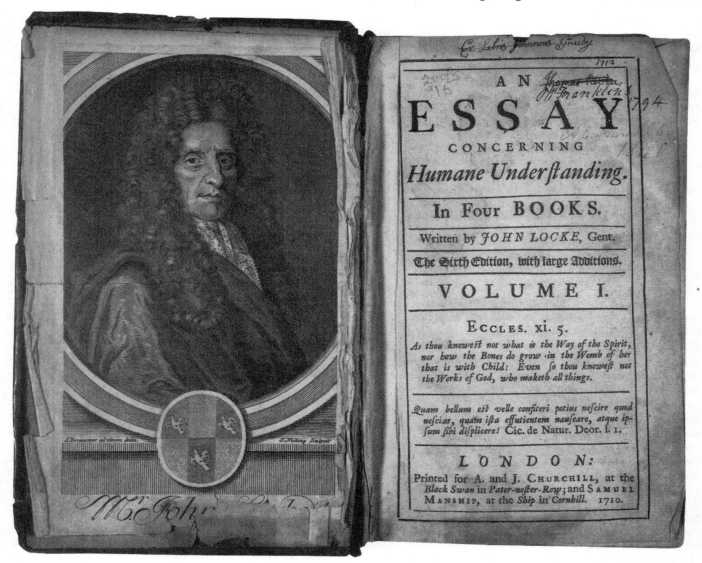

In his lifetime, Locke was prudently wary of admitting authorship of the Two Treatises *and his* Letter concerning Toleration. *Philosophical speculation, however, was safe enough.*

that preceded him—by a legion of thinkers who included James Harrington, John Milton, Henry Neville, John Hampden, to name but a few—and weaved the best of them into a single, comprehensible fabric in the *Two Treatises*. Like the Founders, he held that reason or rationality was men's only means of living alone or in society, and that this attribute of men was as much "endowed by their creator" as were certain unalienable rights. The attempt by a criminal or a magistrate to force man to think or act against his own reason was a violation of the "law of nature." Reason was the antithesis of "innate" ideas, which Locke argued in his *Essay* could not exist, thus robbing the advocates of absolute monarchy of a key

tenet of their arguments. It could be argued that the *Essay* and the *Two Treatises* are affirmations of and companions to each other. By the time the Founders were impelled to compose thoughtful rebuttals to king and Parliament, Locke's works were near-gospel in the colonies. Hardly a library existed—private or college—in 18th-century colonial America that did not boast at least one title by Locke. He had made nearly everything "self-evident."

LOCKE'S IMPORTANCE to the Founders cannot be appreciated without first painting a miniature of his times. As the sun of the Enlightenment slowly burned off the heavy, clinging fog of the Medieval Age, men began

to see the possible in all realms of human thought and action, particularly in politics. They were emerging from the miasma of edict- and sword-enforced ignorance, and they were dazzled. Obstructing their way, or waiting in doctrinal ambushes to pounce on the least hint of blasphemy or treason, were the forces of the Medievalists—or their royalist or secular descendants, whose notion of a stable polity was a monarch wielding absolute, unquestioned dominion over his realm, with a bishop on his right hand ready to field any questions he himself could not answer.

The political fact of Locke's time was that religion was inextricably tied to politics. Locke did not separate the two realms, but he laid the groundwork for it to be accomplished later. To question the political status quo, however, was to question religious orthodoxy—and vice versa.

The genesis of this alliance in Britain was the English Reformation, precipitated by Henry VIII's break with the Roman Catholic Church over his marriage to Anne Boleyn and the establishment of the Church of England in 1534. Leap ahead over nearly a hundred years of roiling English history to the abrupt transition from the Tudor era to that of the Stuarts, marked by the machinations of James I and Charles I to amass more money, power, and influence than Parliament wished to grant them.

There were two civil wars, the first between the Roundheads and Cavaliers, the second between a Presbyterian Parliament and the Independent army of Oliver Cromwell. Cromwell's own brand of "republicanism" began with Pride's Purge of Presbyterians from Parliament by the army (Algernon Sidney refused to vacate his seat, until a soldier put a hand on his shoulder) and the gradual establishment of a dictatorship that nominated and controlled a complaisant "Bare-bones" Parliament. It was Cromwell's Rump Parliament that passed the first Navigation Act in October 1651.

Religious passions moved most of these events. Royal or parliamentary toleration of Catholics, Nonconformists—this time the outlawed Anglicans or Episcopalians—Jews, or Dissenters was viewed as a political act fraught with danger. Catholicism in particular was anathema to most Protestant Englishmen, whatever their sectarian suasion, whether they were well-read lords or gentry, or illiterate publicans or chimney sweeps; they had only to nod across the Channel to France or Spain to prove the consequences of a Catholic monarchy. Papist sympathies from any quarter were regarded as cryptic designs on the liberties and privileges of Englishmen and Parliament. This animus, based partly on bigotry but mostly on demonstrable fact in England's own history and on events on the Continent, would survive well into the 19th century.

Before Locke published his *Two Treatises,* those who championed rights—to life, liberty, and property—floundered on the shoals of custom, precedent, tradition, or convention. Or on Scripture, which the enemies of liberty were as adept in employing as their opponents. Some of the most eloquent and incisive statements in favor of liberty were recorded in the Army Debates of 1647–49, conducted while a Puritan Parliament negotiated with a stubborn Charles I. Both sides of the issues—which included toleration, freedom of conscience, and security of property—brandished their Bibles (ironically, the King James Version, completed in 1611) and assailed each other with book, chapter, and verse in support of myriad positions, accusations, and compromises.

But the revolutionaries had no Locke to show them the way out of the intractable dilemma. When Cromwell died in 1658, the "republic" collapsed tiredly on its own contradictions and for lack of a common moral base. The Rump Parliament invited Charles II—whose father had been beheaded in 1649—to resume the throne. Countless Puritans rushed to conform to the Anglican Church. If they could not agree on a moral base, at least England would have a moral authority.

But history was to repeat itself less than 30 years later.

ENTER JOHN LOCKE, philosopher. Most portraits of him stare intensely back at the viewer, challenging one to be as thoughtful or serious as he, or daring one to be fatuous or insincere. In the first instance, one would gain a friend, even if he disagreed with you; in the second, one would gain a disdainful enemy or, worse, an enemy who would dismiss you and never think of you again. Locke was a retiring man who grew to believe that ideas had a more profound effect on men's actions, lives, and fates than bullets. He was a dark, thin, plainly-dressed man who preferred quiet, civil conversation to boisterous company. Once he broke up a card game by taking out his notebook and proposing to record the verities of the players.

Locke was a shrewd manager of his money and died a rich man. Even in the most unsettling periods of his life, he kept exact accounts of his financial dealings. He preferred country life to life in London, chiefly because prolonged stays in the city aggravated his asthmatic cough—as did the stress of political crises. Travel for his health, coinciding often with Restoration turmoil, more than once saved his life.

Locke was born in August 1632 and raised in the bucolic setting of rural Somerset near Bristol. He was the son of John Locke, Senior, clerk to the justice of the peace in the parish of Chew Magna. The father served in the Civil War as captain of a troop of horse with the Parliamentarians, and he was also an attorney for the commander of that unit, Alexander Popham. An influential Presbyterian, Popham later arranged to send young Locke to Westminster School in London in 1646.

Raised in a Calvinist household, Locke spent the next six years in this royalist and largely high-church school, mastering Greek and Latin by way of Cicero, Livy, Plutarch, and other classical authors. Charles I was executed in Whitehall Palace Yard, a stone's throw from the school. It is tempting to imagine that Locke witnessed the event. But the school's headmaster was a staunch royalist and opponent of Cromwell. On that somber January 30, the student body was made to pray all day for the tried and convicted king's soul, and it is doubtful that any student was permitted to venture outside Westminster Abbey's enclosure.

It was not until Locke went to Christ Church at Oxford in 1652 that his reading began to venture beyond the college's scholastic curriculum of rhetoric, logic, grammar, moral philosophy, and more classical studies. Oxford had been purged of its royalist faculty and was under firm Calvinist control. As an undergraduate, Locke was obliged to attend two sermons a day and to pray every night with his tutor. His first published work was an ode to Cromwell included in a book of poems issued by the college in 1655. Five years later he would pen, in a similar volume, a poem praising Charles II on the occasion of the restored Stuart's entrance into London.

Locke was made a Fellow of Christ Church the year Cromwell died and would continue his Oxford association until he was ordered expelled in 1684 by Charles II for his suspected role in the Rye House Plot to assassinate the king. Locke had welcomed the Stuart's return, if only because it brought an end to the dour, stifling regime of the Puritans. When a lecturer in Greek, rhetoric, and moral philosophy, he wrote the *Two Tracts on Government,* in which he asserted that a "magistrate"—or a sovereign—had every right to impose conformity on his subjects; since the rituals and times and places of worship were "indifferent," there was no good reason for a subject to resist conformity, as the object of worship was universal. Locke did not believe, at that time, that civil upheaval was justified over what he asserted were picayune differences in the style and content of religious services.

In his future *Two Treatises* and *A Letter concerning Toleration,* Locke was to advance the opposite of this position: That a magistrate's power to impose conformity in "indifferent" matters was not only morally wrong but accomplished little but fraudulent uniformity. Force could not compel a man to be any more or less devoted to his beliefs. The object of worship, God, Locke would maintain, was too important to be the subject of insincerity. Men must find their own way according to their own lights. He would extend this line of reasoning to secular or civil matters. At the time, though, it would not be inaccurate to say that early in his career, Locke was as much a skeptic as was Thomas Hobbes, whose major work, *Leviathan,* he undoubtably read and must have agreed that "sovereign power is not so hurtful as the want of it."

Like many other lukewarm Calvinists then, Locke conformed to the Anglican Church at the Restoration. It was an expedient action and cost him nothing of his convictions; the ceremonies were indifferent." But in the second year of his fellowship, he wrote a friend that "Phansye" ruled the world, and he wondered "where is that great Diana . . . Reason?" He would find it, at first, at Oxford.

Contributing to the development of his later views were Locke's friendships with Robert Boyle (of Boyle's Law fame) and other prominent British empiricists of the time, many of whom would become charter members of the Royal Society of London for the Improving of Natural Knowledge. Boyle, a noted chemist, physicist, and essayist on theological issues, had declined many lucrative clerical appointments to devote himself to scientific investigation and experimentation. This unconventional but respected thinker helped to influence Locke's unconventional decision not to follow the path of most other Christ Church Fellows and take orders for the Church of England, but instead to pursue the study of medicine. Although he never took a medical course and pursued his studies independently, he attained a bachelor's degree in medicine in 1674. His knowledge of the sub-

ject, together with the apparent efficacy of his advice to others on their health, were to garner him a reputation as a physician second only to his reputation as a political theorist.

In 1663, Locke wrote a series of *Essays on the Law of Nature,* which discuss the reality-based ethics he claimed ought to govern the actions of rational men. These *Essays* were a kind of overture to the *Two Treatises* and the *Essay concerning Human Understanding,* as they reveal the development and direction of his thinking. At the same time, he practiced medicine with a Dr. David Thomas of London, a close friend, until 1666.

As a respite from his lecturing duties at Oxford, Locke went abroad in 1664 as secretary to Sir Walter Vane, Charles II's envoy to Frederick William, the Great Elector of Brandenburg. In a letter to John Strachy, a boyhood friend, Locke described Christmas visits to several churches near Cleve, including Catholic ones, and expressed pleasant surprise that so many religious sects could reside peacefully in one town. "I have not met with any so good-natured people, or so civil, as the Catholic priests," he wrote. These were not the ogres he had expected to encounter. His observations abroad would lead him to compose and publish anonymously in 1689 *A Letter concerning Toleration,* perhaps the most important and effective argument for the separation of church and state ever written.

Locke returned from the diplomatic mission in May 1666 and resumed his duties and studies at Christ Church. In July he received a letter from Dr. Thomas, asking him to give medical advice to Anthony Ashley Cooper—later the first earl of Shaftesbury—who was in Oxford to drink the supposedly healthy waters of nearby Astrop. Lord Ashley had fought with the Royalists in the Civil War, then in 1643 went over to the Roundheads and had been a member of Cromwell's Council of State. He was known to his contemporaries, writes Lockean scholar Richard Ashcraft, to be "opposed to religious persecution in general and to popery in particular, and as an advocate of the rights of Dissenters and of Parliament"—that is, he argued in the House of Lords and among friends and idealogues against state-enforced Catholicism, absolute monarchy, and the theory of the divine right of kings. Locke said Shaftesbury was "a

vigorous and indefatigable champion of civil and ecclesiastical liberty."

THE TWO MEN formed such a warm friendship that Locke moved into Shaftesbury's London household the next year and acted as his personal physician and confidential advisor. In 1668 he performed a successful operation on his patron's abscessed liver, saving Shaftesbury's life and earning his constant gratitude.

Shaftesbury was the most important member of the Lords Proprietors of Carolina and appointed Locke secretary of that organization. When it drafted a new constitution for the colony, the two men coauthored a document that provided for an elective assembly and religious freedom. Shaftesbury was named Lord High Chancellor in November 1672, and he subsequently made Locke secretary for the Presentation of Benefices and a year later secretary to the Council of Trade and Plantations.

This last office introduced Locke to the realm of finance and economics; and what he learned during his year-and-a-half-tenure enabled him to offer intelligent advice to Parliament, as it debated the Coinage Act of 1696. In his pamphlet *Some Considerations of the Consequences of the Lowering of Interest and Raising the Value of Money,* Locke argued that laws which lowered interest rates on private loans in favor of debtors amounted to theft. And although he was an original subscriber to the Bank of England (for £500, in 1694), Locke wrote that "I cannot but think a monopoly of money by the bank, as well as a monopoly of merchandising by the Act of Navigation, must prove a great prejudice to the trade of the nation."

While Locke was beginning to take and develop copious notes for his *Essay concerning Human Understanding*—in 1671, after a meeting with a small group of friends who could not agree on why they knew what they knew—the match was struck that would lead to a major political conflagration. Shaftesbury, an implacable advocate of toleration, had been influential in moving Charles II to proclaim, in March 1672, the Declaration of Indulgence, whose purpose was to free Nonconformists and Catholics from political and religious restrictions. Parliament responded by forcing the king to withdraw it, on the rationale that such an edict did not lay within proper royal power. The next year brought the revelation that James, the duke of York and the king's brother, had already converted to Catholicism. Little more than a year before, Charles had signed a secret "first" Treaty of Dover with France; among its provisions was an agreement that should Charles II convert to Catholicism, Louis XIV would give him £200,000 a year for his wars with Spain and Holland and 6,000 troops in the event of an English insurrection against Charles's conversion.

Shaftesbury, who had helped negotiate the "second" Treaty of Dover, a mere pact of alliance with France, now saw the ulterior motive behind the Declaration and began balking at the king's policies. He was dismissed as chancellor in November 1673 and a few months later imprisoned in the Tower of London for a year for having opposed the king and his court party. When he was released, he became the leader of the opposition to the king.

When his term as secretary to the Council of Trade expired (or was terminated), Locke departed for France on a four-year sojourn, ostensibly for his health, which had always been precarious. Or, as some maintain, he was deeply involved in anti-court intrigues in this period—1675–79—and had decided to get out of harm's way. Locke's journals are a record of his travels, medical and scientific observations, and meetings with many of France's intellectual lights. It is plausible that he had a hand in the composition of the anonymously published *A Letter from a Person of Quality to His Friend in the Country,* a pamphlet attributed to Shaftesbury, which suggested a conspiracy by the king, the church, and certain government ministers to extend royal powers and reduce Parliament and the church to money-raising devices for the king. Locke may have left for France if he believed he was suspected of having authored the pamphlet, condemned and burned in November 1675; Locke left in December.

He returned from France in April 1679 in the time to witness the unfolding of the Exclusion Crisis—and undoubtedly contribute to it. After a brief stop at Oxford, he moved back into Shaftesbury's household in London, again as the peer's physician and advisor. In May the Scottish Covenanters rebelled against the crown and the repressive measures of John Maitland, the duke of

Lauderdale and Charles's secretary of state for Scottish affairs. The revolt was eventually put down by James Scott, the duke of Monmouth and Charles's natural son.

Shaftesbury, now a member of the king's new Privy Council, not only pushed through Parliament the landmark Habeas Corpus Act but sponsored a succession of exclusion bills, whose aim was to prevent Charles's Catholic brother from inheriting the throne. Charles dissolved two Parliaments for their attempts to get the bills passed. In this period the opposition "country" party and the pro-monarchy "court" party began to coalesce into what would become known as the "Whig" and "Tory" parties—Scottish and Irish terms of derision respectively for "horse drover" and "outlaw."

In March 1681, Charles opened the third and last Exclusion Parliament; he dissolved it after eight days, when it would not do his bidding. His opponents now grasped that the king wished to rule without a legislature. In July a Shaftesbury supporter, Stephen College, was arrested for having entertained exclusion bill supporters with a "cartoon" depicting Charles's tyranny and his removal by Parliament. When a London jury rejected the charges of treason against him, the crown moved his trial to Oxford, where he was convicted and executed. Shaftesbury was arrested for high treason and again put into the Tower. The crown, reading his seized papers, saw that he was at the center of an "association" or confederacy. Not only did it oppose Charles and his brother, but it advocated the subordination of the throne to Parliament and the resort to a force of arms to accomplish it.

This was a separate conspiracy from the Rye House Plot, and the duke of Monmouth, Lords Russell, Grey, and Essex, and Algernon Sidney were arrested in connection with it. Shaftesbury was acquitted and released from the Tower at the end of the year but knew that he could be rearrested at any time. Subsequently, Charles revoked the charters of the City of London and other corporations and had them rewritten to purge the courts and elective offices of Whig juries and the Whig sheriffs who empaneled them; he replaced them with Catholics, Tories, and other pro-monarchy men. The trials and executions continued with a vengeance. Essex committed suicide, the duke of Mon-

mouth was pardoned and fled to Holland, and Lord William Russell was beheaded. Algernon Sidney, who knew Shaftesbury but not Locke, long ago had refused to leave his seat in Parliament when Cromwell dissolved the Rump in 1653. Now he was tried for treason with a known liar as the sole witness to his crime; the prosecution needed two witness for a conviction. The court turned to Sidney's *Discourses on Government,* finished in prison, and argued that the anti-monarchy pro-liberty tract was proof of a conspiracy. Like Stephen College, Sidney was convicted on what he had written, not what he had done. On the scaffold, he refused to recant his claim that resistance to tyranny was a right, and he was beheaded in November 1683.

Locke, busy fighting the battle of ideas, composed in this period the *Two Treatises of Government.* For a long time scholars believed they were written as an apologia for the Glorious Revolution of 1688. A Lockean scholar, Peter Laslett, in 1960 proved that Locke wrote the essay chiefly in response to the events of 1679–83. Shaftesbury's "association" manifesto was a watered-down version of the *Two Treatises* and not nearly as radical as Locke's work. The *Second Treatise* especially was part answer to the growing despotism of Charles and part answer to a pro-monarchy tract written in 1631, Sir Robert Filmer's *Patriacha,* trotted out in 1680 by Tory idealogues to counter numerous Whig publications. Filmer's fundamental premise was that "men are not naturally free" but that the sovereign was. Locke's fundamental premise was that "every man has a property in his own person. This nobody has any right to but himself." *Nobody* included sovereigns and other men, and a man whose life or property was threatened by force had a right to resist, even as far as armed rebellion—a "treasonous" notion.

Shaftesbury had fled England; he died in Holland in January 1683. Locke probably had already finished the *Two Treatises* before Sidney was executed. He knew most of the men implicated in the Rye House Plot. At Oxford University, all books asserting the right of resistance to tyranny were burned. Watching the course of events, Locke must have concluded that his days as a free man were numbered. After hastily arranging his private affairs, he sailed for Holland and settled in Amsterdam in

September 1683. He would not see England again until he accompanied Princess Mary, wife of William of Orange, to Greenwich in February 1689. William and Mary were proclaimed king and queen the day after his return.

During his five and a half years of exile, Locke lived in Amsterdam, Rotterdam, and Utrecht. The Dutch province contained such a large number of English expatriates that Amsterdam was often called "little London." There were enough of them so that not only did Locke feel at home, but his friends could establish a network of "safe" houses for him to move between to elude the prying eyes of Charles II's spies and later James II's. Kidnapping and murder by the two kings' agents were distinct possibilities. Charles had Locke expelled from Oxford, which itself summoned Locke to return to answer charges of libel, and James II included his name in a list of 85 men to be extradited from Holland to stand trial. Charles died in February 1685, converting to Catholicism on his deathbed. The duke of Monmouth's subsequent rebellion against the accession of James II to the throne was crushed, and Monmouth was beheaded. Judge George Jeffreys embarked upon the Bloody Assizes, sentencing 200 men to death and 800 to slavery in the West Indies.

In his exile, Locke completed the *Essay, A Letter concerning Toleration,* and *Some Thoughts concerning Education.* In addition to these and other minor works, he must have been in correspondence with those who would orchestrate the Glorious Revolution. His ideas influenced the content and purpose of the Declaration of Rights, issued by the Convention Parliament of 1689–90. The Declaration, in effect, set the terms of rule accepted by William and Mary that severely curtailed a sovereign's power over the national purse, the courts, and legislation. The Act of Settlement of 1701 underscored the Declaration in addition to mandating a protestant succession.

ON HIS RETURN to England, Locke set about the publication of his works. His *Essay* and *Educa-tion* were published under his own name. The *Two Treatises* and *Toleration,* including two later essays on toleration, however, were published anonymously. Whether this was from modesty or from fear of reprisal by the still powerful Tories has been a subject of speculation; Locke would admit his authorship only in his will, in which he directed that his name appear under the titles of future editions of these works.

While he was in exile, Locke, with grave panache, declined offers from friends to plead on his behalf to the king for a pardon, saying that he did not think he had committed any action for which he needed to be pardoned. With equal verve, he declined King William's offer in 1689 of the ambassadorship to the Elector of Brandenburg on the grounds of his health and his inexperience in diplomatic affairs, adding that he would be at a disadvantage for being "the soberest man in the Kingdom"; he had abstained from liquor most of his life. He did accept the post of commissioner of appeals in excise and later served as a commissioner on the Board of Trade until 1700. These positions allowed him to stay home and oversee the publication of his works. His powers of persuasion influenced the government's coinage policies, and his connections in Parliament and the book trade convinced Parliament to let the ancient Licensing Act lapse without renewal in 1695, thus ending press censorship and the Stationers Guild's monopoly on bookprinting.

His last major conflict was over *The Reasonableness of Christianity,* published in 1695. It was furiously assailed by theological authorities, and Locke was embroiled in the controversy until his death. "Locke's version of Christianity," writes Lockean scholar David Wootton, "appeared to leave no place for the doctrines of original sin or the Trinity. Its stress upon reason seemed to make revealed truth subject to human judgement."

Locke, friends with many of the prominent men of his age, corresponded with such figures as William Penn, James Blair, and Isaac Newton. But there was only one woman in his life. He spent his last years as a permanent guest of Sir Francis and Lady Masham, in Oates, Essex. Lady Masham, whom he had met in 1681 when she was Damaris Cudworth, seemed to be his intellectual equal—and an early, unrequited romantic interest. She was the daughter of Ralph Cudworth, a noted Cambridge philosopher. Locke had converted her from her father's Platonism to his own Aristotelianism. Perhaps she was the only person whose agreement he treasured.

He was sitting in a chair at Oates, listening to her read from the Psalms, when he died quietly in October 1704.

WITHOUT LOCKE, there likely would have been no American Revolution; or, if there had been one, it would have suffered the fate of the English republic of the mid-17th century and collapsed into a heap of grand but unconnected and unsupportable ideas. But even though Locke sits at his age's pinnacle of political thinkers who championed life, liberty, and happiness, neither he nor his predecessors and contemporaries, nor even many who followed him, could imagine a politics without a monarch. The Founders were descendants of colonists who had carved a civilization out of a wilderness without the guidance of kings, bishops, or parliaments; in fact, had accomplished that feat despite their hindrances and obstructions. Thus, the Founders could imagine a politics without a monarch, without royal prerogatives, without parliamentary privileges, and insist, among many other things, upon a separation of church and state. To their credit, they built upon Locke's thought, and more than once they acknowledged their debt to him.

Ed Cline, *novelist and essayist, has probed Jefferson the bibliosavant for this journal, as well as Patrick Henry, Anthony Wayne, Edmund Pendleton, and (in the Autumn 1997 issue) Samuel Johnson.*

Brazil's African Legacy

John Geipel *on how the enforced diaspora of the slave trade shaped South America's largest nation.*

It was the seventeenth-century Jesuit preacher and missionary, Frei Antônio Vieira, who said that Brazil had 'the body of America and the soul of Africa' and this description continues, to some extent, to hold true. In Vieira's day, Africans and their offspring—black and mulatto, slave and free—far outnumbered Europeans in Portugal's South American colony.

Three centuries on, although the African element in the population is much diluted, Brazil's economic, demographic, genetic and cultural debt to Africa remains inestimable. From the colony's very infancy in the early sixteenth century, the contribution of Africa to the population and development of Brazil has been prodigious and pervasive and few aspects of Brazilian society and civilisation have remained untouched by its influence.

Over the four centuries of Portuguese involvement in the Atlantic slave trade, an estimated 10 to 15 million Africans were transported to the European colonies in the Americas. Of these, over 3.5 million were taken to Brazil, many arriving after the growth of the coffee industry in the mid-nineteenth century. Even after the Atlantic slave trade to Brazil was declared illegal in 1850, contraband 'Black Gold' continued to be smuggled across the ocean.

The first Africans were herded ashore in north-east Brazil in the year 1538. The decision to exploit imported and unpaid black labour had been prompted partly in response to a Papal Bull of 1537, which forbade the enslavement of the indigenous 'Indians' (though this was soon to be totally disregarded), and partly because the African's more robust constitution, greater immunity to the white man's diseases and conditioning to hard, physical work in a tropical environment made him more suitable than the native as potential slave material. Besides, the Portuguese were long familiar with the African in the role of chattel.

The slave trade and the consequent miscegenation between Portuguese and black Africans had begun in Europe over half a century before Cabral's discovery of Brazil in 1500. Indeed, the mingling of the two peoples had begun centuries earlier—with the Carthaginians, the Romans and the Moors, all of whom brought large contingents of slaves, servants and mercenaries from sub-Saharan Africa to the Iberian peninsula. Systematic exploitation of an unpaid African labour force by the Portuguese, however, began in earnest in the mid-fifteenth century, when slaves from Guinea were transported to the Alentejo and the Algarve and to the sugar mills of Madeira. This traffic reached such a scale that, by the turn of the sixteenth century, one in ten of the inhabitants of such towns as évora was of African descent, while Lisbon, was one of several cities with an African quarter.

The bulk importation of African slaves to Brazil thus perpetuated a tradition already deeply rooted in Portugal. The blood of Africa ran in the veins of many Portuguese colonial dynasties. As Gilberto Freyre (the sociologist who, writing in the 1930s and 40s, did so much to reconstruct the relationship between master and slave in colonial Brazil) suggests, the affection displayed by many Brazilian planters to their black chattels may be attributed to an ingrained respect for 'Gente de Cor' (People of Colour) dating back to the time of the Moors.

Compared with the Visigoths who had preceded them as overlords of Iberia, the Moors—themselves of hybrid Afro-Asiatic stock—were racially colourblind and did not discriminate against other monotheists ('People of the Book', meaning Christians and Jews) on the basis of ethnic origin or pigmentation. Moreover, as a consequence of five centuries of Arab occupation of their former homeland, the Portuguese in Brazil were long familiar with the Islamic religion practised by many of their African slaves.

From the 1580s, the importation of Africans to Brazil increased dramatically. After the initial expansion of the sugar industry, blacks soon constituted over two-thirds of the population of the north-east. A century later, the discovery of gold in Minas Gerais further increased the demand for slave labour. Meanwhile, in the *sertão* (hinterland) of the north-east, *Pretos* (blacks), *Pardos* (mulattos) and *Cafuzos* (Afro-Indian halfbreeds) formed the majority population of what would become the state of Piauí, where the traditional ranching skills of such West African pastoralists as the Fulani played a prominent role in the development of the region's nascent cattle industry.

Despite the importance to Brazil's economy of African mineworkers, stockmen, stevedores and domestics, by the mid-eighteenth century these groups were vastly outnumbered by the fieldhands working the *engenhos* or sugar mills. At the height of the sugar boom, 40 per cent of Brazil's slave population was involved in the cultivation of the cane. It was this group, largely composed of Bantu tribesmen obtained in sub-equatorial Africa, which endured the most severe and inhumane conditions—but which also contributed most to the popular culture of Brazil.

By contrast, in the urban centres, a burgeoning class of skilled black and mulatto artisans was well established by the 1750s: tailors, coopers, boilermakers, joiners, shipwrights, caulkers, stonemasons, blacksmiths and bakers. Many of these were 'forros' freedmen who had obtained manumission either by purchase (often through mutual-aid societies, some of which were organised on the basis of tribal affiliation), by completion of contract, or by the munificence of a liberal master. Many of these trades had long been practised in Africa, and black craftsmen were able to complement European techniques with those of their own traditions.

By the start of the sixteenth century, Brazil's population of African birth or descent already topped 20,000, with Africans being imported at a rate of 8,000 per year and making up 70 per cent of the labour force. The Portuguese, in common with the rival Western European slaving nations, did not confine their activities to particular parts of the African continent, but ranged far and wide in their insatiable quest for 'Ebony Flesh'. By Vieira's time, the bulk of the slaves destined for Brazil were obtained in the Senegambian region, from where many were 'processed' on the Cape Verde archipelago before being shipped across the Atlantic in hulks known mordantly as 'tumbeiros' (hearses), for as much as half their human cargo would frequently perish during the ocean crossing.

In the seventeenth century, the supply of slaves came mainly from Angola and the 'Contra Costa' (Indian Ocean coast) of Africa, including Madagascar, as far north as Zanzibar, where Portuguese slaving activities overlapped and competed with those of the Arabs. For a century and a half following the Portuguese recovery of Luanda from the Dutch in 1648, Angola provided an inexhaustible reservoir of human merchandise. During the eighteenth century, 70 per cent of the slaves shipped to Brazil were obtained in Angola; indeed, so massive was the human haemorrhage from its shores that large areas of the country remained virtually depopulated for generations.

Unlike the more urbanised Guinea (or 'Sudanese') blacks, who were highly valued as house servants, the bulk of the Bantu obtained in Angola and Mozambique were put to work on the *fazendas* (plantations) of Brazil. It was here that an Angolan Bantu language, Kimbundu, became the lingua franca of the fazendas and missionaries were obliged to learn this language in order to catechise the newly arrived African *boçais*—an opprobrious name similar in sense to the North American 'Guineabird' or 'Salt-water Nigger'.

The opening up of the diamond deposits in the early eighteenth century increased the demand for blacks skilled in the techniques of prospecting, metallurgy and extraction. Many of these Africans were obtained in the Gold Coast (Ghana) and Dahomey (Benin) region of Guinea; known collectively as 'Minas' (from the fort of El Mina from which the majority were shipped out). They were often more familiar with mining methods than their masters and their contribution to the economy of both Portugal and Brazil was incalculable.

At the start of the Brazilian Empire in 1822, a demographic survey revealed that Gente de Cor constituted over two thirds of Brazil's total population—20 per cent of which still had slave status. The traffic of slaves was at its most intense between 1825–1850; during the nineteenth century, some 32 per cent of the total number of Africans imported since the start of the trade arrived in Brazil. It was these comparative late-comers who were to leave their indelible imprint on the culture of their new home.

During the eighteenth and nineteenth centuries, with the undiminished demand for unpaid labour, the Slave Coast of Nigeria became the primary source—whence the late survival in Brazil of traditions rooted in the culture of the Yoruba and the Fon (better known in Brazil by their alternative African nicknames, Nagô and Gegê).

Many of the slaves were purchased as war captives from neighbouring tribes—often after they had been deliberately incited by Europeans to fight one another; others were criminals, debtors or outcasts; while many, such as the hereditary caste of slaves of the Yoruba, already had slave status in their native community. The actual purchase was made, not by the *negreiros* or traders themselves, but by intermediaries, either white '*degredados*' (exiled criminals) who had 'gone native' or half-castes who were themselves the slaves of Portuguese planters. In Angola, after its recovery from the Dutch the Portuguese established a Chartered Colony, which despatched conquistadores to levy feudal dues in the form of slaves for export from the tribal chiefs of the interior.

Unlike some of the Spanish-American colonies, such as Cuba and Colom-

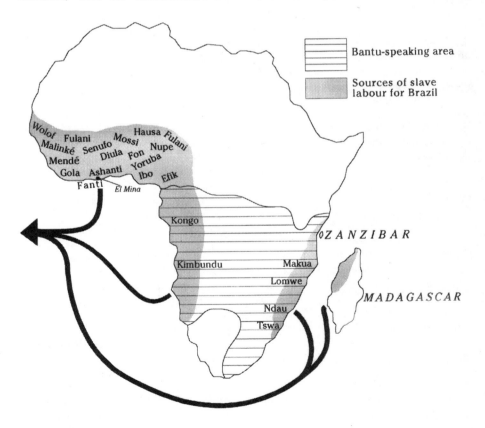

Enforced exodus: this map shows the main tribal groupings from which the slaves and others were drawn in the transatlantic crossings to Brazil.

bia, where detailed records of the slave trade were preserved, much of the documentary evidence of the Brazilian trade was destroyed in 1891, when the liberal Republican minister and abolitionist from Baía, Rui Barbosa, ordered it to be consigned to the flames. However, statistics for the period 1817–70, made by British consuls in the major ports of Brazil, were retained in the archives of the British Foreign Office. These help to identify the general geographical—if not the specific tribal—origins of the slaves imported throughout much of the nineteenth century; while the investigations conducted earlier this century by the anthropologist, Raimundo Nina Rodrigues and his disciple, Artur Ramos, filled in many details of the African background on the basis of identifiable tribal traditions surviving in Brazilian popular culture.

One of the first to stress the importance of acknowledging and evaluating the African contribution to the economy and civilisation of Brazil was the German naturalist, Karl Friedrich Philipp von Martins, whose prize-winning essay on this hitherto neglected subject was published in 1844. This need was also emphasised by the literary critic, Sílvio Romero, who concluded that: 'We owe much more to the Negro than to the Indian; he entered into all aspects of our development', and by such influential commentators as Afonso Celso and the black historian, Manuel Querino, whose many publications stimulated further research into the nation's African heritage.

The survival of African cultural traditions in Brazil must be attributed both to the direct links with the mother continent, which were maintained until the late nineteenth century, and to the fact that, as mortality was high and fertility low among the slave population, levels of imported Africans remained much higher, and for much longer, than in English-speaking North America. In contrast to Protestant Anglo-America, where slaves of similar tribal origin were deliberately kept apart in order to make communication—and potential insurrection—more difficult, the Catholic colonial countries did not enforce this segregation policy so that African tribal identities were able to survive relatively intact.

Maintenance of African cultural traditions in Brazil was also made possible by the establishment there of *quilombos,* communities of maroons or runaway slaves located in the more inaccessible parts of the sertão. The earliest of these were already in existence by the mid-seventeenth century. During the disruptions caused by the thirty years of Dutch occupation of north-east Brazil (1624–54), when the Portuguese struggled to dislodge the interlopers, many more quilombos were founded in the Brazilian interior—this where the frequent occurrence of African place-names testifies to their wide distribution. Some of these 'Black Republics' comprised several *mocambos* or townships, each under the control of an African-style chieftain. The most renowned was Palmares, in the state of Alagoas, the so-called 'Black Troy', which held out for over fifty years until its final surrender to the Portuguese in 1697, when the paramount chief, Zumbi, and his followers committed mass suicide rather than succumb to slavery. Palmares was one of the last of the quilombos to succumb to the relentless wars of attrition waged by the colonial authorities against these well organised, well defended and self-sufficient renegade strongholds.

These fugitive communities, although not exclusively black (they also attracted many Cafuzos, dispossessed Indians and disaffected whites and mulattos) employed many of the agricultural techniques and other traditions of Africa, and many were still used as places of refuge for half a century after the fall of Palmares.

Despite the essential Bantu traditions derived from the cultures of sub-equatorial Africa, which predominated in the *senzalas* (slave quarters) of the plantations and in the quilombos, the influence of other African peoples persisted, on a more local scale, in specific parts of Brazil.

In Baía, for example, the most significant African retentions are those of the Nagô and the Gegê. Many of the dishes associated with Baían cuisine are of Nagô inspiration, such as *acarajé* (kidney bean paste fried in dendê palm oil), the sweet cakes of maize or rice flour known as *aberém* and the chicken, shrimp and garlic ragout, *xinxim,* popularly associated with Oxum, the Yoruba Goddess of Waters. The liturgical language of the syncretic Afro-Brazilian religion, *candomblé,* was an archaic form of Yoruba, passed down orally by successive generations of *babalaôs* or priests. (Elsewhere in Brazil, similar cults are known by such Bantu names as *quimbanda* and *macumba.*) In the hagiology of candomblê, the gods of Guinea (the *orixás*) fuse with the Christian saints; Xangô, Thunder God of the Yoruba, is identified with St Jerome, while his brother, Ogun, God of Blacksmiths, is merged with St Anthony.

In the mid-nineteenth century, groups of so-called 'Agudas' (Brazilian slaves, largely of the Muslim faith) were 'repatriated' to Yorubaland, where they were rapidly assimilated. This Transatlantic connection has been maintained up to our own time by such institutions as the Centro de Cultura Afro-Brasileira and the University of Baía, the only faculty in the Americas which has a chair in Yoruba. It is also significant that one of Brazil's most widely acclaimed touring music groups bears the Yoruba name of *Oludun.*

Specific Nagô sects, often commemorating places in Nigeria, such as Ifé, legendary cradle of the Yoruba, continued to survive in Brazil. Membership of these so-called 'nations' was by no means confined to those who claimed Nagô descent, but also attracted many adherents of other ethnic background, including whites. The multi-racial membership of these sects further emphasised the contrast between race relations in Brazilian society and those of Protestant Anglo-America.

Other distinctive African stocks were recognised during and long after the colonial period in Brazil. These included the Mandinga (from Mali and Senegambia), whose name is synonymous with witchcraft in much of Ibero-America, and the Fula, whose name is applied in Brazil to a light-skinned 'Cabra' or mulatto as a reminder of the fair complexions of the West African Fulani. Other African peoples continued to be remembered in the names of such black batallions of the Brazilian army as the Minas (from Ghana) and the Ardras (from Benin).

It was, however, the Islamicised blacks, known collectively in Brazil by the Yoruba name, Malê, who, while numerically inferior to the largely Bantu and Nagô masses, were to have the greatest impact on the ultimate destiny of Brazil's slave population: for it was they who spearheaded the insurrections which punctured the eighteenth and nineteenth centuries and accelerated the end of bondage.

Outstanding and most influential among the various peoples classed as Malê were the Hausa of northern Nigeria, a highly urbanised nation whose so-called 'holy war' against the white oppressor was a continuation of the *ji-*

had against the infidel which was part of Islamic tradition. In Brazil, many of these Malê, despite having obtained their freedom, remained unassimilated and aloof from white society. Besides the Hausa, the Mandinga and the Fula were solidly Muslim, while many of the Nagô had converted to Islam long before their arrival in Brazil.

The Hausa, esteemed as house slaves for their imposing bearing and courteous manners, were frequently superior, in both intellect and erudition, to their masters and many, notably the *alufás* (imams), were literate in the Ajami (Arabic) script and well versed in the Koran.

The most spectacular of the slave insurrections, such as the 1835 'Malê Uprising', were fomented and organised by these highly motivated people whose primary objective—alongside casting off the yoke of slavery—was to prosyletise their fellow Africans, many of whom had either adopted Catholicism or continued to observe their atavistic forms of worship. The crusading spirit of Islam was thus a dominant and unifying factor in the slave revolts that spread terror through a white population for whom the Haitian revolution of 1791 was still a fresh memory. When the uprising was finally put down, its ringleaders were either executed or exiled to Africa. Although many of these uprisings were well organised, the sheer size of the country meant that they could not be co-ordinated as they had been in the compact geographical setting of Haiti. Threatening though they were on a local scale, the Brazilian slave insurrections were much easier to isolate, contain and extinguish than their successful Haitian exemplar. Moreover, they could not boast a charismatic, supra-regional leader of the stature of Toussaint L'Ouverture or of Antonio Maceo, the mulatto general who waged guerilla war against the Spanish in Cuba in the 1870s.

In 1850, fifteen years after the Malê Uprising, the slave trade was officially abolished in Brazil, one of the last former European colonies in the Americas to do so. Pressure to emancipate their slave population had been exerted on the Brazilians by both the British and the French since the early days of the empire, and in 1831 Dom Pedro had agreed to declare that all Africans entering the ports of Brazil were free.

Abraham Lincoln's Emancipation Proclamation of 1862 added further im-petus to the movement in Brazil and in 1871 a '*Lei do Ventre Livre*' (Law of the Free Womb) was passed, granting freedom at birth to every child born of a slave. A Brazilian Anti-Slavery Society was founded under the presidency of Joaquim Nabuco in 1880, with the backing of the Emperor and such black abolitionists as Luis Gonzaga Pinto da Gama, José do Patrocínio (author of an influential anti-slavery novel, *Motto Moqueiro*) and Antônio Bento, editor of the journal, *Redemption,* and organiser of an 'underground railroad', a network of escape routes which enabled slaves to flee from servitude into the mountain and jungle depths of the interior.

In contrast to the prominent role of Afro-Brazilians in the emancipation movement, mulattos were conspicuously under-represented. Indeed, many Creoles (Brazilian-born blacks) and mulattos were themselves slave-owners who stood to lose a great deal from abolition, and black leaders such as André Robouças expressed deep regret at the disinterest and lack of involvement of their racial half-brothers, especially as many of the earlier insurrections, such as the Baía uprising of 1798 (again inspired by the Haitian Revolution) had been led by mulatto intellectuals, craftsmen and artisans. In 1885, a step closer to full emancipation was taken, with the proclamation of a law freeing all slaves aged sixty and above, and in 1888 the Aurea Decree liberated all 1.5 million still in bondage.

Today, 109 years after the end of slavery in Brazil, and despite the immigration of other, chiefly European and Asian, ethnic groups, an estimated 30–40 per cent of the Brazilian population (ie: upwards of 70 million souls) is still of direct or partial African descent. In the state of Baía alone, the landfall of the majority of Africans in the north-east, the percentage of blacks and mulattos remains, even today, as high as 70 per cent, much as it was in the eighteenth century at the height of the sugar boom.

The demographic pattern, however, is dynamic rather than static; the Afro-Brazilian population is far from uniform and its density continues to vary greatly between regions.

While only 5 per cent or less of the country's 'coloured' population is estimated to be of unbroken African descent, the African element in Brazil's ethnic composition is still visible, as is the indelible African influence on popular culture, from the decorative arts to folklore, cuisine, herbal medicine, music and dance—including the all-pervasive *samba,* whose Bantu name means 'belly button' and which began life, as did so many other traditional Brazilian dances, on the sugar and coffee fazendas. The African influence manifests itself in spectacular form in such institutions as the *Congadas* and *Maracatus*—dance re-enactments of African regal processions—which have become such an integral part of the country's carnival parades.

In candomblé macumba and other Afro-Brazilian religious cults—despite the influence of European Spiritualism and the Catholic veneer—the ancestral gods of Guinea live on, in dual Afro-Catholic guise, while the African influence on the variety of Portuguese spoken in Brazil is demonstrable. This consists not only of a compendious vocabulary derived mainly from Kimbundu and (notably in Baía) Yoruba, but also of details of syntax and word usage and in the soft and sensuous pronunciation of what is often referred to as 'Portuguese with Sugar.'

While it may no longer be possible, as it was in Nina Rodrigues' day, to attribute individual aspects of Brazilian civilisation to specific sources in Africa, it is this deep and ineradicable influence, the legacy of five centuries of intimate and almost continuous contact with the mother continent, which has given Brazilian popular culture so much of its unique identity.

FOR FURTHER READING:

Gilberto Freyre, *The Masters and the Slaves: A Study in the Development of Brazilian Civilization* (University of California Press, 1986); Vincent Bakpetu Thompson, *The Making of the African Diaspora in the Americas, 1441–1900* (Longman, 1987); Roger Bastide, *African Religions of Brazil* (University of Baltimore Press, 1978): José Honório Rodrigues, *Brazil and Africa* (University of Berkeley Press, 1965); Leslie Bethell (ed) *Colonial Brazil* (University of Cambridge Press, 1991); Joseph E. Holloway (ed) *Africanisms in American Culture* (University of Indiana Press, 1990).

John Geipel is the author of several books on anthropological linguistics. His latest contribution, on the secret language of the Gypsies of Spain, appears in Languages and Jargons, *edited by Roy Porter and Peter Burke, (Polity Press, 1996).*

Unit Selections

7. **Descartes the Dreamer,** Anthony Grafton
8. **A New Light on Alchemy,** Zbigniew Szydlo and Richard Brzezinski
9. **Declaring an Open Season on the Wisdom of the Ages,** Robert Wernick
10. **Witchcraft: The Spell That Didn't Break,** Owen Davies
11. **Blacks in the Gordon Riots,** Marika Sherwood
12. **The Passion of Antoine Lavoisier,** Stephen Jay Gould
13. **The First Feminist,** Shirley Tomkievicz
14. **Napoleon the Kingmaker,** Philip Mansel
15. **Napoleon in Egypt,** Bob Brier

Key Points to Consider

❖ What did Descartes contribute to modernity?

❖ Why were the alchemists called the forerunners of modern chemistry?

❖ What was the political agenda of the *Encyclopedia*?

❖ Although the Age of Reason tried to eliminate all superstition, why were there still many accusations of witchcraft?

❖ Why did black men and women join the anti-Catholic protests that rocked London in 1780?

❖ Describe how and why France's greatest scientist, Antione Lavoisier, was victimized by the French Revolution.

❖ Does Mary Wollstonecraft's feminism compare to today's version? Why or why not?

❖ Why was Napoleon feared rather than applauded by his fellow monarchs?

❖ Why was Napoleon's invasion of Egypt in 1798 to have important consequences?

 **Links**   **www.dushkin.com/online/**

These sites are annotated on pages 4 and 5.

This unit explores facets of the Age of Reason (the seventeenth century) and the Enlightenment (the eighteenth century). These two phases of Western tradition had much in common. Both placed their faith in science and reason, both believed in progress, and both were skeptical about much of the cultural baggage that was inherited from earlier periods. Yet each century marked a distinctive stage in the spread of rationalism. In the seventeenth century, a few advanced thinkers, such as John Locke and René Descartes, attempted to resolve the major philosophical problems of knowledge—that is, to develop a theoretical basis for the new rationalism. The eighteenth century saw in the work of Immanuel Kant and David Hume continuation of that theoretical enterprise. But there was a new development as well: Voltaire, Denis Diderot, and others campaigned to popularize science, reason, the principles of criticism, and the spirit of toleration. Increasingly, the critical attitudes engendered by rationalism and empiricism in the seventeenth century were brought to bear upon familiar beliefs and practices in the eighteenth century.

Several articles in this unit show the advance of critical reason. "Descartes the Dreamer" profiles the seventeenth-century thinker who epitomized the new rationalism, while the essay "Declaring an Open Season on the Wisdom of the Ages" shows how Jean d'Alembert and Denis Diderot used the *Encyclopedia* to advance the cause of Enlightenment. In "The First Feminist," Shirley Tomkievicz reviews Mary Wollstonecraft's life and her arguments for "enlightened" treatment of women.

The new attitudes were often troublesome, even revolutionary. During the seventeenth and eighteenth centuries no tradition seemed safe from criticism. Even the Bible was searched for contradictions and faulty logic. Universities and salons became intellectual battlegrounds where the classists confronted the modernists. The struggle went beyond a mere battle of books. Powerful religious and political institutions were subjected to the test of reason and often were found wanting. The goal was to reorganize society on a rational or enlightened basis and to develop a new morality based on reason, not religious authority.

Of course, rationalism was not confined to the these centuries, as any reader of Aristotle or St. Thomas Aquinas can attest. Nor did the influence of the irrational disappear during the Age of Reason. The period witnessed a great European witch craze and a millennarian movement in England. And those who doubt that irrational attitudes could surface among the rationalists need only read about the craze for phrenology or Sir Isaac Newton's interest in alchemy and Blaise Pascal's mysticism. Two articles, "A New Light on Alchemy" and "Witchcraft: The Spell That Didn't Break," highlight the irrational thinking of this period.

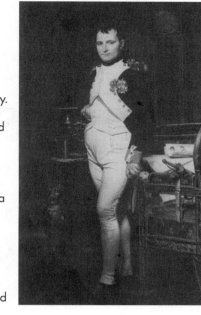

As for the Enlightenment, many have questioned how deeply its ideals and reforms penetrated society. On occasion, radical ideas and social change produced unanticipated consequences as we see in Marika Sherwood's account of the anti-Catholic Gordon riots. Sometimes the peasants stubbornly resisted the enlightened legislation passed on their behalf. And we are hardly surprised to learn that the enlightened despots on the Continent stopped short of instituting reforms that might have lessen their authority, or else they manipulated education and the arts in order to enhance their own power. Nor did modern rationalism cause the great powers to rein in their ambitions, as the international wars of the period demonstrate.

And while the doctrines of the Enlightenment many be enshrined in the noblest expressions of the French Revolution, it also witnessed mass executions and systematic efforts to suppress freedom of speech. The excesses of the Revolution are exemplified by the senseless execution of France's most brilliant scientist (see Stephen Jay Gould's article, "The Passion of Antoine Lavoisier"). In "Napoleon the Kingmaker" Philip Mansel shows how Napoleon rearranged the monarchies of Europe while reverting to some of the ideas of the Old Regime. And, as we see in Bob Brier's essay, "Napoleon in Egypt," even though Napoleon's invasion of Egypt was defeated, he helped create modern Egyptology.

In the last century, with its mass atrocities, world wars, and nuclear weapons, it was difficult to sustain the Enlightenment's faith in reason. But even before our recent disillusionments, rationalism provoked a powerful reaction—Romanticism. In contrast to the rationalists, romantics trusted emotions and distrusted intellect; they were not interested in discovering the natural laws of the universe, but they loved nature as a source of inspiration and beauty. They were preoccupied with self-discovery, not social reform; and they often drew upon medieval experience for their images and models. Rationalism has, however, survived and lives on in our modern programs of education and social uplift under the concept called liberalism.

Rationalism, Enlightenment, and Revolution

Descartes the Dreamer

No single thinker has had a more decisive influence on the course of modern philosophy—and general intellectual inquiry—than René Descartes (1596–1650). On the 400th anniversary of Descartes's birth, **Anthony Grafton** *considers the forces that shaped the man and his thought.*

by Anthony Grafton

All philosophers have theories. Good philosophers have students and critics. But great philosophers have primal scenes. They play the starring roles in striking stories, which their disciples and later writers tell and retell, over the decades and even the centuries. Thales, whom the Greeks remembered as their first philosopher, tumbled into a well while looking up at the night sky, to the accompanying mockery of a serving maid. His example showed, more clearly than any argument could, that philosophy served no practical purpose. Those who take a different view of philosophy can cite a contrasting anecdote, also ancient, in their support: after drawing on his knowledge of nature to predict an abundant harvest, Thales rented out all the olive presses in Miletus and Chios. He made a fortune charging high rates for them; better still, he showed that scholar rhymes with dollar after all.

At the other end of Western history, in the 20th century, Ludwig Wittgenstein held that propositions are, in some way, pictures of the world: that they must have the same "logical form" as what they describe. He did so, at least, until he took a train ride one day with Piero Sraffa, an Italian economist at Cambridge. Making a characteristic Italian gesture, drawing his hand across his throat, Sraffa asked, "What is the logical form of that?" He thus set his friend off on what became the vastly influential *Philosophical Investigations,* that fascinating, endlessly puzzling text which the American philosophers of my youth took as their bible, and to the exegesis of which they brought a ferocious cleverness that would do credit to any seminarian. If Helen's face launched a thousand ships, Sraffa's gesture launched at least a hundred careers.

In each case—and in dozens of others—the story has passed from books to lectures to articles and back, becoming as smooth and shiny in the process as a pebble carried along by a swift-flowing stream. In fact, these stories have become talismans of sorts: evidence that the most profound ideas, the most rigorous analyses, have their origins in curious, human circumstances and strange, all-too-human people. Such anecdotes accessibly dramatize the heroic originality and rigor of philosophers—qualities that one cannot always appreciate only by studying their texts, slowly and carefully.

It seems appropriate, then, that no philosopher in the Western tradition has left a more fascinating—or more puzzling—trail of anecdote behind him than the Frenchman René Descartes. Like Wittgenstein's philosophy, Descartes's began from curious experiences; but in his case the provocation was—or was remembered as—nothing so banal as a train ride.

Early in his life, Descartes became a soldier, serving two years in the Dutch army, before joining the Bavarian service. He writes that in the late fall of 1619, while stationed in the German city of Ulm, he "was detained by the onset of winter in quarters where, having neither conversation to divert me nor, fortunately, cares or passions to trouble me, I was completely free to consider my own thoughts." He refused all company, went on solitary walks, and dedicated himself to an exhausting search for . . . he did not quite know what. Suddenly he stumbled on what he called "the foundations of a marvellous science." After an almost mystical experience of deep joy, Descartes fell asleep, in his close, stove-heated room. He then dreamed, three times.

In the first dream, terrible phantoms surrounded him. His efforts to fight them off were hindered by a weakness in his right side, which made him stagger in a way that struck him as terribly humiliating. Trying to reach a chapel that belonged to a college, he

From *The Wilson Quarterly,* Autumn 1996, pp. 36–46. © 1996 by Anthony Grafton. Reprinted by permission.

found himself pinned to the wall by the wind—only to be addressed by someone who called him by name, promising that one "M.N." would give him something (which Descartes took to be a melon from another country). The wind died, and he awoke with a pain in is left side. Turning over, he reflected for some time, slept again, and dreamed of a clap of thunder. Waking, he saw that his room was full of sparks. In the third dream, finally, he found two books, which he discussed with a stranger. The second book, a collection of poems, included one about the choice of a form of life—as well as some copperplate portraits, which seemed familiar.

Waking again and reflecting, Descartes decided that these dreams had been divinely sent. He connected them, both at the time and later, with the discovery of the new method that would ultimately enable him to rebuild philosophy from its foundations. Paradoxically, Descartes, the pre-eminent modern rationalist, took dreams as the basis for his confidence in his new philosophy—a philosophy that supposedly did more than any other to deanimate the world, to convince intellectuals that they lived in a world uninhabited by occult forces, among animals and plants unequipped with souls, where the only ground of certainty lay in the thinking self.

Like Wittgenstein, Descartes enjoys a tribute that modern philosophers rarely offer their predecessors. He is still taken seriously enough to be attacked. Courses in the history of philosophy regularly skip hundreds of years. They ignore whole periods—such as the Renaissance—and genres—such as moral philosophy, since these lack the qualities of rigor, austerity, and explanatory power that win a text or thinker a starring position in the modern philosophical heavens. But Descartes continues to play a major role. In histories of philosophy, he marks the beginning of modernity and seriousness; he is, in fact, the earliest philosopher after ancient times to enjoy canonical status. Students of Descartes can rejoice in the existence of an excellent *Cambridge Companion to Descartes,* edited by John Cottingham, two helpful Descartes dictionaries, and even a brief and breezy *Descartes in Ninety Minutes*—as well as in a jungle of monographs and articles on Descartes's epistemology and ethics, physics and metaphysics, through which only the specialist can find a path. (One standard

anthology of modern responses to Descartes's work extends to four thick volumes.) Descartes still provokes.

In a sense, moreover, he provokes more now than he did 20 years ago. In the last generation, developments in a wide range of disciplines—computer and software design, primate research, neurology, psychology—have made the question of how to define human consciousness more urgent, perhaps, than it has ever been. What would show that the computer or an ape thinks as humans do? Can one prove that the measurable physiological phenomena that accompany mental states should be identified with them? How can physical events cause mental ones, and vice versa? And who should settle such questions: philosophers, or scientists, or both in collaboration?

New interdisciplinary programs for the study of consciousness or artificial intelligence provide forums for the debate—which remains fierce—on these and other issues. And the debates are, if anything, becoming fiercer. Successes in solving particular problems—such as the creation of a machine genuinely able to play chess, rather than the man disguised as a machine unmasked by Poe—excite some of the specialists responsible for them to declare victory: if a computer has a mind, then the mind is a computer. Stalwart opponents swat these optimists with rolled-up newspapers, insisting that vast areas of mental and emotional experience—like the pain caused by the rolled-up newspaper—undeniably exist and matter even though they have no counterpart in computer models. From whatever side they come, a great many of the contributions to these debates start with a reference to, or amount to, a sustained attack on Descartes.

It is not hard to explain why this Frenchman, who has been dead for three and a half centuries, still seems modern enough to interest and irritate philosophers who otherwise feel contempt for most of their predecessors. He felt and wrote exactly the same way about his own predecessors.

Descartes, as is well known, began his career as a philosopher in a state of radical discontent with the resources of the intellectual disciplines. He described this state with unforgettable clarity, moreover, in the autobiography with which he began his most famous text, his *Discourse on the*

Method (1637). Born in 1596, Descartes lost his mother as a baby and saw little of his father, a councilor in the *parlement* of Brittany at Rennes. For almost a decade, beginning around the age of 10, he attended the Jesuit college of La Flèche at Anjou. Here, he recalled, he made a comprehensive study of classical literature and science. He read—and wrote—much fine Latin, debated in public, learned how to produce an *explication du texte.* He knew all the clichés that humanists used to defend the classical curriculum, and he recited them with palpable irony: "I knew . . . that the charm of fables awakens the mind, while memorable deeds told in histories uplift it and help to shape one's judgment if they are read with discretion; that reading good books is like having a conversation with the most distinguished men of past ages."

But all this contact with traditional high culture left Descartes unconvinced. Knowledge of literary traditions and past events might give a young man a certain cosmopolitan gloss, but it could not yield profound and practical knowledge: "For conversing with those of past centuries is much the same as travelling. It is good to know something of the customs of various peoples, so that we may judge our own more soundly and not think that everything contrary to our own ways is ridiculous and irrational, as those who have seen nothing of the world ordinarily do. But one who spends too much time travelling eventually becomes a stranger in his own country; and one who is too curious about the practices of past ages usually remains quite ignorant about those of the present."

The humanists of the Renaissance had praised the Greeks and Romans, who did not waste time trying to define the good but made their readers wish to pursue it with their powerful rhetorical appeal. Descartes recognized fluff when he heard it: "I compared the moral writings of the ancient pagans to very proud and magnificent palaces built only on mud and sand. They extol the virtues, and made them appear more estimable than anything else in the world; but they do not adequately explain how to recognize virtue, and often what they call by this fine name is nothing but a case of callousness, or vanity, or desperation, or parricide." So much for the soft, irrelevant humanities—still a popular view in American and English philosophy departments. Descartes, in other words, was the first, though hardly the last, philosopher to treat his discipline as if it should have the austere rigor of a natural science.

Even the study of mathematics and systematic philosophy, however—at least as Descartes encountered them in his college—had proved unrewarding. The mathematicians had missed "the real use" of their own subject, failing to see that it could be of service outside "the mechanical arts." And the philosophers had created only arguments without end: "[philosophy] has been cultivated for many centuries by the most excellent minds, and yet there is still no point in it which is not disputed and hence doubtful." All previous thinkers, all earlier systems, seemed to Descartes merely confused.

Descartes insisted that most of philosophy's traditional tools had no function.

He thought he knew the reason, too. All earlier thinkers had set out to carry on a tradition. They had taken over from their predecessors ideas, terms, and theories, which they tried to fit together, along with some new thoughts of their own, into new structures. Predictably, their results were incoherent: not lucid Renaissance palaces, in which all surface forms manifested the regular and logical structures underneath them, but messy Gothic pastiches of strange shapes and colors randomly assembled over the centuries. Such theories, "made up and put together bit by bit from the opinions of many different people," could never match the coherence of "the simple reasoning which a man of good sense naturally makes concerning whatever he comes across."

Descartes's "marvellous science" would be, by contrast, all his own work, and it would have the "perfection," as well as the explanatory power, that more traditional philosophies lacked. To revolutionize philosophy, accordingly, Descartes "entirely abandoned the study of letters." He ceased to read the work of

others, turned his attention inward, and created an entire philosophical system—and indeed an entire universe—of his own. He hoped that this would make up in clarity and coherence for what it might lack in richness of content. And the first publication of his theories, in the form of the *Discourse* and a group of related texts, made him a controversial celebrity in the world of European thought.

As Wittgenstein, 300 years later, cleared the decks of philosophy by insisting that most of its traditional problems had no meaning, so Descartes insisted that most of philosophy's traditional tools had no function. Like Wittgenstein, he became the idol of dozens of young philosophers, who practiced the opposite of what he preached by taking over bits of his system and combining them with ideas of their own. Unlike Wittgenstein, however, he also became the object of bitter, sometimes vicious criticism, from both Protestant and Catholic thinkers who resented the threat he posed to theological orthodoxy or simply to the established curriculum. No wonder that he, unlike his opponents, remains a hero in the age that has none. What characterizes modernity—so more than one philosopher has argued—is its state of perpetual revolution, its continual effort to produce radically new ideas and institutions. Modern heroes—from Reformation theologians such as Martin Luther to political radicals such as Karl Marx—established their position by insisting that traditional social and intellectual structures that looked as solid and heavy as the Albert Memorial would dissolve and float away when seen from a new and critical point of view. The Descartes who wrote the *Discourse* belongs to this same line of intellectual rebels, and in this sense he is deservedly regarded as the first modern philosopher.

Again like Wittgenstein, Descartes refused to take part in normal or in academic high society. Though he devoted a period at the University of Poitiers to study of the law, he made little effort to follow a career as a lawyer—a path chosen by many intellectuals at the time. Though admired by patrons and intellectuals in France and elsewhere, he took little interest in court or city. He did not spend much time in Paris, where in his lifetime the classic French literary canon was being defined on stage and

in the Academy and where the fashionable gossiped brilliantly about literature, history, and sex.

Descartes, who contributed so much to the development of that classic French virtue, clarity, kept aloof from his colleagues in the creation of the modern French language. He lived most contentedly in Holland, sometimes in towns such as Leiden and Deventer but often in the deep country, where he had at most one or two partners in conversation—one was a cobbler with a gift for mathematics—and led an existence undisturbed by great excitements. He only once showed great sorrow, when his illegitimate daughter Francine, who was borne by a serving maid named Hélène in 1635, died as a young child. And he only once departed from his accustomed ways: when he moved to the court of that eager, imperious student of ideas, texts, and religions, Queen Christina of Sweden. There he became mortally ill when she made him rise at four in the frozen northern dawn to give her philosophy lessons. He died at the age of 53, a martyr to intellectual curiosity, in February 1650.

Descartes's "marvellous science" portrayed a whole new universe: one that consisted not, like that of traditional philosophy, of bodies animated by a number of souls intimately connected to them, and related to one another by occult influence, but of hard matter in predictable motion. He cast his ideas not in the traditional form of commentary on ancient texts and ideas, but in the radically antitraditionalist one of systematic treatises that did not cite authorities—other than that of Descartes's own ability to reason. He said that he saw no point in weaving together chains of syllogisms, as the Scholastics of the Middle Ages had, in the vain hope that major and minor premises of unclear validity, drawn at random from old texts and swarming with unexamined assumptions, could somehow yield new and important conclusions. He did not try to protect his weaker arguments from attack by covering them with a thick, brittle armor plating of quotations from ancient and modern sources in the manner of the Renaissance humanists, who saw philology as the mainstay of philosophy.

Descartes, instead, claimed that he could build entirely on his own something new, coherent, and symmetrical.

He liked to compare his work to that of the great town planners of his time, who saw the ideal city as a lucid walled polyhedron surrounding a central square, rather than an irregular, picturesque embodiment of centuries of time and change. The "crooked and irregular" streets and varied heights of the buildings in old cities suggested that "it is chance, rather than the will of men using reason, that placed them so," he said. Coherence, uniformity, symmetry attracted him: the Paris of the Place des Vosges rather then the palaces and alleys of the older parts of the city.

Descartes saw mathematics as the model for the new form of intellectual architecture he hoped to create. For he himself, as he discovered later than stereotypes would lead one to expect, was a very gifted mathematician, one of the creators of modern algebra and the inventor of analytical geometry. Like a mathematician, he tried to begin from absolutely hard premises: ideas so "clear and distinct" that he could not even begin to deny them. In these, and only in these, he found a place to stand. Descartes could imagine away the physical world, the value of the classics, and much else. But he could not deny, while thinking, the existence of his thinking self. Cogito, ergo sum.

From this narrow foothold he began to climb. He proved the existence of God in a way that he himself found deeply satisfactory though many others did not: the idea of God includes every perfection, and it is more perfect to exist than not to exist. Hence God must exist—and be the source of the innate faculties and ideas that all humans possess. He worked out the sort of universe that God would have to create. And he devised, over the course of time, a system that embraced everything from the nature of the planets to that of the human mind, from the solution of technical problems in mathematics to the circulation of the blood.

Wherever possible, precise quantitative models showed how Cartesian nature would work in detail: he not only devised laws for the refraction and reflection of light, for example, but also designed a lens-grinding machine that would apply them (and prove their validity). Parts of his system clanked and sputtered. His elaborate cosmology—which interpreted planetary systems as whirlpools, or vortices, of matter in motion—was technically outdated before it appeared. It could not account for the mathematical details of planetary motion established by Tycho Brahe and Johannes Kepler. Nonetheless, the rigor and coherence of his system inspired natural philosophers on the Continent for a century and more after his death.

The reception of Descartes's philosophy was anything but easy or straightforward. At the outset of his career as a published writer, in the *Discourse on the Method,* he invited those who had objections to his work to communicate

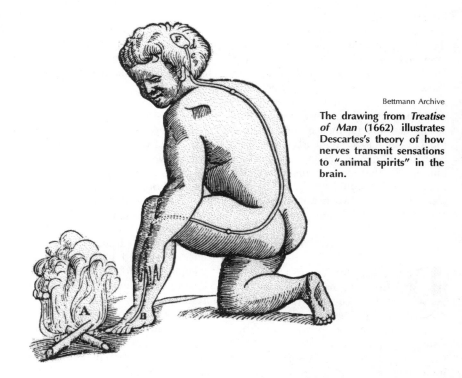

The drawing from *Treatise of Man* (1662) illustrates Descartes's theory of how nerves transmit sensations to "animal spirits" in the brain.

them to him for reply. He circulated his *Meditations* for comment before he published them in 1641, and printed them along with systematic objections and his own replies. Thomas Hobbes, Marin Mersenne, Pierre Gassendi, and others now known only to specialists pushed him to define his terms and defend his arguments. At the same time, his thought became controversial in wider circles. Descartes long feared this outcome. Both a good Copernican and a good Catholic, he was appalled by the condemnation of Galileo in 1633. This led him both to delay publication of his treatise *The World* and to try to devise a metaphysics that would prove his natural philosophy legitimate.

But once his work reached print, Descartes could not avoid controversy. In 1639, his supporters in the faculty of the University of Utrecht began to praise his new philosophy, holding public debates about his theories. The influential theologian Gisbert Voetius defended traditional theology, not only against Cartesianism but against Descartes, whose beliefs and morality Voetius attacked. Descartes found himself forced to defend himself a series of pamphlets. He lost some sympathizers—such as the scholar Anna Maria van Schurmann, one of a number of women with whom he discussed theological or philosophical issues.

In the 1640s, Descartes's political and legal situation became extremely serious, and his life in the Netherlands increasingly exhausting and disturbing. Nor did he always agree with those who considered themselves his followers. Ironically, if inevitably, Descartes's philosophy mutated into Cartesianism—one more of the philosophical schools whose competing claims had driven the young Descartes to try something completely different. Some academic Cartesians—as Theo Verbeek and others have shown— even used his philosophy along with others in a deliberately eclectic way their master would have condemned.

Nonetheless, until recent years philosophers generally thought they had a clear idea both of what Descartes meant to do and about why he framed his enterprise as he did. The question of consciousness, of the nature of the mind and its relation to the body, provides a good example of how Descartes has generally been read. Earlier philosophers, drawing on and adding to a tradition that went back to Aristotle, explained life and consciousness in a way that varied endlessly in detail but not in substance. A whole series of souls, hierarchically ordered, each of them equipped with particular faculties, accounted for organic life in plants, movement in animals, and consciousness in humans. The number and quality of faculties possessed by each being corresponded to its position in the hierarchical chain of being, which determined the number and kinds of souls that being possessed. And the well-established nature and location of these faculties in the body could be used to show how body and soul were intimately and intricately connected. It made perfectly good sense to assume—as the astrologers, then almost as fashionable as now, regularly did—that celestial influences, acting on the four humors in the body, could affect the mind. No one could establish an easy, clear division between mind and body, man and nature.

Descartes, by contrast, drew a sharp line, here as elsewhere, both between his views and traditional ones and between physical and mental processes. He proved, as he insisted he could, that mind and body were in fact separate. Descartes could imagine that he had no body at all, but he could not imagine that he, the one imagining, did not exist. The mind, in other words, was fundamentally different from the body. Bodies had as their defining properties hardness and extension. Their other attributes—such as color and texture—were merely superficial, as one could see, for example, by melting a lump of wax. The material world, accordingly, could be measured, divided, cut. The mind, by contrast, was clearly indivisible; when conscious, one always had access to all of it. Descartes divided human beings, accordingly, into two components: a material, extended body, mobile and mortal, and an immaterial, thinking soul, located somewhere within the body but at least potentially

immortal. He redefined the struggles between different souls which Saint Augustine had so influentially described in his *Confessions* and of which others regularly spoke as struggles between the body and the soul. These took place, Descartes argued, in a particular organ: the pineal gland, within the brain, the one point where soul and body interacted. He held that animals could not have minds, at least in the sense that human beings do. And the firm distinction he made between the physical plane that humans share with other beings and the mental operations that attest to their existence on more than a physical plane continues to irritate philosophers—just as his sharp distinction between the real world of solid matter in motion and the qualitative, unreal world of perception and passion once enraged T. S. Eliot and Basil Willey, who held him guilty of causing the 17th century's "dissociation of sensibility."

Descartes's position in the history of thought has seemed, in recent years, as easily defined as his innovative contributions to it. By the time he was born, in 1596, intellectual norms that had existed for centuries, even millennia, were being called into question. The discovery of the New World had challenged traditional respect for the cosmology and philosophy of the ancients. The Protestant Reformation had destroyed the unity of Christendom, offering radically new ways of reading the Bible. The Scholastic philosophers who dominated the faculties of theology in the traditional universities, though all of them worked within a common, basically Aristotelian idiom, had come into conflict with one another on many fundamental points, and some humanists claimed that their vast Gothic structures of argument rested on misunderstandings of the Bible and Aristotle.

Some thinkers looked desperately for moorings in this intellectual storm. Justus Lipsius, for example, a very influential scholar and philosopher who taught at both Calvinist Leiden and Catholic Louvain, tried to show that ancient Stoicism, with its firm code of duties, could provide an adequate philosophy for the modern aristocrat and military officer. Others began to think that there were no moorings to be found—and even to accept that fact as welcome, since it undermined the dogmatic pretensions

that led to religious revolutions and persecutions. The philosophy of the ancient Skeptics, in particular, offered tools to anyone who wished to deny that philosophers could attain the truth about man, the natural world, or anything else.

Skepticism, as Richard Poplin and Charles Schmitt have shown, interested a few intellectuals in the 15th century, such as Lorenzo Valla. But it first attracted widespread interest during the Reformation. Erasmus, for example, drew on skeptical arguments to show that Luther was wrongly splitting the Catholic Church on issues about which humans could never attain certainty. The major ancient skeptical texts, the works of Sextus Empiricus, appeared in Latin translation late in the 16th century—just as the Wars of Religion between French Calvinists and Catholics were reaching their hottest point. Michel de Montaigne, the great essayist whom Descartes eagerly read and tacitly cited, drew heavily on Greek Skepticism when he mounted his attacks on intellectual intolerance. To some—especially the so-called Politiques, such as Montaigne, who was not only a writer but one of the statesmen who negotiated religious peace in France at the end of the 16th century—Skepticism came as a deeply desirable solution to religious crisis. To others, however—especially to Catholic and Protestant philosophers who still felt the need to show that their religious doctrines not only rested on biblical authority but also corresponded to the best possible human reasoning—Skepticism came as a threat to all intellectual certainties, including the necessary ones.

Descartes tried on principle to doubt everything he knew. (He called his method, eloquently, one of "hyperbolic doubt".) But he found, as we have seen, that there were some things even he could not doubt, and many others found his arguments convincing. Accordingly, Descartes appears in many histories of philosophy above all as one of those who resolved a skeptical crisis by providing a new basis for physics, metaphysics, and morality. Similarly, he appears in many histories of science, alongside Francis Bacon, as one of those who created a whole new method for studying the natural world.

For the last 20 years or so, however, this view of Descartes's place in the history of thought has begun to undergo scrutiny and criticism. Not only students of consciousness but historians of philosophy and science have begun to raise questions about Descartes's isolation in his own intellectual world. For all his insistence on the novelty of his views and the necessity for a serious thinker to work alone, he always looked for partners in discussion.

And this was only natural. "Even the most radical innovator," write the historians of philosophy Roger Ariew and Marjorie Grene, "has roots; even the most outrageous new beginner belongs to an intellectual community in which opponents have to be refuted and friends won over." Descartes, moreover, not only belonged to a community, as he himself acknowledged; he also drew, as he usually did not like to admit, from a variety of intellectual traditions.

For example, Stephen Gaukroger, whose intricately detailed new intellectual biography of Descartes elegantly balances close analysis of texts with a rich recreation of context, finds an ancient source for Descartes's apparently novel notion that certain "clear and distinct" ideas compel assent. The core of the Jesuit curriculum Descartes mastered so well was formed by rhetoric, the ancient art of persuasive speech. Quintilian, the Roman author of the most systematic ancient manual of the subject, analyzed extensively the ways in which an orator could "engage the emotions of the audience." To do so, he argued, the orator must "*exhibit* rather than *display* his proofs." He must produce a mental image so vivid and palpable that his hearers cannot deny it: a clear and distinct idea.

Gaukroger admits that Roman orators saw themselves first and foremost as producing such conviction in others, while Descartes saw his first duty as convincing himself. But Gaukroger elegantly points out that classical rhetoric, for all its concern with public utterance, also embodied something like Descartes's concern with the private, with "self-conviction." The orator, as Quintilian clearly said, had to convince himself in order to convince others: "The first essential is that those feelings should prevail with us that we wish to prevail with the judge."

Descartes's doctrine of clear and distinct ideas is usually described as radi-cally new. It turns out, on inspection, to be a diabolically clever adaptation to new ends of the rhetorical five-finger exercises the philosopher had first mastered as a schoolboy. Gaukroger's negative findings are equally intriguing: he interprets Descartes's famous dreams as evidence not of a breakthrough but of a breakdown, and he argues forcefully that Skepticism played virtually no role in Descartes's original formulation of his method and its consequences.

Several other studies have revealed similarly creative uses of tradition in many pockets of Descartes's philosophy. As John Cottingham has shown, Descartes more than once found himself compelled to use traditional philosophical terminology—with all the problematic assumptions it embodied. Despite his dislike of tradition, he also disliked being suspected of radicalism, and claimed at times not to offer a new theory but to revive a long-forgotten ancient one—for example, the "*vera mathesis*" ("true mathematical science") of the ancient mathematicians Pappus and Diophantus. No one denies the substantial novelty of Descartes's intellectual program; but students of his work, like recent students of Wittgenstein, show themselves ever more concerned to trace the complex relations between radicalism and tradition, text and context.

Descartes's dreams—and his autobiographical use of them—play a special role in this revisionist enterprise. His earliest substantial work, composed in the late 1620s but left unfinished, takes the form of *Rules for the Direction of the Mind;* his great philosophical text of 1641 bears the title *Meditations*. In structure as well as substance, both works unmistakably point backward to his formation in a Jesuit college. There he had not only to study the classics and some modern science but to "make" the *Spiritual Exercises* laid down for Jesuits and their pupils by the founder of the Jesuit order, Ignatius Loyola. These consisted of a set of systematic, graded exercises in contemplation, visualization, and meditation. Students—and candidates for membership in the order—had to reconstruct as vividly as they could in their minds the Crucifixion, Hell, and other scenes that could produce profound emotional and spiritual effects in them. These exercises were intended to enable those who did them to discipline their minds and spirits, to identify and rid themselves of their besetting weaknesses, and finally to choose the vocation for which God intended them. Visions—and even mystical experiences—regularly formed a controlled part of the process, as they had for Ignatius himself. The similarity between these exercises in spiritual self-discipline and Descartes's philosophical self-discipline is no coincidence. Here too Descartes transposed part of the education he thought he had rejected into the fabric of his philosophy.

In seeing visions as a form of divine communication—evidence of a special providence that singled recipients out as the possessors of a Mission—Descartes remained firmly within the Jesuit intellectual tradition. He was, in fact, far from the only product of a good Jesuit education to trace his own development in minute interpretative detail. Consider the case of his near contemporary Athanasius Kircher—another mathematically gifted young man, who studied in Jesuit schools in south Germany before becoming the central intellectual figure in baroque Rome. Kircher's interests were as varied as Descartes's were sharply defined: he spelunked in volcanoes, experimented with magnets, reconstructed the travel of Noah's Ark, and studied languages ranging from Coptic to Chinese, with varying degree of success. But he defined the core of his enterprise with Cartesian precision, if in totally un-Cartesian terms, as an effort to decipher the ancient philosophy encoded in the hieroglyphic inscriptions on Egyptian obelisks. This effort attracted much criticism but also received generous papal support. Ultimately it inspired some of Bernini's most spectacular Roman works of sculpture and architecture, in the Piazza Navona and before the church of Santa Maria sopra Minerva.

Descartes would have found most of Kircher's project risible. Yet they had something vital in common. Kircher, like Descartes, tried to prove the rigor and providential inspiration of his work by writing an autobiography. Kircher's dreams and visions played as large a role in this work as his colorful and sometimes terrifying experiences. Like Descartes, he saw his unconscious experiences as evidence that God had set him on earth to carry out a particular plan. His accidental encounter with a book in which Egyptian hieroglyphs were reproduced and discussed exemplified—he thought in retrospect—the sort of special providences by which God had led him in the right direction. Evidently, then, Cartesian autobiography was actually Jesuit autobiography. Brilliant style, concision, and lucidity set off the beginning of the *Discourse on the Method* from Kircher's Latin treatise. But the enterprises were basically as similar as the larger enterprises they were meant to serve were different. And Descartes's dreams not only make a nice story to adorn the beginning of a lecture but actually shed light on the origins of his central intellectual enterprise.

In effect, then, Descartes has come back to new life in recent years—in two radically different ways. The Descartes who appears in so many studies of the philosophy and physiology of mind—the radical innovator, owing nothing to his predecessors, who devised the brutally simple theory about "the ghost in the machine"—seems hard to reconcile with the Descartes now being reconstructed by historians: the complex, reflective figure, whose relation to tradition took many different forms, and whose system embodied foreign elements even he did not recognize as such. Gaukroger's book marks a first and very rewarding effort to bring the two Descartes together. But the task will be a long one. It may prove impossible to fit Descartes the dreamer into traditional genealogies of modern thought—or to establish a simple relation between his theories of intelligence and current ones. Descartes lives, a troubling ghost in the machine of modern philosophy.

ANTHONY GRAFTON *is the Dodge Professor of History at Princeton University. He is the author of* Joseph Scaliger: A Study in the History of Classical Scholarship *(1983–1993),* Forgers and Critics: Creativity and Duplicity in Western Scholarship *(1990), and* Defenders of the Text: The Traditions of Scholarship in an Age of Science, 1450–1800 *(1991). His study,* The Tragic Origins of the German Footnote, *appeared in 1997.*

A New Light On Alchemy

Fools' gold, Dr. Faustus—traditional images of a Renaissance black art. But was there more to it than that? **Zbigniew Szydlo** and **Richard Brzezinski** offer an intriguing rehabilitation.

In June 1897 the French journal *La Nature* reported that the United States Assay office had, on April 16th, purchased the first ever gold ingot manufactured from silver. Six months later, an article in a popular newspaper related that the inventor, Dr. Stephen H. Emmens, was producing enough gold to bring him at the Assay Office a profit of $150 a week'. Emmens, an American of British descent, bragged that he had finally mastered the alchemists' art and could produce gold commercially. He let

slip that his Argentaurum' process worked by the action of high pressure and intense cold on silver, but was eventually exposed as a fraud when he claimed that his process was endorsed by a leading physicist, Sir William Crookes. By 1901 Emmens was nowhere to be traced.

Three centuries earlier, in 1590s Prague, an unknown alchemist of Arabic origin made a flamboyant appearance in a city with a reputation as the alchemical capital of Europe. After courting

merchants and bankers, he invited twenty-four of the wealthiest to a banquet, during which he promised to multiply gold. He obtained 100 gold marks from each guest, and placed the coins in a large crucible with a mixture of acids, mercury, lead, salt, eggshells and horse dung. But, as he prepared to operate the bellows of his furnace, there was a tremendous explosion which left the guests spluttering in a fog of fumes. By the time the smoke had cleared, the alchemist had vanished, along with the 2,400 gold marks.

Such stories of fraudsters form the modern stereotype of the alchemist, and alchemy is widely seen as little more than the art of changing base metals into gold. With hindsight we know the alchemists were wasting their time: it is impossible to transmute' elements by chemical means, and nothing short of bombardment by neutrons in a nuclear reactor will produce gold from lead, and then only in microscopic amounts.

Although modern chemists are prepared to admit that the alchemists invented many of the chemical processes in use today, alchemy is still often condemned as mumbo-jumbo, and at worst, bundled in with astrology and necromancy as an occult pseudo-science. No wonder then that alchemy was dismissed in 1831 by Thomas Thomson as the 'rude and disgraceful' beginnings of chemistry.

But is this view of alchemy justified? When we hear that some of the greats of science, Sir Isaac Newton (1642–1727) and Robert Boyle (1627–91—of Boyle's law fame) had a keen interest in alchemy, perhaps it is time to think again. When we examine more closely the obscure texts of alchemy and venture behind the baffling terminology and mystical allusion, we see revealed a long and ancient line of philosophers and experimenters searching for secrets far more precious than gold.

The origins of alchemy go back at least four millennia to ancient Mesopotamia, India, China and Egypt and the first reasoned attempts to make sense of the diversity of nature. Aristotle, the tutor of Alexander the Great, brought many of these ideas together when he proposed that all worldly substances were made up of four elements: air, earth, fire and water. A fifth element, the ether or quintessence (from Latin *quinta essentia,* fifth essence) was the stuff of the heavens.

A refinement to this picture was made by Arab alchemists in the eighth century AD, in particular by Jabir ibn Hayyan, known in Europe as Geber. He proposed that all metals were formed of mercury and sulphur mixed in various proportions. White metals had very little sulphur, and yellow metals like gold, had more. It seemed like common sense, and was an open invitation for attempts at gold-making.

Increasingly alchemy gained a mystical side—perhaps from frustration at failed experiments. Into it came a strange concoction of Christian, Gnostic and neo-Platonic ideas. Adepts began to believe that experiments would only work when they were in a state of spiritual elevation achieved through prayer.

Central to the mysteries of alchemy was the belief that ancient texts contained forgotten secrets of nature. The most definitive of these texts was the *Tabula Smaragdina* or Emerald Tablet, which, according to legend, had been discovered by Alexander the Great in the Egyptian tomb of Hermes Trismegistos (thrice-great'), the Greek counterpart of the Egyptian god of wisdom and magic, Thoth. The Emerald Tablet was inscribed with thirteen axioms. Unfortunately, they were rather difficult to understand. The riddle-like language of the fourth is typical: Its father is the sun, its mother the moon; the wind carries it in its belly, its nurse is the earth'. This cryptic style was emulated by the alchemists, who christened themselves sons of Hermes' or Hermetic philosophers.

It is impossible here to go into the full world picture the alchemists had developed by the sixteenth century; but the key to it was *panvitalism*—the idea that the universe and everything in it was alive: animals, plants and minerals. Animals had the shortest lives but most complicated structures; minerals, the longest lives and simplest forms—that they were alive seemed logical after observations of volcanoes erupting, and crystals growing.

Minerals were believed to grow from seeds—the equivalent of plant seeds and human semen. These grew deep in the earth and rose to the surface, maturing as they moved. Depending on the path taken, they developed into different types of rocks. If a young mineral rose quickly along a poor route it emerged in a 'corrupt' form, such as lava; if it rose slowly along a pure and

Mansell Collection

The elixir of life—or a charlatan's potion? A late 16th-century illustration of an alchemist's workshop.

perfect vein it matured into gold. Even until the early twentieth century, English farmers were convinced that stones were growing in the ground and rising up like weeds that periodically needed be removed.

When a true alchemist, as opposed to a quack, was attempting to make gold he was not merely lusting for wealth: gold, because of its rarity, lack of reactivity, and glowing lustre was the mineral world in its ultimate state of perfection. By discovering how to make gold, the alchemist would, it was thought, also have the means of perfecting the plant and animal worlds. In order to produce gold in the laboratory, alchemists attempted to replicate and speed up the natural processes thought to take place deep in the earth. Their main goal was to discover the mysterious substance through which gold travelled on its way to the surface—this material they knew as the Philosopher's Stone. When found, the Stone would be the means of bringing perfection to the human world, giving health and eternal salvation to the fortunate alchemist. In effect, the search for the Philosopher's Stone was much like the quest for the Holy Grail.

The Philosopher's Stone was a major goal of alchemy, but to claim it was the only one is like saying the Grand Unified Theory is the sole aim of physics, or Fermat's Last Theorem was the same to mathematics. Alchemy had the general aim of making sense of nature in all its complexity. To be sure, there were other concrete goals: the *alkabest* or universal solvent which could dissolve all substances, and the universal medicine or Elixir of Life, which would cure all diseases and was related to the Philosopher's Stone. More bizarre, and verging on the occult was *palingenesis*—the reincarnation of plants and animals from their ashes; and attempts to generate miniature human beings (*homunculi*) from semen incubated in rotting horse dung.

Alchemy had already been given a sizeable kick in the direction of a practical science by the extraordinary Swiss physician Paracelsus—or to give his full name, Philippus Theophrastus Aureolus Bombastus von Hohenheim (1493–1541). After travels to the east, and work as a military surgeon, Paracelsus declared that most traditional medicines were useless, so he devised his own, with spectacular results. When appointed physician to the city of Basel in 1527,

he celebrated by publicly burning the works of Galen and Avicenna, the established authorities on medicine.

The only way to learn anything about nature, said Paracelsus, was to go out and observe it at first hand. Only the Bible was infallible, everything else was open to question. Paracelsus disputed Aristotle's four elements theory because fire was nowhere mentioned in Genesis. Borrowing from Geber's theory of metals, he decided that there were three fundamental substances: sulphur, mercury and salt—though he defined them in a broader sense than the modern materials of these names.

Paracelsus' revolutionary ideas spawned a new school of medical alchemists. Many of them were attracted to Prague and the liberal court of the German emperor, Rudolf II, who sponsored a bustling community of proto-scientists and artists. Among Rudolf's alchemical protégés, and shining out above them was a Polish doctor, Michal Sçdziwój (latinised as Sendivogius). Recognised by his contemporaries as one of the greats of early European natural philosophy, he has now slipped back into obscurity. Sendivogius was to signal the next remarkable transformation of alchemy.

Michael Sendivogius (1556–1636) has suffered more than most from the poor reputation of alchemy. Until recently, his life was known only in legendary accounts, replete with tales of spectacular transmutations, imprisonment by jealous rulers and improbable escapes from dungeons and burning towers. In the contemporary record Sendivogius emerges as a very different man. Born in Sacz, Poland, his name appears on the registers of Altdorf and Leipzig universities and in 1591 he matriculated from Vienna University. After serving as a courtier and doctor of medicine at Rudolf's court in Prague, he returned to Poland where he was taken into the confidence of King Zygmunt III. He became involved in the Polish metallurgical industry, and helped set up several factories in the Czestochowa and Silesia regions. He travelled regularly to the German empire on secret diplomatic missions, taking the opportunity to maintain contact with leading academics such as Johann Hartmann, Europe's first professor of chemistry (appointed in 1609).

Sendivogius' most influential book was published in Prague in 1604 as *De*

lapide pbilosopborum (On the Philosophers' Stone), but was soon retitled *Novum lumen cbymicum* (A New Light of Alchemy). Over the next two centuries it was to go through at least fifty-six editions in Latin, German, French, English, Russian and Dutch. Sir Isaac Newton owned a copy, now in the British Library, which has marginal notes in his handwriting, and corners turned down to mark passages. The great French chemist, Antoine Laurent Lavoisier, also had a copy—now at Cornell University and marked with his bookplate. What was it about this work that gave it such a distinguished following?

As was common with alchemical tracts, the author of *A New Light of Alchemy* concealed his name in an anagram: *Divi Leschi Genus Amo*—I love the divine race of the Lechites' (i.e. Poles). Yet the book is surprisingly easy to read and is largely devoid of mystical terminology, quite unlike the opaque writings of Paracelsus. The book is a remarkable exposé of the world-view of Renaissance alchemy, which Sendivogius states had developed greatly beyond the wisdom of the ancients.

In his preface to the first English edition (1650), the translator, John French, a successful doctor of medicine, could hardly have praised Sendivogius' book more highly:

> In that treatise of his thou shalt see the mystery of Deity, and Nature unfolded . . . . So that if anyone should ask me, What one book did most conduce to the knowledge of God and the Creature, and the mysteries thereof; I should speake contrary to my judgement, if I should not, next to the Sacred Writ, say Sandivogius.

Alongside his explanation of the workings of nature, much of which went back to traditional alchemical ideas, Sendivogius had put something quite new:

> Man was created of the Earth, and lives by vertue of the Aire; for there is in the Aire a secret food of life. . . . whose invisible congealed spirit is better than the whole earth.

For the first time Sendivogius revealed that air is a mixture, not a single fundamental substance as proposed by Aristotle. This was a great step. The implications to alchemy were momentous.

By the mid-sixteenth century, the alchemists were convinced there was a 'universal spirit'—a vapour or soul—pervading all matter. It was in this that the life-substance of all entities (including minerals) was believed to be located. Before Sendivogius nobody had managed to identify this universal spirit with a real substance. Sendivogius' 'aerial food of life' seemed to be the true Elixir of Life—sought after by alchemists for centuries.

Sendivogius saw the 'aerial food' percolating through all life, by way of an innocent-looking, colourless, crystalline solid: saltpetre (nitre or potassium nitrate). By observing over time the main source of saltpetre—farmyard soils—Sendivogius became convinced that the 'food of life' was condensing out of the air and growing into living saltpetre crystals. Saltpetre's life-giving power was visible in fertilizers and dynamically demonstrated in gunpowder, of which it was the key ingredient. Saltpetre also seemed to have other miraculous properties: it was used in medicines and freezing mixtures and in the manufacture of the acid, *aqua regia* (the 'queen of waters') which could dissolve gold.

'Aerial nitre'—what modern chemists would call oxygen—seemed to be the key to nature; in its gaseous form, it made all animal life possible; condensed into solid form, as saltpetre (or nitre), it gave life to plants and minerals. It was, in Sendivogius' words: 'Our water that wets not our hands, without which no mortal can live, and without which nothing grows or is generated in the world'. To the great satisfaction of the Hermetic philosophers, Sendivogius' aerial nitre also seemed to be the solution to the fourth riddle of the Emerald Tablet—'the wind carries it in its belly, its nurse is the earth'. Sendivogius' aerial nitre theory was a landmark breakthrough in the understanding of nature. Alchemy was never to be the same again.

The study of the nature of air quickly became a major topic of scientific enquiry. Research was, however, soon interrupted by the horrors of the Thirty Years' War of 1618–48, and Sendivogius himself was brought to the verge of bankruptcy. But a number of central European scientists fled to the relative safety of England, and through contacts like Robert Fludd (1574–1637) and Sir Kenelm Digby (1603–65), the Sendivogian theory received a wide audience in England. Thanks to the so-called 'Invisible College' interest in air survived the English Civil Wars and Cromwell's Commonwealth. By the 1660s air and its properties had grown into a key field of research at Oxford University. The chief experimenters included Robert Hooke (1635–1703), John Mayow (1641–79), and, of course, Robert Boyle. Although they made no mention of the anonymous man who had inspired their research, the influence of Sendivogius is clear in their writings, and it would be appropriate to call them the 'Oxford Sendivogians'.

Even with these great minds at work, the composition of air was to defy the investigators for nearly two centuries. Air contains one-fifth oxygen and four-fifths nitrogen, but the smaller quantities of carbon dioxide and water vapour make its chemical behaviour highly complex and difficult to understand. The subject was confused for many decades by the German 'Phlogiston' theory of about 1700, which was a radical departure from Sendivogian views. But Sendivogius' influence was still in evidence in 1732, when one of the earliest (and greatest) teachers of chemistry, the Flemish author, Herman Boerhaave, restated the importance of Sendivogius' discovery:

HT Archives

Holding up the mirror to nature: the frontispiece to *Utriusque Cosmi . . .* (1617) by Robert Fludd, one of the disseminators of Sendivogius' theories in the West.

Air possesses a certain occult virtue which cannot be explained by any of those properties previously investigated. That in this virtue the secret food of life lies hidden, as Sendivogius clearly said, some chemists have asserted. But what it really is, how it acts, and what exactly brings it about is still obscure. Happy the man who will discover it!

And happy he was. When Joseph Priestley isolated 'dephlogistigated air' in 1774, he tried breathing some of it. He found that his 'breast felt peculiarly light and easy for some time afterwards'. He went on:

Who can tell, but that, in time, this air may become a fashionable article in luxury. Hitherto only two mice and myself have had the privilege of breathing it . . . . Nothing I ever did has surprised me more, or is more satisfactory.

In fact, Priestley was probably not the first person to breathe pure oxygen.

In 1621 an unusual event took place in London. A vessel rowed by twelve oarsmen sailed from Westminster to Greenwich *under water*. The voyage was witnessed by James I and thousands of Londoners. This, the first recorded submarine, was constructed by the Dutch inventor and alchemist Cornelis Drebbel (1572–1633), one of the great lost figures of Renaissance science. Drebbel had become internationally famous after building a perpetual motion machine (which, in fact, was solar-powered); and from about 1604, he worked for James I, building a variety of automata, refrigerators, barometric devices, and probably the first microscope seen in England (1621).

Much of the interest in Drebbel's submarine lay not in its construction and military potential—but in an air-freshening technique that Drebbel had devised, and kept a close secret. The great Robert Boyle described Drebbel's vessel in his *New Experiments Physico-Mechanicall, Touching the spring of the Air, and its effects* (Oxford, 1660). Boyle was especially curious about a 'Chymicall liquor, which he [Drebbel] accounted the chiefe Secret of his submarine Navigation'. Boyle interviewed Drebbel's son-in-law, and discovered that when the air in the submarine became stuffy, Drebbel 'would by unstopping a vessel full of this liquor, speedily restore it to the

troubled Air such a proportion of Vitall parts, as would make it againe, for a good while, fit for respiration'. Although Boyle describes Drebbel's secret substance as a 'liquor', several other writers of the period insist it was a gas. But could it have been oxygen?

In his *Treatise on the Elements of Nature* (1608), Drebbel gives a clue to how he might have manufactured oxygen. In a passage on the origin of thunder, he writes: 'Thus is the body of the saltpetre broken up and decomposed by the power of the fire and so changed in the nature of the air'. This suggests he was aware that heating saltpetre causes it to give off a gas—and realised that this gas was the same substance that allows humans to breathe.

Modern scientists have not been comfortable with the idea that Drebbel isolated oxygen over 150 years before Lavoisier. The idea of a gas did not yet exist (the term was coined by van Helmont in the 1640s); and formal techniques for experimenting with gases were only developed around 1700 by the Englishman, Stephen Hales. Even so, behind the complex medieval terminology of spirits, vapours and exhalations, it is clear that the alchemists understood more about gases than we give them credit for. It had been known for centuries that breathing or burning things in an enclosed space reduces the quality of air, and glass apparatus had made big advances by about AD 1150 when pure alcohol was first obtained in Italy by distilling wine. In practice, there is no reason why Drebbel could not have used oxygen in his submarine, even if he did not understand the full chemical significance of what he had done.

It is likely that Drebbel learnt how to produce oxygen from Sendivogius. Drebbel belonged to a scientific and artistic elite that was already by the sixteenth century, cosmopolitan. Such men travelled Europe seeking wealthy patrons and most of them knew each other. Drebbel visited Rudolf's court at Prague in 1594 and again in 1610–11, and it was here that he may have met Sendivogius, and found out how to manufacture the 'secret food of life' by heating saltpetre.

But if Sendivogius discovered how to make oxygen in around 1600 and Drebbel used it in a practical way in 1620 why is it that nobody knows about it today? How is it that Priestley, Scheele and Lavoisier got all the credit in the

1770s? In part the answer is that the alchemists were highly secretive and believed only the worthy should be enlightened. They wrote in an obscure style so that only the 'sons of Hermes', who were prepared to spend years in study, would be able to understand their texts. Making such knowledge public, they said, was 'casting pearls before swine'. There was also the danger that the knowledge would fall into the wrong hands and be used for evil ends.

Despite its essentially honest objectives, alchemy was, even in its own time, viewed with contempt and regarded as little removed from magic and astrology. It was banned by universities, popes and kings, and Ben Jonson lampooned it furiously in *The Alchemist* (1610). The respected figures of medicine generally ignored the subject. The Imperial Count Palatine Michael Maier (1569–1622) was different.

Maier had known Sendivogius since they had studied together at Altdorf University in 1594, and got to know him better when he was employed as doctor at the Imperial court from 1609 until 1611. Maier had initially been highly sceptical about alchemy, but through Sendivogius he became a committed alchemist and one of its most ardent champions. Along with Sendivogius, Maier seems to have played a key role in the formation of secret philosophical societies, the details of which are only now beginning to emerge. In his 1617 book *Atalanta Fugiens,* Maier wrote that alchemy was the 'noblest of the scholarly disciplines, directly after theology, for its subject matter is the investigation of the greatest secrets of God's creation'.

Alchemy was also accorded respect by Robert Boyle, the archetypal enemy of Aristotelian beliefs, and often described as the world's first true scientist. Boyle believed in the possibility of transmuting base metals into gold, and was influential in obtaining Parliamentary repeal of the Act against gold multipliers in 1689. Sir Isaac Newton was another closet alchemist. In spite of his pioneering work in the 'respectable' sciences—mechanics, optics and calculus—it has recently emerged that Newton spent the bulk of his career secretly attempting to decipher the mysterious texts of alchemy.

There was another problem that prevented Sendivogius' theories from becoming common knowledge: the church.

Hermetic philosophy was knowledge about nature in addition to that in the Bible. To have openly identified a 'spirit of life' that corresponded to a real substance was risking censure. Copernicus had dared publish his theory only on his death bed; Galileo published and got into serious trouble with the Inquisition; Darwin dreaded the church's reaction, and refused to discuss his ideas in public. Sendivogius got over the problem by publishing anonymously, but then took little credit for his discovery.

Today, the identification of a 'food of life' in air by a now obscure Polish alchemist may appear to be of only trivial interest, yet the repercussions on the progress of science were profound. Sendivogius shone a bright new light on alchemy, away from attempts at gold-making towards the investigation of air. By doing so, he set in motion an explosion of protoscientific enquiry which was to end when Lavoisier identified and named oxygen in 1779. With that event, chemistry in its modern form was born.

Sendivogius still does not hold the historical status and respect he deserves; neither does alchemy. In an unscientific age, the alchemy of the hermetic philosophers was the closest there was to a science. But alchemy was more than just a predecessor to chemistry—it was a 'living chemistry'—the study of which encompassed the entirety of nature. Lavoisier has been called the father of chemistry. It is perhaps time that alchemy was acknowledged as the mother of chemistry, rather than just a wayward cousin.

FOR FURTHER READING

John Read, *Prelude to Chemistry* (London, 1936); E.J. Holmyard, *Alchemy* (London, 1957, reprinted Dover Publications, 1990); Betty Joe Dobbs, *The Foundations of Newton's Alchemy or the "Hunting of the Greene Lyon"* (Cambridge University Press, 1975); Z.R.W.M. von Martels, *Alchemy Revisited* (E.J. Brill, 1990); P. Rattansi & A. Clericuzio (Editors), *Alchemy and Chemistry in the 16th and 17th Centuries* (Kluwer Academic Publishers, 1994).

Zbigniew Szydlo, is a chemistry teacher at Highgate School, London, and author of Water which does not wet Hands: The Alchemy of Michael Sendivogius. *(Polish Academy of Sciences, Warsaw, 1994). Available from Chthobios Books, Hastings, tel: 01424-433302. Price £22.50.*

Richard Brzezinski is a science and history writer and editor. He is author of The Army of Gustavus Adolphus *(2 vols, Osprey 1991, 1993).*

Declaring an Open Season on the Wisdom of the Ages

Under the stewardship of scholars Diderot and d'Alembert, the 18th-century's
Encyclopédie championed fact and freedom of the intellect

By Robert Wernick

Most everyone in Paris 250 years ago was aware of the band of voluble, enthusiastic men scurrying around town, piling up notes and editing documents for a gigantic publishing enterprise with which they intended to change the world. It was to be called the *Encyclopédie, ou Dictionnaire raisonné des sciences, des arts et des métiers* (Encyclopedia, or Classified Dictionary of Sciences, Arts and Trades), the *Encyclopédie* for short. It took all human knowledge for its province, it took a quarter of a century to complete, it sold enough copies to justify its being called among the very earliest commercial best-sellers of modern times, and it did change the world.

This past winter, a giant exhibition celebrating the opening of new quarters for the Bibliothèque Nationale in Paris, and showcasing library treasures including the *Encyclopédie,* demonstrated just how this was done. The first two volumes of the *Encyclopédie,* which took five years to assemble, appeared in two very handsome and very expensive folio volumes in 1751; the first subscribers had only to open to page 1 to see that something very new was loose in the world. There was the first article, on the letter *A,* starting off quietly enough with

a historical summary of the letter and its ancestors, the Greek alpha, the Hebrew aleph. Then the authors of the entry went on to turn the batteries of scorn on previous authorities who had laid

down the law on the subject, like the ancient scholar Covaruvias. These authorities had explained that the letter *A* constituted the first sound made by boy babies after being born, it being the

Encyclopédie, Bibliotheque Nationale, Paris.

The Encyclopedists strove to explicate the details that underlay human endeavor. This engraving depicts the lost-wax method for casting figurative sculpture.

The appearance of the *Encyclopédie* in the mid-18th century coincided with nascent industrialization. The compendium documented emergent technologies, from the washing of molten ore (above) to printing.

first vowel in the syllable *mas,* root of the Latin adjective *masculinus.* Girl babies, the authorities averred, uttered an *e* sound, root of *feminina.* The Encyclopedists (as Diderot and his collaborators have come to be known), disregarding authority, insisted on referring to the behavior of some live babies and reported that they "make different vowel sounds, depending on how wide they open their mouths." A reader of 1997 is unlikely to find anything unusual or objectionable in this observation. But in 1751 it was a war cry of revolt. The Encyclopedists were proclaiming, in an insidiously mocking way, that direct observation of brute fact took precedence over the accumulated pile of ancient wisdom.

Denis Diderot, who wrote most of the *A* article, was never happier than when he could summon up all the ponderous columns of authority that had been tramping down the centuries and blow them away with one gust of rational thought. A few dozen pages after *A,* he found himself dealing with the *Ag-*

nus Scythicus, or Scythian lamb. The names of the authorities roll along like caissons: Scaliger, Kircher, Sigismond, Hesberetein, Hayton the Armenian, Surius, Fortunius Licetus, André Lebarrus, Adam Olearius, Olaus Vormius, "and an infinity of other botanists." All of them had gone on repeating in their learned treatises the same description of this plant growing on the steppes east of the Black Sea. A remarkable plant not only shaped like a sheep but growing a darkish down all over its body, it was said to make excellent garments and also to be the source of a cure for spitting up blood.

It took centuries of solemn repetition before another botanist, named Kempfer, took the trouble to visit the steppes and discover that there was no such thing as an *Agnus Scythicus.* He found only an outsize but otherwise ordinary fern with a kind of dusky fuzz on its leaves. Reflecting on this episode of human folly, said Diderot, will be far more useful to the mind than the Scythian lamb ever was to the lungs. It was open season on the wisdom of the ages.

The *Encyclopédie* was not at all an ambitious project to start with. It had begun back in 1745 when a printer and entrepreneur named André-François Le Breton formed a consortium to finance a French translation of the popular and widely admired *Cyclopaedia* of the Englishman Ephraim Chambers. This was the latest, and in many ways the best, of the compendiums of human knowledge that had been coming out in a more or less steady stream since a scholar in Athens created the form in the second century B.C. Le Breton's was a very modest project, involving a small capital outlay. But the undertaking soon ran into difficulties, partly because the thrifty publishers hired unskilled translators, with the result that no one could understand what they turned out.

They then called in two of the brightest young lights of the Parisian intellectual world, the all-around man of letters Denis Diderot—described in a police report as "a very bright and extremely dangerous fellow"—and the mathematician Jean d'Alembert. These two saw a chance of turning the project into a manifesto of the new age, the new way of thinking.

They never pretended to have invented the new way of thinking, they were only systematizing it, publicizing it, letting it loose to spread its rays of enlightenment and disperse the clouds of ancient superstition. They traced this intellectual revolution back a century and a half to the great Francis Bacon, Lord Chancellor of England. It was Bacon, said d'Alembert, who first recognized the necessity of experimental physics, which is the basis of the modern scientific-technological world. It was Bacon who wrote in his *Novum Organum* (1620) that it was not enough simply to observe nature. It was necessary to put nature to the question, that is to say, to create experiments under controlled conditions, an approach that has since become known as the scientific method.

Bacon could not shake off all the shackles of the old ways of thinking all by himself. He was taken in, like everybody else, by the Scythian lamb. But he was far ahead of his time in insisting that accurate investigation of the phenomena of the world took precedence over ancient officially approved dogma.

Following Baconian principles, the *Encyclopédie* dealt with the random pieces of vulgar reality on the same level as the broad tenets that held them together. You didn't need a witch doctor or the abstract speculations of Aristotle or Thomas Aquinas to tell you how the Universe worked. In the *Encyclopédie* it was all set out in crystal-clear prose and engravings. You could learn how to solve mathematical problems and analyze human emotions, how to construct a coal mine, cast an equestrian statue of Louis XIV, fight a duel, make soap. You could consult an entry on how to perform a bladder operation (restraining your patient first in a special surgical chair) or an article on how to study a flea under a microscope. What was new about the *Encyclopédie's* method was that it mixed the theoretical with the practical. Indeed it had no use for theory without practical application: that was the secret weapon which unleashed the scientific-technological-industrial revolution of modern times.

Everything started with facts, and no fact was beneath the notice of Diderot and d'Alembert. Hence their insistence that the volumes of illustrative plates were as important as the volumes of text. They tried to bring everything up to date, to show just how the world was being run at the very moment. It was this more than anything else that distinguished this encyclopedia from its predecessors.

The editors and authors of the *Encyclopédie* were perfectly willing to devote 20 pages to *l'ame,* the soul, in a long account of metaphysical and epistemological speculation. They also devoted 15 pages to the machine manufacture of stockings, one of the principal industrial products of their day, showing in text and engravings all 86 steps in the process.

Previous encyclopedists had aimed to summarize the arts and sciences. But Diderot and company added a significant word to their title—*métiers,* trades and crafts—insisting that no sharp line could be drawn between theory and practice. Such a line had been drawn as a matter of course in the pre-Baconian past, when the idea of treating the human soul and stockings on the same level of seriousness would have seemed obscene. Aristotle and Thomas Aquinas could reason as well as anyone who ever lived, but it would never have occurred to them to reason about the humdrum tools of daily life.

Diderot, as managing editor of the project, kept a strict eye on his collaborators, even when he had to spend four months in jail, to make sure they were accurate and up to date. He had Louis-Jacques Goussier, the superb draftsman who did more than 900 of the plates, spend six weeks in paper mills, six months in ironworks and glassworks, a month watching anchors being made. It would take more than 20 years to get out the first edition: 71,818 articles arranged alphabetically in 17 volumes, plus 11 volumes containing 2,885 illustrative plates. New editions, revised editions, supplementary editions, rival editions, would go on appearing for another half-century.

There may have been as many as 300 men (and one anonymous woman) who collaborated on writing the articles of the original *Encyclopédie.* They came from different backgrounds; of those whose backgrounds can be identified, 15 percent were doctors, 12 percent were administrative officials, 8 percent were priests, 4 percent were titled nobility, 4 percent were merchants or manufacturers. They included famous scientists and famous writers like Voltaire and Montesquieu.

Diderot, 34 years old when he started the work, was the son of a provincial artisan and wrote more than 5,000 of the articles himself. He got fairly substantial lump-sum payments from the businessmen who were underwriting the project—royalties for authors were unknown in those days—but there were many contributors who worked for no monetary compensation whatever, among them the good-tempered and indefatigable Chevalier Louis de Jaucourt. A learned aristocrat with a noble lineage back to the early Middle Ages, he wrote no less than 17,000 articles.

One of them was the last entry under Z, an article on Zzuéné about which there was nothing to say but that it was a city on the eastern bank of the Nile in upper Egypt not far from Ethiopia. That left the author free to embark on a paean to the completion of the great *Encyclopédie.* In the writer's eyes, this very accomplishment had been foretold by Lord Bacon, who had predicted an assemblage of scholars who would engage in an "admirable conspiracy" to flood with light the world of the arts and sciences. "A time will come," said Bacon, "when philosophers will undertake this effort. Then will arise, from the dark realm of the sophists and the envious, a dark swarm which, seeing these eagles soaring and being unable either to stop or to follow their rapid flight, will try by their vain croakings to belittle their accomplishment and their triumph."

The croakings were not long in coming. The printing of books, at least legally, in France (as was the case in the whole world of the mid-18th century, except for England and Holland) depended like most other aspects of life on what the French called *privilége.* A tight little cartel had the monopoly, and each work they printed had to receive a *privilége*

Omnivorous contributors reported on everyday life, too. The entry on fencing tried to estimate casualties.

Encyclopédie, Bibliotheque Nationale, Paris.

or license, signed by the king, which indicated his gracious permission.

The king could hardly be expected to put his seal of approval on misleading or subversive works. And there was no lack of authorities to point out that the Encyclopedists made many factual errors, often borrowed (some said plagiarized) the work of others and wrote in a tone that was subversive from the word go. After the introduction, a foldout sheet contained a sort of table of contents in the form of an allegorical tree of knowledge, showing how all human understanding flowed up the one trunk of Reason and out into many branches.

This was a perfectly traditional device, except that in traditional books the root of the tree was Revealed Religion, or Theology. In the *Encyclopédie's* tree, Theology was only one branch of the limb called Metaphysics, and it in turn was divided into twigs labeled Religion, Superstition, Divination and Black Magic. It was higher up on the tree, but no thicker or more handsome than the twigs farther down, such as differential Algebra, Spelling, Heraldry, Hydrostatics, Instrumental Music, Drapery, Syntax, Clock-making, Fireworks.

A Jesuit publication, the *Journal de Trévoux* accused the Encyclopedists of favoring freedom of thought. Why, it was asked, were there so many articles devoted to obscure pagan deities and so few to kings and saints? Why did Abbé Mallet, the priest who wrote the article on Noah's Ark, spend no time at all on

the Ark's spiritual significance and so much time on ignoble calculations of how big the vessel must have been to hold all those animals, how many man-hours Noah and his sons must have spent cleaning out the mountains of daily manure, how many extra sheep and cattle had to be brought aboard to provide food for the wolves and lions? Pope Clement XIII put the *Encyclopédie* on the Index [of prohibited books] in 1759 and ordered all Catholics who owned a copy of the work to have it burned by a priest, or be excommunicated.

The Encyclopedists might face the threat of jail—or hellfire. They were accused of atheism, free thought, political subversion, corruption of morals. Hitherto, said a bishop, "Hell has vomited its venom drop by drop. Today there are torrents of errors and impieties."

The French government, faced with increasing pressure from defenders of traditional values, took a course, common to all governments, of playing both sides of the board. With one hand it condemned. In 1752, the King's Council ordered the first two volumes of the *Encyclopédie* "to be and remain suppressed." In 1759, the government revoked the license that allowed the *Encyclopédie* to be printed.

With the other hand, it quietly signaled to the Encyclopedists to go on doing just what they were doing. This was possible because the man in charge of suppressing the work was actually devoted to its principles. He was Chrétien-

Guillaume de Lamoignon de Malesherbes, a very cultivated and very brave man who 33 years later would again stick his neck way out by undertaking the defense of Louis XVI at the trial that condemned him to death. During the *Encyclopédie's* early years he was Directeur de la Librairie, the official charged with overseeing the production and distribution of books in France. He was one of the enlightened aristocrats who were convinced that the whole system of *privilèges* and thought control on which the old order was based was both irrational and hopelessly inefficient.

While he acceded to decrees revoking the *Encyclopédie's* permit, he also found time to give Diderot advance warning of a police raid. And Malesherbes offered his own cellar as a safe hiding place for all the thousands of pages of Diderot's notes and drafts until the police were back in their barracks. He found in the arsenal of French government administrators a pleasant little weapon known as *Permission tacite*. This loophole meant that, for instance, while there might be a decree forbidding the printing of the *Encyclopédie* in France, the publishers might, by greasing the palm of a printer in the Swiss city of Neuchâtel arrange a sleight of hand. They could issue the last ten volumes in Paris with fraudulent title pages, stating the printer to be one Samuel Faulche & Compagnie in Switzerland.

Malesherbes realized that the *Encyclopédie* and all it represented in the way of freedom of thought and experimental physics, formed the wave of the future. So did La Breton and other far-sighted, greedy and unscrupulous printer-booksellers, who understood that the new thirst for science and knowledge that was spreading through the world was a potential gold mine. They had stumbled onto a best-seller.

It was a stupendous undertaking. The making and merchandizing of books was still, in the 18th century, a handicraft industry, offering deluxe products to the tiny minority of the population that was both literate and rich. Everything had to be done by hand. The production of paper involved an army of homeless itinerant laborers, who turned ragpickers after the harvest was done, and armies of skilled artisans to turn the rags into paper and then print and bind the volumes.

The quantity of paper needed for the *Encyclopédie* was enormous. Printing only the first volume in the quarto edition called for more than a million pieces of paper, and there were 36 volumes in the quarto edition. There were times when the supply of paper ran low; the work was nearly brought to a halt. Even with a steady supply of paper, it took five months of hard labor by five compositors and 20 pressmen to turn out a volume. A barrel of ink cost as much as a printing press, and a bad walnut crop in the south of France or a revolution in the American Colonies might cause the price of ink to skyrocket.

Very little information has survived of the actual details of book publishing before the 19th century. The *Encyclopédie* is an exception. Prof. Robert Darnton of Princeton discovered about 30 years ago in Switzerland a treasure trove in the form of 50,000 business documents and letters in the archives of the Société typográphique de Neuchâtel, an important publisher of French books in the 18th century. From them he was able to construct, in an admirably thorough and thoroughly enjoyable book called *The Business of Enlightenment*, a full picture of how a work like the *Ency-*

The developing science of medicine intrigued the Encyclopedists: diagram depicts the arterial system.

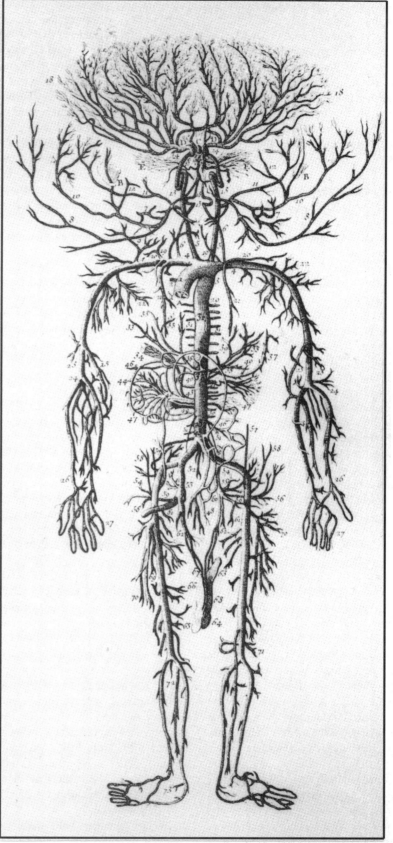

Encyclopédie, Bibliotheque Nationale, Paris.

clopédie was created, manufactured and sold in those years.

It is not a pretty picture. As far as trade practices and merchandising are concerned, it must be admitted that modern publishing houses, so often denounced for their cross commercialism, are paragons of honesty and integrity compared with their forebears of the courtly 18th century. Publishers routinely lied, cheated, swindled, bribed, conspired and spied. They also often mangled and distorted their authors' texts: an article in the Encyclopédie might take a different slant depending on whether it was offered for sale in a Catholic or in a Protestant country.

Diderot came to think that his own work, after it had passed through all these dirty hands, was a "monstrosity." When he was asked to collaborate on a revised version of the work, he replied in a few words of colloquial French best translated as "Get lost."

The fact remained that, for all the wrangling and the mendacities and the troubles with the law, the volumes kept coming out—for the very good reason that the bottom line always showed a more than healthy profit. The publishers made money on a scale that had never been seen before in the book business, and that would not be seen again till the arrival of mechanized publishing and cheap pulp paper in the middle of the next century.

By 1789 almost 25,000 sets of authorized folio, quarto and octavo editions printed more or less legally in Paris, Lyon, Geneva, Neuchâtel, Bern, Lausanne, Lucca and Leghorn had been sold throughout Europe. At an average of 30 volumes per set, that makes three quarters of a million books—an extraordinary figure for the time.

The first folio edition was terribly expensive, affordable only by very rich people like government ministers, archbishops, Russian princes, German princelings. But as fiercely competitive publishers poured out less-expensive quarto and octavo editions, the Encyclopédie came to be read by more and more thousands of more or less ordinary people. It was still far beyond the reach of most of the population. A skilled locksmith or printer would have had to cough up the equivalent of fifteen and a half weeks' wages for the cheapest octavo edition. If Diderot had to buy it, it would have taken four and a half weeks of his pay for the project. Still, the publishers had judged that there was a huge untapped market for books like this; their profits went up all around.

No one can tell how many people actually read the Encyclopédie but by the standards of the time it was surely very considerable. Everyone in Europe who wanted to keep up with current knowledge and current standards had to read it, or at least say he did.

Apparently few if any copies got to Colonial America. But American revolutionaries had imbibed the 18th-century intellectual discourse that created the Encyclopédie. Benjamin Franklin was acting in the spirit of the philosophes when, after sages had been speculating for untold centuries about the nature of lightning, he put a kite up in the sky in an effort to find out.

Jefferson was following the Encyclopedic rules when he heard that pious people were saying that shellfish found at the top of mountains in fossilized form must have been put there by Noah's flood. Jefferson didn't buy the deluge explanation. He took time out to calculate that if all the moisture suspended in the earth's atmosphere were to be condensed into water, the oceans still would not rise halfway up the mountains.

By the time the French Revolution broke out in 1789, Diderot and d'Alembert and many original contributors were dead. However, a new generation had come along to digest the enormous mass of new theoretical and technical knowledge that was piling up year after year. The new Encyclopedists were less philosophical, more technical and more specialized than the old. The new version in 229 volumes that came out between 1781 and 1832 was called the Encyclopédie Méthodique (Methodical Encyclopedia). But the Encyclopedists' aims and their methods were in fact basically the same.

Their enemies were quick to proclaim, and have proclaimed ever since, that the Encyclopedists were responsible for the French Revolution, the Reign of Terror, the guillotine and all the horrors of the modern world. Their friends were equally quick to give them credit for the rise of liberty, universal suffrage, freedom of the press and all the progress of the modern world.

The Encyclopedists had no common political program, and their direct influence on political and social events was probably very small. Darnton's analysis of the account books shows that most of the sales went to people very much like the Encyclopedists themselves, upper-class people brought up in a world of privilege and unchallenged authority. An edition that sold 338 copies in the placid provincial town of Besançon where the population of 28,000 consisted largely of priests, professors, lawyers, officials and landholders, sold only 28 in Lille (pop. 61,000). In that city, the inhabitants were starting to build factories that would change the face of the world, but the people building them were too busy to read anything beyond their balance sheets.

Keenly aware of change, the Encyclopedists had little more prescience than anyone else of how the change was coming. They lived at the dawn of the Industrial Age but could scarcely grasp what would come of it. The technology they admired and illustrated so lovingly was a highly developed handicraft, mostly devoted to luxury goods like stockings and watches. They were not themselves revolutionaries, though their belief in free inquiry and their contempt for irrational authority must have had considerable influence on revolutionaries.

When the revolution in France did come, dismantling the whole vast structure of privilege at one swoop, they had different opinions about it, responded in different ways and had different fates. Some were guillotined, some were pressed into service to make saltpeter and cannon, and to create a rational system of weights and measures. The naturalist Daubenton was asked to dissect a rhinoceros from the former king's menagerie for revolutionary leaders eager to disseminate knowledge.

The great mathematician Condorcet, who had hailed the revolution but had voted against the death penalty for the king, was forced to flee for his life. It was while hiding from the authorities that he wrote his classic demonstration that the progress of knowledge proved that "nature has placed no limit to our hopes" and that the human race was bound to approach ever closer to perfection. Wandering in the country, and starving, he ordered an omelet in a country inn, and when they asked him how many eggs he wanted in it, he faced one of those unexpected practical problems that pop up in times of great social change. He was a marquis by birth, and there would have been no reason for him at any time in his life to see the inside of a kitchen. He answered at random, a dozen, raising doubt as to the reality of his claim to being an unemployed worker. He was thrown into jail and died there, perhaps having swallowed the poison he had hidden in his ring in order to avoid the guillotine.

Most of the surviving Encyclopedists were content to wait out the revolution, and eventually got jobs at universities and government institutes, continuing to amass and channel and analyze the immense flood of knowledge pouring at an ever increasing rate over the earth.

Whatever happened to the individual Encyclopedists, the Encyclopédie itself survived. The solemn old volumes may sit unread in libraries, but some of the livelier articles are continually being reprinted in anthologies of 18th-century prose.

Few people today share the Encyclopedists' ingenuous faith that human knowledge could be satisfactorily summarized in 28 volumes or in 229 (as the last *Encyclopédie* numbered) or that greater diffusion of knowledge must lead to greater happiness for mankind.

But in a sense the Encyclopédie has been triumphant. The spirit of Lord Bacon, the combination of free curiosity and empirical evidence, roams unchecked over most of the world. When the Catholic Church, which once ordered the Encyclopédie to be burned, wished to settle the question of whether the Shroud of Turin really wrapped a crucified man 19 centuries ago or was created by an artist some centuries later, it did not rely on consultation of ancient authorities, as Pope Clement XIII surely would have done. It sent the Shroud to a laboratory. This is just what Diderot would have advised.

A frequent contributor [to] Smithsonian, Robert Wernick writes from Paris for part of the year. He reported recently on the restoration of a chateau in the French countryside.

HT Archives

Witchcraft: The Spell That Didn't Break

Owen Davies argues that a widespread belief in witchcraft persisted in eighteenth- and nineteenth-century rural Britain despite the influence of the Enlightenment.

THE ADVENT OF industrialisation and the rise of the so-called 'Enlightenment' during the eighteenth century has often been portrayed as a watershed in British cultural life. Advances in the field of science and medicine are presumed to have rapidly dispelled 'superstitious' beliefs, as the spread of rational knowledge gradually trickled down to the masses. The dark days of the witch-trials were left behind and the people were freed from the everyday fear of the witch. However, historians are starting to realise that the history of witchcraft does not end with the execution of the last witch or the legal denial of their existence.

The Witchcraft Act of 1736 repealed the English Statutes against witchcraft of 1563 and 1604, and also the Scottish Statute of 1563 (the Irish statute of 1587 remained fossilized in legislation until its belated repeal in 1821). From thenceforth the law dictated that

> no Prosecution, Suit, or Proceeding, shall be commenced or carried on against any Person or Persons for Witchcraft, Sorcery, Inchantment, or Conjuration, or for charging another

ABOVE: 'The ride through the murky air'—a 19th-century illustration to Harrison Ainsworth's 'The Lancashire Witches' shows a literary image of witchcraft.

with any such offence, in any Court whatsoever in Great Britain.

The Act further made it an offence to 'pretend' to exercise or use any kind of witchcraft or sorcery. For the legislature at least, the concept of witchcraft, which had brought hundreds of innocent people to the gallows over the previous two centuries, was now a mere pretence, a false belief consigned to the dustbin of history. But the passing of the Act did not signify the mass rejection of witchcraft. Many educated and eminent people like Dr Samuel Johnson and William Blackstone, one of the foremost legal minds of the eighteenth century, continued to believe that there was such a thing as witchcraft. Not only did the irrefutable word of the Bible plainly speak of witches, but some of the most respected men of the previous century had expressed their belief in witchcraft. However, although Methodists and Scottish Presbyterians continued to fear the threat of Satan and his earthly vassals, and condemned the Act of 1736, by the mid-eighteenth century the intellectual classes had comfortingly convinced themselves that witches no longer existed. Yet little thought was actually given to explaining why they had disappeared. As Dr Samuel Johnson observed, nicely dodging the issue, 'Why it ceased, we cannot tell, as we cannot tell the reason of many things'. In newly 'enlightened' Britain it was thought best not to dwell too much on the dubious events of the recent past.

Educated people like Dr. Johnson continued to believe that there was such a thing as witchcraft.

Although witchcraft became a matter of private debate among the middle and upper classes, it remained a reality for a large portion of the population. While for the ruling elites of early modern England and Scotland witchcraft had been seen as a satanic threat to their moral and spiritual authority, for much of the labouring population, both before

and after 1736, witchcraft was essentially an economic crime. Up until the second half of the nineteenth century, the way of life for many in rural areas had not changed fundamentally for two hundred years. The majority of people were still part of an agrarian economy, and a large portion of the population was involved in some form of husbandry to supplement their income or diet. Other than the very meagre relief provided by the Poor Law, there was no safety-net to fall back on when serious misfortune struck. Thus the illness of a family member or of a pig or cow could cause considerable hardship and lead to suspicions of witchcraft. Most staple foodstuffs such as butter, cheese and bread continued to be produced within the home or farmstead, and when these failed witchcraft might also be blamed. When people suspected witchcraft, they often looked no further than their neighbours to find the culprit. Relations between neighbours were close-knit and intense, but far from harmonious. Borrowing, begging and trespass were continual sources of friction. There was little privacy and gossip was rife. In such an environment personal conflicts were bound to occur frequently.

From the 1680s onwards, the number of witch-trials heard in English and Welsh courts diminished to a trickle, and the last execution for witchcraft was in 1684. In Scotland, too, the number of trials began to decline around the same time, though the courts remained more willing to accept evidence against witches, and exercised little restraint in their sentencing. Thus a serious outbreak of accusations occurred in 1697, resulting in the execution of seven supposed witches, and the very last witch to be burnt was in 1722. The decline in indictments some thirty years before the repeal of the witchcraft laws was not, as has sometimes been assumed, an expression of declining belief. There is no evidence to suggest that there was a decrease in the number of complaints made to justices. Instead, as the trials became a legal embarrassment, justices increasingly dismissed complaints outright or dealt with them informally.

For the majority of the population who continued to consider witchcraft a serious threat, there must have been a good deal of frustration at the withdrawal of the justices and the courts from the arena. Yet the evidence would suggest that people were very slow to

HT Archives

'Credulity, superstition and fanaticism—a medley.' An engraving by William Hogarth mocks the continuing resistance to rationalism in the Age of Reason.

HT Archives

The fatal 'swimming' of suspected witch Ruth Osborne in Hertfordshire in 1751 led to the hanging of Thomas Colley for her murder. But 5,000 had seen her die.

realise that there was no longer a general consensus concerning the need to suppress witches. Right up until the late nineteenth century magistrates up and down the country continued to receive requests for the arrest of suspected witches. In May 1870, for example, Mr Lushington, a magistrate at the Thames police court, was asked by a poor woman to arrest a neighbour named Biddy Coghlan for being a witch. The plaintiff had a hen that had died after laying a few abnormally small eggs, and Coghlan was held responsible. Not surprisingly, Lushington had little time for such complaints, and told the complainant to go about her business.

In the absence of a legal means of trying witches, people continued to resort to the trial by water, otherwise known as witch-swimming. This had been employed throughout the seventeenth century under quasi-official sanction. It was not, in fact, a legally recognised form of proof, but it was often accepted as such by judges and juries. The suspected witches had their thumbs tied to their toes, and a rope bound round their waists. They were then thrown into a pond or river to see whether they would sink or float. If the water rejected them and they floated, this was deemed a divine sign that they were guilty. If, however, they sank, then

God had embraced them, thereby proving their innocence. Swimming must have been a terrifying ordeal for those subjected to it. Both before and after the actual immersion the victims were often subjected to much violent abuse, and many of those who 'proved' their innocence by sinking nearly drowned anyway. These witch-swimmings continued to occur fairly frequently up until the early nineteenth century and could attract hundreds of people. In 1737, for instance, a woman was swum in the River Ouse, at Oakley in Bedfordshire. A large crowd gathered, including the vicar of Oakley, and there were cries of 'A witch! Drown her! Hang her!'. Quite often magistrates, or some other passing 'gentleman', would intercede and stop the proceedings, but legal action was rarely taken against those who organised such brutal events, unless someone died. One of the few prosecutions occurred in Hertfordshire in 1751 when Thomas Colley stood trial for the murder of Ruth Osborne who was swum in a pond near Tring. A crowd, which one witness estimated as being some five thousand strong, gathered to see the swimming, and a collection was even held to recompense the organisers. Tragically, Osborne died from her repeated immersions, and Colley was subsequently hanged for his role in the affair.

The Tring case was widely reported in the press at the time, and became something of a national sensation. It provided ample proof of the strong hold that witchcraft still held over the minds of the people. Yet there was an undoubted reluctance on the part of the authorities to get involved in any way in what they considered 'vulgar' affairs. As a result there was no campaign against the continued persecution of supposed witches. This led to the wholly unsatisfactory situation whereby some of those accused of witchcraft actually volunteered to undergo the ordeal by water because local justices were deaf to their pleas for succour. This is exactly what happened to an old woman of Stanningfield, Suffolk, in 1792. She pleaded with Sir Charles Davers and the Rev. John Ord to protect her against charges of witchcraft that had 'very much disordered her head'. They said they could no nothing, however, and so she decided to let herself be swum before the community in order to clear her name. Her husband and brother complied with her request as they feared she would otherwise kill herself, and they held the rope at her swimming to ensure that she was not mistreated. Fortunately she sank, though she was dragged out 'almost lifeless'.

It is important to realise that throughout the early modern period recourse to the law was just one of several options that victims of witchcraft could choose. People did not go running to the courts every time they considered themselves bewitched. So after 1736 the pattern of response to witchcraft was not that different. Some went to those intriguing magical practitioners known as cunning-folk to be cured. A counter-spell such as a witch-bottle might be employed. Numerous examples of these have been found dating from the seventeenth to the twentieth century. In its simplest form a witch-bottle consisted of a bottle filled with the bewitched person's urine. Into this was put some sharp objects such as thorns, pins or nails. The bottle was then sealed, and either buried in the ground, placed under the hearth-stone, or heated in a fire. The bottle represented the witch's bladder, and the thorns and pins were meant to cause him or her such excruciating pain that they would be forced to remove their spell. However, the most potent method of breaking witches' power was to scratch them in order to draw blood. Since this constituted a physical assault, some who employed it found themselves in court for their violent actions. It is these cases, arising from the act of scratching, which form the bulk of what are effectively witch-trials in reverse. These were court cases in which accused witches were no longer appearing as defendants charged with a capital crime, but as prosecutors seeking legal retribution against those who assaulted them. Most of these prosecutions were heard before the summary court of petty sessions, although some were deemed serious enough to be brought before the quarter sessions or assizes.

A general trawl of secondary sources and a brief random sampling of newspapers from England and Wales has revealed over seventy reverse witch-trials from the mid-eighteenth century to the early twentieth century, as well as nu-

HT Archives

A Devonshire village 'wise man' of the late 19th century: such 'cunning folk' were consulted about counter-charms when witchcraft was suspected.

In the mid-nineteenth century among rural folk 'belief in witchcraft is all but universal'

merous prosecutions involving cunning-folk. The majority of these date from the nineteenth rather than the eighteenth century, partly because there was greater concern over the continued belief in witchcraft then, and also because the introduction of a professional police force facilitated the lodging of official complaints. Indeed, a systematic survey of nineteenth-century Somerset newspapers has uncovered twenty-six reverse witch-trials from that county alone, and no doubt several more went unrecorded. Based on these samples I would suggest that the number of such cases from England, Wales and Scotland probably number well over two hundred. If we further consider that these represent only those assaults which came to court, then we get some idea of the continued level of violence against suspected witches in an age when agents of the British Empire were complaining of the 'heathen' behaviour of many of its co-

lonial subjects. The comparison was not lost on everyone. In the mid-nineteenth century the educationalist, James Augustus St John, bemoaned how

> here in England, in the midst of our civilization, with the light of Christianity, ready to pour into the meanest and darkest hovels [violence against witches was] still prevailing in our rural districts, while the belief in witches is all but universal.

There were numerous women with the scars to prove it. In 1935 a doctor from Poole, Dorset, wrote about an old woman of his acquaintance whose back and chest were covered with scars from being scratched. At the time of the assault she had twenty-two wounds that required stitching up.

The source of the majority of these assaults lay in the prolonged and inexplicable illness of family members. For all the advances in the understanding of human biology, the medical profession's ability to cure remained rudimentary. Until the development of aspirin and antibiotics during the twentieth century, doctors and vets could provide little comfort for a wide range of human and animal medical conditions. Some seri-

ous illnesses, such as internal cancers, remained undiagnosable, and so appeared mysterious to both doctor and patient. When people fell ill, witchcraft was not usually suspected straight away, and general practitioners were called in to apply their medicines. It was only if their treatment failed to provide any significant relief that suspicions sometimes grew that there might be some supernatural cause. A cunning-man or-woman might then be consulted to identify the witch responsible and to instruct on the best course of action. One example amongst many that could be given to illustrate this process occurred in 1854. A man from Heavitree near Exeter fell ill, and went to be treated by the local Poor Law Union surgeon. Finding little relief in the medicine given to him he discontinued his attendance and went to consult a 'wizard doctor'. This gentleman told him that the 'Union doctor was a consummate fool, and did not know what was the matter with him, for he was "bewitched"', and for the large sum of thirty shillings he provided him with a charm that would break the witch's spell.

Most of the rest of the reverse witch-trials resulted from the death or illness of horses, cattle and pigs, from the failure of domestic food processing, or from poor fishing catches. Admittedly, only one case involving fishing has been found, but further newspaper research in

The last straw was a bewitched pudding that swelled so much in the pot it was impossible to remove.

counties with large fishing communities would probably reveal more. The case was heard by a court in Peterhead, Scotland, in September 1872, and concerned a man who drew blood from his wife to ensure that he would have a good catch of herring. In several instances people experienced a series of inexplicable misfortunes. Thus in 1895 a poor, elderly woman of Long Sutton, Lincolnshire,

A coven of witches: a familiar image of a cult that was all too real for many rural people. From 'The Lancashire Witches'.

was assaulted by a farming couple for having supposedly bewitched their cows, pigs, hens, and butter. The last straw was a bewitched pudding that swelled so much in the pot that it was impossible to remove. Although people continued to interpret misfortune in terms of witchcraft, and individuals continued to be subjected to violent attack for being witches right up until the early decades of the present century, from the late nineteenth century onwards the cultural environment in which witchcraft functioned was undergoing a profound transformation. The mechanisation of agriculture, the opening up of a global market for meat and wheat, severe agricultural depression, emigration, and urbanisation led to the fracturing of communal relations across the country. The local production of foodstuffs declined. Bread, butter, milk and cheese were now being brought in and sold by burgeoning retail outlets. People became increasingly divorced from the traditional agricultural rhythm of life. Once largely self-sufficient communities became wholly dependent on goods produced outside the community. As a result, the everyday toing and froing among neighbours buying, borrowing and begging from each other, which helped foster intimate neighbourhood relations, became less frequent. While communities were losing their cohesion

and becoming less introspective, life in general was also becoming more financially secure. The spread of trade unionism, the beginnings of the welfare state—particularly the advent of old age pensions in 1909—the rise of personal insurance, and the eventual setting up of wage boards, meant that the impact of those misfortunes which had often led to accusations of witchcraft was lessened. Witchcraft gradually ceased to serve a function for those who believed in it, and although stories of witches continued to be told and-believed in, fewer and fewer people attracted the reputation of being witches as the social circumstances which produced accusations dwindled. However, while the long-held popular tradition of witchcraft was becoming obsolete, a new phase in the modern history of witchcraft was beginning.

During the late nineteenth century there occurred what has been described as the 'Occult Revival'. This was a renewed learned interest in ceremonial magic that grew out of the Masonic movement, and which was encouraged by the popularity and influence of spiritualism. There had been a small number of erudite, experimental magicians throughout the eighteenth and nineteenth centuries, but what defined the Occult Revival was the shift from solitary to collective magical practice, coupled with the formulation of a new magical tradition bringing together ancient pagan beliefs and the Christian occult philosophies of early modern Europe. To legitimise the credentials of this new brand of occultism, some occultists claimed that they were the inheritors of a secret pagan movement. Powerful support for this nascent tradition was provided by the work on witchcraft by the respected Egyptologist Margaret Murray. In 1921 her book, The Witch-Cult in Western Europe, was pub-

lished. In it she argued that those persecuted as witches in the past were not Devil worshippers but members of a pre-Christian religion who gathered together at 'sabbaths' to venerate and supplicate a horned god. This notion of a pagan witch-cult was further developed by the founder of the modern witchcraft movement, Gerald Gardner. This freemason and spiritualist was a great admirer of Murray's work, and in a series of books published after the Second World War, he set out to trace the history of this ancient religion that came to be called 'Wicca', and to formulate a ritual structure for new members.

However, the concept of witchcraft propounded by the neo-magicians of late nineteenth- and early twentieth-century Britain was very different from the popular experience of witchcraft. There is absolutely no evidence in the modern historical record that those accused of witchcraft were pagan worshippers. In the opinion of those who accused and assaulted them, witches were guilty of malice and spite, not of subversive religious practices. A growing number of Wiccans are accepting this historical fact, and are distancing themselves from the Gardnerian claims for an inherited witchcraft tradition. Those who continue to claim for their religion people labelled as witches in the past, should remember that those who carried the scars of popular persecution were often God-fearing, churchgoing folk who would probably have been as horrified to be embraced as a pagan as scratched for a witch.

FOR FURTHER READING

Bob Bushaway, *Tacit, Unsuspected, but still Implicit Faith: Alternative Belief in Nineteenth-Century Rural England, in* Tim Harris (ed.), *Popular Culture in England, c. 1500-1850* (Macmillan, 1995); Ronald Hutton, *The Triumph of the Moon: A History of Modern Pagan Witchcraft* (Oxford University Press, forthcoming); Ralph Merrifield, *The Archaeology of Ritual and Magic* (Guild Publishing, 1987); James Sharpe, *Instruments of Darkness: Witchcraft in England 1550-1750* (Hamish Hamilton, 1996).

Dr. Owen Davies is the author of Witchcraft, Magic and Culture, 1736-1951 (Manchester University Press, 1999).

Blacks in the Gordon Riots

Marika Sherwood *trawls contemporary reports of the anti-Catholic protests that rocked London in June 1780 to reveal the black men and women who took part, exploring their motives and punishments for doing so.*

The evident Decay of Trade, the enormous Increase of Taxes to carry on a ruinous War against our Colonies, joined with a Perfect Hatred against the secret Advisers and Promoters of it . . . the Ministry has laid too many Burthens on the People to be borne with Patience. I only wonder they have been quiet so long . . .' wrote 'A Detester of ill-grounded Accusations' to the *Public Advertiser* on July 24th, 1780. The 'they' were the Londoners who had rioted during the first week of June 1780.

The poor of London, as well as the not-so-poor, had many other reasons for discontent. For them the city was an unsavoury, unsanitary and grossly overcrowded place, where footpads and robbers were a constant menace and 'justice' was often meted out on the evidence of paid informers. The many gaols housed the bankrupts, the criminals and the political discontents: some 200 'crimes' merited capital punishment. There was resentment against war-profiteering and against the numbers of the Government's 'placemen' and pensioners. Those not liable to taxes were liable to impressment, into both the army and the navy, whose thirst for men seemed unquenchable. Employment was insecure and irregular and 'combining' to attempt to obtain better wages and conditions was illegal.

The city was home to French, Dutch, Irish and Jewish immigrants, as well as an unknown number of people of African descent. The majority of the Afri-

cans probably arrived in the city as the servants of returning plantation owners and colonial merchants, of the captains of vessels in the slave and colonial trades and of the wealthy and even not-so-wealthy households which had either bought them or received them as gifts from those involved in the trade. Some might have been second- or even third-generation Londoners as Britain had been involved in the trade in slaves since the sixteenth century. Others were black Americans who, having fought on the British side in the War of Independence, had been granted their freedom and had fled to Britain.

In such conditions it is hardly surprising that the riots of 1780, named after the leader of the Protestant Association, Lord George Gordon, should have transmuted from anti-Roman Catholic insurrection to a political riot lasting some days. The mob voiced no demands, but it was the symbols of authority and repression that the people burnt down: the gaols, the homes of judges and magistrates and the Lord Chief Justice; and the grossly unpopular Blackfriars bridge tollhouses; pawnshops, crimping houses (where impressed men were kept prior to embarkation) and spunging houses (which held debtors at the pleasure of their creditors). Only the presence of the military prevented the sacking of the Bank of England. The black flag, used as a symbol of defiance in the Highland Clearances, was seen in the streets, sometimes emblazoned with a red cross, whose significance it has not yet been

possible to determine. A total of 285 rioters were killed by the military; hundreds were wounded and 450 were taken prisoner.

Edmund Burke had warned the Government that

> If I understand the temper of the publick at this moment a very great part of the lower, and some of the middling people of this city, are in a very critical disposition, and such as ought to be managed with *firmness and delicacy* . . .

Was it his advice that resulted in fewer hangings than might have been expected? Gordon was found not guilty and freed.

The riots took place during the first week of June; before the end of the month the trials of 326 rioters began at the London and Southwark courts. Among those indicted were John Glover, who 'with a great number of disorderly persons' was charged with 'riotous and tumultuous assembly, and assaulting Newgate and setting loose the prisoners and setting fire to and destroying the prison'. Other reports in the indictment include the demolition of the house of Richard Akerman, one of the turnkeys of the prison. Similarly charged was Benjamin Bowfey. Another rioter tried on June 28th was Charlotte Gardiner, who, with some others, had been indicted for 'riotous assembly' and for demolishing the dwelling house of John Lebarty (sic) of St Catherine's Lane. Lebarty was an Italian, who 'kept a public house and a slop shop', and might well have been a Roman Catholic. On July 14th, Charlotte Gardiner was found guilty. Three days later John Glover and Benjamin Bowfey were also found guilty. These three were among the fifty-nine rioters with capital convictions—but only Charlotte Gardiner was among the twenty-one who were actually executed. All three were described as 'black' in the records.

What can we learn about black people residing in London in 1780 and about attitudes towards them from the trial reports? It must be borne in mind that slavery was not illegal in Britain at this time and that a few slaves were sold both at auction and privately in the major cities. Profits from the trade in enslaved Africans and from slave-worked farms and plantations in the Americas poured into British coffers. There was not yet a concerted movement against the trade, though both John Wesley and the Quakers had spoken out against it. While some were antagonistic to the presence of blacks in Britain, a few others were so horrified at the treatment meted out to their slaves by some British owners that they began legal proceedings to attempt to clarify the position and rights of slaves and owners. Lord Mansfield, the Chief Justice, consistently ruled that these slaves were not entitled to wages and that as they had not been 'hired servants they were not entitled to poor relief should their circumstances change. Nevertheless, some—we do not know what proportion—were set free, and had even formed 'a club to support those who are out of place'.

From the reports in ten newspapers and from monthly and annual journals we learn almost nothing about Charlotte Gardiner. Those who gave evidence against her did not claim to have known her personally. All described her as having been a leader in the looting and burning of Lebarty's premises. She was said to have offered no defence and no one is reported as speaking on her behalf. We do not know what motivated her: was she anti-Catholic for some reason (eg, ill-treatment by a previous Roman Catholic owner/employer), or was she one of the many Londoners unable to find work and with grievances about the conditions in which she was forced to survive? At the execution; on July 11th, Charlotte is unanimously described as being 'almost in rags'. *The Public Advertiser* described her as showing 'great penitence . . . (and) appeared to be much affected'.

When the bodies of the three hanged that day for the destruction of Lebarty's premises were cut down, 'their bodies were delivered to their friends'. *The Political Magazine* for 1780 contradicted this report by stating that 'several blacks' had applied for her body, declaring that they wanted to give her a 'decent Christian burial'. But rumours had reached Sheriff Pugh that the blacks' real intention was to exhibit her body for money. He therefore refused to release her body which he then had 'interred at St Schulchre's at his own expense' (probably St Sepulchre's, Newgate).

Of John Glover the records tell us more. He had been the servant of a lawyer, 'Counsellor' John Philips, of Brookes Street, for twelve years. Glover's master thought enough of his servant to give evidence on his behalf at the trial on July 11th: Glover was on the streets, Philips declared, and carrying a gun barrel, as he had been instructed to fetch it. He was a 'quiet, honest, sober servant', who had been trusted with large sums of money. Two witnesses to the demolition of Newgate spoke on Glover's behalf: one was a watchmaker Daniel Saville of Snowhill, who testified that he had 'seen a black very active in the mob, but it was not the prisoner'. The second man, James McMahon, a soldier, gave similar evidence. Though the Recorder pointed out at the close of the trial that 'the first witness (against Glover) had prevaricated a good deal from what he had sworn before the magistrate', the jury found Glover guilty.

However, Counsellor Philips petitioned the king on behalf of his manservant. By searching the Old Bailey records Philips had discovered that the two men who had given evidence against Glover had criminal records, which should have disqualified them from giving evidence. Had this been known at the time, Philips claimed, and the Recorder agreed, Glover 'might have (had) a good chance' of being acquitted by the jury'. Glover was duly reprieved and given 'his Majesty's pardon, on condition of absenting himself from this kingdom for three years'. As Philips had stated in his deposition that 'Captain Pultney of the man-of-war *Sylph* who knows the prisoner would be glad to have him as crew', Glover might well have ended up serving in the Royal Navy. What became of him is unknown.

Benjamin Bowfey, described by one of the newspapers as a 'Mulatto man',

was also found guilty of a capital offence. Some witnesses claimed they had seen Bowfey in the crowd around Akerman's house; others stated that they had seen him *in* Akerman s house. A police constable swore that, on searching Bowfey's room, he found some silk stockings, a handkerchief, a pocketbook and a key with Akerman's name on it. The reports in the newspapers vary; some claim that when he was arrested Bowfey was wearing a pair of Akerman's silk stockings. Grace Roberts, who lived in the same house as Bowfey, stated on his behalf that he had been at home from 9pm on the night in question. 'Robert à Cape, a black servant in the same house', claimed that Bowfey had spent the night with him, but on examination it was found that he was referring to the following night. Although a Dr Saunders, John Northington and 'some others' gave him 'a good character', Bowfey was sentenced to death.

A few days later Bowfey won the first of many respites. He wrote to the court, to Lord Earlsbury, an exemployer, and to Alderman Woolridge, asking for help. Though preserved in the State Papers, the first two letters (written by an amanuensis?), are illegible. From General Honeywood's letter to Lord St Germain we learn that Bowfey had been his footman for some years; Honeywood had 'thought him a very honest and very foolish fellow. And having a taste for cooking I recommended him to work in the kitchen at St Albans Tavern where I am afraid that he got into very idle company and being very silly was by them drawn into that very abominable riot.' The General also asked Alderman Woolridge to intervene on Bowfey's behalf. Woolridge, who was also a magistrate, wrote to the court that he had interviewed Bowfey, who claimed that a Mr Lloyd, an American, had paid him 'and some others who were in the mob one guinea for their trouble . . . The life of this poor wretch', the Alderman continued, 'is of little consequence to the Public, he appears to me to be so compleatly ignorant as to have been a very proper subject for an artful villain to have worked upon.'

Some two weeks later, on August 8th, 1780, by which time more respites had been issued, the Lord Mayor, Brackley Kennet, wrote to the court, noting that Alderman Woolridge had 'solicited a pardon three times' for Bowfey. He had been making enquiries about Bowfey's

Mr Lloyd. It seems Lloyd, formerly in the Guards, had gone abroad to avoid being arrested. The following day it was announced that 'his Majesty has been pleased to respite the execution of Benjamin Bowfey . . . until further signification of his Majesty's Pleasure'. We do not know how long Bowfey languished in prison; was he perhaps transported to Australia? (He is not on the list of convicts on the First Fleet.)

It is impossible to extrapolate from the lives of these three London blacks to the city's black population as a whole. However, it would certainly seem that all three were free. The two men were workers, but nothing is said about Charlotte Gardiner's employment. What was unusual about them in the context of the other accused was that most of the other prisoners were petty tradesmen and craftsmen, or those with other-than-domestic skills. This probably bears out the contention that, as far as is known at present, most blacks had been brought to this country as domestic servants.

It should also be remembered that blacks had been prohibited from taking apprenticeships in the city since 1731. This prohibition appears to have been due to one black apprentice, John Satia, being admitted to the Freedom of the City of London when he had completed his apprenticeship with William Attey, 'Citizen and Joyner'. As a Freeman he would have been entitled to vote in the City of London elections. There was a debate in the Court of Aldermen regarding Satia, initiated after he had been granted his Freedom. This resulted in a decision that his admission (as a Freeman) should not be 'for the future drawn into precedent and that no Nigros or other Blacks be at any time hereafter admitted into the freedom of this City'. An order to this effect was issued on September 14th, 1731. Thus it seems that while some Aldermen harboured no racial prejudices they nevertheless acquiesced in their peers' racist demands (or were perhaps just outvoted).

While we learn little about the black population from the trial, we learn far more about the relationship of (some) whites to blacks. Interestingly, the newspaper and other accounts do not even invariably mention that Gardiner, Glover and Bowfey were black. The term 'black'

was more often used than 'negro', and the word 'mulatto' was also used to describe Bowfey and another man, McDonald. McDonald, hanged with Charlotte Gardiner, was described by *The London Chronicle* as 'with short black hair, and very hard featured, his face almost approaching to a Mulatto'. Benjamin Bowfey, described by some as a 'black', was stated by witnesses to have smooth hair and might thus have been 'mulatto', or possibly an Indian. It would seem, therefore, that neither the reporters nor the populace were very clear—or concerned—about ethnicity. It should also be noted that the newspapers did not take the obvious opportunity to revile black people; there is no comment whatsoever about colour, ethnicity or stereotypes. Nor are the accounts of the trials of the three blacks inordinately lengthy, or sensationalist: they are treated no differently from other rioters.

The reports of the trials indicate that there was a considerable attempt to ensure that there were no cases of mistaken identity, which might perhaps indicate that the population was not expected to be able to tell one black from another. Thus Ross Jennings, witness against Bowfey, is asked 'How can you be sure that this is the black you saw?' He replies that the 'smoothness and the dress of his hair is not common in one of his complexion'. Another witness, also questioned about this, noted Bowfey's hair as making it easy to identify him. At the trial of Glover, it is pointed out to a witness, the turnkey William Sheppard, that as he had never been in 'a country where blacks are the inhabitants', he was only 'accustomed to see blacks by accident'. How then could he recognise Glover, whom he would have seen in the darkness illuminated only by the fires? Sheppard admitted he saw 'several Blacks and Tawnies' outside the prison, but maintained that he recognised Glover's face. Another turnkey, William Lee, was also pressed as to whether he could recognise Glover and what he actually saw in Glover's hand. Lee replied that Glover was 'not a black, but a copper-coloured person'. (It is these two witnesses whom Counsellor Philips proved to have been ex-convicts; now they were prison guards.)

We do not know how the state found witnesses against the rioters. Was there, for example, an element of coercion? (According to a note in the Alchin Papers at the Corporation of London, those summoned to give evidence were bound over to the extraordinarily high sum of £40 to give evidence at the Sessions.) Were they among the hundreds arrested but not charged? Saville and McMahon, witnesses who refused to identify Glover, both stated that on hearing that a black man had been arrested, they went to the jail to see if they could recognise him. Had they gone to the jail voluntarily? If so, what had motivated them to go specifically to identify a black person? Whatever the case, neither appears to have known Glover, yet they spoke up for him. As we have noted, a neighbour of Bowfey's also spoke on his behalf, as had some whites, including a doctor.

Finally, one has to laud the lengths to which General Honeywell and especially Counsellor Philips went to help a past and present employee. Bowfey was also able to elicit the support of an Alderman and the Lord Mayor. While it is known that the City's Council was not in support of Government policies, there could have been no political advantage to be gained from supporting a man like Benjamin Bowfey, an insignificant tavern worker.

FOR FURTHER READING:

Peter Fryer, *Staying Power: the History of Black People in Britain,* (Pluto Press, 1984); J. Paul de Castro, *The Gordon Riots,* (Oxford University Press, 1926); Nicholas Rogers, 'Crowd and People in the Gordon Riots', in E. Hellmuch (ed) *The Transformation of Political Culture,* (Oxford University Press, 1990) George Rudé, *Idology and Popular Protest, Lawrence & Wishart,* (London, 1980); Peter Linebough, *The London Hanged: Crime and Civil Society in the 18th Century,* (Allen Lane, 1991) This is the only book to detail the cases of the three blacks; however, I believe some of Linebough's data is incorrect: e.g., Bowfey was clearly not hanged on June 20th; having been in Philips' service for twelve years, it is impossible for Glover to have arrived in Britain as a result of the American War of Independence.

Marika Sherwood is a Research Fellow at the Institute of Commonwealth Studies and author of Kwame Nkrumah: The years abroad 1935–1947 *(Freedom Publications, 1996).*

The Passion of Antoine Lavoisier

With its revolution, France founded a rational republic and lost a great scientist

Stephen Jay Gould

Stephen Jay Gould teaches biology, geology, and the history of science at Harvard University.

Galileo and Lavoisier have more in common than their brilliance. Both men are focal points in a cardinal legend about the life of intellectuals—the conflict of lonely and revolutionary genius with state power. Both stories are apocryphal, however inspiring. Yet they only exaggerate, or encapsulate in the epitome of a bon mot, an essential theme in the history of thinking and its impact upon society.

Galileo, on his knees before the Inquisition, abjures his heretical belief that the earth revolves around a central sun. Yet, as he rises, brave Galileo, faithful to the highest truth of factuality, addresses a stage whisper to the world: *eppur se muove*— nevertheless, it does move. Lavoisier, before the revolutionary tribunal during the Reign of Terror in 1794, accepts the inevitable verdict of death, but asks for a week or two to finish some experiments. Coffinhal, the young judge who has sealed his doom, denies his request, stating, "La république n'a pas besoin de savants" (the Republic does not need scientists).

Coffinhal said no such thing, although the sentiments are not inconsistent with emotions unleashed in those frightening and all too frequent political episodes so well characterized by Marc Antony in his lamentation over Caesar: "O judgment! thou are fled to brutish beasts, And men have lost their reason." Lavoisier, who had been under arrest for months, was engaged in no experiments at the time. Moreover, as we shall see, the charges leading to his execution bore no relationship to his scientific work.

But if Coffinhal's chilling remark is apocryphal, the second most famous quotation surrounding the death of Lavoisier is accurate and well attested. The great mathematician Joseph Louis Lagrange, upon hearing the news about his friend Lavoisier, remarked bitterly: "It took them only an instant to cut off that head, but France may not produce another like it in a century."

I feel some need to participate in the worldwide outpouring of essays to commemorate the 200th anniversary of the French Revolution. Next month, on July 14, unparalleled displays of fireworks will mark the bicentenary of the fall of the Bastille. Nonetheless, and with no desire to put a damper on such pyrotechnics, I must write about the flip side of this initial liberation, the most troubling scientific story of the Revolution—the execution of Antoine Lavoisier in 1794.

The revolution had been born in hope and expansiveness. At the height of enthusiasm for new beginnings, the revolutionary government suppressed the old calendar, and started time all over again, with year I beginning on September 22, 1792, at the founding of the French republic. The months would no longer bear names of Roman gods or emperors, but would record the natural passage of seasons—as in *brumaire* (foggy), *ventose* (windy), *germinal* (budding), and to replace parts of July and August, originally named for two despotic Caesars, *thermidor.* Measures would be rationalized, decimalized, and based on earthly physics, with the meter defined as one ten-millionth of a quarter meridian from pole to equator. The metric system is our enduring legacy of this revolutionary spirit, and Lavoisier himself was the guiding force in devising the new weights and measures.

But initial optimism soon unraveled under the realities of internal dissension and external pressure (the powerful monarchists of Europe were, to say the least, concerned lest republican ideas spread by export or example). Governments tumbled one after the other, and Dr. Guillotin's machine, invented to make execution more humane, became a symbol of terror by sheer frequency of public use. Louis XVI was beheaded in January, 1793 (year one of the republic). Power shifted from the Girondins

Reprinted with permission from *Natural History*, June 1989, pp. 16, 18, 20, 22–25. © 1989 by the American Museum of Natural History.

to the Montagnards, as the Terror reached its height and the war with Austria and Prussia continued. Finally, as so often happens, the architect of the terror, Robespierre himself, paid his visit to Dr. Guillotin's device, and the cycle played itself out. A few years later, in 1804, Napoleon was crowned as emperor, and the First Republic ended. Poor Lavoisier had been caught in the midst of the cycle, dying for his former role as tax collector on May 8, 1794, less than three months before the fall of Robespierre on July 27 (9 Thermidor, year II).

Old ideas often persist in vestigial forms of address and writing, long after their disappearance in practice. I was reminded of this phenomenon when I acquired, a few months ago, a copy of the opening and closing addresses for the course in zoology at the Muséum d'Histoire naturelle of Paris for 1801–2. The democratic fervor of the revolution had faded, and Napoleon had already staged his *coup d'etat* of 18 Brumaire (November 9, 1799), emerging as emperor de facto, although not crowned until 1804. Nonetheless, the author of these addresses, who would soon resume his full name Bernard-Germain-Etienne de la Ville-sur-Illon, comte de Lacépède, is identified on the title page only as C^{en} Lacépède (for *citoyen,* or "citizen"—the democratic form adopted by the revolution to abolish all distinctions of address). The long list of honors and memberships, printed in small type below Lacépède's name, is almost a parody on the ancient forms; for instead of the old affiliations that always included "member of the royal academy of this or that" and "counsellor to the king or count of here or there," Lacépède's titles are rigorously egalitarian—including "one of the professors at the museum of natural history," and member of the society of pharmacists of Paris, and of agriculture of Agen. As for the year of publication, we have to know the history detailed above—for the publisher's date is given, at the bottom, only as "l'an IX de la Rèpublique."

Lacépède was one of the great natural historians in the golden age of French zoology during the late eighteenth and early nineteenth century. His name may be overshadowed in retrospect by the illustrious quartet of Buffon, Lamarck, Saint-Hilaire and Cuvier, but Lacépède—who was chosen by Buffon to complete his life's work, the multivolumed *Histoire naturelle*—deserves

a place with these men, for all were *citoyens* of comparable merit. Although Lacépède supported the revolution in its moderate first phases, his noble title bred suspicion and he went into internal exile during the Terror. But the fall of Robespierre prompted his return to Paris, where his former colleagues persuaded the government to establish a special chair for him at the Muséum, as zoologist for reptiles and fishes.

By tradition, his opening and closing addresses for the zoology course at the Muséum were published in pamphlet form each year. The opening address for year IX, "Sur l'histoire des races ou principales variétés de l'espèce humaine" (On the history of races and principal varieties of the human species), is a typical statement of the liberality and optimism of Enlightenment thought. The races, we learn, may differ in current accomplishments, but all are capable of greater and equal achievement, and all can progress.

But the bloom of hope had been withered by the Terror. Progress, Lacépède asserts, is not guaranteed, but is possible only if untrammeled by the dark side of human venality. Memories of dire consequences for unpopular thoughts must have been fresh, for Lacépède cloaked his criticisms of revolutionary excesses in careful speech and foreign attribution. Ostensibly, he was only describing the evils of the Indian caste system in a passage that must be read as a lament about the Reign of Terror:

> Hypocritical ambition, . . . abusing the credibility of the multitude, has conserved the ferocity of the savage state in the midst of the virtues of civilization. . . . After having reigned by terror *[regné par la terreur]*, submitting even monarchs to their authority, they reserved the domain of science and art to themselves [a reference, no doubt, to the suppression of the independent academies by the revolutionary government in 1793, when Lacépède lost his first post at the Muséum], and surrounded themselves with a veil of mystery that only they could lift.

At the end of his address, Lacépède returns to the familiar theme of political excesses and makes a point, by no means original of course, that I regard as the central structural tragedy of the nature of any complex system, including organisms and social institutions—the

crushing asymmetry between the need for slow and painstaking construction and the potential for almost instantaneous destruction:

> Thus, the passage from the semisavage state to civilization occurs through a great number of insensible stages, and requires an immense amount of time. In moving slowly through these successive stages, man fights painfully against his habits; he also battles with nature as he climbs, with great effort, up the long and perilous path. But it is not the same with the loss of the civilized state; that is almost sudden. In this morbid fall, man is thrown down by all his ancient tendencies; he struggles no longer, he gives up, he does not battle obstacles, he abandons himself to the burdens that surround him. Centuries are needed to nurture the tree of science and make it grow, but one blow from the hatchet of destruction cuts it down.

The chilling final line, a gloss on Lagrange's famous statement about the death of Lavoisier, inspired me to write about the founder of modern chemistry, and to think a bit more about the tragic asymmetry of creation and destruction.

Antoine-Laurent Lavoisier, born in 1743, belonged to the nobility through a title purchased by his father (standard practice for boosting the royal treasury during the *ancien régime*). As a leading liberal and rationalist of the Enlightenment (a movement that attracted much of the nobility, including many wealthy intellectuals who had purchased their titles to rise from the bourgeoisie), Lavoisier fitted an astounding array of social and scientific services into a life cut short by the headsman at age fifty-one.

We know him best today as the chief founder of modern chemistry. The textbook one-liners describe him as the discoverer (or at least the namer) of oxygen, the man who (though anticipated by Henry Cavendish in England) recognized water as a compound of the gases hydrogen and oxygen, and who correctly described combustion, not as the liberation of a hypothetical substance called phlogiston, but as the combination of burning material with oxygen. But we can surely epitomize his contribution more accurately by stating that Lavoisier set the basis for modern chemistry by recognizing the nature of elements and compounds—by finally dethroning the ancient taxonomy of air, water, earth, and fire as indivisible elements; by identifying gas, liquid, and solid as states of aggregation for a single substance subjected to different degrees of heat; and by developing quantitative methods of defining and identifying true elements. Such a brief statement can only rank as a caricature of Lavoisier's scientific achievements, but this essay treats his other life in social service, and I must move on.

Lavoisier, no shrinking violet in the game of self-promotion, openly spoke of his new chemistry as "a revolution." He even published his major manifesto, *Traité élémentaire de chimie,* in 1789, starting date of the other revolution that would seal his fate.

Lavoisier, liberal child of the Enlightenment, was no opponent of the political revolution, at least in its early days. He supported the idea of a constitutional monarchy, and joined the most moderate of the revolutionary societies, the Club of '89. He served as an alternate delegate in the States General, took his turn as a *citoyen* at guard duty, and led several studies and commissions vital to the success of the revolution—including a long stint as *régisseur des poudres* (director of gunpowder, where his brilliant successes produced the best stock in Europe, thus providing substantial help in France's war against Austria and Prussia), work on financing the revolution by *assignats* (paper money backed largely by confiscated church lands), and service on the commission of weights and measures that formulated the metric system. Lavoisier rendered these services to all governments, including the most radical, right to his death, even hoping at the end that his crucial work on weights and measures might save his life. Why, then, did Lavoisier end up in two pieces on the *place de la Révolution* (long ago renamed, in pleasant newspeak, *place de la Concorde*)?

The fateful move had been made in 1768, when Lavoisier joined the infamous Ferme Générale, or Tax Farm. If you regard the IRS as a less than benevolent institution, just consider taxation under the *ancien régime* and count your blessings. Taxation was regressive with a vengeance, as the nobility and clergy were entirely exempt, and poor people supplied the bulk of the royal treasury through tariffs on the movement of goods across provincial boundaries, fees for entering the city of Paris, and taxes on such goods as tobacco and salt. (The hated *gabelle,* or "salt tax," was applied at iniquitously differing rates from region to region, and was levied not on actual consumption but on presumed usage—thus, in effect, forcing each family to buy a certain quantity of taxed salt each year.)

Moreover, the government did not collect taxes directly. They set the rates and then leased (for six-year periods) the privilege of collecting taxes to a private finance company, the Ferme Générale. The Tax Farm operated for profit like any other private business. If they managed to collect more than the government levy, they kept the balance; if they failed to reach the quota, they took the loss. The system was not only oppressive in principle; it was also corrupt. Several shares in the Tax Farm were paid for no work as favors or bribes; many courtiers, even the King himself, were direct beneficiaries. Nonetheless, Lavoisier chose this enterprise for the primary investment of his family fortune, and he became, as members of the firm were called, a *fermier-général,* or "farmer-general."

(Incidentally, since I first read the sad story of Lavoisier some twenty-five years ago, I have been amused by the term farmer-general, for it conjurers up a pleasantly rustic image of a country yokel, dressed in his Osh Kosh b'Gosh overalls, and chewing on a stalk of hay while trying to collect the *gabelle.* But I have just learned from the *Oxford English Dictionary* that my image is not only wrong, but entirely backward. A farm, defined as a piece of agricultural land, is a derivative term. In usage dating to Chaucer, a farm, from the medieval Latin *firma,* "fixed payment," is "a fixed yearly sum accepted from a person as a composition for taxes or other moneys which he is empowered to collect." By extension, to farm is to lease anything for a fixed rent. Since most leases applied to land, agricultural plots become "farms," with the first use in this sense traced only to the sixteenth century; the leasers of such land then became "farmers." Thus, our modern phrase "farming out" records the original use, and has no agricultural connotation. And Lavoisier was a farmer-general in the true sense, with no mitigating image of bucolic innocence.)

I do not understand why Lavoisier chose the Ferme Générale for his investment, and then worked so assiduously in his role as tax farmer. He was surely among the most scrupulous and fair-minded of the farmers, and might be justifiably called a reformer. (He opposed the overwatering of tobacco, a monopoly product of the Ferme, and he did, at least in later years, advocate taxation upon all, including the radical idea that nobles might pay as well.) But he took his profits, and he provoked no extensive campaign for reform as the money rolled in. The standard biographies, all too hagiographical, tend to argue that he regarded the Ferme as an investment that would combine greatest safety and return with minimal expenditure of effort—all done to secure a maximum of time for his beloved scientific work. But I do not see how this explanation can hold. Lavoisier, with his characteristic energy, plunged into the work of the Ferme, traveling all over the country, for example, to inspect the tobacco industry. I rather suspect that Lavoisier, like most modern businessmen, simply jumped at a good and legal investment without asking too many ethical questions.

But the golden calf of one season becomes the shattered idol of another. The farmers-general were roundly hated, in part for genuine corruption and iniquity, in part because tax collectors are always scapegoated, especially when the national treasury is bankrupt and the people are starving. Lavoisier's position was particularly precarious. As a scheme to prevent the loss of taxes from widespread smuggling of goods into Paris, Lavoisier advocated the building of a wall around the city. Much to Lavoisier's distress, the project, financed largely (and involuntarily) through taxes levied upon the people of Paris, became something of a boondoggle, as millions were spent on fancy ornamental gates. Parisians blamed the wall for keeping in fetid air and spreading disease. The militant republican Jean-Paul Marat began a campaign of vilification against Lavoisier that only ended when Charlotte Corday stabbed him to death in his bath. Marat had written several works in science and had hoped for election to the Royal Academy, then run by Lavoisier. But Lavoisier had exposed the emptiness of Marat's work. Marat fumed, bided his time, and waited for the season when patriotism would become a good refuge for scoundrels. In January 1791, he launched his attack in *l'Ami du Peuple* (the Friend of the People):

> I denounce you, Coryphaeus of charlatans, Sieur Lavoisier [coryphaeus, meaning highest, is the leader of the chorus in a classical Greek drama] Farmer-general, Commissioner of Gunpowders. . . . Just to think that this contemptible little man who enjoys an income of forty thousand livres has no other claim to fame than that of having put Paris in prison with a wall costing the poor thirty millions. . . . Would to heaven he had been strung up to the nearest lamppost.

The breaching of the wall by the citizens of Paris on July 12, 1789, was the prelude to the fall of the Bastille two days later.

Lavoisier began to worry very early in the cycle. Less than seven months after the fall of the Bastille, he wrote to his old friend Benjamin Franklin:

> After telling you about what is happening in chemistry, it would be well to give you news of our Revolution. . . . Moderate-minded people, who have kept cool heads during the general excitement, think that events have carried us too far . . . we greatly regret your absence from France at this time; you would have been our guide and you would have marked out for us the limits beyond which we ought not to go.

But these limits were breached, just as Lavoisier's wall had fallen, and he could read the handwriting on the remnants. The Ferme Générale was suppressed in 1791, and Lavoisier played no further role in the complex sorting out of the farmers' accounts. He tried to keep his nose clean with socially useful work on weights and measures and public education. But time was running out for the farmers-general. The treasury was bankrupt, and many thought (quite incorrectly) that the iniquitously hoarded wealth of the farmers-general could replenish the nation. The farmers were too good a scapegoat to resist; they were arrested en masse in November 1793, commanded to put their accounts in order and to reimburse the nation for any ill-gotten gains.

The presumed offenses of the farmers-general were not capital under revolutionary law, and they hoped initially to win their personal freedom, even though their wealth and possessions might be confiscated. But they had the misfortune to be in the wrong place (jail) at the worst time (as the Terror intensified). Eventually, capital charges of counter-revolutionary activities were drummed up, and in a mock trial lasting only part of a day, the farmers-general were condemned to the guillotine.

Lavoisier's influential friends might have saved him, but none dared (or cared) to speak. The Terror was not so inexorable and efficient as tradition holds. Fourteen of the farmers-general managed to evade arrest, and one was saved as a result of the intervention of Robespierre. Madame Lavoisier, who lived to a ripe old age, marrying and divorcing Count Rumford, and reestablishing one of the liveliest salons in Paris, never allowed any of these men over her doorstep again. One courageous (but uninfluential) group offered brave support in Lavoisier's last hours. A deputation from the Lycée des Arts came to the prison to honor Lavoisier and crown him with a wreath. We read in the minutes of that organization: "Brought to Lavoisier in irons, the consolation of friendship . . . to crown the head about to go under the ax."

It is a peculiar attribute of human courage that when no option remains but death, criteria of judgment shift to the manner of dying. Chronicles of the revolution are filled with stories about who died with dignity—and who went screaming to the knife. Antoine Lavoisier died well. He wrote a last letter to his cousin, in apparent calm, not without humor, and with an intellectual's faith in the supreme importance of mind.

> I have had a fairly long life, above all a very happy one, and I think that I shall be remembered with some regrets and perhaps leave some reputation behind me. What more could I ask? The events in which I am involved will probably save me from the troubles of old age. I shall die in full possession of my faculties.

Lavoisier's rehabilitation came almost as quickly as his death. In 1795, the Lycée des Arts held a first public memorial service, with Lagrange himself offering the eulogy and unveiling a bust of Lavoisier inscribed with the words: "Victim of tyranny, respected friend of the arts, he continues to live; through genius he still serves humanity."

Lavoisier's spirit continued to inspire, but his head, once filled with great thoughts as numerous as the unwritten symphonies of Mozart, lay severed in a common grave.

Many people try to put a happy interpretation upon Lagrange's observation about the asymmetry of painstaking creation and instantaneous destruction. The collapse of systems, they argue, may be a prerequisite to any future episode of creativity—and the antidote, therefore, to stagnation. Taking the longest view, for example, mass extinctions do break up stable ecosystems and provoke episodes of novelty further down the evolutionary road. We would not be here today if the death of dinosaurs had not cleared some space for the burgeoning of mammals.

I have no objection to this argument in its proper temporal perspective. If you choose a telescope and wish to peer into an evolutionary future millions of years away, then a current episode of destruction may be read as an ultimate spur. But if you care for the here and now, which is (after all) the only time we feel and have, then massive extinction is only a sadness and an opportunity lost forever. I have heard people argue that our current wave of extinctions should not inspire concern because the earth will eventually recover, as so oft before, and perhaps with pleasant novelty. But what can a conjecture about ten million years from now possibly mean to our lives—especially since we have the power to blow our planet up long before then, and rather little prospect, in any case, of surviving so long ourselves (since few vertebrate species live for ten million years)?

The argument of the "long view" may be correct in some meaninglessly abstract sense, but it represents a fundamental mistake in categories and time scales. Our only legitimate long view extends to our children and our children's children's children—hundreds or a few thousands of years down the road. If we let the slaughter continue, they will share a bleak world with rats, dogs, cockroaches, pigeons, and mosquitoes. A potential recovery millions of years later has no meaning at our appropriate scale. Similarly, others could do the unfinished work of Lavoisier, if not so elegantly; and political revolution did spur science into some interesting channels. But how can this mitigate the tragedy of Lavoisier? He was one of the most brilliant men ever to grace our history, and he died at the height of his powers and health. He had work to do, and he was not guilty.

My title, "The Passion of Antoine Lavoisier," is a double-entendre. The modern meaning of *passion,* "over-mastering zeal or enthusiasm," is a latecomer. The word entered our language from the Latin verb for suffering, particularly for suffering physical pain. The Saint Matthew and Saint John Passions of J. S. Bach are musical dramas about the suffering of Jesus on the cross. This essay, therefore, focuses upon the final and literal passion of Lavoisier. (Anyone who has ever been disappointed in love—that is, all of us—will understand the intimate connection between the two meanings of passion.)

But I also wanted to emphasize Lavoisier's passion in the modern meaning. For this supremely organized man—farmer-general; commissioner of gunpowder; wall builder; reformer of prisons, hospitals, and schools; legislative representative for the nobility of Blois; father of the metric system; servant on a hundred government committees—really had but one passion amidst this burden of activities for a thousand lifetimes. Lavoisier loved science more than anything else. He awoke at six in the morning and worked on science until eight, then again at night from seven until ten. He devoted one full day a week to scientific experiments and called it his *jour de bonheur* (day of happiness). The letters and reports of his last year are painful to read, for Lavoisier never abandoned his passion—his conviction that reason and science must guide any just and effective social order. But those who received his pleas, and held power over him, had heard the different drummer of despotism.

Lavoisier was right in the deepest, almost holy, way. His passion harnessed feeling to the service of reason; another kind of passion was the price. Reason cannot save us and can even persecute us in the wrong hands; but we have no hope of salvation without reason. The world is too complex, too intransigent; we cannot bend it to our simple will. Bernard Lacépède was probably thinking of Lavoisier when he wrote a closing flourish following his passage on the great asymmetry of slow creation and sudden destruction:

Ah! Never forget that we can only stave off that fatal degradation if we unite the liberal arts, which embody the sacred fire of sensibility, with the sciences and the useful arts, without which the celestial light of reason will disappear.

The Republic needs scientists.

The First Feminist

*In 1792 Mary Wollstonecraft wrote a book to prove that her sex
was as intelligent as the other: thus did feminism come into the world.
Right on, Ms. Mary!*

Shirley Tomkievicz

The first person—male or female—to speak at any length and to any effect about woman's rights was Mary Wollstonecraft. In 1792, when her *Vindication of the Rights of Woman* appeared, Mary was a beautiful spinster of thirty-three who had made a successful career for herself in the publishing world of London. This accomplishment was rare enough for a woman in that day. Her manifesto, at once impassioned and learned, was an achievement of real originality. The book electrified the reading public and made Mary famous. The core of its argument is simple: "I wish to see women neither heroines nor brutes; but reasonable creatures," Mary wrote. This ancestress of the Women's Liberation Movement did not demand day-care centers or an end to women's traditional role as wife and mother, nor did she call anyone a chauvinist pig. The happiest period of Mary's own life was when she was married and awaiting the birth of her second child. And the greatest delight she ever knew was in her first child, an illegitimate daughter. Mary's feminism may not appear today to be the hard-core revolutionary variety, but she did live, for a time, a scandalous and unconventional life—"emancipated," it is called by those who have never tried it. The essence of her thought, however,

is simply that a woman's mind is as good as a man's.

Not many intelligent men could be found to dispute this proposition today, at least not in mixed company. In Mary's time, to speak of *anybody's* rights, let alone woman's rights, was a radical act. In England, as in other nations, "rights" were an entity belonging to the government. The common run of mankind had little access to what we now call "human rights." As an example of British justice in the late eighteenth century, the law cited two hundred different capital crimes, among them shoplifting. An accused man was not entitled to counsel. A child could be tried and hanged as soon as an adult. The right to vote existed, certainly, but because of unjust apportionment, it had come to mean little. In the United States some of these abuses had been corrected—but the rights of man did not extend past the color bar and the masculine gender was intentional. In the land of Washington and Jefferson, as in the land of George III, human rights were a new idea and woman's rights were not even an issue.

In France, in 1792, a Revolution in the name of equality was in full course, and woman's rights had at least been alluded to. The Revolutionary government drew up plans for female education—to the age of eight. "The education of the

women should always be relative to the men," Rousseau had written in *Emile*. "To please, to be useful to us, to make us love and esteem them, to educate us when young, and take care of us when grown up, to advise, to console us, to render our lives easy and agreeable; these are the duties of women at all times, and what they should be taught in their infancy." And, less prettily, "Women have, or ought to have, but little liberty."

Rousseau would have found little cause for complaint in eighteenth-century England. An Englishwoman had almost the same civil status as an American slave. Thomas Hardy, a hundred years hence, was to base a novel on the idea of a man casually selling his wife and daughter at public auction. Obviously this was not a common occurrence, but neither is it wholly implausible. In 1792, and later, a woman could not own property, nor keep any earned wages. All that she possessed belonged to her husband. She could not divorce him, but he could divorce her and take her children. There was no law to say she could not grow up illiterate or be beaten every day.

Such was the legal and moral climate in which Mary Wollstonecraft lived. She was born in

From *Horizon*, Spring 1972. © 1972 by Forbes, Inc. Reprinted by permission of *American Heritage* magazine, a division of Forbes, Inc.

London in the spring of 1759, the second child and first daughter of Edward Wollstonecraft, a prosperous weaver. Two more daughters and two more sons were eventually born into the family, making six children in all. Before they had all arrived, Mr. Wollstonecraft came into an inheritance and decided to move his family to the country and become a gentleman farmer. But this plan failed. His money dwindled, and he began drinking heavily. His wife turned into a terrified wraith whose only interest was her eldest son, Edward. Only he escaped the beatings and abuse that his father dealt out regularly to every other household member, from Mrs. Wollstonecraft to the family dog. As often happens in large and disordered families, the eldest sister had to assume the role of mother and scullery maid. Mary was a bright, strong child, determined not to be broken, and she undertook her task energetically, defying her father when he was violent and keeping her younger brothers and sisters in hand. Clearly, Mary held the household together, and in so doing forfeited her own childhood. This experience left her with an everlasting gloomy streak, and was a strong factor in making her a reformer.

At some point in Mary's childhood, another injustice was visited upon her, though so commonplace for the time that she can hardly have felt the sting. Her elder brother was sent away to be educated, and the younger children were left to learn their letters as best they could. The family now frequently changed lodgings, but from her ninth to her fifteenth year Mary went to a day school, where she had the only formal training of her life. Fortunately, this included French and composition, and somewhere Mary learned to read critically and widely. These skills, together with her curiosity and determination, were really all she needed. The *Vindication* is in some parts long-winded, ill-punctuated, and simply full of hot air, but it is the work of a well-informed mind.

Feminists—and Mary would gladly have claimed the title—inevitably, even deservedly, get bad notices. The term calls up an image of relentless battle-axes: "thin college ladies with eyeglasses, no-nonsense features, mouths thin as bologna slicers, a babe in one arm, a hatchet in the other, grey eyes bright with balefire," as Norman Mailer feelingly envisions his antagonists in the

Women's Liberation Movement. He has conjured up all the horrid elements: the lips with a cutting edge, the baby immaculately conceived (one is forced to conclude), the lethal weapon tightly clutched, the desiccating college degree, the joylessness. Hanging miasmally over the tableau is the suspicion of a deformed sexuality. Are these girls man-haters, or worse? Mary Wollstonecraft, as the first of her line, has had each of these scarlet letters (except the B.A.) stitched upon her bosom. Yet she conformed very little to the hateful stereotype. In at least one respect, however, she would have chilled Mailer's bones. Having spent her childhood as an adult, Mary reached the age of nineteen in a state of complete joylessness. She was later to quit the role, but for now she wore the garb of a martyr.

Her early twenties were spent in this elderly frame of mind. First she went out as companion to an old lady living at Bath, and was released from this servitude only by a call to nurse the dying Mrs. Wollstonecraft. Then the family broke up entirely, though the younger sisters continued off and on to be dependent on Mary. The family of Mary's dearest friend, Fanny Blood, invited her to come and stay with them; the two girls made a small living doing sewing and handicrafts, and Mary dreamed of starting a primary school. Eventually, in a pleasant village called Newington Green, this plan materialized and prospered. But Fanny Blood in the meantime had married and moved to Lisbon. She wanted Mary to come and nurse her through the birth of her first child. Mary reached Lisbon just in time to see her friend die of childbed fever, and returned home just in time to find that her sisters, in whose care the flourishing little school had been left, had lost all but two pupils.

Mary made up her mind to die. "My constitution is impaired, I hope I shan't live long," she wrote to a friend in February, 1786. Under this almost habitual grief, however, Mary was gaining some new sense of herself. Newington Green, apart from offering her a brief success as a schoolmistress, had brought her some acquaintance in the world of letters, most important among them, Joseph Johnson, an intelligent and successful London publisher in search of new writers. Debt-ridden and penniless, Mary set aside her impaired constitution and wrote her first book, probably in the

space of a week. Johnson bought it for ten guineas and published it. Called *Thoughts on the Education of Daughters,* it went unnoticed, and the ten guineas was soon spent. Mary had to find work. She accepted a position as governess in the house of Lord and Lady Kingsborough in the north of Ireland.

Mary's letters from Ireland to her sisters and to Joseph Johnson are so filled with Gothic gloom, so stained with tears, that one cannot keep from laughing at them. "I entered the great gates with the same kind of feeling I should have if I was going to the Bastille," she wrote upon entering Kingsborough Castle in the fall of 1786. Mary was now twenty-seven. Her most recent biographer, Margaret George, believes that Mary was not really suffering so much as she was having literary fantasies. In private she was furiously at work on a novel entitled, not very artfully, *Mary, A Fiction.* This is the story of a young lady of immense sensibilities who closely resembles Mary except that she has wealthy parents, a neglectful bridegroom, and an attractive lover. The title and fantasizing contents are precisely what a scribbler of thirteen might secretly concoct. Somehow Mary was embarking on her adolescence—with all its daydreams—fifteen years after the usual date. Mary's experience in Kingsborough Castle was a fruitful one, for all her complaints. In the summer of 1787 she lost her post as governess and set off for London with her novel. Not only did Johnson accept it for publication, he offered her a regular job as editor and translator and helped her find a place to live.

Thus, aged twenty-eight, Mary put aside her doleful persona as the martyred, set-upon elder sister. How different she is now, jauntily writing from London to her sisters: "Mr. Johnson . . . assures me that if I exert my talents in writing I may support myself in a comfortable way. I am then going to be the first of a new genus. . . ." Now Mary discovered the sweetness of financial independence earned by interesting work. She had her own apartment. She was often invited to Mr. Johnson's dinner parties, usually as the only female guest among all the most interesting men in London: Joseph Priestley, Thomas Paine, Henry Fuseli, William Blake, Thomas Christie, William Godwin—all of them up-and-coming scientists or poets or painters or philosophers, bound together by left-wing political views. Moreover, Mary was successful in her own writing as well as in editorial work. Her *Original Stories for Children* went into three editions and was illustrated by Blake. Johnson and his friend Thomas Christie had started a magazine called the *Analytical Review,* to which Mary became a regular contributor.

But—lest anyone imagine an elegantly dressed Mary presiding flirtatiously at Johnson's dinner table—her social accomplishments were rather behind her professional ones. Johnson's circle looked upon her as one of the boys. "Wollstonecraft" is what William Godwin calls her in his diary. One of her later detractors reported that she was at this time a "philosophic sloven," in a dreadful old dress and beaver hat, "with her hair hanging lank about her shoulders." Mary had yet to arrive at her final incarnation, but the new identity was imminent, if achieved by an odd route. Edmund Burke had recently published his *Reflections on the Revolution in France,* and the book had enraged Mary. The statesman who so readily supported the quest for liberty in the American colonies had his doubts about events in France.

Mary's reply to Burke, *A Vindication of the Rights of Men,* astounded London, partly because she was hitherto unknown, partly because it was good. Mary proved to be an excellent polemicist, and she had written in anger. She accused Burke, the erstwhile champion of liberty, of being "the champion of property." "Man preys on man," said she, "and you mourn for the idle tapestry that decorated a gothic pile and the dronish bell that summoned the fat priest to prayer." The book sold well. Mary moved into a better apartment and bought some pretty dresses—no farthingales, of course, but some of the revolutionary new "classical" gowns. She put her auburn hair up in a loose knot. Her days as a philosophic sloven were over.

Vindication of the Rights of Woman was her next work. In its current edition it runs to 250-odd pages; Mary wrote it in six weeks. *Vindication* is no prose masterpiece, but it has never failed to arouse its audience, in one way or another. Horace Walpole unintentionally set the style for the book's foes. Writing to his friend Hannah More in August,

1792, he referred to Thomas Paine and to Mary as "philosophizing serpents" and was "glad to hear you have not read the tract of the last mentioned writer. I would not look at it." Neither would many another of Mary's assailants, the most virulent of whom, Ferdinand Lundberg, surfaced at the late date of 1947 with a tract of his own, *Modern Woman, the Lost Sex.* Savagely misogynistic as it is, this book was hailed in its time as "the best book yet to be written about women." Lundberg calls Mary the Karl Marx of the feminist movement, and the *Vindication* a "fateful book," to which "the tenets of feminism, which have undergone no change to our day, may be traced." Very well, but then, recounting Mary's life with the maximum possible number of errors per line, he warns us that she was "an extreme neurotic of a compulsive type" who "wanted to turn on men and injure them." In one respect, at least, Mr. Lundberg hits the mark: he blames Mary for starting women in the pernicious habit of wanting an education. In the nineteenth century, he relates, English and American feminists were hard at work. "Following Mary Wollstonecraft's prescription, they made a considerable point about acquiring a higher education." This is precisely Mary's prescription, and the most dangerous idea in her fateful book.

"Men complain and with reason, of the follies and caprices of our Sex," she writes in Chapter 1. "Behold, I should answer, the natural effect of ignorance." Women, she thinks, are usually so mindless as to be scarcely fit for their roles as wives and mothers. Nevertheless, she believes this state not to be part of the feminine nature, but the result of an equally mindless oppression, as demoralizing for men as for women. If a woman's basic mission is as a wife and mother, need she be an illiterate slave for this?

The heart of the work is Mary's attack on Rousseau. In *Emile* Rousseau had set forth some refreshing new ideas for the education of little boys. But women, he decreed, are tools for pleasure, creatures too base for moral or political or political privilege. Mary recognized that this view was destined to shut half the human race out of all hope for political freedom. *Vindication* is a plea that the "rights of men" ought to mean the "rights of humanity." The human right that she held highest was

the right to have a mind and think with it. Virginia Woolf, who lived through a time of feminist activity, thought that the *Vindication* was a work so true "as to seem to contain nothing new." Its originality, she wrote, rather too optimistically, had become a commonplace.

Vindication went quickly into a second edition. Mary's name was soon known all over Europe. But as she savored her fame—and she did savor it—she found that the edge was wearing off and that she was rather lonely. So far as anyone knows, Mary had reached this point in her life without ever having had a love affair. Johnson was the only man she was close to, and he was, as she wrote him, "A father, or a brother—you have been both to me." Mary was often now in the company of the Swiss painter Henry Fuseli, and suddenly she developed what she thought was a Platonic passion in his direction. He rebuffed her, and in the winter of 1792 she went to Paris, partly to escape her embarrassment but also because she wanted to observe the workings of the Revolution firsthand.

Soon after her arrival, as she collected notes for the history of the Revolution she hoped to write, Mary saw Louis XVI, "sitting in a hackney coach . . . going to meet death." Back in her room that evening, she wrote to Mr. Johnson of seeing "eyes glare through a glass door opposite my chair and bloody hands shook at me. . . . I am going to bed and for the first time in my life, I cannot put out the candle." As the weeks went on, Edmund Burke's implacable critic began to lose her faith in the brave new world. "The aristocracy of birth is levelled to the ground, only to make room for that of riches," she wrote. By February France and England were at war, and British subjects classified as enemy aliens.

Though many Englishmen were arrested, Mary and a large English colony stayed on. One day in spring, some friends presented her to an attractive American, newly arrived in Paris, Gilbert Imlay. Probably about four years Mary's senior, Imlay, a former officer in the Continental Army, was an explorer and adventurer. He came to France seeking to finance a scheme for seizing Spanish lands in the Mississippi valley. This "natural and unaffected creature," as Mary was later to describe him, was probably the social lion of the moment, for he was also the author of a best-selling novel called *The Emigrants,* a far-fetched account of life and love in the American wilderness. He and Mary soon became lovers. They were a seemingly perfect pair. Imlay must have been pleased with his famous catch, and—dear, liberated girl that she was—Mary did not insist upon marriage. Rather the contrary. But fearing that she was in danger as an Englishwoman, he registered her at the American embassy as his wife.

Blood was literally running in the Paris streets now, so Mary settled down by herself in a cottage at Neuilly. Imlay spent his days in town, working out various plans. The Mississippi expedition came to nothing, and he decided to stay in France and go into the import-export business, part of his imports being gunpowder and other war goods run from Scandinavia through the English blockade. In the evenings he would ride out to the cottage. By now it was summer, and Mary, who spent the days writing, would often stroll up the road to meet him, carrying a basket of freshly gathered grapes.

A note she wrote Imlay that summer shows exactly what her feelings for him were: "You can scarcely imagine with what pleasure I anticipate the day when we are to begin almost to live together; and you would smile to hear how many plans of employment I have in my head, now that I am confident that my heart has found peace. . . ." Soon she was pregnant. She and Imlay moved into Paris. He promised to take her to America, where they would settle down on a farm and raise six children. But business called Imlay to Le Havre, and his stay lengthened ominously into weeks.

Imlay's letters to Mary have not survived, and without them it is hard to gauge what sort of man he was and what he really thought of his adoring mistress. Her biographers like to make him out a cad, a philistine, not half good enough for Mary. Perhaps; yet the two must have had something in common. His novel, unreadable though it is now, shows that he shared her political views, including her feminist ones. He may never have been serious about the farm in America, but he was a miserably long time deciding to leave Mary alone. Though they were separated during the early months of her pregnancy, he finally did bring her to Le Havre, and continued to live with her there until the child was born and for some six months afterward. The baby arrived in May, 1794, a healthy little girl, whom Mary named Fanny after her old friend. Mary was proud that her delivery had been easy and as for Fanny, Mary loved her instantly. "My little Girl," she wrote to a friend, "begins to suck so manfully that her father reckons saucily on her writing the second part of the Rights of Woman." Mary's joy in this child illuminates almost every letter she wrote henceforth.

Fanny's father was the chief recipient of these letters with all the details of the baby's life. To Mary's despair, she and Imlay hardly ever lived together again. A year went by; Imlay was now in London and Mary in France. She offered to break it off, but mysteriously, he could not let go. In the last bitter phase of their involvement, after she had joined him in London at his behest, he even sent her—as "Mrs. Imlay"—on a complicated business errand to the Scandinavian countries. Returning to London, Mary discovered that he was living with another woman. By now half crazy with humiliation, Mary chose a dark night and threw herself in the Thames. She was nearly dead when two rivermen pulled her from the water.

Though this desperate incident was almost the end of Mary, at least it was the end of the Imlay episode. He sent a doctor to care for her, but they rarely met again. Since Mary had no money, she set about providing for herself and Fanny in the way she knew. The faithful Johnson had already brought out Volume I of her history of the French Revolution. Now she set to work editing and revising her *Letters Written during a Short Residence in Sweden, Norway, and Denmark,* a kind of thoughtful travelogue. The book was well received and widely translated.

And it also revived the memory of Mary Wollstonecraft in the mind of an old acquaintance, William Godwin. As the author of the treatise *Political Justice,* he was now as famous a philosophizing serpent as Mary and was widely admired and hated as a "freethinker." He came to call on Mary. They became friends and then lovers. Early in 1797 Mary was again pregnant. William Godwin was an avowed atheist who had publicly denounced the very institution of marriage. On March 29, 1797, he nevertheless went peaceably to church with Mary and made her his wife.

The Godwins were happy together, however William's theories may have been outraged. He adored his small stepdaughter and took pride in his brilliant wife. Awaiting the birth of her child throughout the summer, Mary worked on a new novel and made plans for a book on "the management of infants"—it would have been the first "Dr. Spock." She expected to have another easy delivery and promised to come downstairs to dinner the day following. But when labor began, on August 30, it proved to be long and agonizing. A daughter, named Mary Wollstonecraft, was born; ten days later, the mother died.

Occasionally, when a gifted writer dies young, one can feel, as in the example of Shelley, that perhaps he had at any rate accomplished his best work. But so recently had Mary come into her full intellectual and emotional growth that her death at the age of thirty-eight is bleak indeed. There is no knowing what Mary might have accomplished now that she enjoyed domestic stability. Perhaps she might have achieved little or nothing further as a writer. But she might have been able to protect her daughters from some part of the sadness that overtook them; for as things turned out, both Fanny and Mary were to sacrifice themselves.

Fanny grew up to be a shy young girl, required to feel grateful for the roof over her head, overshadowed by her prettier half sister, Mary. Godwin in due course married a formidable widow named Mrs. Clairmont, who brought her own daughter into the house—the Claire Clairmont who grew up to become Byron's mistress and the mother of his daughter Allegra. Over the years Godwin turned into a hypocrite and a miser who nevertheless continued to pose as the great liberal of the day. Percy Bysshe Shelley, born the same year that the *Vindication of the Rights of Woman* was published, came to be a devoted admirer of Mary Wollstonecraft's writing. As a young man he therefore came with his wife to call upon Godwin. What he really sought, however, were Mary's daughters—because they were her daughters. First he approached Fanny, but later changed his mind. Mary Godwin was then sixteen, the perfect potential soul mate for a man whose needs for soul mates knew no bounds. They conducted their courtship in the most up-to-the-minute romantic style: beneath a tree near her mother's grave they read aloud to each other from the *Vindication*. Soon they eloped, having pledged their "troth" in the cemetery. Godwin, the celebrated freethinker, was enraged. To make matters worse, Claire Clairmont had run off to Switzerland with them.

Not long afterward Fanny, too, ran away. She went to an inn in a distant town and drank a fatal dose of laudanum. It has traditionally been said that unrequited love for Shelley drove her to this pass, but there is no evidence one way or the other. One suicide that can more justly be laid at Shelley's door is that of his first wife, which occurred a month after Fanny's and which at any rate left him free to wed his mistress,

Mary Godwin. Wife or mistress, she had to endure poverty, ostracism, and Percy's constant infidelities. But now at last her father could, and did, boast to his relations that he was father-in-law to a baronet's son. "Oh, philosophy!" as Mary Godwin Shelley remarked.

If in practice Shelley was merely a womanizer, on paper he was a convinced feminist. He had learned this creed from Mary Wollstonecraft. Through his verse Mary's ideas began to be disseminated. They were one part of that vast tidal wave of political, social, and artistic revolution that arose in the late eighteenth century, the romantic movement. But because of Mary's unconventional way of life, her name fell into disrepute during the

nineteenth century, and her book failed to exert its rightful influence on the development of feminism. Emma Willard and other pioneers of the early Victorian period indignantly refused to claim Mary as their forebear. Elizabeth Cady Stanton and Lucretia Mott were mercifully less strait-laced on the subject. In 1889, when Mrs. Stanton and Susan B. Anthony published their *History of Woman Suffrage,* they dedicated the book to Mary. Though Mary Wollstonecraft can in no sense be said to have founded the woman's rights movement, she was, by the late nineteenth century, recognized as its inspiration, and the *Vindication* was vindicated for the highly original work it was, a landmark in the history of society.

Napoleon the Kingmaker

With his own elaborate imperial court, with his family ensconced on thrones across the continent, and with his overthrow of several historic republics, Napoleon brought Europe to a pinnacle of monarchism, argues **Philip Mansel.**

The period after 1789 has been so often labelled an age of revolution that its character as an apogee of monarchy has been ignored. Yet, unlike those of 1830 and 1848, the revolution of 1789 inspired more revulsion than imitation abroad. From Naples to St Petersburg rulers previously interested in reforms reverted to conservatism. The Habsburg monarchy, under Joseph II in the vanguard of Enlighten-ment, became a citadel of censorship and repression: in 1798 a Viennese crowd attacked the house of the first am-bassador from the French Republic sim-ply for flying the Tricolour. England was swept by Loyalist movements con-vinced of the truth of Thomas Rowland-son's famous cartoon of 1792, *The Contrast,* which depicted 'British Lib-erty' above the caption 'National Pros-perity and Happiness', in contrast to the figure of 'French Liberty' representing 'National and Private Ruin' and 'Misery'.

Russia provides the clearest example of the increase in authoritarian monar-chy. An emphasis on discipline and or-der replaced Catherine's efforts to promote local initiative and participa-tion. In 1796–97, in the first year of Paul I's reign, according to one of his secre-taries, he issued 48,000 orders, rules and laws. The new Tsar also initiated the re-turn to grandeur which was a feature of nineteenth century courts, after the fash-ion for such royal retreats as the Her-mitage, the Trianon, and Joseph II's pavilion in the Augarten. On May 4th, 1797, the imperial ambassador Count Cobenzl wrote that Paul I had multiplied:

> . . . so far as it has been possible the occasions for grand etiquette and rep-resentation on the throne. It is unbe-lievable to what degree Paul I loves great ceremonies, the importance which he attaches to them and the time which he employs for them.

No mere brushing of the lips, but full formal kissing of the imperial hand, was demanded from his officials. The central moment of his day, whatever the tem-perature, was the guard parade. It was at once an endurance test, the chief cere-mony of state and a means by which Paul I exerted direct control over his of-ficers and his empire. During his reign three regiments and his own 2,400

H T Archives

Thomas Rowlandson had presented a forthright contrast between liberty in Hanoverian Britain and Jacobin France in the early 1790s. Though Napoleon hid some of the anarchy beneath the restored trappings of monarchy, few argued that the ills Rowlandson had pointed to were alleviated under the Empire.

 This article first appeared in *History Today,* March 1998, pp. 39-46. © 1998 by History Today, Ltd. Reprinted by permission.

'Gatchina troops' were added to the Imperial Guard. According to his biographer Roderick McGrew, Paul 'pointed society, with the state in the vanguard, towards a severely hierarchical and essentially militarised mode of organisation'.

Thus when Bonaparte seized power in 1799, while much of Europe had been conquered by the armies of the French Republic, the powers united against it in the Second Coalition were more monarchical and conservative than before. Earlier than is generally thought, the First Consul Bonaparte aligned himself with this monarchical trend, acquiring in succession a guard (1799), a palace (1800), court receptions and costumes (1800–02), a household (1802–04), a dynasty (1804), finally a nobility (1808).

By January 3rd, 1800, the Garde des Consuls, created in November 1799, numbered 2,089—more than Louis XVI's Garde Constitutionelle of 1792. From the beginning it was an elitist unit with taller men, more splendid uniforms, and privileges of pay and rank over line units. On February 10th, 1800, escorted by his guard, Bonaparte moved into the Tuileries palace. He soon established what his architect Pierre Fontaine called 'the magnificence due to his rank'. The weekly, later monthly, reviews which Bonaparte held in the Tuileries courtyard, riding a white horse which had once belonged to Louis XVI, inspired widespread admiration, not least from Paul I. According to one English visitor 'their presence alone maintains public tranquility and causes a sensation'. An Austrian later called such a review 'the finest military spectacle it is possible to see'. In the autumn of 1800, as he withdrew from the Second Coalition, Paul I suggested that Bonaparte make the throne of France hereditary in his family.

The Hofburg, rather than Versailles, was the model for the regular receptions which Bonaparte began to hold in the Tuileries, and after the autumn of 1802 at St Cloud. Rank at the French court was now based on service to the state rather than noble birth, and was revealed by space not time; by which room an officer or official could enter in the state apartments, rather than what time a courtier could enter the king's bedroom. Officers down to the rank of captain were admitted into the fourth room before the Salle des Consuls, field officers into the third, generals into the second, ambassadors into the first. The English

traveller, J.G. Lemaistre, who attended one of these receptions, wrote on March 7th, 1802: 'persons used to courts all agree that the audience of the First Consul is one of the most splendid things of the kind in Europe'. Bonaparte both employed 'all the requisites of show, parade, form and etiquette', and received 'flattery and cringing attention'.

Bonaparte's costume, as well as his guard and his receptions, revealed his monarchical ambitions. Heavily embroidered official uniforms were created in December 1799 for the consuls and ministers, and in May 1800 for prefects and senators. At a reception in the Tuileries after Bonaparte's review of the guard in March 1802, J.G. Lemaistre admired his 'grand costume of scarlet velvet richly embroidered with gold' and 'the handsome uniforms and commanding figures of the soldiery . . . the consular guards are the handsomest men I ever saw, scarcely any are less than six feet high'. He also wrote of foreign visitors, 'everyone not in uniform is in the full dress of the old court'.

For Bonaparte's court was already in some ways more old-fashioned than other courts. 'The full dress of the old court', which was imposed at the receptions for foreigners and Frenchmen without official positions, was more common in 1802 than it would be after 1814 under the Restoration. Foreigners bought their court dress in Paris, since elsewhere on the Continent it had, with a few exceptions, been abandoned. In 1800, in a gesture revealing desire at once for trade, splendour and peace, the city of Lyon had presented the First Consul with a cherry velvet *habit à la française,* embroidered with olive branches in gold and silver thread. Bonaparte wore this costume in preference to his official First Consul's uniform at the Te Deum for the signature of the Concordat with the pope at Nôtre Dame on April 18th, 1802, and subsequently on other state occasions. He later devised a special lace and velvet court costume for himself, *the petit costume de l'Empereur,* such as no other monarch possessed. Costume was an instrument of power. When a group of men dared visit the Second Consul Cambacérès, future Archichancelier de l'Empire, in black tail coats, he asked: 'Are you in mourning? I would like to express my sympathy for the loss you have suffered'.

The proclamation of the empire in May 1804, the establishment of the

households of the Emperor, the Empress and the Imperial Family in July, the coronation by the pope in December of that year, were confirmations of an existing monarchical reality. From the start members of the old nobility—Segur, Talleyrand, Rohan, La Rochefoucauld—were among the court officials, as they had been among the first government officials nominated in 1800.

Napoleon never wavered on such gains of the Revolution as equality before the law, religious toleration, the confiscation and sale of ecclesiastical property, and careers open to talents (although between 1805 and 1814 the proportion of non-nobles in court office fell by half). However, at the same time as he extended French territory by force of arms, Napoleon extended the principle of monarchy by imperial decree. He personally organised the destruction of the last city states in Europe. Already in 1797, after a thousand years, Venetian independence had been abolished on his orders; Genoa also lost its independence forever in 1805, when the Ligurian Republic was annexed to the French Empire. In 1805, when Napoleon crowned himself king in Milan cathedral, the Italian Republic became the Kingdom of Italy with its own viceroy, Eugène de Beauharnais, its own court and nobility. One of the best surviving examples of a Napoleonic palace interior can be seen in Venice, in what is now the Museo Correr on the Piazza San Marco: from 1807 to 1814 it served as one of Napoleon's palaces as King of Italy. In 1805 another ancient urban republic, Dubrovnik, which had recently experienced a commercial renaissance, was also abolished and annexed to the Kingdom of Italy.

The same year the Republic of Lucca—a free city since the twelfth century—became 'a principality under Napoleon's brother-in-law Felix Baciocchi, who was crowned in pomp in Lucca cathedral on July 14th, 1805. In 1806, acting as self-appointed overlord of Europe, Napoleon transformed the Batavian Republic, one of the bastions of European bourgeois life, into the Kingdom of Holland, under his brother Louis-Napoleon. Despite murmurs from the citizens, the great symbol of seventeenth-century urban prosperity and independence, the Town Hall of Amsterdam, became a Royal Palace, as it still is; one of the building's attractions was that the square in front could contain 5,000 soldiers to subdue any potential popular disturbance. Meanwhile, King Louis-Napoleon introduced court costumes for the first time into the Netherlands: 'the intention seems to be to compensate them for never having worn embroidery in this country' wrote Stanislas de Girardin, a chamberlain of Napoleon.

In 1806, Napoleon transformed another great commercial city, Frankfurt, self-governing since the twelfth century, into the capital of a Grand Duchy under the last Archbishop Elector of Mainz, whom Napoleon had appointed Prince Primate of the Confederation of the Rhine. His heir was Eugene de Beauharnais, so that the expected second son of Napoleon I could become King of Italy. The same year, again acting as self-appointed overlord of Europe, the Emperor of the French elevated his allies, the rulers of Bavaria, Württemberg and Saxony, to the rank of King, and the rulers of Baden and Hesse-Darmstadt to that of Grand Duke. Absorbing free cities, and independent ecclesiastical and noble territories, these monarchs enjoyed more power during and after the Napoleonic era than they had under the Holy Roman Empire. Further extensions of monarchy occurred when the Septinsular republic of the Ionian islands, established by the Second Coalition in 1799, was annexed to the French Empire in 1807, as were the free cities of Hamburg, Lubeck and Bremen in 1810.

Foreign conquests not only helped Napoleon extend monarchy in Europe but also helped him strengthen monarchy within his empire. Both the territorial titles of the *noblesse d'empire* created in 1808, and the domains and revenues assigned with them, were based on locations outside France. Hugues Maret, the Emperor's trusted Ministre secrétaire d'Etat, for example, became Duke of Bassano in northern Italy, while Joseph Fouché, Minister of Police, became Duke of Otranto in the Kingdom of Naples. In 1810, Napoleon married the Archduchess Marie Louise, the last of the nine marriages—to the Houses of Bavaria (twice), Baden, Württemberg, Hohenzollern-Sigmaringen, Salm-Salm, von der Leyen and Arenberg—by which he connected members of his family, his marshals or their relations, with dynastic Europe.

The imperial household, rather than the Senate, the Corps Legislatif and the Conseil d'Etat, became the power-centre of the state, the *Etiquette du Palais Im-*

E T Archives

The Treaty of Tilsit, signed on July 7th, 1807, confirmed Napoleon's mastery of Europe, following the diplomatic wooing of Tsar Alexander I (centre) and humiliation of Queen Louise and King Frederick William III of Prussia.

périal a clearer guide to the power structure than the written constitution. The Emperor's *lever* and *coucher* became, critical moments, as Louis XVI's had not been, used by ambitious courtiers, such as the chamberlain Stanislas de Girardin (who was ultimately successful), to restate their candidacy for a prefecture. In 1810 dukes obtained the *entrée* to the throneroom, while presidents of sections in the Council of State lost it. Count Regnault de Saint Jean d'Angély, Secretary of State of the Imperial Family, wrote to Cardinal Fesch on October 4th, 1810:

> . . . the ministers and grand officers of the Empire are also part of the Household of the emperor . . . This practice is consistent with the practice of the former French monarchy and the current practice of the other courts of Europe.

By September 1813 so many chamberlains were serving as officers in the army or prefects in the *departements* that not enough were available for duty at court. In addition the Emperor used his ADCs to check and control the power and patronage of the Minister of War. Ultra-monarchical etiquette was used to assert the Emperor's superiority over the Senate, the Corps Legislatif and the city of Paris—even, to the Repre-

sentatives' fury, during the Hundred Days. Echoing many Parisians, Madame de Boigne wrote of Napoleon that she had never seen a monarch treat the public so cavalierly—by his failure to salute or bow to his subjects. Stendhal, who often attended court between 1810 and 1814 as 'inspector of the furniture and buildings of the crown', wrote in 1818 of

> . . . this court devoured with ambition [whose] pestilential air . . . totally corrupted Napoleon and exalted his armour propre to the state of a disease . . . he was on the point of making Europe one vast monarchy.

Indeed by 1812, Napoleon owned forty-four palaces, from Rome to Amsterdam, more than any other monarch; when the restoration begun in 1808 had been completed, he was also planning to use Versailles, which he inspected several times. As one of his secretaries Baron Meneval wrote, he saw himself as 'the pillar of royalty in Europe'. On January 18th, 1813, he wrote to his brother Jerome that his enemies, by appealing to popular feeling, represented 'upheavals and revolutions . . . pernicious doctrines.'

In Napoleon's opinion his fellow monarchs were traitors to 'their own cause' when in 1813 they began to desert the French Empire, or in 1814 refused to accept his territorial terms for peace. However, like the Kaiser in 1914, he over-estimated their commitment to authoritarian monarchy. Most monarchs admired Napoleon's genius, his skill at taming the Revolution, the excellence of his guard and army, the splendour of his court and palaces. They were ready to imitate Napoleonic models in those domains and to travel long distances to pay him court at Erfurt in 1808, Paris in 1809 and Dresden in 1812. In 1811 Metternich, a particular admirer of Napoleonic autocracy, thought of using French troops to suppress the Hungarian constitution. In 1813 both the King of Prussia and the Emperor of Austria dreaded war and hesitated to appeal to popular nationalism.

However, most monarchs feared Napoleonic expansion more than they admired Napoleonic autocracy. Moreover, there was a monarchical alternative to Napoleon I. In Vienna, Saint Petersburg and London there flourished what Count S. Uvarov, future minister of education in Russia, but long resident in Vienna, called 'that sort of open conspiracy . . . that great war machine . . . the secret alliance of European opinion against the France of the time'. He was referring to networks of dedicated opponents of French expansion, united by feelings of European solidarity. They included the great writer Madame de Staël; Baron von Stein the Prussian reformer; Baron von Armfelt, a confidante of Alexander I; Count Pozzo di Borgo, one of his ADCs and the oldest and most implacable enemy of Napoleon since their youth on the island of Corsica; General Moreau, Napoleon's rival of 1800–04; and in Austrian service the great publicist, later called 'the Secretary of Europe', Friedrich von Gentz. They helped push Austria to attack the Napoleonic Empire in 1809, the Tsar to maintain resistance in 1812, and Bernadotte to join, that year, what Madame de Staël called 'the European cause.'

Some of these enemies of Napoleon had personal connections with the Bourbon emigre government which, from 1798 if not before, both the British and Russian governments had kept as a reserve card in their plans for redrawing the map of Europe. As Pitt had told the House of Commons in 1800, the British government considered: 'the Restoration of the French monarchy . . . as a most desirable object because I think it would afford the strongest and best security to

this country and to Europe'—although it was never a *sine qua non* of peace.

The reappearance of the Bourbon dynasty on the European stage owed less to respect for its dynastic rights than to its commitment to France's traditional frontiers. This renunciation of territorial expansion, first evident at the Treaty of Aix-la-Chapelle in 1748, was maintained throughout the reign of Louis XVI (Vergennes wrote to Louis XVI in 1777, 'France as it is now constituted should far more fear than desire additional territory') and was repeatedly asserted in Louis XVIII's proclamations and letters. Even Napoleon, who continued to insist on retaining Antwerp and the 'natural frontiers', called a return to the 'old frontiers' 'inseparable from the reestablishment of the Bourbons'. This was the principal reason why Britain supported the Bourbons with money, asylum for Louis XVIII after 1807, assistance in distributing his proclamations in France and active encouragement for his nephew the Duc d'Angouleme behind British lines in south-west France in March 1814.

Like both Catherine II and Paul I, Tsar Alexander I remained more sympathetic to the Bourbon cause than is generally believed. His court, like the Swedish, went into mourning for the Bourbon prince, the Duc d'Enghien, executed on Napoleon's orders in 1804, and refused to recognise Napoleon's imperial title until 1807. Although opposed to fighting a war for the sole object of the restoration of the King of France, in 1805 he considered the restoration of a Bourbon with a constitution 'highly desirable'. Throughout the years of peace with Napoleon after the Treaty of Tilsit in 1807, the Russian government continued diplomatic contacts with, and paid a subsidy to, Louis XVIII.

In a private audience in May 1813, Alexander I told the Comte de La Ferronays, a representative of Louis XVIII, that he was prepared to consider supporting a Restoration, once allied armies had crossed the Rhine: 'Let us let circumstances do the work. I know better than anyone, believe me, that the reestablishment of legitimacy is the only base on which one can establish the peace and tranquility of Europe'. To Louis XVIII he wrote 'we need patience, circumspection and the greatest secrecy'.

Pozzo di Borgo was one of several royalist ADCs of the Tsar at allied head-

quarters from January to June 1814. In April, assisted by the growth of anti-Napoleonic feeling in France, and the Tsar's secret inclination, Pozzo insisted on the restoration of the Bourbons and Napoleon's abdication. It may have been Pozzo who suggested Elba, an island he knew well, as Napoleon's compensation.

As the Bourbons had found during their emigration, so Napoleon learnt in 1814: territorial interests mattered more than blood connections to what Marshal Bernadotte called 'the family of kings'. To Napoleon's surprise, after 1814 Francis I of Austria showed no more support for the dynastic interests of his grandson the King of Rome than the Bourbons of Spain, Naples or Parma had done, after 1793, for those of their French cousins. Francis I wrote to Metternich of Napoleon's exile to Elba (formerly subject to his brother the Grand Duke Ferdinand III of Tuscany);

> The island of Elba does not please me, for it is a loss to Tuscany; they give to others what belongs to my family, which cannot be allowed in future, and Napoleon remains too near to France and Europe.

The Empress Marie Louise was more loyal, but concerned above all to gain Parma as an independent sovereignty for herself: *'Parme ou rien est ma devise'*. Hence her switch of loyalties from husband to father in autumn 1814.

Napoleon I had hoped to link the sense of solidarity of the monarchs of Europe to the French Empire. Instead it had been turned against the Empire in the European coalition of 1813–15. From Moscow to London, consciously rivalling the monuments of the Napoleonic Empire, monarchs built triumphal arches, temples of victory and war memorials celebrating their victory over Napoleon. The picture by Peter Krafft of 'The Commander-in-Chief Prince Schwarzenberg presenting to Emperor Franz I, Emperor Alexander I and King Frederick William III captured French troops and standards after the Battle of Leipzig, October 18th, 1813', the Battle of the Nations which, more than Waterloo, marked the end of the Napoleonic Empire, is the finest memorial to 'Coalition Europe'. It was painted in 1817 for the Military Invalids Hospital of Vienna as a dynastic, artistic, humanitarian and European riposte to the similar picture by Baron Gerard, once on the ceiling of the hall of the Council of State in the Tuileries: 'Count Rapp presenting the banners of the defeated Russian Imperial Guard to Napoleon I on the battlefield of Austerlitz, December 2nd, 1805'. Fewer dead and wounded are depicted; three monarchs instead of one are shown; and they are humbly dismounted rather than, like Napoleon, portrayed on horseback.

After 1815 the monarchies of Europe owed relatively little, apart from a reinforced sense of Francophobia, to the Napoleonic Empire and epoch. The Napoleonic legend was a legend, not a political reality. None of Napoleon's innumerable changes to the map of Europe lasted, except for certain frontiers created for some of his German allies. All Napoleonic constitutions were abolished. Rather than continuing the military autocratic style and regime of Napoleon, many monarchs adopted liberal constitutions, based on the 1814 charter of Louis XVIII. By 1821 such constitutions had spread across half of the German Confederation; by 1848 to Spain, Piedmont and Prussia. Napoleon's most immediately important legacy was nei-

ther his guard, nor his court, nor his nobility, the majority of whom rallied to his successors, nor even perhaps the Code Napoleon, but his dynasty.

After 1815, the Bonapartes continued to function as a dynasty. Indeed, because of the plebiscites of 1804 and 1815 endorsing Napoleon I, they considered themselves, as Joseph Bonaparte wrote to La Fayette in 1830, more legitimate than the Bourbons. The son of Napoleon's admirer Lady Holland found in Rome in 1828 that Jerome-Napoleon, former King of Westphalia, kept 'the best mounted and most princely looking establishment' in the city, and 'will not go out where he is not received as a king'. As they had done at the Tuileries, in Rome the Bonapartes quarrelled over who had the right to a royal armchair at Madame Mére's family dinners; in the end she stopped giving them.

In addition to its internal French political programme of plebiscites and strong government, the dynasty was committed, in Europe, to reversing the two main legacies of the European coalition: the territorial settlement of 1814–15 and the Congress system. This was

one reason for Louis-Napoleon's popularity and rise to power in 1848. It would be Napoleon III who, by the wars into which he led the French Empire against Russia in 1854, Austria in 1859 and Prussia in 1870, destroyed the alliance between the monarchs of Europe which had overthrown his uncle.

FOR FURTHER READING:

Louis Bergeron, *L'Episode Napoléonien* (Editions du Seuil, 1972); Charles J. Esdaile, *The Wars of Napoleon* (Longman, 1995); Pierre-Francois-Léonard Fontaine, *Journal*, 2 vols, Ecole Nationale Superieure des eaux-Arts, 1987; Paul W. Schroeder, *The Transformation of European Politics 1763–1848* (Oxford University Press, 1994).

Philip Mansel's *latest book is* Constantinople: City of the World's Desire 1453–1924 *(Penguin 1997). He is currently working on a history of Paris between 1814 and 1848. He is editor of* The Court Historian, *newsletter of the Society for Court Studies.*

Napoleon IN EGYPT

The general's search for glory led to the birth of Egyptology.

by **Bob Brier**

TWO HUNDRED YEARS AGO NAPOLEON BONAPARTE WAS IN EGYPT AND WAS NOT ENJOYING HIS TOUR. HIS FLEET HAD BEEN SUNK AT ABOUKIR BAY, HE HAD SUFFERED HIS FIRST DEFEAT ON LAND AT ACRE, AND HIS MEN WERE DYING OF THE PLAGUE. AMID THIS DISASTER, ONE OF HIS ENTOURAGE, GEOFFROY ST.-HILAIRE, WROTE HOME,

Here I once again find men who think of nothing but science; I live at the center of a flaming core of reason. . . . We busy ourselves enthusiastically with all the questions that are of concern to the government and with the sciences to which we have devoted ourselves freely.

St.-Hilaire, a 26-year-old naturalist, was unconcerned that he was in the middle of a war 2,000 miles from home. He was doing what he liked to do best—studying exotic animals. St.-Hilaire had followed Bonaparte to Egypt, which the 29-year-old general hoped to conquer for France, striking a fatal blow to England's economy by seizing control of the land trade route to India.

Bonaparte also had plans for his own career:

Europe presents no field for glorious exploits; no great empires or revolutions are to be found, but in the East where there are six hundred million men. . . . My glory is declining. This little corner of Europe is too small to supply it. We must go East. All the great men of the world have there acquired their celebrity.

Bonaparte would be a new Alexander the Great, but there was far more to the young general than military ambition. Yes, he would colonize Egypt, but he

© Chester Higgins

St.-Hilaire

would also reveal to Europe the hidden Orient. He would study and record every aspect of Egypt. To this end, he brought with him more than 500 civilians, including about 150 biologists, mineralogists, linguists, mathematicians, chemists, and other scholars. Nothing like it had ever been done before. The results of their labors would appear in the monumental 20-volume *Description de l'Égypte*, completed in 1828, and in the course of their research Egyptology was born.

The scientists Bonaparte assembled included the best minds of France. Bonaparte himself was a member of the mathematics section of the Institut de France, the most important French scholarly organization, and early in his career he proudly signed his name *"Bonaparte, membre de l'Institut."* He

was familiar with learning and the finer things in life. During his successful Italian campaign of 1796–1797 he had befriended the chemist Claude Louis Berthollet and the mathematician Gaspard Monge. Berthollet taught Bonaparte some chemistry, and Monge helped the young general select Italian art works, which were confiscated, brought back to Paris, and displayed in the Musée Napoleon (later the Louvre).

When Napoleon sailed for Egypt, Berthollet and Monge accompanied him, along with even greater luminaries: mathematician Jean Baptiste Joseph Fourier, mineralogist Déodat Guy Gratet de Dolomieu, and well-known botanical artist Pierre Joseph Redoute. One of the older savants was the artist Dominique Vivant Denon, who had also assisted Bonaparte in selecting art on the Italian campaign; he later became the first curator of the Louvre. Although these established men were important, most members of the commission were in their early twenties or even younger. These scholars formed the Scientific and Artistic Commission of Egypt; some of the senior members were professors at prestigious schools like the École Polytechnique in Paris, and they brought their most promising students with them on the trip of their lives.

THE FLEET LANDED AT ALEXANDRIA on July 1, 1798, and almost immediately the savants were left to fend for themselves. There was a war to fight and the generals were too preoccupied with getting supplies for their troops to worry about the scholars. So Monge, Fourier, Denon, and the students had to scrounge for themselves.

Reprinted with the permission of *Archaeology* Magazine, Vol. 51, No. 3 (May/June 1999), pp. 44-53. © 1999 by the Archaeological Institute of America.

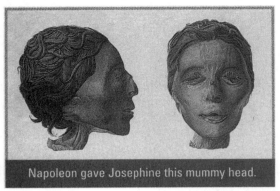

Napoleon gave Josephine this mummy head.

photo © Chester Higgins

Conditions at Alexandria were squalid, and some of the men went to nearby Port Rashid (ancient Rosetta) looking for better accommodations. Once Cairo was secured they would be summoned and established in permanent quarters.

During their first month in Egypt, the French fought the two most important battles of the campaign. Both are misnamed: The Battle of the Pyramids was fought in a melon field at Embabba nearly ten miles from the pyramids, and the Battle of the Nile was fought not on the Nile but at Aboukir Bay.

The Battle of the Pyramids, fought three weeks after the landing at Alexandria, established Napoleon's military superiority over the Mamluks, Egypt's elite fighting class. The Mamluks were superb horsemen, skilled with sabres and pistols, but they were no match for a disciplined professional army. The French army formed squares, with rifles at the sides, artillery at the corners, and cavalry within. The Mamluks pranced in front of them in their silk pantaloons, vests, and turbans decorated with feathers and jewels. The French could see the pyramids in the distance and, just as the battle was about to begin, Napoleon declared, "Soldiers, from these heights 40 centuries look down upon you." Given that hieroglyphs had not been deciphered and the chronology of the pharaohs was virtually unknown except from the Bible, his estimate of the age of the pyramids turned out to be remarkably accurate, only about four centuries off. The Mamluks, led by Murad Bey, charged with sabres and pistols drawn; the French waited until they were nearly upon them and then blew them away.

Napoleon had little time to enjoy his victory. Ten days later his entire fighting fleet was destroyed by England's Admiral Horatio Nelson. The fleet's 13 ships were anchored in a line close to shore at Aboukir Bay, a few miles from Alexandria. At 2:00 A.M. on August 1, Nelson sailed into Aboukir Bay and decided to fight then and there. With no soundings to guide him, he sailed between the French fleet and the shore. The French, believing this impossible, had left their landward cannons unprepared for battle, and Nelson fired broadside after broadside into their ships. Admiral Bruyes aboard the French flagship *L'Orient,* having lost both his legs to cannon fire, was seated in a chair with tourniquets on the stumps, still giving orders, when a cannonball hit him. Captain Casabianca assumed command, though himself badly wounded, and fought on in the burning ship to the end. When the fire on *L'Orient* reached her powder magazine the ship exploded with a deafening roar that could be heard 50 miles away. When the ship sank, much of the savants' scientific instrumentation, surveying equipment, and supplies went with it.

In spite of this setback, the savants settled into their tasks. The senior men, Monge, Berthollet, and a one-legged general named Louis Cafarelli, in charge of financial and administrative matters, were housed in the palace of Hassan Kashef in Cairo. The botanists set up their experiments in the garden of Qassim Bey's palace. St.-Hilaire was ecstatic about the space and was soon involved in helping set up chemistry labs and collecting mineral, botanical, and zoological specimens. The Egyptian chronicler Abd al-Rabman al-Jabarti described with wonder the library they set up in the house of Hassan Kashef:

The administrators, astronomers, and some of the physicians lived in this house in which they placed a great number of their books and with a keeper taking care of them and arranging them. And the students among them would gather two hours before noon every day in an open space opposite the shelves of books, sitting on chairs arranged in parallel rows before a wide long board. Whoever wishes to look up something in a book asks for whatever volumes he wants and the librarian brings them to him. Then he thumbs through the pages, looking through the book and writes. All the while they are quiet and no one disturbs his neighbor. When some Muslims would come to look around they would not prevent them from entering. Indeed they would bring them all kinds of printed books in which there were all sorts of illustrations and maps of the countries and regions, animals, birds, plants, histories of the ancients, campaigns of the nations, tales of the prophets including pictures of them, their miracles and wondrous deeds, the events of their respective peoples and such things which baffle the mind.

MORE IMPORTANT to the expedition than the laboratories and collections were the workshops under the direction of Nicolas-Jacques Conte. An artist and engineer, Conte had an uncanny ability to design and build almost anything that was needed. Once, when lead was in short supply and the artists needed pencils, he used graphite, thus inventing the modern pencil—the *crayon Conte.* He made replacements for the scientific instruments lost at Aboukir Bay and elsewhere and also made a study of the contemporary manufacturing of various products in Cairo so what was useful could be duplicated in his workshops. According to Napoleon, Conte was capable of creating "the arts of France in the deserts of Arabia." Monge said he had "all the arts in his hands and all the sciences in his head." To Berthollet he was "the pillar of the expedition."

A month after the Battle of the Pyramids, on August 22, 1798, Bonaparte formed the Institut d'Égypte, modeled after the Institut de France. Its goals were to enlighten Egypt; advise the Egyptian government; and study the country's history, industry, and natural phenomena. Bringing savants on a military expedition was certainly in the spirit of the Enlightenment, as were the goals of the institute, but Bonaparte's main concern was clearly practical. His savants had skills that would be useful to an army far from home. Many were civil engineers who could build bridges and forts; others could manufacture whatever the army might need. At the institute's first session, on August 23, Bonaparte, its vice-president, suggested six research topics:

1) *How can the bread ovens be improved?*
2) *How can the Nile water be purified?*
3) *Are windmills practical for Cairo?*
4) *Can beer without hops be brewed in Egypt?*
5) *Are the raw materials for gunpowder available in Egypt?*

6) What is the legal system in Egypt, and what improvements do the citizens want?

The savants were also free to investigate topics of their own, and even the dullest engineer was more eager to explore the temple of Dendera than study bread ovens. (They did report that reeds and safflower stalks would fuel the ovens better than the wood used in France.)

Of all the memoirs published by members of the expedition, by far the most popular was Denon's *Travels in Upper and Lower Egypt*. At 55, Denon was the oldest on the expedition, but was always in the middle of things. When Napoleon instructed General Desaix to pursue the retreating Mamluks south, Denon saw it as a chance to sketch the monuments of Upper Egypt and went along. He was constantly asking Desaix for more time to draw the temples and tombs. In the Valley of the Kings, Denon was overwhelmed by the tombs and the vibrant colors of the paintings in them, but was told they had to press on:

How was it possible to leave such precious curiosities without taking a drawing of them? How to return without a sketch to show? I earnestly demanded a quarter of an hour's grace: I was allowed twenty minutes. One person highlighted me while another held a taper to every object that I pointed out to him, and I completed my task prescribed with spirit and correctness.

Denon's excitement was contagious, and soon General Desaix became his fellow archaeologist, as Barthelemy Mery's epic poem notes:

Desaix now far from the sky of Idumia commends the exploits of the army to the engraving tool,
and the same hand that harasses Mamluks during a day's respite, captures monu ments in
wonderful work to commemorate his remarkable journey.

While exploring the Valley of the Kings, Denon came upon a relief of a scribe writing on a scroll. Unaware, despite his education, that Egyptians wrote on papyrus and that travelers had already brought papyri back to Europe, Denon congratulated himself on being "the first who had made this important discovery." This reveals a great deal about both Denon and early Egyptology and explains his excitement when local

Description de l'Égypte, photo © Chester Higgins

Ruins of the city of Antinoöpolis, built by Hadrian where his lover Antinous drowned, no longer exist. This engraving by Napoleon's savants is one of the few records of the site.

guides brought him a mummy with a papyrus rolled up under its left arm:

I turned pale . . . my voice failed me . . . so great was my fear of destroying it, that I knew not what to do with my treasure; I was afraid to touch this book, the most ancient of books at this day known; I dared confide it to no person, deposit it no where; all the cotton of the quilt that served me for a bed did not seem sufficient to embalm it with sufficient softness.

IN SPITE OF HIS ALMOST PATHOLOGICAL ENthusiasm, Denon made some reasonable observations about ancient Egypt. The papyrus he so treasured was a Book of the Dead, a series of spells and prayers intended to ensure that the deceased would be resurrected in the next world. Denon noticed that a section of the text ended in the middle of a line and that the space to the left of the writing had been left blank. From this he correctly deduced that the writing was from right to left. (Right to left was the more common direction of writing, but ancient Egyptian could also be written from left to right.)

Denon returned to France with Bonaparte, a full two years before the rest of the savants, so he had a head start on publishing. His *Travels in Upper and Lower Egypt,* which appeared in 1802, was a sensation, going through more than 20 editions in various languages. It was the first relatively accurate depiction of Egypt that Europe had seen. Prior to that, Richard Pococke's *Description of the East, and Some Other Countries* (1743–45) and Fredrik Norden's *Voyages d'Égypte et de Nubie* (1755) were the primary references, and neither author was an artist.

Denon's illustrations were clearly a step up, but while generating interest they were not the beginning of Egyptology. It was the younger men Denon left behind who measured and drafted the monuments with the precision of engineers. This was the start of scientific archaeology. One of the youngest, René-Edouard Devilliers, an 18-year-old engineering student, brought his books with him, and in October 1798 Monge tested him and pronounced him a civil engineer. For most of the campaign he teamed up with the 21-year-old engineer Prosper Jollois; as far as one can tell from their memoirs, they forgot about bridges and roads and fell in love with antiquity. Between letters home complaining about bad food and poor accommodations, they mapped, drew, and described dozens of monuments in detail.

Denon had quickly sketched the now-famous zodiac ceiling at Dendera temple, but Jollois and Devilliers, retracing his route south, drew it carefully and accurately which was far from easy. The ceiling on which were carved hundreds

The Roots of Egyptology

Napoleon's savants recorded ancient monuments throughout Egypt. Clockwise from upper left: scholars measuring a colossal hand of Ramses II at Memphis; the artist Dutertre standing with his sketch pad before a statue of Ramses II at Karnak; savants measuring the Sphinx; Duterte, beneath an umbrella, drawing the Great Temple of Amun at Karnak; the artist Cecile sketching the tomb of Paheri at El-Kab (here the self-conscious artist makes himself the focus of the depiction rather than the monument).

Description de l'Égypte and Travels in Upper and Lower Egypt (Sphinx): photos © Chester Higgins

An English cartoon shows Napoleon's savants trapped by the Mamluks atop a Roman column honoring Pompey the Great.

of details of the sky as the Egyptians saw it had been blackened by soot from the fires of centuries of squatters who had lived in the temple. The pair recorded the temples at Philae, Esneh, Edfu, and Kom Ombo, and sketched the colossi of Memnon and Luxor temple. Jollois was not impressed with ancient construction techniques and noted that the temple walls were irregular, some slanting inward, others outward.

Their greatest adventure, however, was in the Valley of the Kings. The valley had been drawn by Pococke, but to skilled draftsmen his work seemed amateurish. Not only did Jollois and Devilliers produce the first professional map of the valley, they discovered a new tomb. When Napoleon's forces entered Egypt there were 11 open tombs in the valley; exploring the valley's remote western branch, the young engineers

found the tomb of Amenhotep III. Its walls had been damaged by centuries of flooding, and much of the painted plaster lay on the ground, too fragile to be removed. Small antiquities, such as figurines of servants intended to wait on the king in the next world, littered the floor of the pharaoh's tomb, and the boys took some as royal souvenirs. Four that Devilliers brought back to France are still owned by his descendants. A small green schist head of Amenhotep III that they discovered is now in the Louvre.

While the artists and engineers measured and drew monuments, the naturalists amassed collections of minerals, insects, birds, and plants. These collections became a major point of contention when it was time to leave Egypt. Plague and an inability to replace troops had doomed the expedition from the moment Nelson sank the French fleet. In 1801 the British, under General Hutchinson, dictated terms of surrender, article 16 stipulating that all antiquities and the savants collections become British property. Bonaparte was in France, having left Egypt two years before when he saw that the campaign was a lost

Reading the ROSETTA STONE

UNEARTHED BY THE FRENCH in July 1799, the Rosetta Stone bears three inscriptions, Greek, hieroglyphic, and demotic (the Egyptian script used for mundane transactions). Napoleon's savants realized the stone was the key to deciphering the ancient Egyptian language because the last line of Greek, which they could read, said the three inscriptions contained the same text (dating to 196 B.C., it praises Ptolemy V for reducing taxes on priests). Comparison of them would unlock the Egyptian writings. But the decipherment was not as easy as scholars had expected, primarily because everyone made the same mistaken assumption that the hieroglyphic inscription was purely ideographic, with hieroglyphs standing only for concepts. Thus, scholars concentrated on the demotic text because they believed it alone was an alphabetic script and would provide a close parallel to Greek text. The idea that a script had to be either totally alphabetic or totally ideographic was firmly entrenched by the time the stone was discovered.

The British physician and physicist Thomas Young made the first crucial breakthrough around 1814. He realized that the demotic was a mixture of phonetic and symbolic signs. Then, using the phonetic values obtained from the demotic, he figured out phonetic values for some of the hieroglyphs. He knew from the Greek and demotic texts that King Ptolemy's name appeared repeatedly and deduced that it was inside the ovals in the hieroglyphic text. The name for these ovals, cartouche, is the French word for cartridge—given by the soldiers who saw them carved on temple walls and thought they looked like ammunition.

Young's discovery was crucial, but it would be another decade before the Egyptian language was truly deciphered. Even Young, who first deciphered the phonetics of the name in the cartouches, was a victim of the entrenched assumption that hieroglyphs were

pictorial. He thought the non-Egyptian name Ptolemy was the exception to the rule. It would be Jean Francois Champollion in 1822 who realized that hieroglyphs were both ideographic and phonetic. With the cracking of the code, Egyptologists could now read the history of the country they had been studying for decades.

BRITISH MUSEUM CONSERVATORS have given the Rosetta Stone its most thorough cleaning since it arrived at the museum in 1802, according to an *Art Newspaper* report (February 1999). The familiar appearance of the three-quarter-ton monolith—black stone with white inscriptions—has changed considerably. To make the inscriptions more legible, they were filled with white chalk, perhaps in 1847. Much of the chalk had been lost by 1980, when it was replaced with a water-soluble white paint. During the recent cleaning, conservators removed this white paint and found beneath it ink dating from 1799, the year the stone was discovered by a French officer serving in Egypt. Copies of the inscriptions had been printed then directly from the stone. In some of the incisions, traces of a light red iron-earth pigment were discovered under the ink. Curator Richard Parkinson told the *Art Newspaper* that it seems likely that when the stone was originally erected the inscriptions were filled with light red pigment, making them stand out from the gray surface. That the stone is, in fact, gray rather than black became apparent when layers of protective wax were removed. The wax, applied decades ago, had darkened from airborne dirt and the hands of museumgoers who couldn't resist touching the stone.

The newly cleaned stone will be the centerpiece of a British Museum exhibition titled "Cracking the Codes: The Rosetta Stone and Decipherment," opening July 10 and running through January 2000.—B.B.

The zodiac ceiling was so impressive that in 1821 a French expedition went back and dynamited it out.

cause. Departing secretly by night, he had left a letter placing General Kleber in charge, but Kleber was assassinated a few months later by a religious fanatic. The next and last commander-in-chief was the highly eccentric general Abdullah Menou, who had converted to Islam so he could marry a bathkeeper's daughter and was little respected by either French or British. The distraught scientists pleaded with Menou to defend their collections. Menou protested vehemently, calling the English "common thieves" for wanting to take the scientists' collections. Edward Clarke, a Cambridge mineralogy professor present at the negotiations, wrote in a letter to his friend Reverend William Otter,

We found much more in their possession than was represented or imagined... Statues, Sarcophagi, Maps, MSS., Drawings, Plans, Charts, Botany, Stuffed Birds, Animals, Dried Fishes, &c. Savigny, who has been years in forming the beautiful collection of Natural History for the Republic, and which is the first thing of the kind in the world, is in despair. Therefore, we represented it to General Hutchinson, that it would be the best plan to send him to England also, as the most proper person to take care of the collection and to publish its description, if necessary. This is now agreed to by all parties.

When the other French naturalists heard that Savigny was going to England, they offered to go as well. These men had risked their lives, endured hardships, and were not easily separated from their trophies. Many realized that their academic careers would be forever established if they published their findings. In the end, the naturalists were permitted to return to France with their collections.

LETTING DRAWINGS, paintings, rocks, and plants go was one thing, but the Rosetta Stone—the key to the decipherment of hieroglyphs—was quite something else. The French had unearthed the Rosetta Stone at the port of el-Rashid in July 1799 as

Description de l'Égypte, photo © Chester Higgins

The zodiac ceiling from the Dendera temple represents the night sky. It is now in the Louvre.

they were strengthening the foundations of a fort. Lieutenant Bouchard, the officer in charge, realized that the stone was important, and by August it was being studied in Cairo. The 47-inch-tall, 30-inch-wide stone slab bore three inscriptions, of which one was Greek, which the savants could read (inscribed in 196 B.C., it praises King Ptolemy V for reducing taxes on priests). They immediately realized they had the key to deciphering the ancient Egyptian language, because the last line of Greek said that the inscriptions were the same text in "sacred and native and Greek characters." The top inscription is in "sacred" characters (hieroglyphs), while the middle is in the "native" script used in the late period (after about 600 B.C.) for mundane transactions (known as demotic from the Greek word for people). Thus there are only two languages on the Rosetta Stone—Egyptian (written in two forms) and Greek.

By the time of the French surrender in 1801, the existence of the Rosetta Stone was known throughout the scholarly world. When the treaty was signed, the British were not about to let it go to France. In an attempt to protect it, General Menou claimed that the stone was

not the property of the French government, but his private property and that as an officer he should be permitted to keep it. Clarke, who was party to the negotiations, was adamant that the stone should go to England:

I was in Cairo when the capitulation began. There I learned from the Imperial consul, that the famous inscription which is to explain the Hieroglyphics was still at Alexandria. I then intended to write to General Hutchinson and Lord Keith on the subject, to beg it might be obtained for the University of Cambridge, or the British Museum, as I know full well, we have better Orientalists than the French and a knowledge of eastern languages may be necessary in some degree towards the decipherment of these inscriptions.

Ultimately the stone was taken to England and placed in the British Museum.

ALTHOUGH THE ROSETTA STONE WAS the key to modern Egyptology, the publications of the scientists on the expedition were almost as important. When they returned to France, Bonaparte became first consul and authorized funds for the publication of the *Description de l'Égypte*. The work was to cover everything—the ancient monuments, natural history, and modern country (ca. 1800), and was to include the first comprehensive map of Egypt. Edmé Jomard, one of the expedition's young engineers, was named editor and was soon soliciting drawings, paintings, and research papers from his colleagues. As the submissions accumulated and the years passed, it became evident that the project would be larger than anyone had anticipated. In all it took 20 years to complete, and many who had participated in the campaign were dead by the time the final volume was published.

One thousand sets of the *Description* were printed, each containing nearly 1,000 large engravings. A small army of engravers transferred the savants drawings to copper plates, but eventually they realized that if something was not done to speed the process they would never complete the work. Once again, Conte saved the day inventing a machine to engrave the skies mechanically for the plates with views of monuments. It even had a little adjustable wheel so it could be programmed for clouds. Nearly a million large sheets of handmade paper were needed for the publication, and five paper manufacturers were kept busy on the project. Five massive volumes of engravings depicted antiquities, three natural history, and two modern Egypt. Because Bonaparte ordered that the maps should "remain under the seal of a state secret," that volume was the most problematic. Even after his exile they were considered secret, delaying their publication until 1828.

The antiquities volumes of the *Description* set the standard for Egyptological publications for nearly a century. Jollois and Devillier's rendering of the zodiac ceiling of the Dendera temple was so impressive that in 1821 a French expedition went back, dynamited it out, and brought it back to France, a worthy replacement for the Rosetta Stone they had so reluctantly relinquished. The illustrations in the volumes, drawn not by professional artists but by architects and engineers, were the first accurate depictions of Egyptian monuments Europe had ever seen. Though unable to translate the inscriptions they copied, they were aware that

Description de l'Égypte, photo © Chester Higgins

The *Description de l'Égypte* frontispiece features a pastiche of the most important monuments studied during Napoleon's Egyptian campaign, including the Rosetta Stone, colossi of Memnon, Luxor and Karnak temples, and the Sphinx.

their work would have long-lasting effects if it led to decipherment; indeed, it would be the foundation of modern epigraphy. Often the illustrators drew themselves into their sketches, and many can be seen at work in the drawings of the *Description*. My favorite, a curly-headed artist with a monumental ego, Cecile, drew himself into a dozen of his own engravings. In France the

Description set off a wave of Egyptomania in everything from furniture to women's fashion.

One important legacy of Napoleon's savants is their record of the city of Antinoöpolis, built by the Roman emperor Hadrian on the site where his lover, Antinous, drowned himself in the Nile. The savants realized it was the best-preserved Roman city in Egypt and returned to it four times to document every detail of its ruins. Their account and illustrations in the *Description de l'Égypte* are our only record of the city which was dismantled in the nineteenth century to build a sugar refinery in the village of El-Sheikh 'Ibada.

Thirty-four of Napoleon's scholars died in Egypt, many of the plague, some in battle. In later decades, others would return to Egypt to complete the description begun by the savants, and the French would dominate Egyptian archaeology for a century. In 1859 a group of French scholars working in Egypt founded the Institut Égyptien, a direct descendant of Napoleon's Institut d'Égypte. Among those present was 84-year-old Gaspard Monge, president of the first institute and the last surviving savant of Bonaparte's Egyptian campaign.

BOB BRIER *is a professor of philosophy at the C.W Post Campus of Long Island University.*

Unit Selections

16. **Arkwright: Cotton King or Spin Doctor?** Karen Fisk
17. **Samuel Smiles: The Gospel of Self-Help,** Asa Briggs
18. **Giuseppe Garibaldi,** Denis Mack Smith
19. **Conversations with Malthus,** Suzanne Rickard
20. **The Age of Philanthropy,** Gertrude Himmelfarb
21. **Women Murderers in Victorian Britain,** Judith Knelman
22. **'The White Man's Burden'? Imperial Wars in the 1890s,** Lawrence James

Key Points to Consider

❖ What were Richard Arkwright's principal contributions to the industrialization of England?

❖ What was the model for success in nineteenth-century England?

❖ Discuss Giuseppe Garibaldi's contributions to the unification of Italy.

❖ Why was Robert Malthus vilified in the nineteenth century?

❖ Why did Victorians take such an interest in philanthropy?

❖ Discuss the public and press reactions to women murderers in the nineteenth century. Why did these cases draw such interest?

❖ What is suggested by "the white man's burden"? What does the term reveal about nineteenth-century imperialism?

 **Links** | **www.dushkin.com/online/**

16. **Anthony S. Wohl/Vassar College**
    http://www.stg.brown.edu/projects/hypertext/landow/victorian/race/rcov.html
17. **Historical U.S. Census Data Browser**
    http://fisher.lib.virginia.edu/census/
18. **Society for Economic Anthropology Homepage**
    http://sea.agnesscott.edu

These sites are annotated on pages 4 and 5.

The early years of the nineteenth century were marked by the interplay of two powerful though opposite forces—change and continuity. The French Revolution and industrialization proved the impetus for political, economic, and social changes in Western civilization. The ideals of the French Revolution remained alive in France and inspired nationalistic movements in other parts of Europe. Industrialization brought material progress for millions, particularly the burgeoning middle class, but often at the expense of the unskilled workers who were victims of low wages and an impersonal factory system. Shifting demographic patterns created additional pressures for change. It had taken all of European history to reach a population of 180 million in 1800. Then, in the nineteenth century, the European population doubled, causing major migrations on the continent from the countryside to the cities, and sending waves of emigrants to America, Australia, and elsewhere. By 1919 about 200 million Europeans had migrated.

But forces of continuity also lingered on. Notwithstanding the impact of industrialism, much of Europe remained agrarian, dependent upon peasant labor. Christianity remained the dominant religion and the institution of monarchy retained the loyalty of those who wanted to preserve an orderly society. In addition, millions of Europeans, having lived through the crises of the French Revolution and Napoleonic eras, were willing to embrace even the most repressive, reactionary regimes if they could guarantee peace and stability.

The interaction of tradition and change raised vital new issues and generated conflicts in politics and thought. Of necessity the terms of political dialogue were redefined. The century was an age of ideologies: conservatism, with its distrust of untested innovations and its deep commitment to order and traditions; liberalism, with its faith in reason, technique, and progress; various forms of socialism, from revolutionary to utopian, each with its promise of equality and economic justice for the working class; and nationalism, with its stirring demand, at the same time unifying and divisive, that the nationalities of the world should be autonomous. Even Darwinism was misappropriated for political purposes. Transformed into Social Darwinism, it was used to justify the domination of Western nations over their colonies. Popular misconceptions of evolution reinforced prevailing notions of male supremacy.

In sum, the nineteenth century, for those who enjoyed economic and political status, was the "Golden Age" of human progress. For the rest, many of whom shared the materialist outlook of their "betters," it was a time of struggle to attain their fair share of the fruits of progress.

Several articles in this unit explore the dynamics of change in the nineteenth century. Economic forces and related ideologies are covered in "Arkwright: Cotton King or Spin Doctor?" "Giuseppe Garibaldi," and "Conversations with Malthus." Middle-class values, which reached their heights in this century, are treated from diverse perspectives in "The Age of Philanthropy" and "Women Murderers in Victorian Britain." " 'The White Man's Burden'? Imperial Wars in the 1890s" surveys the racial theories, economic impulses, and national rivalries that drove late nineteenth-century imperialism.

Arkwright: Cotton King or Spin Doctor?

Was Richard Arkwright really the mechanical genius of the Industrial Revolution?
Karen Fisk *questions his record as Britain's first cotton tycoon.*

Sir Richard Arkwright (1723–92) is usually credited with revolutionising the technical basis of cotton production between 1768 and 1792, transforming it from a cottage industry to one of worldwide proportions. Apart from developing machinery to do the work, he is credited with creating the factory system, earning him such titles as a 'founding father' of the Industrial Revolution and the 'father of the factory system'. Undoubtedly an inspirational figure of the eighteenth century, he emerged from a working-class background and achieved immense wealth. However, closer scrutiny of the evidence raises uncertainties about the traditionally accepted view of Arkwright, the mechanical genius, and his technical achievements.

Indeed, it appears that Arkwright's first patent was obtained by simply improving existing spinning frames. Having trained as a barber, Arkwright was unlikely to have possessed the technical skills required to produce these machines himself. It therefore seems curious that Arkwright achieved such recognition for the invention, which proved a catalyst to all the events that followed. So how and why has Arkwright been made the Cotton King?

Until the early eighteenth century, most of Britain's cloth was made from wool in areas where there were both sheep and ample water for the various processes, such as the West Country, Yorkshire and Lancashire; with most of the manufacture being carried out in the workers' homes. The system had lasted for centuries, but in 1702 a major turning point occurred when Thomas Cotchett, an elderly barrister, together with the engineer George Sorocold, built a silk mill powered by a waterwheel on the Derwent at Derby. This mill has good claim to the title of being the first factory, in the sense that it was a single establishment with complex machinery, a source of power, and accommodation for a number of workers. Sir Thomas Lombe, a wealthy silk merchant of Norwich and London, made considerable additions to Cotchett's mill in 1717, which established the pattern of textile factories. The transformation within and around Derbyshire that this heralded was unique, not only for its radical repercussions for textile production and business, but in a wider sense that was to alter the course of modern society.

Later inventions, such as the 'Flying Shuttle' by John Kaye of Bury in 1733, further promoted the textile industry to new heights. The demand for yarn became so greatly increased that it became impossible to meet it merely by hand labour. A machine for carding cotton had been introduced into Lancashire in 1760, and, in 1761, the Society for the Encouragement of Arts and Manufacturies offered a price of £50 for a successful spinning machine. Until 1767, spinning continued to be wholly by the old-fashioned jersey wheel. It was later in this year that James Hargreaves completed and patented the 'Spinning Jenny'. The jenny was, however, applicable only to the spinning of cotton for weft, being unable to give the yarn the degree of strength required in the longitudinal threads, or warp.

At his uncle's insistence, the highly-motivated Arkwright received more education than was customary for someone of his class. Eager to improve his lot of life, Arkwright made the most of his opportunities and soon realised that there was a fortune to be made, quite apart from a prize to be won, from designing an efficient spinning machine.

In 1768 Arkwright employed John Kaye, a clockmaker from Warrington, to assist in the construction of wooden models in an attempt to produce a workable machine. Arkwright was not alone in taking up the challenge. Lewis Paul and John Wyatt conducted many experiments between 1736 and 1745 and probably came closest in their attempts to invent a spinning machine, while Thomas Highs, a reedmaker at Leigh, was another who unsuccessfully attempted to design such a machine. Highs had also employed John Kaye to help him and it seems possible that Kaye copied some of Highs' ideas which he conveyed to Arkwright. Most of these early designs were similar and it was simply a matter of time before one person made a breakthrough in achieving the correct specifications. Arkwright may simply have modified certain components of Highs' basic attempt in achieving this goal.

Besides requiring considerable technical assistance, Arkwright could not have continued his spinning venture without adequate financial support. His business sense told him that his invention had more than just local potential, as it could be used in power-driven factories. However, a factory required much more capital than Arkwright possessed. His frame still needed perfecting and considerable investment would be necessary to make his venture a commercial success. Furthermore, to protect his ideas from being

This article first appeared in *History Today,* March 1998, pp. 25-30. © 1998 by History Today, Ltd. Reprinted by permission.

stolen and to ensure profit, he needed to take out a patent. Where a patent was granted, the holder alone had full entitlement to it for fourteen years. The machines could either be sold, or the holder could sell licences allowing other manufactures to use his invention. Anybody using the design without a licence or agreement was liable to prosecution. But patents themselves were costly to take out as legal fees had to be met and, again, Arkwright could not afford to patent his invention without further financial backing which he set about raising.

John Smalley, a publican and paint merchant of Preston, and David Thornley, a merchant of Liverpool, became Arkwright's first backers. Soon after the expansion of the partnership Thornley died, which is the reason his name rarely appears in history books. John Smalley's name appears as a witness to Arkwright's first patent declaration. Shortly afterwards, however, the three associates must have run into difficulties as the partnership was enlarged to include Samuel Need and Jedediah Strutt. Both Need and Strutt had extensive connections with the textile industry. Need was probably the wealthiest hosier in Nottingham, while Strutt had established a flourishing hosiery trade centred in Derby. Together they masterminded the spinning project, ensuring that it became a profitable enterprise.

What is clear from this summary of Arkwright's quest to invent a successful spinning machine is that, in contrast to the traditional view of a struggling lone inventor and genius, the highly ambitious young man sought and received considerable assistance in achieving his goal. The new associates began their venture in a Nottingham Mill, which was driven by horses as had been envisaged in the patent. However, this method soon became too expensive, as well as unfeasible for production on a large scale. Arkwright resolved to use waterpower, an initiative he is often credited with pioneering but which had in fact already proved successful, notably in the Cotchett and Sorocold mill of 1702 and Thomas Lombe's Derby silk mill of 1717. The trials of the new spinning frame showed sufficient promise for the partners to take the momentous decision to erect a mill powered by a waterwheel and in 1771 a site at Cromford, near Matlock, was leased.

Arkwright took out a second patent for a series of adaptions and inventions to augment his existing machinery in 1775. The whole process of yarn manufacture, including carding, drawing, roll-ing and spinning, was now performed by a beautifully arranged succession of operations on one machine. The grant of this further patent removed every obstacle to providing an efficient supply of yarn to meet demand. Whatever the future held for Arkwright, the prosperity of cotton manufacture was guaranteed.

As the rapid increase of power-driven machines produced yarn more cheaply, English merchants were able to capture a large proportion of the world market for cotton cloth. More mills were established in England and Scotland to meet the demand, in turn creating greater demands for wood, iron, leather, bricks, timber and so on needed to make the machines and mills and the fuel to run them. Of course, other developments in iron manufacture and steam engine design contributed, but the expanding cotton industry stimulated technological advances in most areas. For example, expanding coal production enabled mines to meet the demands of the new coke furnaces used for smelting. The introduction in 1776 of the steam pumping-engines of James Watt enabled colliery owners to mine deeper coal seams. Iron was the master material of the early Industrial Revolution. Developments in Shropshire in 1709 by Abraham Darby introduced pig- and cast-iron, while Henry Colt established the manufacture of wrought iron. Between 1740 and 1850, iron produced in Britain alone rose from 17,000 to 1.4 million tons annually.

The meteoric development of the textile industry is still, however, the most dramatic story of the Industrial Revolution. In a few decades, the textile mills became the biggest employer of labour in Britain. All this, happening within a period of about fifty years, created great changes within the lifetime of a single individual. In Derbyshire, people who had been self-employed, or who had been outworkers in their own home, found themselves living in new villages such as Cromford, and working in large mills owned by a single employer. A new industrial community was developed, which was to change the face of society for ever.

Unexpected difficulties soon arose for Arkwright, for in the late 1770s he found he was running short of water to power his mill. When he first moved to Cromford, probably only the water frames (the spinning frame driven by water), and some of the winding frames were power-driven. As one after another of the preparatory stages was mecha-

Courtesy of the Museum of the Lancashire Textile Industry.

A full-size water frame worked by Cromford Mill. The site was chosen, stated Arkwright in 1780, as 'a place affording a remarkable fine Stream of Water . . . in a Country very full of inhabitants vast numbers of whom & small Children are constantly Employed in the Works'.

nised, hand processes were replaced by systems needing power. The site of the mill was also enlarged and this, too, meant more energy would have been required. Attempts were made to combat the water problem. The level of the pond supplying the mill was raised, generating a higher fall of water. In the meantime, Arkwright investigated the possibility of using steam power which had already proved successful in other industries at that time.

Evidence indicates that a steam engine was used to drive spinning machines at Papplewick near Nottingham in 1788. The majority of written accounts state that Papplewick was the first textile factory to use steam power for spinning cotton. The introduction in 1712 of the steam pump invented by Thomas Newcomen, later to be refined by James Watt in 1776, was first used in collieries to put out water. Water power, meanwhile, was in use at Derby's silk mill long before Arkwright was even born. Again we must ask why Arkwright has been granted such individual recognition for his role in the textile revolution.

Without a business-like approach and certain leadership qualities, Arkwright could not have made his immense fortune. He did not, however, have an easy relationship with his partners and made many enemies. He began expanding his empire by building several additional cotton mills. He licensed his patents to cotton spinners in the North and Midlands. His achievements inspired others to attempt similar projects. Little is known about the licences which the partners sold to allow rivals to construct their machines. Gordon and Pares, the partnership which built the mill at Calver in 1780, paid £2,000 for using the first patent, £5,000 for the second, and an annual payment of £1,000 thereafter. However, other manufacturers felt that Arkwright charged excessively for the privilege and this encouraged them to use his designs without seeking permission.

Arkwright decided to take steps to protect himself, and began approaching spinners who had infringed his carding patent. Three submitted and paid up. However, deciding to take nine more to trial, he discovered that the Lancashire manufacturers had organised resistance. Already in 1772 they had attempted to set the first patent aside on the grounds that Arkwright was not the original inventor. This was unsupported by evidence and the case ended with a verdict which confirmed the validity of the patent.

In 1781, Arkwright's second patent, obtained in 1775, was again attacked by the Lancashire manufacturers. A legal decision was obtained against him, not on the grounds of prior invention, but because he had not given an accurate description of the machinery in the specification. Descriptions and pictures of ten machines were given in the patent. The opening and cleaning machines depicted in the patent were never used, and no satisfactory machine for doing this was made until Snodgrass adapted the threshing machine to produce the 'scutcher' in 1808, while about the same time, William Strutt, son of Jedediah, invented the 'devil' at Belper. The devil began the process of opening and loosening the cotton which had been tightly compressed into a bale for trans-shipment. The scutcher also cleaned out the seeds and dirt. At Cromford this must have been done by women beating the cotton with sticks and picking out dirt by hand until it was ready for carding (disentangling the cotton fibres in their natural state and beginning to lay them parallel).

Arkwright succeeded in having the 1781 verdict reversed four years later. In June of the same year, several other cotton spinners, particularly those in Lancashire, went to court again. A formidable array of witnesses was brought against Arkwright. Amongst them emerged Thomas Highs, who for the first time claimed the credit for the roller-spinning invention.

John Kaye, the clockmaker from Warrington, whom Highs had employed before 1768, was summoned to prove that he had communicated Highs' ideas to Arkwright. At the same trial, James Hargreaves' widow claimed that he had invented the 'crank and comb' (the answer to successful carding) thirteen or fourteen years earlier, and others claimed they had used it before 1775. Robert Pilkington gave evidence that he and Richard Livesay had made a carding engine in 1770 with the carding arranged in strips, thus preceding Arkwright by five years. Consequently, in June 1785, Arkwright lost the case and the rights to his patent. He tried to have the case re-opened the following November: he failed and finally the patents were freely available to all.

So why is it that Arkwright is acknowledged above all his peers? One deserving reason is that he cared about the welfare of his workers. Shift work was practised in most of these early mills and Cromford was no exception, with machinery running day and night. To contemporaries, this seemed wonderful, as did the fact that children could also earn a livelihood.

Mindful of the well-being of his employees, Arkwright built rows of cottages for his workers. The best example of this housing is North Street in Cromford, situated less than one mile from his mills. A school was founded for the

Courtesy of the History Today Archives.

Women's work, factory style: carding, drawing and roving—an engraving from *Cotton Manufacture in Great Britain* by Edward Baines.

children of his staff, churches and chapels were built with Sundays left free from work for church attendance, and the Greyhound Inn was also constructed for the local community. Farms were established for the provision of fresh vegetables, and loans were advanced to those wishing to buy a cow. In 1790, the right to hold a Saturday market was secured, and fairs were held twice yearly.

Arkwright was strict about the employment of children. He did not employ parish apprentices, nor any child under the age of ten, and no children were admitted into the mills until they could read. However, the pressure of parents to get their children mill work resulted in a lowering of standards. Consequently, children were taken on if they could read any small words at all.

Arkwright deserves credit for these early enlightened efforts which have been overshadowed by the malpractices of some later cotton masters of Lancashire. Many employed children at the age of five or six. The youngest began picking up waste cotton from the floor and going under machines in order to clean dust and dirt from the machinery. Bad health and stunted growth were often the price for those working in such cramped conditions.

Not everyone approved of the rapid changes, and mills were frequently under attack from rioters, or Luddites as they became known, who were opposed to the mechanised system which brought unemployment to those involved in hand-spinning. Lancashire mills, particularly, incurred trouble and many were destroyed by fire. However, the location of Arkwright's mills was generally remote from towns, with the risk of industrial unrest kept to a minimum. It was also said that within an hour, loyal supporters from his villages could gather together over 6,000 men, 1,000 guns and several cannons. Considered an understanding and fair employer, Arkwright was held in high esteem amongst the population at Cromford, which no doubt contributed to the expansion of his cotton empire.

On April 14th, 1781, Samuel Need died, ending the cotton partnership. John Smalley was paid over £3,000 by the remaining partners, and may also have been given a licence to build waterframes. He subsequently constructed a three-storey mill at Holywell. Jedediah Strutt bought land at Belper where he built three mills, and this was to become one of the largest cotton spinning sites in the country. Strutt also purchased land at Milford, and the famous warehouse was begun in which the Strutts experimented with a fireproof structure. His son William was the first man to design and build multi-storey fireproof buildings, the iron-framed construction and machinery being more ambitious than anything undertaken by Arkwright.

Establishing more mills in Derbyshire, Yorkshire, Worcestershire and Manchester, Arkwright began to expand throughout the country. He also opened a mill in Scotland after a visit took him to Lanark to see the Falls of Clyde. Here he realised their great potential as a source of water power. Further inventions, such as Samuel Crompton's Spinning Mule of 1779, helped the cotton trade continue to develop more rapidly than any other industry of its time in spite of the general economic depression and the American War of Independence. In 1751, Britain's export of cotton goods was valued at £46,000. By 1800 this had risen to £5,400,000 and by 1861 to £46,800,000—more than a thousandfold increase in value. Judged by the numbers employed, the Arkwright empire was the largest in the country. By 1782, he estimated his workforce at over 5,000.

In 1786 Arkwright was knighted by George III. In the following year, he reached the pinnacle of his social ambition when he was made High Sheriff of Derbyshire. To match his new rank, in 1789, Sir Richard bought a large estate around Cromford on which he built Willersley Castle. Arkwright had become socially acceptable where it mattered and this is no doubt another factor contributing towards his recognition as a great pioneer industrialist.

But, throughout his life, he had suffered from violent asthma and on August 3rd, 1792, aged sixty, a complication of disorders brought about his death. He was buried a week later at Matlock Church; the funeral procession was watched by a crowd of 2,000. Sir Richard's final resting place lies beneath the altar of a small chapel he had begun to build at Smelting Green Mill, close to Cromford Bridge. Arkwright's only son, thirty-seven-year-old Richard, inherited the greater part of his fortune. Included in this was the entire cotton-spinning empire. The younger Arkwright had been involved in cotton production for the whole of his working life, and was well qualified to inherit his father's legacy. However, within a year of his father's death, he had relinquished control of much of it, selling the mills at Nottingham and Wirksworth, retaining only the Cromford and Masson Mills.

Arkwright can perhaps be regarded as the first industrial tycoon in Britain. He was able to adapt other people's techniques and was an effective raiser of funds from other investors. Despite numerous setbacks, his sheer determination and commitment were a key factor in what was accomplished. He was not afraid to take risks. His perseverance, business sense and leadership must be seen as the driving force behind his success. James Hargreaves did not possess the vision required to create a lucrative business, while Samuel Crompton lacked Arkwright's commercial ability.

The debates surrounding Arkwright continue. However, the remarkable expansion which occurred in the eighteenth-century textile revolution is unquestionable. Without his contributions, the textile revolution might never have developed in Derbyshire from the domestic into the mill-based industry that played such a central role in the Industrial Revolution.

FOR FURTHER READING:

Brian Bailey, *Britains Industrial Past,* Whittet Books, London, 1985; R.S. Fitton, *The Arkwrights—Spinners of Fortune,* Manchester University Press, 1989; R.S. Fitton & A.P. Wadsworth, *The Strutts and the Arkwrights,* Manchester University Press, 1973; Richard L. Hills, *Richard Arkwright and Cotton Spinning,* Priory Press, London, 1973; Frank Nixon, *The Industrial Archaeology of Derbyshire,* David and Charles, Newton Abbot, Devon, 1969.

Karen Fisk is a freelance textile designer.

Samuel Smiles: The Gospel of Self-Help

Victorian Britain's prophet of honest toil was far from being the crudely complacent reactionary, as he has sometimes been caricatured.

Asa Briggs

Asa Briggs is Provost of Worcester College, Oxford, and author of The BBC, The First Fifty Years *(Oxford University Press, 1985).*

Self-help was one of the favourite mid-Victorian virtues. Relying on yourself was preferred morally—and economically—to depending on others. It was an expression of character even when it did not ensure—even, indeed, when it did not offer—a means of success. It also had social implications of a general kind. The progressive development of society ultimately depended, it was argued, not on collective action or on parliamentary legislation but on the prevalence of practices of self-help.

All these points were made succinctly and eloquently, but none of them originally or exclusively, by Samuel Smiles whose *Self-Help* appeared in one of the golden years of mid-Victorian Britain, 1859, the year that also saw the publication of John Stuart Mill's *Essay on Liberty* and Charles Darwin's *The Origin of Species*. Mill examined the attractions of individuality as well as the restraints on individualism: Darwin explored struggle as well as evolution, or rather explained evolution in terms of struggle. Neither thinker escaped attack. Smiles by contrast was not looking for argument and counter-argument. He believed that he was expounding not something that was new or controversial but something that was old and profoundly true, a gospel, not a thesis; and that behind that gospel was a still more basic gospel, the gospel of work.

Smiles did not claim that all his contemporaries practised self-help. He rather extolled the virtues of self-help as part of an 'old fashioned' but 'wholesome' lesson in morality. It was more 'natural,' he admitted, to be 'prodigal' than to be thrifty, more easy to be dependent than independent. What he was saying had been said by the wisest of men before him: it reflected 'experience, example and foresight'. 'Heaven helps them who help themselves.'

As far as individuals were concerned, Smiles was anxious to insist on the value of perseverance, a favourite word of one of his heroes, George Stephenson. 'Nothing that is of real worth,' he insisted, 'can be achieved without courageous working. Man owes his growth chiefly to that active striving of the will, that encounter with difficulty, which he calls effort; and it is astonishing to find how often results apparently impracticable are then made possible.' As far as society was concerned, 'national progress was the sum of individual industry, energy and uprightness' as 'natural decay' was of 'individual idleness, selfishness and vice. What we are accustomed to decry as great social evils will, for the most part, be found to be but the outgrowth of man's perverted life.' 'The spirit of self-help is the root of all genuine growth in the individual; and exhibited in the lives of many, it constitutes the true source of national vigour and strength. Help from without is often enfeebling in its effects, but help from within invariably invigorates. Whatever is done for men and classes to a certain extent takes away the stimulus and necessity of doing for themselves; and where men are subjected to over-guidance and over-government, the inevitable tendency is to render them comparatively helpless.'

Smiles adopted the phrase *Self-Help,* which proved to be very difficult to translate into other languages, from a lecture by the American reformer and prophet, R. W. Emerson, delivered in 1841; and while Smiles' own book first appeared in 1859, its contents had first been delivered by Smiles in lectures to Leeds working men fourteen years before—one year, indeed, before the passing of the repeal of the corn laws. While the book belonged unmistakably to mid-Victorian Britain, the message, therefore, was an early-Victorian transatlantic message, delivered in years not of relative social harmony in Britain but of social conflict. The point is of crucial importance in any discussion of Victorian values in the 1980s. Smiles emerged not from a conservative but from a radical background, the background of Chartism, and the Anti-Corn Law League. He was not encouraging Leeds working men to be quiescent or deferential but to be active and informed. Richard Cobden was one of his heroes. Another was the radical Joseph Hume, and both figured prominently in *Self-Help*. Smiles knew them both personally, and in a letter to Cobden in 1841 he had described the extension of the suffrage as 'the key to all great changes, whose object is to elevate the condition of the masses.'

Smiles' direct political involvement was limited, however, after the 1840s, and he settled down during the next decade to the more complacent view, which he expressed in 1852, that 'as men grow older and wiser they find a little of good in everything . . . they begin to find out that truth and patriotism are not confined to any particular cliques or parties or factions.' Indeed, he moved well to the right of Cobden, and by the late-Victorian years, when new political causes, radical or socialist of which he disapproved were being canvassed, what he had had to say had come to sound 'conservative', as it has done to late-twentieth-century defenders of 'Victorian values'.

Yet there is a difference in the response. Whereas late-Victorian rebels attacked Smiles for his cheerful economics, claiming—unfairly—that he was interested only in individual advancement reflected in material success, late-twentieth-century defenders have praised him primarily for his hard economic realism. In particular, Sir Keith Joseph, himself writing from a Leeds vantage point, in the introduction to a new and abridged edition of *Self-Help* (1986), has set out to rehabilitate Smilesian trust in the *entrepreneur* and 'the virtues that make him what he is'. While describing *Self-Help* as 'deeply expressive of the spirit of its own times', he does not note that these were changing times and that modes of economic organisation and responses to 'entrepreneurship' were very different by 1904, the year when Smiles died, from what they had been when *Self-Help* was published.

Smiles was born not in Leeds but in Haddington, a few miles east of Edinburgh, seven years before the birth of Queen Victoria, and he took a medical degree from Edinburgh University. His first book was called *Physical Education: or the Nurture and Management of Children,* and was published in 1838, the year he moved to Leeds. There is an evident Scottish strain in his writing before and after, although curiously it is less apparent in *Physical Education* than in some of his other work. It was, after all, Robert Bruce who had had attributed to him the motto 'if at first you don't succeed, try, try, try again', and Calvin who had provided Scotsmen with a religion which made the most of austerity and vocation.

In more modern times Thomas Carlyle, born seventeen years before Smiles,

Upward mobility—this 1861 cartoon shows a 'Lancashire working-man living rent free in his own home', the fruits of diligence and temperance.

had described life as 'a scene of toil, of effort, of appointed work', and had extolled 'the man who works' in the warmest language: 'welcome, thou art ours; our care shall be of thee'. The mill-owner economist, W. R. Greg, writing one year after the publication of *Self-Help*, praised Carlyle above all others for 'preaching upon the duty and dignity of work, with an eloquence which has often made the idle shake off their idleness and the frivolous feel ashamed of their frivolity. He has proclaimed, in tones that have stirred many hearts, that in toil, however humble, if honest and hearty, lies our true worth and felicity here below'.

Smiles himself took as one of his examples of perseverance in *Self-Help* Carlyle's prodigious effort to rewrite the first volume of his *French Revolution* after a maid had used the manuscript to light the kitchen and parlour fires: 'he had no draft, and was compelled to rake up from his memory facts, ideas and expressions, which had long been dismissed'. No one could have appreciated this experience more than Smiles who was a prodigious writer who followed up *Self-Help* with many volumes, including three related works *Character* (1871), *Thrift* (1875) and *Duty* (1880). He also produced a history of his publisher, John Murray and 'his friends' in 1891.

Self-Help was full of anecdotes. Essentially it was a case-book drawing its material, including some of its most apposite quotations, from personal biographies. 'Our great forefathers still live among us in the records of our lives', he claimed, again very much as Carlyle had always claimed. 'They still sit by us at table, and hold us by the hand'. There was more than a touch of Victorian hero worship here. Yet Smiles always broadened the range to include the humble as well as the great, extending the range as far as he possibly could in his *Life and Labour* (1887). Biographies offered demonstrations of 'what men can be, and what they can do' whatever their station. 'A book containing the life of a true man is full of precious seed. It is still a living voice'. And much as he made his own living out of books, Smiles maintained that living examples were far more potent as influences than examples on paper. His book *Thrift* took as its motto a phrase from Carlyle 'Not what I have, but what I do is my kingdom'. He might have chosen instead

Emerson's motto, 'The importance of man as man . . . is the highest truth'.

Smiles himself was a lively phrasemaker, interlacing his anecdotes, which by themselves were memorable and well set out, with short phrases that linger in the mind—'he who never made a mistake never made a discovery'; 'the tortoise in the right road will beat a racer in the wrong'; 'the nation comes from the nursery'. Such phrases bind together the whole text of *Self-Help* which is far more readable—as it is pertinent—today than the verse of Martin Tupper's *Proverbial Philosophy* (1838), the popularity of which (on both sides of the Atlantic) reached its peak during the 1850s. It is far more readable too than most of the many other Victorian books designed to inspire young men like the anonymous *Success in Life* (1852), the original idea of which had been suggested by 'an American publication', perhaps John Todd's *Hints Addressed to the Young Men of the United States* (1845), which included one chapter on 'industry and economy' and another on 'self-government and the heart'. Smiles himself acknowledged a debt to G. L. Craik's *Pursuit of Knowledge under Difficulties* (1831), published by Charles Knight who specialised in diffusing knowledge. Indeed, he had been so inspired by it, Smiles wrote, that he learnt some of its key passages by heart.

The transatlantic element in the self-help literature demands a study of differences as well as of influences. There were to be many American 'success' books aiming, as Smiles aimed, at large audiences, some of the first of which were influenced, as Smiles was, by the cult of phrenology. The later line of descent can be traced through books, which move from phrenology to popular psychology, like J. C. Ransom's *The Successful Man in his Manifold Relations with Life* (1887), A. E. Lyon's *The Self-Starter* (1924), Dale Carnegie's *How to Win Friends and Influence People* (1936), C. E. Poppleston's *Every Man a Winner* (1936) and Norman Vincent Peale's *The Power of Positive Thinking* (1955). Yet many of these authors are slick where Smiles was sturdy, and consoling where he was inspiring. Few would have had much sympathy either with Smiles' attack on 'smatter knowledge'. Such 'short-cuts', he explained, as learning French or Latin in 'twelve lessons' or 'without a master', were 'good for nothing'. The

would-be learner was more to blame than the teacher, for he resembled 'the lady of fashion who engaged a master to teach her on condition that he did not plague her with verbs and particles'.

One American with whom Smiles has sometimes been compared is Horatio Alger (1832–99) after whom a twentieth-century American business award was named. In his own lifetime Alger's sales were spectacular, though his books took the form of stories rather than biographies or homilies. *Ragged Dick* was one title, *Upward and Onward* another. The *genre* has been well described as 'rags to riches stories', although the twentieth-century award was endowed more generally to honour a person who had 'claimed the ladder of success through toil and diligence and responsible applications of his talents to whatever tasks were his'.

There are as many myths about 'Holy Horatio' as Alger himself propounded. In fact, he allowed a far bigger place to luck (sponsors appearing by magic at the right time and place) than Smiles ever could have done, and he grossly simplified the nineteenth-century social context, particularly the city context, in which poor people found or failed to find their chances. As the late-nineteenth-century American institutional economist, Richard T. Ely, put it neatly, 'if you tell a single concrete workman on the Baltimore and Ohio Railroad that he may get to be president of the company, it is not demonstrable that you have told him what is not true, although it is within bounds to say that he is far more likely to be killed by a stroke of lightning.'

Smiles was less concerned with social 'mobility' than with mental and physical 'effort', but he, too, could be accused of living in a land of myth when he exclaimed that 'energy accomplishes more than genius'. It was a favourite mid-Victorian statement, however, which implied a contrast between what was happening then and what had happened before, and between what was happening in Britain and what was happening elsewhere. By stating it so simply Smiles actually did influence *entrepreneurs*, few of whom depended on great intellects or on deep and systematic study. William Lever, for example, fittingly born in 1851, was given a copy of *Self-Help* by his father on his sixteenth birthday, and treasured it so much that he in turn gave copies to young men he employed in his works at Port Sunlight. On the front page of one such copy the words are inscribed, 'It is impossible for me to say how much I owe to the fact that in my early youth I obtained a copy of Smiles' *Self-Help*.'

Andrew Carnegie (1835–1919) would have made no such comment. Yet his own biography not only proclaimed many Smilesian virtues, but might well have provided the basis for an Alger true story. Carnegie was born in a tiny weaver's cottage at Dunfermline, and he had his first real break in life when he became a messenger boy in a Pittsburgh telegraph office at a salary of $2.50 a week. In 1901, when he had sold his steel business for $480 million, he became the richest man in the world. 'It's a God's mercy I was born a Scotsman,' he declared in a remark that might have appealed to Smiles, 'for I do not see how I could ever have been contented to be anything else.'

The testimonials Smiles himself received from readers of his books often came from people very differently placed from Lever or Carnegie. Thus, a working man in Exeter told him that his books had 'instructed and helped him greatly' and that he wished 'every working man would read them through and through and ponder them well'; a surgeon in Blackhealth declared that *Self-Help* had given 'fresh energy and hopefulness to his career'; and an emigrant to New Zealand exclaimed that self-help had 'been the cause of an entire alteration in my life, and I thank God that I read it. I am now devoted to study and hard work, and I mean to rise, both as regards my moral and intellectual life. I only wish I could see the man who wrote the book and thank him from my heart'.

There was at least one late-Victorian socialist, a man who was himself capable of inspiring 'the millions', who was deeply impressed by Smiles. Robert Blatchford, pioneer of *Merrie England,* wrote an essay on *Self-Help* after Smiles' popularity had passed its peak in which he condemned fellow-socialists who spoke mockingly of Smiles as 'an arch-Philistine' and of his books as 'the apotheosis of respectability, gigmanity and selfish grab'. Blatchford himself considered Smiles 'a most charming and honest writer', and thought *Self-Help* 'one of the most delightful and invigorating books it has been my happy fortune to meet with'. He paid tribute to

Smiles' indifference to worldly titles, honour and wealth, and declared that the perusal of *Self-Help* had often forced him 'to industry, for very shame'.

The prolific rationalist writer Grant Allen, a leading spokesman of the late-Victorian revolt, took a very similar view. In a little book published in 1884 called *Biographies of Working Men* he asserted his debt to Smiles and made explicit what many of Smiles' critics then and since failed to see in Smiles' work. 'It is the object of this volume', Grant Allen began, 'to set forth the lives of working men, who through industry, perseverance and high principle, have raised themselves by their own exertions from humble beginnings. Raised themselves! Yes, but to what? Not merely, let us hope, to wealth and position, nor merely to worldly respect and high office, but to some conspicuous field of real usefulness to their fellow men.' Smiles made the same point in *Self-Help*. He would not have shared Allen's view, however, which brings out clearly the difference between the mood of the 1850s and the 1880s, that 'so long as our present social arrangements exist . . .

the vast mass of men will necessarily remain workers to the last, [and] no attempt to raise individual working men above their own class into the professional or mercantile classes can ever greatly benefit the working classes as a whole'.

Nonetheless, on certain social matters, Smiles had often expressed radical views. Like many people trained as doctors he was deeply concerned with public health. As Mary Mack has pointed out, Jeremy Bentham had used medicine as a source of *analogy* for the understanding of morals and legislation, and Smiles, who as a young man met Edwin Chadwick and Dr Southwood Smith, Bentham's disciples, never believed that the environment should be left uncontrolled if it threatened the private health not only of the deprived but of people and power and influence. Smiles supported measures, too, to deal with the adulteration of food. Drawing a distinction between economic and social *laissez-faire*—and he was not alone in this—he was fully aware of the presence in mid-Victorian society not only of Adam Smith's beneficent invisible hand

A 'Punch' cartoon of 1858 attacking the adulteration of food—one of the areas where Smiles decidedly did not believe in the principle of laissez-faire.

but of a 'terrible Nobody'. Indeed, Charles Dickens could not have written more forcefully than Smiles did:

> When typhus or cholera breaks out, they tell us that Nobody is to blame. That terrible Nobody! How much he has to answer for. More mischief is done by Nobody than by all the world besides. Nobody adulterates our food. Nobody poisons us with bad drink... Nobody leaves towns undrained. Nobody fills jails, penitentiaries, and convict stations. Nobody makes poachers, thieves, and drunkards. Nobody has a theory too—a dreadful theory. It is embodied in two words: laissez-faire—let alone. When people are poisoned with plaster of Paris mixed with flour, 'let alone' is the remedy... Let those who can, find out when they are cheated: *caveat emptor.* When people live in foul dwellings, let them alone, let wretchedness do its work; do not interfere with death.

Like many other believers in economic *laissez-faire* Smiles was prepared to use the machinery of the law to provide a framework for dealing with abuses:

> Laws may do too much... but the abuse of a thing is no proper argument against its use in cases where its employment is urgently called for.

Throughout the whole of his life Smiles was far too active a Victorian to believe that *vis inertiae* was the same thing as *laissez-faire.* Nor was he ever tempted, as many Americans were, into the entanglements of social Darwinism. There is no reference to Herbert Spencer in his *Autobiography,* which appeared in 1905, one year after his death, and only one reference to Darwin. One of the lecturers he had heard at Edinburgh, he observed *en passant,* had already expounded very similar views 'or at all events had heralded his approach'.

There was another subject which fascinated Smiles and which he believed required very positive state intervention—national education. He had forcefully urged the need for a national system in Leeds in 1850, and he paid tribute in his *Autobiography* to W. E. Forster, MP for neighbouring Bradford, who 'by a rare union of tact, wisdom and common sense, introduced and carried his measure [the 1870 Education Act] for the long-wished education of the English people. It embodied nearly

all that the National Public School Association had so fruitlessly demanded years before'.

In pressing for nationally provided primary education in Leeds in 1850 and later, Smiles had been drawn into controversy with Edward Baines, editor of the *Leeds Mercury* and one of the most vociferous advocates, then and in 1870, of education managed by voluntary agencies and not by the state. In the course of a continuing controversy Smiles had no doubts about his own position. There were no analogies between education and free trade in commodities, he pointed out:

> The classes who the most require education are precisely those who do not seek it. It is amongst the utterly uneducated that the least demand exists. In the case of bread it is very different. The consumer wants it, knows he wants it, and will give every present consideration for it.

A further false analogy, he thought, was between education and the freedom of the press:

> Nobody proposes to establish newspapers for everybody, supported by the government, and the want of such a Press is not felt. But let it be shown that it is of as much importance to the interests of society that everybody should have a newspaper as that everybody should be educated, and then the analogy may be admitted... but not till then.

It was through his philosophy of education that Smiles blurred any divisions that others might have made between 'self-help' for the individual and 'mutual self-help' for the group. He always attached even more importance to adult— or continuing—education than to school education, necessary though the latter was. The process which started at school had to be followed through: 'the highest culture is not obtained from teacher when at school or college, so much as by our ever diligent self-education when we have become men.' Such education could be fostered in groups like the group of young working men he had addressed in Leeds. There were possibilities of other forms of 'mutual self-help' also, for example friendly societies. Indeed, in *Thrift* Smiles made as much as he could of the mutual insurance principle. He could never have been accused of neglecting 'welfare', provided that it did not lead to dependence.

The doctrine of 'honest toil' could have a radical cutting-edge, as in this 1858 'Punch' cartoon of the working man 'enlightening' the 'superior' (but idle) classes.

The Smiles message was not merely a transatlantic one. It made its way round the world, sometimes to the most unlikely places. It was translated into Dutch and French, Danish and German, Arabic and Turkish, 'several of the native languages of India' (in the words of a happy publisher) and Japanese. Victorian values, it was implied, were universal values, and there was confidence in their power to change societies. The Japanese, in particular, treasured it, and many of them continue to treasure it. 'The English work forms an octavo of moderate size,' *The Times* wrote; 'in Japanese it is expanded into a book of fifteen hundred pages.' This was no handicap to its sale, for it seemed as useful as looms and steam engines. In Latin America the Mayor of Buenos Aires is said to have compared Smiles with Rousseau and to have added 'Alexander the Great slept with his Homer, Demosthenes and Thucydides, and every notable man of the times should have at hand the social gospel'.

The universalism was restricted, however, although it went with the universalism of steam power and railways, in particular. Smiles had become secretary of a railway company in 1845 and he wrote *The Life of George Stephenson*

two years before *Self-Help*. Nonetheless, he ended *Self-Help* with a chapter which introduced a word which was at least as difficult to translate from English into other languages as 'self-help' itself—the word 'gentleman'. Hippolyte Taine, convinced that the three syllables 'gentleman' summed up the whole history of English society, felt that the syllables expressed all the distinctive features of the English upper-class—a large private income, a considerable household of servants, habits of ease and luxury and good manners, but it also implied qualities of heart and character. Smiles, however, felt that:

> For Englishmen a real 'gentleman' is a truly noble man, a man worthy to command, a disinterested man of integrity, capable of exposing, even sacrificing himself for those he leads; not only a man of honour, but a conscientious man, in whom generous instincts have been confirmed by right thinking and who, acting rightly by nature, acts even more rightly from good principles.

Taine's reference to Mrs. Craik's novel *John Halifax, Gentleman* (1856) is a practical illustration of the extension of the old ideal of the gentleman in a

new nineteenth-century society. He might have referred instead to the last pages of *Self-Help*, where Smiles chose a 'grand old name' to express the kind of character he most wanted to see in action. Smiles drew out the 'grand old name' of the gentleman from its upper-class context. It had no connection with riches and rank, he argued, but with moral worth.

The equipoise of society rested on such ideological balances as well as on the balance of interests. From the 1870s onwards, however, both kinds of balance broke down. Britain was never again the same.

FOR FURTHER READING:

Samuel Smiles, *Self-Help* (first edition 1853, Penguin Books with an introduction by Keith Joseph, 1986); Asa Briggs, *Victorian People* (Penguin Books, 1985); Grant Allen, *Biographies of Working men* (1884); J. Burnett, editor, *Useful Toil: Autobiographies of Working people from the 1820s–1920s* (Penguin Books, 1974); T. Travers, *Samuel Smiles and the Pursuit of Success in Victorian Britain* (Canadian Historical Association, 1971); M. D. Stephens and G. W. Roderick, *Samuel Smiles and Nineteenth-Century Self-Help in Education* (Nottingham Studies, 1983).

Giuseppe Garibaldi

*Infrequently does a historian acquire the reputation of synonymity with the history of the country he or she has studied, but **Denis Mack Smith** has accomplished this fact with his work and writing on Italy. This is a portrait of Italy's hero of the risorgimento in which the author deftly combines an assessment of the achievement with all the colour of Garibaldi's personal idiosyncracies.*

Denis Mack Smith

Tough cookie; a heroic image of Garibaldi at Caprera, the remote island to which he eventually retired, having played a major role in steering Italy towards unification.

Giuseppe Garibaldi is one of the great men of the nineteenth century. He was a remarkably successful admiral and general. He was the very prototype of patriotic hero, but also a great internationalist, and later in life one of the pioneers of Italian socialism. Connecting all his activities was the fact that he was a liberator by profession, a man who spent his life fighting for oppressed peoples wherever he found them, however naive his analysis of oppression. Whatever he did, moreover, was done always with passionate conviction and boundless enthusiasm, and this makes his character the more striking and attractive.

Garibaldi's career was dazzlingly full of colour and incident; but behind the public personality was someone of simple good nature and amiability, a lovable and fascinating person of transparent honesty whom men would obey unhesitatingly and for whom many were glad to die. In his time he was probably the most widely known and loved figure in the world. He appealed directly to the common people, just because he himself was the embodiment of the common man: as a radical democrat and humanitarian he believed above all else in liberty and social justice. Yet, at the same time, he was quite exceptional in character, a real individual and non-conformist, whether in his religion, his clothes, his personal habits, or in the events of his extraordinary life.

Garibaldi lived from 1807 to 1882. He was born in Napoleonic France and all his life, like Cavour, spoke Italian imperfectly. By trade he followed his father and became a sea-captain. He knew the Black Sea and also the China seas. He served in ships of Italy and France, and also of the United States and Peru, and even for a time with the Bey of Tunis; and he also captained the first screw-propelled steamer to fly the Italian flag. Twice in his life he was a schoolmaster, at Constantinople and Montevideo. Once at least he was a commercial traveller, and once he worked in a candle factory on Staten Island. He married three times. For several years he was engaged to a wealthy and talented English-woman, and subsequently he proposed unsuccessfully to another. In the course of his various wanderings he claimed British as well as United States citizenship; sat as an elected deputy in the French assembly; and was offered a command by Lincoln in the American civil war. In sum, it was a more than ordinarily variegated and dramatic life, and this provided a fitting back-cloth for his flamboyant character.

Garibaldi first became a household name with his defence of Rome in 1849. Before then, however, and this is most important for understanding his temperament and influence, he had been for half his adult life a guerrilla leader in the political bear-garden of Brazil and Argentina. When he returned from South America to Europe he brought back a novel and successful type of warfare. A few irregulars, by breaking the accepted conventions of war, could acquire a high nuisance-value in foreign-occupied Italy.

The South American influence is seen in the gaucho costume that Garibaldi carried to the end of his life— the cloak or poncho, and the red shirt which came from the slaughter houses of Buenos Aires. Following the gaucho example, his Italian armies were able to live in hostile territory by lassoing stray animals and barbecueing them in the open. The hard democracy of the pampas, furthermore, had taught Garbaldi to treat all men as equals, and many Italians were subsequently to learn through him a new freedom of behaviour, to give up obsequious habits of hand-kissing and caste apparel and deferential forms of speech. Italy also learnt by the same means a dangerous praxis of government, one not without analogues in Italian history but which had been developed to a fine art in a land where the caudillo

and the pronunciamento were accepted as normal.

Garibaldi came back to Europe with a confirmed love of fighting. He never was able to resist the call of battle, especially where honour was to be plucked or people delivered. All too easily he convinced himself that he was fighting for humanity and liberty in general. From earliest boyhood his actions and daydreams show his fixation on becoming a hero and making the world a freer and healthier place. Surprisingly unambitious himself, he offered his services alternately to king and republic, to one caudillo after another, even on one occasion to the Pope. Such a simple soul inevitably became the catspaw of more selfish and less idealistic factions, in Italy as in Uruguay and the Rio Grande. Himself a man of complete integrity, he was also credulously quixotic, a romantic Arthurian knight who rushed in to support some causes which later he had reason to regret.

Garibaldi's importance in the history of Italy is firstly as a soldier, and secondly as a patriotic legend. At a time when statesmen were silent and impotent, he, with a single-minded and simple-minded belief in victory, had the brute courage to act; and it was the kind of action that ennobled his country, publicised her grievances and potentialities, and cheered and emboldened the laggards and the sceptics among his countrymen.

For example, in 1848, with only a few score men, he dared to take on the might of Austria in a private war. In 1849 his defence of the Roman republic kept liberal Europe breathless with admiration, and proved that some Italians at least knew what to fight for and loved what they knew. His retreat from Rome subsequently furnished an abundance of martyrs to feed the cult of patriotism, and gave Italy her one risorgimento heroine in the South American creole, Anita. These feats were enough to make him celebrated. But eleven years later, in 1860, Garibaldi on his own initiative set off with a thousand men for Sicily, and in a few months conquered almost half of Italy; only to hand it over without fuss to his great enemy Cavour, and return voluntarily, a king-maker, into humble private life.

Compared with this quite extraordinary achievement, his other military exploits were not so momentous. It is true that in the Austrian wars of 1859 and

1866, though very poorly equipped by the government, he proved himself the only Italian general who had enough skill and character to earn the respect of his opponents. But he failed in three separate attempts at a march on Rome, and the jealousy of the regular army, coupled with the strong personal and political dislike of almost all Italian statesmen, contrived to make him henceforward an isolated figure.

When present politics merged into past history, Garibaldi's importance in the risorgimento was to be deliberately played down by the Establishment. The army disliked him for his outstanding military success, the Church for his heresies, Cavour and the deputies for his political insubordination, the middle classes for his threat of social revolution. Even Mazzini broke with him over his obstinate disobedience and individualism. The official historians of Italy, therefore, in their subsequent effort to develop a justification for the triumph of Piedmont and conservatism, made him out to be unserious as a character, and merely marginal in his contribution to victory.

Nor did he himself leave much reliable documentary evidence in his wake for the benefit of later historians. His several versions of autobiography were fanciful—one was written in hendecasyllabic verse—and sometimes even contradictory. There were no close disciples to annotate his every movement, and his letters were those of an extrovert who obstinately spoke of other things than his own mental processes. The guerrilla armies upon whom his fame depended inevitably melted away and left no archives; and, in any case, his battles had been mostly impromptu combinations without any prearranged plan that could be re-created. Hence the romantic legends of the one hand, and official denigration of the other, both equally untrustworthy.

Yet Garibaldi it was, along with Mazzini, who succeeded in accustoming the rest of Europe to the idea of an Italian nation, and he it was who forced Cavour to go faster and further than seemed possible or desirable on any rational analysis. It was his uncritical and unshakeable confidence in unification that finally converted the sceptical statesmen in Turin, and his constant refusal to count the cost brought about almost the only military victories in the saga of national rebirth. He had discovered the secret of inspiring untrained volunteers with an enthusiasm that moved mountains and frontiers. Along with Gordon he is the supreme leader of irregulars in partisan warfare. Through him the common people were won over to a cause that might otherwise have seemed in their eyes remote and profitless; or at least he helped to obscure their vision of what was happening until they were too late to intervene and stop it.

If Garibaldi was mistrusted by the new ruling classes of Italy whom he had helped into power, it was partly because he remained this type of popular hero. His main backers, apart from certain radical financiers such as Adriano Lemmi and the armament firm of Ansaldo, were not politicians but ordinary people whose imagination was fired by his panache and his genuine altruism. The illiterates who voted uncomprehendingly for Italy in the plebiscites often did so because told that this was to support 'Don Peppino' or 'Galubardu'. The concept of Italy for these people was at best a vague abstraction, at worst a meaningless word.

The risorgimento, like all revolutions, was the work of a small, perhaps very small, minority. Again and again Garibaldi had to lament that Neapolitans, Venetians and Romans in turn stirred hardly a finger to 'liberate' themselves from 'foreign' or priestly rule. His volunteers were mostly made up of townsmen from the north, with a nucleus of simple adventurers; they were chiefly professional men and students hoping to avoid their examinations. Often he bewailed this unpromisingly narrow basis of recruitment. The peasants who formed the great majority of Italians, though personally moved by his heroism in adversity, were usually neutral or hostile. His army was sometimes treated as a band of brigands. Villages could bar their gates against him; the local inhabitants often refused him information while acting as unofficial spies for the Austrian soldiery; and he even found some who made no concealment of welcoming a return to Austrian rule.

The fact was that admiration for Garibaldi's person seldom went with

any desire to share the hardships which he undertook on the nation's behalf. 'The Italians have too much individual egoism and too little love of their country,' he complained:—'this hermaphrodite generation of Italians whom I have so often tried to ennoble, little though they deserve it.' Patriotism certainly existed, but it was really strong only among remarkable individuals. Usually it was a generalised, rhetorical feeling, skin-deep, and falsified by other sentiments. Noisy patriotic demonstrations could thus be a compensation, making amends for earlier frigidity. In particular, the widespread—but quite exceptional—popular insurrection in Sicily was partly a mere grudge-war against the Neapolitan overlords, partly a peasants' revolt that cut across politics and had nothing to do with patriotic feeling.

As soon as Garibaldi was in retirement, and once he too, like the separatists and peasants in Sicily, was in opposition to the new Italy which they had together helped into existence, he became the natural focus of many of these

Two *Punch* cartoons satirise Garibaldi's dealings with Victor Emmanuel and Pope Pius IX. Preferring royal dictatorship to a parliamentary system, Garibaldi in his relationship with the monarch, showed none of the hostility he felt towards the Catholic faith.

same discontents, the natural outlet and expression of a general disillusionment. When the romantic cult of Garibaldi grew up in the collective subconscious, it was in part a boost for national morale during a period of disappointment. His exploits were to be sometimes exaggerated in compensation for the dreary showing made by the national army between 1848 and 1866. A legend appeared, compounded by romantic storytellers such as Dumas who liked a good tale as much as the truth.

In this phase of his life Garibaldi became a kind of idealised symbol of the millennium, a sanctified representative of that different and more glorious national revolution which should have taken place but had not. In Naples and Sicily he had been credited with magic powers; and in the more sober north women held up their children for him to bless, even for him to baptise. Garibaldi's image replaced that of God in many a humble peasant's cabin, and his haircut *alla nazzarena* helped this illusion. Prostrate with arthritis, he was carried in solemn procession through the streets of Milan and Palermo, and it seemed like the catafalque of a miracle-working saint.

Abroad, too, he was the object of an extravagant adulation. When injured by a bullet in 1862, twenty-three surgeons from all over the world were sent to see him by zealous enthusiasts. Passionate love-letters arrived secretly from wives of members of both House of Commons and House of Lords, and Cavour knew what he was doing when he slyly sent authenticated locks of the hero's hair to London for distribution to the faithful. Garibaldi's daughter religiously kept even his nail clippings, and a host of relics was preserved for the edification of those who came on pilgrimage in the weekly packet-boat to Caprera.

The 1860s found this ex-dictator of the Two Sicilies in more or less continual opposition, and this did much to weaken popular allegiance to the state and so store up dangers for the future. Naturally he resented that his project for an Italian revolution had been obstructed by the politicians and then captured and drastically watered down. As long ago as the 1830s he had fled into exile after being condemned to death by the king's government. Again, after his retreat from Rome, he had been arrested and exiled for another four years. Three times subsequently did the national army move against him to stop his conquest of Rome, and in one engagement they crippled him for life. But this made him only yet more of a popular hero, and unprecedented mass ovations misled his not very subtle or critical mind into dangerous deeds of insubordination. Laconic communiques were issued from Caprera criticising various aspects of government policy. Parliament he condemned as the seat of corruption and gerrymandering, as a rubber stamp for ministerial autocracy, a fraud designed by the clever lawyers who specialised in oratorical dexterity and corridor intrigue. 'Give us battles, not liberties,' was his cry to the king; for behind 'liberties' he discerned a contrivance by parliament to prefer an oligarchy of wealth and intellect at the expense of the common people.

What made this attitude particularly dangerous was that Garibaldi understood from the king that he might rely on royal support in subverting the normal constitutional government of the country. Sometimes he was even positively encouraged to rebel, and this led directly to his tragic wounding at Aspromonte. Victor Emanuel engaged in private political activity behind the backs of all of his successive Prime Ministers, just as he commonly appointed or dismissed them without any reference to parliament; and in such monarchical irresponsibility is the key to many involved moments in modern Italian history.

For example, the king came to blows frequently with Cavour over the morals and politics of the Court; whereas on the other hand, Garibaldi was someone he could appreciate—a bluff, frank, soldierly man, with a firm sense of loyalty and without the subtle finesse and secondary aims of a politician. Garibaldi was always genuine, and what he said rang true, even if it was silly; whereas Cavour and his successors were guilefull and dissembling almost from habit. Moreover, they used parliament to control the king, while Garibaldi on the contrary preferred a royal dictatorship over parliament. Cavour was not only too much a civilian for Victor Emmanuel, who liked people in uniform; he was also too clever; and the king had his own reasons for preferring character to intelligence.

This secret royal favour, when combined with Garibaldi's own lack of brains, his recklessness, his urge towards action and his great popular following, made him a person of great but irresponsible power. The United States Minister wrote back to his government in 1861 that, 'though but a solitary and private individual, he is at this moment, in and of himself, one of the great Powers of the world.' Garibaldi's political views are therefore of peculiar interest.

The first point to be made is that he was too simple and guileless to understand more than the surface of politics. Florence Nightingale, one of his great admirers, was shocked on meeting him to find that he understood very little indeed of the causes he so ardently professed. He was a convinced republican, but also fought for the monarchy; he believed in dictatorship, but all his life fought for freedom and against despotism; he was a bellicose patriot, but also adhered to a pacifist internationalism.

And yet in some convictions he never wavered, for instance in his antipathy to the Catholic faith and his attachment to democracy. He always believed in a wider suffrage and in free and universal education. Unlike the twentieth-century Garibaldians, he thought it criminal folly for a poor country such as Italy to acquire overseas colonies and spend so much on armaments. Repeatedly he addressed memoranda to the Great Powers on the abolition of war and on the means of creating through international arbitration a United States of Europe. For he was a patriot with a difference. 'If Italy ever in her turn threatened the independence of neighbour states, I should regretfully but surely be on the side of the oppressed.' Such a statement would have astonished some of his later disciples.

Garibaldi's combination of idealism and simple good sense can also be traced in his notions on social reform; for here he spoke with genuine knowledge and feeling. By heredity, environment and temperament, he understood the masses as Cavour and Mazzini never did, and if others had shared his understanding, Italy might have been a more stable and tranquil place today. He believed prophetically that 'the great future of Italy lies with her working classes,' and hence that their emancipation and education was an urgent task. Proudly he called himself a socialist; but his socialism was of the heart not of the head; it was based not on class-war but on easing the tension between capital and labour. Though disapproved of by Marx, this sentiment nevertheless was to become an important strand within the Italian socialist movement.

Another trend inside the Italian Left has been towards authoritarianism, and this too goes back to Garibaldi. His own favourite type of warfare had accustomed him to the need for quick and unchallenged decisions, and his preference for autocratic methods became instinctive. Among his volunteers the penalty for disobedience was instant death; and we are told that he would shoot a man without stopping to take the cigar from his mouth.

In politics his aim was always freedom, but people might have to be forced to be free. Whenever he possessed civil authority he chose to be a dictator, and he was hailed as *Duce* by the mob when he appeared on numberless balconies. Too unambitious, unintelligent and uncorrupted to play the Mussolini himself, he advocated a royal dictatorship. Government needed the *fasces*—he employed the very word. And the deputies should be packed off home as a corrupting and disabling element; for Cavour seemed to be setting up a pseudo-constitutional government like that of Louis Napoleon, in which liberty was only a sham. Garibaldi's impatience here with Italian parliamentarism was excessive. He sensed the disease, but was not the man to devise an adequate remedy. Yet in partial explanation it may be remembered that, in 1922, many of the liberals who claimed to inherit from Cavour were also to invoke the *fasces* against a corrupt and anarchical parliamentary regime.

G. M. Trevelyan admirably describes that great moment when the hero of two worlds stepped down from his autocratic position at Naples and retired to a lonely island off Sardinia. For a long time he had been an admirer of Robinson Crusoe, and at Caprera he too could exist free from the intrigue and misgovernment that he thought were ruining his country. Caprera was a barren granite outcrop where he could live a simple life independent of the social obligations and political involvements he so much disliked; and there, not far from that other romantic island of Montecristo, he spent most of his declining days, surrounded by his legitimate and illegitimate children.

With difficulty he built up a farm in this unlikely spot, helped by heavy subventions from his admirers all over the world. His affairs were always entangled, for he was a bad administrator and the farm was singularly unprofitable. But his needs were few. He himself, when in health, would milk the cows. He washed his own shirts, and rarely possessed more than one change of clothing. He had trained himself to cut a coat and trousers by eye. For food he was self-sufficient. Increasingly he became a vegetarian, though to go shooting and spearing fish remained almost his favourite pastime.

He also read books—his small library included Shakespeare, Byron, Plutarch, La Fontaine, Voltaire, Arthur Young on agriculture, and other English books on navigation, agriculture and the art of war. And he wrote too, partly to try to earn his living, partly to stir up the younger generation to emulation of great deeds. The three novels he wrote are dull and absurd to a degree, and his poems are often embarrassing; but he had a genuine love of roughly improvised verse such as may still be found here and there among the Italian peasantry.

Garibaldi died at Caprera in 1882. Always unconventional, he had enjoined his wife to place his body on a pyre of aromatic wood, and to burn him under the open sky in the same pagan, hygienic way he had lived. But the dignitaries of Rome, whom he had always execrated alive, would not be done out of a good funeral, and were revenged on him dead. They argued, as an added touch of irony, that burning would offend people's religious sensibilities. So he was incongruously buried in the presence of dukes and ministers. The world had the last word against him.

His own last word was a Political Testament. To his children and friends he bequeathed his love for liberty and truth. He explicitly condemned the Catholic priesthood and the Mazzinians as the great national enemies. And again he recommended his countrymen to select the most honest man in Italy and make him a temporary dictator. Only when Italians were more educated to liberty, and their country was less threatened from outside and in, should dictatorial rule give way to a regular republican government. Here, in brief, was a neat abstract of the lessons learnt by a simple-minded but strong-hearted soldier during a lifetime of devotion to an ideal.

Conversations with Malthus

Suzanne Rickard meets one of the bogeymen of the nineteenth century and discovers he was not the cold-hearted monster that was often portrayed.

POPULATION MALTHUS', the political economist the Reverend Thomas Robert Malthus, MA, FRS, slipped quietly to his death through heart failure just before Christmas 1834. During his lifetime this mild-mannered Anglican clergyman is said to have 'generated more vituperation, vilification and misunderstanding than that of any comparable figure in the history of social and political thought'. The source of such vituperation goes back to his first published essay, *An Essay on the Principles of Population as it Affects the Future Improvement to Society* (1798).

Malthus's writings on population increase, and particularly his early rejoinder to the speculative writings of the late eighteenth-century political and social philosophers, William Godwin, the Marquis de Condorcet, 'and other writers', brought him immediate notoriety and offended—even outraged—the faith of his peers. The first *Essay,* published anonymously, was, as Malthus admitted, 'written on the spur of the occasion'. It was immediately controversial, questioning the ability of man and Divine Providence to provide for the moderate needs of mankind.

Moderate cloathing [sic], moderate houses, the power of receiving friends, the power of purchasing books, and particularly the power of supporting a family, will always remain objects of rational desire among the majority of mankind.

This was the kind of rational desire Malthus wrote about in a private letter to Godwin in 1798, but many regarded Malthus's writing as anything but moderate.

Malthus published over twenty-five pieces of analytical political economy over a thirty-year period, covering the effects of rent, the state of agriculture, the Poor Law, profit, capital accumulation, the value of currency, the effects of the Corn Laws, the state of Ireland, as well as the principle of population, yet it was his moral and economic views on population that overshadowed other analyses. Malthus challenged the received wisdom that unbounded population growth was desirable since it had the potential to increase demand. In Malthus's view, 'unchecked' population growth resulted in bare subsistence, abject poverty and early death. His arguments have occupied scholars ever since.

Malthus wrote in the first *Essay*:

The power of population is so superior to the power in the earth to produce subsistence for man, that pre-mature death must in some shape or other visit the human race.

Encapsulating Malthus's proposition, Professor Donald Winch wrote recently that Malthus maintained that this law of nature was 'impervious to institutional change and legislative contrivance'. Malthus recognised that biology rather than rationality ruled. As he argued, the

ever-present propensity for population growth to outstrip the means of subsistence . . . placed the happiness and morals of the mass of society under persistent threat.

In an age which refused to acknowledge or tolerate any form of contraception, Malthus's homily was a moralising and sobering discourse.

Shortly after Malthus's death, the Canon of St Paul's Cathedral, the Reverend Sydney Smith, wrote a statement of appreciation about him in a private letter to his friend, Sir Robert Wilmot-Horton, former Benthamite MP for Newcastle-under-Lyme, Governor of Ceylon, and first cousin of the poet, Lord Byron:

Poor Malthus! Everybody regrets him;—in science and in conduct equally a philosopher, one of the most practically wise men I ever met, shamefully mistaken and unjustly calumniated, and receiving no mark of favour from a Liberal Government, who ought to have interested themselves in the fortunes of such a virtuous martyr to truth.

Smith was one of England's wittiest and well-informed clergymen, and had long been a critical admirer of Malthus. In 1802 he wrote in the *Edinburgh Review* in support of Malthus's refutation of William Godwin's utopian visions for a perfect society, and their paths crossed for many years thereafter at social gatherings. Wilmot-Horton, meanwhile, had carefully lobbied Malthus, as a result of their mutual interest in the problems of Ireland, redundant labour, emigration and Catholic Emancipation, bringing these men together in avid conversation and frequent correspondence.

Smith and Wilmot-Horton were not alone in their admiration. Even amongst those contemporaries who disagreed vehemently with various 'Malthusian' propositions, many would have agreed that Malthus was a man of integrity and a seeker of truth. Malthus observed and forced many uncomfortable truths upon society, in particular that rapid population growth ought not be regarded as a Providential blessing but as a potential curse on human happiness. By his systematic reasoning, Malthus gave a new principle and left a legacy—200 years of the population debate. Those contemporaries who drew upon his work included the economists, Nassau Senior and James Mill. John Stuart Mill later defended Malthus's population principles, suggesting that it was Malthus's observations on the economic condition of the labouring classes, and his insistence that improvement was only possible with controls over population growth, which began 'all sound thinking on the subject of wages and mass poverty'.

Malthus was thirty-two years old, a bachelor and a Fellow of Jesus College, Cambridge, when the first Essay was published. He scrupulously revised this work over six editions. The second ap-

HT Archives

Standing room only: In 1851 George Cruikshank illustrated a Malthusian population projection.

Maria Edgeworth described Malthus as a 'man of strict truth, perfect integrity and rational benevolence'.

---

peared in 1803 with a revised title, *An Essay on the Principle of Population; or, a view of its past and present effects on Human Happiness; with an inquiry into our prospects respecting the future removal or mitigation of the evils which it occasions,* and this time it bore his name, 'T.R. Malthus, A.M.'

Thomas Robert Malthus signed himself variously Robert Malthus, T. Robert Malthus, Thos. R. Malthus and T.R. Malthus. Others called him names—Mr. M, Population Malthus, Monster Malthus, Beastly Malthus, Muddleheaded Malthus, Mischievous Malthus, and the Miserable Parson. Some close friends, including his father, called him 'Bob'. His pupils at the East India College apparently called him 'Old Pop'. Offended religionists called him the 'Malthusian Devil'. Marx later called him '[A] shameless sycophant of the ruling classes', but Malthus did not live to hear that charge. Whatever description, the insertion of Malthus's name into conversations rarely failed to provoke reaction.

His views made him extremely unpopular with Romantics and utopian thinkers, and for his sharp perceptions he was demonised. Yet Malthus was a sociable man and very much part of the society of the day. From his desk at his parents' home at Albury in Surrey, Malthus produced the famous *Essay,* outlining the so-called 'Malthusian doctrine', arguing that while population increases geometrically—1,2,4,8,16,32—food supplies increase only arithmetically—1,2,3,4,5,6. He reasoned that such ratios inevitably produce overpopulation, shortages, poverty and potential for social disorder.

He wrote not as a politician nor a romantic, but as a mathematician. Soon after he published the *Essay,* he was regarded as an economic and religious heretic or, alternatively, as a respected authority on population issues and political economy. Poets such as Coleridge, Hazlitt and Southey cast him as a misanthrope, but Malthus neither hated mankind nor avoided human society. Some reforming Tory politicians, including the Evangelical banker-philanthropist Michael Sadler, abhorred Malthus's 1798 view that there was no room at Nature's table for millions upon millions of hungry mouths. William Cobbett labelled him a monster. Certain bishops attacked his views, while others, such as theologians William Otter and William Paley, admired his work and were converted to his way of thinking. Younger economists such as John

McCulloch bitterly opposed him, while David Ricardo respected and expressed great affection for his opponent.

Malthus held his readers' attention by the very force of his ideas and the reasonableness of his personality. James Currie MD (1756-1805), a well-known philanthropist and slavery abolitionist who praised Malthus's 1798 *Essay* in the Prefatory Remarks to his *Life of Robert Burns,* described Malthus, after talking with him at length, as 'a most ingenious and pleasant man'. Maria Edgeworth referred to Malthus as 'the most amiable man—of strict truth, perfect integrity and rational benevolence as all who know him declare', and she was dumbfounded that some represented him as 'a bloodthirsty monster—An Ogre'.

Malthus lived in tumultuous years—the American War of Independence, the French Revolution, the settlement of Australia, the Napoleonic wars. He witnessed the burgeoning effects of the Industrial Revolution shifting populations into towns, changing for ever the balance between town and country. The expansion of population in towns caused obvious problems. The countryside and rural towns, often thought to provide a healthier environment, provided Malthus with first-hand population evidence—births, deaths and marriages. As curate of Okewood Chapel, he had access to parish registers recording baptisms which gave a vital source of raw statistics on 'Malthusian' unchecked population growth. The death registers told another story of premature mortality. As Malthus observed in his *Essay,* 'the sons and daughters of peasants will not be found such rosy cherubs in real life, as described in romances'.

Always a realist, Malthus lived long enough to know that the passage of the first Reform Act of 1832 would force the issue of rent in more ways than one. Rent had economic implications, but it was to have broader electoral and political effects. While he gave copious advice, he did not live to see the harshness and practical operations of the new Poor Law of 1834. Having written on the political and economic circumstances of Ireland in 1809, and given advice in 1827 on emigration from that country, he did not witness the horrendous effects upon population of the potato famine in Ireland in the 1840s. He may have experienced some pangs of pity had he done so, but in light of his forecasts and

calculations on population growth, he may have also said 'I told you so'.

Malthus first began writing in 1796 with another anonymous tract entitled *The Crisis,* criticising prime minister Pitt's administration, and signing himself as 'a Friend of the Constitution', but the essay attracted no publisher. The *Essay* of 1798 was written principally to refute Godwin's equally famous *Enquiry Concerning Political Justice, and its Influence on General Virtue and Happiness,* published in 1793. Godwin's later essay on *Avarice and Profusion* provided the real impetus for Malthus to expound his own arguments questioning Godwin's visions of a perfect society.

Malthus took his *Essay* to Joseph

Malthus's father was an unusual man, a disciple of Rousseau, and an eccentric ambitious for his son.

Johnson, the celebrated Unitarian bookseller and publisher of Gilbert Wakefield, his former tutor. In the light of this well-established friendship, Johnson accepted Malthus's work and put it out as a pamphlet bound 'in boards' at the cost of six shillings. It was a confident move on Malthus' part to leave his work with Johnson who was publisher of some of the leading challengers to most prevailing orthodoxies of the time, including Thomas Paine, William Godwin himself, and his daughter Mary Wollstonecraft.

A young cleric moving in such radical company might seem unlikely until we remember Malthus's father. Thomas Robert Malthus was born at the Rookery, Wotton, Surrey, on February 13th, 1766, to Daniel Malthus (1730–1800) and his wife, Henrietta Catherine *née* Graham (1733–1800). Thomas Robert was the second son and one of seven children and his godfathers were the philosophers, Jean-Jacques Rousseau and David Hume. Daniel Malthus was an unusual man, not religious in an or-

thodox sense, a strict father, a disciple of Rousseau, a thinker, an eccentric ambitious for his clever younger son, who was born with a hare lip and cleft palate. This deformity produced Malthus's noticeable speech defect but it did not impede his ability to converse.

Malthus was schooled at home by his father until he became a pupil of Robert Graves at Claverton near Bath in 1773. In 1782 his father sent the sixteen-year old Malthus to the Unitarian minister, Gilbert Wakefield, to attend briefly the Dissenting Academy in Warrington, and then to study as Wakefield's private pupil at his home at Bramcote in Nottinghamshire. It was a rational educational choice. Wakefield was a Nonconformist, a Classical and Hebrew scholar, who took an enlightened approach towards his pupils, expecting them to communicate freely. This radical thinker was later imprisoned for seditious libel in 1799.

Malthus's interest in politics and political economy was probably sparked and encouraged by Wakefield. And he had no regrets about his brush with Dissent. He wrote in 1784:

> I think I shall never repent having been this little time at Bramcot [sic] before my going to college, for I have, if I am not deceived, got into a more steady and regular way of study.

In the same year, Malthus went up to Jesus College and began his university training. He was ordained into the Church of England in 1788.

In 1793, Malthus was elected a Fellow of Jesus. For the following years, he continued with his curacy, witnessed his sisters' marriages, expanded his circle of friends, writing a little and travelling, observing the state of the poor in his parish and the wider countryside. While he remained a bachelor, notes that he made while in Scandinavia reveal how much he admired women, and how well he understood, at least in theory, the passion between the sexes. Practising what he preached, Malthus married late. He fell in love and wed his 28-year-old cousin Harriet Eckersall in 1804. In 1805, at the age of 39, he became a father. Practising restraint perhaps, and the principles of 'virtuous love', Malthus had three children. In 1805 he was appointed professor of modern history and political economy at the new East India College at Haileybury in Hertfordshire, the earliest chair of political economy in England.

He was a member of numerous illustrious societies, a Fellow of the Royal Society, the Royal Society of Literature, the Political Economy Club, the British Association, the Statistical Society, and he was made a member of the French Institute, the *Academie des Sciences Morales et Politiques',* and the Prussian Royal Academy at Berlin. In his private life he was animated, often humorous in a dry way, with an extraordinary laugh which captivated his friends. On his travels to Scandinavia, his Jesus College travelling companions enjoyed his company and his stamina, commenting on his 'fitful bursts of fancy'. Refusing to bow to the impediment of a hare lip, he apparently used his face to make 'a very comic expression of features' and adopted 'a most peculiar intonation of voice when he was in the vein, . . . often a source of infinite delight and pleasantry to his companions'. He was also a regular at London's King of Clubs gatherings and enjoyed convivial dinners and witty conversations with friends, including his opponent David Ricardo. Malthus liked the theatre, enjoyed playing cricket, skated on winter ice, shot wildfowl, taught pupils, officiated at marriages, and enjoyed family life.

Whether expressed in the first *Essay on the Principles of Population,* or in subsequent editions, Malthus's constant view was that restraint—moral restraint and prudential restraint—provided the ultimate keys to human happiness. He sought acceptance and application of his theory but not public popularity. Malthus, as Donald Winch has reminded us, 'presented himself as a calm and dispassionate seeker after scientific truth in the accepted Newtonian manner'. Malthus was not concerned with personal approval but with truths. When asked by the feminist and economist Harriet Martineau if he was ever stung by criticism, he assured her that he was, 'only just at first . . . never after the first fortnight'.

Close friends were at pains to defend 'Mr Malthus' as a good man. As Miss Martineau remarked,

> the reformers of morality, personal and social, are always subject at the outset to the imputation of immorality from those interested in the continuance of corruption'.

Prolific breeding was the cause of many problems, but Malthus was not adverse to individual babies.

She found Malthus not only inspirational but also a pleasant conversationalist. Miss Martineau was author of, among other works, the highly successful *Illustrations of Political Economy.* She described herself as a 'radical woman' and Malthus's work on political economy was of central importance to her, so much so that some described her unkindly as a 'Malthusian Old Maid'. In her *Autobiography,* she described Malthus as 'a simpleminded, virtuous man, full of domestic affections', and as the 'best-abused man of the age'. She credited him as a man 'who did more for social ease and virtue than perhaps any other man of his time'.

Afflicted by deafness and dreading difficulties in understanding him, Miss Martineau was surprised that she could hear Malthus so well. He did not use her formidable ear trumpet to converse with her. She wrote:

> Malthus was the one whom I heard quite easily without it; Malthus whose speech was hopelessly imperfect . . . his inability to pronounce half the consonants in the alphabet . . . His first sentence, slow and gentle, with the vowels sonorous, whatever might become of the consonants, set me at ease completely . . . his worst letter was 'L'.

Malthus was sometimes accused of loathing babies, a result of his harsh views on the 'rights' of illegitimate children born in the Poor House. In one of her letters, Miss Martineau described a Sunday gathering in 1833 at which she, the Wedgwoods, Erasmus Darwin and the Malthuses cosily read the *Examiner* together. Miss Martineau dandled Mrs. Wedgwood's baby on her knee and Malthus patted the baby's cheeks. Pro-

lific breeding was the cause of many problems, but Malthus was not averse to individual babies, including his own beloved children. Sydney Smith, joking later about the sensitive matter of fecundity, said that 'Philosopher Malthus' was a very good natured man, 'if there are no appearances of approaching fertility [he] is civil to every lady'. Bad Malthus jokes might abound in select company and Smith, a long-time friend, could afford to take such liberties.

Conversations with Malthus were often continued by correspondence. He seemed always to be battling with his 'in' tray, apologising to many of his friends and correspondents for the lateness of his replies. The sum total of his correspondence indicates the breadth and length of his extended conversations. Many wrote and many beat a path to Malthus's door. Hailey House at the East India College was a gracious if modest habitation; his door was always ajar and through it walked a procession of interesting individuals, including the United States ambassador to The Hague, Alexander Everett, author of *New Ideas on Population* (1822). After meeting one of his intellectual heroes, the ambassador remarked he had 'rarely met with a finer specimen of the true philosophic temper, graced and set off by the urbanity of a finished gentleman'.

Malthus's name cropped up in many literary and journalistic allusions, although only one portrait exists. He had met Byron at a soiree in 1813, and he appears at least four times in Byron's long poem *Don Juan,* published in 1820, recalling the exploits of the dissolute Spaniard famous for his heartless seduction of women. For Malthus, who preached late marriage and moral restraint, this must have been an irony. In the 12th Canto, Byron refers to love and cash. 'Without cash, Malthus tells you— "take no brides".' Later, Malthus is accused of procreational hypocrisy, 'And Malthus does the thing 'gainst which he writes'. (Some ill-informed calumnies claimed that Malthus had eleven daughters!) In the 15th Canto, Byron refers to zealous matrons, 'who favour, *malgré* Malthus, generation'. Byron follows with a question, 'Had Adeline read Malthus? I can't tell: I wish she had: his book's eleventh commandment, [which] says 'Thou shalt not marry' unless well'. Byron accused Malthus of 'turning marriage into arithmetic.' Malthus, of course, did nothing of the sort, except to plead for prudent marriages.

Evidence of the influence of faith and religion upon Malthus' principles of population is not difficult to find in his writings, although Malthus's God was a hard God, as were the laws of nature. As Charles Darwin explained in his autobiography, his own theory of evolution by natural selection was inspired by his reading of Malthus's *Essay on the Principles of Population* in 1838—only the fittest survived.

In keeping with Church doctrine Malthus had no sympathy for artificial contraception, regarding such interference as an abomination, encouraging what he termed 'concubinage'. He held a personal idea of a God whose universe worked in particular ways under natural laws and had to grapple with the thought of a benevolent deity who watched benignly over human misery brought on by poverty and fecundity. Such was his struggle that many thought him heretical in his rejection of the biblical injunction 'go forth and multiply'. Virtuous procreation should only match personal resources, not the resources of the state, and Malthus clearly had problems with the view that the Lord would provide, even to the most prayerful poor.

Nonetheless, he wished to believe fervently in the goodness of the Deity. Reconciling the cruelty of the principal law of population with a loving God must have troubled him, and religious sensibilities were close to the surface. His final 'natural' justification for human misery was that it would engender tenderness and sympathy and promote positive activity to remove its causes.

Removed from the sensitivities of population restraints, although directly related to the theories of demand, were the conversations on political economy and related topics conducted between the very different economists Malthus,

the Anglican clergyman, and David Ricardo, the Jewish stockbroker and politician, from their first meeting in 1811. The two men shared friends and acquaintances and many letters passed between them arguing gross and fine economic points. Ricardo and Malthus stayed in one another's homes. Hailey House could not compare with Ricardo's grand Gatcombe Park nor his elegant London townhouse in Upper Brook Street, but the warmth and interchange of views gave them both extraordinary satisfaction. When Ricardo died in 1823, Malthus said that he never loved anyone outside his own family so much:

> Our interchange of opinions was so unreserved, and the object after which we were both enquiring was so entirely the truth and nothing else, that I cannot but think we sooner or later must have agreed.

Shortly before his death, Ricardo wrote to Malthus and expressed his views on their conversations:

> And now, my clear Malthus, I have done. Like other disputants, after much discussion, we each retain our own opinions. These discussions, however, never influence our friendship; I should not like you more than I do if you agreed in opinion with me.

Although Malthus made many amendments to his first *Essay*, taking into account contemporary circumstances, the legacy for Malthus was a constant need to explain himself. He had deduced his principles from David Hume, Robert Wallace, Adam Smith and Richard Price, all men of the eighteenth century, but his ideas were challenged soundly by nineteenth-century economists and intellectuals. Malthus reminded his readers in the Preface to the

1817 edition, the fifth, that the first *Essay* was 'published at a period of extensive warfare, combined, from peculiar circumstances, with a most prosperous foreign commerce'. Times had changed. While Malthus amended and published the sixth and final edition of the *Essay* in 1826, and still had his champions, his work had been too often misinterpreted. In economic terms, he was outflanked by competitors, but the value of his writings have endured.

Malthus died in his 68th year and was buried in Bath Abbey. He left a widow and two surviving children and an accruing legacy of ideas. As his headstone proclaimed:

> One of the best men and truest philosophers of any age or country raised by dignity of mind above the misrepresentations of the ignorant and the neglect of the great. . . . His writings will be a lasting monument to the extent and correctness of his understanding.

For Further Reading:

Patricia James, *Population Malthus: His Life and Times,* (Routledge, 1979.); J.M. *Keynes, Essays in Biography,* (Rupert Hart-Davis, 1951.); T.R. Malthus, *An Essay on the Principle of Population* [using the text of the 1803 edition], selected and introduced by Donald Winch, Cambridge University Press, 1992.); T.R. Malthus, *An Essay on the Principle of Population and A Summary View of the Principle of Population,* (edited with an introduction by Anthony Flew, Penguin Books, 1982); Andrew Pyle (series editor), *Population: Contemporary Responses to Thomas Malthus,* (Thoemmes Press, 1994.); Donald Winch, Malthus, (Oxford University Press, 1987).

Dr Suzanne Rickard works at the History Program, Australian National University, Canberra.

The Age of Philanthropy

by Gertrude Himmelfarb

Civil society has become the rallying cry of liberals and conservatives alike, especially in the wake of the recent reform of the welfare system. The devolution of welfare to the states suggests a further devolution to local authorities, and a still further one to the unofficial but powerful institutions of civil society—families, neighborhood groups, churches, private social-work agencies, philanthropies—all those "voluntary associations" that Alexis de Tocqueville took to be the genius of American democracy.

It is surely presumptuous to quarrel with Tocqueville, yet in one small respect I venture to do so. Tocqueville presented those associations as a unique feature of American society. Although the Americans, he observed in the second volume of *Democracy in America* (1840), "took some of their laws and many of their customs" from the English, own travels suggested to him that "the principle of association was not used nearly so constantly or so adroitly" in England as in America.

Tocqueville had visited England in 1833, just before writing the first volume of *Democracy in America,* and again in 1835, after the publication of that volume and before writing the second. But long before then, indeed almost a century before then, largely under the impetus of the Wesleyan revival, a multitude of associations ("societies," they were often called) had sprung up in England for every conceivable purpose: to establish and endow schools, hospitals, orphanages, and almshouses, and to serve a myriad of other charitable and social functions. In the course of the 19th century many more such societies were founded, suggesting that the English used that "principle of association" at least as "constantly" and "adroitly" as did the Americans. And if the concept of civil

society is extended (as surely it must be) to include the family, here too the English must take pride of place, for not even the Americans could be more reverent of the family, or of the other institutions of civil society, than the Victorians were.

Tocqueville might have contributed to one of the hoarier myths about Victorian society: that it was ruthlessly materialistic, acquisitive, and self-centered. The myth starts with the image of the hard-headed, hardnosed Victorian employer who regarded his workers as instruments of production rather than as human beings, and who exploited them under the cloak of principle, invoking the natural, even divine, laws of political economy. The sole function of government in this laissez-faire system is said to have been the preservation of law and order, which in practice meant keeping the potentially lawless and disorderly lower classes in a state of docility and subjugation. Those who professed a concern for the poor are dismissed as eccentric do-gooders, condescending Lady Bountifuls, or officious philanthropists who pretended to help the poor for their own self-serving motives.

Part of this myth is easily disproved. Neither in principle nor in practice was political economy as rigidly laissez faire as this picture suggests. The first of the factory acts limiting the hours of work for children was passed in 1833; within a decade it was followed by laws limiting the hours of women, and somewhat later, the hours of men. In the course of the century, Parliament enacted scores of other reforms concerning health, sanitation, housing, education, transpor-

The mark of Victorian philanthropy was direct and personal involvement in the day-to-day lives of the poor.

tation, even holidays, while the municipalities assumed responsibility for the water supply, sewage, public baths, street lighting, street cleaning, libraries, and parks. All of these reforms coincided with a period of rapid economic growth, so that by the last quarter of the century the standard of living of the working classes had risen considerably, thus belying the Marxist theory of "immiseration": the idea that capitalism inevitably results in the growing misery and poverty of the proletariat.

Even more remarkable than the improvement in the conditions of the working classes was the enormous surge of social consciousness and philanthropic activity on the part of

From *The Wilson Quarterly*, Spring 1997, pp. 48-55. © 1997 by Gertrude Himmelfarb. Reprinted by permission.

the middle and upper classes. This is not to say that there had been no such consciousness and activity in the previous century. When John Wesley propounded the trinity, "Gain all you can. . . . Save all you can. . . . Give all you can," he gave practical effect to it by taking up collections following the sermon and distributing the money to the poor, setting up loan funds and work projects, and instructing his followers to pay "visitations" to the sick and to prisoners in jail. It is not surprising to find Methodists and Evangelicals prominent in the founding of orphanages, schools, hospitals, friendly societies, and charitable enterprises of every kind. By the late 18th century, the principle of "philanthropy" (still carrying with it its original meaning of "love of mankind") had given rise to full-time philanthropists such as John Howard, who successfully agitated for the reform of the prison system, and Jonas Hanway, who devised the "boarding out" system to remove infants from the poorhouses. Hannah More, preferring moral reformation to philanthropy, characterized this period, not altogether in praise, as "the Age of Benevolence." A London magistrate, deploring the corruption of "virtue" into "good affections," complained, "We live in an age when humanity is in fashion."

That magistrate would have had more to complain of in the 19th century, when the fashion for humanity expressed itself in a score of legislative and administrative reforms as well as a renewed burst of philanthropies and social activities. So far from supplanting private, voluntary efforts, as many people had feared, the government seemed to inspire them to greater exertions. To the French historian and critic Hippolyte Taine, this was yet another of the peculiarities of the English. Citing an article in the *Edinburgh Review* in 1861, he noted that of the £13 million spent on public education in the preceding 21 years, only £4 million was contributed by the state; the rest came from private subscriptions. (Even after the institution of compulsory, publicly supported education in 1870, church-endowed and private schools continued to play a large part in the educational system.) And education was only one of the causes that drew upon private funds:

> There are swarms of societies engaged in good works: societies for saving the life of drowning persons, for the conversion of the Jews, for the propagation of the Bible, for the advancement of science, for the protection of animals, for the suppression of vice, for the abolition of tithes, for helping working people to own their own houses, for building good houses for the working-class, for setting up a basic fund to provide the workers with savings banks, for emigration, for the propagation of economic and social knowledge, for Sabbath-day observance, against drunkenness, for founding schools to train girls as schoolteachers, etc., etc.

What was even more remarkable, Taine observed, was that an Englishman regarded this kind of "public business," as "*his* business," feeling obligated to contribute to the "common good" and bringing to it the same conscientious attention a Frenchman brought to his private business affairs.

Two decades later Taine would have had more societies to add to his roster and more reason for astonishment. The 1880s saw a veritable explosion of social concerns and activities. In 1884, the journal of the leading philanthropic association, the Charity Organisation Society, reported: "Books on the poor, poverty, social questions, slums and the like subjects, rush fast and furious from the press. The titles of some of them sound like sentimental novels." That same year, Beatrice Potter (better known as Beatrice Webb, the Fabian) wrote in her diary: "Social questions are the vital questions of today: they take the place of religion."

There was, in fact, a religious, almost revivalist tone in this accession of social consciousness. Webb has left a memorable description of what she called the "Time-Spirit" of this period. The spirit was a compound of two elements: the first, a religious dedication to the service of others, inspired not by orthodox religion or a belief in God but by a secular religion, the "Religion of Humanity"; the second, the faith in science, the idea that the welfare of society could best be promoted by scientific, rational, organized means.

To one degree or another, these elements manifested themselves in the multitude of philanthropic enterprises, reform movements, humanitarian societies, research projects, publications, and journalistic exposes that flourished in the last quarter of the century. Some were overtly religious, such as the Salvation Army and the Christian Social Union. But many more exhibited the kind of sublimated, secularized "religion" described by Beatrice Webb. In this respect, the time-spirit of late-Victorian England was in notable contrast to that of earlier periods. Most of the reformers earlier in the century, such as the Evangelicals, who led the movement for the abolition of the slave trade, had been inspired by a firm religious creed; they were reformers, one might say, because they were devout Christians. Many of the later reformers were less devout but no less ardent in pursuing worthy causes. Just as they redoubled their moral zeal to compensate for their loss of religious faith, so they redoubled their humanitarian zeal as well. Humanitarianism became, in effect, a surrogate religion. This quasi-religious spirit was evident even in the socialist organizations such as the Fabian Society, which was professedly secular, or the Social Democratic Federation, which was ostensibly Marxist.

The scientific aspect of the time-spirit also took many forms. For socialists (in the Fabian Society, Social Democratic Federation, and Socialist League), science meant the rational, planned organization of the economy and society. For social workers (in the Charity Organisation Society), it meant the rational, planned organization of charity and relief. For settlement-house workers (in Toynbee Hall), it meant the education and edification of the working classes. For social researchers (such as Charles Booth and Seebohm Rowntree), it meant the systematic investigation and analysis of the different classes of the poor, their material and moral conditions, their problems and prospects of improvement.

It was this combination of religiosity and rationality that informed the social consciousness of the late Victorians. Critics at the time complained that the Religion of Humanity had the effect of diluting and distorting religion, replacing the old stern Puritanism with "a vapid philanthropic sentiment . . . a creed of maudlin benevolence." In fact, the new humanitarianism was neither vapid nor maudlin. The God of Humanity proved to be as stern a taskmaster as the God of Christianity. The Charity Organisation Society instructed its social workers that "scientific" charity should not be "indiscriminate" or "promiscuous," distributed without regard to need or worth, lest it contribute to the very evil it was designed to remedy, the pauperization and demoralization of the poor. True humanitarianism was an exercise in doing good, not feeling good—doing good to others, even if it meant curbing one's own spontaneous, benevolent impulses.

The dispensers of charity, no less than the recipients, were held to high standards. They were expected to give generously of their time and resources and to have a sustained personal involvement in their work. This was not "checkbook philanthropy," satisfied merely by the contribution of money (although such contributions were expected, in small amounts as well as large, since the organizations were entirely dependent on private funds). Nor was it the kind of "telescopic" philanthropy satirized by Charles Dickens in the character of Mrs. Jellyby, in *Bleak House,* who was so preoccupied with the natives of Borrioboola-Gha that she neglected her own children. Nor was it professional philanthropy in the current sense, where everyone from the director of the charity to fund raisers, social workers, and clerks is a salaried employee, paid to do a job quite like any other.

Victorian philanthropists, social workers ("visitors," as they were called), settlement-house residents, even researchers, were personally involved in the day-to-day lives of the poor with whom they were concerned. And while they brought to their work a spirit of professionalism, seeking to dispense charity or conduct their inquiries "scientifically," they also brought to it the dedication of unpaid, voluntary workers giving a good deal of their time, their energy, and their money to the welfare of those less fortunate than themselves.

Philanthropy was inspired by the dual motive: to serve others and to fulfill a moral need. When Beatrice Webb started work as a visitor for the Charity Organisation Society, she weighed the relative importance of the "moral facts" and "economic facts" involved in charity, "the relationship of giver and receiver," and "the moral effect on the person who receives." She concluded that it was "distinctly *advantageous to us* to go amongst the poor," not only to have a better understanding of their lives and problems but because "contact with them develops on the whole our finer qualities, disgusting us with our false and worldly application of men and things and educating in us a thoughtful benevolence." In some instances, she recognized, benevolence might take the form of "pharisaical self congratulation." But the real philanthropist would not be guilty of this, for he would be too aware of the "mixed result" of his work (if indeed it had any result) "to feel much pride over it."

Today, such statements are often taken as evidence of the elitist, authoritarian, self-serving nature of philanthropy. But they can as well be taken as evidence of a self-sacrificing, even self-abasing spirit, a belief that the "privileged," no less than the poor, had spiritual needs, that they had to "give" (as Wesley said), as much as the poor had to receive, and that what they had to give was of themselves. Even the Fabian socialist Walter Besant paid tribute to the principle of the "new philanthropy," as he called it: "Not money, but yourselves."

Two criticisms are commonly made of Victorian philanthropy. The older, more familiar one is that even at the time such philanthropy was obsolete and irrelevant, that the social and economic problems of late-Victorian England could not be solved by private, voluntary efforts but required either substantial legislative and administrative action by the state or radical structural changes in the economy. Philanthropy was not only inadequate but counterproductive, since it distracted attention from real remedies for all-too-real problems. From the beginning, the argument goes, and certainly by the end of the 19th century, industrialism and urbanism had created social evils that were beyond the scope of individuals. Poverty, unemployment, bad housing, overcrowded slums, and unsanitary conditions were neither the result of a failure of character on the part of workers nor of a lack of good will on the part of employers and landlords. Therefore they could not be solved or even alleviated by well-disciplined workers, well-intentioned employers, or well-wishing philanthropists.

More recently, criticism has taken another turn. The gravamen of the charge now is that philanthropy is all too often a self-serving exercise on the part of philanthropists at the expense of those whom they are ostensibly helping. Philanthropy stands condemned, not only as ineffectual but as hypocritical and self-aggrandizing. In place of "the love of mankind," philanthropy is now identified with the love of self. It is seen as an occasion for social climbing, for joining committees and attending charity balls in the company of the rich and the famous. Or as an opportunity to cultivate business and professional associations. Or as a way of enhancing one's self-esteem and self-approbation by basking in the esteem and approbation of others. Or as a method of exercising power over those in no position to challenge it. Or as a means (a relatively painless means) of atoning for a sense of guilt, perhaps for riches unethically acquired. Or as a passport to heaven, a record of good works and virtues to offset bad works and vices. Or (the most recent addition to this bill of indictment) as a form of "voyeurism" an unseemly, perhaps erotic interest in the private lives of the lower classes.

This kind of criticism is often advanced as a corollary to the "social control" thesis. Just as Victorian values are said to have been an instrument for the pacification of the working class, so Victorian philanthropy is described as a device for the subjugation of the even more vulnerable class of the very poor. By discriminating between the "undeserving" and the "deserving" poor, the dispensers of charity managed to keep the former in a condition of servility in the workhouse while forcing the latter into the labor market on terms set by the employers. Thus profits were secured, the status quo was maintained, discontent was suppressed, and revolution was averted.

The difficulty with the "social control" thesis is that it can be neither proved nor refuted, since any empirical fact can be interpreted in accord with it. If some philanthropists and reformers advocated a system of free, compulsory education, it can be said that they did so only because educated workers were more productive than uneducated ones; if others opposed such a system (ostensibly out of a distrust of any kind of state-controlled education), it was to keep the poor in a state of ignorance and submission. By this mode of reasoning, any philanthropic enterprise, regardless of its nature, purpose, or effect, can be disparaged and discredited.

The other familiar argument, that philanthropy was no solution to the problem of poverty, would have been conceded by Victorians, who never made any such claim, if only because they did not believe that poverty was a "problem" that could be "solved." At best they thought it could be alleviated, and this only for some individuals or groups, in certain circumstances, and in particular respects. The entire purpose of Charles Booth's monumental study, *Life and Labour of the People in London* (1891–1903), was to break down the category of "poor" into distinctive "classes," analyzing each of them in terms not only of income but also of the regularity of their work and earnings, their living and working conditions, their habits and moral qualities. The effect was to distinguish the various problems that went under the umbrella term "poverty," and thus the specific remedies—not "solutions"—appropriate to those specific problems.

This "disaggregation," as we would now say, was typical of Victorian social reformers and philanthropists, who were perfectly aware of the special and limited nature of their enterprises. The Charity Organisation Society, which tried to coordinate the activities of the many philanthropic groups, made a great point of distinguishing between the functions of private charity and public relief. Where the Poor Law was directed to the relief of the indigent, charity should be reserved for those who were needy but not actually destitute, who were generally employed and might even have some resources such as savings or possessions but who had temporary problems that, unless alleviated, might lead to pauperism. Relief, in short, was meant for paupers; charity for the poor. And neither relief nor charity would "solve" the problem of poverty; at most they would alleviate it.

Nor did the reformer Octavia Hill have any illusions about solving the housing problem when she embarked upon her housing projects. She hoped that the principles she established for her houses—that tenants pay their rent promptly, that "rent collectors" (in effect, social workers) respect the privacy of the tenants and assist them unobtrusively, and that the houses include such "amenities" as ornaments and gardens as well as essential utilities—would be applied on a larger scale by private owners and institutions. But she also knew the limitations of her financial resources, the relatively small number of families she could accommodate, and, more important, the particular kinds of workers she wanted to accommodate. She made it clear that her houses were not meant for the artisans who could afford the "model dwellings" erected by the Peabody Trust and other building societies, nor for the vagrants who found refuge in the "common lodging houses," but rather for the "unskilled laborers" who constituted the bulk of the industrious, thrifty working people."

Latter-day critics, who fault the Victorians for not solving the problems of poverty and housing, use such words as "vague" and "illogical," "ambivalent" and "ambiguous," "transitional" and "half-way house," to describe the ideas and projects of these philanthropists, reformers, and thinkers. The implication is that Victorian England can be understood only as a prelude to the welfare state (or, as some historians would prefer, to socialism); anything short of that is regarded as naive and futile. If most Victorians objected to a large extension of state control, if they preferred small measures of reform to large ones and local laws and regulations to national ones, if they persisted in expending their energy and resources on private, voluntary efforts, it could only be, so it is supposed, because of a failure of imagination, or a weakness of will, or a commitment to an outmoded ideology or vested interest.

Although Victorian philanthropists did not believe that there were comprehensive solutions to most social problems, they did believe that some problems could be alleviated and that it was the duty of the more fortunate to do what they could to relieve the conditions of the less fortunate. This was the moral imperative that made philanthropy so important a part of Victorian life. But there was another moral imperative: that every proposal for alleviation produce moral as well as material benefits—at the very least that it not have a deleterious moral effect. This was the common denominator that linked together public relief and private charity, settlement houses and housing projects, socialist organizations and temperance societies. Whatever was done for the poor was meant to enable them to do more for themselves, to become more self-reliant and more responsible—to bring out, as Green said, their "better selves." "Charity," wrote the secretary of the Charity Organisation Society, "is a social regenerator. We have to use Charity to create the power of self-help."

The Victorians were avowedly, unashamedly, incorrigibly moralists. They were moralists in their own behalf—they engaged in philanthropic enterprises in part to satisfy their own moral needs. And they were moralists in behalf of the poor, whom they sought not only to assist materially but also to elevate morally, spiritually, culturally, and intellectually—and whom, moreover, they believed capable and desirous of such elevation. Just as it is demeaning to the working classes to suggest (as some historians do) that work, thrift, prudence, sobriety, and self-help were middle-class values imposed upon them from above, so it is demeaning to the philanthropists to say that they promoted these values solely for their own ulterior motives. In any case, whatever their motives (and there were surely self-serving, self-aggrandizing, self-satisfied individuals among them), the values they commended to the poor were those they cherished for themselves and for their own families. It was no small achievement that people of very different political and philosophical dispositions, engaged in very different philanthropic enterprises, should have agreed on this: that the poor had the will to aspire to these same values and the ability to realize them.

GERTRUDE HIMMELFARB, *a former Wilson Center Fellow, is professor of history emeritus at the Graduate School of the City University of New York. Her books include* On Looking into the Abyss: Untimely Thoughts on Culture and Society *(1994),* Poverty and Compassion: The Moral Imagination of the Late Victorians *(1991), and* The De-Moralization of Society: From Victorian Virtues to Modern Values *(1995), from which this essay is partly adapted.*

Women Murderers in Victorian Britain

Women as perpetrators of crime, rather than its victims, were
figures of especial fascination and loathing in the Victorian popular press.
Judith Knelman delves deeper.

The domestication of women early in the reign of Queen Victoria—inspired largely by her example—made it especially difficult for the English to believe that women would harbour, let alone indulge, murderous impulses. By this time the popular press had, through its sensational treatment of such figures, defined the murderess as a cold-blooded monster who operated by stealth and was particularly attracted to poison as a weapon. Such women, having betrayed the trust of their nearest and dearest, could not be understood as women, and so they were loudly derided as traitors to their sex. The crude woodcuts of nineteenth-century broadsides often showed a freshly hanged female figure being gawked at by an assembly of her moral superiors. Newspapers were more reliable but not much less subtle in their depiction of murderesses.

From about 1830, newspapers faithfully recorded all the physical and psychological details they could muster of the few women who were prosecuted for murder. Before that, newspaper reports of murder cases were fairly short and to the point, the point usually being that an execution date had been set. But these could be supplemented with colourful, sometimes poetic and often fictitious accounts in the form of broadside ballads chanted and sold in the streets.

This is not to say that male murderers did not attract the notice of the sensational press. Leaving aside infanticide, which was rather less stigmatised than other kinds of murder, men were responsible for about 85 per cent of recorded homicides. Most, but not all, of the best-selling subjects among murder broadsides and pamphlets were men. However, sharing the honours with the likes of William Corder, James Rush, François Courvoisier, John Thurtell, James Greenacre, Daniel Good and George Manning were Manning's wife, Maria, whose lover they killed because he reneged on a *ménage à trois* arrangement they had made and Constance Kent, a well-brought-up young woman

who at the age of sixteen slit her young stepbrother's throat and dropped him into a privy to punish her stepmother. Male murderers were more often written and sung about than female murderers because there were more of them.

The simple rarity and unexpectedness of killings by women go a long way to account for the attention paid to murderesses. Moreover, there was not the same conflict in the cultural presentation of a male murderer. While male villainy was dismissed as an unfortunate regression, the same sort of behaviour in females, particularly when it was directed at males, was condemned as a hideous perversion.

Deviant behaviour by men was deplorable; deviant behaviour by women was unacceptable. Violent women were depicted as fiends or monsters who could not be allowed to remain alive. A forerunner of Lorena Bobbitt, for example, Ann Crampton, was hanged in Durham in 1814 though her victim lived to describe his experience in court. She was guilty of 'cutting and maiming' him for being unfaithful to her and seems in retrospect to have been a rather pathetic figure, plain, middle-aged and jealous. A broadside issued in 1814 describing 'a most cruel and bloody Transaction' is quite explicit about what she did:

Mrs. Cut cock's come to gaol,
Keep her Wolf, and do not fail;
Of the Jade make an example,
For it you have reason ample.
Keep her upon bread and water,
This audacious Mother's Daughter;
When the world was first created,
And the living creatures mated,
They were order'd all to breed,
But thinks she, I'll stop your speed;
So determined on her prey,
Swept the whole concern away.
Who the Man is I can't tell
But my Lady bears the Bell;
For crimes among all women kind
Such another I can't find.

Gentleman, take care be sure,
Keep you fast the Stable door;
For it seems mischief in common,
Is transacted by the woman;
Turnkey, take a stick and bang he,
Damn her a b___h I would not hang her
Neither, but I'd have an end,
Such as with old shoes they mend;
And I'd take especial care,
How she ever_____.
Any more while in existence,
Shoe makers lend your assistance;
For no excuse can be made,
For the conduct of this Jade;
If she'd really took his life,
With a razor or a knife;
That I freely would forgiven,
But this job I can't by Heaven.

This broadside, despite its levity, clearly articulates the attitude of the male establishment to women who threatened their dominance; punish them in such a way as to make an example of them. Men insisted on defining women as devoted to their care, and were regularly incensed to find the definition disproved.

Even worse were women who killed in cold blood. Esther Hibner, who starved and otherwise abused her young needlework and weaving apprentices with the result that more than one of them died, was ridiculed by the press when she was tried and hanged in 1829. Eliza Ross, hanged in 1832 for smothering an old woman so that she could sell the body to an anatomist

was (reasonably enough) reviled as sub-human.

Broadsides tended to focus on murders that stood out as especially horrifying. If they dealt with infanticide, it was not to describe an ordinary case of suffocation but something more violent, something that would make the mother stand out for her lack of human feeling—like a bundle of charred bones found buried in the garden. Every so often a broadside of this theme would appear, with details that were probably invented to sell at a particular time and in a particular place. But such things undoubtedly did happen. There seems to have been no attempt to come to terms with the economic realities that drove new mothers to such unnatural action, only grim satisfaction at the opportunity for retribution.

Other female horrors described by broadsides, perhaps but not necessarily embroidered for dramatic effect, involved the murder of stepchildren (by sticking pins into their hands, hanging, boiling, or roasting in the oven) and elderly parents (usually by poison). And there was always husband-poisoning.

The appetite of the masses for crime news was later indulged by newspaper proprietors, who found, despite their propaganda to the contrary, that crime paid. The papers had to stick to facts, but fortunately there was a good supply of raw material. From the 1840s to the end of the century in England unusual murders abounded. As detective work became more effective, the stories filled out, and the public was able—and more than willing—to follow a case in many chapters from inquest to execution.

News of sensational crimes spread like wildfire in the nineteenth century as literacy increased. In the 1840s it was the staple of the popular Sunday newspaper, and, once the stamp tax was lifted in 1855, of the daily penny and then (from 1868) the halfpenny newspaper. By the 1850s, church schools, dame schools, mechanics' institutes and various philanthropic associations had spread literacy sufficiently that the middle and working classes between them were able to support an army of new, cheap magazines and newspapers that grew even stronger once the paper duty was abolished in 1861. After the Second Reform Bill engaged the masses politically in 1867 there was no stopping the cheap press.

Although the Victorian press was attempting to bridge the gap between the 'otherness' of remote events and the everyday world of the reader, to expand reality to include what was seen and heard by others, it tended to treat crime as a fiction while presenting it as a fact. Marguerite Diblanc, for example, an excitable Belgian cook who in 1872 strangled her Park Lane mistress and then fled to Paris, was depicted by English newspapers as an amazon.

For most of the nineteenth century the press made violent women ugly, 'masculine', old-looking, and, in general, inhuman. Some may have been, but clearly others were victims of circumstances. However, even the few papers that agitated in the 1840s for more humanitarian treatment of the poor did not extend their sympathy to desperately poor murderesses. The general reading public found it inconvenient to make the connection between the desperation of poverty and the 'remedy' of murder. Indeed, far from being regarded as a contributing factor, poverty seems to have been, to some, an offence in itself. 'I can't make out whether we have any business on the face of the earth, or not', says Dickens's Toby (in The Chimes), speaking of the poor:

I get so puzzled sometimes that I am not even able to make up my mind whether there is any good at all in us, or whether we are born bad. We seem to do dreadful things; we seem to give a deal of trouble; we are always being complained of and guarded against. One way or another, we fill the papers.

Toby was oversimplifying, but news reports are black and white in more ways than one. Literature, more like life, has many shades of grey. So even when fictional criminals were presented as bad, they could be attractive, passionate or sympathetic women—'round', in E.M. Forster's terms. Such a presentation was much less likely in straight factual reporting, which was 'flat' or two-dimensional.

Broadsides and newspapers depicted the murderess as a monster because she had behaved in an extremely unnatural way. She was an outsider who refused to abide by the rules of society. Literature, because it can flesh out characters, tends to look into the circumstances that trigger peculiar behaviour.

It was from broadsides that the idea of news as a commodity for the general public came into its own in England. By the 1830s probably between two-thirds and three-quarters of the working classes could read at least a little, i.e. well enough to make their way past the huge headlines ('Execution!', 'Horrid Murder', 'Sorrowful Lamentation', 'Inhuman Murder', 'The Last Dying Speech and Confession of. . . .') through the print under the chilling woodcut illustrations. Murder and execution broadsides were immensely popular and well circulated for the good reason that they highlighted events on which attention was focussed at a particular time: a murder, trial, confession or execution—that people were talking about. The broadsides, fixed on walls in homes, inns and coffee houses or outdoors on posts, were as much about entertainment as information.

Though deviant women could be dismissed in the press as subhuman, a sensitive novelist could come close to justifying the destructive impulse by showing through characterisation and plot how it developed. Dickens showed Nancy to be an abused wife in *Oliver Twist* (1837) but he did not go so far as to make her kill Bill Sykes. Decades later, in *Tess of the d'Urbervilles* (1891), Thomas Hardy forced readers to see Tess, though she is a fallen woman and then a murderess, as a poor creature hopelessly trapped in an abusive relationship, and the despicable Alec d'Urberville as deserving of his fate. His depiction of Tess's hanging—of scarcely more moment than the swish of a horse's tail against a fly—is so wrenching that its dimension as angry criticism of society's intolerance and callousness is unmistakable.

Hardy's heroine is based partly on a woman whom he saw hanged in Dorchester in his boyhood for the murder of her abusive husband. Coverage in the local press at the time of her execution included a leading article about the 'ignominious end' and 'well-merited fate' of the 'wretched criminal' for 'the deliberate murder of poor Anthony Brown, by the hand of his own wife'. Though the extenuating circumstances that underlay this case are in hindsight painfully obvious, most press reports condemned Martha Brown at the time. Similarly, in 1807 Martha Alden slit her drunken husband's throat because, she claimed, he had threatened to beat her when he arrived home. She may have been defending herself, but she was depicted as a raging animal, driven by passion.

The typical nineteenth-century murderess was a young girl who had killed her newborn, illegitimate baby. Such a deed was not terribly shocking, and as the century progressed, it tended to be treated increasingly leniently by the criminal justice system. As news, it was routine; as literature, it endured in the work of Scott (*The Heart of Midlothian*, 1818) and George Eliot. Like Hardy, Eliot, in her first full-length novel, reconstructed a murder case to show what pressures might drive a woman to kill. In *Adam Bede* (1859) we meet Hetty Sorel long before her seduction and subsequent pregnancy, and we see how impossible it would be for her to maintain a child. Her story is based on an 1802 case that Eliot happened to hear about and, in a more general sense, on other cases that resulted in the execution of desperate young women for whom infanticide seemed the only possible answer. These cases were all dispatched in short order by the press and the justice system.

True crime was recognised as a rich source of material by many nineteenth-century novelists, not all of them social reformers. The Newgate novelists of the 1830s, chief among them Edward Bulwer-Lytton, made popular a fictionalised form of criminal biography. So-called 'penny dreadfuls' often picked up themes from the *Newgate Calendar*. Then came the sensation novels of the 1860s, tales of mistaken identity, murder and mystery. In their sensation novels, Dickens and Wilkie Collins picked up setting, plot details and characters from recent murders, though they did not reconstruct whole cases. They gave female deviancy an aura of glamour that it seldom had.

Although—or perhaps because—deviancy was shocking, the Victorians, reined in by an exacting and repressive social code, were fascinated by it. As Punch put it, in a satirical vein:

> . . . upon the apprehension of a criminal, we notoriously spare no pains to furnish the nation with his complete biography; employing literary gentlemen, of elegant education and profound knowledge of human nature, to examine his birthplace and parish register, to visit his parents, brothers, uncles and aunts, to procure intelligence of his early school days, diseases which he has passed through, infantile (and more mature) traits of character, etc . . . we employ artists of eminence to sketch his likeness as he appears at the police court, or views of the farmhouse or back kitchen where he has perpetrated the atrocious deed . . . we entertain intelligence within the prison walls with the male and female turnkeys, gaolers, and other authorities, by whose information we are enabled to describe every act and deed of the prisoner, the state of his health, sleep, and digestion, the changes in his appearance, his conversation, his dress and linen, the letters he writes, and the meals he takes. . . .

The use of the generic pronoun by no means suggests that female criminals escaped this sort of scrutiny. To the (male) purveyors of information, the female criminal mind was even more fascinating than the male. How extreme deviants came to act as they did was a question that the Victorians were prepared to spend time and money on exploring.

Many of them visited Madame Tussaud's Exhibition, a fixture on Baker Street in London since 1835, for its Separate Room, which was dubbed by Punch in 1846 'the Chamber of Horrors'—a name that has stuck. This room, separated from the rest of the display so as not to offend the sensibilities of delicate female visitors, featured lifelike wax figures of notorious criminals, many of them made from death masks after their execution.

Those who would not be satisfied with replicas attended trials, sometimes for an admission fee, or visited prisons. In 1849, curious Londoners were reported to by applying to Newgate Prison for permission to visit so that they could catch a glimpse of the Mannings, and there were similar attempts in Bristol when Sarah Thomas, a servant who had murdered her mistress, was awaiting execution. Executions were the biggest draw: as *Punch* bitingly suggested, the buildup in the press made people feel that they would be missing something if they did not attend.

Newspaper and broadside accounts of female hangings suggest that such events were more riveting than male hangings. A murderess was presented as a sort of witch figure so as to preserve the Victorian norm of femininity. Gentle, submissive, passive, self-sacrificing, delicate creatures do not strangle babies with their bare hands and drop them into the river; they do not bash in their mistress's head for giving one order too many; nor do they poison friends and relatives so as to obtain a little extra income.

It was widely believed that murderesses were such hardened creatures that they resisted confession and penitence, and it does appear to be the case that proportionately they were less ready than men to concede their guilt at the eleventh hour. Broadsides of adamant women like Mary Ann Burdock (1835) emphasise their inhumanity. When a women did repent publicly, as did Har-

riet Parker, who in 1848 asphyxiated two children to get back at their philandering father, she became fascinatingly fragile and human again, and her behaviour on the scaffold was scanned for what it revealed of her humanity. Forgiveness, however, was a possibility in the next world but not in this one.

FOR FURTHER READING:

V.A.C. Gatrell, *The Hanging Tree: Execution and the English People 1770–1868* (Oxford University Press, 1994); Mary Hartman, *Victorian Murderesses: A True History of Thirteen Respectable French and English Women Accused of Unspeakable Crimes* (Schocken Books, 1977); Vir-

ginia Morris, *Double Jeopardy: Women Who Kill in Victorian Fiction* (University of Kentucky Press, 1990); Victor E. Neuberg, *Popular Literature: A History and Guide* (Penguin, 1977); Leslie Shepherd, *The History of Street Literature* (David & Charles, 1973); Lucia Zedner, *Women, Crime, and Custody in Victorian England* (Clarendon Press, 1991).

Judith Knelman is Associate Professor of Journalism in the Faculty of Information and Media Studies at the University of Western Ontario. Her new book Twisting in the Wind: The Murderess and the English Press *is published by University of Toronto Press.*

'The White Man's Burden'? Imperial Wars in the 1890s

Lawrence James *looks at the mélange of racial theory, economic interest and Boys' Own 'derring-do' that fuelled European ambitions for a 'place in the sun'.*

Lawrence James

Lawrence James is the author of The Iron Duke: a military biography of the Duke of Wellington *(Weidenfeld and Nicholson, March 1992). He is working on a biography of Allenby and a general history of the British Empire.*

Lords of the earth? The Asante King Prempe and his mother making submission to the British expeditionary force—a *Graphic* illustration of 1896.

In the summer of 1900, Colonel James Willcocks led a small army of troops to Kumasi in what today is Ghana to fight the Asante King Prempe who had defied his new British overlords. During the march, Willcocks was approached by a village headman who claimed the Haussa soldiers had broken down his people's huts in their search for firewood and demanded compensation. Willcocks investigated the story, found it untrue and had its teller seized and brought before him. 'All he had to say', recalled Willcocks, 'was that I was his "good father", and I accordingly treated him as a good father does his child'. Like a naughty schoolboy whose mischief had been uncovered and punished by a firm but benign headmaster, the headman bore no grudges, later telling Willcocks he was a 'devilish fine fellow'.

This incident, and for that matter the campaign of which it formed a small part, are instructive, shedding light on contemporary attitudes towards empires and their subject races. Willcocks, a professional soldier with twenty years experience waging the small wars of empire, was proceeding against a native prince who had broken faith. His duplicity and that of the headman were reminders that those whom Kipling characterised as 'sullen, new caught peoples, half devil and half child' needed sharp lessons before they could be set along the road to moral and physical regeneration. Moreover, Willcocks revealed by his treatment of the headmen that he possessed that gift, claimed by many others like him, British and French, of a profound understanding of the native mind which enabled him to see through the fraud, treat its perpetrator appropriately and at the same time win his respect.

While readers today may be repelled by all that is implicit in this anecdote, their counterparts in the 1890s would have seen it as an amusing incident in the irresistible advance of European civilisation across Asia and Africa. This decade witnessed the heyday of self-confident, often self-congratulatory and always aggressive imperialism in which Britain, France, Germany, Italy, Japan and the United States conquered and annexed in the name of civilisation.

This unprecedented spate of expansion was seen as the culmination of a natural historical progression. Nations that had now reached what Cecil Rhodes believed was the highest state of civilization were taking control over those which had lagged behind, or races, like the Asante, who were considered unfit to manage their own affairs. This process was inevitable and beneficial for all concerned. 'The future of Africa under any form of European tutelage must be better than the dark and evil nightmare of the past' concluded the *Dublin Review* after delegates to the 1885 Berlin Conference had sanctioned the continent's division among the European powers.

The work was soon underway in Africa and in some areas the results looked promising. Technical and cultural progress advanced side by side in the

French Ivory Coast where a report of 1896 described the laying of telegraph and telephone lines through the bush. Most important was the spread of French taught in recently established schools where, allegedly, the pupils were proud to be mastering the language of their new rulers. Using their new tongue, they would learn, among other things, about the achievements and superiority of French civilisation and in time feel themselves a part of French culture.

Credit for the transformation of the Ivory Coast was given to a governor who was 'benevolent, fatherly and firm'. This model of enlightened imperialism had its equivalents elsewhere, although Frenchmen in general were dismissive of British civilisation, which they regarded as inferior to their own. For their part the British assumed the superiority of their own moral qualities which uniquely qualified them to govern. 'The British race', proclaimed Joseph Chamberlain, the future Colonial Secretary in 1885, was 'the greatest of governing races that the world has ever seen' and for this reason alone it was Britain's 'mission' to protect and enlarge her empire. In America, ardent imperialists followed a similar moral imperative; in 1900 Senator A.J. Beveridge announced that 'the civilisation of the world' was the God-given 'mission of our nation'. This was the opinion of Kipling, who believed in the brotherhood of all Anglo-Saxon nations. He aired the general view of their duty to uplift and civilise in his poem *The White Man's Burden,* which was an appeal to the American people after the annexation of the Philippines.

Those who shouldered the burden or undertook its French equivalent, the *'mission civilisatrice,'* had first to win over the hearts and minds of subject races and persuade them that what was being done was to their ultimate advantage. Marshal Lyautey, a soldier-administrator who had developed his theories in Indo-China during the 1890s, favoured what he called displays of 'our care and welfare for their [the natives] moral and material interests'. 'It is', he wrote:

> . . . in the moral sphere, the most noble, the highest and the purest one, that the most worthy work of France and her tradition is associated with the destiny of Moroccans—not as a subject people—but as a people who are benefiting thanks to our Protectorate,

from the fullness of their natural rights and the satisfaction of their moral needs.

These sentiments were echoed by Kipling who celebrated the conquest of the Sudan in 1898 with a poem whose theme was the British promise to build a university in Khartoum:

> They do not consider the Meaning of
>   Things;
> They consult nor creed nor clan.
> Behold, they clap the slave on the back,
> And behold he ariseth a man!
> They terribly carpet the earth with dead,
> And before their cannon cool,
> They walk unarmed by twos and threes
> To call the living to school.

This was reassuring since nearly 11,000 Sudanese had been killed by artillery, machine-gun and rifle fire during the recent battle of Omdurman. Such blood-letting was unparalleled in a colonial war of this period, but it had been necessary, argued the *Daily Mail's* war correspondent, G. W Steevens, to secure the 'downfall of the worst tyranny in the world' and to provide the Sudan with 'immunity from rape, torture and every extreme of misery'. His readers would have required no such reminder since the two-year campaign had been presented by the press as a contest between benign civilisation and brutal barbarism. The contrast was nicely shown in two *Daily Graphic* illustrations: a line drawing which portrayed a medical orderly tending a wounded Sudanese and a photograph of the bones of Jaalin tribesmen massacred at the orders of the Khalifa Abdullah.

And yet the Sudanese had fiercely resisted Kitchener's invasion. Wherever they went in the 1890s, the imperial powers had to overcome determined opposition before they could lay the foundations for their 'civilised' order. Even conquered people could display an alarming recidivism which some found inexplicable. Frederick Selous, colonist and big-game hunter, reflecting on the 1896 Ndebele uprising in Rhodesia, concluded that armchair imperialists were wrong to expect gratitude 'when we free a tribe of savages from what we consider a most oppressive and tyrannical form of government, overthrow the power of witch-doctors and take measures to safeguard life and property'. The evidence suggested not, and only the most condign chastisement, resolutely and repeatedly applied, would teach the natives 'the uselessness of rebelling against the white man'.

The dogma of the swift, annihilating response was outlined in forthright terms by General Sir Francis Younghusband who had spent much of the 1880s and 1890s putting it into practice:

> The moment there is a sign of revolt, mutiny or treachery, of which the symptoms not unusually are a swollen head, and a tendency to incivility, it is wise to hit the Oriental straight between the eyes, and to keep on hitting him thus, till he appreciates exactly what he is, and who is who.

Politicians, aware that the public could easily misunderstand the nature of these applications of main force, had to be more circumspect. Chamberlain told the Commons in 1895 that, 'expeditions, punitive or otherwise' were 'the only way we can establish peace between contending native tribes in Africa' and 'the only system of civilising and practically of developing the trade of Africa'. Like the nanny's smack or the caning delivered by the schoolmaster, war was a means of inducing the purblind or recalcitrant to accept what was best for their long-term interests.

The application of this simple doctrine revealed a gulf between the high-minded ideals of imperialism and the realities of empire-building. Columns of heavily-armed troops penetrated disaffected districts, chivvied rebels or resisters, burnt crops and villages and slaughtered or carried off livestock. Many found the work distasteful, others justified it on the grounds that barbarous methods were the only ones that would make a lasting impression on barbarous minds. One officer, in his published version of the mini-campaign fought against mutinous Sudanese askaris in Uganda in 1898–99, omitted details of the killing of the mutineers, families and was privately deeply ashamed of what he called a 'hateful' type of warfare. In French territories it took the form of the *razzia,* a systematic programme of destruction and looting designed to induce terror. During the suppression of the Maji Maji revolt of 1905–06 in German East Africa 75,000 died, nearly all the victims of an artificially created famine. Similar methods were employed by American troops in 1900 during the suppression *of* the Filipino revolt. Asked by

a Senate investigating committee to defend the burning of villages, General Robert P. Hughes answered, 'These people are not civilised'.

Hughes' reprisals against the Filipinos had been the response to that most exasperating form of native resistance, guerrilla warfare. In conventional conflicts, imperial armies relied on overwhelming firepower and the all-too-common attachment of many Asian and African generals to the traditional tactic of the headlong charge, often by warriors who had convinced themselves that they had supernatural protection from bullets. On the way to relieve the Peking legations in 1900, Captain Jellicoe, then commander of a naval landing party, was amazed by the Boxer onrush:

> Without any hesitation they charged a Maxim and were literally mown down—coming on at a jog trot and

collapsing when hit. They often stopped a few yards off and went through gesticulations for rendering themselves immune from bullet wounds.

Nevertheless over-confident, neglectful or rash commanders could suffer defeats. The Italians were trounced at Adowa in 1896 by an Ethiopian army which, unusually, had a sprinkling of machine guns and modern artillery, and two small French columns were overwhelmed in southern Chad in 1898–99. The chances of such disasters occurring had been reduced by the Brussels agreement of 1890 by which the European powers banned the import of modern weaponry into Africa.

Climates, fevers and intestinal distempers caused more casualties than native weaponry, modern or antiquated. Three thousand men, a third of the army,

Co-option of the white Dominions into Britain's imperial mission was an important psychological element in the enterprise—this *Punch* cartoon of the famous 1897 Spithead Naval Review captures perfectly the sentiment, with the British lion taking the young cubs out for the 'proudest moment of my life'.

Brand loyalty: the mingling of empire derring-do and product promotion at the end of the Victorian era was one of the most visible expressions of the way imperialism penetrated popular culture—as in this Pattison's whisky advertisement touching, in questionable taste, on the victories of the Sudan campaign.

died from diseases during the 1894–95 French campaign against the Hovas of Madagascar and only twenty-five from enemy action. Meticulous logistical planning prevented losses on this scale and, whenever possible, native troops and locally recruited auxiliaries were deployed in torrid or febriferous regions. Jollre's detachment of 380 which captured Timbuktu in 1894 contained only twenty-eight Frenchmen. British campaigns in East and West Africa were fought by black troops, Sudanese mercenaries and Sikhs borrowed from the Indian army. White officers and NCOs always commanded and, as a precaution, manned machine guns which were the key to victory on the imperial battlefield. In 1905 there was one machine gun to every 130 men in the German army in East Africa, a far higher proportion than would have been considered necessary in Europe.

Black, Egyptian, Arab, Indian and Indo-Chinese troops did most of the donkey work in the imperial wars of the 1890s. Their European officers prided themselves in their skill in choosing those races and tribes who were the most warlike and responsive to training and discipline. Furthermore, many believed that their ability to command rested on inner qualities, unique to their race.

French colonial officers fancied that they established a rapport with their men through *baraka,* an interior charisma possessed by Muslim holy men that brought the owner luck and the reverence of others. British officers attributed their power of leadership to character, that amalgam of bravery, selflessness, adherence to duty, team spirit and prowess in games that had been instilled in them by the post-Arnoldian public schools. These institutions produced young men who were ideally suited to command and govern; in 1911 a Guards officer insisted that 'Public School spirit and public spirit are almost synonymous'.

It was not a sense of public duty alone that impelled young officers to seek service on imperial frontiers. Many were drawn to the colonies through a love for adventure, high rates of pay, an addiction for sport, especially shooting game, and the chance to make a name for themselves that would guarantee rapid promotion. 'When one once started on *safari*—i.e. the line of march in Africa, one never knows where it may lead to' wrote one subaltern during the 1898 Uganda campaign. For Kitchener, Haig,

The Boer War in South Africa (above, a British heliograph crew in the field, 1899) excited unprecedented jingoism at home, though not necessarily with the troops. The British soldiers suffering heavy casualties and privations at the hands of the Boers, might well have had a sardonic word or two for the spectacle, left, of 'Arts Tribute to Arms'—an 'installation' to celebrate the relief of Mafeking prepared (complete with British lion and bust of Baden-Powell) by South Kensington Art Students.

Joffre and Gallieni the path led to high command while others, like Wingate, Lugard and Lyautey, stepped sideways and became high-ranking administrators.

All warrior preconsuls were unshaken in their belief that they were following a creed that was morally right. In many cases, they were impatient with political control exercised from afar by men ignorant of the day-to-day realities in areas where European power was still precarious. Some, particularly those anxious to make a career for themselves and win public attention, acted off their own bat or defied their political masters. In the early 1890s *commandant supérieur,* Louis Archinard, followed his own initiative and launched a series of offensives, including one against Timbuktu, that caused an exasperated official in Paris to complain about the 'State within a State' created in West Africa by a handful of disobedient officers. Lugard followed his own judgement rather than Chamberlain's and, in 1902, went ahead with preparations for a campaign in Northern Nigeria despite Colonial Office misgivings. Most famously, Rhodes engineered a *coup de main,* the Jameson Raid, against the Transvaal in 1895–96 in the belief that he was serving the best interests of the British Empire and with it the cause of civilisation in southern Africa which he believed would never be promoted by the Boers.

The insubordination and temerity of these men were excused by their domestic partisans, particularly newspaper proprietors and editors. Imperial wars sold newspapers and weekly illustrated journals like the *Graphic.* The 1890s witnessed a rapid expansion of newspaper readership with the appearance of a new type of daily designed to attract the working and lower-middle class. Heavily reliant on a sensational style, the new press paid special attention to imperial wars which were given extensive coverage with front-line reports and pictures. Recent extensions of the international telegraph network now made it possible for the public to read up-to-the-minute news of wars, even in the most distant lands; details of the 1896 Rhodesia campaign took less than a day to reach London from Bulawayo. Soldiers welcomed war correspondents, but cautiously for they had an uncomfortable knack of exposing blunders. 'Remember I can make or mar you' one journalist warned an uncooperative young officer during a NorthWest Frontier campaign.

Press treatment of imperial wars was vivid. During July, 1896, *Daily Graphic* readers saw spirited line drawings of scenes of fighting in the Sudan and on-the-spot sketches of the bodies of murdered settlers in Rhodesia. Most satisfying for those who accepted the empire as an agent of civilisation was a pencil drawing of Muslim chiefs swearing on the Quran to renounce slavery, watched by Royal Niger Company officers.

Each imperial war produced a crop of instant books, either compiled by war correspondents or written by officers who had taken part, like Winston Churchill, whose account of the Malakand campaign was published in 1897. Much imperial literature was directed at the young, produced to encourage patriotism and give examples of the manly courage demanded of those who served the empire. G. A. Henty was the prolific master-wordsmith of this genre. His tales of imperial wars were fast moving, picaresque adventures in which every page is crammed with incident. Issues are presented starkly; in *With Buller in Natal* (1900), the Boers are dismissed as 'an ignorant race, a race almost without even the elements of civilisation, ignorant and brutal beyond any existing white community'. By contrast, Henty's young heroes combine 'pluck' with resourcefulness, a way with the natives and true sportsmanship.

Imperial lessons were taught in thee schoolroom. In 1896 the *Practical Teacher* advocated regular lessons in elementary schools on the British Empire in which pupils would learn about the supremacy of the Royal Navy; the names of colonies and trade routes. Adults were reminded of such facts in advertisements; under a headline 'The two Greatest Navies in the World', Players Navy Cut tobacco displayed the product together with the numbers of British warships and sailors. During the Boer War copywriters went wild and fighting men in khaki endorsed mustard, tobacco, cigarettes, beef extracts and patent cure-alls. This was an attempt to cash in on the enormous public excitement aroused by the war in South Africa. Its early and dramatic phases dominated newspapers (headlines included 'Koorn Spruit Ambush' and 'More Deeds of Derring-Do') and newsreel footage was shot of troops on campaign for showing in cinemas.

Later when the war resolved itself into a tedious anti-guerrilla campaign, public concern waned and the views of opponents of the war made some headway. During the 1890s there had been those, mainly on the left, who were apprehensive about imperialist principles and critical of the methods used in imperial wars. Reports of the fighting in Rhodesia and war artists' drawings of horsemen galloping down fleeing natives provoked Irish and radical MPs to make charges of inhumanity and there was disquiet about stories of Kitchener riding in triumph into a captured Sudanese town followed by emirs laden with chains. Other, equally distressful incidents like the use of firing squads carrying out the execution of captured rebels to test the effectiveness of different types of ammunition on the North-West Frontier in 1895 were deliberately kept secret for fear of public outcry. The public did hear, in 1902, of the trial and execution of Lieutenants Morant and Handcock for the multiple murders of Boer POWs, a crime which left one senior officer fearful that the Boer War would 'degenerate into pure savagery'. Sometimes the civilisers came close to embracing the very vices they were fighting to extirpate.

Imperial wars of the 1890s aroused great public interest, most of it emotional and transient. Disappointed and enraged Italians rioted when they heard the baleful news of Aduwa; New York theatre goers cheered the popular song *Unchain the Dogs of War* as American fleets sailed for Cuba and the Philippines; and the British public swung between mass despondency and delirium during the Boer War. There was exhilaration of another kind in Khartoum when nationalist Egyptian officers heard news of British defeats in South Africa in 1899 which seemed to them to mark an end to a decade of European invincibility. Indian nationalists likewise took heart from the news of Japan's victories over Russia in 1905.

Domestic patriotic hysteria never travelled to the imperial front line. A Scottish volunteer yeomanry man in South Africa noticed that soldiers never sang the jingoistic songs so popular at home. Another yeomanry man discovered in Cape Town a book kept to record the comings and goings of young patriots like himself. It contained one entry that read: 'Reason for Joining: Patriotic Fever; Reason for Leaving: Enteric Fever'. There was always a gap between rhetoric and reality in the imperial wars of civilisation against barbarism.

FOR FURTHER READING:

The best general account of this subject is V. J. Kiernan, *European Empires from Conquest to Collapse, 1815–1960* (Fontana); Winston Churchill's *The Malakand Field Force, My Early Life* and *The River War* and Richard Meinertzhagen's *Kenya Diary* (Eland books) give valuable insights. Something of the flavour of war in the 1890s can be gained from old copies of the *Graphic* and *Illustrated London News* and the mood of popular imperialism is reflected in the boys' stories of G. A. Henty and Captain Brereton which are still plentiful in second-hand bookshops.

Unit Selections

Key Points to Consider

❖ What were some of Albert Robida's predictions for the future?

❖ Why should the Versailles Treaty be reexamined?

❖ How did the British reshape the Middle East after World War I?

❖ Describe school reform in Germany under the Nazis.

❖ How did Japan change as a result of Western-style constitutionalism, and what have been some of the results?

❖ Why did the U.S.–Soviet atomic rivalry never lead to a nuclear war?

❖ Is the United States still seen as the greatest world power of the millennium?

 **Links**   **www.dushkin.com/online/**

These sites are annotated on pages 4 and 5.

The nineteenth century ended with high hopes for the future of Western civilization. Popular novelists foresaw air travel, television, visual telephones, records, and space travel, and even the construction of a new continent in the Pacific. Technology would liberate those living in this century from most of their burdens, or so argued the futurists of the time. There were skeptics of course: Mark Twain punctured the pious hypocrisies of Westerners who presumed that their Christianity and technology demonstrated their superiority over the heathens of the non-Western world. And a few writers questioned whether humans would be any happier, even with all the material benefits that the future promised.

Even before this glittering future could be realized, turn-of-the-century artists and thinkers brought forth an alternative vision of far greater originality. They set in motion a period of unprecedented cultural innovation and artistic experimentation, out of which emerged modern music, theater, literature, art, and architecture. Never before had there been so many cultural manifestos: Fauvism, Cubism, and Futurism. In "When Cubism Met the Decorative Arts in France," Paul Trachtman traces the lasting influence of one such movement. In philosophy it was the age of pragmatism, positivism, and Bergsonism. On the intellectual frontier, Alfred Binet, Ivan Pavlov, and Sigmund Freud reformulated the premises of psychology. Advanced work in experimental science concentrated on radioactivity and the atom, setting the stage for Albert Einstein's abstract theories.

Thus, in the years before World War I, the West was able to point to unrivaled accomplishments. Aristocrats and the middle class were confident of the future because they were eminently satisfied with the present.

In hindsight, all this seems a great illusion. We can now see how such illusions blinded Europeans to the coming war. Millions of lives were lost in World War I, which was a showcase for the destructive forces of European technology. The war dashed the hopes of an entire generation and contributed to revolutions in Russia, Germany, and Austria, the breakup of the Ottoman Empire, the collapse of the international economy, and the emergence of totalitarian dictatorships: all factors that, in turn, brought on World War II.

Robert Hendrick's article, "Albert Robida's Imperfect Future," describes the accurate predictions of the technological future. The essays "Two Cheers for Versailles" and "How the Modern Middle East Map Came to Be Drawn" trace many current problems to the international politics of the World War I settlement. In "Nazism in the Classroom," Lisa Pine explores fascism in Germany. "Six Days to Reinvent Japan" recounts the U.S. role in establishing Western-style constitutionalism in Japan after World War II. John Lewis Gaddis, in "Face-Off," examines the political and military tensions between the United States and Russia that led to the cold war. The article "The Future That Never Came," by Mitchell Reiss, explains why the U.S.–Soviet rivalry did not produce a nuclear war. "Mutable Destiny: The End of the American Century?" questions whether the United States will be able to keep its hegemony.

Albert Robida's Imperfect Future

A 19th-century French novelist's vision of the future included not just television, air transport and women in the workplace, but also biological warfare and population crises. **Robert Hendrick** examines the predictions of Albert Robida.

Who, before the First World War, most accurately predicted to the public the shape of the world that we now live in? Who best foresaw the scientific and technological miracles that we take for granted? At the same time, who most clearly perceived and warned of the environmental and ecological dangers that would accompany these advances? And finally, who predicted the close cooperation between science and the military that would result in biological, chemical, and other doomsday weapons? The answer to all four questions is the same person.

It is a good bet that most people would answer with the name of Jules Verne. The recent publication of Verne's 'lost' novel, *Paris in the Twentieth Century,* 131 years after it was written, has drawn considerable public attention primarily because Verne predicted the automobile and mass transit systems. Although Jules Verne is not a bad response, there is a much better one. For while Verne guessed correctly about some aspects of our civilisation, he did not fully perceive what our world would be like, nor did he publish his futuristic predictions in his own lifetime. The man who most clearly and accurately predicted the shape of the technological revolution that has marked the twentieth century was not Verne (nor H.G. Wells), but rather a now-forgotten French writer and illustrator named Albert Robida (1848–1926).

At the end of the last century, Robida was a well-known Parisian illustrator who for a dozen years edited the popular magazine *La Caricature,* and who pub-lished thousands of amusing, satirical drawings reflecting *la belle époque* in his own and in scores of other French magazines and newspapers. A prodigious worker, he wrote and illustrated eighty books on subjects ranging from travel, to histories of France, to children's stories. He even found time to illustrate 169 books by other authors. His drawings were carefree and fanciful; they had many of the qualities of humour and observation which have made Gary Larson's *Far Side* cartoons so successful today. Contemporaries especially enjoyed his depictions of young women whose gay, effervescent vitality and innocent eroticism was similar to the women in the posters of Jules Chéret, which were so popular they were stolen off walls as soon as they were hung. It was a style that fitted the times and made both men wealthy.

But Robida was best known for three novels he wrote between 1882 and 1892 which predicted what life would be like in the mid-twentieth century. These books were an offshoot of a new literary genre, the 'scientific novel', begun by Jules Verne in the 1860s. In this genre, scientific knowledge and technology played a major role in the development of the plot. Robida was to be the most successful of Verne's emulators, but his novels of anticipation differed from Verne's in two key ways.

Firstly, while Verne knew much more science and based all his fictional technology on known facts (he had filled 25,000 note cards with scientific information), Robida had a kind of intuitive sixth sense that allowed him to guess where technological advances would lead without being able to explain the scientific principles involved in their development. Robida just assumed scientists would be able to create the inventions he envisioned. He let his imagination run wild and in the process more accurately predicted the technological and social developments of our contemporary world than any other forecaster of his time.

Secondly, while the deluxe editions of Verne's novels were profusely illustrated by professional artists, their drawings tended to rely on the massive size of machinery and weapons to impress and overwhelm the reader. Robida, on the other hand, used his own whimsical drawings to illustrate his novels and he has been described as the most gifted and original artist in the history of science fiction. Like Chéret, Robida realised that appealing drawings, especially of pretty girls, sell products; in this case, his own novels. On the title page of *Le vingtième siècle,* for example, while the background depicts all kinds of marvellous technological developments, the shapely, hourglass figure of a young woman dominates the drawing.

It is the unerring accuracy with which Robida predicted the technological, scientific, and even social advances of our century that makes his work so remarkable. Among the more important of his predictions were giant-screen television sets, with multiple programmes to select from; radio; twenty-four-hour worldwide news coverage in 'real time'; video telephones; college courses given on television; rapid air transportation and transcontinental air routes; bullet trains; rain making; shopping by telephone; 'test tube' babies; genetic engineering; fast food outlets; the development of national park systems and prison reform.

Robida also predicted the economic, political and social emancipation of women, even to the extent of foreseeing revolutions in dress such as the miniskirt and tight-fitting jeans. On a negative note, he foresaw the formation of the military-industrial complex, the use of chemical and biological warfare, the need to develop gas masks and the vast ecological and environmental destruction caused by the advance of science and technology in the industrialised world.

The first of Robida's futuristic novels, *Le vingtième siècle* appeared in fifty installments in his magazine in 1882, and was then published in a book edition in 1883 that was reissued five times over the next decade. Set far in the future in the early 1950s, its rather simplistic plot revolves around the humorous attempts of a multi-millionaire banker, Raphael Ponto, to find a career for his charming but scatterbrained ward, Helene (the aforementioned young woman on the title page). His efforts fail because Helene lacks both interest and vocational skills. All ends well, however, when she marries Ponto's son.

But it wasn't the plot that attracted Robida's readers. They were more interested in his humour (which could be biting—especially when he satirised social practices), his lively and highly-imaginative drawings and most of all by his promise that the future would be one of unending progress. Both his text and pictures expressed the conviction that the future of civilisation would be one of constant scientific and technological advance. In this optimistic view, Robida perfectly caught the dominant faith in progress that marked his period. At this time, many French scientists were encouraging the public to believe that science was uncovering all nature's secrets; just two years after *Le vingtième siècle* was published, the chemist Marcelin Berthelot assured the French public that there were no more scientific mysteries left. Meanwhile, Louis Pasteur's successes in combatting anthrax, swine fever and rabies made Berthelot's claim seem valid and Robida's predictions extremely convincing.

Robida envisioned a world where every middle-class family would own one or two airships. One illustration shows his design for a holiday home; the higher structure is the 'garage' for the family's airships. Interestingly, he did not mention the possibility of the automobile; when cars became common, he detested their noise and fumes. Robida's middle-class family would also have four or five servants, would own homes in the city and in the country, have access to rapid transportation systems, and would own all the electrical appliances we are familiar with today—except computers. Because of the rapid strides being made by scientists such as Pasteur, whose work was reported and followed in the daily newspapers, none of these predictions of future technological wonders seemed quite as outlandish to Robida's readers as we might at first suspect.

There were, however, some less enlightened aspects of his futuristic vision—in particular, from our perspective his views of women and of the working class seem totally nonprogressive. In *Le vingtième siècle,* women have won full political and social freedom and all careers are open to them, they are even depicted operating their own stock exchange. But throughout the novel Robida, who was a devoted husband who occasionally collaborated with his daughter in his publications, ridicules women. He portrays them as lazy, stupid, or insecure, mainly because they try to take advantage of the rights they have won. Their real sin, in his eyes, is that they have become 'masculinised'. Like virtually all men of his class in the period, Robida believed that a woman's place was in the home. Jules Verne was no different. For example, in 1893 he urged the young women at a girls school in Amiens to devote their intellectual abilities to creating 'a pleasant family home and hearth'.

Nor did Robida care for the working classes, who are depicted in his novels when they are mentioned at all, as either servants or thieves. These negative views of the ability of women to function outside the home and the fear of the working classes were deeply ingrained in his bourgeois readers. But aside from these two, to our eyes, somewhat jarring notes, *Le vingtième siècle* remains an optimistic and amazingly accurate vision of life in the second half of the twentieth century.

Robida was also among the first to recognise that science and technology have two faces and that their positive aspects are inevitably linked to negative impacts. Dreams of progress, he began to feel, should not blind one to the environmental nightmares that technological advances can produce. Such a point seems obvious to us today after accidents in the nuclear-power industry, oil spills, acid rain, ozone depletion and so forth. But it was not at all understood by Robida's progress-happy contemporaries. By 1887 he began to worry about environmental issues and about the possible misuse of science by scientists for their personal gain.

The first reflection of these concerns was in his futuristic vision of the alliance of science and technology with the military. *La guerre au vingtième siècle (The War of the Twentieth Century)* first appeared in instalments in *La Caricature* and was published in book form in 1887. In this novel, Robida produced the first modern vision of technological warfare ever published. He predicted the use of submarines, tanks, planes and other weapons we now, unhappily, take for granted.

What was most modern about this novel was his premonition of the use of science by the military in the production of chemical and biological weapons. *La guerre* was part of a new literary genre that emerged in England, France and Germany in the 1870s in which the novelist described an imaginary invasion of his country in the near future. William Le Queux and E. Phillips Oppenheim in England both grew rich writing dozens of these potboilers. These futuristic novels reflected current European international tensions and described existing weapons systems. But Robida was alone in describing the enlistment of the sciences in the fictional creation of new weapons for the future. Although H. G. Wells would later incorporate futuristic weapons into *The War of the Worlds,* he saw them as fanciful weapons developed by alien cultures. In other words, he did not foresee that they could or would be produced on earth. Robida's chemical and bacteriological weapons were much more realistic and accurate in their prediction of the future. Nevertheless, Robida's drawings were so fanciful, *La guerre* conveys no sense of terror or even alarm to the reader. In fact, the benign quality of his art probably goes a long way toward explaining why Robida has slipped into obscurity; his readers simply did not take them seriously, even when he used them to convey a warning.

Late in 1891, Robida began publishing, again in serial form, the last of this trilogy of futuristic novels, *La vie électrique (The Electric Life)*. Published in single-volume form in 1893 and reissued four times over the next decade, La vie electrique was a sequel to *Le vingtième siècle*. While the characters are all new, the setting remains the same with all the miracles of science and technology he created in the earlier novel still intact. The plot is as unsophisticated as that of its predecessor. Set in 1956, it focuses on the attempts of a wealthy scientist and manufacturer, Philox Lorris, to break up the love affair of his son, Georges, with the not-terribly-bright Estelle. Of course, he fails; as in the earlier novel, love finds a way and Estelle and Georges are married.

Once again, it was not the plot that attracted his readers, but rather Robida's vision of a futuristic world of continual scientific and technological progress. In the beginning of *La vie électrique*, Robida's picture of science was what his readers had come to expect: television, airships, video phones, and so forth. He reflected the impact of Darwinism on the general public when he referred to 'the great law of selection' which could be used 'to establish, by a carefully studied selection process, a true superior race'; a position that heralded the eugenics movement that was just getting under way. Using the immense public adulation of Louis Pasteur as his inspiration, Robida had Lorris organise a massive effort to develop a 'microbe of health' which would counteract the diseases faced by humans. This colossal optimism about the power of science was captured by Robida through Georges Lorris' complaint to his father that the nineteenth century had made so many strides there was nothing left to invent or discover. Taken aback by his

son's *naiveté*, Lorris responds with a statement that perfectly captured the late nineteenth-century public's faith in science: 'We are only at the first stammerings of science; the next century will laugh at us'.

Yet as the novel progresses, a darker view of science emerges. At the same time that Lorris is searching for the microbe of health', he is also making a fortune developing and selling weapons such as artillery shells filled with asphyxiating and paralysing gases and biologically dangerous organisms. As was the case with Jules Verne toward the end of his career, Robida was clearly beginning to worry about the ability of scientists for doing evil as well as good.

He expresses great concern over environmental dangers toward the end of *La vie électrique*. His drawings begin to depict industrial waste destroying the quality of the air and rivers and killing wildlife. Lorris admits that because of the advance of science: 'Our air is dirty and polluted . . . Our rivers carry virtual purees of the most dangerous bacilli; our streams swarm with pathogenic ferments'.

At the end of the book, Robida shows he has become ambivalent about the future that science and technology promise. If science can furnish man with 'powerful weapons in the great struggle of life against death,' it also provides him with the 'most formidable means of destruction'. Ultimately, Robida surrenders to what seems to him to be the uncontrollable march of scientific advances: 'Let us bow before the sovereign power of science!'

That resigned acceptance of both aspects of science was probably the most accurate prediction he ever made. Science and technology can both cure and destroy. Science today seems more a mysterious force of progress and, at the

same time, appears more uncontrollable than it ever did to Robida. Yet he deserves credit for being one of the first to recognise the two faces of progress. Robida's own disillusionment with science and technology was symbolised by the fact that when the French government held a competition for projects for the Universal Exposition to be held in 1900, he suggested not a science fiction version of a city of the future, but rather the re-creation of a medieval town. The government accepted his plan for Vieux Paris. Old Paris was one of the most successful attractions of the Exposition.

FOR FURTHER READING:

There is very little on Robida in French and even less in English. None of his novels have been translated into English. A listing of his publications and illustrations can be found in Philippe Brum, *Albert Robida (1898–1926)* (Editions Promodis, 1984). The material below either mentions Robida or would be of interest to those who find the topic appealing. Marc Angenot, 'Albert Robida's Twentieth Century', *Science-Fiction Studies*, 10 (1983); I.F. Clarke, *Voices Prophesying War, 1763–1984* (Oxford University Press, 1966); Arthur B. Evans, *Jules Verne Rediscovered: Didacticism and the Scientific Novel* (Greenwood Press, 1988); Arthur B. Evans, Science Fiction', in Pierre L. Horn (ed.), *Handbook of French Popular Culture* (Greenwood Press, 1991); Anthony Frewin, *One Hundred Years of Science Fiction Illustration, 1840–1940* Jupiter Books, 1974).

Robert Hendrick *is Professor of History at St John's University, New York, and a contributor to L. Grinstein, C. Biermann, R. Rose (eds) Women in the Biological Sciences: A Biobibliographic Sourcebook (Greenwood Press, 1997).*

When Cubism Met the Decorative Arts in France

From side tables to the dazzling dress designs of Sonia Delaunay, an exhibition at the Portland Museum in Maine surveyed the scene

Paul Trachtman

Paul Trachtman's most recent SMITHSONIAN *article was about the computer artist Charles Csuri (February 1995). He writes from New Mexico.*

When we invented Cubism, we had no intention whatsoever of inventing Cubism," said Pablo Picasso, many years later. "We wanted simply to express what was in us." What was in Picasso and his contemporaries was a voracious, if not violent, appetite for new forms of intellectual, cultural and industrial life that were shaping a nascent 20th century. The decorative and flowing Art Nouveau, along with the vibrant and emotional expressiveness of the Impressionist painters—a last flowering of 19th-century Romanticism—was cast aside for the new ideas of Freud and Einstein, stripping bare the human psyche and the physical universe. When a prominent collector objected to Picasso's use of house paint in some 1912 paintings, the artist told his Paris dealer, "Perhaps we shall succeed in disgusting everyone, and we haven't said everything yet."

At first, there wasn't much of a public to disgust. Early critical responses to the new Cubist art ranged from "ugly" to "grotesque," but only a few people actually looked at it, even in Paris. Gertrude Stein, an American writer in Paris who was doing away with grammar as Picasso did away with perspective and anatomy, recorded the young painter's ire at his critics: "Picasso said to me once with a good deal of bitterness, they say I can draw better than Raphael and probably they are right, perhaps I do draw better but if I can draw as well as Raphael I have at least the right to choose my way and they should recognize it, that right, but no, they say no."

Yet, despite its early limited influence, the new style spread from the artists' studios to the salons and then into popular culture in a relatively short time. By the 1920s, about the same time that the Spanish philosopher José Ortega y Gasset was declaring modern art "antipopular" and predicting that it "will always have the masses against it," a modern geometric style of decorative arts, drawn partly from Cubism, was inspiring French designers of clothing, furniture, lamps, clocks, dinnerware, even architecture. By the mid-1920s, the new Art Deco style had spread into almost every aspect of popular life. Its influence would soon be seen in the United States as well, in the sleek geometric facades of movie palaces, roadside diners and gas stations, and the stripped-down fashions of the flapper era. By 1925, when an international exposition of decorative and industrial arts was staged in Paris, a critic could see Cubism's influence in epochal terms, writing: "With the Exposition des Arts Décoratifs a new style is established to take its place with the historic periods. To the Renaissance, the Jacobean, the Georgian, the Rococo and the Colonial is added the Modern."

The popularity of Cubism in the decorative arts caught the attention of Kenneth Wayne, a young curator at the Portland Museum of Art in Maine, who went on to organize the museum's show "Picasso, Braque, Léger and the Cubist Spirit, 1919–1939," which [ran] through October [1996]. One part of the show set the objects of Art Deco design alongside paintings and sculptures of the Cubists from the years between the two world wars. And in doing so, it offers a rare chance to see the Cubists from a different angle, a fresh perspective.

The first Cubist brushstrokes appeared in Picasso's historic painting *Les Demoiselles d'Avignon,* made in 1907. A composition that combines elements of realism, primitive form and geometric abstraction, it depicts five nude figures gathered around a small arrangement of fruits. It was not yet Cubism but certainly pointed the way with faces inspired by African masks or broken down into geometric forms, with breasts and torsos represented by diamonds, rectangles and triangles along with more natural orbs and curves. Perspective was diminished in the flat planes of the painting, and the background fractured, as if the scene were reflected in a broken mirror. What was indeed reflected in this painting was the legacy of Paul Cézanne (SMITHSONIAN, April 1996), his flattened landscapes and still lifes expressing the elemental forms and planes of nature.

Georges Braque met Picasso around this time, and in 1909 they began a collaboration that could be called the invention of Cubism. Henri Matisse, seeing some Braques the year before, rather scornfully coined the term "Cub-

From *Smithsonian*, July 1996, pp. 45-51. © 1996 by Paul Trachtman. Reprinted by permission of the author.

ism." For the next few years, Braque and Picasso maintained a close but private relationship, showing each other their new paintings and constructions. These works were part of their visual dialogue, and it was often hard to tell which artist painted which. They rarely exhibited in the Paris salons, but other artists, visiting their studios and glimpsing their work, were converted to the new style.

Fernand Léger, fascinated with the machines and designs of industrial society, found in Cubism an ideal technique to express his own vision of modern life. Juan Gris, more intrigued with the landscape of his own mind than the outer world, gave Cubism its purest, most mathematical form, using a compass and ruler to plot out his paintings. Others, including Matisse and the young Mexican painter Diego Rivera, who came to Paris in 1912, had brief flirtations with the Cubist style. The sculptor Jacques Lipchitz cast Cubist images in bronze. "What began as a rarefied pictorial style," says Kenneth Wayne, "became a popular language." To understand this language, it helps to clear away the layers of interpretation that have been added over the years. "Mathematics, trigonometry, chemistry, psychoanalysis, music and whatnot have been related to Cubism to give it an easier interpretation," Picasso once complained. "All this has been pure literature, not to say nonsense, which brought bad results, blinding people with theories."

The show Wayne has put together includes more than 100 paintings, sculptures, prints and decorative objects made in the two decades after World War I, when Picasso and Braque emerged from their hermetic, prewar collaborations into a Cubism that could delight the senses. Among the paintings in the show one finds two Braque still lifes with a bright, decorative air: his *Pipe and Basket* of 1919 and 1927's *Still Life with Pears, Lemons and Almonds.* The later work seems an almost playful throwback to the still lifes of Cézanne, with the table slightly tilted and everything just about to slip off. There is also Picasso's *Harlequin Musician* of 1924, a vibrant play of form and color in a figure that may represent the artist himself. "Picasso identified with the harlequin figure," one critic observed, "because it's an entertainer, a trickster, a figure on the fringes of society, and that's how he saw himself."

One of the most striking paintings in the show is Fernand Léger's *Two Women,* made in 1922 when the artist turned to human rather than purely industrial forms in the hope of coming closer to life, albeit life with a metallic sheen. He was seeking a Cubism the working class could understand, his wife recalled.

The decorative objects in the show are displayed in two large alcoves, where one can clearly see the influence of the artists on popular style and fashion. A vivid example of this influence is the ceramic vase made by Robert Lallemant in the late '20s; its jagged edges and geometric motifs use the same Cubist vocabulary as the canvases on the walls near it. A folding screen by decorator Jean Dunand and a pair of side tables by Pierre Chareau exhibit a Cubist play of planes, as if blurring the distinction between flat and three-dimensional space.

In its emphasis on geometric forms, Cubism was often mistaken as a rejection of nature and the landscape altogether. But Picasso declared, "One cannot go against nature; it is stronger than the strongest man."

The bold, geometric clothing designs of Sonia Delaunay, a painter who once collaborated on fashions with Coco Chanel, are another highlight of the Portland Museum show. Delaunay, like Picasso, designed costumes for Diaghilev's avant-garde Ballet Russes, but her successes in the world of textiles and fashion took Cubism off the stage and into the streets, ready to wear.

Her dresses first appeared in Paris just before the war, in 1913–14, when she wore them to the Bal Bullier, a popular dance hall where artists and poets tried out new dances like the fox-trot and the tango. Delaunay's dresses were made from geometric scraps of various fabrics, combining taffeta and tulle, flannel and silk, in bright, contrasting colors, from violet and green to scarlet and blue. She dressed her husband, Robert, also a painter, with similar style. One account describes him as wearing "a red oat with blue collar, a green jacket, sky-blue waistcoat, a tiny red tie, black pants, red socks, black-and-yellow shoes." By the war's end, Delaunay could sell her designs from her own Paris boutique and attract such famous customers as the Hollywood actress Gloria Swanson. By 1923 her geometric patterns were being printed by a French silk manufacturer. Soon after, her garments could be found in London and New York department stores.

The Portland show is significant not only for its content but for its location as well. Small and medium-sized museums around the country are becoming more important to our cultural life at a time when great blockbuster shows are ever more costly and difficult to mount. "There will always be the blockbusters," says Wayne, "but the smaller museums are doing interesting things that draw on their own strengths." Wayne arrived at the Portland Museum of Art only a year ago, fresh out of Stanford graduate school, and was asked to organize a major exhibition for this summer. "I've been sprinting ever since," he says.

The show at the Portland Museum is an invitation to take another look at what the Cubists were up to. It was a sociable world where Cubists and other young artists rubbed shoulders. Picasso went horseback riding with Matisse; Modigliani sketched Picasso in a restaurant; and avant-garde writers, composers and painters all gathered together at cafés, salons and dinner tables.

Even the lines between fine art and the decorative arts were in question. Duchamp hung hardware on gallery walls. Sonia Dulaunay made Cubist-inspired dresses. Le Corbusier painted still lifes and also designed houses, which he defined as machines for living in. Léger saw machines as objects of beauty.

The Cubists and their friends were taking their cues from their environment: from the landscape, the streets, the materials of everyday life. "When one crosses a landscape by automobile or express train, it becomes fragmented," Léger said. "A modern man registers a hundred times more sensory impressions than an eighteenth-century artist. . . . The compression of the modern picture, its variety, its breaking up of forms, are the result of all this." Painting, he declared, "has never been so truly realistic, so firmly attached to its own period as it is today." To claim realism for the geometric Cubist compositions may seem like a bit of avant-garde hyperbole, but Léger was being quite literal. "We live in a geometric world," he asserted. The Cubists were painting their experience of the world, a world in which "rupture and change crop up unexpectedly."

In its emphasis on geometric forms, Cubism was often mistaken as a rejection of nature and the landscape altogether. Ortega y Gasset described the modern painter as willfully blind to nature: "He shuts his eyes to the outer world and concentrates upon the subjective images in his own mind." But this is hardly what Léger or Picasso had in mind. On one of the rare occasions when he really spoke about his art, Picasso declared, "One cannot go against nature; it is stronger than the strongest man." Gertrude Stein recalled his bringing back some early Cubist paintings of a Spanish village after a trip to Spain in 1909: "Picasso had by chance taken some photographs of the village that he had painted and it always amused me when every one protested the fantasy of the pictures . . .[he wanted to show them] that the pictures were almost exactly like the photographs." It was as if Picasso saw Cubism out of one eye, reality with the other.

It was not the details but the emotions, the feeling of life and nature that Picasso was after. "The painter goes through states of fullness and evacuation," he said. "That is the whole secret of art. I go for a walk in the forest of Fontainebleau. I get 'green' indigestion. I must get rid of this sensation into a picture. Green rules it. A painter paints to unload himself of feelings and visions."

Léger sometimes seemed to doubt that he could ever paint with the vividness of the real machinery all around him. Once recalling a showing of his paintings at an annual Paris exhibition, the Salon d'Automne, he wrote: "I had the advantage of being next to the Aviation Show, which was about to open. I jumped over the barrier, and never had such a stark contrast assailed my eyes. I left vast surfaces, dismal and gray, pretentious in their frames, for beautiful, metallic objects, hard, permanent, and useful, in pure local colors; infinite varieties of steel surfaces at play next to vermilions and blues. The power of geometric forms dominated it all."

Cubism was not the only new art movement that flourished in the avant-garde movement. There were the Futurists, the Surrealists, the Dadaists, and there was Matisse who ignored them all.

The vividness Léger found in the Aviation Show had its match in the life of the Paris avant-garde. Looking back, we tend to think of the Cubists only in terms of their art, as though they were making their painting in a vacuum. But they were living in an exciting milieu, and the artists and their lives often provided the raw material of Cubism. A few anecdotes, like old snapshots, give only a faded impression of the time: Gertrude Stein observed that Picasso often got new ideas from writers, not from other painters. Jean Cocteau was one of those writers. Soon after they met, Picasso asked Cocteau to pose for him. In turn, Cocteau invited Picasso to join him and the composer Erik Satie in collaborating on costumes and sets for the ballet *Parade*. "Picasso was the great encounter for me," Cocteau wrote of his visits to the painter's studio. "How my heart pounded as I hurried up those stairs." Marcel Duchamp, who made his second sale of a painting to the dancer Isadora Duncan, knew the writers, too. "The amusing thing about the literary people of that time," he recalled, "was that, when you met two authors, you couldn't get a word in edgewise. . . . One was torn between a sort of anguish and an insane laughter."

Like Gertrude Stein, the young American writer Ernest Hemingway was in Paris and became intrigued by the painters. Hemingway claimed that he studied the Cézannes at the Louvre to improve his writing style and said he could see Cubist images in the nightlife of a Paris street. There were no sewers, and at night tank wagons pumped out the cesspools of the old apartment buildings. "The tank wagons were painted brown and saffron color," he wrote, "and in the moonlight when they worked the rue Cardinal Lemoine their wheeled, horsedrawn cylinders looked like Braque paintings."

Cubism was not the only new art movement that flourished in this avant-garde hothouse. There were the Futurists, the Surrealists, the Dadaists, and there was Matisse who ignored them all. But it was Cubism that had the greatest impact on the popular mind, producing a new visual consciousness.

The Cubists' view of things became more understandable as the world was fractured by World War I. In fact, the war was a kind of alchemy through which a modern consciousness was formed from its elements. As the French mobilized, Gertrude Stein was with Picasso at a telling moment. "I very well remember at the beginning of the war being with Picasso on the boulevard Raspail when the first camouflaged truck passed," she wrote. "It was at night, we had heard of camouflage but we had not yet seen it and Picasso amazed looked at it and then cried out, yet it is we who made it, that is Cubism."

It wasn't only the camouflage that was Cubist. The French novelist Louis-Ferdinand Céline portrayed the war, as seen by a young soldier, in images a Cubist well might have painted. When Picasso described his pictures as "a sum of destructions," he was talking about esthetics, not war. "I do a picture—then I destroy it," he said. "In the end, though, nothing is lost: the red I took away from one place turns up somewhere else." But a Cubist esthetic that defined the creative process in terms of destructions seemed less strange after the shock of World War I. Céline's soldier, and many others, saw both armies as madmen "shut up on earth as if it were a looney bin, ready to demolish everything on it, Germany, France, whole continents, everything that breathes, destroy, destroy. . . ." As Gertrude Stein saw it, people "were forced by the war to recognize Cubism."

As the war ended, French designers did more than recognize it. They helped to popularize it. Their "capricious geometry" was set in concrete mansions, embodied in tubular steel furniture, printed onto wallpaper and textiles, even embroidered into women's shoes. One innovation of the Cubist painters, the arresting surface textures and odd materials in some of their canvases and collages, was seized on with gusto by the designers. Braque had painted still lifes with oils and sand on canvas, for example, and Picasso produced collages with dishcloth fabric, pins and nails. Then the designers rushed in, adding exciting new contrasts and materials as well as new forms to popular decor and fashion.

Sonia Delaunay's postwar couture sometimes combined fur, wool and silk. Le Corbusier introduced a leather and metal chaise longue molded to fit the

When Picasso painted a portrait, he wanted us to see a face not as God created it but as Picasso created it. He rearranged it so we would see what he had made.

human body. Interior designer Marcel Guillemard dreamed up a Cubist cabinet and bar made of metal tubing and square panels stacked in pivoting sections that could swing out at various angles; it would fit right in with the plastic cubes and sectional furniture found in today's shopping malls. Others achieved their effects with new and sometimes improb-

able juxtapositions of materials. Jacques Le Chevallier designed a desk lamp of aluminum and plastic, cut into trapezoids and rectangles, with adjustable metal flaps for the shade. And Pierre Legrain's faceted, geometric clock was made of metal and sharkskin.

The Cubists kept on painting after the war, although heading in different directions. While Braque mostly stuck to his still lifes and Léger began to explore biomorphic forms, Picasso pursued several other styles along with Cubism, including Neoclassicism and Surrealism, and sometimes put them all into the same painting. By then the Cubist spirit was alive and well in the world, and the original Cubists knew that they had been seen, if not always understood. And that was what they were really after. When Picasso painted a portrait, for example, he wanted us to see a face not as God created it but as Picasso created it. He rearranged it so we would see what he had made. As he quipped about one of his Cubist portraits, "I had to make the nose crooked so they would see it was a nose."

Two Cheers for Versailles

Mark Mazower *looks back to the much maligned Versailles Treaty and finds we still live in the continent it created.*

THE VERSAILLES TREATY settlement was, from the moment of its birth, unloved as few creations of international diplomacy have been before or since. Hitler and Churchill were united in its condemnation; so were commentators from the American anti-Soviet diplomat and historian George Kennan to the British Marxist E.H. Carr. One is hard put to find a school textbook with anything good to say about the achievements of the Paris peacemakers. Yet curiously we still live in the world they shaped: were the foundations laid more carefully by them than we like to think? The argument that the defects of Versailles led to the outbreak of another world war is commonplace; yet one might as easily argue that its virtues underpinned the peace after 1945.

Some suggest that Versailles was based on principles inconsistently applied. The charge is obviously true. The right of national self-determination was granted at Germany's expense, and the *Anschluss* with Austria, which Social Democrats in Vienna wanted in 1918, was prevented by the Great Powers and only achieved after the Nazis broke the League of Nations system and marched in twenty years later. But international affairs are not a matter of logic alone, and the principle of consistency must be matched against considerations of power politics or geography. National self-determination could never have been applied across the board; the basic issue is whether a better principle existed for the re-ordering of Europe.

More serious an accusation is that the peace settlement was not so much inconsistent as ineffective: it was based upon an inaccurate appraisal of the European balance of power and deprived of the means of its own defence by American withdrawal and British indifference. At Paris the Great Powers ignored the fact that the almost simultaneous collapse of Germany and Russia had produced an anomalous situation in eastern Europe. The French, who of all the Great Powers felt most immediately threatened, thought the only safeguard of their own security—if the League was not to be equipped with an army of its own—was alliance with grateful clients like the Baltic states, Poland, Czechoslovakia, Romania and Yugoslavia. But it should have been obvious that the newly independent states formed there would be unable alone to ensure stability in the region once these two Great Powers reasserted themselves. The Treaty of Brest Litovsk of early 1918 had shown what intentions the Germans of the *Kaiserreich* harboured in that area; after 1939, Hitler's New Order pushed the principle of German (and Russian) hegemony one brutal stage further. But this is less an argument against the Versailles settlement itself than against the refusal of the Great Powers who sponsored it to back it up with armed force before 1939.

Thirdly, it is often felt that the whole approach to Germany after the Treaty was flawed. The enemy was humiliated but not crushed, burdened by reparations yet unopposed when it rearmed and marched into the Rhineland. It is true that the contrast is striking with the policies pursued towards Germany after the Second World War when long-term economic assistance was provided and by governments not the markets, and when the *Bundeswehr* was quickly incorporated within west European defence arrangements. But the economic problem after 1919 was not so much reparations as the shaky structure of international lending and, in particular, the shock of the world depression. The Allies were helped to learn from the mistakes of the inter-war era by the Cold War, which divided Germany, and made Europe's German problem a question of reunification rather than of territorial expansion and *revanche* in the East.

Finally, there is the accusation common to conservatives and Communists alike that the Versailles peace settlement was overly ideological. For some, it was an extension of nineteenth-century liberal moralising, a combination of British utilitarianism and American idealism—a basically philosophical approach to the world which lacked realism or understanding of the political passions which animated people in Europe.

Alternatively, it was—behind the veil of noble sentiments—an anti-Communist crusade whose liberalism masked a fundamentally reactionary and deeply conservative goal: the containment, if not the crushing, of Bolshevism. Outflanked gradually by other more determined and forceful anti-Communist movements of the right, European liberals lost their enthusiasm for defending the Versailles order and sat back to watch fascism take over the task of saving Europe from red revolution.

One question, however, confronts the critics of Versailles: what were the alternatives? It was not, after all, as if the Powers had willed this new liberal order of independent, democratic nation-states into existence. They had certainly not been fighting the Great War to this end. On the contrary, as late as 1918 most Entente diplomats still favoured the preservation of the old empires in central Europe in the interests of continental stability. Of course, after 1919 the conflicts and tensions produced by the new

This article first appeared in *History Today*, July 1999, pp. 8-14. © 1999 by History Today, Ltd. Reprinted by permission.

Europe 1919 and 1999: the borders drawn at Versailles have been subjected to many challenges and conflicts over the last eighty years, but have in large part endured.

states of the region made many people nostalgic for what the Austrian writer Stefan Zweig, looking back to the Habsburg era, called 'the world of yesterday'. Fragmentation since the war seemed to have harmed the region both politically and economically, especially once the world depression forced countries into an impoverished self-sufficiency.

Yet it was a rare blend of nostalgia and *realpolitik* which lay behind much of the antipathy to Versailles. The makers of America's new role in Europe after 1945, for example, who had grown up looking closely at these problems, held Versailles responsible for the instability of interwar Europe. Adolf Berle, Roosevelt's assistant secretary of state between 1938 and 1944, believed that French generals had been responsible for breaking up the Austro-Hungarian Empire and wanted some kind of reconstitution of that entity to ward off the Russians. Hitler, he advised the presi-

dent on the eve of Munich, was perhaps 'the only instrument capable of re-establishing a race and economic unit which can survive and leave Europe in balance.'

George Kennan, a younger man but more influential than Berle in defining the Cold War policy of containment, took a very similar view in the late 1930s. In his despatches from Prague he wrote:

It is generally agreed that the breakup of the limited degree of unity which the Habsburg Empire represented was unfortunate for all concerned. Other forces are now at work which are struggling to create a new form of unity . . . To these forces Czechoslovakia has been tragically slow in adjusting herself . . . The adjustment— and this is the main thing—has now come.

It did not take long for someone as astute as Kennan to realise that the Nazi New Order was not going to stabilise

central Europe in the way the Habsburgs had done. But the reason for this, in his mind, was not the apparently obvious one that Hitler's whole upbringing had turned him into a German nationalist critic of the Austro-Hungarian monarchy. It was, rather, what Kennan conceived as the excessively democratic character of Hitler's Germany and the limited involvement of Germany's aristocracy in the Third Reich. More aristocratic government was Kennan's answer to Europe's problems. It is hard to imagine a more far-fetched or unrealistic approach—the Habsburgs were marginalised between the wars even by Hungary's reactionary regent Admiral Horthy, and the most successful Habsburg aristocrat of that era was the bizarre and premature proponent of European union, Count Coudenhove-Kalergi. Perhaps only an American conservative intellectual like Kennan could have taken the prospect of a Habsburg restoration seriously. European conservatives, closer to the ground, had fewer illusions. 'The Vienna to Versailles period has run its course,' wrote the historian Lewis Namier in February 1940.

> Whatever the weaknesses of the system created in 1919, a return to previous forms is impossible. They have been broken, and broken for good.

It was not aristocrats that had kept the old empires together but dynastic loyalty, and this had vanished.

If dynasticism no longer offered an alternative principle to the Versailles order, then what of the rival ideologies of right and left? This was where root-and-branch critics of Versailles had to bite the bullet. Most anti-Communists between the wars had no difficulty in swallowing the idea of an authoritarian revision of the Versailles settlement. What made them hesitate was a quite different proposition; the reality of life under the Nazi New Order. The difference between a right tolerable to most conservatives and an extreme and ideological fascism was that, for instance, between King Alexander's royal dictatorship in Yugoslavia, and Ante Pavelic's genocidal *Ustase* state in Croatia, or between King Carol's Romania and that of the Iron Guard, with its bloody pogroms, in the winter of 1940-41. Above all, the New Order was based on the idea of German racial superiority, and few anti-Communists could stomach this once they saw what it meant in terms of practical politics.

If one agreed with Namier that 'no system can possibly be maintained on the European Continent east of the Rhine which has not the support either of Germany or of Russia,' then the only ideological alternative to Nazism was Communism, or more precisely the extension of Russian rule westwards into Europe. Just as Versailles's critics on the right had seen Germany's move east after 1933 as confirmation of their own prejudices, so critics on the left similarly interpreted the course of events after 1943 as a happy necessity. Historians like E.H. Carr saw this as realism replacing the idealism of Versailles. It was apparently not felt to be realistic to point out that all the historical evidence pointed to the unpopularity of Communism among the majority of the populations who now had to endure it. In only one country in central Europe, Hungary, had a Bolshevik regime held power for any length of time before 1945, and that still brief experience—the Bela Kun regime of 1919—had only confirmed how unpropitious the soil was for such experiments. Today we are unlikely to see Communism as an attractive alternative to the principles embodied in the Versailles order: yesterday's 'realism' looks riddled with its own form of wishful thinking.

One of the reasons Bela Kun fell from power in 1919 was that he had not understood the strength of Hungarian nationalist feeling. So long as it had appeared to Hungarians that Bolshevik Russia might help them get back their traditional lands, they were prepared to tolerate Kun. But once it appeared that the Allies would not let this happen, Kun lost any popularity he had once enjoyed and he was easily defeated. The power of nationalism was the chief force to emerge from the First World War in Europe, and was the main political factor facing the architects of a new post-war settlement. From our perspective at the century's end, it hardly looks as though fascism and Communism were able to handle European nationalism better than the peacemakers at Versailles. Hitler's New Order proceeded by ignoring all nationalisms except the German, and lost Europe in consequence. Communism believed that eventually nationalist antipathies would vanish, subsumed within an internationalist struggle: but time ran out for the Communists before this happened. If we want to find guidance in the past for how to tackle the problems of nationalism that remain in Europe, we cannot do better than return to the diplomats who gathered in Paris eighty years ago.

In the Bukovina (a former province of the Habsburg empire), Paris seemed very far away in the spring of 1919. But events were occurring there which help us chart the trajectory of antisemitic violence from the unorganised pogroms of the nineteenth century to the more systematic population engineering of the twentieth. A manifesto was posted up in the village of Kamenestie, written in Romanian:

> Order to all the Jews in the village. Those Jews who are still in the village are asked to go to the city or somewhere else. You can leave in good condition [sic] and without fear in ten days. It will be made unbearable for those who stay beyond the limit.

Throughout the little villages of the Bukovina, pogroms were taking place in late 1918. 'Following the example of the neighbouring villages,' runs an account from Petroutz,

> The peasants decided to drive the Jews out of this place. On the night of November 17th, they attacked the Jewish families Hermann, Feller and Schubert, broke doors and windows and took away everything they found. A scroll of the Law was torn to pieces by the marauders. After the robbery they burned everything that remained. All three families fled to Suczawa.

The Jews were the chief targets of ethnic violence in the Bukovina, as they were elsewhere in eastern Europe, in Galicia for instance, or in Lithuania. But the war of nationalities could not be reduced to antisemitism: Poles were fighting with Ukrainians, Germans and Lithuanians. Across much of Europe there fell a double shadow: ethnic as well as class war. Bolshevism was contained by a combination of land reform, reformist social democracy and the military defeat of the Red Army in the Russo-Polish war. But the nationalist enmities and suspicions which exploded into violence as the First World War ended, and which generated casualties on such a scale that some historians have compared them with the violence which erupted under Nazi rule after 1941, these proved harder to tackle.

Ethnic civil war emphasised in the most unmistakable way that the peacemakers in Paris were not sketching their maps on a *tabula rasa*. On the contrary, they were as much responding to circumstances as shaping them. East European critics of Great Power arrogance often forget today how far the Versailles settlement was brought into being, not by the Powers, but by local nationalist elites and their supporters. New nations were pressing their claims on paper, in the streets and by force of arms, as the war approached an end. Serb, Croat and Slovene delegates issued the Corfu Declaration in July 1917 and declared the new tripartite Yugoslav nation 'a worthy member of the new Community of Nations.'

The Provisional People's Government of the Polish Republic proclaimed 'the authority of Polish democracy' in its November 1918 manifesto. The Czech National Committee seized power in Prague as early as October 28th of the same year in the name of the infant Czechoslovak state. Much of the subsequent fighting from the Baltic to the Balkans was designed to conquer as much territory as possible for the new states, to see off rival claimants and to settle scores with Jews, Germans, Muslims and other hated, despised or feared peoples. Between 1920 and 1923, the Treaty of Sevres was signed, scrapped and replaced by the Treaty of Lausanne as the struggle between Greece and Turkey shifted first one way then the other, culminating eventually in the forced population exchange of some two million people.

It is to the credit of the Versailles peacemakers that they confronted the problem of ethnic violence head on. They were aware of the chief defect of the Wilsonian principle of national self-determination—namely that if it was interpreted territorially and not merely as a grant of cultural autonomy, then on its own it ruled out either an equitable or a geographically coherent settlement of the problems of central and eastern Europe. No one, after all, was proposing to give the Kashubians, the Polesians, the Pomaks, or any of the other small ethnic groups of the region a state of their own. They, and several other larger peoples like the Jews, the Ukrainians and the Macedonians, would remain under the rule of others. In other words, the creation—or better, the recognition—of nation-states at Versailles was accompanied by its inescapable shadow, the problem of minorities.

Fearful in particular that Poland's appetite for territory might destabilise the whole area, the Powers obliged the reluctant Poles to sign a treaty granting the country's very sizeable minority population certain rights. The Polish treaty formed the basis for a series of similar treaties imposed in 1919 and 1920 upon most of the states of central and eastern Europe. The result was that for the first time an international organisation—the League of Nations—assumed the right to intervene in a member state's internal affairs on behalf of minority populations.

This right, however, was very limited and scarcely used at all by the League. Most countries feared doing away with the idea that a state was sovereign within its own borders, and even the Great Powers who had sponsored the Minority Rights Treaties trod warily. They had resisted calls to universalise the regime of minority rights on the grounds that 'the League cannot assume to guarantee good government in this matter throughout the world'. By 1929 they were very reluctant to act at all against member states accused of rights violations. British foreign secretary Austen Chamberlain warned that,

> We have not reached such a degree of solidarity in international affairs that any of us welcome even the most friendly intervention in what we consider to be our domestic affairs.

This attitude discouraged the most dynamic lobbyists for Europe's minorities, the Germans and the Jews. Until 1933, they worked together in the European Congress of Nationalities to try to give the Minorities Treaties teeth. Thereafter their paths diverged. But Hitler's rise to power can be seen in the context of the failure of the League to protect Europe's minorities. Where the League's rather timid use of international law had failed, the Nazis used force; their 'solution' involved forced population transfer, resettlement and ultimately genocide. And after 1944 many of these instruments were turned on the Germans themselves as they were driven out of Poland and the former Habsburg lands.

Yet we should not write off the peacemakers of Versailles too quickly. Despite the horrors of the 1940s, which virtually eliminated both the Jews and the Germans from much of eastern Europe, many minorities remained across the region. However, instead of building on the League's tentative efforts to construct an international regime of minority rights, the architects of the post-war order enshrined in the United Nations deliberately retreated from the problem and tried to dress up its reluctance to deal with it with meaningless persiflage about 'human rights'. As a result, when issues of minority rights came to the fore after the collapse of Communism in eastern Europe in the decade after 1989, most obviously in the context of the disintegration of Yugoslavia, the international community possessed no coherent strategy for tackling the problem.

The consequences have been all too visible in Bosnia and Kosovo. The United Nations was less equipped to tackle the fundamental problem of minority rights than its predecessor, the League, had been. It delivered food and tried to keep the peace without a clear doctrine of what kind of peace it should keep. The contrast between the self-confident and articulate liberal universalism of the 1920s and the post-modern evasions of the 1990s was all too conspicuous. In Kosovo, too, the contrast with the Versailles generation does not flatter our own times. NATO intervention in Kosovo could, as articulated somewhat optimistically by Tony Blair, be interpreted as marking a new doctrine of foreign affairs, according to which state sovereignty may be overridden to prevent massive violations of minority rights. Yet, NATO's attacks on the Serbs, in the absence of any UN mandate, do not indicate any great confidence in international law and institutions. The United States, which has been leading the charge, is, after all, opposed to the creation of an International Criminal Court. If inter-war Europe suffered because international guarantees were never acted upon, we may suffer in the 1990s through military action taken without any reference to international law at all, the late twentieth-century equivalent of gunboat diplomacy handled by a post-Holocaust generation of politicians.

The very least, then, that we can say for Versailles is that it recognised and articulated the major problems for European stability at that time. What was more, there was no palatable alternative to the nation-state then, or since. Where the peace was found wanting between the wars was in the will to uphold it. Today NATO is turning itself into the kind of force which the peacemakers of 1919 lacked. But do its political masters have a clear grasp of what kind of Europe they wish to defend? They could do worse than cast their eyes back to the work of their predecessors eighty years ago.

For Further Reading

I. Claude, *National Minorities: An International Problem* (Harvard, 1955). James Headlam-Morley, *A Memoir of the Paris Peace Conference*, 1919 (London, 1972). J. Harper, *American Visions of Europe* (Cambridge, 1996). C. Fink, *'Defender of Minorities': Germany in the League of Nations 1926–1933* (Central European History, 5:4, 1972). R. Brubaker, *Nationalism Refrained: Nationhood and the National Question in the New Europe* (Cambridge, 1996). E. Kulischer, *Europe on the Move: War and Population Changes*, 1917–1947 (New York, 1948).

Mark Mazower is a Visiting Professor of History at Princeton University. He is the author of *Dark Continent: Europe's Twentieth Century* (1998).

How the Modern Middle East Map Came to be Drawn

When the Ottoman Empire collapsed in 1918, the British created new borders (and rulers) to keep the peace and protect their interests.

David Fromkin

Lawyer Historian David Fromkin is the author of a prizewinning book entitled A Peace to End All Peace.

The dictator of Iraq claimed—*falsely—that until 1914 Kuwait had been administered from Iraq, that historically Kuwait was a part of Iraq, that the separation of Kuwait from Iraq was an arbitrary decision of Great Britain's after World War I.* The year was 1961; the Iraqi dictator was Abdul-Karim Qasim; and the dispatch of British troops averted a threatened invasion.

Iraq, claiming that it had never recognized the British-drawn frontier with Kuwait, demanded full access to the Persian Gulf and when Kuwait failed to agree, Iraqi tanks and infantry attacked Kuwait. The year was 1973; the Iraqi dictator was Ahmad Hasan al-Bakr; when other Arab states came to Kuwait's support, a deal was struck, Kuwait made a payment of money to Iraq, and the troops withdrew.

August 2, 1990. At 2 A.M. Iraqi forces swept across the Kuwaiti frontier. Iraq's dictator, Saddam Hussein, declared that the frontier between Iraq and Kuwait was invalid, a creation of the British after World War I, and that Kuwait really belonged to Iraq.

It was, of course, true, as one Iraqi dictator after another claimed, that the exact Iraq-Kuwait frontier was a line drawn on an empty map by a British civil servant in the early 1920s. But Kuwait began to emerge as an independent entity in the early 1700s—two centuries before Britain invented Iraq. Moreover, most other frontiers between states of the Middle East were also creations of the British (or the French). The map of the Arab Middle East was drawn by the victorious Allies when they took over these lands from the Ottoman Empire after World War I. By proposing to nullify that map, Saddam Hussein at a minimum was trying to turn the clock back by almost a century.

A hundred years ago, when Ottoman governors in Basra were futilely attempting to assert authority over the autonomous sheikdom of Kuwait, most of the Arabic-speaking Middle East was at least nominally part of the Ottoman Empire. It had been so for hundreds of years and would remain so until the end of World War I.

The Ottomans, a dynasty, not a nationality, were originally a band of Turkish warriors who first galloped onto the stage of history in the 13th century. By the early 20th century the Ottoman Empire, which once had stretched to the gates of Vienna, was shrinking rapidly, though it still ruled perhaps 20 million to 25 million people in the Middle East and elsewhere, comprising perhaps a dozen or more different nationalities. It was a ramshackle Muslim empire, held together by the glue of Islam, and the lot of its non-Muslim population (perhaps 5 million) was often unhappy and sometimes tragic.

In the year 1900, if you traveled from the United States to the Middle East, you might have landed in Egypt, part of the Ottoman Empire in name but in fact governed by British "advisers." The Egyptian Army was commanded by an English general, and the real ruler of the country was the British Agent and Consul-General—a position to which the crusty Horatio Herbert Kitchener was appointed in 1911.

The center of your social life in all likelihood would have been the British enclave in Cairo, which possessed (wrote one of Lord Kitchener's aides) "all the narrowness and provincialism of an English garrison town." The social schedule of British officials and their families revolved around the balls given at each of the leading hotels in turn, six nights out of seven, and before dark, around the Turf Club and the Sporting

From *Smithsonian* magazine, May 1991, pp. 132–134, 136, 138–148. © 1991 by David Fromkin. Reprinted by permission of the author.

Club on the island of El Gezira. Throughout Egypt, Turkish officials, Turkish police and a Turkish army were conspicuous by their absence. Outside British confines you found yourself not in a Turkish-speaking country but in an Arabic-speaking one. Following the advice of the *Baedeker*, you'd likely engage a dragoman—a translator and guide—of whom there were about 90 in Cairo ("all more or less intelligent and able, but scarcely a half of the number are trustworthy").

On leaving Egypt, if you turned north through the Holy Land and the Levant toward Anatolia, you finally would have encountered the reality of Ottoman government, however corrupt and inefficient, though many cities—Jerusalem (mostly Jewish), Damascus (mostly Arab) and Smyrna, now 1zmir (mostly Greek)—were not at all Turkish in character or population.

Heading south by steamer down the Red Sea and around the enormous Arabian Peninsula was a very different matter. Nominally Ottoman, Arabia was in large part a.vast, ungoverned desert wilderness through which roamed bedouin tribes knowing no law but their own. In those days Abdul Aziz ibn Saud, the youthful scion of deposed lords of most of the peninsula, was living in exile, dreaming of a return to reclaim his rights and establish his dominion. In the port towns on the Persian Gulf, ruling sheiks paid lip service to Ottoman rule but in fact their sheikdoms were protectorates of Great Britain. Not long after you passed Kuwait (see map) you reached Basra, in what is now Iraq, up a river formed by the union of the great Tigris and Euphrates.

A muddy, unhealthy port of heterogeneous population, Basra was then the capital of a province, largely Shiite Arab, ruled by an Ottoman governor. Well north of it, celebrated for archaeological sites like Babylon and Nippur, which drew tourists, lay Baghdad, then a heavily Jewish city (along with Jerusalem, one of the two great Jewish cities of Asia). Baghdad was the administrative center of an Ottoman province that was in large part Sunnl Arab. Farther north still was a third Ottoman province, with a large population of Kurds. Taken together, the three roughly equaled the present area of Iraq.

Ottoman rule in some parts of the Middle East clearly was more imaginary than real. And even in those portions of

the empire that Turkish governors did govern, the population was often too diverse to be governed effectively by a single regime. Yet the hold of the Turkish sultan on the empire's peoples lingered on. Indeed, had World War I not intervened, the Ottoman Empire might well have lasted many decades more.

In its origins, the war that would change the map of the Middle East had nothing to do with that region. How the Ottoman Empire came to be involved in the war at all—and lost it—and how the triumphant Allies found themselves in a position to redesign the Middle Eastern lands the Turks had ruled, is one of the most fascinating stories of the 20th century, rich in consequences that we are still struggling with today.

The story begins with one man, a tiny, vain, strutting man addicted to dramatic gestures and uniforms. He was Enver Pasha, and he mistook himself for a sort of Napoleon. Of modest origins, Enver, as a junior officer in the Ottoman Army, joined the Young Turks, a secret society that was plotting against the Ottoman regime. In 1913, Enver led a Young Turk raiding party that overthrew the government and killed the Minister of War. In 1914, at the age of 31, he became the Ottoman Minister of War

Though he was blamed for Gallipoli, Winston Churchill was put in charge of reorganizing the entire Middle East.

himself, married the niece of the sultan and moved into a palace.

As a new political figure Enver scored a major, instant success. The Young Turks for years had urgently sought a European ally that would promise to protect the Ottoman Empire against other European powers. Britain, France and Russia had each been approached and had refused; but on August 1, 1914, just as Germany was about to invade Belgium to begin World War I, Enver wangled a secret treaty with the kaiser pledging to protect the Ottoman domains.

Unaware of Enver's coup, and with war added to the equation, Britain and France began wooing Turkey too, while the Turks played off one side against the other. By autumn the German Army's plan to knock France out of the war in six weeks had failed. Needing help, Germany urged the Ottoman Empire to join the war by attacking Russia.

Though Enver's colleagues in the Turkish government were opposed to war, Enver had a different idea. To him the time seemed ripe: in the first month of the war German armies overwhelmingly turned back a Russian attack on East Prussia, and a collapse of the czar's armies appeared imminent. Seeing a chance to share in the spoils of a likely German victory over Russia, Enver entered into a private conspiracy with the German admiral commanding the powerful warship *Goeben* and its companion vessel, the *Breslau,* which had taken refuge in Turkish waters at the outset of hostilities.

For years the real ruler of Egypt was Lord Kitchener, a general, whose main concern was for the Suez Canal.

During the last week of October, Enver secretly arranged for the *Goeben* and the *Breslau* to escape into the Black Sea and steam toward Russia. Flying the Ottoman flag, the Germans then opened fire on the Russian coast. Thinking themselves attacked by Turks, the Russians declared war. Russia's allies, Britain and France, thus found themselves at war with the Ottoman Empire too. By needlessly plunging the empire into war, Enver had put everything in the Middle East up for grabs. In that sense, he was the father of the modern Middle East. Had Enver never existed, the Turkish flag might even yet be flying—if only in some confederal way—over Beirut and Damascus, Baghdad and Jerusalem.

Great Britain had propped up the Ottoman Empire for generations as a buffer against Russian expansionism. Now with Russia as Britain's shaky ally, once the war had been won and the Ottomans overthrown, the Allies would be able to reshape the entire Middle East. It would be one of those magic moments in history when fresh starts beckon and dreams become realities.

"What is to prevent the Jews having Palestine and restoring a real Judaea?" asked H. G. Wells, the British novelist, essayist and prophet of a rational future for mankind. The Greeks, the French and the Italians also had claims to Middle East territory. And naturally, in Cairo, Lord Kitchener's aides soon began to contemplate a future plan for an Arab world to be ruled by Egypt, which in turn would continue to be controlled by themselves.

At the time, the Allies already had their hands full with war against Germany on the Western Front. They resolved not to be distracted by the Middle East until later. The issues and ambitions there were too divisive. Hardly had the Ottoman Empire entered the war, however, when Enver stirred the pot again. He took personal command of the Ottoman Third Army on the Caucasus frontier and, in the dead of winter, launched a foolhardy attack against fortified positions on high ground. His offensive was hopeless, since it was both amateurishly planned and executed, but the czars generals panicked anyway. The Russian government begged Lord Kitchener (now serving in London as Secretary of State for War) to stage a more or less instant diversionary action. The result was the Allied attack on the Dar-

British camel unit jogs down the Jordan Valley; Prince Faisal and T. E. Lawrence often used camels in guerrilla raids on Turks.

danelles, the strait that eventually leads to Constantinople (now Istanbul).

Enver soon lost about 86,000 of his 100,000 men; the few, bloodied survivors straggled back through icy mountain passes. A German observer noted that Enver's army had "suffered a disaster which for rapidity and completeness is without parallel in military history." But nobody in the Russian government or high command bothered to tell the British that mounting a Dardanelles naval attack was no longer necessary. So on the morning of February 19, 1915, British ships fired the opening shots in what became a tragic campaign.

Initially, the British Navy seemed poised to take Constantinople, and Russia panicked again. what if the British, having occupied Constantinople, were to hold onto it? The 50 percent of Russia's export trade flowing through the strait would then do so only with British permission. Czar Nicholas II demanded immediate assurance that Constantinople would be Russia's in the postwar world. Fearing Russia might withdraw from the war, Britain and France agreed. In return, Russia offered to support British and French claims in other parts of the Middle East.

With that in mind, on April 8, 1915, the British Prime Minister appointed a committee to define Britain's postwar goals in the Middle East. It was a committee dominated by Lord Kitchener through his personal representative, 36-year-old Sir Mark Sykes, one of many

remarkable characters, including Winston Churchill and T. E. Lawrence, to be involved in the remaking (and remapping) of the Middle East.

A restless soul who had moved from school to school as a child, Sykes left college without graduating, and thereafter never liked to stay long in one spot. A Tory Member of Parliament, before the war he had traveled widely in Asiatic Turkey, publishing accounts of his journeys. Sykes' views tended to be passionate but changeable, and his talent for clever exaggeration sometimes carried over into his politics.

As a traditional Tory he had regarded the sultan's domains as a useful buffer protecting Britain's road to India against Britain's imperial rivals, the czar chief among them. Only 15 months earlier, Sykes was warning the House of Commons that "the disappearance of the Ottoman Empire must be the first step towards the disappearance of our own." Yet between 1915 and 1919, he busily planned the dismantling of the Ottoman Empire.

The Allied attack on the Dardanelles ended with Gallipoli, a disaster told and retold in books and films. Neither that defeat, nor the darkest days of 1916–17, when it looked for a while as though the Allies might lose the war, stopped British planning about how to cut up the Turkish Middle East. Steadily but secretly Sykes worked on. As the fight to overthrow the Ottoman

Empire grew more intense, the elements he had to take into account grew more complex.

It was clear that the British needed to maintain control over the Suez Canal, and all the rest of the route to their prized colonial possession, India. They needed to keep the Russians and Germans and Italians and French in check. Especially the French, who had claims on Syria. But with millions of men committed to trench warfare in Europe, they could not drain off forces for the Middle East. Instead, units of the British Indian Army along with other Commonwealth forces attacked in the east in what are now Iraq and Iran, occupying Basra, Baghdad and eventually Mosul. Meanwhile, Allied liaison officers, including notably T. E. Lawrence, began encouraging the smallish group of Arabian tribesmen following Emir (later King) Hussein of the Hejaz, who had rebelled against the Turks, to fight a guerrilla campaign against Turkish forces.

Throughout 1917, in and near the Hejaz area of Arabia (see map), the Arabs attacked the railway line that supported Turkish troops in Medina. The "Arab Revolt" had little military effect on the outcome of the war, yet the fighting brought to the fore, as British clients and potential Arab leaders, not only Hussein of the Hejaz, but two of his sons, Faisal and Abdullah. Both were deadly rivals of Ibn Saud, who by then had become a rising power in Arabia and a client of the British too.

British officials in Cairo deluded themselves and others into believing that the whole of the Arabic-speaking half of the Ottoman Empire might rise up and come over to the Allied side. When the time came, the Arab world did not follow the lead of Hussein, Abdullah and Faisal. But Arab aspirations and British gratitude began to loom large in British, and Arab, plans for the future. Sykes now felt he had to take Arab ambitions into account in his future planning, though he neglected those of Ibn Saud (father of today's Saudi king), who also deserved well of Britain.

By 1917 Sykes was also convinced that it was vital for the British war effort to win Jewish support against Germany, and that pledging support for Zionism could win it. That year his efforts and those of others resulted in the publication of a statement by Arthur James Balfour, the British Foreign Secretary, expressing Britain's support for the es-

tablishment of a Jewish national home in Palestine.

The year 1917 proved to be a turning point. In the wake of its revolution Russia pulled out of the war, but the entrance by the United States on the Allied side insured the Allies a victory—if they could hold on long enough for U.S. troops to arrive in force. In the Middle East, as British India consolidated its hold on areas that are now part of Iraq, Gen. Edmund Allenby's Egyptian-based British army began fighting its way north from Suez to Damascus. Lawrence and a force of Arab raiders captured the Red Sea port of Aqaba (near the point where Israel and Jordan now meet). Then, still other Arabs, with Faisal in command, moved north to harass the Turkish flank.

By October 1918, Allenby had taken Syria and Lebanon, and was poised to invade what is now Turkey But there was no need to do so, because on October 31 the Ottoman Empire surrendered.

As the Peace Conference convened in Paris, in February 1919, Sykes, who had been rethinking Britain's design for the Middle East, suddenly fell ill and died. At first there was nobody to take his place as the British government's overall Middle East planner. Prime Minister David Lloyd George took personal charge in many Middle East matters. But more and more, as the months went by, Winston Churchill had begun to play

a major role, gradually superseding the others.

Accordingly, early that year the ambitious 45-year-old politician was asked by the Prime Minister to serve as both War Minister and Air Minister. ("Of course," Lloyd George wrote Churchill, "there will be but one salary!") Maintaining the peace in the captured—and now occupied—Arab Middle East was among Churchill's new responsibilities.

Cheerful, controversial and belligerent, Churchill was not yet the revered figure who would so inspire his countrymen and the world in 1940. Haunted by the specter of a brilliant father, he had won fame and high office early, but was widely distrusted, in part for having switched political parties. Churchill's foresighted administration of the Admiralty in the summer of 1914 won universal praise, but then the botched Dardanelles campaign, perhaps unfairly, was blamed on him. As a Conservative newspaper put it, "we have watched his brilliant and erratic course in the confident expectation that sooner or later he would make a mess of anything he undertook." In making Churchill minister of both War and Air in 1919, Lloyd George was giving his protege' a try at a political comeback.

By the end of the war, everyone was so used to the bickering among the Allies about who was going to get what in the postwar Middle East that the alter-

After the final surrender of the Turks, on October 31, 1918, the question was: How to administer the remains of the Ottoman Empire?

native—nobody taking anything—simply didn't enter into the equation. Churchill was perhaps the only statesman to consider that possibility. He foresaw that many problems would arise from trying to impose a new political design on so troubled a region, and thought it unwise to make the attempt. Churchill argued, in fact, for simply retaining a reformed version of the Ottoman Empire. Nobody took him seriously.

After the war, a British army of a million men, the only cohesive military force in the region, briefly occupied the Middle East. Even as his real work began, however, Churchill was confronted with demands that the army, exhausted from years of war, be demobilized. He understood what meeting those demands meant. Relying on that army, Prime Minister Lloyd George had decided to keep the whole Arab Middle East under British influence; in the words he once used about Palestine: "We shall be there by conquest and shall remain." Now Churchill repeatedly warned that once British troops were withdrawn, Britain would not be able to impose its terms.

Lloyd George had predicted that it would take about a week to agree on the terms of peace to be imposed on the defeated Ottoman Empire. Instead it took nearly two years. By then, in Churchill's words, the British army of occupation had long since "melted away," with the dire consequences he predicted.

In Egypt, demonstrations, strikes and riots broke out. In Arabia, Ibn Saud, though himself a British client, defeated and threatened to destroy Britain's protégé Hussein. In Turkey, the defeated Enver had long since fled the country to find refuge in Berlin. From there he journeyed to Russia, assumed leadership of Bukhara (in what is now the Uzbek Republic of the USSR) in its struggle for independence from Moscow, and was killed in battle against the Red Army of the Soviet Union in 1922. Turkish nationalists under the great Ottoman general Mustafa Kemal (later known as Kemal Ataturk) rebelled against the Allied-imposed treaty and later proclaimed the national state that is modern Turkey

In Palestine, Arabs rioted against Jews. In what is now Saddam Hussein's Iraq, armed revolts by the tribes, sparked in the first instance by the imposition of taxes, caused thousands of casualties. "How much longer," the outraged London *Times* asked, "are valuable lives to be sacrificed in the vain endeavour to impose upon the Arab population an elaborate and expensive administration which they never asked for and do not want?"

By the end of 1920, Lloyd George's Middle East policy was under attack from all sides. Churchill, who had warned all along that peacetime Britain, in the grip of an economic collapse, had neither the money, the troops, nor the

Prime Minister Lloyd George (right) sought full control of the Middle East.

will to coerce the Middle East, was proved right—and placed even more directly in charge. On New Year's Day 1921 he was appointed Colonial Secretary, and soon began to expand his powers, consolidating within his new department responsibility for all Britain's domains in Arabic-speaking Asia.

He assembled his staff by combing the government for its ablest and most experienced officials. The one offbeat appointment was T. E. Lawrence. A young American journalist and promoter named Lowell Thomas, roaming the Middle East in search of a story, had found Lawrence dressed in Arab robes, and proceeded to make him world-famous as "Lawrence of Arabia." A complex personality, Lawrence was chronically insubordinate, but Churchill admired all the wonderful stories he'd heard of Lawrence's wartime exploits.

Seeking to forge a working consensus among his staff in London and his men in the field, Churchill invited them all to a conference that opened in Cairo on March 12, 1921. During the ten-day session held in the Semiramis Hotel, about 40 experts were in attendance. "Everybody Middle East is here," wrote Lawrence.

Egypt was not on the agenda. Its fate was being settled separately by its new British proconsul, Lord Allenby. In 1922 he established it as an independent kingdom, still largely subject to British control under terms of a unilateral proclamation that neither Egypt's politicians nor its new king, Fuad, accepted.

Early planning for postwar Middle East fell to Sir Mark Sykes, whose work grew in complexity as rival Allied and Arab claims evolved.

All Britain's other wartime conquests—the lands now called Israel, the West Bank, Jordan and Iraq—were very much on the agenda, while the fate of Syria and Lebanon, which Britain had also conquered, was on everybody's mind. In the immediate aftermath of the war, it was control of Syria that had caused the most problems, as Lloyd George tried to keep it for Britain by placing it under the rule of Lawrence's comrade-in-arms, Prince Faisal, son of Hussein. After Syria declared its independence, the French fought back. Occupying all of Syria-Lebanon, they drove Faisal into exile. The French also devised a new frontier for Lebanon that invited eventual disaster, as would become evident in the 1970s and '80s. They refused to see that the Muslim population was deeply hostile to their rule.

Churchill, meanwhile, was confronted by constant Arab disturbances in Palestine. West of the Jordan River, where the Jewish population lived, Arabs fought against Jewish immigration, claiming—wrongly, as the future was to show—that the country was too barren to support more than its existing 600,000 inhabitants. Churchill rejected that view, and dealt with the Arab objections to a Jewish homeland by keeping—though redefining—Britain's commitment to Zionism. As he saw it, there was to be a Jewish homeland in Palestine, but other homelands could exist there as well.

The 75 percent of Palestine east of the Jordan River (Transjordan, as it was called, until it became Jordan in 1950) was lawless. Lacking the troops to police it and wanting to avert additional causes of strife, Churchill decided to forbid Jews from settling there, temporarily at least.

Fittingly while still War and Air Minister, Churchill had devised a strategy for controlling the Middle East with a minimum number of British troops by using an economical combination of airpower and armored cars. But it would take time for the necessary units to be put in place. Meanwhile tribal fighting had to be contained somehow. As the Cairo conference met, news arrived that Abdullah, Faisal's brother, claiming to need "a change of air for his health," had left Arabia with a retinue of bedouin warriors and entered Transjordan. The British feared that Abduilah would attack French Syria and so give the French an excuse to invade Transjordan, as a first step toward taking over all Palestine.

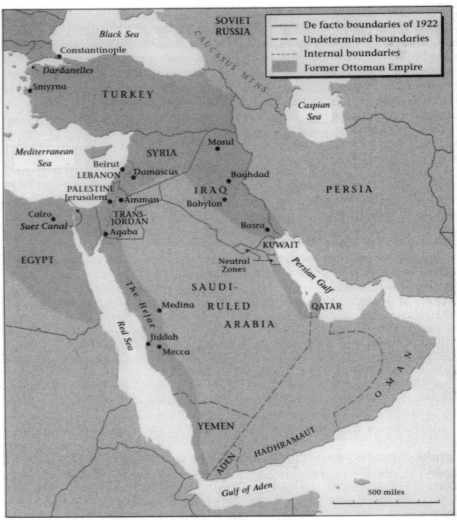

Map shows the Middle East redrawn by the British as of 1922. Iraq has just been created out of three more or less incompatible Ottoman provinces. Part of Palestine has become Transjordan (today's Jordan), which is still ruled by one of Abdullah's descendants.

As a temporary expedient Churchill appointed Abdullah as governor of a Transjordan to be administratively detached from the rest of Palestine. He charged him with keeping order by his prestige and with his own bedouin followers—at least until Britain's aircraft and armored cars were in place. This provisional solution has lasted for seven decades and so have the borders of Transjordan, now ruled over by Abdullah's grandson, Hussein, the Hashemite King of Jordan.

The appointment of Abdullah seemed to accomplish several objectives at once. It went part way toward paying what Lawrence and others told Churchill was Britain's wartime debt to the family of King Hussein, though Hussein himself was beyond help. Too stubborn to accept British advice, he was losing the battle for Arabia to his blood rival, Ibn Saud.

Meanwhile Prince Faisal, Britain's preferred Arab ruler, remained in idle exile.

Other chief items on the Cairo agenda were the Ottoman territories running from the Persian Gulf to Turkey along the border of Persia, which make up present-day Iraq. Including what were suspected—but not proved—to be vast oil reserves, at a time when the value of oil was beginning to be understood, these territories had been the scene of the bloodiest postwar Arab uprisings against British rule. They caused so many difficulties of every sort that Churchill flirted with the idea of abandoning them entirely, but Lloyd George would have none of it. If the British left, the Prime Minister warned, in a year or two they might find that they had "handed over to the French and Americans some of the richest oil fields in the world."

144

As a matter of convenience, the British administered this troubled region as a unit, though it was composed of the three separate Ottoman provinces—Mosul, Baghdad and Basra, with their incompatible Kurdish, Assyrian Christian, Jewish, Sunnl Muslim, and Shiite populations. In making it into a country, Churchill and his colleagues found it convenient to continue treating it as a single unit. (One British planner was warned by an American missionary, "You are flying in the face of four millenniums of history . . .") The country was called Iraq—"the well-rooted country"—in order to give it a name that was Arabic. Faisal was placed on the throne by the British, and like his brother Abdullah in Transjordan, he was supposed to keep Iraq quiet until the British were ready to police it with aircraft and armored cars.

One of the leftover problems in 1921 was just how to protect Transjordan's new governor, Abdullah, and Iraq's new king, Faisal, against the fierce warriors of Ibn Saud. In August 1922 Ibn Saud's camel-cavalry forces invading Transjordan were stopped outside Amman by British airplanes and armored cars. Earlier that year, the British forced Ibn Saud to accept a settlement aimed at protecting Iraq. With this in mind, the British drew a frontier line that awarded Iraq a substantial amount of territory claimed by Ibn Saud for Arabia: all the land (in what is now Iraq) west of the Euphrates River, all the way to the Syrian frontier. To compensate Ibn Saud's kingdom (later known as Saudi Arabia) the British transferred to it rights to two-thirds of the territory of Kuwait, which had been essentially independent for about two centuries. These were valu-able grazing lands, in which oil might exist too.

It is this frontier line between Iraq, Kuwait and Arabia, drawn by a British civil servant in 1922 to protect Iraq at the expense of Kuwait, that Iraq's Saddam Hussein denounced as invalid when he invaded.

In 1922, Churchill succeeded in mapping out the Arab Middle East along lines suitable to the needs of the British civilian and military administrations. T.E. Lawrence would later brag that he, Churchill and a few others had designed the modern Middle East over dinner. Seventy years later, in the tense deliberations and confrontations of half the world over the same area, the question is whether the peoples of the Middle East are willing or able to continue living with that design.

Nazism in the Classroom

Lisa Pine *looks at how lessons in the classroom were perverted in the service of the Third Reich.*

Whilst most governments seek, or have sought, to imbue their nation's youth with correct values and ideals, those regimes of an authoritarian nature have attempted to do so with greater thoroughness—in part, to create a consensus for their rule and ideology. This is clearly demonstrated, for example, by the way in which Mussolini's regime reformed the education system in Italy, introduced state textbooks and set up youth organisations in order to instil Italian youth with Fascist ideology.

In Austria, too, the clerico-fascist regime of 1934–38 attempted to inculcate its beliefs in Austrian youth by similar means. But perhaps the most striking example of this type of youth manipulation through ideological 'education' was the Nazi regime, which introduced sweeping reforms into the German school system reinforced by the activities of its youth groups, the Hitler Youth and the League of German Girls. It went so far as to utilise school textbooks as propaganda tools, with which to disseminate its ideology.

The socialisation of youth was already a prominent part of educational activity during the nineteenth century, when the publishers of children's literature and textbooks clearly recognised that they could be used to shape a child's view of the world by disseminating social values. Story books, as well as history books, were used to diffuse positive social values, but also more negatively to disseminate racist values

by means of stereotyping, with such tales as *The Story of Little Black Sambo* (1899). Racial stereotyping in school books was based upon distorted generalisations, as well as pseudo-scientific and religious justifications, and was reinforced by the use of vivid descriptions and illustrations. This kind of indoctrination was seized upon eagerly by the Nazi government.

The Nazi *Weltanschauung* or 'world view' served as the basis of all educational activity in the Third Reich and became an instrument of justification and legitimisation for the actions of the regime. The concepts of racial superiority, 'national community' and leadership stood at the centre of the Nazi *Weltanschauung*, and were directly applied to principles of education which was no longer aimed at benefiting the individual, but instead, was directed towards the creation of an entire generation of German youth that would be strong, prepared for sacrifice, and willing to undertake its responsibilities towards the 'national community', a notion based upon mass emotion, not rationality. As such, children were pedagogic objects, subjected to the arbitrariness of the system.

In *Mein Kampf* Hitler had already laid out his ideas about education and what it should entail. He claimed that the highest task of education was to consist of the preservation, care and development of the best racial elements. Education, in the Nazi state, was understood in terms of racial selection, so that only the élite would reproduce. This

was, of course, reflected in all policy, not just educational policy. Young 'Aryan' children had to be made aware of the differences between people who fitted into the 'national community' and those who did not. In Hitler's words: 'No boy and no girl must leave school without having been led to an ultimate realisation of the necessity and essence of blood purity'.

In December 1934, Wilhelm Frick, the Minister of the Interior, announced that 'the political task of the school is the education of youth in the service of nation and state in the National Socialist spirit'. Similarly, according to Bernhard Rust, the Minister of Education, the purpose of school textbooks was to achieve 'the ideological education of young German people, so as to develop them into fit members of the national community . . . ready to serve and to sacrifice'.

To this end strict censorship was imposed upon the publishing industry. Certain titles 'blacklisted' by Josef Goebbels, the Minister of Propaganda, were removed from circulation as 'alien' or 'decadent' literature. Censorship was implemented by Philipp Bouhler, the Director of the Party Censorship Office, in conjunction with Bernhard Rust at the Ministry of Education. At first, publishers often reprinted pre-Nazi schoolbooks, with only slight amendments, such as the insertion of swastika flags and Party slogans. However, by the late 1930s, when new writing and illustrations serving the regime became more widely available in greater quantities,

 This article first appeared in *History Today,* April 1997, pp. 22-27. © 1997 by History Today, Ltd. Reprinted by permission.

school textbooks were employed more blatantly to represent Nazi ideals. Old textbooks were replaced by new editions which incorporated the central tenets of Nazi ideology. These were written by authors approved by the Ministry of Education and the National Socialist Teachers' Association. Whilst some of these were by named authors, others were anonymous. For example, many primers and readers were compiled and edited by 'an expert team of German educators'.

The lack of subtlety of approach in the regime's unashamed utilisation of schoolbooks for propaganda purposes revealed itself, for example, in primers, where the first page consisted of the words *'Heil Hitler'*, with children portrayed raising their arms in the Hitler salute. A picture of Hitler usually appeared on the frontispiece, sometimes alone, but more usually showing him with a child or group of children.

Primers contained numerous stories and poems about Hitler, who was portrayed as an omniscient, generous and benevolent man. One such piece entitled 'A Happy Day' from the *German Reader for Elementary Schools* (1936) describes the mounting excitement of school children in their anticipation of a visit by Hitler to their village.

Nazi symbols were often used in conjunction with domestic themes in order to make them familiar and more accessible to small children. An illustrated story, in a primary school reader entitled *My First Book* (1935), shows children helping their mother decorate their home with a swastika flag, roses and a painting of a swastika. Here, a political message was delivered through familiar, familial channels of consciousness. Another story in the *German Reader for Elementary Schools* (1938) about unemployment and its effects on family life was also used to political effect. It tells of a distressed mother whose husband is unemployed. The family are experiencing severe financial hardship, and can afford only potato soup for dinner, instead of meat. The father has been shot in the foot during the First World War and has not worked since. In this story, the Nazi regime rescues the family from the clutches of poverty and misery, by specifically helping the war-wounded man. The story ends with the father returning home triumphantly one day, with the news that he has a job starting the next day, working with 200 others on the construction of a new bridge.

This brings tremendous joy to the family and meat back to their dinner table.

The theme of young children 'helping the *Führer*' appears in numerous textbooks from 1939 onwards, when the government was clearly concerned about shortages of raw materials and the war effort. One story tells of a boy who collects old materials for recycling from his home and the homes of his relatives. Another, in a book entitled *Happy Beginnings* (1939), with an illustration of a family sitting around the dinner table, deals with the *Eintopf*. This was the 'one-pot' dish that German families were encouraged to eat instead of their usual meal on one Sunday of each month, in order to save money which was instead to be donated to the needs of the state. In this story, one of the children tells her parents that she used to think that the *Eintopf* meant that there was a large pot outside the town hall, and that all the people went there to eat. Her brother laughs at her, but their father admonishes him, saying that the girl at least now understood what the *Führer* meant. There is a knock at the door and the collector appears. One of the children is told to go and fetch the money, and to give double that day, as it is the father's birthday. This story explained the political significance of the *Eintopf*, using the family context to instil the message.

In *Fables for Lower Saxony* (1939), a mother asks her daughters to fetch potatoes from the cellar in baskets to fill up a sack for the Winter Relief Organisation, whose motto was 'no one shall go hungry, no one shall freeze'. They bring up three baskets of potatoes and ask if this is enough. Their mother tells them to bring up another basket, as the sack is not yet full, emphasising that they should be pleased to make sacrifices for the Winter Relief Organisation and, hence, the state.

The Nazi idealisation of the mother features heavily in the textbooks of the period. There were ordinary stories of children preparing a special treat for their mother's birthday or for Mother's Day, aimed at young children, but in reading books for older children, depictions of the mother could be found under the sub-heading of 'heroes of everyday life'. This sense of the mother being raised to a heroic position was one that the regime clearly wished to instil in children. For example, one schoolbook includes a play for Mother's Day, in which four councillors are portrayed,

contemplating ways to relieve the mother of her many burdens and duties. Just as they are considering the possibility of finding someone to help the mother, a woman appears at the door. The councillors ask her if she is a wife and mother, to which she replies that she is. They then ask her if she takes care of her family, to which she answers that she does—from dawn to dusk. However, when the suggestion is made that some assistance might lighten her burden, she firmly rejects the idea, claiming that mothers love their domain and are happy to toil from early in the morning until late at night for their families. After she goes, the councillors conclude their session by deciding that 'mothers do not want to be relieved' of their tasks and duties.

Bucolic life, untainted by the depravities of urbanisation was accorded a special significance during the Third Reich. The Nazi 'Blood and Soil' doctrine defined the strength of the nation in terms of an idealisation of peasant values and the sacredness of the German soil. The regime excoriated many aspects of life in the big cities, not least the tendency of young couples to limit the size of their families. Urbanisation leading to the 'death of the nation' was a recurrent theme.

This comes across especially strongly in certain textbooks, such as *Country Folk and Agricultural Work* (1939), aimed specifically at pupils in rural areas, to demonstrate to them their own importance and value in maintaining a healthy nation. The rural family was portrayed as the 'archetype of a true family'. Textbooks went to great lengths to show that what was regarded as a family in the big cities, was often not a true family, but a distorted image of one. A husband and wife living in a city, without children, but with domestic pets instead, could be described at best as a 'household', but not as a 'family'.

Another aspect of rural family life that was deemed positive by the Nazi regime was the inclusion of the grandparents in the home. In this extended family, both the grandmother and grandfather had their roles and duties to perform. The other advantages of emphasising their presence was to make children more aware of their ancestry.

All this related back to the issue of German blood. Much use was made of genealogy and family trees to establish purity of race. On this theme, there were texts entitled, for instance, 'You and Your Ancestors', which asked pupils: 'Do you know what kind of blood runs through your veins? Do you know your father and your mother, and have you yet seen the ancestry of your forefathers?' One writer of such a text claimed to have traced his own family tree back to around 1500, and to therefore know what blood type flowed through his veins. The presentation of ancestral knowledge in an exciting and colourful manner highlighted its importance, encouraging pupils to take an interest in their own ancestry and to consider the fact that one day they themselves would be the ancestors of a future family—as branches of a family tree would continue to grow. In addition to the pupils' books, there were a number of aids to teachers which suggested ways in which these issues could and should be taught. Another approach used, apart from actively involving children in their own ancestry, was the inclusion of numerous poems and stories about heredity, blood and kinship.

The main benefit to be derived from genealogical activities was awareness, both of an individual's own traits, and, more importantly, of his membership of the 'blood community' of the German nation. Of course, the ramifications of this went much further, by suggesting that those of non-German blood, or who could not definitively prove to be of German blood, were 'inferior'. Fundamentally, the purpose of such texts was to highlight the sense of continuity between children, their parents, their grandparents, their great-grandparents and so on. They emphasised the idea of blood flowing from the past, to the present and the future, pulsing in the veins of a family generation after generation. One book sought to demonstrate the inheritance and transmission of family characteristics through the generations by considering the composer Johann Sebastian Bach. It illustrated Bach's family tree, in order to show that in his family there were no fewer than thirty-four 'musically competent' people, of whom approximately half were 'outstandingly gifted'. This particular example was part of a comprehensive chapter dealing with heredity, race and family. Within this context, blood was the most important symbol, for 'German blood' was the guarantee of the future of the nation.

The Nazi preoccupation with 'the order of nature' formed the basis of a number of texts. For example, in one story, a husband and wife decide to exchange roles. The husband takes over the cooking, whilst the wife goes out into the fields to do his work. After a disastrous day for the man—who previously thought his wife had the easy option in staying at home and cooking—he tells her that it is better 'not to reverse the order of nature'. The implications of this are crystal clear in relation to Nazi ideology.

In a similar vein—but more related to Nazi pseudo-scientific racial thought—was a fable appearing in the *German Reader for Secondary Schools* (1942), whose substance was as follows: A cuckoo meets a nightingale in the street. The cuckoo wants to sing as beautifully as the nightingale, but claims that he cannot do so because he was not taught to sing when he was young. The nightingale laughs and says that nightingales do not *learn* to sing, but are *born* with the ability to sing. The cuckoo, nevertheless, believes that if only he could find the right teacher, his offspring will be able to sing as beautifully as the nightingale. His wife has a clever idea. She decides to lay an egg in the nest of a hedge sparrow. When the mother hedge sparrow returns to her nest, she is surprised to see the strange egg, but decides to take care of it as if it were her own. When the eggs hatch, a young cuckoo emerges among the fledgling sparrows. He is nourished and cared for in exactly the same way as them, but he does not grow into a hedge sparrow. In fact, the older he grows, the more noticeable his differences become. When he tries to sing, he cannot. Despite growing up in the nest of a hedge sparrow, he grows up to be a true cuckoo.

This story was used to pose the questions: 'What is more important? The race from which one stems, or the nest in which one grows up?' The issues raised in this fable are particularly significant, reflecting both the debate about inherited versus acquired characteristics, and the rudiments of Nazi racial ideology.

Racism and anti-Semitism also permeated biology and 'racial science' textbooks which aimed to point out to children the distinctions between the 'Aryan' race and 'inferior' races, for example, by means of craniology. There were also readers, such as *The Poisonous Mushroom* (1938), in which a whole array of anti-Semitic imagery was used, with caricatures, graphic illustrations and vivid descriptions of Jews as hideous, hook-nosed seducers of 'Aryan' women, Christ-slayers and money-grabbing usurers. 'The Jew' was portrayed as 'the Devil in human form'. In many secondary school books, anti-Semitic quotations by Hitler and other Nazi leaders were interspersed with folklore and nationalist literature. This type of racial indoctrination was, of course, just one small part of the Nazis' attempt to create popular consensus for their anti-Semitic policies culminating in the 'Final Solution'.

History lessons were a way of exciting children's sense of national pride and concern about the continued existence of the German state and nation, and about future glories to match—or even to exceed—those of the nation's great heroic past. History was to be looked at 'with the eyes of blood' and its primary function was to serve the 'political, intellectual and spiritual mobilisation of the nation'. Nazi history textbooks often dealt with German history only. Great rulers of Germany's past, such as Frederick the Great, were used to stress heroic leadership, ceaseless service to the state, military successes, and, of course, parallels to Hitler.

The ultimate triumphs of Nazism were given considerable priority in the history textbooks of the period, such as *Nation and Leader: German History for Schools* (1943). The issues of care and protection of the race found their way into history textbooks quite extensively too. Themes such as 'national renewal' were not uncommon in the history books of the Nazi era. Historical atlases showed Germany's greatness in her most historically important and expansive periods, and especially in the Third Reich.

Arithmetic books of the Nazi era also indoctrinated children by pervading the curriculum in a well-established tradition, echoing the religious bodies of the early nineteenth century, which based numerical tasks upon biblical content, and curricula in capitalist societies in the late nineteenth and early twentieth centuries, with textbook calculations based upon stocks and shares and profit-making. The Nazis used arithmetic exercises to propagate their racial and political ideas. The following example, from a standard 1941 textbook is overtly loaded with discrimination against the 'hereditarily ill'. Pupils were given the information that:

> Every day, the state spends RM 6 on one cripple; RM $4\frac{1}{4}$ on one mentally-ill person; RM $5\frac{1}{2}$ on one deaf and dumb person; RM $5\frac{3}{5}$ on one feeble-minded person; RM $3\frac{1}{2}$ on one alcoholic; RM $4\frac{4}{5}$ on one pupil in care; RM $2\frac{1}{20}$ on one pupil at a special school; and RM$\frac{9}{20}$ on one pupil at a normal school.

Using this, pupils were to answer questions such as 'What total cost do one cripple and one feeble-minded person create, if one takes a lifespan of forty-five years for each?' and 'Calculate the expenditure of the state for one pupil in a special school and one pupil in an ordinary school over eight years, and state the amount of higher cost engendered by the special school pupil'.

This was typical of the way in which data regarding state expenditure on 'hereditarily ill' or 'inferior' people was used in 'education'. The implications of such exercises are patent.

The Nazi regime was not original in its desire to indoctrinate children from an early age and to use school textbooks for this purpose. However, it did so in conjunction with the rest of its policies and with its own specific motivations in mind. Its concern was to create a racially 'pure' 'national community', in which the development of the individual was of little or no importance. That the Nazi regime used school textbooks so widely and blatantly for the dissemination of its ideology, shows distinctly the lengths to which it was willing to go in order to influence the society it sought to create.

FOR FURTHER READING:

L. Pine, 'The dissemination of Nazi ideology and family values through school textbooks', *History of Education* (1996), vol. 25, No. 1, 91–109; W. Marsden, 'Rooting racism into the educational experience of childhood and youth in the nineteenth- and twentieth-centuries', *History of Education* (1990), vol. 19, No. 4, 333–353; C. Kamenetsky, *Children's Literature in Nazi Germany* (Ohio University Press, 1984); G. Blackburn, *Education in the Third Reich: Race and History in Nazi Textbooks* (State University of New York Press, 1985); M. Burleigh and W. Wippermann, *The Racial State: Germany 1933–1945* (Cambridge University Press, 1991).

Lisa Pine is Lecturer in Modern History at the University of Luton and author of Nazi Family Policy, 1933–1945 *(Berg, 1997).*

Six Days to Reinvent Japan

Fifty years ago, in postwar Tokyo, General Douglas MacArthur gave a group of young Americans the assignment of drafting a new constitution for Japan. The resulting democratic charter has ordered Japanese political life ever since. Our author tells the story of this unusual "constitutional convention."

by Alex Gibney

On February 2, 1946, amid the ruins of postwar Japan, *His Butler's Sister,* starring Deanna Durbin, opened at the Ginza Subaruza in downtown Tokyo. The film, a musical comedy in which a temporary maid falls for her sophisticated boss, was the first American movie approved for showing by the office of the Supreme Commander of the Allied Powers (SCAP), General Douglas MacArthur. The Japanese audiences—who were supposed to be impressed by the film's democratic sentiments—were instead stunned by the sumptuous gowns, well-stocked refrigerators, and other emblems of material wealth that the characters in the film took for granted. Their world was so remote and alien to the viewers in the Ginza Subaruza that the movie seemed almost like science fiction.

But just a few blocks away, something even more fantastic was taking place: General MacArthur, the de facto emperor of Occupied Japan, was preparing orders to revise the fundamental principles of the Japanese state.

Two days later, at his direction, General Courtney Whitney assembled 25 American men and women—military officers, civilian attachés, researchers, and interpreters—in the Dai Ichi Insurance building, across the moat from the Imperial Palace. "Ladies and gentlemen," Whitney boomed, "we will now resolve ourselves into a constitutional convention . . . entrusted . . . with the historically significant task of drafting a new constitution for the Japanese people."

The Americans intended to change the 57-year-old Meiji charter that had allowed a militaristic regime to arise in Japan. They hoped thereby to establish a peace-loving democracy and a legal structure guaranteeing the rights of the Japanese people.

They did their work well. Fifty years later, the constitution they drafted—including the famous "no war" clause of Article Nine and the guarantees of civil rights and democratic freedoms—remains fully in force. Remarkably, during all those years, the Japanese have never seen fit to amend the document.

That may now be changing. During the Cold War, the United States served as Japan's military shield and economic sponsor. With the struggle over, and with Japan prosperous and at peace, some Japanese, as well as a number of Americans, have begun to wonder if the time has not come to alter the constitution's Article Nine, which renounces war and "the threat or use of force as a means of settling international disputes." Is the United States, which has 45,000 troops stationed in Japan, now stuck with a costly and unnecessary military burden? Does the constitutional provision allow Japan to evade its international responsibilities? Is it time, as some contend, for Japan to become a "normal" country again?

There are even more basic questions. Doubts persist among many Japanese and foreign observers as to whether Japan is truly a full-fledged democracy. Because democracy was imposed from above, not demanded from below, by the Japanese people, many maintain that powerful special interests, including big industry, the government bureaucracy, and the Liberal Democratic Party itself, effectively undermined the best efforts of the American framers.

Yet the fact remains that the Japanese people have not cast off their American-drafted constitution. And the reason is clear: most Japanese deeply believe in its principles. This belief was especially strong in 1946, when the rubble and twisted metal throughout Japan's great cities gave proof of a failed political system. Defeated in war, the Japanese were ready for a General MacArthur, acting like a new emperor, to transform the system that had led to such catastrophe.

MacArthur did not accomplish the task by himself, of course. It helped that the men and women to whom he gave the assignment of revising the constitution were idealistic amateurs, uninhibited by extensive special knowledge of Japan and fervently convinced that the

From *The Wilson Quarterly*, Autumn 1996, pp. 72–80. © 1996 by Alex Gibney. Reprinted by permission.

principles of liberal democracy were universal truths.

Buoyed by their nation's victory in war, the members of SCAP's Government Section exuded a self-confidence that almost equaled their commander's. As is well known, MacArthur lacked neither vainglory nor the will to make history. Perhaps because of both, he was willing to sanction occupation policies that seemed to fly in the face of his conservative principles. The policies proclaimed in his name included busting trusts, purging businessmen and politicians tainted by connections with the wartime regime, initiating land reform, bolstering the power of labor unions, and releasing Communists from jail.

The Potsdam Declaration proclaimed by the Allies in 1945 called for the Japanese government to "remove all obstacles to the revival and strengthening of democratic tendencies among the Japanese people" and to establish "freedom of speech, of religion, of thought, as well as respect for fundamental human rights." Those under MacArthur's command who saw Potsdam as a license to effect a social revolution in Japan could be certain of his support, so long as giving "power to the people" was part of a military program of dismantling the governmental machinery behind Japan's war effort.

The members of MacArthur's Government Section were convinced that the very nature of the Meiji Constitution, written in 1889 by the great 19th-century statesman Ito Hirobumi, had encouraged Japan's militarism. The charter's goals were summed up by the slogan "Fukoku Kyohei" ("Rich Nation, Strong Military"). In a hurry to modernize Japan and so protect it from the weapons of the Western powers, Ito traveled all over the world in search of models for a constitution that would adapt modern Western statecraft to the Japanese character, in a way that would centralize power (no time for democracy in the push to modernize) and unify a weak and isolated country of feuding domains (*han*) around a nationalistic symbol.

The charter Ito gave Japan combined the Prussian constitution of Otto Von Bismarck (which is why Japan's parliament bears the German name Diet) with the mystical allure of the Japanese emperor (a legendary descendant of Japan's

"mother," the Sun Goddess Amaterasu) who—until he was resurrected by Ito—had been a purely ceremonial figure in Kyoto. By moving the 16-year-old Emperor Mutsuhito to Tokyo from the old imperial capital, dressing him in a military uniform, and making him the sovereign of the Japanese state (with the ceremonial name "Meiji," meaning "enlightened rule"), Ito and his fellow modernizers from the western domains of Satsuma and Choshu had been able to create a strong national symbol and to design a form of government that looked like a parliamentary democracy.

But, in practice, as political scientist Chalmers Johnson has noted, Ito's constitution neither permitted real democracy—which many educated citizens had begun to demand—nor bestowed real power upon the emperor. While the constitution gave the emperor the power to declare war and peace, conclude treaties, and appoint key officials, the actual levers of power were operated by the men behind the throne—advisers such as Ito (who also became prime minister) and, later, Japan's wartime cabinet ministers. Responsible to the emperor, not the Diet, they "were basically beyond the law," Johnson observed.

After the war, when the American occupiers made it clear that they wanted changes in this political system, Prime Minister Shidehara Kijuro appointed a distinguished group of jurists, the Matsumoto Committee, to consider a few modifications to Ito's constitution. But when an enterprising Japanese journalist revealed details of the committee's secret first draft on the front page of Japan's *Mainichi Shimbun,* readers—most of them extremely bitter toward the existing system—were shocked at how superficial the proposed changes were. The Matsumoto Committee, believing that the militarists had abused a Meiji Constitution that was fundamentally sound, thought that constitutional revision meant little more than dusting off the old furniture. General MacArthur had other ideas.

When General Whitney relayed MacArthur's order for them to draft a new constitution for Japan, his young subordinates could not believe it. "I was flabbergasted," recalled Colonel Charles Kades, the popular deputy chief of SCAP's Government Section who was selected to chair the Constitution Steering Committee (and

who died in June 1996 at the age of 90). He was even more astonished when Whitney told them how much time they had to complete their work: a mere six days.

The story of their mission mocks the portentous stereotypes of nation building. Kades and the others given this daunting assignment were not learned philosopher-statesmen. They were intelligent, educated men and women who, owing to the urgency of the military's assignment and the might of their nation, found themselves in a peculiar position of power. Their inexperience might even have been an advantage, making them more willing, perhaps, than constitutional scholars or "experts" on Japan to institute the dramatic political changes deemed necessary by the Allies in general, the Americans in particular, and many of the Japanese themselves. Guided by their native idealism, they set out to transform Japan into a Western-style democracy and a beacon of pacifism—in MacArthur's words, "the Switzerland of Asia."

The men and women chosen for this task of "creative destruction" were a diverse lot. They included a doctor, a novelist, a former congressman and governor of Puerto Rico, a newspaperman, a foreign service officer, two academics, and five lawyers. Though they held views that ran the political spectrum, most were liberals who had supported President Franklin Roosevelt's New Deal and were sympathetic to the use of government to promote social equality. They also shared a faith in the American way, and they espoused it with an almost missionary zeal. "We felt that what we knew about American experience could be imposed and replicated almost totally in Japan," says Milton Esman, now an emeritus professor of government at Cornell University, then a 24-year-old with a freshly minted Ph.D. from Princeton.

The brash confidence of the drafters was in part a reflection of their ignorance of Japan. "My knowledge was zero," Kades candidly admitted. "Before I arrived, I knew nothing about Japan except that which one would glean from a local American newspaper." Indeed, there was a disdain in the Government Section for anyone—such as the old "Japan hands" in the State Department—who had special knowledge of, or affection for, Japan which might make them reluctant to implement radical social changes.

It was clear to the Americans that the Japanese government did not represent the wishes of the Japanese citizenry. "There were ultra-nationalists in the cabinet at the time," said Kades, "whereas it was clear from the press and the radio and the letters to the editors that the Japanese people wanted to swing to the left. Not to the left of center, but from the extreme right toward the center."

To reinvent Japan, these foreign founders had precious little to work with. There were a few translations of published draft constitutions, drawn up by independent Japanese groups and political parties, that the Americans had collected or that had arrived, unbidden, in the Dai Ichi building. There was a dog-eared copy of a vague State Department directive about democracy. And Colonel Kades clutched a handwritten note from MacArthur advising the committee of his wishes. These included retaining the emperor, ending the "feudal" rights of peerage, abolishing war as a sovereign right of the nation, and patterning the budget after "the British system." "I don't think any of us had any idea what the British system was," Kades said, and any resemblance the final draft had to it was, he added, "purely coincidental."

"I thought, 'my goodness, we have to have some prototypes,' " recalls Beate Sirota Gordon, who, at 22, was the youngest member of the Government Section and—other than the translators—the only one able to speak Japanese. She commandeered a jeep and driver and set out through the bombed-out ruins of Tokyo in search of constitutions from various countries. Under orders to keep the operation secret, Sirota drove from library to library, taking only a few constitutions from each place, because she "didn't want to make the librarians suspicious." She returned with more than a dozen constitutions, and spread them out on a table for her colleagues.

Supervising the "constitutional convention" was a Steering Committee made up of Kades, Lieutenant Colonel Milo Rowell, a conservative Republican lawyer from Fresno, California, and Alfred Hussey, a navy commander and Harvard-trained lawyer from Plymouth, Massachusetts. They divided the members of the "convention" into seven committees.

In drafting a new charter, the Americans tried to preserve some of the character of the old one. They did not try to force an American-style president and congress on Japan. Rather, they retained the form of a parliamentary system while insisting that both houses of the old bicameral Diet be popularly elected. (In the Meiji Constitution, the upper house had been composed of members of the imperial family, nobles, and imperial appointees.) To forestall abuses of power by the cabinet and unofficial "advisers" to the throne, the new system had the prime minister elected by the lower house, and the entire cabinet responsible to the Diet, not the emperor, as under the Meiji Constitution.

The Committee on the Emperor, Treaties and Enabling Provisions—led by Richard Poole, one of the younger members of the Government Section (and now a retired foreign service officer)—had the important job of defining the emperor's new constitutional role. "We didn't want him to be just window dressing," Poole says. Nor did they want him to retain the power he had under the Meiji Constitution. They finally arrived at the formula that the emperor was "the symbol of the state and the unity of the people, deriving his position from the will of the people with whom resides sovereign power."

That the emperor should continue to have a role was of the greatest concern to the conservative Japanese government, which regarded the imperial institution as essential to the Japanese polity. But in the United States and among U.S. allies, there was considerable pressure to abolish the institution and to try Emperor Hirohito himself as a war criminal. Fearing that "blood would flow in the streets" if Hirohito were deposed, MacArthur unilaterally decided to keep the emperor. But he was to be stripped of all semblance of power. The constitution that emerged stipulated that the emperor "shall not have powers related to government." His role was to be purely symbolic.

Yet even as a mere symbol, the emperor remained a problem because he was identified so closely with Japan's militarism and aggression. The solution was to have the Japanese, in the new charter, renounce forever the right to wage war. Kades assigned himself the task of writing Article Nine, the "no war" provision.

The origin of the idea for Article Nine is still a mystery. Though some credit Prime Minister Shidehara, the emperor, or even Kades (who casually mentioned the idea to General Whitney during a car ride to see Shidehara), most informed observers agree that the inventor was probably MacArthur. He, in any case, was the only man with the authority and the audacity to insist on its inclusion. "MacArthur was concerned with his place in history," says Esman, who believes that the general was motivated primarily by his titanic ego. He thought history would take keen and admiring interest in a military man who "was able to induce a society like Japan to renounce armaments."

In Kades's view, Article Nine stemmed partly from a pragmatic concern: MacArthur's fear that Japan might be the battleground for an American-Soviet confrontation if Japan were not "neutral." But Article Nine also resulted from "sheer idealism," said Kades. "MacArthur decided that he might be able to change the course of history, by changing the nature of Japan."

In writing the provision, Kades made a critical change in MacArthur's wording in his handwritten directive, one that looms large even today. MacArthur had written: "Japan renounces [war] . . . even for preserving its own security." Kades struck out that last clause because he "didn't feel it was practical to forbid a nation's self-defense." That stroke of a pen, along with some minor Japanese changes in the text that Kades approved, gave "the color of respectability" (in his words) to the establishment of Japan's Self-Defense Forces—a rather large military body allowed to defend Japan from external attack but prohibited from foreign deployment. (For this reason, Japan provided no troops in the Persian Gulf War.)

Next to Article Nine, the most radical constitutional changes were made by the Committee on Civil Rights. Imagining the reaction of the conservative Japanese Government, the Steering Committee, as an inside joke, staffed this committee with the Government Section's most ardent leftists. Among them was Beate Sirota, a recent graduate of Mills College who had grown up in Japan, spoke fluent Japanese, and was determined to right the social wrongs—particularly, those suffered by women—that she had perceived as a child. She was assigned to the Civil Rights Committee, Kades later said, precisely because "she knew what it was like to live in a police state." Inside the committee, she was given the job of dealing with women's rights, as well as with academic freedom.

In drafting the charter's section on women's rights, Sirota was largely on her own. The Steering Committee provided no initial guidance. The U.S. Constitution had no equal-rights provision. There was nothing about women's rights in any of the State Department directives. And the various constitutions proposed by the Japanese political parties had nothing meaningful on the subject. So this part of Japan's national charter was simply invented on the spot by an idealistic young woman who felt strongly that fundamental injustices inflicted on Japanese women needed to be corrected. "The idea that a woman couldn't decide whom she wanted to marry . . . that she couldn't divorce a man . . . that she really had no rights as far as property was concerned . . . was very disturbing to me," she says.

To prevent any misinterpretation or evasion, Sirota made her first draft pointedly specific. Expectant and nursing mothers were to be guaranteed public assistance, for instance, and not only was there to be universal compulsory education but "school supplies shall be free." The assorted rights were proclaimed in terse one- or two-sentence paragraphs. "I wanted them to be like bullets," she recalls.

Not to be outdone, the other members of the Civil Rights Committee drafted a plan that gave workers the right to organize, to bargain collectively, and to strike, as well as the right "to earn a living." They also drafted constitutional guarantees of freedom of speech, due process, and "economic liberty." Many of the rights set down by the committee became part of the constitution, but others were modified by Kades, the Steering Committee, Whitney, or MacArthur himself.

As for Beate Sirota's "bullets" for women's rights, Kades decided that "meritorious though they might be, the provisions were the concern of statutory regulation and not constitutional law." Sirota confronted the colonel in the hall outside the conference room. She was certain that—given the weight of tradition and male domination of the government—the failure to be specific meant that women would never get equal

rights. Why couldn't Kades—for whom Sirota had the highest regard and affection—understand? She leaned against him and began to cry. Kades was a bit taken aback. No military handbook had prepared him for this spontaneous display of deep emotion by a subordinate. But it changed no one's mind. While Kades and the Steering Committee left Sirota's broad guarantees of social security and women's rights in the constitution, they removed all of her carefully aimed "bullets."

On February 13, nine days after General Whitney told the men and women of the Government Section about their historic mission, he, Kades, Rowell, and Hussey drove to the foreign minister's residence and presented the American draft of Japan's new constitution to Shigeru Yoshida, the foreign minister (and a future prime minister), and two other government representatives. The Japanese were stunned. Instead of making a few minor changes, the Americans had turned the Meiji Constitution on its head—taking power from the emperor and his advisers and giving it not only to the Diet but to women, intellectuals, and labor unions.

After huddling among themselves for half an hour, the Japanese officials apologized to the Americans for keeping them waiting in an adjacent garden. Whitney replied with a brutal but meaningful quip: "Don't worry, we've been enjoying your atomic sunshine." As if on cue, a B-29 flew by, rattling the windows of the foreign minister's residence. "It certainly had a persuasive element," Kades recalled.

Faced with the unmatched force of an occupying power, and the threat that MacArthur would present the new constitution directly to the Japanese people (who were likely to embrace it), Prime Minister Shidehara, Yoshida, and the others agreed to present the American version to the Diet as a Japanese draft. Though few were fooled about the document's origins (one Japanese journalist said it "smelled of butter," meaning it was distinctively American), the constitution was approved by both houses of the Diet on November 3, 1946, in the form of an amendment to the 1889 constitution. It went into effect on May 3, 1947.

Besides clarifying the nation's political system, spelling out with whom political power rested and from whom it

came, the new constitution proclaimed a vastly expanded list of popular rights, including not only those enshrined in the U.S. Constitution but equality of the sexes and the right of labor to bargain and act collectively.

The document's idealism struck a responsive chord in a devastated populace eager to put the immediate past behind it. To those whose lives had been shattered by war, some of them living in tin-roofed shacks amid the rubble of Tokyo, the permanent peace offered by Article Nine was strongly appealing. And to Japanese used to living under the wartime regime's unchecked powers, the guarantees of personal rights and freedoms were also very welcome.

Still, the new constitution *was* being imposed by a foreign power. Milton Esman never imagined that the charter would outlast the occupation, which ended in 1952. Today, he credits its lasting popularity to the disparate groups—women, intellectuals, teachers, and labor unions—that fought against any basic changes that might encourage militarism or limit freedom of expression.

The fact of the matter is that many of the democratic ideas contained in the "MacArthur Constitution" were not foreign to many Japanese. Even during the Meiji era, as proved by the discovery of model constitutions in village farmhouses all over Japan, educated citizens were reading the works of Locke, Spencer, and Rousseau, and pressing their government for greater popular representation and individual rights. Their ideas had simply been suppressed by Japan's rulers—men whose power was buttressed by a constitution and a system of government that strengthened the state at the expense of freedom and democracy. The "MacArthur Constitution" was an attempt to fix that.

Ironically, the Americans themselves were partly responsible for weakening the very democratic reforms that the constitution encouraged. With the advent of the Cold War and the fall of China to Mao Zedong's Communists, and the election of a Republican majority in the U.S. Congress, American occupation policy in Japan changed. Instead of shoring up all of the new constitution's reforms, the architects of U.S. foreign policy focused on building up Japan as a bulwark against communism in Asia. In practice, that meant bolstering

Courtesy of The National Archives

The effort to democratize Japan did not end with the new constitution. A Tokyo newspaper in 1950 organized a fair near Osaka that featured replicas of American landmarks, including a paper-mâché U.S. Capitol.

conservative forces within the Japanese political economy while undermining more liberal forces, such as labor unions. The occupation command sent clear signals—through aggressive "red purges" and the banning of strikes—that the democratic traditions embedded in the constitution should not be carried to "extremes."

While the Americans' ignorance of Japan may have helped them to make sweeping constitutional changes, it was a disadvantage when it came to understanding how the new democratic principles would be implemented. As a result, the Diet remained weaker than intended and, as Kades admitted to me, because the Government Section never understood the unique power of Japan's bureaucracy in relation to the Diet, the unsympathetic bureaucracy was able to undermine many of the democratic reforms.

Still, the constitution made a great difference. The drafters could not have foreseen the extraordinary impact that Article Nine was to have on Japan—and the world. "It never occurred to us," recalled Kades, "that [because of Article Nine] Japan would not have to spend enormous amounts of money on defense and therefore could channel that money into economic recovery and become an economic superpower."

Today, Japan has grown so used to its military dependency on the United States that it sometimes has difficulty charting its own course in world affairs. A 1994 report by a nongovernmental commission in Japan urged that the nation assume a larger international role, including taking a greater part in United Nations peacekeeping operations. In recent years, stung by criticism of its failure to send troops to take part in the 1991 Persian Gulf War, Japan has bent Article Nine to send unarmed soldiers to assist international peacekeeping efforts in Cambodia, Mozambique, and Rwanda. Increasingly, though, both inside and outside Japan, there are calls for Japan to amend its "Peace Constitution."

Yet Japan, constrained by its own history, has not done so. Inside Japan, there is still great popular resistance to strengthening the military. And among other nations, there is also strong resistance. Many in South Korea, North Korea, China, Taiwan, and Southeast Asia have not forgotten the brutality of Japan's military aggression in World War II. When Japanese prime minister Ryutaro Hashimoto visited the controversial Yasukuni shrine to the spirits of the country's military heroes in Tokyo July [1996], there were immediate protests

from China, the two Koreas, and other Asian countries.

In the post-Cold War world, Japan is trying gradually to define its proper role. If the Japanese do amend Article Nine so as to be able to fulfill their international responsibilities, they will have to find a way to mollify the fears of Asia's other powers, lest the specter of a revived Japanese militarism prompt a destabilizing arms race in the region.

The other radical constitutional change that Charles Kades and his cohorts made—the guarantees of civil rights and freedoms—has also proven a lasting legacy. Until recently, Japan was the only country in Asia where the people enjoyed freedom of speech, freedom of the press, and the right to a fair trial; where unions had the right to organize, and where women were at least constitutionally assured of equality with men.

That last guarantee—of sexual equality—has not, to be sure, turned Japan into a fully egalitarian society. Although the enfranchisement of women and the constitutional guarantees of women's rights, including the right to own property and the right to divorce, were tremendous advances, Japanese culture, with its tradition of female subservience, has proven resistant to change.

And that points up the central contradiction of Japan's democratic constitution: it was bestowed as a gift from above rather than achieved through strong popular demand. As a document drafted by foreign amateurs in less than a week, it was a remarkable accomplishment, and it has served Japan well in the half-century since. But its weakness was also the weakness of the occupation: it was democracy by directive. Nevertheless, the constitution was not rejected. As the Japanese have more and more made it their own, it has grown stronger. The constitution's origins still matter, but what matters more is how the Japanese continue to interpret and adapt it to fit the needs of their own changing society.

ALEX GIBNEY, *a writer and documentary producer, was the executive producer of the Emmy Award-winning 10-part PBS series "The Pacific Century." He is completing a book about the American authors of the Japanese constitution.*

The Future That Never Came

In August the world will solemnly mark the 50th anniversaries of Hiroshima and Nagasaki. Their devastation in 1945 inaugurated an age fraught with doomsday anxieties: the fear of Armageddon, of uncontrolled proliferation, and, more recently, of nuclear terrorism. Yet even before the Cold War began to fade, many countries were quietly retreating from the nuclear temptation. Mitchell Reiss explains why—and what can be done to encourage the trend.

Mitchell Reiss

Mitchell Reiss, a Wilson Center Guest Scholar, was special assistant to the U.S. national security advisor from 1988 to 1989. He is the author of Bridled Ambition: Why Countries Constrain Their Nuclear Capabilities, *published by the Woodrow Wilson Center Press and distributed by Johns Hopkins University Press. He is currently writing and consulting on the relationship between technology and foreign policy.*

Half a century ago, World War II ended in two blazing flashes of heat, light, and devastation. The radioactive clouds that rose over Hiroshima and Nagasaki on those two fateful days in August 1945 cast a dark shadow over what historian John Lewis Gaddis has called "the long peace" that followed. Within seven years, the United States tested a fusion device 1,000 times more powerful than the atomic explosive that flattened Hiroshima and killed more than 100,000 Japanese. By then, the Soviet Union also possessed its own atomic bomb and would soon explode a thermonuclear bomb. It seemed a foregone conclusion that many other countries, in the quest for national security and international military and technological prestige, would seek and, inevitably, obtain nuclear weapons.

During the darkest periods of these 50 years, there seemed to be only one question on many people's minds: when and where would the next Nagasaki occur? Few could have believed that every advanced country in the world would not want the bomb, and few would have imagined that such a "winning weapon" would not again be used in military conflict. Yet despite the wars and innumerable crises that have embroiled the nine countries known or believed to have acquired nuclear weapons (India, Israel, and Pakistan remain officially mute on the point), and despite the creation of nuclear warheads numbering in the tens of thousands, not one of these weapons has been used in war since Nagasaki. Never before in military history have countries exercised such restraint with the destructive power at their disposal.

Nor have nuclear arms proved to be the irresistible temptation that many feared they would be. Not only have nations such as Germany and Japan eschewed them, but some countries that possessed either the weapons or the means to build them have quietly (and without much fanfare in the press) retreated. Even North Korea, the greatest saber rattler of recent years, has avoided all-out confrontation on its suspected nuclear weapons program.

Instead of the dreaded global nuclear conflagration, the 50 years since Nagasaki have provided the world with an unexpected nuclear education. These weapons have proved much less useful and far more costly than anybody expected. The imperative now is to recognize these lessons and to apply them in the post–Cold War world.

To the nuclear physicists of the early 1940s, the future had an ominous cast. Scientists working on the wartime Manhattan Project quickly recognized the dangers of unbridled postwar competition in atomic arms. They knew far better than their political masters that science knows no borders and that the American nuclear monopoly could not last.

The Manhattan Project itself was a cooperative venture among the United States, the United Kingdom, Canada, and scientists from France. Its distinguished international cast, including Denmark's Niels Bohr, Germany's Hans Bethe, Hungary's Leo Szilard, and Italy's Enrico Fermi, was a living example of the cosmopolitan nature of scientific inquiry. The United States might keep its own atomic secrets (and even that proved impossible), but it was inevitable that other countries—perhaps many others—would eventually penetrate the mysteries of the atom on their own. The British physicist James Chadwick, whose experiments in the early 1930s revealed the inner structure of the atom, described his thoughts during the war: "I realized that a nuclear bomb was not only possible—it was inevitable.... Everybody would think about them before long, and some country would put them into action."

Even before the end of the war, these fears prompted Leo Szilard and other scientists working at the Metallurgical Laboratory of the University of Chicago, where history's first controlled-fission chain reaction took place in a squash court under Stagg Field in December 1942, to propose that the United States share its special knowledge with the world through a supranational organization. In return for receiving the peaceful benefits of the atom—chiefly, "energy too cheap to meter," in the phrase of the day—these nations would forgo autonomous nuclear research and development projects. The alternative was almost too horrifying to contemplate. Philip Morrison, a physicist who worked on the Manhattan project, wrote immediately after the war: "If we do not learn to live together so that science will be our help and not our hurt, there is only one sure future. The cities of men on earth will perish."

The first two decades of the nuclear age seemed to bear out some of the worst fears of the scientists. The poet W. H. Auden declared the postwar era an "age of anxiety." The bone-chilling prospect of a hundred Hiroshimas prompted policymakers to give serious thought to dispersing America's population to the countryside and even to building cities underground. The world-renowned British philosopher and pacifist, Bertrand Russell, was so alarmed by the nuclear peril that he recommended in 1946 that the United States launch an atomic attack against the Soviet Union if Moscow refused to help form a world government.

At first, hopes ran strong that atomic energy could be placed under international control. In a speech at the United Nations in June 1946, financier Bernard Baruch, the U.S. representative to the United Nations Atomic Energy Commission (UNAEC), proposed to transfer control of all the world's "dangerous" atomic activities, including fuel-production facilities, to just such a supranational authority. "Nondangerous" activities, such as the use of radioactive isotopes in medical research, would remain in national hands, monitored by the new agency. But only after these controls were in place would the United States relinquish the bomb. This plan, which now seems either hopelessly utopian or thoroughly cynical, was a serious attempt to prevent global disaster. "Let us not deceive ourselves: we must elect world peace or world destruction," Baruch declared.

The Baruch plan foundered on growing Soviet-American tensions. The Soviets offered a fundamentally different plan: the United States would eliminate its nuclear stockpile within three months, and an international control scheme would be developed in later negotiations. Two years of desultory political jousting followed before the UNAEC suspended its work in frustration. After Moscow exploded its first atomic device in August 1949, several years earlier than expected, most remaining enthusiasm for international control died, as did most talk in the U.S. scientific community of "one world or none."

Other countries, it was recognized, soon would be able to uncover the technological mysteries for themselves. As German physicist Werner Heisenberg warned in February 1947, the development of atomic bombs was "no longer a problem of science in any country, but a problem of engineering." In 1950, tens of millions of people around the world signed the Stockholm Appeal, a petition demanding that atomic bombs be outlawed as "weapons of terror and the mass destruction of whole populations." Audiences in the United States flocked to see *The Day the Earth Stood Still* (1951), a Hollywood Cold War fantasy in which a benevolent visitor from outer space lands a flying saucer in Washington to warn humanity of its peril: the human race will destroy itself and perhaps the universe if it does not bring an end to the arms race.

Great Britain became the third member of the atomic club in October 1952, detonating a bomb on board a ship near the Monte Bello Islands off the coast of Australia. (No Americans were invited to observe the test, in retaliation for Washington's curtailment of the flow of nuclear information to London after World War II. The test, declared the British defense minister, showed that Britain was "not merely a satellite of the United States.") Later that month, at Enewetak Atoll in the Pacific, the United States exploded the world's first hydrogen bomb. It was built despite the opposition of some top nuclear scientists, including Enrico Fermi and J. Robert Oppenheimer, who objected that such a "superbomb" could serve only as a weapon of genocide, not as a useful military device. "Mike," as it was called, gouged out a crater three miles wide and half a mile deep. Less than a year later,

the Soviet Union exploded its own crude H-bomb. The arms race was on in earnest.

Inaugurating their famous "doomsday clock" in 1947, the scientist-editors of the *Bulletin of the Atomic Scientists* had set the minute hand at seven minutes to midnight; after the Mike test it edged five minutes closer. President Dwight D. Eisenhower, concerned about the growing cost of the U.S. defense effort and by the inability of the Western European countries to muster sufficient military forces to counter the Soviet threat, authorized in 1953 a "New Look" defense strategy. By emphasizing the use of battlefield (tactical) nuclear weapons to repel an attack, the New Look accelerated "vertical" proliferation: the enlargement of superpower arsenals. Now there would be nuclear artillery shells, demolition mines, and short-range missiles.

At the outset of Ike's presidency, 20 countries possessed independent nuclear-research projects that might allow them eventually to build the bomb. Eisenhower won worldwide applause in December 1953 when he announced his Atoms for Peace initiative before the United Nations. Coupling partial disarmament with the expansion of peaceful uses of the atom around the world, he proposed that the United States, Soviet Union, and United Kingdom "make joint contributions from their stockpiles of normal uranium and fissionable material to an International Atomic Energy Agency (IAEA)." This would have the effect of reducing the amount of material available for the manufacture of weapons—though it would handicap the Soviet Union more than the United States. The IAEA would act as a kind of nuclear-materials bank for countries with peaceful nuclear-energy programs.

By the time the IAEA came into existence in 1957, however, Eisenhower's original disarmament idea was all but forgotten. The IAEA, based in Vienna, was now designed to promote the peaceful uses of atomic energy and to act as a watchdog to ensure that nuclear technology was not diverted to military ends, an important function that it still performs today.

Another potential route to disarmament was a ban on nuclear testing. The idea gained impetus when American H-bomb tests at Bikini atoll in 1954 showered radioactive fallout over a broad swath of the Pacific, forcing the highly

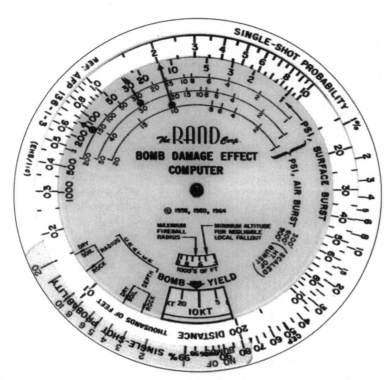

A Cold War artifact: defense specialists used the Bomb Damage Effect Computer to estimate such things as the extent of fallout and the size of fireballs produced by bombs of different sizes.

publicized evacuation of several islands. To the horror of the world, the crew of the *Lucky Dragon,* a Japanese tuna trawler that chanced to be nearby, contracted radiation sickness, and one of the men died. In Japan fear spread that fish, a staple of the national diet, had become contaminated. Forty million Japanese signed petitions calling for the abolition of nuclear weapons. Traces of fallout were later found in milk and other substances in the United States and elsewhere.

The public's sudden awareness of radioactivity raised a new kind of alarm, the threat of insidious nuclear contamination. The preoccupation with poisoning was reflected in such things as Nevil Shute's 1957 best seller *On the Beach,* with its eerie portrait of Australians carrying on as they await an invasion of deadly fallout produced by a world war that has destroyed the Northern Hemisphere.

Led by Indian prime minister Jawaharlal Nehru, the Non-Aligned Movement denounced the nuclear powers and demanded a total ban on nuclear testing. In January 1958, a petition signed by 11,000 scientists from around the world calling for an end to nuclear tests was presented to UN Secretary-General Dag Hammarskjöld. But the agreement that emerged five years later, the Limited Test Ban Treaty, prohibited tests only in the atmosphere, in outer space, and underwater. Because underground tests were still permitted, the treaty did little to slow either nuclear testing or the bomb's spread. The chief U.S. test-ban negotiator, Averell Harriman, later lamented that it was merely an environmental-protection measure.

Meanwhile, other hurdles to nuclear proliferation, such as scientific expertise and engineering competence, were being lowered; the global diffusion of civilian nuclear research and power reactors by the United States, Great Britain, France, and (with much tighter controls) the Soviet Union was another cause for concern.

Nuclear power plants have no direct use in bomb making, but possession of the technology allows a country to develop a cadre of trained scientists and engineers with the skills and knowledge to develop fuel reprocessing and other technologies needed to make a bomb. A 1958 American study, *1970 Without Arms Control,* predicted that "by 1970, most nations with appreciable military strength will have in their arsenals nuclear weapons—strategic, tactical, or both."

Two years later, in February 1960, an explosion in the Sahara made France the fourth member of the nuclear club. The British scientist and writer C. P. Snow predicted that "within, at the most, 10 years, some of these bombs are going off. . . . That is the certainty."

Speaking before the United Nations in 1963, President John F. Kennedy voiced the apprehension felt by many of his contemporaries: "I am haunted by the feeling that by 1970 . . . there may be 10 nuclear powers instead of four, and by 1975, 15 or 20. . . . I see the possibility in the 1970s of the president of the United States having to face a world in which 15 or 20 or 25 nations may have these weapons. I regard that as the greatest possible danger and hazard."

In 1964, China became the world's fifth nuclear power. By this time, every country that was technically competent to build nuclear arms, save Canada, had done so. China's test, the first by a member of the developing world, accelerated international efforts to halt the bomb's spread. New treaties restricting weapons in space and in Latin America were drawn up. In the United Nations, the Eighteen-Nation Disarmament Committee abandoned its work on comprehensive disarmament and turned instead to nonproliferation. Its efforts led to the Treaty on the Nonproliferation of Nuclear Weapons (NPT), signed by 61 countries in 1968.

Under the NPT, the non-nuclear states pledged to forswear nuclear weapons and to accept IAEA safeguards on their peaceful nuclear programs. The members of the nuclear club formally agreed not to help other countries to arm themselves. (China and France, however, did not sign the treaty until the 1990s.) In Article VI, they agreed to pursue negotiations on "cessation of the nuclear arms race at an early date, and to nuclear disarmament." The day the treaty was signed, July 1, 1968, the United States and Soviet Union announced the beginning of the Strategic Arms Limitations Talks (SALT).

But several countries that had no intention of swearing off the atom did not sign the NPT. With French help, Israel had developed a nuclear capability years earlier. In India, Prime Minister Lal Bahadoor Shastri had concluded in 1964 that China's nuclear blast left him no option but to permit research on "peaceful" nuclear explosives. On May 18, 1974, the Indians got their bomb. (Prime Minister Indira Gandhi received news of the successful test in code words: "the Buddha smiles.") From China and India, the chain reaction led to Pakistan. Prime Minister Zulfikar Ali Bhutto had already vowed that his country would acquire nuclear weapons if India did, even if his people had "to eat grass or leaves, even go hungry" to free up the necessary resources. New Delhi's nuclear test energized Pakistan's quest for an "Islamic bomb." South Africa decided that it too needed nuclear arms. The world appeared well on its way to fulfilling Kennedy's nightmare vision.

II.

The Cold War, however, ended not with the expected bang but a whimper—or at least a long, exhausted exhalation. Its passing has eased the world's most extreme anxieties about the nuclear age. Less than a decade ago, Armageddon seemed even more imminent to some than it had in Kennedy's day. "The world is moving inexorably toward the use of nuclear weapons," wrote a commentator in the *Journal of the American Medical Association* during the early 1980s, expressing a fairly common view. By 1984, the editors of the *Bulletin of the Atomic Scientists,* alarmed by the Reagan administration's military build-up and by the superpowers' increasingly bellicose rhetoric, had inched their famous minute hand to three minutes to midnight, as close to apocalypse as it had been since the early 1950s. Visions of "nuclear winter," a new nightmare scenario of how the world would slowly die in the aftermath of a nuclear war, terrified the public, much as *On the Beach* had 30 years before. Critics warned that the arms race was propelling the world toward disaster.

Then, suddenly, it was over.

The disintegration of communism and of the Soviet Union itself after the Berlin Wall fell in November 1989 brought the quickest imaginable end— short of war itself—to the old fears. True, there had been significant change before 1989. Modest arms-control agreements during the 1970s that placed ceilings on certain categories of nuclear systems were replaced in the latter half of the 1980s with ambitious agreements

that cut deeply, such as the 1987 Intermediate-Range Nuclear Forces Treaty. But today the superpowers can't disarm fast enough to suit themselves.

In the fall of 1991, George Bush and Mikhail Gorbachev announced sweeping reciprocal unilateral reductions in deployed tactical nuclear weapons. The 1991 START I Treaty virtually halved the number of U.S. and Soviet strategic nuclear warheads. If START II is fully implemented, the superpowers will cut their strategic nuclear arsenals by more than 80 percent from their Cold War peak. The United States and Russia will dismantle more than 15,000 warheads. The chief drag on disarmament now is not military or political but technical: the limited number of U.S. and Russian facilities equipped to dismantle these warheads and safely and securely store the leftover nuclear material.

Yet there has scarcely been time to celebrate. From the allied victory in the Persian Gulf War, barely more than a year after the fall of the Berlin Wall, came the sobering discovery that Saddam Hussein's Iraq was well advanced on a secret project to build an atomic bomb. In late 1992, the IAEA uncovered (with the help of U.S. spy satellite imagery) another case of nuclear cheating, this time in communist North Korea. Earlier this year, news reports suggested that Iran was perhaps only five years away from developing a bomb, much closer than previously estimated. According to a 1988 study chaired by veteran military analysts Fred C. Iklé and Albert Wohlstetter, 40 countries will be able to produce nuclear weapons by 2000.

To borrow the metaphor used by R. James Woolsey, former director of the U.S. Central Intelligence Agency, the Soviet bear may be dead, but the forest is still full of poisonous snakes. The sprawling nuclear archipelago of the former Soviet Union, a complex of laboratories and factories employing almost one million physicists, chemists, metallurgists, engineers, and technicians, could well turn out to be a breeding ground for new nuclear snakes. Highly skilled scientists now earn less in a month than what an American teenager brings home after a day working the cash register at McDonald's. The temptations of going to work for a foreign power or even a terrorist group must be considerable.

Amid squalid military and deteriorating political conditions in Russia, there is also reason to worry about the safety and security of stockpiles of nuclear warheads and the fissile materials that can be used to make bombs. This is not an idle fear. To take one especially rich cache of bomb material out of circulation, operatives in a covert U.S. effort code-named "Project Sapphire" spirited 600 kilograms of highly enriched uranium (HEU), enough for perhaps 30 to 40 nuclear bombs, from a storage site in a remote and desolate corner of Kazakhstan. (However, 300 kilograms of HEU stored nearby was inexplicably left behind.) Nuclear smuggling from the former Soviet Union to the European black market is well documented. In one of the most alarming cases, police in the Czech Republic acting on an anonymous tip last year seized six pounds of highly enriched uranium, about one-sixth the amount needed for a bomb. Three men were arrested at the time, but who was behind the plot and where the uranium was bound remain a mystery.

But the great and still largely unrecognized surprise is that contrary to what scientists, statesmen, and ordinary people have assumed since Hiroshima and Nagasaki, the countries of the world have not rushed to arm themselves with nuclear weapons. Some have recognized the drawbacks and limitations of these weapons; others have gone so far as to conclude that they are a liability.

While the news media have focused with grim fascination on the new nuclear-nightmare scenarios of the post–Cold War world, several countries possessing nuclear weapons programs or harboring nuclear ambitions have, almost unnoticed, stepped back from the brink. They have slowed, halted, or even reversed their activities. Even North Korea, the most xenophobic and isolated country in the world, recently agreed to measures that promise over the course of 10 to 12 years to eliminate its ability to build nuclear weapons. These developments are without precedent in the nuclear age.

Very often people talk about the perils of proliferation as if nothing has changed during the course of the world's long experience with nuclear weapons. But this half-century of "mutual assured destruction" between the superpowers as well as nuclear crises in Cuba in 1962, the Middle East in 1973, and during the

The Nuclear World

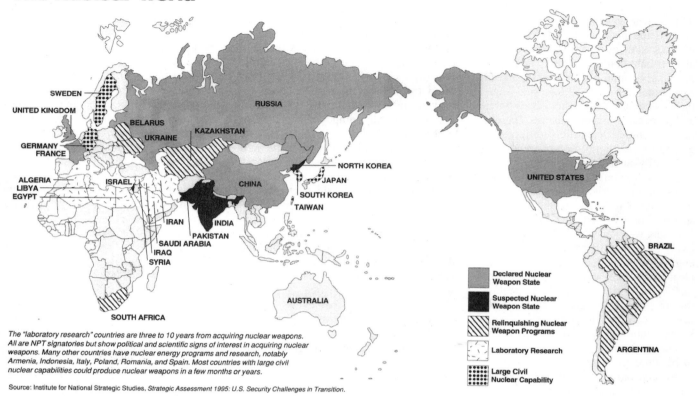

The "laboratory research" countries are three to 10 years from acquiring nuclear weapons. All are NPT signatories but show political and scientific signs of interest in acquiring nuclear weapons. Many other countries have nuclear energy programs and research, notably Armenia, Indonesia, Italy, Poland, Romania, and Spain. Most countries with large civil nuclear capabilities could produce nuclear weapons in a few months or years.

Source: Institute for National Strategic Studies, *Strategic Assessment 1995: U.S. Security Challenges in Transition.*

India-Pakistan clash of 1990 have provided the world with a profound nuclear education. The fact that an arsenal of some 30,000 strategic and tactical nuclear weapons could not preserve the Soviet Union, and may even have hastened its collapse, has raised new questions about the value of nuclear arms. The deep cuts scheduled by Moscow and Washington, moreover, have lowered the weapons' prestige value.

The stunningly large (and unexpected) bills that have started to fall due from the arms race also give other nations pause. The cost of dismantling nuclear weapons, storing excess plutonium and other dangerous materials, and repairing the environmental damage caused by more than 50 years of weapons research and production is huge. The United States will have to spend between $30 billion and $100 billion to clean up various installations, including production facilities at Rocky Flats, Colorado, Hanford, Washington, and Savannah River, South Carolina. In the former Soviet Union, the bill could reach $300 billion, although it is unlikely that anywhere near that amount will be found. And who knows what other costs of this radioactive legacy re-

main to be discovered? It is equally difficult to gauge the "opportunity costs" incurred by having generations of skilled scientists, engineers, and technicians devote their talents to building bombs instead of the gross national product.

All of these lessons have bred new attitudes toward nuclear weapons. In December 1991, when the Soviet Union was in its death throes, the world was confronted with the uncomfortable reality that three countries it had scarcely heard of—Ukraine, Belarus, and Kazakhstan—with leaders whom it hardly knew, now each possessed the means to devastate the United States, Europe, or any other target they chose. Thousands of Soviet tactical and strategic nuclear weapons were located on these three countries' soil. Yet each of them agreed to surrender these arms over the next few years.

Quickest to act was Belarus, site of more than 1,000 nuclear weapons. Stanislav Shushkevich, a physicist-turned-antinuclear activist after the 1986 Chernobyl disaster, used his largely ceremonial position as chairman of the Belarus Supreme Soviet to push a more rapid withdrawal than even Moscow

wanted. In the West there was dread that the Muslim leaders of Kazakhstan might transfer some of its fearful nuclear inheritance—including 104 huge SS-18 intercontinental ballistic missiles, each code named "Satan"—to their radical coreligionists in the Middle East. Eager for U.S. aid and investment and wary of angering Moscow, Kazakhstan pledged in 1992 to return the SS-18s and other weapons to Russia.

Ukraine was a little more recalcitrant. The country's stolid president, former Communist Party ideology chief Leonid Kravchuk, understood that the weapons would not be terribly helpful in defending Ukraine or improving its appalling economic conditions. But they could be bartered for Ukrainian membership in useful international organizations such as the North Atlantic Treaty Organization's Partnership for Peace. Ukraine's assent was finally purchased in 1994 at the cost of hundreds of millions of dollars in U.S. denuclearization assistance and, among other things, Russian promises to forgive Ukraine's multibillion-dollar oil and gas debt and to provide fuel for the country's nuclear power plants.

For each of these three countries the nuances were slightly different, but the fundamental calculations were essentially the same. Their leaders recognized that nuclear weapons are largely irrelevant to the most pressing problems of the late 20th century: civil war, ethnic and tribal conflict, mass migration, AIDS, economic backwardness, and international terrorism. More and more, these weapons appear to be elaborate and expensive anachronisms. There is not even much scientific prestige to be gained by building a bomb—now, after all, a 50-year-old technique.

A nuclear arsenal rarely promotes domestic prosperity, fosters better relations with neighbors, enhances national security, or wins international prestige. Nuclear weapons programs are more likely to siphon off scarce scientific and engineering talent, trigger a costly nuclear arms race with a regional adversary, sow mistrust among allies, inhibit the transfer of sensitive technologies needed for economic development, and invite international ostracism. This "winning weapon," moreover, turns out to be almost too terrible to use.

That is one reason why the popular fear of nuclear terrorism, while not wholly unrealistic, is greatly exaggerated. Nuclear blackmail is a staple of international spy thrillers such as Dominique Lapierre and Larry Collins's *Fifth Horseman* (1980), in which Libya's Muammar Qaddafi tries to force the United States to support the establishment of a Palestinian state by threatening to blow up New York City. But terrorists and leaders of "rogue" nations face many of the same constraints limiting others who seek to promote a political agenda. Would a nuclear blast advance their cause, or would it unify a horrified international community against them? If one is bent on violence, isn't it far easier to strike at a symbolic target with conventional means? The terrorists who attacked the World Trade Center, after all, made their explosive from a mixture of fertilizer and diesel fuel. This is not to mention the still-daunting technical tasks of manufacturing and safely handling a nuclear bomb.

Only one country in history has unilaterally and voluntarily eliminated its own fully developed nuclear arsenal: South Africa. That it was done virtually without fanfare or international acclaim and headlines is regrettable, since South Africa's experience illustrates some of the new realities of nuclear weapons. Immediately after becoming president in September 1989, F. W. de Klerk ordered that the country's nuclear weapons program, including an arsenal of six nuclear devices that had taken a decade to build, be dismantled. By July 1991, the highly enriched uranium from the warheads had been removed and melted down and most of the non-nuclear components had been destroyed.

These extraordinary steps were part of a much larger design. The coming transfer of power to the black majority certainly helped sway de Klerk, but so did South Africa's growing sense of security from external threats following the negotiated removal of Cuban troops from Angola in December 1988 and the dwindling of Soviet influence in southern Africa. A nuclear arsenal, moreover, would hinder South Africa's efforts to become a respected member of the international community.

The power of international opinion is not merely a matter of rhetoric. Countries that insist on maintaining nuclear programs pay a price in the international arena. They are excluded from international organizations such as the IAEA. They may be denied loans and other assistance by the World Bank and other multilateral institutions, as well as the Japanese and some other aid givers. They are also subject to formal and informal embargoes on the transfer of a variety of sensitive technologies, ranging from supercomputers to civilian nuclear power plants to induction furnaces used in the fabrication of high-tech metals. Some countries (such as Belarus) now clearly hope that there may be as much prestige to be gained from forgoing nuclear weapons as from possessing them.

International standing was a powerful consideration in the slightly less dramatic December 1991 decision by two long-time rivals, Argentina and Brazil, to accept international safeguards on all their nuclear activities. During the 1980s, both countries seemed intent on producing nuclear bombs—more for prestige purposes, apparently, than because one posed any threat to the other. Although relations between the two countries improved in mid-decade, the breakthrough came in the late 1980s with the accession to power of two dynamic civilian leaders, Carlos Menem in Argentina and Fernando Collor in Brazil. The two presidents were eager to carve out larger roles on the international stage (and in the international economy) for their countries, and, not incidentally, for themselves. And that meant currying favor with the international community, especially the United States. Brazil, in addition, faced a threat from its long-time financial supporter, Germany, to cut off economic assistance by 1995 if Brasília did not abandon its nuclear pretensions.

Whereas Argentina's Raul Alfonsín could declaim to popular approval in the mid-1980s that he would break before he would bend to the wishes of the United States and the industrialized West, his successor, Carlos Menem, stated that he would much prefer Argentina to be the last country in the First World rather than the first country in the Third World. (The Argentine foreign minister put the idea more colorfully when he declared that he wanted ties between Argentina and the United States as intimate as *"relaciones carnales."*) For Argentina and Brazil, the price of full admission to the international community was placing their nuclear programs under IAEA safeguards.

The United States had a hand in all of these success stories, directly cajoling, convincing, or coercing some countries and more indirectly influencing others through its support for international export controls, the NPT, and IAEA safeguards. But Washington probably played its most important role in May 1990, when the world may have come as close to nuclear war as it had since the 1962 Cuban missile crisis.

That spring, the explosive issue of Kashmir was again agitating India and Pakistan. Amid strikes, bombings, and assassinations by Muslim separatists and fundamentalists in the Indian state of Kashmir, Indian prime minister V. P. Singh ordered a crackdown. Singh's government accused the Pakistanis of aiding their Muslim brethren; there was an exchange of hot rhetoric and before long there were military maneuvers along the India-Pakistan border. In May, U.S. intelligence concluded that Pakistan had assembled nuclear bombs. President Bush instantly dispatched Deputy National Security Advisor Robert Gates to mediate.

In Islamabad, Gates was blunt: "Our military has war-gamed every conceivable scenario between you and the Indians, and there isn't a single way you win," he informed Pakistan's leaders.

Gates then visited New Delhi, where he warned that Indian air strikes against insurgent training camps in Pakistan-held Azad Kashmir might prompt Islamabad to use nuclear weapons immediately rather than as a last resort to save the regime. Gates was successful; both sides pulled their troops back.

In the annals of nonproliferation, however, the story of India and Pakistan must be counted a draw rather than a success. The two countries have not halted their nuclear programs, even though over the years they have exercised some self-restraint. India has not detonated a nuclear device since its first explosion more than 20 years ago. Pakistan has never conducted a nuclear test and reportedly stopped producing weapons-grade uranium in 1990 when President Bush cut off U.S. military and economic aid to Islamabad. Neither country has deployed nuclear weapons or ballistic missiles or even officially declared that it has nuclear weapons.

Nevertheless, the subcontinent remains a potential nuclear flash point. India can assemble 15 to 25 nuclear weapons on short notice and Pakistan can assemble six to eight, probably within a few days, according to U.S. government estimates. If nuclear war ever breaks out in the world, many defense analysts believe, the Indian subcontinent is the most likely location.

A more familiar "draw" is Israel, whose opaque nuclear posture was perfectly expressed by strategist Yigal Allon's remark in the mid-1960s: "Israel will not be the first to introduce nuclear weapons in the Middle East, but it will not be second either." Although widely suspected of having as many as 200 nuclear weapons, Israel has neither deployed nor detonated one, although some observers believe it was behind a mysterious flash in the South Atlantic detected by a U.S. satellite in September 1979.

Even nonproliferation success stories remain unfinished. Backsliding may yet occur; political commitments can be renounced and legal obligations can be flouted. Nuclear recidivism is a possibility, with North Korea the most likely candidate. A small number of countries will undoubtedly persevere in seeking to acquire nuclear arms or holding onto those they already have. Nuclear weapons are still thought by some to confer international status

and enhance national security. For others, they remain useful tools for intimidating neighbors and regional rivals. These countries will pay the price of being hated in return for being feared.

There are military defenses against such transgressors—the United States, for example, is developing ballistic missile defenses. But nuclear weapons can be delivered by boat, truck, or several other means. Over the long term the most effective defenses are political.

III.

For four weeks this spring, delegates from 172 countries will meet in New York City to decide the fate of the Nuclear Nonproliferation Treaty. The conference can be seen, in effect, as a global referendum on the nature of the international system for the next century.

The absence of any solid security architecture to replace the Cold War's bipolar system has already contributed to a general unease in the world. Regional tensions have increased in many areas; ancient antagonisms, ethnic strife, and religious hatreds have resurfaced, literally with a vengeance in some cases. Without vigorous international regimes to control the spread of nuclear arms and other weapons of mass destruction, the world will certainly become an even more dangerous place.

Since it took effect in 1970, the NPT has been the most important means of easing nuclear anxieties around the world. It provides countries with reasonable assurances that their neighbors, potential rivals, and enemies are not arming themselves with the world's ultimate weapon.

Along with the inspection and verification system provided by IAEA safeguards (which would end with the NPT's demise), the treaty is a vital strand in a web of interlocking, overlapping, and mutually reinforcing political pledges and legal commitments. This web also includes strict export controls that deny sales of sensitive technologies, such as supercomputers, that can be helpful in building nuclear weapons; nuclear weapons-free zones, such as those established in Latin America and the South Pacific (and soon to be created in Africa); strong multilateral alliances; ballistic missile defenses to protect U.S. and allied forces; and "negative" and "positive" security assurances, which

are vows by the nuclear powers that they will not use or threaten to use nuclear weapons against other countries and will come to their defense should they face nuclear aggression.

The NPT and the IAEA safeguards system are not panaceas and they are certainly not fail-safe. They do not *determine* decisions by countries on whether to acquire nuclear weapons. But this harsh truth overlooks the positive influence they do exert. Submitting to comprehensive IAEA safeguards and taking NPT membership are earnests of the intent not to develop nuclear weapons. Although the sincerity and durability of these pledges may be questioned in some cases, such as Iraq, Iran, and North Korea, they are an accurate barometer of the nuclear intentions of the vast majority of countries.

Many of the states not possessing nuclear weapons that will participate in this spring's conference complain that the nuclear powers have not kept their side of the original bargain, notably their promise to share the benefits of peaceful nuclear technology—chiefly nuclear power. They are threatening to block the treaty's renewal or extend it only for a limited period. They believe, as Ambassador Makarim Wibisono of Indonesia, the leader of the 77-member Non-Aligned Movement at the NPT conference, observes, that "efforts to combat the danger of proliferation have been used to preserve and promote a technological monopoly in the hands of nuclear supplier states and relegate the developing countries to a position of continued dependency." Some of the nonnuclear states also want speedier superpower disarmament, or even a firm target date for the total elimination of nuclear arsenals.

At the heart of all of these concerns is the worry that if the treaty is extended indefinitely and unconditionally this spring, the non-nuclear states will lose a valuable (and, for many countries, their only) means of leverage in their quest for wider technology transfer and nuclear disarmament. But the consequences of following through on their "nuclear extortion" would be very serious for these countries: without an NPT, their security would be at far greater risk than that of the states with nuclear weapons.

Anything less than the extension of the treaty indefinitely (or for a very long time) would be a failure. Even if the

NPT is not canceled outright but only extended for a short period, countries such as South Korea, Japan, and Germany would be tempted to hedge their bets against the treaty's eventual collapse by increasing their ability to build bombs. Analysts at the RAND Corporation have dubbed this ratcheting up of nuclear potential "virtual proliferation."

Total collapse of the NPT would have more clear-cut results. Gradually but inexorably, the bomb would spread. Perhaps the treaty's demise would galvanize the leading states to devise new institutions and arrangements to halt proliferation. But a failure to agree on extension would itself suggest a breakdown in the global consensus against proliferation.

The stakes ultimately go beyond nuclear weapons. The treaty's demise would cripple efforts to restrain the spread of other weapons of mass destruction. Specialists warn that it could doom the Chemical Weapons Convention, which has been signed but not yet ratified by many countries, and vastly complicate efforts to strengthen the verification provisions of the Biological and Toxin Weapons Convention. (The Central Intelligence Agency estimates that 25 countries currently have programs to build nuclear, chemical, or biological weapons.) Even under the best of circumstances, controlling these weapons in the future will probably prove even more difficult than the regulation of nuclear arms. A world that cannot agree on the latter will be very unlikely to achieve the former.

IV.

In the early 1960s, a young physicist named Herman Kahn published a provocative book on thermonuclear war challenging the world to "think about the unthinkable." But it turned out that war, even with thermonuclear weapons, was easy to contemplate. The truly unthinkable challenge, as Kahn's critics noted, was to map out a realistic path toward a nuclear-free world. Until recently, this kind of thinking was casually dismissed, left to the liberal fringes of the peace and disarmament community. Hard-headed professional nuclear strategists, armed with their RAND Corporation "bomb wheels"—which allow them to estimate the size of the crater and the extent of the fallout from a blast

Thinking about the Unthinkable, Again

Some U.S. analysts argue a new military strategy is needed to deal with nuclear threats in the post–Cold War world. In the National Interest *(Winter 1993–94),* **Eliot Cohen** *of the School for Advanced International Studies at Johns Hopkins University offers one such view.*

Three forces have come together to increase the danger of proliferation in the 1990s. First, over the decades technological know-how has diffused, putting nuclear potential within the range of a number of states. Second, the collapse of the Soviet Union has created a vast pool of scientists available for hire to work on such programs. It has also, in all likelihood, made nuclear material, including weapons, available for sale to potential proliferators. At the same time, the implosion of the Soviet state has removed from the world stage a major military power that had come to see the benefits of preventing nuclear proliferation. Third, and ironically, the Persian Gulf War has made it clear that no country can match the United States in a conventional conflict. To a hostile general staff, nuclear weapons look increasingly attractive as means of deterring either the Yankees or (more likely) their local clients, who provide the necessary bases from which American military power operates.

It is hard to see how any American strategy, no matter how clever the conception or assiduous the implementation, could do more than meliorate the fundamental problem. . . .

Of course it makes sense to pursue marginal remedies [such as anti-missile defenses and more aggressive efforts to help dismantle the Russian nuclear arsenal] as energetically as possible. . . . But both technically and politically they can achieve only limited success. The problem of detecting mobile missiles during the Gulf War offers a good example. Even if American pilots had received instantaneous warning of Scud launches (and some did, when they witnessed the actual firing of the missiles), they simply could not locate the launchers with suf-

ficient accuracy to bring weapons to bear on them. . . . If ever the United States manages to defeat the ballistic missile, the low-flying (and soon, stealthy) cruise missile will prove a more difficult challenge yet. As for the talk of pre-emptive war, would that the United States were willing to engage in it, should the need arise. But really, who can imagine a president authorizing a large-scale, unilateral air and possibly ground attack against a country that has done no direct harm to the United States or its allies? The days of Osirak-type raids on a single, easily located and above-surface nuclear facility are over. Secrecy, camouflage, deception, and dispersion will make pre-emption a far more extensive and uncertain operation than ever before.

It is altogether proper to be gloomy about the proliferation problem. In addition to undertaking [other measures], the American government needs to prepare itself, materially, organizationally, and psychologically, for the day after the first nuclear weapon is used in anger. . . . The material preparation requires, among other things, a renewal of investment in the development of sophisticated nuclear weapons which the United States might use to destroy a nascent nuclear arsenal. It is technically feasible to develop nuclear weapons that could do useful work against such limited targets, without incinerating cities or blasting into the air large quantities of radioactive dust. The organizational preparation entails a kind of war planning unfamiliar to the armed forces in the recent past—crippling, punitive strikes against opponents whom the United States cannot disarm, or sudden, preemptive blows thrown at very short notice. The psychological preparation will prove the most difficult of all, however, for it will require a confession that none of the cleverly conceived arms-control efforts (export controls, buy-back plans, and international agreements) will do more than defer the dark day on which, for the first time since Nagasaki, a country uses an atomic bomb as a weapon of war.

of a given nuclear yield—preferred instead to discuss throw weights, MIRVs, and the seemingly ever-gaping "window of vulnerability."

Yet some especially visionary (or cynically calculating) politicians envisioned a different future. In January 1986, Mikhail Gorbachev called for

a nuclear-free world by 2000. Nine months later at Reykjavík, Iceland, Ronald Reagan, the quintessential Cold Warrior, called for the elimination of all nuclear weapons (although his horrified advisers quickly qualified his statements). In 1988, Prime Minister Rajiv Gandhi of India proposed before the

UN's Special Session on Disarmament a phased disarmament that would lead to a world without nuclear weapons by 2010. Recently a number of retired senior U.S. officials, including former secretary of defense Robert McNamara and General Andrew Goodpaster, former supreme allied commander in Europe, have urged that the United States dedicate itself to the elimination of all nuclear weapons.

In fact, under both domestic law and international treaty, the United States is already obligated to eliminate all of its nuclear weapons. The legislation that established the U.S. Arms Control and Disarmament Agency in 1961 and Article VI of the NPT both stipulate this goal. Is it really a desirable one?

Even among the dry policy analysts, there is serious discussion of moving toward a nuclear-free world. The end of the U.S.-Soviet rivalry, it is said, has vastly reduced the need for nuclear weapons. Their role in the Pentagon's war planning, for example, has greatly diminished. The United States, moreover, is highly unlikely ever to be the first to use these weapons in a conflict. Indeed, one former U.S. official argues that Washington would not likely use them even if the United States were attacked first. Nuclear weapons, in other words, are moving toward obsolescence.

At the other extreme, strategic analyst Kenneth N. Waltz of the University of California at Berkeley contends that "more might be better." The further spread of nuclear weapons to many countries might have a stabilizing influence on international life, he believes.

Waltz's thinking is based on the Cold War experience of deterrence, the "balance of terror" that helped keep the peace between the United States and the Soviet Union. "The likelihood of war decreases as deterrent and defensive capabilities increase," Waltz argues. "New nuclear states will feel the constraints that present nuclear states have experienced."

Waltz's theory has been much discussed among academics during the past decade, and its flaws have been thoroughly vetted. It is not at all clear, for example, that other countries could reconstruct the same delicate balance of deterrence—and even the Soviet-American stand-off was full of perils. There are many other difficulties: a nuclear power might, for example, have an incentive to strike pre-emptively at a neighbor just developing a bomb. And as the number of nuclear powers rises, so does the chance of a classic "madman scenario" or, more likely, a fatal error in the more mundane command-and-control systems of the weapons.

Yet there is some wisdom in Waltz's argument, at least insofar as it applies to the *current* line-up of nuclear powers. Nuclear weapons do generally promote prudence and caution, in their possessors as well as in others. They deter others from using not only nuclear arms but perhaps chemical and biological weapons as well. Under some circumstances, they may even prevent conventional warfare among the states possessing nuclear weapons.

There are, in other words, benefits to be reaped from these ultimate weapons. But these benefits would survive even if the United States and other nuclear powers vastly reduced their arsenals. Borrowing a page from India and Pakistan, it may be possible to move to what specialists call "non-weaponized" deterrence. It is too late to "disinvent" the bomb, and impossible to lock its "secrets" away. But nuclear weapons can be taken off alert, deactivated, and disassembled. Such a step would greatly lengthen the "nuclear fuse." It would fall short of total nuclear disarmament. It could, however, be a significant way station on the long road toward a goal that seemed hopelessly utopian only a short while ago. Before it can be reached, we will need to reduce the role and number of nuclear weapons in international affairs and, ultimately, render them irrelevant to political life.

On this path to zero, perhaps the greatest danger is not from the spread of the weapons themselves but from our forgetting how very different they really are. For this reason, Harold Agnew, the former director of the Los Alamos National Laboratory, once suggested that a nuclear bomb be detonated in an isolated part of the ocean once each decade with world leaders in attendance. Then they would hear, see, and *feel* its awesome power. The danger is that as the echoes of Hiroshima and Nagasaki grow more distant with the passing of time, the devastation and unspeakable horror of those events may fade from our collective memories. We forget at our peril.

Face-Off

East-West tension defined the Cold War, but its legacy is the victory of hope over fear

By John Lewis Gaddis

The Cold War began to end 10 years ago, not with any great decision grandly proclaimed but with a hapless official spokesman fumbling his lines. On Nov. 9, 1989, Gunter Schabowski, Berlin district secretary for the ruling East German Communist Party, was *supposed* to announce a decision by his bosses to allow a limited and controlled flow of East Germans through the Berlin Wall, to take effect the next day. This concession would, they hoped, relieve the pressures on the German Democratic Republic that had been mounting throughout the summer and fall, as Mikhail Gorbachev made it increasingly clear that the Soviet Union would no longer prop up its fellow Marxist-Leninist regimes in Eastern Europe. Schabowski slipped up on a detail, however, telling a televised press conference that the new rules were to take effect "immediately, without delay."

Within hours, excited East Berliners had overwhelmed the border guards, forced open the crossing points, and surged into West Berlin, forbidden territory for as long as most of them could remember. Soon they were dancing on top of the wall, chipping away at it with hammers and crowbars, and then quite literally toppling it with bulldozers and backhoes. The very symbol of a continent divided for almost half a century—indeed of a world so divided—came tumbling down, almost overnight.

Nobody on either side had anticipated this: The wall had seemed as permanent a fixture of the Berlin landscape as the Cold War had appeared to be within the post-World War II international system. That such a forbidding structure proved so fragile surprised everyone. But even then, few who witnessed the wall's collapse would have guessed what was soon to come: that the division of Germany would disappear within a year, or that in just over two years the Soviet Union itself would cease to exist.

Today we take for granted what astonished us then: We assume, far more easily than we should, that the process that began with the opening of the Berlin Wall and ended with the Soviet Union's essentially peaceful breakup could *only* have happened in the way that it did. History works like that: Our view of the past is so much clearer than our vision of the future that we tend to forget that the past once had a future, and that it was just as opaque to those who lived through it as our own future is for us today. My college students were between 8 and 11 years old when the Berlin Wall came down. They've known only a pitifully weak Russia that cannot keep its borders secure, its military intact, its economy afloat, or its prime ministers in office. How, they wonder, could such a country have ever caused Americans and their allies to fear for their future?

I suggest, as an answer, a short time-machine trip. Set the dial first for November 1989, the anniversary we're commemorating, to get a sense of the unexpectedness of what happened and of the euphoria it produced. Then go back in 10-year intervals from that event. A very different picture emerges.

November 1979: Jimmy Carter is in his third year as president of the United States, and the mood is anything but euphoric. The American Embassy staff has just been taken hostage in Tehran, following the overthrow of a longtime friend, the shah of Iran. In Nicaragua, the Sandinistas have deposed the Somoza regime, an even older ally. The Soviet Union under Leonid Brezhnev has deployed a new generation of SS-20 missiles aimed at European targets and is openly encouraging Marxist revolutions in what Carter's national-security adviser, Zbigniew Brzezinski, has called an "arc of crisis" running from Southern Africa to Southeast Asia. The Russians are on the verge of invading Afghanistan and are threatening to crack down on Poland, where the Solidarity trade union movement is only beginning to test its capacity for resistance. Still reeling from defeat in Vietnam, the disruptions of Watergate, and a continuing energy crisis, Americans are confronting the prospect of double-digit inflation and unemployment. Détente is dying, if not dead, and a highly visible Committee on the Present Danger has been insisting that if nothing is done to reverse these trends, the credibility of the United States as a superpower will not survive. Ronald Reagan has announced his intention to run for the

 From *U.S. News & World Report*, October 18, 1999, pp. 39-46. © 1999 by U.S. News & World Report. Reprinted by permission.

The East-West Divide

The Cold War dominated politics for 40 years

■ **MARCH 1946.** Former British Prime Minister Winston Churchill warns the world, during a speech in Fulton, Mo., that an "iron curtain" is descending across Europe.

■ **APRIL 1948.** Start of Marshall Plan, a U.S.-sponsored economic program to aid 16 European nations ravaged by World War II.

■ **JUNE 1948.** Soviet troops block all road, rail, and water traffic between West Berlin and the West. U.S., Britain, and France airlift 2.3 million tons of food and supplies to the city for 15 months.

■ **APRIL 1949.** North Atlantic Treaty Organization (NATO) sets up common defense alliance to counter-weigh Soviet forces in Eastern Europe.

■ **AUGUST 1949.** Soviet Union tests its first atomic bomb.

■ **OCTOBER 1949.** China turns Communist under Mao Zedong's leadership.

■ **JUNE 1950.** North Korean troops invade South Korea. U.S. and 16 other United Nations countries fight alongside South Korea until July 1953 armistice.

■ **JUNE 1953.** Soviet troops quell anti-Communist revolts in East Germany.

■ **MAY 1955.** Warsaw Pact signed by Soviet Union and seven Eastern European countries to ensure unified command against NATO.

■ **NOVEMBER 1956.** Soviet tanks crush national rebellion against communism in Hungary. Thousands flee to the West.

■ **MAY 1960.** American U-2 reconnaissance plane shot down over Sverdlovsk, Russia. Pilot Francis Gary Powers survives and in August is sentenced to 10 years' confinement in U.S.S.R. In 1962 Powers is exchanged for Soviet spy Rudolf Abel.

■ **APRIL 1961.** U.S.-sponsored invasion of Cuba by 1,500 Cuban exiles opposed to Fidel Castro fails at Bay of Pigs. Between 1962 and 1965, Cuba releases captured prisoners in exchange for $53 million worth of food and medicine.

■ **APRIL 1961.** Soviet cosmonaut Yuri Gagarin gains worldwide fame as first man to travel in space aboard the Vostok 1 spacecraft.

■ **AUGUST 1961.** East Germany erects Berlin Wall to stem increasing flight of its citizens to the West.

■ **OCTOBER 1962.** President John Kennedy orders naval blockade of Cuba to prevent Soviet shipments of nuclear missiles. Threat of nuclear war recedes when Soviet Premier Nikita Khrushchev halts work on launch sites and removes missiles already in Cuba.

■ **AUGUST 1963.** Nuclear Test-Ban Treaty prohibits nuclear-weapons tests in the atmosphere, underwater, and in space.

■ **AUGUST 1964.** Congress authorizes expansion of U.S. involvement in Vietnam after North Vietnamese torpedo boats attack two American destroyers.

■ **AUGUST 1968.** Troops from the Soviet Union, East Germany, Poland, Hungary, and Bulgaria invade Czechoslovakia to prevent political reforms.

■ **FEBRUARY 1972.** President Richard Nixon reopens severed ties with China during 10-day official visit.

■ **MAY 1972.** SALT I agreements curtail Soviet and U.S.

nuclear-arms race by limiting antiballistic missile systems.

■ **APRIL 1975.** Vietnam War ends as Communist North Vietnamese forces occupy Saigon without resistance.

■ **DECEMBER 1979.** Soviet Army invades Afghanistan on Christmas Day. Soviets suffer 60,000 casualties in nine-year war against Afghan guerrillas.

■ **SEPTEMBER 1980.** Independent trade union, Solidarity, founded in Poland under Lech Walesa.

■ **MARCH 1985.** Mikhail Gorbachev launches economic and political restructuring program dubbed "perestroika."

■ **NOVEMBER 1989** Fall of Berlin Wall. East German government opens the country's borders with West Germany.

■ **OCTOBER 1990.** East and West Germany reunify under NATO auspices and with Soviet approval.

■ **DECEMBER 1991.** Soviet reformer Gorbachev resigns from office. The Soviet Union collapses, ending 74 years of Soviet communism.

---

presidency, precisely with a view to restoring it.

November 1969: The United States is mired in an unwinnable war in Southeast Asia. Although Richard Nixon's new administration has promised gradually to withdraw American troops, some 500,000 remain in Vietnam—most disillusioned about their mission, many demoralized and on drugs, and some even challenging the authority of their officers. The Air Force is secretly bombing enemy sanctuaries in Cambodia, while at home antiwar protests have mounted to such an extent that Nixon has had to ask the "silent majority" of Americans to help him avoid national humiliation. The Soviet Union has overtaken the United States in the production and deployment of intercontinental ballistic missiles, thereby ending an American

Flashpoints. *East Berlin, 1953: Workers clash with riot police. Prague, 1968: Soviet tanks crush Czechoslovakia's hopes for reform.*

superiority in strategic weaponry that had prevailed since the beginning of the Cold War. In striking contrast to the Americans' failure in Vietnam, the Soviet Union has crushed Alexander Dubcek's reform movement in Czechoslovakia and has threatened to respond similarly to such experiments elsewhere. China, still in the

throes of Chairman Mao Zedong's Great Cultural Revolution, is preparing for nuclear war—not with the United States, as one might have expected, but with its erstwhile ideological ally. How would the Americans react, a Soviet diplomat has discreetly inquired in Washington, if the Russians were to launch a pre-emptive strike against the Chinese?

November 1959: Soviet space achievements—the first ICBM, the first artificial Earth satellite—have caused a crisis of confidence in the United States, where an aging Dwight Eisenhower is presiding over a country seriously worried about its apparent inferiority in science and technology. The Soviet leader is the ebulliently bumptious Nikita Khrushchev, who is claiming to be turning out rockets "like sausages," capable of devastating any point on the face of the Earth. He has challenged the exposed position of the United States and its allies in West Berlin, has exploited growing anti-American sentiment in the Middle East, and has just returned from a highly publicized visit to the United States, where he repeated his frequent prediction that America's grandchildren would live under communism. Just to the south, a young guerrilla fighter and occasional baseball player named Fidel Castro has come to power in Cuba—with the result that the former playground for American gangsters and vacationers already seems well along the path that Khrushchev has laid out.

November 1949: Joseph Stalin is alive and in command inside the Kremlin, while Harry S. Truman is president of the United States. The Soviet Union has consolidated its post–World War II sphere of influence in Eastern Europe, forcing the United States to respond with the Truman Doctrine, the Marshall Plan, and most recently the North Atlantic Treaty Organization—an unprecedented peacetime commitment to the defense of an increasingly desperate Western Europe. The Russians have just exploded their first atomic bomb, several years earlier than expected, and Truman is under pressure to respond by building thermonuclear weapons with a thousand times the destructive power of the device the Americans had dropped, only four years before, on Hiroshima. Mao has proclaimed the People's Republic of China and will soon depart for Moscow to forge a Sino-Soviet alliance, thereby confirming communist control over most of the Eurasian continent. Allegations of espionage within the United States are creating an atmosphere of near hysteria, which Sen. Joseph McCarthy will soon exploit and which his critics will name for him. Meanwhile, George Orwell has published *1984*, a profoundly pessimistic vision of survival in an apparently endless Cold War.

What this brief trip through time suggests is that for anyone living in November of 1949, 1959, 1969, or 1979, the Cold War's outcome would not have been at all clear. If anything, it looked as though the Soviet Union and its allies might win: There was a remarkable gap between what people *thought* was hap-

Confrontation. *The Soviet Union closed all land routes from the West to Berlin in 1948. Britain and the United States responded with a massive airlift.*

pening and what we now know to have happened. Fears outweighed hopes for so long that when the latter actually prevailed it was a completely unexpected development.

It's now the historians' task to explain this triumph of hopes over fears. It helps to have partial access to Soviet, Eastern European, and Chinese archives. Before the Cold War ended, the American public had more than enough information from Western sources to expose the shortcomings of the United States and its allies, but historians could only hint at those that may have existed on the other side. We now know much more, and what emerges is a pattern of brutality, shortsightedness, inefficiency, vulnerability, and mistrust within the Marxist-Leninist world that dates back to the earliest days of the Cold War.

Just as important, though, is our knowledge of how the Cold War turned out. The view from inside any historical event is bound to be limited—and the Cold War was an unusually protracted event. We have a better sense now of where it's going to fit within the long sweep of history. And we can see, more clearly, why so much of what the West feared never came to pass.

A list of such fears, for an American at the end of 1949, might well have included the following: that, as Orwell's novel suggested, authoritarianism could be the wave of the future; that, as the Marshall Plan and NATO implied, Europe was in danger of becoming a Soviet sphere of influence; that, as Mao's victory seemed to indicate, international communism was a coordinated, monolithic movement; that, as the Soviet atomic bomb appeared to show, a new and far more devastating world war

loomed on the horizon; that, as the spy cases revealed, the nation's most closely held secrets were transparent to the enemy. Today, half a century later, we can see how each of these fears became hopes, and then accomplishments, and then the means by which the West prevailed in the Cold War.

■ **Authoritarianism.** It was not at all unreasonable in 1949 to have feared the eventual triumph of authoritarianism: Democracy and capitalism had hardly enhanced their reputation during the 1930s, and the United States and Great Britain had defeated Nazi Germany in World War II only by collaborating with Stalin's Soviet Union. There were plenty of people who, during those difficult years of Depression and war, saw at least a short-term denial of liberties as a necessary evil and found a certain allure in a vision of socialism they hoped would overcome the shortcomings of capitalism. But as postwar economic recovery proceeded, it began to reward lateral rather than hierarchical forms of organization: Only the decentralized, largely spontaneous market system could make the millions of decisions required each day if the supply and demand of goods and services was to be kept in balance. And with freedoms so obviously suppressed in the authoritarian East even as they flourished in the democratic West, it became increasingly hard to see how coercion could ever lead to equity. It was no coincidence, then, that as the Cold War neared its end, democracies were replacing, rather than succumbing to, dictatorships. Or that the first modern examples of what Marx understood a proletarian revolution to be— a spontaneous mass movement led by workers and intellectuals, aimed at achieving liberty and justice—occurred only in Eastern Europe in 1989 and in the Soviet Union in 1991.

■ **Spheres of influence.** We can now see, as a consequence, that the spheres of influence the United States and the Soviet Union maintained in Europe were always asymmetrical: The first existed by invitation, the second by imposition. Stalin may well have expected the Europeans to welcome him as a liberator at the end of World War II, but when that did not happen—largely because his regime's reputation preceded its armies—he could establish his authority only by imposing it. But that caused the Europeans beyond his reach to invite the Americans to remain as a counterweight. Europe was divided, as a result, but there was dissimilarity in the division: Washington's sphere of influence arose by consent; Moscow's by denying it. That distinction made all the difference in how the Cold War came out, because it allowed the NATO countries to legitimize the American presence through free elections that repeatedly ratified it. No such opportunities existed within the Warsaw Pact: hence the ease with which it fell apart in 1989–90 when the only glue that had kept it together—Moscow's determination to use force—itself dissolved.

■ **International communism.** The consolidation of Soviet authority in Eastern Europe, together with Mao's victory in China, caused many Americans in 1949 to worry that the Kremlin commanded not only the traditional resources of a great state but also the subversive capabilities of a purposefully expansionist ideology. If Marxism-Leninism continued to advance as it had since the end of World War II, then the Western democracies could find themselves surrounded by hostile communist states. What happened instead, though, was that as communists took over states, the states took over the communists. Quarrels over how to align a common ideology with dissimilar national interests led first the Yugoslavs, and then the Chinese, and then the Poles, Hungarians, and Czechs, to challenge Moscow's authority. By the 1970s the American diplomat W. Averell Harriman could point out, with total accuracy, that it was the *Soviet Union* that now found itself surrounded by hostile communist states. And by the end of the 1980s, so little was left of the international communist movement that it was difficult to remember why the West had ever feared it in the first place.

■ **The bomb.** The Soviet atomic bomb also alarmed the West in 1949, but its effect over the long run was to make war with the United States not more likely but less so. The single most important characteristic of the Cold War—

Setting the Record Straight

Archives slowly yielding their secrets

There is much we still don't know—and may never know—about the Cold War. But once-secret documents are providing a glimpse into key events and showing that some of what we do know—or think we know—is wrong. Among the findings:

■ Moscow secretly deployed 100 nuclear warheads in Cuba during the 1962 missile crisis, making the era's most dangerous standoff even scarier in retrospect.

■ President Eisenhower in 1957 gave U.S. military commanders *advance* permission to use nuclear weapons if they were in danger of being overwhelmed by a Soviet attack and could not reach him.

East-bloc archives have provided the most important new revelations, showing that communism wasn't a monolith:

■ Stalin reluctantly approved North Korea's June 1950 attack on the South (Kim Il Sung pestered him with 48 telegrams), believing the United States would not respond militarily. Stalin may have been motivated more by intramural competition with Mao Zedong, newly victorious in China, than by the global struggle with the United States. U.S. officials thought the attack was a Soviet foray that had to be met head on, a misjudgement that led to America's re-armament and eventual involvement in Vietnam.

In many other instances, Moscow's clients called the tune (or tried to), says Christian Ostermann, director of the Woodrow Wilson Center's Cold War International History Project:

■ East German leader Walter Ulbricht was the driving force behind the Berlin Wall, not a hesistant Soviet Premier Nikita Khrushchev.

■ Former Polish leader Wojciech Jaruzelski has long maintained he imposed martial law in 1981 to forestall a Soviet invasion. A Soviet general's diary indicates the opposite: Jaruzelski pleaded fruitlessly for Moscow to intervene, fearing he could not handle the challenge posed by Solidarity alone.

But the communist threat was no chimera:

The U.S. Venona code-breaking project and KGB archives belatedly removed any doubt that dozens of Moscow spies penetrated the U.S. government and the scientific community. While not every U.S. communist in the '30s and '40s was a spy, the U.S. party actively helped the Soviet Union. But Joe McCarthy isn't vindicated. By the time he began sounding off on the issue, Moscow had already cut ties to U.S. Communists. "What is vindicated is the much broader and more general . . . anticommunism of the postwar period," says historian John Haynes.

Also vindicated: fears about KGB dirty tricks. *The Sword and the Shield,* a new book based on secret KGB archives, details how Moscow tried to smear U.S. leaders ranging from Martin Luther King Jr. to President Reagan, obsessed over famous Soviet dissidents and planned sabotage in America and Europe.

—*Warren P. Strobel*

the reason we attach the adjective to the noun—is that it went on for so long with such high levels of tension without ever producing a direct military clash between its major antagonists. The obvious explanation is nuclear weapons, which expanded the potential arena of military conflict to such an extent that the superpowers had no way of fighting each other with any assurance of keeping their own territories insulated from the resulting violence. Since wars had

mostly arisen, in the past, over the *protection* of territory, this was a fundamental change in the way nations thought about, and used, military force. The Cold War may well be remembered as the point at which the costs of hot wars, at least among the great powers, became too exorbitant, the benefits too problematic, and the issues that had always before provoked such wars too insignificant. The fact that the Soviet Union collapsed with its military power intact is as eloquent an indication as one might want of such power's ultimate irrelevance.

■ **Espionage.** Even the spies look less sinister now than they did in 1949, despite the fact that we now know there were more of them than anyone then suspected. For the Cold War also changed our thinking about secrecy. Whereas the idea in the past had been to *conceal* information from enemies, a paradoxical side effect of ICBMs was the reconnaissance satellite, from which very little could be concealed. The Americans and the Russians soon saw the benefits of this new technology and agreed tacitly to tolerate it: Neither side made any effort to shoot down such spies in space, as a well-known spy in the sky, U-2 pilot Francis Gary Powers, had been shot down over the Soviet Union in 1960. The strategic arms limitation agreements of the 1970s could hardly have worked without overhead surveillance. But if transparency made sense when it came to the arms race, might it have at earlier stages of the Cold War? We know little, as yet, about how Stalin used the information his spies provided. There is reason to sus-

---

United at last.
Doing what was for more than 40 years unthinkable, East Berliners used crowbars and sledgehammers to tear down the wall on Nov. 9, 1989.

---

pect, though, that on balance it reassured him by minimizing the possibility of surprise, just as reconnaissance satellites did for a subsequent generation of Cold War leaders. If that is the case, then some future historian may well revise what we think of the spies as well, finding that even in those deep fears there was some hope.

The world has spent the past half-century having its worst fears not confirmed. That is a big difference from the way in which it spent the first half of this century, when the opposite happened. No one could have anticipated, in 1900, that the next five decades would see unprecedented violence, including two world wars, a nearly successful effort to wipe out an entire people, and the invention of the most lethal form of military technology in human history.

But it is equally the case that few people at the beginning of 1950 could have imagined that the five decades to follow would witness great-power peace—that, although the world was hardly free from violence and injustice during the second half of the 20th century, the record was decidedly preferable to that of the first half. Fears did become hopes, although it took us a while to begin to realize what was happening. With the dancing feet, and then the hammers and crowbars, and then the bulldozers and backhoes at the Berlin Wall, however, a certain amount of progress in human affairs became difficult to deny.

John Lewis Gaddis is Robert A. Lovett professor of history at Yale University. His most recent book is We Now Know: Rethinking Cold War History.

Mutable Destiny

The End of the American Century?

By Donald W. White

In 1918, when the European powers were in the last throes of the Great War, Oswald Spengler published *The Decline of the West* in which he argued that the continental bastion of world power since 1500 was in decline. At the time, his claim seemed fantastic. A long spell of successful world hegemony had dazzled Europeans into thinking that they were exempt from the possibility of following the paths of the failed civilizations of history. It was true that the war brought an end to the German, Austro-Hungarian, and Ottoman Empires, but the Western European powers of Great Britain, France, the Netherlands, and Belgium emerged from the war with empires of greater land area than ever before—dominating some two-thirds of the world's land surface. Spengler espoused a theory that every culture passes through a life-cycle similar to that of a human being: a culture is born, grows to vigorous youth, becomes complacent in middle age, and ages until it declines and fades away. He conceived a colorful metaphor and was prescient that the European world order and the empires than enforced it were doomed. All these empires, indeed, are no more, as the recent return of Hong Kong by the United Kingdom to China reminds us. Yet Spengler's theory does not enable one to predetermine history

DONALD W. WHITE teaches history at NYU and is author of *The American Century: The Rise and Decline of the US as a World Power*

or, in particular, to know the fate of the United States. Societies, unlike living organisms, have no biological code, and no historical law guarantees their demise. What individuals and societies believe and do matters in the continuity of history; each generation, ultimately, creates its own history.

When the United States was still approaching the zenith of its power, in 1914, the publisher Henry Luce wrote his well-known essay, "The American Century," presenting to Americans a shining symbol of national preeminence and helping them take their bearings in a world where American power would loom large. Though rival writers followed with alternative characterizations of the century, suggesting "The Century of the Common Man," "The People's Century," or "The Democratic Century," the American Century received lasting attention. Many presidents, philosophers, historians, and journalists have employed the expansive imagery of the phrase, including Bill Clinton—the last US president of the twentieth century— in his second inaugural address as he described how the United States became the world's mightiest industrial power, won great victories in two world wars, and waged a successful global Cold War.

The notion of the American Century represented the policy implication that the United States should act as a preeminent power—what Luce called the most vital nation in the world—exemplifying its values of capitalist free enterprise, cultural exchange, humani-

tarian foreign aid, political freedom, equality of opportunity, and self-reliance. This century was, of course, never entirely American—many non-American peoples shared the world during this timespan—but for America, the twentieth century was an era of preeminence like that of Alexander the Great's Hellenistic Empire of the fourth century BC, the Roman Empire of the first century, the Chinese and Mongol Empire of the thirteenth century, or the British Empire of the nineteenth century. The American Century idea resembled Rome's *Pax Romana* or Britain's "White Man's Burden," and it expressed similar expectations and hubris. In the twilight of the closing century, we may take a broad view of the United States as a world power, examining the nation's remarkable rise to preeminence, its recent relative decline, and its prospects on the eve of a new century.

THE DAWN OF DOMINANCE

Historians debate exactly when the United States became a world power, but a common idealized explanation is that it was almost exactly one hundred years ago when, on a May morning in 1898, Admiral George Dewey's warships steamed triumphantly into Manila Bay to defeat the Spanish fleet, winning a decisive victory in the ten-week Spanish-American War. While any rise to geopolitical preeminence is a process rather than an event, the victory prompted President William McKinley to pronounce the United States a world power, but he had other evidence as well. Already in 1880, Americans produced 28.6 percent of the world's industrial output, and the United States had surpassed Britain as the world's largest industrial nation. The United States was also developing a favorable balance of trade by exporting manufactures, along with agricultural produce and natural resources. It began to build a first-class steel and steam navy. Additionally, the United States joined European nations in amassing a far-flung empire, from Puerto Rico to the Philippines to the Panama Canal Zone. As the historian Frederick Jackson Turner observed, the closing of the American frontier was turning Americans away from their preoccupation with the North American continent and driving them to conquer new lands abroad.

By the outbreak of the First World War, the United States had truly become a Great Power. The country presented formidable economic competition to Europe, accounting for over 35 percent of the world's industrial production and suddenly overtaking Great Britain as the center of global finance. By the end of the war, the United States had built up a navy that rivaled the size of the British Navy, the world's largest. Material power, however, did not imply the internationalism espoused by President Woodrow Wilson. Rejecting lasting political involvement in world affairs, Americans as a whole shunned participation in the League of Nations and sought to return to so-called normalcy.

After the close of the Second World War, the United States came to dominate the world scene as a superpower. Although its supremacy was challenged by the Soviet Union, the United States was nevertheless an entity of enormous, unprecedented power and reach. It was a unified, continental nation, so rich in natural resources that it produced almost two-thirds of the world's oil and controlled the world petroleum market. The United States had a large population, expanded by immigrants and their descendants, that ascribed to an ethic of hard work and persistence, and no nation could match America in the educational level and technical skill of its work force. The United States led the world in scientific and technological innovation in everything from transistors, air

conditioning, and televisions to atomic energy. Furthermore, the US economy produced an estimated 50 percent of world GDP: one country was producing about as much as the rest of the world combined, a level of relative economic production unprecedented in the modern world since Britain had led the Industrial Revolution. Americans possessed 70 percent of the world's automobiles, 83 percent of its aircraft, 50 percent of its telephones, and 45 percent of its radios. The American standard of living was the highest in the world, twice as high as that of developed nations such as Great Britain when measured in per capita income. In addition, the US military in 1945 consisted of a navy larger than the rest of the world's navies combined, the largest air force, the best-equipped army, and a nuclear capability of unmatched destructive capacity.

But beyond this powerful combination of material strengths, the United States enjoyed a unique consensus among its people. Americans emerged from the biggest war in world history in triumph over fascism and in leadership of the Allies. American leaders talked about the nation's power and the responsibility it conferred on the people because their failure to accept that responsibility after the earlier world war had been disastrous. The people in general believed in their nation, supporting its leaders and their international policies. This unity encompassed both the left and the right, it was largely bipartisan, and it was defined by intellectuals in many fields. This national consensus effected a great transformation in outlook—that the United States should no longer be isolated from the world, but deeply involved in it.

This new perspective continued during the expansion of a world role that was one of the extraordinary occurrences in history. America's world role became manifested in a post-war alliance system that enveloped the globe from the Western Hemisphere to Western Europe to the Middle East and on to Southeast Asia, Australia, New Zealand, and Japan. At its height in the 1950s and early 1960s, the alliance system incorporated distant and scattered old empires, newly independent states, and peoples of different religions, races, and ethnicities in diverse regions from tropical to arctic. The alliances by no means constituted a traditional empire, but within their frontiers, the United

States was the great center of trade, the world's banker nation, and the provider of the key international currency, the dollar. The American people shared their fortune by distributing charitable aid abroad in unprecedented quantities through programs such as the Marshall Plan and the Peace Corps. Food, clothing, movies, machinery, and science made the American name known everywhere. US military power was pledged to defend allied states, which eventually required foreign strategic outposts, naval ports and fleets, air bases, and missile launch cites.

THE ONSET OF DOUBT

The focus of this massive international activity was confronting expansive communism, an effort which embroiled the United States in costly Cold War crises from Berlin to South Vietnam. In 1975, Daniel Bell of Harvard University declared that the "American Century lasted scarcely 30 years.... It foundered on the shoals of Vietnam." He was equally harsh in his criticism of failed US policy: "There is no longer a Manifest Destiny or mission. We have not been immune to the corruption of power. We have not been the exception." Was Bell premature in his declaration of the end of the American Century?

The US failure to resolve the Vietnam War challenged the notion of US supremacy and prompted many to question whether the nation could sustain its superpower status. The United States employed massive force in Vietnam—dropping more tons of bombs on Vietnam than it did in every theater of the Second World War—but North Vietnam and the Viet Cong survived and triumphed. In the end, the United States lost a war for the first time in its history, and it lost the war as a superpower to a small peasant country, one President Lyndon Johnson had characterized as a fourth-rate power.

But America's time of troubles did not end with the final US evacuation from Vietnam in the spring of 1975. Before the end of the war, the United States had developed a deep trade deficit. After chalking up annual trade surpluses beginning in the 1890s and unprecedented surpluses after the Second World War, US trade was in the red in 1971. Since then, the country has sustained yearly trade deficits. This deficit was in the kinds of goods that Americans once exported to the world: not only in natural resources like oil and gas, but in machinery, automobiles, telecommunications, clothes, and iron and steel goods. The United States also began to buy more than it sold from most regions of the world, including Canada and Mexico, Germany and Western Europe, Japan, China and East Asia, and eventually Russia, Eastern Europe, and the former Soviet republics.

Since the 1970s, the US share of world economic activity has declined significantly. have stagnated for a generation, and American expectations have diminished.

The trade deficit weakened confidence in the dollar, which was devalued against other currencies in 1971 and headed into a long-term decline against the German mark and the Japanese yen. The trade and currency crises preceded the United States becoming a debtor nation. The United States had been a creditor since early in the century, and, after the Second World War, it developed capital resources far beyond those of any other country, but by 1985, the United States was a debtor again, and it remains the biggest debtor nation in history. US overseas investment dwindled and foreign investment increased at home, with corporations, real estate, financial institutions, and government securities being swallowed up by wealthy foreign buyers. Symbolizing this new indebtedness, Japanese companies purchased notable American landmarks in the 1980s such as Columbia Studios in Hollywood, CBS Records, and New York's Rockefeller Center.

It is significant that, after rising over the course of American history, the US share of world output began to fall

steadily. By the 1970s, it had fallen to 30 percent of world GDP, and by the 1990s, to 20 percent or less—less than half of what it had been at its peak and less than it was at the time of the Spanish-American War, when the United States first emerged as a world power.

America's decline from preeminent military and economic power after the Vietnam War corresponded to a breakup of the old consensus regarding its international role. Adherents to the old social consensus held to patriotic notions of American power and the glory of global exertion, while New Left protesters and the counterculture vehemently rejected the assumptions of the American Century as immoral and exploitative. Politically, the nation changed form having a patriotic trust in government, its leaders, and its foreign policies to a skepticism which was exasperated by President Johnson's deception during the buildup in Vietnam and by the Watergate scandal that brought down the Nixon White House. Economically, the nation evolved away from an orientation of production toward one of consumption, both in maintaining consumer lifestyles and in waging or preparing for war. Socially, the national popular consensus surrendered to divisions among groups of diverse ideologies, ethnicities, and parties who, in seeking to overcome past injustices of segregation or oppression, came to focus on what separated them rather than on what united them.

DECLINE OR STABILITY

Disagreement over whether America will rise to greater heights of power or is in decline reflects the difficulty of comprehending these biggest of historical questions. Perhaps, as some historians suggest, it is impossible to perceive an event as large as the rise or decline of a preeminent power while it is happening. It is easier to gauge relatively short-term spans of political or business cycles to determine how a society is faring because the conditions of prosperity and employment are more immediate to individual circumstances.

Debate over American decline was rekindled by the historian Paul Kennedy of Yale University, who published *The Rise and Fall of the Great Powers* in 1987. Kennedy believed that America's role as a world power was declining and would continue to decline. His book en-

gaged in prophecy or future history, projecting the future of the great powers to the year 2000 based on their past since 1500. Joseph Nye of Harvard University, however, in his 1990 book *Bound to Lead,* argued that America, with plenty of resources to assure its global leadership, was still by far the dominant world power and that this dominance should continue to grow.

In evaluating these arguments, one should bear in mind that relative decline is different from absolute decline. The case for absolute decline is a hard one to prove: the United States remains a continental nation, blessed with resources, and the home of new immigrants like those who have invigorated the country throughout its history. The United States remains the world's greatest military power, it still has the world's largest economy, and it represents a prime example of democratic government. Finally, America did win the Cold War.

But since the 1970s, the US share of world economic activity has declined significantly. have stagnated for a generation, and American expectations have diminished. Perhaps it is not meaningful to compare America today with the soaring heights it once achieved after the Second World War: its position then was extraordinary, in part a function of the ruin of the other powers. Though Americans may look back on the immediate postwar years with some emotion or pride, we might be reluctant to accept those times as a benchmark against which we can measure our present condition. But to fail to recognize the significance of those times would be like ignoring the *Pax Romana* or Britain's Victorian Age because they were once extraordinary times.

Another argument can be made that the United States has revived in power in the 1990s, economically, militarily, and culturally. Although no one would argue that America is as powerful relative to the rest of the world as it was in the 1950s, it still appears to be a leader in the new international economy and remains a vital example of democracy. In addition, though Japan and Germany seemed invulnerable ten years ago, and the United States seemed an indebted and unproductive giant, Japan and Germany have recently experienced recession or sluggish growth with high unemployment.

Japan remains the world's biggest creditor and most successful trader, while the United States continues to suffer towering trade deficits and remains the world's greatest debtor. As a debtor, the United States finds it difficult to afford the accouterments of global leadership—foreign aid, prodigious embassy staffs, information agency installations, and military presence.

Historians who point to a recent American decline are correct, but prophecies of America's impending demise as a leading force in the world remain untested and unproved.

The reserves of US military strength that had vastly increased throughout the cold war remain available for use in the 1990s, but the United States has experienced constraints in maintaining an enormous defense establishment to support troops in foreign bases, a global navy and air force, and an extensive nuclear arsenal. Although the United States has abandoned bases from the Philippines to Germany and has cut military spending substantially, the partial dismantling of this military, particularly the nuclear arsenal, is a positive and natural development after the Cold War.

In the exchange of culture, the United States still dominates with the popularity of American habits, clothing, and fads—Marlboro cigarettes, McDonald's burgers, T-shirts and NFL jerseys, Hollywood movies, and television (not the sets, which the United States has practically stopped manufacturing, but the prime-time programming, from the classic *I Love Lucy* to *Baywatch*).

So why the sense of loss? Perhaps America's current sense of drift is a product not of American failure but of success: America overcame devastating economic downturns and went on to defeat both fascism and communism.

America stands, it follows, on the eve of the twenty-first century with no great crusades left.

But complacency can mask social divisions over real international issues and over America's world view. There is a lost consensus over America's role in the world. What does America stand for in the post-Cold War world? For what does it seek to be known? By its status as sole remaining military superpower? By its industry and trade? By its art, music, and popular culture? The end of the Cold War opens great opportunities for peace, growth, and general welfare, but it has not ended war or eliminated international conflict over issues of economic competition, poverty, the environment, immigration, and nationality. America's future prospects depend on a new consensus, but a consensus for what?

BACK IN THE SADDLE

When Henry Luce concluded his essay declaring that the twentieth century was American, he was careful to write that this was only a first American Century, leaving open the expectation for more. Is American preeminence at an end?

Great empires of history *do* decline and *have* declined, as Spengler showed, but no law of history allows accurate predictions of when or how these declines take place: at the end of the American Revolution in 1783, many Britons bemoaned the condition of their empire, which seemed to have entered a period of decline after its triumph in the Seven Years War in 1763. In Parliament, Edmund Burke declared after the British defeat at Yorktown that Britain had lost "her empire on the ocean, her boasted, grand, and substantial superiority which made the world bend before her!" Along with the loss of trade and of "happiness at home," the war had reduced Britain from "the most flourishing empire in the world to one of the most unenviable powers on the face of the globe." Lord George Germanine, Lord North's Minister of War, maintained that "from the instant when American independence should be acknowledged, the British empire was ruined." How wrong these doomsayers were. Britain went on to expand its industry and its trade into every region and to spread the English lan-

guage and system of law, becoming the global superpower of the nineteenth century—until its eventual decline in the twentieth century.

Every one of the hegemonic empires of the past has eventually declined or fallen into oblivion. The Egyptian, Persian, Greek, Roman, Chinese, and British Empires have vanished. That thought is daunting, but decline is not the immutable·law of history that Spengler thought it was. The United States has not ceased to be a world power. It has declined in power from a position of preeminence and is not about to take up again the role of a preeminent power with its costs and burdens. It simply cannot afford a role of this global scope as a debtor nation, although this condition can be reversed. There does not now appear to be any call for a Russian, Chinese, German, or Japanese Century, and the United States could emerge in the leadership vacuum.

The United States can remain a leader by rebuilding within. It should seek to reemphasize the health of its democracy and the productive capability of its society as the primary objectives of nationhood.

The United States has within its power the ability to harness resources once lavished on consumption and military preparedness for productive purposes, and, to the extent that the United States has carried out this reconversion, it has slowed its relative decline. Within a thriving society, founded on equal opportunity for all people, the challenges of poverty, unemployment, welfare costs, and even affirmative action can best be addressed. Martin Luther King's 1968 book, *Where Do We Go From Here?* posed two alternative paths for human history in its subtitle: "Chaos or Community?" Political equality has been achieved, he wrote; economic opportunity for all has not. He did not foresee the economic downturn that followed the prosperity of the postwar years, but he looked for an economy that would bring benefits to majority and minority alike, for one can not truly prosper without the other. The question he asked and the vision he presented are just as relevant today.

Yet rebuilding within is not enough. The United States has to be engaged fully in the world as it becomes increasingly interdependent. More dependent on foreign technology, materials, and capital than ever before, the United States has to reconcile its own values and interests with those of developed nations as well as rising powers like China, India, Indonesia, and Brazil. The United States certainly can no longer afford to choose between internationalism and isolationism, for the latter is no longer a realistic option. The United States, rather, must determine what kind of internationalism it will practice. One compelling option would be for the United States to use international organizations such as the United Nations as essential instruments of policy and to throw its weight behind them. Therein lie the mechanisms for peacemaking and for sharing the burdens the United States had once borne alone in its preeminence. The example of a leading power putting its full support behind cosmopolitan internationalism might have enormous, though not immediately apparent, benefits for the United States and other countries. Despite the argument that working within a multilateral framework would display weakness, the cultivation of meaningful international cooperation may leave the United States in a stronger position in terms of its material strength, internal cohesion, and international legitimacy.

Those who point to a recent American decline are correct, but prophecies of America's impending demise as a leading force in the world remain untested and unproved. The United States has declined from the position of preeminent power it had reached in the middle years of the twentieth century. Future historians may well record that this extraordinary era of American preeminence was when the United States had its greatest influence on the world's peoples, nations, and history. The American Century—the era of American preeminence—may be ending, but not the history of America in the world, which remains for Americans and their international partners to make. The goals and ideals that will guide the United States through the next century of its history may be the nation's founding principles themselves. Frederick Jackson Turner once wrote, "Other nations have been rich and prosperous and powerful. But the United States has believed that it had an original contribution to make to the history of society by the production of a self-determining, self-restrained, intelligent democracy." The power of that moral example of America may be the most enduring meaning of America in the world.

Unit 5

Key Points to Consider

❖ What are some differences of the recent Millennium celebrations as compared with those of the past?

❖ Discuss the fears or nightmares that arose as we approached the Millennium. What impact did St. John's writing about the Apocalypse have in the West?

❖ Discuss the contributions of Albert Einstein, who was chosen *Time*'s "Man of the Twentieth Century." Do you agree or disagree with the selection? Why or why not?

❖ What are the conflicts that exist between Western and Muslim values? How do these conflicts affect the status of Muslims living in the West?

❖ What are the major problems in dealing with the situation in the Balkan nations?

❖ Why do you think some nations are richer than others? What is the connection between education and the wealth of nations?

❖ What, according to Thomas Sowell in "Whither Western Civilization?" are Western civilization's major accomplishments and shortcomings? What, in his opinion, are its future prospects?

DUSHKIN ONLINE   Links   www.dushkin.com/online/

These sites are annotated on pages 4 and 5.

Looking to the future, after the recent Millennium celebrations, the West contemplates the new twenty-first century. This time the prospects for disillusionment seem slight, for there is little optimism about the current or future prospects of Western civilization. Indeed, with the development and spread of nuclear weapons in the non-Western world, we are forced to consider the possibility that our civilization could destroy itself in an instant. Of course, like our ancestors a century ago, we can point to continued progress, particularly in science and technology. But, unlike our predecessors, we are attuned to the potential for the unforeseen disruptions and disasters that can accompany such innovations.

Our ambivalence about technology is paralleled by our growing recognition that we can no longer depend upon an unlimited upward spiral of economic growth as seen in the recent erratic swings of the stock markets around the world. In the course of the last century, other visions have eluded us, including the hope that we could create a just and equal society through drastic and rapid social reorganization. Most of the great revolutionary promises of the age have not been met. Nor do we see that elimination of repressive social and moral taboos will produce an era of freedom and self-realization. By now most areas of human conduct have been demystified (and trivialized), and confusion rather than liberation seems to be the immediate result. Finally, modernism, that great artistic and intellectual movement of the century's early years, has exhausted itself. For decades avant-garde experimentation had challenged established styles and structures in art, music, architecture, and literature, creating an ever-changing "tradition of the new," to borrow Harold Rosenberg's phrase. Avant-gardism presumes the existence of cultural norms to be tested, but now we find ourselves in the so-called postmodern condition, "a kind of unregulated marketplace of realities in which all manner of belief systems are offered for public consumption." Old beliefs and new are in a continuous process of redefinition.

These developments have contributed to an uncommon degree of self-consciousness in our culture. Seldom in any era have people been so apprehensive about the future of civilization and the prospects for humanity. The articles in this concluding section convey some current optomistic as well as some pessimistic concerns. "Exhibiting the Nation" and "A Brief History of Relativity" look forward to progress, while "The Way the World

Ends" and "The Viral Superhighway" describe a bleak future, whether from the Last Judgment or from disease. "Folly & Failure in the Balkans" focuses on widespread tribalization, a trend that pits culture against culture, religion against religion, and ethnic group against ethnic group. These tensions are often aggravated by the unprecedented mass migrations of our time, a topic covered in "Belonging in the West." The unequal distribution of the world's wealth can also sow seeds of conflict. "The Poor and the Rich" attempts to explain why some nations are richer than others. Along these lines, "Who's Top?" considers the possible link between education and the wealth of nations. Given all these complications, many have raised doubts about the future of nation-states. That theme is addressed in the report "Falling Tide: Global Trends and U.S. Civil Society," which is pessimistic about the future of liberal democratic governments. In the last article, Thomas Sowell speculates about the broader long-term prospects for Western civilization in his report "Whither Western Civilization?"

Exhibiting the Nation

In the Royal Historical Society Gresham lecture, delivered in November 1999, Asa Briggs looks at the continuities and contrasts between 1851, 1951 and 2000.

IT IS A PRIVILEGE to be delivering this lecture on the eve of a wide range of millennial celebrations, including the opening of the Millennium Dome. It provides an opportunity for pondering on the meaning of 'celebration' as well as of memory, myth and history. My aim is to go backwards in time as well as forwards—governments and oppositions now greatly prefer the latter—and to seek to establish what I believe are necessary perspectives.

The year 2000 is still in the future, and it is impossible to evaluate the 'Millennium Experience', without having yet experienced it. The year 1851 seems far back in a controversial Victorian past. The Festival of Britain, about which considerably less has been written, seems to us almost equally far back in time. Though thousands of people remember it, its initiators and most of its organisers are dead.

Historians have never treated it as they treated the Great Exhibition: as the dividing date between early and mid-Victorian England, in the familiar tripartite division of the reign. Nonetheless, those who planned it judged it to be an event of substantive historical importance. The Chairman of the Festival Council, General Ismay, a friend of Churchill, was particularly clear about this and echoed Churchillian language when he addressed a meeting at the Guildhall on June 8th, 1949:

> We are determined that 1951 will be not only the Centenary of the Great Exhibition of 1851, but that it will itself be a landmark in our island story for all time.

The theme of the Exhibition was 'Britain's Contribution to Civilisation, Past, Present and Future, in the Arts, Science and Technology'.

There was a direct link between 1851 and 1951. The first headquarters of the Festival organisation were in the same rooms in the Royal Society of Arts where the 1851 Exhibition had first been planned; and it was the Royal Society of Arts, in the middle of the War in 1943, which had first raised the question of celebrating 1851 and prompted the

---

The Great Exhibition was a culmination, not an advent; it had a long and tangled history behind it.

---

setting up of a Committee to consider the form that any celebration should take. When the issue of a post-war celebration was raised in public, in a letter to *The Times* in September 1945 and in the same month in a leader in the *News Chronicle*, 1851 was taken as the inspiration. The editor of the *News Chronicle*, Gerald Barry, who was to become Director General of the Festival, pressed the case for an International Exhibition in Britain, which would afford, he said,

'an opportunity for assembling in London an international collection of exhibits in the fields of the arts and of science and of technology representing developments . . . which have taken place in the world behind the cultural blackout of the War' and provide a 'powerful stimulus to both manufacturers and designers, as well as a challenge to engineers and architects'.

It would be 'the means, too, of attracting to this country not only traders with millions of pounds at their disposal but large numbers of foreign tourists who would spend their money in the country and, we may hope—would be encouraged to repeat their visits in future years.' There was no need for an Exhibition to attract them in unprecedented numbers. Tourism, which had been given a boost in 1851 before the 'ism' was invented, was to develop its own history and organisation. What Barry had suggested was not to be the form of the Festival which he himself was to direct in 1951. It was to be British, demonstrating to the world, as Lord Ramsden, chairman of the first official committee, put it, 'the recovery of the United Kingdom from the effects of War in the moral, cultural, spiritual and material fields'. For the Board of Trade it followed on naturally from a 'Britain Can Make It' Exhibition in 1949. Once, however, its overall supervision passed from the President of the Board of Trade, Sir Stafford Cripps, into the willing hands of Herbert Morrison, who set up a Great Exhibition Centenary Committee in December 1947, it began to be thought of also as a 'tonic to the nation'. This phrase was to serve as the title of an admirable book edited by Bevis Hillier and Rayner Banham, which was commissioned by Roy Strong to accompany a fascinating Festival exhibition in the Victoria and Albert Museum a quarter of a century after it ended.

The vantage points in time and space from which we view exhibitions and festivals are bound to influence how we see them as much as our own preoccupations and prejudices. Strong was aware that this was so in planning an exhibition about the Festival for 1976, the centenary of another great exhibition, the American centennial in Philadelphia.

The 1976 exhibition and the book accompanying it provide the one subsequent evaluation of the 1951 Festival in the terms that its initiators and organisers would have approved of, while at the same time offering an anthology of contemporary and retrospective opinions of all kinds on the Festival, friendly and hostile, immediate and retrospective. The buzz adjective of the day was 'contemporary', but the chosen theme was broader than that, and while Brian Aldiss, the science fiction writer, could call the Festival 'a memorial to the future'—many people who visited it still think and feel in that way—in the first instance it was a memorial to the past. In the completed Festival buildings there was a miniature display commemorating the Great Exhibition, devised by Hugh Casson and James Gardner, accompanied by a spoken description of the scene at the opening ceremony on May 1st, 1851.

I begin in 1851, as they did, emphasising three points about it. First, the Great Exhibition was a culmination rather than an advent; it had a long and tangled history behind it, as the Festival did. Second, what was being specifically exhibited in the Crystal Palace in 1851 was not the nation but 'all the nations'; it was a universal exhibition. Third, the first decisions relating to the Exhibition, as was the case also in 1951, but unlike those relating to the Dome 2000, concerned what was to be displayed inside it, not what would house them. Nonetheless, it was Joseph Paxton's miracle of glass and iron, designed late in the day on a precious piece of blotting paper, that won the supreme award offered through the Exhibition itself, and by the time that it closed he was the nation's hero, a hero of self-help who graduated through dream as much as through work from lily pond at Chatsworth to palace

Raising the roof: the construction of the Great Exhibition building was eagerly followed by the press, including the *Illustrated London News* which carried this illustration on December 11th, 1850.

in Hyde Park. When the Exhibition ended he was knighted by the Queen. There was romance in him as well as in his creation.

There was no such hero in 1951, when there were many architects for many pavilions—among them Casson himself. Basil Spence, Maxwell Fry and Jane Drew, and Ralph Tubbs who designed the Dome of Discovery, then the largest dome in the world, a symbolic 365 feet in diameter. The Millennium Dome is proudly proclaimed as the largest structure of its kind in the world, covering 20 acres and capable of housing two Wembley stadiums or thirteen Albert Halls.

The 2000 theme, 'Time to Make a Difference', looks at time in a totally different way from Albert, Honorary President of the Great Exhibition—and he was far more than a President—for whom establishing historical perspectives was of fundamental importance. To me the key words in the influential address on the Great Exhibition which he delivered at a gargantuan banquet in the Mansion House on March 21st, 1850, related not to design, but to time and place. He spoke of 'our present era' as 'a period of the most wonderful transition' and described the object of the Exhibition as 'the presentation of a true test and living picture of the point of development at which the whole of mankind has arrived in this great task'. Albert did not hesitate to add that the Exhibition would mark 'a new starting point from which all nations will be able to direct their further exertions'.

A group of colleagues, including Henry Cole and Lyon Playfair had something to teach him, and both Cole and Playfair were described inadequately as Prince Consorts in miniature. Cole, satirised often at the time, has had many tributes paid him in recent years, most of them offered since 1951, although as an undoubtedly eminent Victorian two substantial volumes were devoted to him two years after his death in 1882, *Fifty Years of Public Work of Sir Henry Cole KCB accounted for in his Deeds, Speeches and Writings*. 'Whatsoever thy hand findeth to do, do it with thy might' was the text on its frontispiece.

Playfair is now the more neglected of the two by historians, if not in Scotland. Yet through Peel he had met the Prince before the Exhibition, and it was his system of classifying objects in the Great Exhibition that prevailed and not that of the Prince.

A pupil of the great German chemist Justus von Liebig, Playfair was to be involved, like Cole, in the aftermath of 1851 as a partner as much as in the prelude leading up to it, and he too had a distinguished Victorian biographer, Wemyss Reid, who described his life, 'lived without ostentation and without parade', as 'undoubtedly one of the fullest and most useful lives of his time. It was emphatically a life of work, and of work not for the accumulation of wealth or the achievement of fame, but for the acquiring of truth and the service of his fellow men'.

There were other important figures among Albert's colleagues, a diverse group, but the Prince held them together while bringing to his own task a 'sense of service' as much as—though this was not absent—a desire for princely fame. Like Playfair, he was deeply interested in science, and like Cole he was anxious to raise aesthetic standards. Yet it was Cole's idea that there should be a Royal Commission to prepare the Exhibition, a crucial idea that was implemented in January 1850. With Albert as Chairman, it placed the Exhibition in what Jürgen Habermas has called 'the public sphere' and in what the liberal-minded Lord Carlisle called in 1850 'an arena [differ-

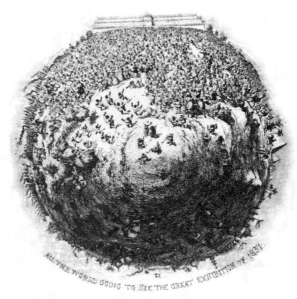

HT Archives

George Cruikshank produced several cartoons showing most of the world flocking to Hyde Park.

ent from 'the crowded saloon' or 'the heated theatre'], where all ranks may mingle, where all [including 'the workmen and workwomen of the world'] may learn and all may profit from what they see'.

In March 1850 Albert found exactly the right words, blessed by the Archbishop of Canterbury, to move his hearers. It was Albert too who encouraged the Archbishop of Canterbury to 'invoke the blessing of Almighty God' on the whole Exhibition undertaking in a short prayer at the Opening Ceremony. 'We acknowledge, O Lord, that Thou has multiplied on us blessings which Thou mightest most justly have withheld.' 'Both riches, and honour come of Thee, and Thou reignest over all'.

Words were never enough, however, and in the Mansion House, where both the Archbishop and Albert spoke there were gutta purcha models of home products—Irish linens, Scots plaid and Welsh leeks. There were symbols too, for Exhibitions are always replete with symbols and icons. Above the Prince's chair were two huge figures representing Peace and Plenty. The first would have been highly appropriate in 1951 after six years of war and with the atomic bomb in the background, the latter not. There was ample austerity after 1951; meat rationing was not abolished until 1954.

Back in 1851 not everyone enjoyed what even by Victorian standards could be called 'plenty'. Nor was peace secured: not far round the corner was the

Crimean War. But what were called, however misleadingly the 'hungry forties' were now past, and so were the revolutions of 1848. It was not entirely rhetorical in 1851 to dwell on peace as well as on work. *Paxton vobiscum* 'The tree of trees to be planted [in the Palace], wrote *Punch*, 'is a gigantic olive that is expected to take root, an olive strengthened, sheltered and protected by the glass walls and roof that admit the commercial trophies of all the world—a veritable Peace Congress, manufactured by the many coloured hands of the human family. We do not see why there should not be an Order of the Olive. Will Prince Albert think of it.' Doubtless he would have liked to have done. What *Punch* had in mind, however, was the advance of free trade which both Cobden and Peel, who died before the Exhibition opened, believed would afford the best opportunities for peace. The factory-produced steam engines on display were described as 'England's arms of conquest . . . the trophies of her bloodless war'.

Albert spoke of 'our present era as a period of the most wonderful transition' and gave as the object of the Exhibition the presentation of a true test and living picture of the point of development at which the whole of mankind has arrived in this great task'. He added that the Exhibition marked a 'new starting point from which all nations will be able to direct their further exertions'. The Great Exhibition charted the culmination of the first British-dominated stages of industrialisation.

It was not only the building, therefore—and, like the Queen, Albert loved the Crystal Palace and visited it regularly in 1851 during the course of its construction—but the symbols and some at least of the objects inside, satirised as well as praised, that carried with them both messages and a sense of romance. Among comments made by visitors to the Crystal Palace was that of the historian Thomas Babington Macaulay: 'I made my way into the building; a most gorgeous sight . . . beyond the dreams of the Arabian romances. I cannot think that the Caesars ever exhibited a more splendid spectacle'. In the sharpest of contrasts, William Morris found everything ugly in what has been described as 'the Great Victorian Collection'.

Macaulay, along with Gladstone, devised Latin inscriptions for Exhibition medals—there were no financial prizes—and Charles Babbage, often described as the father of the computer, was angry with the Royal Commission which turned the Exhibition from a Royal Society of Arts project into a great state occasion for not showing any interest in his massive calculating machine.

In 1951, when the Victorian revival was only in its first stages, the country and the world had still not entered the computer age. There was a strong interest in history and as part of the Festival there was an outstanding exhibition of books, organised by the National Book League, and presented in the Victoria and Albert Museum. It was described in the official catalogue of the Festival as 'perhaps the greatest collection of literary treasures ever shown in one place collected from national libraries and private collections'. Over 60,000 people visited it to see amongst other treasures Caxton's first printings in the English language, Coverdale's Bible and the first quartos of *Hamlet* and *Richard II*. Curiously, the writer of the Exhibition catalogue chose a musical metaphor to describe it, calling it 'an oratorio' which would 'inspire many and convert some to faith in . . . the future'. This was not to be the language, let alone the technology, of 1999.

Most of the group of people associated with the 1951 Festival did not use this earnest language. Indeed, one of the favourite words of the group of people associated with the 1951 Festival was 'fun'. There had been no shortage of fun in 1851, but it was for the most part on the sidelines, and in the sideshows, like Batty's Hippodrome or Wylde's Globe in Leicester Square; in the mass of ephemera connected with it; and, above all, in the press. The key figure in the planning and devising of the 1951 Festival, Barry, knighted like Paxton after it was over, entered the scene through journalism, and they appreciated, as did Herbert Morrison, the importance of emphasising the fun element, what Morrison called the 'jolly', in all the Festival publicity.

By temperament, too, as well as by policy, most of the members of the Festival's Executive Committee wanted to enjoy themselves as much in planning the Festival as they expected the public to enjoy themselves when it opened. Barry himself commented on an early draft of a Festival plan in April 1949 that 'we must avoid being too serious and too historical, even possibly at some sacrifice of continuity'. The plan had been drafted by Ian Cox, described in the official guide to the Exhibition as 'the man who devised the theme of the Exhibition'. Cox wanted the Festival pavilions together to tell a consecutive story, and so they were to do. There was to be an 'educative' element. But Barry, like most of the so-called 'theme convenors' of the separate pavilions, wanted there to be an entertainment element also. 'People simply will not go to an exhibition', he told Cox, 'to learn a lesson, however perfectly it may be told. Offered a choice between the *Express* and *Mirror* they choose the *Mirror* in the rate of ten to one'.

The *Daily Mirror* supported the Festival wholeheartedly from its inception, whereas many other newspapers, including the *Daily Telegraph* and the *Evening Standard* did not. 'It's Britain's great day', the *Mirror*'s headline ran on the day of the opening May 3rd, with a side heading 'And it'll be just as good on TV'. By then it could quote one of its readers noting that the 'Tory press' too was now saying 'what a wonderful show it is'.

The South Bank site, recommended by the architect Sir William (later Lord) Holford, was exciting, particularly at night, and incorporated the Festival Hall. Alternative sites might have been Battersea Park, where a Festival funfair was organised, Wormwood Scrubs—or even the Crystal Palace site at Sydenham. Morrison visited the Tivoli Gardens in Copenhagen in 1950, and this was the kind of South Bank that he wanted, a palace, in the words of *The People* where 'for a few shillings the workers can have a glorious time till nearly midnight'. Already in 1948 Barry had stated in a memorandum on Battersea Park, that 'something more imaginative and civilized than a mere conglomeration of giant racers, dodgems and sideshows can be devised—something on the lines of the famous Tivoli Gardens'. There was a Scandinavian influence at work here as there was, of course, in home design and furniture design. 1851 had been 'cluttered'; 1951 was to be open, cheerful and, above all, in bright colours.

Paradoxically, the Festival, while delighting in what it called 'the new', stimulated a burst of research on the Great Exhibition of 1851 which fostered a Victorian revival, given a further impetus with the foundation of the Victorian Society in 1958. Research on the Exhibition was represented not only in British books, like the Stationery Office publication by G. H. Gibbs-Smith, or C. R. Fay's *Palace of Industry* (1951), an engaging idiosyncratic study of 'the Exhibition and its fruits', but, after a delay of twenty years, a learned German monograph, U. Haltern's *Die Londoner Weltausstellung*.

The historiography is interesting, but before it unfolded, Osbert Lancaster, though not a historian, identified some of its salient features in a 1951 Preface to an unchanged reprint of the text of Christopher Hobhouse's *1851 and the Crystal Palace*, first published in 1937 and still the best single book on the subject. 'There is no better way of studying the fluctuations of the twentieth-century *Zeitgeist*', Lancaster wrote, 'than to compare the attitudes adopted by the various generations to the Victorian era.' There was a long spell when 'the Victorian age was a fit subject for contemplation only if it were never taken seriously' and 'for more than thirty years the Crystal Palace had been regarded as the funniest of all the Victorian jokes. . . . Those were the days when a comedian had only to murmur "Albert the Great" to bring down any moderately sophisticated house.'

Hobhouse, whose cast of mind was 'predominantly late-eighteenth-century Whig' and who was 'insulated from current prejudices', actually enjoyed researching on 1851. The quality that he shared with the Victorian public was 'gusto'. 'The reader', Lancaster concluded, 'is left in no doubt that had Hobhouse had the opportunity of inspecting it he would have enjoyed the Exhibition itself just as wholeheartedly as the Duke of Wellington or any of the three million or so Victorians who went through the turnstiles'.

Lancaster's Preface has a Betjemanesque twist to it. But there was a still more serious strand in another historiographical by-product of 1951. Studying the history of the Great Exhibition encouraged also the study of other exhibitions. The subsequent bibliography is extensive, leading up to B. Bennett's *The Anthropology of World Fairs* (1984) and Paul Greenhalgh's *Ephemeral Vistas* (1988).

Not Britain, but the world, post-imperial, post-colonial, is now the context. The exhibitions are now being treated less as particular events staged at particular times, as episodes in a sequence and as versions of a genre. The sequence is real enough—for the nineteenth-century Paris, 1855; London, 1862; Paris, 1867; Vienna, 1873; Philadelphia, 1876; Chicago, 1893; Paris, 1889 and 1900, to pick out only a few, with the last, Paris, 1900, being hailed at the time and since as 'the Exhibition of the Century'.

The exhibition genre has never been subject to entirely fixed rules, and lessons have been learnt at one Exhibition and profited from in the next. There has been, in consequence, a variety of different technologies of display and as wide a range of articles being displayed.

The variety began with the buildings themselves, symbolic as well as practical, most of them ephemeral, some surviving, none designed to be eternal. The Crystal Palace, dismissed by John Ruskin as 'a greenhouse larger than ever greenhouse was built before', not only won the medal for the category of 'civil engineering, architecture and building contrivances' but the supreme prize of the Great Exhibition, the Great Medal. Yet because of its prefabricated parts, it could have been just as rapidly constructed at Birmingham as in Hyde Park or in Sydenham: in Dicken's phrase it could be 'put up like a bedstead'. The engineers who constructed the parts, Fox Henderson and Company, were involved too in constructing the roofs of Birmingham and New Street Stations— and of Paddington.

The next exhibition in London—held in 1862—had no new symbolic build-ing. The *Art Journal* called Francis Fowke's structure a 'wretched shed'. An officer in the Royal Engineers, Fowke had designed far more interesting Victorian things than a building, among them 'a portable bath to pack up like a book' and a 'collapsing camera'. Abroad the main buildings came in all shapes and sizes; there was another Crystal Palace—in this case far worse—in New York in 1853, before the first Crystal Palace had been moved—in modified form—from Hyde Park to Sydenham. And there was to be more than one nineteenth-century dome. Vienna, twenty years later, had a dome proudly described as being twice the size of that of St. Peter's in Rome. Chicago, 1893,

> 'Far from making a rung on the ladder of progress, this might be the furthest pinnacle we can reach'.

could not beat that; the best it could do was to include a dome in its administrative building which was said to be exceeded in size only by that in the Vatican.

Many exhibitions have sought to devise their own symbolic icons. Paris in 1889 had the Eiffel Tower, still there; London in 1951 had the Skylon, quickly destroyed. Such features all had their critics. When the Eiffel Tower was projected, a group of French writers, including Dumas and de Maupassant, called it a 'horror'. They 'loathed the prospect of a dizzily ridiculous tower dominating Paris like a gigantic black factory chimney'. In 1951 the Skylon, usually compared with a giant cigar, was described by the poet George MacBeth, as 'the finicky skylon, confessing its failure on legs'.

That is not how many people remembered it. For them it had been exciting to move 'upstream' and 'downstream' on the Festival site with the Skylon ris-ing high above them. Things looked new. Yet for the architects 1951 was a culmination, the climax of activity for what the MARS (Modern Architecture Research Group) group of 'modern' British architects had been striving to do since the formation of the group in 1933. Along with Casson, Tubbs, Fry and Misha Black, the Group had been dedicated to communicating the aesthetics of 'modern architecture' to a wide public. The Festival gave them their great opportunity.

It was not only architects and designers who pointed out that the Festival did not initiate a genuinely 'new style'. The brilliantly acerbic Marghanita Laski, writing in the *Observer* in July 1952 suggested that all was now over:

> This time last year when our Festival was flaunting its pretty gaiety, we knew already that far from making a rung on the ladder of progress, this might be the furthest pinnacle we could reach. It was this underlying ... apprehension that gave our Festival such poignancy and strangely, such delight.

There had also been a political change: Churchill was back in power. The election of 1951 has received more attention from historians than has the Festival. Herbert Morrison, who had risen to power in politics from a secure London base, had seen a successful Festival as a major Labour achievement. The political situation must be compared with that in 1851, when there had been no Labour Party. Nor did working men have the vote, and a Central Working Classes Committee, chaired by the Bishop of Oxford, which was part of the Royal Commission's organisation, had been dissolved. According to Cole, the Conservative leader Lord Stanley would have 'bolted' if it had been given equal status with other committees. Nonetheless, the Committee included the former Chartists William Lovett and Henry Vincent, and though it was dissolved there was a sense, throughout the Exhibition and after, that working men and women were at the centre of it. As one writer, anxious not to sound patronising, put it, writing in the *Journal of Psychological Medicine and Mental Pathology*, 'elevated and enlightened in the scale of humanity, the labouring classes, not only in England, but in every other country besides, are feeling their moral ascendancy more powerfully than ever'. One label attached to the Exhibition was 'the Great Parliament of Labour'.

Labour history still shaped Labour politics in 1951, but in 1999, for a 'new' Labour government taking over the idea of the Millennium Dome from its Conservative predecessor—Michael Heseltine had been its main promoter—it is the future of the country rather than its history that is of supreme interest to it, and the government believes that the future rather than the past will interest those who 'come to Greenwich, the Home of Time'. The phrase is geographical, not historical.

Economic history remains fundamental. The official *Economic Survey* for 1951, the fifth in a series, was itself an optimistic document. Published in April 1951, the month before the Festival opened, it extolled achievements in every aspect of the nation's life. 'Productive equipment had been extended and modernised, even though severe restrictions on investment still had to be maintained. Personal consumption had been raised by 5 per cent or so above the 1947 level, though supplies of meat and sugar both remained well below pre-war.' It is the 'thoughs' rather than the percentages which now stand out.

So, too, does the reference to coal in a sentence which noted that 'industrial production last year was 30 per cent greater than in 1947' but went on 'and with the notable exception of coal... the most serious of the shortages which afflicted industry four years ago had been successfully overcome'.

In 1851 coal had been displayed at the Exhibition as much as glass. One particular block of coal weighing twenty-four tons was displayed outside the Palace alongside a statute of Richard Coeur de Lyon. In 1951, too, inside the Power and Production Pavilion was a representation of a coal mine describing how coal was found and mined. By 2000 a sequence of pit closures and pit strikes had pointed to the end of coal, which had played such a crucial role in Britain's economic history. Symbolically in 1993 the Queen's traditional gift of coal to needy pensioners was dropped.

In 1999, one of the fourteen exhibition zones within the Millennial Dome is concerned with fuel and power, although the first zone, labelled 'Mind', has as its theme 'the creative power inherent in us all'; Zone 4 is still called 'Work', however, although the imperative attached to it is 'Explore a new

world of work and consider how you can learn and use new skills'. The next zone is called Learn. 'Creativity is the key. School is just the beginning. Open your mind to life-long learning'. For all the obvious contrasts between learning through the Network in 2000 and learning in 1851 before the Education Act of 1870 set up locally controlled elementary schools, it is the methods of physical work in 1851 and 2000 that contrast most sharply—huge machines to excavate soil, huge cranes to raise the Ferris wheel. Already, of course, there were cranes in 1851, but work on the riverside site would have been speeded up had there been what we now consider to be essential equipment.

> It has been difficult to secure sponsorship for the Spirit Zone in the Dome, and to agree on what role the Church of England should have. There were no doubts in 1851 or 1951.

It is essential to draw long-term comparisons and contrasts, and in this context to compare, for example, the *Illustrated London News* and *Punch* in 1851 and 1951. It was in the *ILN* that Paxton's sketch of his building first appeared for the public to contemplate. *Punch's* editor Jerrold coined the words 'Crystal Palace', and in 1951 it published a large scale Festival of Punch, beginning with details of a Bouverie Street Exhibition which made fun of many of the pavilions, adding to them A Gallery of Calm Assumptions. Part III was called 'The Festival Charivari' and included articles on 'Old England, Roast Beef of' and 'Pomp for all Circumstances'.

Like much of *Punch*, these articles induced nostalgia. There was no analy-

sis. The advertisements, however, were in many respects more revealing than the articles and cartoons. Thus, the 1951 Schweppivaria advertisement described the role of Mr. Schweppes, forty-seven years older than Mr Punch, in making 'Britain Fit for Festivals'. In 1851 Schweppes had been Sole Purveyors. In 2000 no Millennium Experience would be possible without the financial support of a National Lottery Grant, and the Camelot consortium that won the franchise for the National Lottery, created in 1994—a Lottery would have been anathema both in 1851 and in 1951—had as one of its constituent elements Cadbury Schweppes.

Other long-term comparisons can be drawn. While it has proved extremely difficult to secure sponsorship for the 'Spirit Zone' in the Millennium Dome—or to agree in a multi-religious society on what role the Church of England should have, there were no doubts in 1851 or 1951. Two very different archbishops of Canterbury, Dr Sumner and Dr Fisher, gave the same message in 1851 and 1951. In 1851 Sumner told an audience in the Guildhall that 'Whilst we are ministers of religion we are at the same time citizens and ... as citizens and as patriots we take a lively interest in whatever tends to promote the national prosperity'. In 1951 on the day of the closing of the Festival a broadcast by Archbishop Fisher took the place of an official closing ceremony on the South Bank. 'I think the Festival has been a good thing for all of us', he pronounced, 'and has brought encouragement just when it was needed. ... It has been a real family party and I am glad to know that almost everywhere the Church has helped to make it so'.

No long-term comparisons and contrasts would be complete if they did not cover the monarchy. In 1851 the liberal *Daily News* wrote proudly 'of our true-born Queen, seated on her dais, amid all that is rich and rare in the Crystal Palace' blending 'the prestige of regal state and modern intellectual power with [the] simple holiday reminiscences of our olden time'. The royal message in 1949, delivered by King George VI at the Guildhall, should be compared with Albert's message in York a hundred years before:

> As we look forward to the year 1951, each one of us can share in the anticipation of an event which may be

outstanding in our lives. The motives which inspire the Festival are common to us all—pride in our past and all that it has meant, confidence in the future which holds so many opportunities for us to continue our contribution to the well being of mankind and thanksgiving that we have begun to surmount our trials.

The Queen and I trust that every family in all parts of the country will share in this great Festival so that all of us may join in showing that Britain lives on, now as ever taking her rightful place among the Nations of the world.

What that place was it was for others to say.

I do not know what Queen Elizabeth, who as a princess opened the Royal Fes-tival office at the Society of Arts in May 1948, will say any more than I know what will constitute the 'Millennium Experience'. The company managing it has only one shareholder, Lord Falconer of Thornton, and time alone will tell what he has to say of it also, or Jenny Page, his Chief Executive. The person closest to Morrison in 1951, Max Nicholson, is still with us. He was to pursue his interests after 1951 in ecology and environment, at the heart of the planetary issues that often carry with them a sense of foreboding, even doom, rather than hope. At the millennium, timed through a Christian calendar, the millenarial hopes of 1851 and 1951 are not in abundant evidence. Only believers in a 'new age' show confidence. *Time* magazine devoted a number to 'millen-nium madness' in 1999, bearing on its cover the words 'The End of the World? Will Computers Melt Down? Will Society?'

I end, I hope appropriately, with a Low cartoon of November 1950, which shows Morrison and Barry as helpless captives in the stocks in a funless seventeenth-century Cromwellian England. 'There's one consolation', Barry tells Morrison, 'the Sunday observances of today can't last for more than 300 years'. That is the sort of time span we need, not quite as long as Macaulay's, when we move into a new millennium.

Asa Briggs's most recent publication is *The Age of Improvement* **(2nd ed, Longman 2000).**

The Way the World Ends

The third millennium approaches, bringing with it visions of peace, apocalyptic terror—and a stream of new books about the last days. What the Bible says about the end of time, and how prophecy has shaped our world.

By Kenneth L. Woodward

THE CHRISTIAN BIBLE begins with the creation of the world, before time itself began. It closes with a harrowing vision of the world's end, when time will be no more. For most of Western history, when the world began has been a matter of curiosity. But predicting when the world will *end* has been an all-consuming passion.

Of all the books of the Bible, none has fired the imagination of the West more than the last: the mysterious Apocalypse. The four horsemen of the apocalypse, the heavenly book with seven seals, the beast with the mark of 666, the Whore of Babylon, the deceitful Antichrist—these are just a few of the powerful and troubling images that Revelation injected into Western art and consciousness. Its prophecies have been of even greater consequence: the return of the Jews to the Holy Land, the millennial kingdom of Christ on earth, the Battle of Armageddon and the promise of a new heaven and earth have justified numerous wars and revolutions and inspired utopias and religious sects of every sort.

Millennial dreams and apocalyptic nightmares are never far below the surface of the American psyche—especially now, as the third millennium approaches. Of course, few people seriously think the apocalypse will come at 12:01 on New Year's Eve; some of those who do will descend on Jerusalem at the year-end with millennial expectations, putting Israeli police on high alert (see "Millennium Madness"). The deeper and more interesting phenomenon is the enormous role prophecy has played in Western religious and popular culture. A

NEWSWEEK Poll found that 40 percent of American adults do believe that the world will one day end, as Revelation describes, in the Battle of Armageddon. Every choir that sings "The Battle Hymn of the Republic " or the Salvation Army's "Onward, Christian Soldiers" resurrects martial images and themes from Christian prophecy. In the 1970s, the best-selling book of the decade was Hal Lindsey's apocalyptic "The Late Great Planet Earth," with 28 million copies sold by 1990. More recently, a series of "Left Behind " novels by Tim LaHaye and Jerry Jenkins based on Christian prophecies, including two published this year, have sold more than 9 million copies. Among academics, studies of the apocalyptic tradition have produced dozens of new books. "Over the past 30 years," says Bernard McGinn, a medieval specialist at the University of Chicago Divinity School, "more scholarship has been devoted to apocalypticism than in the last 300."

Like Christians and Jews, Muslims also see an apocalyptic end to the world: there will be natural calamities, followed by the war of Armageddon led by the "hidden" imam, a descendant of Muhammad, and Jesus against the forces of evil, led by Dajjal, an Antichrist figure. After a millennium of peace, both Jesus and the imam will die and the final judgment will take place. For Hindus and Buddhists, time is cyclical, and so the world renews itself after each cycle but never ends.

Christian apocalypticism—the vision of the endtimes—comes from a mysterious book written by John, a Christian prophet living in exile on the island of Patmos toward the end of the first cen-

tury. His intention was to warn the fledgling Christian communities of Asia Minor against compromising with the Roman Empire and its cult of the divine emperor. His message, though, took the form of a personal revelation from Christ filled with mythic beasts, avenging angels and terrifying tribulations for humankind amid clashing cosmic forces. Much suffering would come to the world, John prophesied, before Christ himself would return to defeat his human adversary, the Antichrist, in the Battle of Armageddon. Christ would then establish a millennial kingdom on earth for the just. Then, after a final clash with Satan, Christ would pass judgment on all the living and the dead. For the just, there would be a heavenly Jerusalem—a new heaven and a new earth. But the precise meaning of John's figurative revelation was hidden in strange and forbidding symbols that Christians have tried to decipher ever since.

"The whole of Western history can be read through the prism of John's Apocalypse," says historian McGinn, coeditor of a recent three-volume Encyclopedia of Apocalypticism. In the 12th century, for example, the Crusaders saw the recapture of Jerusalem from the Muslims as a defeat of the Antichrist. Christopher Columbus set sail thinking his voyage to India would hasten the return of Christ to earth. For the same reason, Oliver Cromwell readmitted Jews to England after the English civil war, thinking his victory would establish the New Jerusalem on British soil. Isaac Newton wrote a book on the Biblical prophecy, hoping to prove that "the world is governed by providence." In

From *Newsweek*, November 1, 1999, pp. 66-74. © 1999 by Newsweek, Inc. Reprinted by permission.

Puritan New England, America's greatest theologian, Jonathan Edwards, studied John's Apocalypse and calculated that the millennium of Christ's kingdom on earth would begin in the year 2000.

"Apocalypticism"—the belief that God will shortly intervene in history, destroy the wicked and initiate his own kingdom on earth—did not begin with John of Patmos. Jesus himself was a Jewish prophet "who taught and expected the end of the world as he knew it," argues New Testament scholar Bart D. Ehrman in his new book, "Jesus: Apocalyptic Prophet of the New Millennium." The apostle Paul, writing two decades after the death of Jesus, expected to witness Christ's return to earth. But the Gospel of Matthew, reflecting views of Christians some 60 years later, has Jesus warning his disciples to look out for signs of the endtimes—among them, wars and famines and earthquakes. But he also warned that "the end is not yet."

Whether John's Apocalypse (the word means "unveiling") is a foretelling of the future or a symbolic interpretation of the then current situation of Christians has long vexed church theologians. Early Christianity had revived the long-dormant spirit of Hebrew prophecy, and in doing so relied on Jewish precedents. Much of John's arcane imagery is borrowed from Ezekiel, Zachariah and especially the dreams of Daniel. He also uses numbers as a code for letters. Thus the beast whose number is 666 translates to Nero, the mad emperor who had persecuted Christians; his seven heads refer to the first seven Roman emperors. Similarly, the number 1,000 does not denote a period of 10 centuries but symbolizes an indefinite period of long duration.

In short, most contemporary Biblical scholars now believe that John was not predicting a distant future. Rather, he was locating the trials of the first-century churches within a wider cosmic battle between Christ and Satan. Like the earlier prophets, he wanted Christians to know that the faithful would be rewarded and their oppressors punished.

For as long as the early church suffered persecution, John's vision of a divine rescue was both compelling and consoling. By the third century, however, John's Apocalypse was widely considered unworthy of being included among the canonical books of the Bible. Jerome and other church fathers thought that John's endtimes vision encouraged religious fanaticism (reading it, one

bishop led his flock out to the desert to await the end) and that his anti-Roman polemics provoked unnecessary civil discord. Augustine defined what soon became the official Catholic position: John's Revelation should not be interpreted literally or as future-telling, but as an allegory of the everyday struggle between good and evil, the church and the world. On that basis, the Apocalypse was officially accepted as Scripture.

Even so, medieval Christians wanted to know where they stood on God's timetable. They had no clocks or watches, no universal calendar to record the passing of the centuries, much less mark the end of the first millennium. But they did have an abundance of wars, famines and natural calamities—precisely the signs that Jesus said would signal the endtime. Medieval society lived in the shadow of imminent apocalypse, but this apprehension often spurred missionary action. Convinced that Christ's return was near, Pope Gregory I (590–604) sent a group of monks north to convert England where its leader, Augustine, became both the first Archbishop of Canterbury and a saint.

The Middle Ages were rich in speculations by learned monks about where their own age stood in relation to the endtimes. Chief among these was Joachim of Fiore, who claimed that a personal revelation had unlocked the secret of John's Apocalypse as the key to the whole Bible. In essence, Joachim found that all of history was divided into three progressively more spiritual epochs: the age of the Father (the period of the Old Testament), the age of the Son (the period since Christ) and a soon-to-come age of the Holy Spirit, in which new religious orders would renew the church and through it purify the entire human race. His own age, he saw, was one of transition and crisis: the Antichrist, he believed, was already alive in Rome and his defeat would bring about the end of the present era in 1260.

Joachim's scheme of progressively purer ages influenced millenarian movements for the next 700 years. Never mind that he—and others—miscalculated specific dates. What mattered was his vision of a purified world, which appealed to spiritual reformers of every stripe. Radical followers of Saint Francis (whom some saw as the sixth angel of John's Apocalypse) proposed the abolition of property and other institutions in favor of a pure communist society. In

the 16th century a group of Anabaptists, convinced the millennium was near, took over the town of Leiden. John, their leader, proclaimed himself king and messiah. Through terror, he abolished private ownership of money, instituted polygamy and banned all books but the Bible. In the late 19th century, early Marxists could claim this radical tradition as a precursor of true communism.

Indeed, millenarian dreams were a constant problem for Europe's established churches. When a visionary friar informed Pope Benedict XIV that the Antichrist had arrived and was already 3 years of age, the pope was visibly relieved. "Then I shall leave the problem to my successor," he said. What made the Apocalypse of John so enduring is that any hated or revered figure could be identified as one of the mythic players in his symbolic endtimes scenario. For some in the late Middle Ages, it was Emperor Frederick II; for Frederick's supporters it was Pope Innocent IV, whose name could be translated into the dread mark of the beast—666. For many Christians it was Muhammad or the Turks in general, whose armies threatened to devour Europe. Eventually, Napoleon, Hitler, Stalin and even Mikhail Gorbachev (who seemed to have the "mark of the beast on his forehead") entered the list of Antichrists.

Martin Luther was the first to identify the papacy as such with the Antichrist. At first he discounted the value of John's Apocalypse. But then he saw in it a revelation of the Church of Rome as the deceiving Antichrist who secretly served Satan. For him, the papacy was the "synagogue of Satan" and "the kingdom of Babylon and of the true Antichrist"—a view that was to become dogma for all Protestant churches. "By 1641," writes historian Eugen Weber in his brilliant new book, "Apocalypses," "a clergyman could be denounced to [the English] Parliament for declaring that the pope was not Antichrist."

The Puritans who settled Massachusetts were driven by prophecy as well. Having endured a transatlantic exodus, they began to see their theocratic colony as a real, if as yet imperfect, model of the New Jerusalem prophesied by John. They were, it seemed to many of them, participants with God in creating a millennial kingdom of God on earth. Eventually, many of their descendants came to believe in a revised endtimes script: Christ would return after—not before, as

Millenium Madness

For those who see the Bible as a literal blueprint and 2000 as an apocalyptic pivot,
these are days of portents, hopes—and fears

By John Leland

FOR MOST OF the 1990s, the man who called himself only Elijah was one of Jerusalem's lesser curiosities, an American who claimed to be the Biblical prophet. He called himself a witness from the Book of Revelation, predicting that 2000 would usher in the end of the world. Then in the last year he attracted a small following from among the thousands of Christians, many of them American, who have lately flocked to the city to be on hand for the prophesied return of Christ. For Israeli authorities, Elijah was no longer a harmless eccentric. In this most tense of nations, which expects 3 million visitors during the millennial year, officials fear that some may try to hasten the Second Coming by sparking a violent conflict. Elijah was asked to leave the country. "We don't expect masses of cults coming over," says an Israeli police officer who declined to be identified. "The majority will be innocent pilgrims. But we have to be prepared."

For millions of Americans the prophecies found in Revelation are not literary allegories but a blueprint of the events to come—if not in 2000, then soon enough. According to a new NEWSWEEK Poll, about 18 percent of Americans expect the end-times to come within their lifetime. This translates to roughly 36 million people—not just fringe extremists but your office mate, mail carrier or soccer coach. Or your U.S. representative: House Majority Whip Tom DeLay has a wood carving in his office that reads THIS COULD BE THE DAY, a phrase widely used to refer to the Rapture.

The Rev. Jerry Falwell recently announced that the Antichrist was "probably" already among us. Speaking to NEWSWEEK last week, Falwell avoided setting a date for the big day—"That's usually the tragedy of these surges of prophecy preaching"—but applauded what he sees as a grass-roots rise in endtimes sermons. "There are happenings today: the approach of one world government, the global-nation syndrome that is so prevalent today, the cashless society," he said. "There are many who believe that we could be in the last century." Tapping this spirit, a rash of best-selling novels and movies—including the stealth-hit film "The Omega Code," which grossed $2.4 million in its opening weekend this month after being marketed strictly through Christian networks—has rechanneled the last days as popular entertainment. Monitoring all these rumblings, the FBI is warning local police departments to be on the lookout for increased militia activities as the new year approaches. As many as 239 Web sites, by one recent count, are multiplying millennial scenarios. "Doomsday sayers aren't standing on street corners proclaiming the end of time," says Ted Daniels, director of the one-man Millennium Watch Institute in Philadelphia. "Instead they've all gone on the Internet."

In his small, nondenominational End Time Ministries in Elizabeth, N.J., the Rev. Al Horta is one of the keepers of the apocalyptic faith. The signs, he believes, are all around: wars, school shootings, AIDS, earthquakes, the Y2K bug. The founding of the state of Israel in 1948—an oft-cited precondition for Armageddon—means to Horta that we are "of the generation" and "in the season" that will see Christ's return. Carmen Lanier, 39, a member of the New Hope Revival Church in Columbus, Ga., concurs. For her, these "last days" are a time to get right with God. As "things get darker on the earth and the perversion of man increases," she says, she and other faithful will be "emboldened" to minister to lost souls. "I will have the power of Jesus Christ," she says. "I will be able to heal the sick, to speak to the dead." For those not saved in the Rapture, she envisions a world sunk in "complete madness, a period of darkness, a horrible time to be alive."

Yet among Christian communities, the coming millennium has inspired a surprisingly low count of doomsday survivalist cults, says J. Gordon Melton, a researcher at the University of California, Santa Barbara. After two decades of studying Christian schisms, splinter groups and rogue denominations, Melton finally concluded that the millennium is a bust, apocalypse-wise. Except for the odd group hoarding water or fretting over the Y2K computer bug, the Armageddon wires have been surprisingly quiet. "I expected to have a field day with millennial groups," he says. "And there was nothing."

But for true believers, ground zero for apocalyptic zealotry remains the city of Jerusalem. There are already about 100 Christians living on the Mount of Olives, the spot where the Bible says Jesus will return to earth. On a recent Jerusalem evening, an American named Brother David led five congregants in an ecstatic prayer vigil, singing and speaking in tongues. David once had a ministry in Brooklyn, N.Y., but he sold everything 18 years ago to launch his House of Prayer group in Jerusalem, where he expects to be on hand for the day of days. "I feel the Lord's re-

---

When asked if they think Jesus will return to the earth during their lifetimes, 18% of American adults answer yes

---

turning," he told NEWSWEEK, "and the millennium is to be the time of his coming." He hastens to distance his sect from those who would commit violence. Such groups, he says, "are not Christians, they are cults. Nobody I know would do any violence. But with these cults, well, you never can tell."

Even among such dedicated millennialists, the deadline of all deadlines remains fungible. History has not been kind to prophets who fixed a date for Christ's return, only to see it pass. After one 19th-century believer sold his worldly possessions, his son sued him for squandering his inheritance. For modern would-be prophets, maybe it's just too soon to know. Some doomsayers are already looking ahead to 2033, the second millennium of the Crucifixion and the Resurrection. And why not? In this game, you only have to be right once.

With Anne Underwood, Matt Rees, Jill Jordan Sieder and Andrew Murr

John wrote—his American saints had established a millennial society. This optimistic vision was well expressed in 1832 by revivalist Charles Grandison Finney, a president of Oberlin College. He thought that if the church helped converts to be educated, given just wages and thus regenerated in body as well as in soul, then "the millennium may come in this country in three years."

Others were more pessimistic. In 19th-century America, as in 14th-century Europe, the country was overrun with visionaries, reformers and prophets. Among the most creative was Joseph Smith, who concluded at an early age that the entire Christian enterprise was a corruption of what used to be. In 1823, he reported angelic revelations, telling him to gather a group of latter-day saints in preparation for Christ's return to earth. (Mormons believe he will appear in Independence, Mo., as well as in Jerusalem.) Twenty years later, Baptist convert William Miller concluded, after extensive study of Biblical prophecy, that Christ would return in 1843, then changed it to Oct. 22, 1844. Thousands of believers withdrew from their churches in anticipation. When Christ failed to appear, Miller's movement was shattered. But a remnant under Ellen White reinterpreted the spiritual meaning of the prophesied date and formed the Seventh-day Adventists.

Catholics, too, received prophecies and warnings of the endtimes in the 19th century. They came in a series of apparitions of the Virgin Mary at Lourdes and other European sites. After her appearance to Catherine Laboure in Paris in 1830, the church struck a "miraculous" medal for distribution among the faithful. On it was an image of the Virgin appearing as "the woman clothed with the sun," a figure straight out of John's Apocalypse.

Although John's prophecies were aimed at Christians, they have also had enormous significance for Jews. According to one ancient tradition, the Antichrist will be Jewish, but the predominant emphasis in Christian prophecy is on the return of the Jews to the Holy Land and the rebuilding of the Jerusalem temple as a prelude to the Jews' conversion to Christ. This view made Christian fundamentalists, for whom prophecy fulfilled is proof of the Bible's literal truth, one of Zionism's strongest supporters over the last century. It also explains why the creation of the state of Israel in 1948 excited fresh expectations that the countdown to Armageddon had surely begun.

Jews, of course, have their own apocalyptic traditions built around the coming of the messiah. One view, espoused by the great medieval philosopher Maimonides, is that the messiah will be an exceptional but human being who will preside as king over a free Israel for a thousand peaceful years, according to God's covenant with his people. The other, more mystical view, says philosopher Shaul Magid, of the Jewish Theological Seminary in New York, is that "flesh will no longer exist and there will be pure spiritual reality." Talmudic tradition divides history into three ages of 2,000 years each: an age of confusion (from creation to Abraham), the age of Torah (from Abraham on) and the age of redemption (approaching the coming of the messiah). This year on the Jewish calendar is 5760, leaving 240 years in which the messiah could come.

Christian fundamentalism owes much of its continuing power and appeal to the belief that the prophecies of John, Daniel and other Biblical writers forecast a sequence of specific historical events. But fundamentalists have also shown a remarkable capacity to add to the stock of apocalyptic portents. Since the Antichrist must have the means for controlling the world, many new technological advances are now seen as ominous signs: Social Security numbers, bar codes, ATMs, international organizations like the United Nations and the European Common Market, and—most recently— the World Wide Web. As a newly elected president, George Bush set off alarms among many Biblical literalists when he announced in 1990 his ambition to create a "new world order." Could he be, some fundamentalists wondered, the cat's-paw for the Antichrist?

Whether fundamentalists and other "prophetic" Christians will suffer in the endtimes remains for them a matter of some dispute. They have built an escape clause into the endtimes scenario: "the rapture." This means that at a trumpet's blast, all true Christians will suddenly ascend halfway to heaven the moment Christ begins his descent. Cars will be driverless, planes will be pilotless and children will lose parents if they are among the secret elect. Others think that even the elect will suffer at least part of the seven years of hell on earth that God plans for the wicked. At least one church, in North Hollywood, has taken steps to preserve its property should its officers disappear during the rapture. The church's insurance companies have agreed to delay premium payments for seven years, when the raptured officers return.

Of those who say they believe in the Bible's endtime prophecies, few are likely to translate those beliefs into such direct action. Nor, with a robust economy, are there too many signs of millenarian social unrest. Next month authors LaHaye and Jenkins will publish yet another volume, a nonfiction title that asks, "Are We Living in the End Times?" Clearly, the answer is "Not yet"; the last in their fiction series is planned for the year 2003. For most Americans, it appears, the Biblical account of the endtimes continues to resonate because there are few competing narratives. Even nuclear annihilation and ecological implosion can be fit into John's Apocalypse. When Ronald Reagan was president, recalls University of Wisconsin historian Paul Boyer, who has studied modern apocalyptic movements, he suggested that "we may be the generation that sees Armageddon." But on leaving the White House in 1989, Reagan allowed that "America's greatest moment is yet to come." He wasn't thinking of the millennium.

Exiled on his island, John of Patmos never imagined that his apocalyptic writing would become a handbook for interpreting historical events. Like most first-century Christians, he thought the end was imminent. And one can only wonder how he'd react to those throughout history who have used his vision to justify violence, war, paranoia and even hate.

Though widely read for the wrong reasons, John's Apocalypse nonetheless insists on hard truths that no serious believer can discount. One is that sinners have reason to fear a God who, having chosen to create the world, can also choose to destroy it. The second is that the just have reason to hope in a God who stands by those who trust their lives to him. Thinking of the end of the world—like contemplating one's own end—is a painful process. But studying the Apocalypse presumes that even the end of the world is within the province of God. And who's to say that John's mythic battle between Christ and Antichrist is not a valid insight into what the history of humankind is ultimately all about?

With Anne Underwood

A Brief History Of Relativity

What is it? How does it work? Why does it change everything?
An easy primer by the world's most famous living physicist

By Stephen Hawking

Toward the end of the 19th century scientists believed they were close to a complete description of the universe. They imagined that space was filled everywhere by a continuous medium called the ether. Light rays and radio signals were waves in this ether just as sound is pressure waves in air. All that was needed to complete the theory was careful measurements of the elastic properties of the ether; once they had those nailed down, everything else would fall into place.

Soon, however, discrepancies with the idea of an all-pervading ether began to appear. You would expect light to travel at a fixed speed through the ether. So if you were traveling in the same direction as the light, you would expect that its speed would appear to be lower, and if you were traveling in the opposite direction to the light, that its speed would appear to be higher. Yet a series of experiments failed to find any evidence for differences in speed due to motion through the ether.

Professor Hawking, author of A Brief History of Time, *occupies the Cambridge mathematics chair once held by Isaac Newton.*

The most careful and accurate of these experiments was carried out by Albert Michelson and Edward Morley at the Case Institute in Cleveland, Ohio, in 1887. They compared the speed of light in two beams at right angles to each other. As the earth rotates on its axis and orbits the sun, they reasoned, it will move through the ether, and the speed of light in these two beams should diverge. But Michelson and Morley found no daily or yearly differences between the two beams of light. It was as if light always traveled at the same speed relative to you, no matter how you were moving.

The Irish physicist George FitzGerald and the Dutch physicist Hendrik Lorentz were the first to suggest that bodies moving through the ether would contract and that clocks would slow. This shrinking and slowing would be such that everyone would measure the same speed for light no matter how they were moving with respect to the ether, which FitzGerald and Lorentz regarded as a real substance.

But it was a young clerk named Albert Einstein, working in the Swiss Patent Office in Bern, who cut through the ether and solved the speed-of-light problem once and for all. In June 1905 he wrote one of three papers that would establish him as one of the world's leading scientists—and in the process start two conceptual revolutions that changed our understanding of time, space and reality.

In that 1905 paper, Einstein pointed out that because you could not detect whether or not you were moving through the ether, the whole notion of an ether was redundant. Instead, Einstein started from the postulate that the laws of science should appear the same to all freely moving observers. In particular, observers should all measure the same speed for light, no matter how they were moving.

This required abandoning the idea that there is a universal quantity called time that all clocks measure. Instead, everyone would have his own personal time. The clocks of two people would agree if they were at rest with respect to each other but not if they were moving. This has been confirmed by a number of experiments, including one in which an extremely accurate timepiece was flown around the world and then compared with one that had stayed in place. If you wanted to live longer, you could keep flying to the

*Space and time,
he discovered,
were as pliable
as rubber bands*

east so the speed of the plane added to the earth's rotation. However, the tiny fraction of a second you gained would be more than offset by eating airline meals.

Einstein's postulate that the laws of nature should appear the same to all freely moving observers was the foundation of the theory of relativity, so called because it implies that only relative motion is important. Its beauty and simplicity were convincing to many scientists and philosophers. But there remained a lot of opposition. Einstein had overthrown two of the Absolutes (with a capital A) of 19th century science: Absolute Rest as represented by the ether, and Absolute or Universal Time that all clocks would measure. Did this imply, people asked, that there were no absolute moral standards, that everything was relative?

This unease continued through the 1920s and '30s. When Einstein was awarded the Nobel Prize in 1921, the citation was for important—but by Einstein's standards comparatively minor—work also carried out in 1905. There was no mention of relativity, which was considered too controversial. I still get two or three letters a week telling me Einstein was wrong. Nevertheless, the theory of relativity is now completely accepted by the scientific community, and its predictions have been verified in countless applications.

A very important consequence of relativity is the relation between mass and energy. Einstein's postulate that the speed of light should appear the same to everyone implied that nothing could

be moving faster than light. What happens is that as energy is used to accelerate a particle or a spaceship, the object's mass increases, making it harder to accelerate any more. To accelerate the particle to the speed of light is impossible because it would take an infinite amount of energy. The equivalence of mass and energy is summed up in Einstein's famous equation $E=mc^2$, probably the only physics equation to have recognition on the street.

Among the consequences of this law is that if the nucleus of a uranium atom fissions (splits) into two nuclei with slightly less total mass, a tremendous amount of energy is released. In 1939, with World War II looming, a group of scientists who realized the implications of this persuaded Einstein to overcome his pacifist scruples and write a letter to President Roosevelt urging the U.S. to start a program of nuclear research. This led to the Manhattan Project and the atom bomb that exploded over Hiroshima in 1945. Some people blame the atom bomb on Einstein because he discovered the relation between mass and energy. But that's like blaming Newton for the gravity that causes airplanes to crash. Einstein took no part in the Manhattan Project and was horrified by the explosion.

Although the theory of relativity fit well with the laws that govern electricity and magnetism, it wasn't compatible with Newton's law of gravity. This law said that if you changed the distribution of matter in one region of space, the change in the gravitational field would be felt instantaneously everywhere else in the universe. Not only would this mean you could send signals faster than light (something that was forbidden by relativity), but it also required the Absolute or Universal Time that relativity had abolished in favor of personal or relativistic time.

Einstein was aware of this difficulty in 1907, while he was still at the patent office in Bern, but didn't begin to think seriously about the problem until he was at the German

University in Prague in 1911. He realized that there is a close relationship between acceleration and a gravitational field. Someone in a closed box cannot tell whether he is sitting at rest in the earth's gravitational field or being accelerated by a rocket in free space. (This being before the age of *Star Trek*, Einstein

*Gravity, he said, could
change the curvature of
space-time*

thought of people in elevators rather than spaceships. But you cannot accelerate or fall freely very far in an elevator before disaster strikes.)

If the earth were flat, one could equally well say that the apple fell on Newton's head because of gravity or that Newton's head hit the apple because he and the surface of the earth were accelerating upward. This equivalence between acceleration and gravity didn't seem to work for a round earth, however; people on the other side of the world would have to be accelerating in the opposite direction but staying at a constant distance from us.

On his return to Zurich in 1912 Einstein had a brainstorm. He realized that the equivalence of gravity and acceleration could work if there was some give-and-take in the geometry of reality. What if space-time—an entity Einstein invented to incorporate the three familiar dimensions of space with a fourth dimension, time—was curved, and not flat, as had been assumed? His idea was that mass and energy would warp space-time in some manner yet to be determined. Objects like apples or planets would try to move in straight lines through space-time, but their paths would appear to be bent by a gravitational field because space-time is curved.

With the help of his friend Marcel Grossmann, Einstein studied the theory of curved spaces and surfaces that had been developed by Bernhard Riemann as a piece of abstract mathematics, without any thought that it would be relevant to the real world. In 1913, Einstein and Grossmann wrote a paper in which they put forward the idea that what we think of as gravitational forces are just an expression of the fact that space-time is curved. However, because of a mistake by Einstein (who was quite human and fallible), they weren't able to find the equations that related the curvature of space-time to the mass and energy in it.

Einstein continued to work on the problem in Berlin, undisturbed by domestic matters and largely unaffected by the war, until he finally found the right equations, in November 1915. Einstein had discussed his ideas with the mathematician David Hilbert during a visit to the University of Gottingen in the summer of 1915, and Hilbert independently found the same equations a few days before Einstein. Nevertheless, as Hilbert admitted, the credit for the new theory belonged to Einstein. It was his idea to relate gravity to the warping of space-time. It is a tribute to the civilized state of Germany in this period that such scientific discussions and exchanges could go on undisturbed even in wartime. What a contrast to 20 years later!

The new theory of curved space-time was called general relativity to distinguish it from the original theory without gravity, which was now known as special relativity. It was confirmed in spectacular fashion in 1919, when a British expedition to West Africa observed a slight shift in the position of stars near the sun during an eclipse. Their light, as Einstein had predicted, was bent as it passed the sun. Here was direct evidence that space and time are warped, the greatest change in our

special relativity

Einstein's 1905 theory claims that light moves through a vacuum at a constant speed relative to any observer, no matter what the observer's motion—with bizarre consequences

relativity and time

A moving clock runs slower than a stationary one from the perspective of a stationary observer

1 A man riding a moving train is timing a light beam that travels from ceiling to floor and back again. From his point of view, the light moves straight down and straight up.

Light

Distance light pulse travels

The observer riding the train thinks the light bulb and mirror are standing still

Mirror

2 From trackside, Einstein sees man, bulb and mirror moving sideways: the light traces a diagonal path. From Einstein's viewpoint, the light goes farther. But since lightspeed is always the same, the event must take more time by his clock.

Distance light pulse travels, as seen by Einstein, is farther

The observer watching the train thinks the light bulb and mirror are moving

More time has elapsed

relativity and length

A moving object appears to shrink in the direction of motion, as seen by a stationary observer

1 The man now observes a light beam that travels the length of the train car. Knowing the speed of light and the travel time of the light beam, he can calculate the length of the train.

Distance light pulse travels, as seen by observer on train

The observer on the train sees only the motion of the light beam

2 Einstein is not moving, so the rear of the train is moving forward from his point of view to meet the beam of light: for him, the beam travels a shorter distance. Because the speed of light is always the same, he will calculate the train's length as shorter—even after he allows for his faster-ticking clock. As the train approaches the speed of light, its length shrinks to nearly zero.

Distance light pulse travels, as seen by Einstein

Someone watching from outside sees the light beam moving but with the motion of the train added

Sources: *World Book Encyclopedia: Einstein for Beginners.*

perception of the arena in which we live since Euclid wrote his *Elements* about 300 B.C.

Einstein's general theory of relativity transformed space and time from a passive background in which events take place to active participants in the dynamics of the cosmos. This led to a great problem that is still at the forefront of physics at the end of the 20th century. The universe is full of matter, and matter warps space-time so that bodies fall together. Einstein found that his equations didn't have a solution that described a universe that was unchanging in time. Rather than give up a static and everlasting universe,

which he and most other people believed in at that time, he fudged the equations by adding a term called the cosmological constant, which warped space-time the other way so that bodies move apart. The repulsive effect of the cosmological constant would balance the attractive effect of matter and allow for a universe that lasts for all time.

This turned out to be one of the great missed opportunities of theoretical physics. If Einstein had stuck with his original equations, he could have predicted that the universe must be either expanding or contracting. As it was, the possibility of a time-dependent universe wasn't

taken seriously until observations were made in the 1920s with the 100-in. telescope on Mount Wilson. These revealed that the farther other galaxies are from us, the faster they are moving away. In other words, the universe is expanding and the distance between any two galaxies is steadily increasing with time. Einstein later called the cosmological constant the greatest mistake of his life.

General relativity completely changed the discussion of the origin and fate of the universe. A static universe could have existed forever or could have been created in its present form at some time in the past.

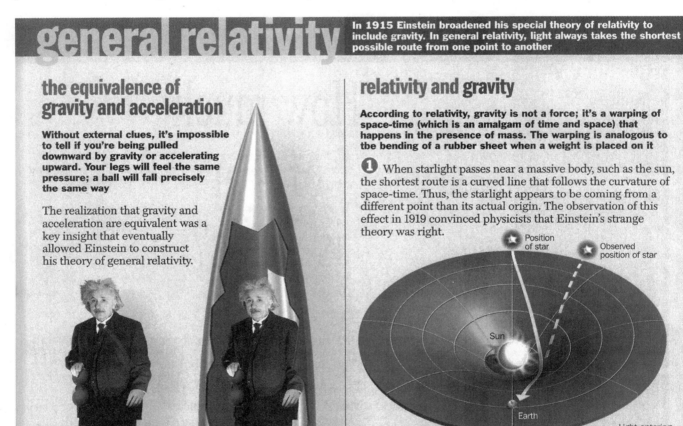

general relativity

In 1915 Einstein broadened his special theory of relativity to include gravity. In general relativity, light always takes the shortest possible route from one point to another

the equivalence of gravity and acceleration

Without external clues, it's impossible to tell if you're being pulled downward by gravity or accelerating upward. Your legs will feel the same pressure; a ball will fall precisely the same way

The realization that gravity and acceleration are equivalent was a key insight that eventually allowed Einstein to construct his theory of general relativity.

relativity and gravity

According to relativity, gravity is not a force; it's a warping of space-time (which is an amalgam of time and space) that happens in the presence of mass. The warping is analogous to the bending of a rubber sheet when a weight is placed on it

1 When starlight passes near a massive body, such as the sun, the shortest route is a curved line that follows the curvature of space-time. Thus, the starlight appears to be coming from a different point than its actual origin. The observation of this effect in 1919 convinced physicists that Einstein's strange theory was right.

Position of star

Observed position of star

Sun

Earth

Light entering the black hole

2 If a mass is concentrated enough, the curvature of space-time becomes infinite. This phenomenon is known as a black hole because a light beam that comes too close will never escape.

TIME Graphics by Ed Gabel and Joe Lertola

On the other hand, if galaxies are moving apart today, they must have been closer together in the past. About 15 billion years ago, they would all have been on top of one another and their density would have been infinite. According to the general theory, this Big Bang was the beginning of the universe and of time itself. So maybe Einstein deserves to be the person of a longer period than just the past 100 years.

General relativity also predicts that time comes to a stop inside black holes, regions of space-time that are so warped that light cannot escape them. But both the beginning and the end of time are places where the equations of general relativity fall apart. Thus the theory cannot predict what should emerge from the Big Bang. Some see this as an indication of God's freedom to start the universe off any way God wanted. Others (myself included) feel that the beginning of the universe should be governed by the same laws that hold at all other times. We have made some progress toward this goal, but we don't yet have a complete understanding of the origin of the universe.

The reason general relativity broke down at the Big Bang was that it was not compatible with quantum theory, the other great conceptual revolution of the early 20th century. The first step toward quantum theory came in 1900, when Max Planck, working in Berlin, discovered that the radiation from a body that was glowing red hot could be explained if light came only in packets of a certain size, called quanta. It was as if radiation were packaged like sugar; you cannot buy an arbitrary amount of loose sugar in a supermarket but can only buy it in 1-lb. bags. In one of his groundbreaking papers written in 1905, when he was still at the patent office, Einstein showed that Planck's quantum hypothesis could explain what is called the photoelectric effect, the way certain metals give off electrons when light falls on them. This is the basis of modern light detectors and television cameras, and it was for this work that Einstein was awarded the 1921 Nobel Prize in Physics.

Einstein continued to work on the quantum idea into the 1920s but was deeply disturbed by the work of Werner Heisenberg in Copenhagen, Paul Dirac in Cambridge and Erwin Schrodinger in Zurich, who developed a new picture of reality called quantum mechanics. No longer did tiny particles have a definite position and speed. On the contrary, the more accurately you determined the particle's position, the less accurately you could determine its speed, and vice versa.

Einstein was horrified by this random, unpredictable element in the basic laws and never fully accepted quantum mechanics. His feelings were expressed in his famous God-does-not-play-dice dictum. Most other scientists, however, accepted the validity of the new quantum laws because they showed excellent agreement with observations and because they seemed to explain a whole range of previously unaccounted-for phenomena. They are the basis of modern develop-ments in chemistry, molecular biology and electronics and the foundation of the technology that has transformed the world in the past half-century.

When the Nazis came to power in Germany in 1933, Einstein left the country and renounced his German citizenship. He spent the last 22 years of his life at the Institute for Advanced Study in Princeton, N.J. The Nazis launched a campaign against "Jewish science" and the many German scientists who were Jews (their exodus is part of the reason Germany was not able to build an atom bomb). Einstein and relativity were principal targets for this campaign. When told of publication of the book *One Hundred Authors Against Einstein,* he replied, Why 100? If I were wrong, one would have been enough.

After World War II, he urged the Allies to set up a world government to control the atom bomb. He was offered the presidency of the new state of Israel in 1952 but turned it down. "Politics is for the moment," he once wrote, "while . . . an equation is for eternity." The equations of general relativity are his best epitaph and memorial.

They should last as long as the universe. The world has changed far more in the past 100 years than in any other century in history. The reason is not political or economic but technological—technologies that flowed directly from advances in basic science. Clearly, no scientist better represents those advances than Albert Einstein: TIME'S Person of the Century.

The Viral Superhighway

Environmental disruptions and international travel have brought on a new era in human illness, one marked by diabolical new diseases

By George J. Armelagos

So the Lord sent a pestilence upon Israel from the morning until the appointed time; and there died of the people from Dan to Beer-sheba seventy thousand men.
—2 Sam. 24:15

SWARMS OF CROP-DESTROYING LOCUSTS, rivers fouled with blood, lion-headed horses breathing fire and sulfur: the Bible presents a lurid assortment of plagues, described as acts of retribution by a vengeful God. Indeed, real-life epidemics—such as the influenza outbreak of 1918, which killed 21 million people in a matter of months—can be so sudden and deadly that it is easy, even for nonbelievers, to view them as angry messages from the beyond.

How reassuring it was, then, when the march of technology began to give people some control over the scourges of the past. In the 1950s the Salk vaccine, and later, the Sabin vaccine, dramatically reduced the incidence of polio. And by 1980 a determined effort by health workers worldwide eradicated smallpox, a disease that had afflicted humankind since earliest times with blindness, disfigurement and death, killing nearly 300 million people in the twentieth century alone.

But those optimistic years in the second half of our century now seem, with hindsight, to have been an era of inflated expectations, even arrogance. In 1967 the surgeon general of the United States, William H. Stewart, announced that victory over infectious diseases was imminent—a victory that would close the book on modern plagues. Sadly, we now know differently. Not only have deadly and previously unimagined new illnesses such as AIDS and Legionnaires' disease emerged in recent years, but historical diseases that just a few decades ago seemed to have been tamed are returning in virulent, drug-resistant varieties. Tuberculosis, the ancient lung disease that haunted nineteenth-century Europe, afflicting, among others, Chopin, Dostoyevski and Keats, is aggressively mutating into strains that defy the standard medicines; as a result, modern TB victims must undergo a daily drug regimen so elaborate that health-department workers often have to personally monitor patients to make sure they comply [see "A Plague Returns," by Mark Earnest and John A. Sbarbaro, September/October 1993]. Meanwhile, bacteria and viruses in foods from chicken to strawberries to alfalfa sprouts are sickening as many as 80 million Americans each year.

And those are only symptoms of a much more general threat. Deaths from infectious diseases in the United States rose 58 percent between 1980 and 1992. Twenty-nine new diseases have been reported in the past twenty-five years, a few of them so bloodcurdling and bizarre that descriptions of them bring to mind tacky horror movies. Ebola virus, for instance, can in just a few days reduce a healthy person to a bag of teeming flesh spilling blood and organ parts from every orifice. Creutzfeldt-Jakob disease, which killed the choreographer George Balanchine in 1983, eats away at its victims' brains until they resemble wet sponges. Never slow to fan mass hysteria, Hollywood has capitalized on the phenomenon with films such as *Outbreak,* in which a monkey carrying a deadly new virus from central Africa infects unwitting Californians and starts an epidemic that threatens to annihilate the human race.

The reality about infectious disease is less sensational but alarming nonetheless. Gruesome new pathogens such as Ebola are unlikely to cause a widespread epidemic because they sicken and kill so quickly that victims can be easily identified and isolated; on the other hand, the seemingly innocuous practice of overprescribing antibiotics for bad colds could ultimately lead to untold deaths, as familiar germs evolve to become untreatable. We are living in the twilight of the antibiotic era: within our lifetimes, scraped knees and cut fingers may return to the realm of fatal conditions.

Through international travel, global commerce and the accelerating destruction of ecosystems worldwide, people are inadvertently exposing themselves to a Pandora's box of emerging microbial threats. And the recent rumblings of biological terrorism from Iraq highlight the appalling potential of disease organisms for being manipulated to vile ends. But although it may appear that the apocalypse has arrived, the truth is that people today are not facing a unique predicament. Emerging diseases have long loomed like a shadow over the human race.

PEOPLE AND PATHOGENS HAVE A LONG history together. Infections have been detected in the bones of human ancestors more than a million years old, and evidence from the mummy of the Egyptian pharaoh Ramses V suggests that he may have died from smallpox more than 3,000 years ago. Widespread outbreaks of disease are also well documented. Between 1347 and 1351 roughly a third of the population of medieval Europe was wiped out by bubonic plague, which is carried by fleas that live on rodents. In 1793, 10 percent of the population of Philadelphia succumbed to yellow fever, which is spread by mosquitoes. And in 1875 the son of a Fiji chief came down with measles after a ceremonial trip to Australia. Within four months more than 20,000 Fijians were dead from the imported disease, which spreads through the air when its victims cough or sneeze.

According to conventional wisdom in biology, people and invading microorganisms evolve together: people gradually become more resistant, and the microorganisms become less virulent. The result is either mutualism, in which the relation benefits both species, or commensalism, in which one species benefits without harming the other. Chicken pox and measles, once fatal afflictions, now exist in more benign forms. Logic would suggest, after all, that the best interests of an organism are not served if it kills its host; doing so would be like picking a fight with the person who signs your paycheck.

But recently it has become clear to epidemiologists that the reverse of that cooperative paradigm of illness can also be true: microorganisms and their hosts sometimes exhaust their energies devising increasingly powerful weaponry and defenses. For example, several variants of human immunodeficiency virus (HIV) may compete for dominance within a person's body, placing the immune system under ever-greater siege. As long as a virus has an effective mechanism for jumping from one per-

son to another, it can afford to kill its victims [see "The Deadliest Virus," by Cynthia Mills, January/February 1997].

If the competition were merely a question of size, humans would surely win: the average person is 10^{17} times the size of the average bacterium. But human beings, after all, constitute only one species, which must compete with 5,000 kinds of viruses and more than 300,000 species of bacteria. Moreover, in the twenty years it takes humans to produce a new generation, bacteria can reproduce a half-million times. That disparity enables pathogens to evolve ever more virulent adaptations that quickly outstrip human responses to them. The scenario is governed by what the English zoologist Richard Dawkins of the University of Oxford and a colleague have called the "Red Queen Principle." In Lewis Carroll's *Through the Looking Glass* the Red Queen tells Alice she will need to run faster and faster just to stay in the same place. Staving off illness can be equally elusive.

THE CENTERS FOR DISEASE CONTROL and Prevention (CDC) in Atlanta, Georgia, has compiled a list of the most recent emerging pathogens. They include:

- *Campylobacter,* a bacterium widely found in chickens because of the commercial practice of raising them in cramped, unhealthy conditions. It causes between two million and eight million cases of food poisoning a year in the United States and between 200 and 800 deaths.
- *Escherichia coli* 0157:H7, a dangerously mutated version of an often harmless bacterium. Hamburger meat from Jack in the Box fast-food restaurants that was contaminated with this bug led to the deaths of at least four people in 1993.
- Hantaviruses, a genus of fast-acting, lethal viruses, often carried by rodents, that kill by causing the capillaries to leak blood. A new hantavirus known as *sin nombre* (Spanish for "nameless") surfaced in 1993 in the southwestern United States, causing the sudden and mysterious deaths of thirty-two people.
- HIV, the deadly virus that causes AIDS (acquired immunodeficiency syndrome). Although it was first ob-

served in people as recently as 1981, it has spread like wildfire and is now a global scourge, affecting more than 30 million people worldwide.
- The strange new infectious agent that causes bovine spongiform encephalopathy, or mad cow disease, which recently threw the British meat industry and consumers into a panic. This bizarre agent, known as a prion, or "proteinaceous infectious particle," is also responsible for Creutzfeldt-Jakob disease, the brain-eater I mentioned earlier. A Nobel Prize was awarded last year to the biochemist Stanley B. Prusiner of the University of California, San Francisco, for his discovery of the prion.
- *Legionella pneumophila,* the bacterium that causes Legionnaires' disease. The microorganism thrives in wet environments; when it lodges in air-conditioning systems or the mist machines in supermarket produce sections, it can be expelled into the air, reaching people's lungs. In 1976 thirty-four participants at an American Legion convention in Philadelphia died—the incident that led to the discovery and naming of the disease.
- *Borrelia burgdorferi,* the bacterium that causes Lyme disease. It is carried by ticks that live on deer and white-footed mice. Left untreated, it can cause crippling, chronic problems in the nerves, joints and internal organs.

HOW IRONIC, GIVEN SUCH A ROGUES' gallery of nasty characters, that just a quarter-century ago the Egyptian demographer Abdel R. Omran could observe that in many modern industrial nations the major killers were no longer infectious diseases. Death, he noted, now came not from outside but rather from within the body, the result of gradual deterioration. Omran traced the change to the middle of the nineteenth century, when the industrial revolution took hold in the United States and parts of Europe. Thanks to better nutrition, improved public-health measures and medical advances such as mass immunization and the introduction of antibiotics, microorganisms were brought under control. As people began living longer, their aging bodies succumbed to "diseases of civilization": cancer, clogged arteries, diabetes, obesity and osteoporosis. Omran was the first to formally recognize that shift in the disease environment. He called it an "epidemiological transition."

Like other anthropologists of my generation, I learned of Omran's theory early in my career, and it soon became a basic tenet—a comforting one, too, implying as it did an end to the supremacy of microorganisms. Then, three years ago, I began working with the anthropologist Kathleen C. Barnes of Johns Hopkins University in Baltimore, Maryland, to formulate an expansion of Omran's ideas. It occurred to us that his epidemiological transition had not been a unique event. Throughout history human populations have undergone shifts in their relations with disease—shifts, we noted, that are always linked to major changes in the way people interact with the environment. Barnes and I, along with James Lin, a master's student at Johns Hopkins University School of Hygiene and Public Health, have since developed a new theory: that there have been not one but three major epidemiological transitions; that each one has been sparked by human activities; and that we are living through the third one right now.

The first epidemiological transition took place some 10,000 years ago, when people abandoned their nomadic existence and began farming. That profoundly new way of life disrupted ecosystems and created denser living conditions that led, as I will soon detail, to new diseases. The second epidemiological transition was the salutary one Omran singled out in 1971, when the war against infectious diseases seemed to have been won. And in the past two decades the emergence of illnesses such as hepatitis C, cat scratch disease (caused by the bacterium *Bartonella henselae*), Ebola and others on CDC's list has created a third epidemiological transition, a disheartening set of changes that in many ways have reversed the effects of the second transition and coincide with the shift to globalism. Burgeoning population growth and urbanization, widespread environmental degradation, including global warming and tropical deforestation, and radically improved methods of transportation have given rise to new ways of contracting and spreading disease.

We are, quite literally, making ourselves sick.

WHEN EARLY HUMAN ANCESTORS moved from African forests onto the savanna millions of years ago, a few diseases came along for the ride. Those "heirloom" species—thus designated by the Australian parasitologist J. F. A. Sprent because they had afflicted earlier primates—included head and body lice; parasitic worms such as pinworms, tapeworms and liver flukes; and possibly herpes virus and malaria.

For 99.8 percent of the five million years of human existence, hunting and gathering was the primary mode of subsistence. Our ancestors lived in small groups and relied on wild animals and plants for their survival. In their foraging rounds, early humans would occasionally have contracted new kinds of illnesses through insect bites or by butchering and eating disease-ridden animals. Such events would not have led to widespread epidemics, however, because groups of people were so sparse and widely dispersed.

Global Warming could allow the mosquitoes that carry dengue fever to survive as far north as New York City.

About 10,000 years ago, at the end of the last ice age, many groups began to abandon their nomadic lifestyles for a more efficient and secure way of life. The agricultural revolution first appeared in the Middle East; later, farming centers developed independently in China and Central America. Permanent villages grew up, and people turned their attention to crafts such as toolmaking and pottery. Thus when people took to cultivating wheat and barley, they planted the seeds of civilization as well.

With the new ways, however, came certain costs. As wild habitats were transformed into urban settings, the farmers who brought in the harvest with their flint-bladed sickles were assailed by grim new ailments. Among the most common was scrub typhus, which is carried by mites that live in tall grasses, and causes a potentially lethal fever. Clearing vegetation to create arable fields brought farmers frequently into mite-infested terrain.

Irrigation brought further hazards. Standing thigh-deep in watery canals, farm workers were prey to the worms that cause schistosomiasis. After living within aquatic snails during their larval stage, those worms emerge in a free-swimming form that can penetrate human skin, lodge in the intestine or urinary tract, and cause bloody urine and other serious maladies. Schistosomiasis was well known in ancient Egypt, where outlying fields were irrigated with water from the Nile River; descriptions of its symptoms and remedies are preserved in contemporary medical papyruses.

The domestication of sheep, goats and other animals cleared another pathway for microorganisms. With pigs in their yards and chickens roaming the streets, people in agricultural societies were constantly vulnerable to pathogens that could cross interspecies barriers. Many such organisms had long since reached commensalism with their animal hosts, but they were highly dangerous to humans. Milk from infected cattle could transmit tuberculosis, a slow killer that eats away at the lungs and causes its victims to cough blood and pus. Wool and skins were loaded with anthrax, which can be fatal when inhaled and, in modern times, has been developed by several nations as a potential agent of biological warfare. Blood from infected cattle, injected into people by biting insects such as the tsetse fly, spread sleeping sickness, an often-fatal disease marked by tremors and protracted lethargy.

A SECOND MAJOR EFFECT OF AGRICULture was to spur population growth and, perhaps more important, density. Cities with populations as high as 50,000 had developed in the Near East by 3000 B.C. Scavenger species such as rats, mice and sparrows, which congregate wherever large groups of people live, exposed city dwellers to bubonic plague, typhus and rabies. And now that people were crowded together, a new pathogen could quickly start an epidemic. Larger populations also enabled diseases such as measles, mumps, chicken pox and smallpox to persist in an endemic form—always present, afflicting part of the population while sparing those with acquired immunity.

Thus the birth of agriculture launched humanity on a trajectory that has again and again brought people into contact with new pathogens. Tilling soil and raising livestock led to more energy-intensive ways of extracting resources from the earth—to lumbering, coal mining, oil drilling. New resources led to increasingly complex social organization, and to new and more frequent contacts between various societies. Loggers today who venture into the rain forest disturb previously untouched creatures and give them, for the first time, the chance to attack humans. But there is nothing new about this drama; only the players have changed. Some 2,000 years ago the introduction of iron tools to sub-Saharan Africa led to a slash-and-burn style of agriculture that brought people into contact with *Anopheles gambiae,* a mosquito that transmits malaria.

Improved transportation methods also help diseases extend their reach: microorganisms cannot travel far on their own, but they are expert hitchhikers. When the Spanish invaded Mexico in the early 1500s, for instance, they brought with them diseases that quickly raged through Tenochtitlán, the stately, temple-filled capital of the Aztec Empire. Smallpox, measles and influenza wiped out millions of Central America's original inhabitants, becoming the invisible weapon in the European conquest.

IN THE PAST THREE DECADES PEOPLE AND their inventions have drilled, polluted, engineered, paved, planted and deforested at soaring rates, changing the biosphere faster than ever before. The combined effects can, without hyperbole, be called a global revolution. After all, many of them have worldwide repercussions: the widespread chemical contamination of waterways, the thin-ning of the ozone layer, the loss of species diversity. And such global human actions have put people at risk for infectious diseases in newly complex and devastating ways. Global warming, for instance, could expose millions of people for the first time to malaria, sleeping sickness and other insect-borne illnesses; in the United States, a slight overall temperature increase would allow the mosquitoes that carry dengue fever to survive as far north as New York City.

Major changes to the landscape that have become possible in the past quarter-century have also triggered new diseases. After the construction of the Aswan Dam in 1970, for instance, Rift Valley fever infected 200,000 people in Egypt, killing 600. The disease had been known to affect livestock, but it was not a major problem in people until the vast quantities of dammed water became a breeding ground for mosquitoes. The insects bit both cattle and humans, helping the virus jump the interspecies barrier.

In the eastern United States, suburbanization, another relatively recent phenomenon, is a dominant factor in the emergence of Lyme disease—10,000 cases of which are reported annually. Thanks to modern earth-moving equipment, a soaring economy and population pressures, many Americans have built homes in formerly remote, wooded areas. Nourished by lawns and gardens and unchecked by wolves, which were exterminated by settlers long ago, the deer population has exploded, exposing people to the ticks that carry Lyme disease.

Meanwhile, widespread pollution has made the oceans a breeding ground for microorganisms. Epidemiologists have suggested that toxic algal blooms—fed by the sewage, fertilizers and other contaminants that wash into the oceans—harbor countless viruses and bacteria. Thrown together into what amounts to a dirty genetic soup, those pathogens can undergo gene-swapping and mutations, engendering newly antibiotic-resistant strains. Nautical traffic can carry ocean pathogens far and wide: a devastating outbreak of cholera hit Latin America in 1991 after a ship from Asia unloaded its contaminated ballast water into the harbor of Callao, Peru. Cholera causes diarrhea so severe its victims can die in a few days from dehydration; in that outbreak more than 300,000 people became ill, and more than 3,000 died.

The modern world is becoming—to paraphrase the words of the microbiologist Stephen S. Morse of Columbia University—a viral superhighway. Everyone is at risk.

Our newly global society is characterized by huge increases in population, international travel and international trade—factors that enable diseases to spread much more readily than ever before from person to person and from continent to continent. By 2020 the world population will have surpassed seven billion, and half those people will be living in urban centers. Beleaguered third-world nations are already hard-pressed to provide sewers, plumbing and other infrastructure; in the future, clean water and adequate sanitation could become increasingly rare. Meanwhile, political upheavals regularly cause millions of people to flee their homelands and gather in refugee camps, which become petri dishes for germs.

More than 500 million people cross international borders each year on commercial flights. Not only does that traffic volume dramatically increase the chance a sick person will infect the inhabitants of a distant area when she reaches her destination; it also exposes the sick person's fellow passengers to the disease, because of poor air circulation on planes. Many of those passengers can, in turn, pass the disease on to others when they disembark.

THE GLOBAL ECONOMY THAT HAS arisen in the past two decades has established a myriad of connections between far-flung places. Not too long ago bananas and oranges were rare treats in northern climes. Now you can walk into your neighborhood market and find food that has been flown and trucked in from all over the world: oranges from Israel, apples from New Zealand, avocados from California. Consumers in affluent nations expect to be able to buy whatever they want whenever they want it. What people do not generally realize, however, is that this global network of food production and delivery provides countless pathways for pathogens. Raspberries from Guatemala, carrots from Peru and coconut milk from Thailand have been responsible for recent outbreaks of food poisoning in the United States. And the problem cuts both ways: contaminated radish seeds and frozen beef from the United States have ended up in Japan and South Korea.

Finally, the widespread and often indiscriminate use of antibiotics has played a key role in spurring disease. Forty million pounds of antibiotics are manufactured annually in the United States, an eightyfold increase since 1954. Dangerous microorganisms have evolved accordingly, often developing antibiotic-resistant strains. Physicians are now faced with penicillin-resistant gonorrhea, multiple-drug-resistant tuberculosis and E. coli variants such as 0157:H7. And frighteningly, some enterococcus bacteria have become resistant to all known antibiotics. Enterococcus infections are rare, but staphylococcus infections are not, and many strains of staph bacteria now respond to just one antibiotic, vancomycin. How long will it be before run-of-the-mill staph infections—in a boil, for instance, or in a surgical incision—become untreatable?

ALTHOUGH CIVILIZATION CAN EXPOSE people to new pathogens, cultural progress also has an ob- vious countervailing effect: it can provide tools—medicines, sensible city planning, educational campaigns about sexually transmitted diseases—to fight the encroachments of disease. Moreover, since biology seems to side with microorganisms anyway, people have little choice but to depend on protective cultural practices to keep pace: vaccinations, for instance, to confer immunity, combined with practices such as hand-washing by physicians between patient visits, to limit contact between people and pathogens.

All too often, though, obvious protective measures such as using only clean hypodermic needles or treating urban drinking water with chlorine are neglected, whether out of ignorance or a wrongheaded emphasis on the short-term financial costs. The worldwide disparity in wealth is also to blame: not surprisingly, the advances made during the second epidemiological transition were limited largely to the affluent of the industrial world.

Such lapses are now beginning to teach the bitter lesson that the delicate balance between humans and invasive microorganisms can tip the other way again. Overconfidence—the legacy of the second epidemiological transition— has made us especially vulnerable to emerging and reemerging diseases. Evolutionary principles can provide this useful corrective: in spite of all our medical and technological hubris, there is no quick fix. If human beings are to overcome the current crisis, it will be through sensible changes in behavior, such as increased condom use and improved sanitation, combined with a commitment to stop disturbing the ecological balance of the planet.

The Bible, in short, was not far from wrong: We do bring plagues upon ourselves—not by sinning, but by refusing to heed our own alarms, our own best judgment. The price of peace—or at least peaceful coexistence—with the microorganisms on this planet is eternal vigilance.

George J. Armelagos is a professor of anthropology at Emory University in Atlanta, Georgia. He has coedited two books on the evolution of human disease: PALEOPATHOLOGY AT THE ORIGINS OF AGRICULTURE, *which deals with prehistoric populations, and* DISEASE IN POPULATIONS IN TRANSITION, *which focuses on contemporary societies.*

Belonging in the West

*Multiple challenges and concerns arise from the presence of
ever-growing Muslim communities within Western society.*

Yvonne Yazbeck Haddad

When Daniel Pipes sounded the alarm: "The Muslims Are Coming! The Muslims are Coming!" in the November 19, 1990, issue of *National Review,* it was clear that Muslims were already here. Indeed, they had become an intregal part of the West. Since that time, Islam, particularly Islamic fundamentalism, has continually been depicted as the next enemy: as a force replacing communism as a challenge to the West.

Consequently, Muslims are often suffered from considerable prejudice. They have been accused of adhering to a religion that is devoid of integrity, that encourages violent passions in its adherents, that menaces civil society and is a threat to our way of life. Muslims are stereotyped as potentially bloodthirsty terrorists whose loyalty as citizens must be questioned. Not one promoter of political correctness has put them on a list of communities to be protected. But Muslims have been victims of hate crimes that include assault, murder, and the burning of mosques in both Europe and North America. As a result, their apprehension about their security and future in Western society has increased.

The Muslim encounter with the West dates back to the beginning of Islam. As Muslims spread into Byzantium and North Africa, they established their hegemony over large areas inhabited by Christian populations. While their expansion into western Europe was halted at Poitiers in 731, Muslims created a thriving civilization in different parts of Spain, Portugal, Sicily, and southern France between the eighth and fifteenth centuries. In the East, Ottoman expansion into Europe was not halted until the failure of the siege of Vienna in 1683. While a significant number of Muslims continued to live in eastern Europe, in Bulgaria, Romania, Albania, and Serbia, the fall of Grenada in 1492 and the Inquisition (which gave Muslims the options of conversion to Christianity, expulsion, or death) all but eliminated a Muslim presence in western Europe. Thus, the recent growth of the Muslim community in Europe and North America has been called the "new Islamic presence."

> *Some Muslim
> scholars have
> admonished Muslims
> to leave the West,
> lest they lose
> their souls.*

Indeed, since the sixteenth century, Muslims have encountered Western cultures as conquering and imperial powers, competing in their quest to subjugate Muslims and monopolize their economic resources. Consequently, some Muslims depict the West as bent on combating Is-

This article first appeared in *The World & I,* September 1997, pp. 50-59. Reprinted by permission of *The World & I,* a
publication of The Washington Times Corporation. © 1997.

lam not only through colonial conquest but through armies of missionaries. They perceive a West that is and ever has been eager to displace or eradicate Muslims. They find evidence in the Reconquista, the Crusades, and, more recently, in Palestine and Bosnia.

LIVING BEYOND THE ISLAMIC STATE

Muslim jurists have offered various opinions about whether it is permissible for Muslims to live outside the jurisdiction of an Islamic state. This issue has been raised during the last two decades, as some Muslim scholars have admonished Muslims to leave the West lest they lose their soul amid its wayward ways. Other jurists have insisted that as long as Muslims are free to practice their faith, they are allowed to live outside the house of Islam, while still others have said that it is Muslims' duty to propagate the faith in their new abode. Thus they not only have the opportunity to share the salvific teachings of Islam but must try to redeem Western society from its evil ways and restore it to the worship of God.

Muslims are repelled by what they see as a degenerate Western society with weak family values.

The question then is often asked: "Given their experience of the West, why do they come?" Surveys show that Muslims move to Europe and North America for the same reasons that other populations have chosen to come: for higher education, better economic opportunities, and political and religious freedom. Others are refugees, the by-product of Euro-American adventures in the world. Thus the first significant group of Muslims to come to France

were North Africans and Senegalese who were recruited to fight in French colonial wars. Immigrants to Britain are from its former colonies and from the ranks of its Asian (Bangladeshi, Indian, and Pakistani) colonial civil servants expelled from Africa by the leaders of newly independent nations. In the Netherlands, the initial Muslim population came from the colonies of Indonesia and Suriname.

The majority of Muslims in Europe were recruited as temporary guest workers to relieve the shortage of labor in the post–World War II reconstruction. The host countries of Germany, the Netherlands, Austria, Britain, Switzerland, and France expected them to leave when their contracts expired. In the 1970s, a recession and growing unemployment prompted European governments to reduce imported labor. Some even provided financial incentives for the laborers to return to their homelands. This policy led to an unintended growth of the Muslim community, as many opted to bring their families and settle for fear that they would not have another opportunity.

In European nations with an official state religion, such as Britain and the Netherlands, Muslims have sought parity with Jews and Catholics who have been given special privileges. But to no avail. Thus, during the Salman Rushdie affair, Muslims sought implementation of the blasphemy law, only to find out that it operates only to protect Anglicanism. In Britain, for example, the school day starts with a Christian prayer. In courts, the oath is taken on the Bible. Town council meetings start with a prayer. Anglican clergy celebrate marriage that is automatically legal without having to go to the registrar. While Catholic and Jewish marriages are recognized, those performed by imams are not. Catholics and Jews obtain state funding to support their parochial schools, but Muslim requests for parity have been denied.

Muslims have fared differently in nations that have historically welcomed immigrants—the United States, Canada,

Here Yet Apart

🐎 *Though an integral part of twentieth-century Western society, Muslims have lately been targets of considerable prejudice.*

🐎 *Many argue that it may not be possible to lead a Muslim lifestyle beyond the borders of an Islamic state.*

🐎 *Both Islamic and European governments have helped build mosques and Muslim centers in the West, in the hopes of blunting the rise of fundamentalism and aiding the assimilation of Muslim immigrants.*

🐎 *Muslims ask whether Western society, which prides itself on liberal democracy, pluralism, and multiculturalism, will be flexible enough to provide for Islamic input into the shaping of its future.*

Latin America, and Australia. Muslim migrant laborers began coming to America in the nineteenth century. While many returned, a few settled permanently and formed the nucleus of what is now the fourth and fifth American-born generation of Muslims. The largest number of Muslims came in the 1970s on a preference visa and were accepted as citizens and given voting rights. Predominantly members of the educated elite, they are doctors, professors, and engineers.

Islam is the second- or third-largest religion in various European nations. It is estimated that there are five million Muslims in France, organized in over 1,000 mosques and prayer halls. They constitute about 10 percent of the population, making Islam the largest religion after Catholicism and with more active adherents than either Protestants or Jews. In Britain, the Muslim population is estimated at about two million, organized in over 600 mosques. The Muslim community of the United States is estimated at five million, about 10 percent of whom are involved in organized religion in over 1,250 mosques and Islamic centers. Canada has about half a million.

It is expected that Muslims will outnumber Jews in Canada and the United States by the first decade of the next

Muslim Legal Expectations

Kathleen Moore

When a truck bomb shattered the Murrah Federal Building in downtown Oklahoma City on April 19, 1995—the worst terrorist act ever on American soil—many in the media and federal law enforcement jumped to the conclusion that an "Islamic fundamentalist" was responsible. Similarly, the downing of TWA Flight 800 and the Olympic Park explosion in Atlanta set off allegations that "Middle Eastern-looking" terrorists were to blame. Those hasty conclusions have proved groundless. However, Muslim defendants have been convicted for the 1993 bombing of the World Trade Center, and a Muslim suspect has been arrested in connection with the attack on traffic near the CIA headquarters in January of that year.

Instantly attributing blame to unknown Muslim terrorists was not just the result of the media and law enforcement officials letting their imaginations run amok. Such images were also conjured up—and in some instances acted upon—by the general public. Some 200 incidents of anti-Muslim harassment were reported in the days immediately following the tragedy in Oklahoma.

Consequently, American Muslim communities mobilized to an unprecedented degree. Existing organizations, such as the American Muslim Council and the Islamic Society of North America, were joined by newly formed groups such as the Council on American-Islamic Relations (CAIR) to defend Muslims' civil rights. Public relations and lobbying efforts and press conferences highlighted not merely the Muslim presence in the United States but also the American Muslims' experiences as targets of discrimination. Thus the rights consciousness of this growing segment of the American population is largely being shaped by Muslims' responses to media distortions and perceived demonization of Islam.

The fears that motivate anti-Islamic sentiment appear to derive from a sense of insecurity that has lurked just beneath the surface of our national life since the fall of the Berlin Wall in 1989. The prospects for world peace would seem to be greater than at any other time in this century, but our doubts about the future seem nevertheless to escalate. This post–Cold War malaise has its consequences for those who fear they may come to take the unenviable place of the "Red menace" in the public mind. Of great concern to many Muslims is the prospect that they will be increasingly subjected to various forms of discrimination in Western countries as negative portrayals of Islam and Muslims take their toll.

The visible effects of these concerns and experiences of mistreatment can be seen in the emergence of rights-advocacy groups that have used a variety of legal strategies to assert Muslim rights. For instance, in the United States, CAIR has conducted media campaigns over the last two years or so to bring to public attention instances where women have been prohibited from wearing the traditional Islamic hijab (head scarf) at work. Cases of harassment involving Muslims who have been taunted with epithets relating to prevalent prejudicial stereotypes have been documented and financially supported through the legal process by these advocacy groups. In Britain, a few muslim activist have (so far, unsuccessfully) pressed the government for greater autonomy, particularly allowing Islamic courts to adjudicate issues of family law separate from the civil court system.

We are now witnessing the emergence of a distinctive Western Muslim identity, carved out of the secular social environment of the West. It would not be accurate, however, to assume that the Muslim identity being forged is uniform or monolithic. In fact, significant distinctions and disagreements exist within Muslim communities that are differentiated by sectarian, ethnic, regional, or generational traits. But it is meaningful to note that there are shared experiences and to recognize that the formulation of this identity is taking place under constraints imposed by the host societies. Muslim legal expectations and interpretations are thus voiced within particular contexts, in response to specific events, cultural characteristics, and historical pressures.

In an idealized sense, Muslims migrated to the United States and Britain with a centuries-old tradition in hand. In this legal framework are the classical traditions of Islamic jurisprudence that offer models for minority living. Historically, these models focus on three essential questions: First, under what conditions are Muslims allowed to live outside Muslim territory? In essence, the answer is only where religious freedom prevails. Second, what responsibilities do Muslim minorities have with respect to their host society? Here, answers are varied. Third, what is the relationship of Muslim minorities, living in places like the United States and Britain, to the global Muslim community as a whole? Again, answers are varied and problematic.

In general, the classical models suggest that if a Muslim minority does not encounter religious freedom and is unable to practice its faith, then it has the options of fighting back (*jihad*) or emigration (*hirah*).

(Continued on next page)

century. The North American community is noted for its ethnic national, linguistic, and secretarian diversity. It includes over a million converts, mostly African Americans. While it is estimated that up to 18 percent of the slaves brought to America were Muslims, most had converted to Christianity by the beginning of this century. The conversion of African Americans to Islam is a twentieth-century phenomenon.

THE MUSLIM EXPERIENCE IN THE WEST

The Muslim experience in the West varies according to the immigrants' background, the nations they came from, their reasons for leaving, and their educational attainments. The host country's policies are also influential: whether it welcomes foreigners and/or grants them citizenship rights, its perceptions of Islam, and its laws governing the relationship between religion and state.

During the eighties, various Muslim countries began laying Islamic foundations in the West by providing funds for the construction of mosques and schools and the teaching of Arabic and Islam. For example, in a two-year period, Saudi Arabia spent $10 million to construct mosques in North America. In

Yet many see these traditions as out of touch with Muslim minorities' realities and in need of revision to fit today's circumstances. Recent calls have been made for the formulation of a "new" jurisprudence in light of changing conditions. A variety of issues have been singled out by the British and American Muslim communities as being crucial.

Some issues are the product of the secular environment in which Muslims live. Do they have rights to religious freedom that require accommodation of their specific needs in the workplace, at school, or in the military? How will Muslims survive as a vibrant religious community in the West? Will they be able to freely and fully participate in its religious landscape and in defining the future as a pluralistic society? How can Muslim children be successfully integrated into the larger society, to function as hyphenated Americans or Britons without abandoning the faith? Can Muslims vote or run for political office in a secular society where the institutions of government are not based on Islamic values? What roles are women permitted to play in public life?

Attendance at mosques and Islamic centers (in the West) has gone up over the last decade or so. Mosques are now not only for prayer at the five prescribed times: They have become community centers and provide facilities for tutoring students in their school subjects, Qur'anic studies, marriage ceremonies, free counseling and mediation, and legal services.

In some of these places, Muslims are listening to those who warn from the pulpit that the encounter with the secular West is destructive and that the only option for Muslim survival is to remain marginal to public life. From this isolationist perspective, the Muslim minority should re-affirm a Muslim identity in isolation, untainted by the materialistic values of the West. This, it is thought, will have the effect of inviting others to Islam by providing an example of an incorruptible "city on a hill" in the midst of moral decay.

On the other side of the debate are the "accommodationists," who struggle to feel at home in the United States and Britain. Muhammad Abduh, an early twentieth-century reformer in Egypt, provides some insight into the accommodationists' position. Abduh gave a *fatwa* (religious legal opinion) permitting Muslims in South Africa to consume meat butchered for People of the Book (i.e., Christians and Jews) when no *halal* meat (i.e., food prepared or butchered in the Islamically prescribed way, similar to the Jewish tradition of kosher) was available.

Accommodationists advise cooperation with non-Muslims, provided that it benefits the Muslim community. As long as the Muslim who lives as minority is at liberty to maintain the "core" of the religion, he may adjust to the host society. Accommodationists argue that diet, as long as it is nourishing, need not comply with stringent Islamic strictures; attire, as long as it is clean and modest, need not be restricting (such as the so-called veil or head scarf is); and the architecture of mosques and Islamic centers need not slavishly imitate Middle Eastern styles as long as the buildings are accessible and functional.

In the last two decades the circumstances of Muslim minorities have come to the attention of various international Islamic organizations, such as the muslim World League, which has established a Fiqh Council, a body that engages in the interpretation of Islamic law to address minority concerns. The council represents a wide variety of Islamic legal schools and advocates what is being called "jurisprudence of necessity" (*fiqh al-darurah*) and "jurisprudence of minority" (*fiqh al-aqalliyah*) to respond to issues of Muslim life in a non-Islamic environment.

Some critics within Islam, though, see this as an effort to impose a "top-down" understanding of Muslim contingencies and reject it in favor of a "bottom-up" approach. Efforts at using American legal rules and then sanctifying them as "Islamic" because they are fair and just can be seen at the local level. For instance, American laws governing marriage, divorce, and child custody, where the woman would, arguably, have greater rights than Islam affords, have been sanctified in places where the *imam* (leader of the mosque) has sanctioned a civil marriage license or divorce decree obtained by a member of his mosque.

The secular legal system has had its effect on Muslim legal consciousness. For example, one leader of a large mosque community in an urban area in the western United States asserts that the process of working out a set of rules to govern Muslim life must be thought of as a jurisprudence of "minority," not because of any specific Islamic tradition but because Muslims are living in the United States, where a significant body of case law on minority relations already exists. To be labeled a minority entitles one to rights. The word *minority* may connote weakness or vulnerability, but it is also a recognized basis for making claims to resources and privilege in America. Thus, it is imperative to accommodate Islamic practices to fit the opportunities provided by the local customs and laws of the community in which they are now a permanent part.

Kathleen Moore is assistant professor of political science at the University of Connecticut.

Germany, Sweden, and the Netherlands—where there are large Turkish and Moroccan communities—the fear of the potential for growth of Islamic fundamentalism among the *marginalized guest* workers led to arrangements with the Turkish and Moroccan governments to supervise the religious affairs of the community. Both governments welcomed the opportunity to blunt the growth of fundamentalism and curtail its dissemination in their countries. The European governments paid for construction of Islamic centers and mosques and imported the religious leaders to lead prayers and provide religious instruction.

Two issues are of paramount importance for both the immigrants and host countries: security and cultural coherence. All nation-states have developed a myth of national identity that has been inculcated in schoolchildren through literature, art, music, assumptions, legends, and a particular understanding of history. These myths have shaped several generations of Europeans and Americans through the cauldron of two wars and created distinctive identities marking the way the West sees itself and what it takes for granted, as well as what it identifies as alien, strange, and weird.

Educated Muslims who emigrated in the postwar period also have a preformed understanding of Western culture based on the experience of colonialism and neocolonialism. Their perceptions have been shaped by watching Western movies and television, which they perceive as imbued with drugs, violence, racism, and pornography. Muslims are repelled by what they see as a degenerate society with weak family values. They condemn premarital or extramarital sex and having children out of wedlock, both of which increase the fragility of marriage and hence the family bond. They believe that Western values concerning parents and children's duties toward one another are lacking. There is too much emphasis on individual freedom and not enough on corporate responsibility.

A primary concern for Muslim immigrants is surviving in what they experience as a hostile environment and safeguarding the welfare of their children. They are fully aware that Europe and the Americas have been shaped by secular Christianity. They seek to maintain the right to practice their faith according to its tenets as revealed to them by God. They are concerned about perpetuation of the faith among their children and preservation of Islamic values. In this context they have sought to have employers provide them with time off to fulfill their religious duties during the day, to attend the Friday prayer at the mosque, fast during the month of Ramadan, and celebrate the two major holidays (Eid al-Fitr and Eid al-Adha). Many are concerned about properly slaughtered meat (halal), while others seek the right to have their children excused from coed athletics and sex education (which they believe promotes promiscuity). They believe that religious freedom should provide the right to wear the head scarf (hijab) for women.

In France, the issue of wearing the hijab took on national significance when several female students were banned from wearing it on the grounds that such behavior is tantamount to proselytizing, a proscribed activity in the secular schools of France. For Muslims, the ban was seen as an anti-Muslim act, since Christians are allowed to wear a cross and Jews a yarmulke, both of which could then be interpreted as an act of propagating a faith.

The issue of the hijab has surfaced in other Western nations under different rubrics. For example, in Canada, feminists championed the banning of head scarfs, which they depicted as a symbol of oppression. Muslim girls who put them on insisted that it was an act of obedience to a divine injunction and therefore protected under the freedom of religion. More important, they viewed it as an instrument of liberation from being a sex object. In the United States, the Council on American-Islamic Relations reported that there was a 50 percent increase in 1996 in the number of incidents of discrimination against women who wear the hijab.

ISLAM IN A PLURAL SOCIETY

The Western experience is also shaping new forms of Islamic organization and administration. The imam not only leads prayer and worship but acts as an ambassador to the host culture, attempting to build bridges to other faith communities and representing Muslims in interfaith events. Moreover, the mosque, besides being a place of congregational prayer, has become a social center where the community meets for a variety of events that help cement relationships and provide for community celebrations. In this center for Islamic knowledge and education Islam is taught to the next generation, which reflects on its meaning in the new environment. The mosque has become an island

While immigrants struggle to maintain their identity, they are increasingly challenged as their children become indigenized into the surrounding culture.

of security and a venue for the sharing of one's experiences. It is not unusual to see people clothed in their ethnic dress for Sunday services, taking advantage of a chance to affirm primary identity in an environment where individuals can be themselves without being under constant scrutiny for conformity.

Some Muslims contemplate the option of returning to their homeland, should conditions of life in the West continue to be unacceptable. Their children, however, have been reared and educated in the West. The West is their homeland. They are bicultural and possess an intimate experience and knowledge of Western society, as well as a knowledge about the culture of the parents as remembered and reinvented in the West. While immigrants struggle to maintain their identity; they are increasingly being challenged and changed as their children become more indigenized into the surrounding culture.

Some Western authors have continued to question whether Muslims are worthy of citizenship in a democratic nation or whether their presence will alter the place where they settle. While some continue to debate whether they belong *in* the West, it is evident that Muslims are part and parcel *of* the West. An estimated ten thousand Muslims currently serve in the armed services of the United States, for example. There are two Muslim chaplains, one in the Navy and one in the Army and plans have been made to appoint one in the Air Force.

Muslims in the West generally favor keeping a low profile for security reasons. They are the latest victims of chauvinism and xenophobia. Events such as the oil embargo of 1973, the Iranian revolution, the holding of American hostages for 444 days, and the Pan Am bombing have created concern among many westerners. Irresponsible and irrational actions such as the bombing of the World Trade Center have heightened fears of Islamic fundamentalism. This has exacerbated the fear of Islam and tapped into a history of misunderstanding and vilification. Thus, Muslims fear they are becoming the new villains on the block, replacing Jews, Gypsies, Italians, and African Americans as objects of odium.

Muslims continue to ask whether Western democracies are liberal enough to include Islamic input into the national consensus, or if they will insist on an exclusively Judeo-Christian culture. Will Western pluralism or multiculturalism be flexible enough to provide for Islamic input into the shaping of the future of Western society? Or will Muslims continue to be marginaiized, ostracized, studied, and evaluated, always judged as lacking, always the "other"?

Yvonne Yazbeck Haddad is professor of the history of Islam and Christian-Muslim relations at Georgetown University.

Folly & Failure in the Balkans

Tom Gallagher examines the sorry story of ethnic conflict in the Balkans, and concludes that foreign interference has needlessly fanned the flames of nationalism.

BISMARCK'S OPINION THAT THE BALkans were not worth the bones of a single Pomeranian grenadier has long been heeded by hard-headed statesmen from Disraeli to Kissinger who warned against active involvement in the region. A sense of fatalism about the ability of local leaders and their populations to aspire to good government and 'civilised' conduct has long coloured Western policy towards southeast Europe.

But the statements and actions of powerful Western leaders in the recent war over Kosovo suggested that a break with past traditions may be occurring. Madeleine Albright, the US Secretary of State, declared to Congress in May that 'the Continent cannot be whole and free as long as its south-east corner is wracked by ethnic tensions and threatened with conflict'. With maps of the region by his side, President Clinton went on television to show the American people where Kosovo was and why the peace of Europe depended on securing justice for deported Kosovo refugees. Britain's prime minister Tony Blair delighted Albanian refugees by promising that they would all be able to return to their homes. Other leaders promised a new Marshall Plan for the region in order to integrate it economically with the rest of Europe.

A look at the role of the great powers in the Balkans over the last two hundred years shows that such clear statements of principles are uncharacteristic. Statesmen have been reluctant to act as peacemakers in the region, at least for extended periods. Altruistic gestures towards oppressed peoples have been

overtaken by the need to preserve a balance of power between states whose interests collide in the region.

The Balkan peninsula is a region where civilisations and social systems have collided and merged for thousands of years. For over four hundred years, the Ottoman Empire headed by a Muslim sultan in Constantinople controlled most of the Balkans. The Ottomans taxed their subject peoples heavily and conscripted their young men to fight in frequent wars. But the west European obsession with ensuring that the religion of the people matched that of the ruler was not shared. The Orthodox Christian Church and the Jews enjoyed freedom of worship. They were allowed to maintain their own courts and judges, applying their own laws to their communities in a whole range of civil matters. Forcible conversions to Islam were rare. But among certain peoples, particularly the Slavs of Bosnia and the Albanians, large-scale conversions took place, not least because of the opportunities for upward mobility in the

---

Intellectuals were encouraged to explore the past and invent glorious historical pedigrees.

Ottoman bureaucracy or the military provided for Muslims.

The autonomy enjoyed by the Orthodox Church preserved cultural values pre-dating Islam, particularly memories of the Byzantine Empire which had lasted until 1453. This sense of religious and historical separation would provide the seedbed for nationalism when the Ottoman empire decayed. A Byzantine heritage was also preserved by influential Greek families, known as the *phanariots*, who administered parts of the Empire on behalf of the Sultan.

The Orthodox Church was a supranational body that was non-national in its doctrines and outlook. Sometimes the harshness of church courts and the exactions of the *phanariots* made ordinary Greeks view the Turks as less onerous oppressors. During the seventeenth century Greek peasants in the Peloponnese welcomed the return of the Turks after periods of Venetian rule marked by heavy taxation and forcible conversion to Catholicism.

Memories of the sacking of Constantinople in 1204 by Crusaders who looted and massacred, desecrating churches and fatally weakening the Byzantine empire, created long-term enmity between western and eastern Christianity. Today in Greece these images of western treachery and barbarism enable opinion formers to appeal for solidarity with fellow Orthodox Serbs and condemn what is seen as Nato aggression first in Bosnia and later in Kosovo.

Two hundred years ago, as the Ottoman empire became enfeebled and corrupt, it was the West which appeared to offer the path to modernisation and re-

This article first appeared in *History Today*, September 1999, pp. 45-51. © 1999 by History Today, Ltd. Reprinted by permission.

newed greatness for local Christian leaders and especially restless intellectuals in the Balkans.

In 1807 the Serbs were the first South Slav people to establish their independence. This achievement encouraged the view among Serb rulers that they were entitled to play the leading role in creating a union of South Slav peoples. When Yugoslavia emerged in 1918, the domineering attitude of the Serb leadership provoked resentment among other peoples, particularly the Croats, who, because of their experience of Austrian Habsburg rule from Vienna, had acquired different governmental traditions and expectations.

Before their current demonisation, the Serbs had long enjoyed a vogue in Europe because of their martial sacrifices in the cause of political freedom as well as the beauty of their poetry. Writers from Goethe and Walter Scott to Rebecca West expressed their admiration for the lyric beauty of Serbian popular songs, while Jacob Grimm ranked Serb poetry alongside that of Homer.

The romantic nationalism pioneered by the German philosopher Herder found a ready audience among restless intellectuals in Eastern Europe. With its emphasis on the unique value of every ethnic group and on each group's 'natural right' to carve out a national home of its own, romantic nationalism was able to undermine the multi-cultural traditions of the Eastern world. When Herder hailed the Slavs as 'the coming leaders of Europe', intellectuals were encouraged to explore the past and all-too-often invent glorious historical pedigrees meant to give reborn nations the inalienable right to enjoy contemporary greatness. If this meant dominating territories shared by more than one ethnic group, then many nationalists justified such a course even if it meant that they were imitating the imperialists whose rule they were seeking to throw off.

The prospects of cultural nationalism were transformed by the French Revolution and Napoleon's humiliation of dynastic empires. The revolution against the traditional political order legitimised a West European concept of nationalism allowing a people to identify with a territory on which they were entitled to establish a state and government of their own.

The appeal of romantic nationalism for European public opinion was first revealed by the Greek War of Independence in the 1820s. Acts of cruelty were committed on both sides but it was the Ottoman atrocities against the Greeks that moved the liberal European conscience. The Ottoman massacre of Greeks on the island of Chios in 1822, immortalised in Delacroix's painting, enabled European public opinion to overrule governments that might have wished to limit Greek ambitions. It was not just Byron, but Shelley, Goethe and Schiller who unleashed a storm of enthusiasm for Philhellenism that cautious governments found hard to stem. In 1824, a series of privately financed loans, which in effect made the City of London the financier of the revolution, proved critical in ensuring Greek success.

One hundred and fifty years later, philhellenism was still a strong enough force to ensure that Greece entered the European Union even though there were nagging doubts about her real commitment to a post-nationalist agenda based upon European integration. In the 1980s and early 1990s Greece would earn the reputation of being arguably the most nationalistic of the Balkan states, under the populist premier Andreas Papandreou. Persistent interference by outside powers in its internal affairs had produced a culture of suspicion and complaint which helped nationalism to flourish.

After Greek independence was achieved in 1832, Great Power interference combined with local factionalism to weaken the prospects of effective government. Russia and Britain in particular had conflicting interests and ambitions in the Balkans. As a multi-national empire in its own right, Russia was hostile to the pretensions of European small state nationalism. But the tsars claimed to be the legitimate successors to the Orthodox Empire at Byzantium and the defenders of east European Christendom.

In 1774 Catherine the Great of Russia extracted from the sultan the right to appoint consuls in the Ottoman empire who could make representations on behalf of its Christian subjects. Between 1787 and 1792, Russia fought a war with Turkey whose aim was to partition the Ottoman empire and establish Russian control of Constantinople and the Bosphorus Straits. For the first time Britain became aware of conflicting British and Russian interests in the Near East. The realisation gave birth to long-standing international tensions as two rival European powers sought to fill the vacuum left by the retreating Ottoman empire on their own terms.

Britain feared that its imperial possessions in India would be threatened if Russia became a Mediterranean power. Thus the Foreign Office became associated with the policy of propping up the Ottoman empire, or at least preventing its slow decline becoming a rapid collapse that might overturn a precarious balance of power.

An anti-Russian coalition headed by Britain waged war in the Crimea in 1853–54 to foil the tsar's bid to partition the Ottoman empire. Thus the only general European conflict in the hundred years between 1815 and 1914 was due to the Eastern Question. An independent Romania emerged afterwards under the sponsorship of France. The victors in the Crimean War chose to sponsor Romania to prevent Russia controlling the mouth of the Danube. The Romanians claimed Latin ancestry and could act as a bulwark preventing a union of South Slav peoples which Britain feared would enable Russia to clinch its ambitions in the eastern Mediterranean.

Thus the precedent was established for map changes in the Balkans in order to satisfy a precarious balance of power rather than to suit the wishes of the local inhabitants. Emerging peoples threw in their fortunes with a Great Power in the hope that they could achieve their territorial goals. Prospects of co-operation between the Balkan peoples diminished as outside powers were prepared to sponsor rival nationalisms for short-term goals. In 1876 the power of events in the Balkans to galvanise international opinion was shown by the reaction in Britain to massacres perpetrated by Turkish forces against Christian Slavs in Bulgaria. William Gladstone, the leader of the Liberal opposition, published his pamphlet *The Bulgarian Horrors and the Question of the East* in September 1876 and by the end of that month it had sold 200,000 copies. He demanded that prime minister Disraeli use Britain's authority to compel the sultan to grant freedom to the Christian Bulgarians.

Gladstone had earlier earned the gratitude of the Greeks when, after serving as governor of the Ionian Islands, he had persuaded the House of Commons to place them under Greek rule. He wished British policy in the Balkans to be guided by moral criteria, challenging the doctrine set down by Palmerston in 1848 when he argued that the furtherance of British interests should be the only object of a British Foreign Secretary . . . [and] that it is in Britain's interest to preserve the balance of power in international affairs.

In 1994, when addressing the House of Commons for the first time as foreign secretary, Malcolm Rifkind repeated the words of Palmerston and said that they would be his motto. Britain was then under fire for pursuing a policy of minimal engagement in the war in Bosnia. Its refusal to support the lifting of the arms embargo which would have enabled the Muslim-led government to defend itself against its Serb adversaries was widely criticised. The government's most vociferous critic was Gladstone's descendant as Liberal leader, Paddy Ashdown, who visited the Bosnian war zone on numerous occasions and argued that Britain was lowering standards of behaviour in the region by refusing to countenance forceful action against Serbs who had subjected the city of Sarajevo to a three-year siege and 'ethnically cleansed' many other areas populated by Muslims.

Gladstone's 'Midlothian campaign' of public speaking on the Bulgarian crisis contained the advocacy of the underdog and the condemnation of aggressors which was to become a hallmark of Balkan crises in the 1990s. Intellectuals, churchmen and ordinary citizens, moved or repelled by Gladstone's rhetoric, entered the fray. The poet Swinburne, who wrote in 1877 that 'the Turks are no worse than other oppressors around the world,' had his counterparts among leading playwrights and television personalities in the late 1990s who argued that there were many Kosovos around the world for whom Nato refused to act.

In 1877 Tennyson's sonnet hailing tiny Montenegro which had repulsed the Ottomans centuries earlier as 'a rough rock-throne of freedom' got much attention. It was accompanied by a long article about Montenegran history written by Gladstone, no other British leader identifying himself as completely with a Balkan cause until Tony Blair's emotional tours of Albanian refugee camps in May 1999. But Gladstone's campaign failed to move his great rival Disraeli. War with Russia appeared imminent in 1877 when, after a Russian victory at the siege of Plevna, Constantinople seemed to lie at its feet. Britain feared an enlarged Bulgaria would become an

extension of Russia and an international conference was held in Berlin in 1878 to arbitrate the dispute.

The diplomatic carve-up of the region that ensued under the cynical guidance of Bismarck ruled out the creation of a viable pattern of states as the Ottoman empire was gradually forced out of Europe. Decisions were made about Macedonia, Bulgaria and Bosnia which would return to disturb the peace of Europe in subsequent decades. Rather than sponsoring a Balkan confederation or large ethnically mixed states where minority rights were protected by international guarantees, the European powers left two South Slav states with unsatisfied national programmes who would clash in wars over the next sixty years: Serbia and Bulgaria. Territory was annexed by the powers to which they had but the flimsiest claim: Bessarabia was taken by Russia despite its mainly Romanian population; while Bosnia had been occupied by Austria-Hungary in 1876. The biggest losers were the region's Muslim peoples, several million of whom were driven out of Serbia, Bulgaria and Bosnia, due to the absence of a powerful protector.

The rise of nationalism in the Balkans had arguably left the region as vulnerable to foreign penetration as it had been before. But communities which had been slow to acquire a national

---

The powers had sponsored small, unstable and weak states, each based on the idea of nationality.

---

identity, such as the Albanians, quickly asserted their own national claims so as not to be overwhelmed by competitors. In Constantinople, western-style nationalism was adopted by modernising sections of the Turkish elite to stave off the complete dissolution of their state. One early result was the persecution of minorities deemed to be acting on behalf of Russia, the first of a series of horrific

massacres being perpetrated against the Christian Armenians in 1896. These culminated under the cover of the First World War in 1915, when as many as a million Armenians were massacred or died in forced evacuations of their territory.

In a bid to protect trading routes, secure military objectives, or establish client states, the powers had sponsored small, unstable and weak states, each based on the idea of nationality. The Balkan states usually had conflicting territorial claims as well as ethnic minorities that had to be assimilated or driven out. They formed unstable local alliances, sought backing from outside powers in order to guarantee security or satisfy national ambitions and, in turn, were used by these powers for their own strategic advantage.

The term 'Balkanisation' has acquired world notoriety to describe the problems arising from such a fragmentation of political power. Two Balkan wars in 1912 and 1913, as Turkey was forced to give up most of its Balkan possessions, degenerated into a bloody scramble for territory among rival states. International arbitration guaranteed an independent Albania in 1913. But the capacity of the Balkans to trigger a wider conflict was shown by the way the great powers went to war following the assassination of the heir to the Austrian throne, Archduke Franz-Ferdinand, in Sarajevo on June 28th, 1914, by local pro-Serb nationalists.

At Versailles in 1919 the victorious Allied states rejected the precedent of the Congress of Berlin and instead sponsored territorially powerful states in the Balkans: Romania, Yugoslavia, and Greece. A new European order based on the national self-determination of peoples and operating under the aegis of the League of Nations was meant to guarantee the peace. But the self-determination principle often only applied where it weakened enemy states such as Austria-Hungary and it was disregarded where its consequences proved unfavourable to the victors. Thus Italy acquired the South Tyrol and parts of the Dalmatian coast where non-Italians predominated. Meanwhile, Yugoslavia excluded the Albanians of Kosovo. The burning of villages in the 1920s followed by the confiscation of land from Albanians in the 1930s, unless they had Yugoslav documents to prove ownership, was a foretaste of future deportations.

The League of Nations lacked the powers to protect minorities in states where insecure majorities which had gained territory as a result of the outcome of a European war often gave subject peoples the grim choice of assimilation or exclusion. Turkey's success in foiling an effort sponsored by the Allies to create a Greater Greece in parts of Asia Minor encouraged other defeated powers to defy Versailles Europe. In 1922 the deportation of 1.3 million Greeks from Asia Minor to Greece and 800,000 Turks in the opposite direction created an ominous precedent.

The mutual hostility which poisoned relations between the East European states encouraged the effective withdrawal of Britain and France from the whole region in the 1930s. The ascendancy of Germany was only challenged in 1939 by Britain and France as the threat to the balance of power became too great to ignore. But the eventual defeat of Nazi Germany only resulted in a swop of tyrannical rulers. In October 1944 Churchill concluded his famous 'Percentages Agreement' with Stalin which assigned the Soviet Union a dominant role in Bulgaria and Romania, and an equal stake for both powers in Yugoslavia, with Britain enjoying a majority stake in Greece. Despite his great services to the cause of freedom, Churchill was prepared to abandon more countries to a tyrannical fate than Chamberlain actually did at Munich in 1938.

During the Cold War, the West identified with bids by countries like Poland and Czechoslovakia to throw off the Soviet yoke. Lech Walesa and Vaclav Havel were seen as the champions of liberty-loving peoples that had been cruelly severed from the West, their natural home. However, the emphasis in the Balkans was in backing a strong leader or strong regional power capable of keeping 'ancient ethnic hatreds' in check and preserving a balance of power that would prevent the superpowers coming to blows there.

Thus Marshal Josip Broz Tito, the architect of Communist Yugoslavia, became a recipient of Western financial and diplomatic support after he broke with Stalin in 1948. Tito was probably the most enlightened Communist ruler the world has ever seen. But he still ran a police state and Western creditors poured money into Yugoslavia without

linking aid to gradual democratisation. Milovan Djilas who went from being Tito's loyal lieutenant to his chief critic, was warning in the 1950s that social democracy and the social market were crucial requirements to prevent the internal tensions which festered under one-party rule, but his long imprisonments produced relatively little concern in the West.

During the last decades of the Cold War the West was even prepared to back Romania's Nicolae Ceausescu, an unsavoury Communist despot, in the mistaken belief that he was a weak link in the chain of Soviet power. But it is not just from the Communist Balkans that the evidence showing a Western preference for authoritarian leaders over democratically-elected ones comes.

After the defeat of the Communists in the 1944–49 Greek civil war, the United States was the main power behind right-wing forces determined to prevent the centre-left opposition winning office. Simultaneously, after going back on a First World War offer to Greece to cede Cyprus, with its Greek majority to Athens, Britain pursued a policy of divide-and-rule which left a bitter legacy of ethnic strife even after it conceded independence in 1960. In 1964, when the moderate left finally won office in Athens, the United States proposed to settle the Cyprus question by partition. When the Greek ambassador in Washington told Lyndon Johnson that such a plan could never be accepted, the president retorted:

> F___ your parliament and your constitution. America is an elephant, Cyprus is a flea. If these two fellows continue itching the elephant, they may just get whacked by the elephant's trunk, whacked good.... If your prime minster gives me talk about democracy, parliament and constitution, he, his parliament, and his constitution, may not last very long.

The US Central Intelligence Agency was implicated in the 1967 military coup which extinguished Greek democracy for seven years, just as it was in the attempted overthrow in 1974 of Archbishop Makarios, the leader of Cyprus, which led to a Turkish occupation and partition of the island.

The liking for improvised, short-term solutions to complex problems that ignore the wishes of local populations and

are enforced by tyrannical leaders characterised the major powers' approach to the Balkans before and after 1945. It produced some of the biggest American and British blunders of the Cold War and has left two well-armed Balkan states, Greece and Turkey, which several times have almost gone to war.

Similarly, the penchant for diplomatic quick-fixes epitomised the West's engagement with Yugoslavia as it dissolved into fratricidal conflict in the 1990s. A new note was apparently struck in the Kosovo conflict in the spring of 1999 as Nato committed itself to undoing the effects of ethnic violence perpetrated on over a million Kosovar Albanians. Nato leaders also promised to abandon the view that the Balkans are a non-European zone of disorder and recurring hatreds by integrating the region with the economic and security structures that brought peace to western Europe after 1945. Time will tell whether these expensive pledges, made in the heat of war, will be redeemed by those who made them or their successors.

The lazy statecraft of external-policy makers has turned the Balkans into a European danger zone. Unless a new approach based on conflict prevention and permitting ill-used Balkan peoples to enjoy the same opportunities as the West emerges from the war in Kosovo, there is every likelihood that Balkan wars and crises will be a feature of the new millennium as they were of the old.

FOR FURTHER READING

Barbara Jelavich, *History of the Balkans* (two volumes; Cambridge University Press 1995); *Unfinished Peace: Report of The International Commission on the Balkans* (Aspen Institute/ Carnegie Endowment For International Peace, 1996); Tim Judah, *The Serbs: History, Myth and the Destruction of Yugoslavia* (Yale University Press, 1997); C.M. Woodhouse, *Modern Greece, A Short History* (Faber 1998). Noel Malcolm, *Kosovo: A Short History* (Macmillan 1998).

Tom Gallagher is Professor of Ethnic Peace and Conflict at Bradford University. His Europe's Turbulent South-East *is to be published in 2000 by Harwood.*

The Poor and the Rich

In recent years, researchers have moved closer to answering the most important question in economics: why are some countries richer than others?

Understanding growth is surely the most urgent task in economics. Across the world, poverty remains the single greatest cause of misery; and the surest remedy for poverty is economic growth. It is true that growth can create problems of its own (congestion and pollution, for instance), which may preoccupy many people in rich countries. But such ills pale in comparison with the harm caused by the economic backwardness of poor countries—that is, of the larger part of the world. The cost of this backwardness, measured in wasted lives and needless suffering, is truly vast.

To its shame, economics neglected the study of growth for many years. Theorists and empirical researchers alike chose to concentrate on other fields, notably on macroeconomic policy. Until the 1980s, with a few exceptions, the best brains in economics preferred not to focus on the most vital issue of all. But over the past ten years or so, this has changed. Stars such as Robert Lucas of the University of Chicago, who last year won the Nobel prize in economics, have started to concentrate on growth. As he says of the subject, "the consequences for human welfare . . .are simply staggering. Once one starts to think about them, it is hard to think of anything else."

Early economists certainly thought about them. Adam Smith's classic 1776 book was, after all, called an "Inquiry into the Nature of Causes of the Wealth of Nations". Many building-blocks for understanding growth derive from him. Smith reckoned that the engine of growth was to be found in the division of labour, in the accumulation of capital and in technological progress. He emphasised the importance of a stable legal framework, within which the invisible hand of the market could function, and he explained how an open trading system would allow poorer countries to catch up with richer ones. In the early 19th century, David Ricardo formalised another concept crucial for understanding growth—the notion of diminishing returns. He showed how additional investment in land tended to yield an ever lower return, implying that growth would eventually come to a halt—though trade could stave this off for a while.

The foundations of modern growth theory were laid in the 1950s by Robert Solow and Trevor Swan. Their models describe an economy of perfect competition, whose output grows in response to large inputs of capital (ie, physical assets of all kinds) and labour. This economy obeys the law of diminishing returns: each new bit of capital (given a fixed labour supply) yields a slightly lower return than the one before.

Together, these assumptions give the neoclassical growth model, as it is called, two crucial implications. First, as the stock of capital expands, growth slows, and eventually halts: to keep growing, the economy must benefit from continual infusions of technological progress. Yet this is a force that the model itself makes no attempt to explain: in the jargon, technological progress is, in the neoclassical theory, "exogenous" (ie, it arises outside the model). The second implication is that poorer countries should grow faster than rich ones. The reason is diminishing returns: since poor countries start with less capital, they should reap higher returns from each slice of new investment.

THEORY INTO PRACTICE

Do these theoretical implications accord with the real world? The short answer is no. The left-hand side of the chart on the next page shows average growth rates since 1870 of 16 rich countries for which good long-term data exist. Growth has indeed slowed since 1970. Even so, modern growth rates are well above their earlier long-run average. This appears to contradict the first implication, that growth will slow over time. It may be that an acceleration of technological progress accounts from this, but this should hardly console a neoclassical theorist, because it would mean that the main driving force of growth lies beyond the scope of growth theory.

What about the second implication— are poor countries catching up? The right-hand side of the chart plots, for 118 countries, growth rates between

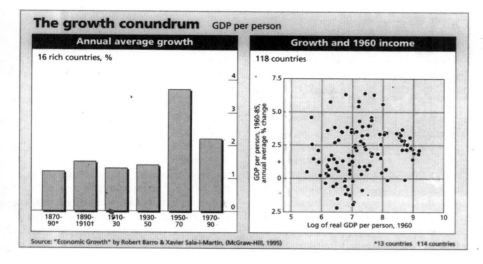

The growth conundrum GDP per person

Annual average growth

16 rich countries, %

1870-90* | 1890-1910† | 1910-30 | 1930-50 | 1950-70 | 1970-90

Growth and 1960 income

118 countries

GDP per person, 1960-85, annual average % change

Log of real GDP per person, 1960

Source: "Economic Growth" by Robert Barro & Xavier Sala-i-Martin, (McGraw-Hill, 1995)   *13 countries †14 countries

1960 and 1985 against their initial 1960 level of GDP per person. If poor countries were catching up, the plots on the chart should follow a downward-sloping pattern: countries that were poorer in 1960 should have higher growth rates. They do not. Indeed, if there is any discernible pattern in the mass of dots, it is the opposite: poorer countries have tended to grow more slowly.

Having arrived at neoclassical growth theory, however, economics by and large forgot about the subject. It had a model that was theoretically plausible, but did not seem to fit the facts. How best to proceed was unclear. Then, after a pause of 30 years, along came "new growth theory".

This new school has questioned, among other things, the law of diminishing returns in the neoclassical model. If each extra bit of capital does not, in fact, yield a lower return than its predecessor, growth can continue indefinitely, even without technological progress. A seminal paper was published in 1986 by Paul Romer (see references at the end). It showed that if you broaden the idea of capital to include human capital (that is, the knowledge and skills embodied in the workforce), the law of diminishing returns may not apply. Suppose, for example, that a firm which invests in a new piece of equipment also learns how to use it more efficiently. Or suppose it becomes more innovative as a by-product of accumulating capital. In either case, there can be increasing, not decreasing, returns to investment.

In this and other ways, new growth theorists can explain how growth might persist in the absence of technological progress. But, they have gone on to ask, why assume away such progress? A sec-

ond strand of new growth theory seeks to put technological progress explicitly into the model (making it "endogenous", in the jargon). This has obliged theorists to ask questions about innovation. Why, for instance, do companies invest in research and development? How do the innovations of one company affect the rest of the economy?

A further divergence from the neoclassical view follows. As a general rule, a firm will not bother to innovate unless it thinks it can steal a march on the competition and, for a while at least, earn higher profits. But this account is inconsistent with the neoclassical model's simplifying assumption of perfect competition, which rules out any "abnormal" profits. So the new growth theorists drop that assumption and suppose instead that competition is imperfect. Attention then shifts to the conditions under which firms will innovate most productively: how much protection should intellectual-property law give to an innovator, for instance? In this way, and not before time, technological progress has begun to occupy a central place in economists' thinking about growth.

In the latest resurgence of interest in growth theory, however, the original neoclassical approach has enjoyed something of a revival. Some economists are questioning whether the "new" theories really add much. For instance, the new theory emphasises human capital; arguably, this merely calls for a more subtle measure of labour than the ones used by early neoclassical theorists. More generally, it is argued that if factors of production (capital and labour) are properly measured and quality-adjusted, the neoclassical approach yields everything of value in the new

theory, without its distracting bells and whistles. So it often proves in economics: the mainstream first takes affront at new ideas, then reluctantly draws on them, and eventually claims to have thought of them first.

THE MISSING LINK

To non-economists, however, both approaches seem curiously lacking in one crucial respect. Whereas in popular debate about growth, government policy is usually the main issue, in both neoclassical and new growth theory discussion of policy takes place largely off-stage. To the extent that government policy affects investment, for instance, either could trace out the effects on growth—but the connection between policy and growth is tenuous and indirect. Each approach may take a strong view about the role of diminishing returns, but both remain frustratingly uncommitted about the role of government.

An upsurge of empirical work on growth is helping to fill this hole—and, as a by-product, shedding further light on the relative merits of the new and neoclassical theories. The nuts and bolts of this work are huge statistical analyses. Vast sets of data now exist, containing information for more than 100 countries between 1960 and 1990 on growth rates, inflation rates, fertility rates, school enrollment, government spending, estimates of how good the rule of law is, and so on. Great effort has been devoted to analysing these numbers.

One key finding is "conditional convergence", a term coined by Robert Barro, a pioneer of the new empirical growth studies. His research has found that if one holds constant such factors as a country's fertility rate, its human capital (proxied by various measures of educational attainment) and its government policies (proxied by the share of current government spending in GDP), poorer countries tend to grow faster than richer ones. So the basic insight of the neoclassical growth model is, in fact, correct. But since, in reality, other factors are not constant (countries do not have the same level of human capital or the same government policies), absolute convergence does not hold.

Whether this is a depressing result for poor countries depends on what determines the "conditional" nature of the catch-up process. Are slow-growing countries held back by government policies that can be changed easily and quickly? Or are more fundamental forces at work?

Most empirical evidence points to the primacy of government choices. Countries that have pursued broadly free-market policies—in particular, trade liberalisation and the maintenance of secure property rights—have raised their growth rates. In a recent paper, Jeffrey Sachs and Andrew Warner divided a sample of 111 countries into "open" and "closed". The "open" economies showed strikingly faster growth and convergence than the "closed" ones. Smaller government also helps. Robert Barro, among others, has found that higher government spending tends to be associated with slower growth.

Human capital—education and skills—has also been found to matter. Various statistical analyses have shown that countries with lots of human capital relative to their physical capital are likely to grow faster than those with less. Many economists argue that this was a factor in East Asia's success: in the early 1960s the Asian tigers had relatively well-educated workforces and low levels of physical capital.

A more difficult issue is the importance of savings and investment. One implication of the neoclassical theory is that higher investment should mean faster growth (at least for a while). The empirical studies suggest that high investment is indeed associated with fast growth. But they also show that investment is not enough by itself. In fact the causality may run in the opposite direction: higher growth may, in a virtuous circle, encourage higher saving and investment. This makes sense: communist countries, for instance, had extraordinarily high investment but, burdened with bad policies in other respects, they failed to turn this into high growth.

The number-crunching continues; new growth-influencing variables keep being added to the list. High inflation is bad for growth; political stability counts; the results on democracy are mixed; and so on. The emerging conclusion is that the poorest countries can indeed catch up, and that their chances of doing so are maximised by policies that give a greater role to competition and incentives, at home and abroad.

But surely, you might think, this hides a contradiction? The new growth theory suggests that correct government policies can permanently raise growth rates. Empirical cross-country analysis, however, seems to show that less government is better—a conclusion that appeals to many neoclassical theorists. This tension is especially pronounced for the East Asian tigers. Advocates of free market point to East Asia's trade liberalisation in the 1960s, and its history of low government spending, as keys to the Asian miracle. Interventionists point to subsidies and other policies designed to promote investment.

Reflecting the present spirit of rapprochement between the growth models, it is now widely argued that this contradiction is more apparent than real. Work by Alwyn Young, popularised by Paul Krugman, has shown that much of the Asian tiger's success can be explained by the neoclassical model. It resulted from a rapid accumulation of capital (through high investment) and labour (through population growth and increased labour-force participation). On this view, there is nothing particularly miraculous about Asian growth: it is an example of "catch-up". Equally, however, the outlines of East Asian success fit the new growth model. Endogenous growth theory says that government policy to increase human capital or foster the right kinds of investment in physical capital can permanently raise economic growth.

The question is which aspect of East Asian policies was more important—which, up to a point, is the same as asking which growth model works best. Although debate continues, the evidence is less strong that micro-level encouragement of particular kinds of investment was crucial in Asia. Some economists dissent from that judgment, but they are a minority. Most agree that broader policies of encouraging education, opening the economy to foreign technologies, promoting trade and keeping taxes low mattered more.

ONE MORE HEAVE

There is no doubt that the neoclassical model of the 1950s, subsequently enhanced, together with the theories pioneered by Mr Romer, have greatly advanced economists' understanding of growth. Yet the earlier doubt remains. Both models, in their purest versions, treat the role of government only indi-rectly. The new empirical work on conditional convergence has set out to put this right. The fact remains that in the earlier theoretical debate between the neoclassical and the new schools, the question that matters most—what should governments do to promote growth?—was often forgotten.

A new paper by Mancur Olson makes this point in an intriguing way. The starting-point for today's empirical work is a striking fact: the world's fastest-growing economies are a small sub-group of exceptional performers among the poor countries. Viewed in the earlier theoretical perspective, this is actually rather awkward. Mr Romer's theories would lead you to expect that the richest economies would be the fastest growers: they are not. The basic neoclassical theory suggests that the poorest countries, on the whole, should do better than the richest: they do not. Neither approach, taken at face value, explains the most striking fact about growth in the world today.

Mr Olson argues that the simplest versions of both theories miss a crucial point. Both assume that, given the resources and technology at their disposal, countries are doing as well as they can. Despite their differences, both are theories about how changes in available resources affect output—that is, both implicitly assume that, if resources do not change, output cannot either. But suppose that poor countries simply waste lots of resources. Then the best way for them to achieve spectacular growth is not to set about accumulating more of the right kind of resources—but to waste less of those they already have.

Marshalling the evidence, Mr Olson shows that slow-growing poor countries are indeed hopelessly failing to make good use of their resources. Take labour, for instance. If poor countries were using labour as well as they could, large emigrations of labour from poor to rich countries (from Haiti to the United States, for instance) ought to raise the productivity of workers left behind (because each worker now has more capital, land and other resources to work with). But emigration does not have this effect.

Data on what happens to migrants in their new homes are likewise inconsistent with the two growth theories. Immigrants' incomes rise by far more than access to more capital and other resources would imply. It follows that labour (including its human capital, entrepreneurial spirit, cultural traits and the rest) was being squandered in its country of origin. When workers move, their incomes rise partly because there is more capital to work with—but also by a further large margin, which must represent the wastage incurred before. Mr Olson adduces similar evidence to show that capital and knowledge are being massively squandered in many poor countries.

This offers a rationale for the pattern of growth around the world—a rationale that, consistent with the recent work on conditional convergence, places economic policies and institutions at the very centre. According to this view, it is putting it mildly to say that catch-up is possible: the economic opportunities for

poor countries are, as the tigers have shown, phenomenal. The problem is not so much a lack of resources, but an inability to use existing resources well. It is surely uncontroversial to say that this is the right way to judge the performance of communist countries (those exemplars of negative value-added) before 1989. Mr Olson's contention is that most of today's poor countries are making mistakes of an essentially similar kind.

The question still remains: what are the right policies? One must turn again to the empirical evidence. That seems a frustrating answer because, suggestive though recent work on conditional convergence may be, such findings will always be contested. Citizens of the world who sensibly keep an eye on what

economists are up to can at least take pleasure in this: the profession has chosen for once to have one of its most vigorous debates about the right subject.

Main Papers Cited

"Increasing Returns and Long-Run Growth". By Paul Romer. Journal of Political Economy, 1986.

"Economic Reform and the Process of Global Integration". By Jeffrey Sachs and Andrew Warner. Brookings Papers on Economic Activity, 1995.

"The Tyranny of Numbers: Confronting the Statistical Realities of the East Asian Experience". By Alwyn Young. NBER working paper 4680, 1994.

"Big Bills Left on the Sidewalk: Why Some Nations Are Rich, and Others Poor". By Mancur Olson. Journal of Economic Perspectives, forthcoming.

World Education League

Who's Top?

Some countries seem to educate their children much better than others. Why? No comprehensive answer has emerged yet but plenty of lessons are being learnt from the tests which reveal the educational discrepancies

A class has 28 students and the ratio of girls to boys is 4:3. How many girls are there? Which of the following is made using bacteria: yogurt, cream, soap or cooking oil? Simple enough questions in any language (the answers, by the way, are 16 and yogurt). But when half a million pupils from around the world were set questions like these, some countries, just like some pupils, did very well and some very badly.

The tests were set for the largest-ever piece of international education research, the Third International Maths and Science Study (TIMSS). Of the 41 nations participating in this first phase, Singapore was teacher's pet: the average scores of its pupils were almost twice those of South Africa, bottom of the class (see table 1).

East Asian countries have overtaken nations such as America and Britain which have had universal schooling for much longer. America came 17th in science and 28th in mathematics. England came 25th in maths and Scotland (whose pupils were tested separately) came 29th. The four richest East Asian economies took the first four places in maths.

Some former communist countries, notably the Czech Republic, Slovakia, Slovenia and Bulgaria, also did significantly better than their richer western neighbours, even though they spend much less on education. Six of the top 15 places in both maths and science went to East Europeans. It seems that how much a country can afford to spend has less than you might think to do with how well educated its children are. American children have three times as much money spent on their schooling as young South Koreans, who nevertheless beat them hands down in tests.

International educational comparisons like the TIMSS study have been subjects of growing academic enthusiasm and criticism since the 1960s (for the controversies, see box "Answering the Critics"). Teachers, though, have been almost entirely hostile and most governments have held themselves aloof from the arguments, fearing embarrassment. A poor showing in the league table would give political op-

2+2=?			1
13-year-olds' average score in TIMSS* (Int average =500)			
Maths		**Science**	
1 Singapore	643	Singapore	607
2 South Korea	607	Czech Republic	574
3 Japan	605	Japan	571
4 Hong Kong	588	South Korea	565
5 Belgium (F†)	565	Bulgaria	565
6 Czech Republic	564	Netherlands	560
7 Slovakia	547	Slovenia	560
8 Switzerland	545	Austria	558
9 Netherlands	541	Hungary	554
10 Slovenia	541	England	552
11 Bulgaria	540	Belgium (F†)	550
12 Austria	539	Australia	545
13 France	538	Slovakia	544
14 Hungary	537	Russia	538
15 Russia	535	Ireland	538
16 Australia	530	Sweden	535
17 Ireland	527	United States	534
18 Canada	527	Canada	531
19 Belgium (W‡)	526	Germany	531
20 Thailand	522	Norway	527
21 Israel	522	Thailand	525
22 Sweden	519	New Zealand	525
23 Germany	509	Israel	524
24 New Zealand	508	Hong Kong	522
25 England	506	Switzerland	522
26 Norway	503	Scotland	517
27 Denmark	502	Spain	517
28 United States	500	France	498
29 Scotland	498	Greece	497
30 Latvia	493	Iceland	494
31 Spain	487	Romania	486
32 Iceland	487	Latvia	485
33 Greece	484	Portugal	480
34 Romania	482	Denmark	478
35 Lithuania	477	Lithuania	476
36 Cyprus	474	Belgium (W‡)	471
37 Portugal	454	Iran	470
38 Iran	428	Cyprus	463
39 Kuwait	392	Kuwait	430
40 Colombia	385	Colombia	411
41 South Africa	354	South Africa	326

*Third International Maths and Science Study †Flanders ‡Wallonia
Source: TIMSS

ponents ammunition, while the studies might be used to accuse ministers of starving their education system (or, possibly, of wasting taxpayers' money on a grand scale).

Now, attitudes are changing, at least among politicians. Over the past ten years or so, governments' desire to know more about how their schools compare with others, and what lessons can be learned from the comparison, have begun to outweigh fear of embarrassment. More countries took part in TIMSS than in its predecessors, and the attention paid to its findings by the world's politicians, educators and the news media was much greater than for previous studies.

POLITICIANS DO THEIR HOMEWORK

President Clinton described the test in his state-of-the-union message in February, as one "that reflects the world-class standards our children must meet for the new era." America's poor overall showing has sparked calls for the adoption of a national curriculum and national standards for school tests—including from Mr Clinton himself. These calls are based on the observation that the coun-

tries which did best in the study tended to have national frameworks of this kind.

In a television interview in December, the French president, Jacques Chirac, described as "shameful" a decision by his education ministry to pull out of an international study of adult literacy which was showing that the French were doing badly. And in Britain last year, Michael Heseltine, the deputy prime minister, brushed aside objections from officials in the Department for Education and Employment, and published the unflattering results of a study he had commissioned comparing British workers with those in France, America, Singapore and Germany—chosen as key economic competitors.

The Germans, in turn, were shocked by their pupils' mediocre performance in the TIMSS tests. Their pupils did only slightly better than the English at maths, coming 23rd out of 41 countries. In science, the English surged ahead (though not the Scots) while the Germans were beaten by, among others, the Dutch, the Russians—and even the Americans. A television network ran a special report called "Education Emergency in Germany"; industrialists accused politicians of ignoring repeated warnings about declining standards in schools.

There are more studies to come. In December the Organisation for Economic Cooperation and Development (OECD), a club of 29 of the world's richest countries, launched its own series of annual reports. The OECD already collects data on how the governments spend their combined $1 trillion annual education budgets, and what proportion of each nation's population reaches a given level of education. The new studies will go much further, comparing how schools, colleges and universities are run in each country and analysing the implications for policymakers.

In some countries, international comparisons are already being used as a catalyst for educational reform. The poor performance of Swedish children in maths, in one study in the mid 1980s, led to the setting up of a new programme of in-service training for teachers. The initial results from TIMSS suggest that Sweden has since pulled itself up to slightly above the international average.

Although Japanese children have repeatedly gained high overall marks in maths tests, some studies have suggested that they are not as advanced in other things, such as analysing data, as they are in basic arithmetic. The Japanese government has started using such

---

Answering the Critics

Cross-country comparisons have long been controversial. Among the doubts: Do tests put an unwarranted premium on certain qualities—speed of recall, mental arithmetic—while ignoring hard-to-measure ones like creative thinking? Were pupils from different countries really comparable? (For instance, in countries where children are made to repeat a year of their education if they fail to reach a certain standard, tests for, say, 13-year-olds may exclude those who have been sent to join a class of 12-year-olds). Were pupils in some countries told that the tests were extremely important, while others were not? Did the tests give an unfair advantage to countries whose curriculum for 13-year-olds happens to include more of the topics included in them?

Wendy Keys of Britain's National Foundation for Education Research, one of the bodies that organised the TIMSS project, says that a number of measures were

taken to answer such criticisms. The score for each country was adjusted to take account of any pupils who were held back a year. Teachers everywhere were given precise instructions on how to explain the tests to pupils, and independent monitors were sent to schools chosen at random. After the results were in, experts in each country looked at how their pupils had done on those questions which most closely matched the curriculum for children of their age.

The results? Broadly, the new study confirmed the relative positions of countries which had taken part in earlier studies. That consistency suggested the original criticisms may have been exaggerated. However, the refinements made in the recent study may overturn one of the theories that has been used to explain why America and Britain, in spite of having had universal education for longer than most nations, do so poorly. This is that they contain an unusually large proportion

of pupils who perform very badly. The comforting implication would be that ordinary pupils do reasonably well but that average scores are dragged down by a so-called "long tail of low achievers".

This explanation was given a colour of plausibility by earlier tests. In those, mediocre scores in Britain and America could be explained away by the failure of the tests to take account of countries where pupils are held back a year. The new version of the test puts that problem right—and the two countries are still doing poorly. Though the mass of results from TIMSS is still being analysed, Dr Keys says there is no sign so far of the "long tail". The implication would be that the average scores of American and British pupils are mediocre because average performance is mediocre, and not because of some peculiarity at the very bottom of the class.

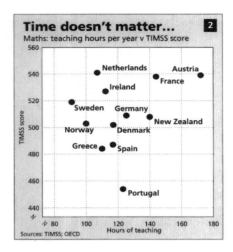

Time doesn't matter... `2`
Maths: teaching hours per year v TIMSS score

Sources: TIMSS; OECD

findings to reform its national curriculum. Hungary, discovering in early studies that its children were among the world's best in maths and science but among the least literate, ordered its teachers to spend more time on reading.

KNOWLEDGE WORKERS

Leaving aside the results of the tests, two main factors lie behind governments' increasing willingness to take part in international education studies to begin with. The first is the growing consensus that education is the key to getting rich—for countries as well as for individuals. It is widely believed that one of the main reasons why tiger economies like Singapore and South Korea have grown so quickly is that their governments have made determined and successful efforts to raise educational standards.

The other factor is value for money. Governments everywhere have woken up to the full economic significance of education just as they are making desperate attempts to rein in public spending. OECD countries already spend about 6% of national income on education; given the pressure to trim budgets there is no prospect that governments will chuck money at schools without checking to see whether standards are improving. Hence the enthusiasm for comparisons. If governments could discover what it is about their education system that helps growth, then perhaps, they hope, they could do better without spending more.

So do the tests help? They do not provide a sure-fire formula of exactly how much should be spent on schools,

how schools should be managed and precisely how each subject should be taught.

All the same, the tests are already proving useful, especially for exposing myths. A popularly-held view has it that "opportunity to learn" is the key to educational success—ie, the more time children spend on a subject, the better they do at it. Alas, the evidence so far is not encouraging for the proponents of this theory. Taking the twelve countries which both took part in TIMSS and also had their average teaching hours measured in the OECD's recent study of school management, there seems little correlation between time spent on a subject and performance of pupils in tests (see chart 2). Young Austrians spend exceptionally long hours on maths and science lessons; for them, it pays off in higher test scores. But so do New Zealand's teenagers—and they do not do any better than, say, Norwegians, who spend an unusually short time on lessons in both subjects.

Next—and of particular interest to cash-strapped governments—there appears to be little evidence to support the argument, often heard from teachers' unions, that the main cause of educational under-achievement is under-funding. Low-spending countries such as South Korea and the Czech Republic are at the top of the TIMSS league table. High-spenders such as America and Denmark do much worse (see chart 3). Obviously, there are dozens of reasons other than spending why one country does well, another badly, but the success of the low-spending Czechs and Koreans does show that spending more on schools is not a prerequisite for improving standards.

Another article of faith among the teaching profession—that children are bound to do better in small classes—is also being undermined by educational research. As with other studies, TIMSS found that France, America and Britain, where children are usually taught in classes of twenty-odd, do significantly worse than East Asian countries where almost twice as many pupils are crammed into each class. Again, there may be social reasons why some countries can cope better with large classes than others. All the same, the comparison refutes the argument that larger is necessarily worse.

Further, the tests even cast some doubt over the cultural explanation for

the greater success of East Asia: that there is some hard-to-define Asian culture, connected with parental authority and a strong social value on education, which makes children more eager to learn and easier to teach. Those who make this argument say it would of course be impossible to replicate such oriental magic in the West.

Yet the results of TIMSS suggest that this is, to put it mildly, exaggerated. If "culture" makes English children so poor at maths, then why have they done so well at science (not far behind the Japanese and South Koreans)? And why do English pupils do well at science and badly at maths, while in France it is the other way around? A less mystical, more mundane explanation suggests itself: English schools teach science well and maths badly; French schools teach maths better than science; East Asian schools teach both subjects well.

Apart from casting doubt on some widely-held beliefs, do international comparisons have anything constructive to say? So far, the conclusions are tentative, but some answers are emerging.

TEACHING THE TEACHERS

As well as getting pupils to sit tests, the TIMSS researchers monitored the way lessons were taught in each country. Eventually this should point to which teaching method tends to be most successful, though the data are still being worked on. Meanwhile, other researchers have been searching for common factors among those countries

...nor does money `3`
State spending per pupil*, $'000 PPP 1993

	0 1 2 3 4 5 6 7	Maths	Science
Switzerland		8	25
United States		28	17
Germany		23	18
Denmark		27	34
France		13	28
England	†	25	10
Japan		3	3
South Korea		2	2
Czech Rep.		6	2
Hungary		14	9

TIMSS ranking

*Sources: TIMSS; OECD *Secondary †Average for whole of Britain*

whose schools seem to turn out well-educated pupils.

Julia Whitburn of Britain's National Institute of Economic and Social Research has studied the way maths is taught in Japan and Switzerland, two countries which are different in many ways but whose pupils seem to do consistently well at in the subject. She noted a number of common factors:

- Much more time is spent on the basics of arithmetic than on more general mathematical topics such as handling data;
- Pupils learn to do sums in their heads before they are taught to do them on paper; calculators are usually banned;
- Standardised teaching manuals, which are tested extensively in schools before being published, are used widely;
- A method known as "whole-class interactive teaching" is used widely. The teacher addresses the whole class at once, posing questions to pupils in turn, to ensure they are following the lesson. American and British schools have been criticised for letting pupils spend much of their time working in small groups, with the teacher rushing from one group to the next to see how they are doing. Ms Whitburn notes that in Japan and Switzerland this method is only used in teaching arts and crafts;
- Finally, great efforts are made to ensure that pupils do not fall behind. Those that do are given extra coaching.

Learning, though, is not a one-way street. Just as western countries are busy seeking to emulate Japanese schools, schools and universities in Japan are coming under pressure from employers to turn out workers with the sort of creativity and individuality that the Japanese associate with western education. And just as American and British politicians are demanding that schools copy their more successful oriental counterparts and set their pupils more homework, the South Korean government is telling schools to give pupils regular homework-free days, so they can spend more time with their families—just like western children. Perhaps in education there is such a thing as a happy medium.

Falling Tide

Global Trends and US Civil Society

By Francis Fukuyama

Modern liberal states require healthy civil societies for their long-run stability—under a system of limited government, society must be self-organizing to fulfill a variety of social needs. Furthermore, the democratic process requires citizens to organize if they are to represent their passions and interests effectively in the political marketplace. Civil society presupposes social capital—the norms and values that permit cooperative behavior on the part of groups.

The assertions that American civil society is ailing and that American social capital has been depleted have been put forward in recent years, most notably by Robert Putnam. While the case for decline in American associational life has not been proven, there are [a] number of trends that indicate a lower stock of social capital among at least parts of American society. International comparisons of civil society reveal interesting and often paradoxical trends, but suggest that perhaps the United States is not alone in facing problems in the values and associations on which healthy democratic government depends.

Individualism and hostility to authority are deeply ingrained themes in American political culture. Nevertheless, Alexis de Tocqueville and many other acute observers of American social life have noted that Americans often unite in voluntary social groups to achieve social and political objectives. This is not the paradox it seems to be—for most Americans, individualism

FRANCIS FUKUYAMA is Hirst Professor of Public Policy and Director of George Mason University's International Transactions Program

means hostility to *ascribed* social status, coupled with the belief that individuals should be free to choose their own social attachments. American individualism has seldom involved hostility to community life altogether. The individualism embedded in the US Declaration of Independence and the US Constitution, as well as in the Lockean tradition of liberalism on which these documents are founded, is counterbalanced by a sectarian Protestant tradition that fosters cooperation in small voluntary organizations. The secular voluntary associations—non-governmental organizations (NGOs), labor unions, and activist groups—which today comprise American civil society are the heirs of this religious heritage.

THE PUTNAM DEBATE

Any contemporary discussion of the state of American civil society must begin with the controversy engendered by Robert Putnam's 1995 article "Bowling Alone." In a now familiar argument, Putnam relied on a wide variety of empirical measures of social capital and argued that America's traditional "art of association" has been in decline since the mid-1960s.

Putnam relies on two sorts of data. The first is survey data concerning numbers and types of organizations to which respondents belong and their attitudes about trust, other people's honesty, and the like. The second type of data concerns the numbers of groups in various regions or countries and their membership trends over time. Together, these statistics are taken as indicators of social capital.

The survey data on trust shows an unambiguous decline between the early 1960s and the early 1990s. The largest declines concern trust in public institutions,

such as Congress, the President, and "government" in general. In 1960, 70 percent of Americans polled said that they expected their government to "do the right thing." By 1990, only 19 percent shared that sentiment. Levels of interpersonal trust have exhibited similar, though somewhat less dramatic, trends. In 1965, 58 percent of Americans indicated that they trusted their fellow citizens. By 1991, that majority had dwindled to a 37 percent minority.

Putnam also cites declines in the memberships of organizations such as the Boy Scouts, the Red Cross, parent-teacher associations, and the so-called "animal organizations"—traditional service groups such as the Elks, the Kiwanis, and the Lions—that were an important aspect of social life in earlier generations, especially for men. The data on group memberships is ambiguous, however, and subject to what are perhaps insuperable problems of measurement.

Putnam has been criticized on both empirical and normative grounds. Numerous scholars have pointed to a significant number of surveys showing that groups and group membership may have actually *increased* over the time period covered by Putnam, particularly for younger Americans. Other academics suggest that many important qualitative aspects of civic engagement are not reflected in the available data. It is entirely possible, for example, that people are more actively involved in a smaller number of organizations. One recent study of civic engagement in Philadelphia pointed to the fact that while expressed cynicism is up, time spent by people in community organizations has increased.

Data on declining groups and group membership may be misleading for other reasons as well. First, newly formed groups tend to be poorly organized and

Table 1: (1980—1990)

% Change in Group Memberships

	US	Japan	German	Italy	Britain	France	Sweden
Social Welfare	−3.8	0.3	−5.7	0.6	−2.9	1.7	0.8
Religious Orgs.	−8.7	−1.7	2.6	3.5	−7.9	1.7	0.8
Educational/Cultural	5.5	2.1	5.9	3.3	2.5	−2	0.0
Trade Unions	−4.8	−3.5	−1.6	−2.2	−5.4	1.7	0.8
Political Parties	1.2	−0.8	−1	−0.7	0.3	0.4	−3.1
Community Action	3	−1	1.7	2.3	2.3	1.7	−1.9
Professional Assoc.	−1.4	−2.4	−0.3	2.9	−0.2	−4.5	5

Change in % of people who say they would

	US	Japan	German	Italy	Britain	France	Sweden
claim false benefits	−12.7	2.1	−0.5	−17.4	−9.3	−6.1	−4.8
cheat on taxes	−0.1	5.1	−13.1	−17.8	−3.3	2.3	−12.2
buy stolen goods	−3	6.1	−10.4	−9.1	−4.7	13.8	−3
lie for own interest	0.4	1.1	−11.6	−18.8	−7.4	−8.9	1.2
accept bribes	−1.5	6.7	−2.6	10.4	−5.6	16.7	0.4

(University of Michigan, World Values Survey)

hence less likely to keep good statistical information on themselves or to be included in surveys of group membership. Researchers learned of the membership decline among the Freemasons and Shriners only because those groups are well-established and keep good records. Much less is known, on the other hand, about the many informal support groups that formed in response to the AIDS epidemic over the past decade and a half. In addition, for a large number of informal social networks, no data exists at all. Alcoholics Anonymous, for example, deliberately refuses to keep membership statistics. In a society with a constant level of group turnover, available data would always tend to show decline because of the lack of data on newer groups.

THE BAD APPLE EFFECT

Group membership statistics do not fully measure the effects of associations on civil life. Not all groups contribute positively to society. Some—such as the Ku Klux Klan, organized crime, or the Nation of Islam—breed distrust and hatred or are actively engaged in criminal activity. In addition, groups with more benign purposes can nonetheless be problematic from the standpoint of democratic governance. Mancur Olson has argued that societies—particularly modern welfare states—tend to accumulate rent-seeking interest groups whose

primary goal is to win state subsidies for their members, a dynamic that contributes to economic and political stagnation. Several observers have argued that there can be such a thing as "too

Expressions of cynicism and distrust have dramatically displaced respect for authority in American popular culture, suggesting some sort of erosion of civil society.

much civil society." In a highly politicized society where interest groups are actively represented, the political process is often not focused on the national interest and can become mired in socially inefficient, special-interest politicking. The expansion of well-organized, well-funded interest-group lobbying in Washington over the past few decades would hardly have given Tocqueville—or any other proponent of American democracy—cause to celebrate.

To measure the social capital derived from association accurately, one must distinguish between groups that produce negative and positive externalities. While all groups require some degree of social capital to operate, hate groups actively destroy trust and social capital outside of their membership. On the other hand, some organizations contribute to social capital by building bonds of trust that benefit society at large. As the German sociologist Max Weber noted, America's historical Puritan ethic mandated honesty not simply toward other members of one's religious community, but toward all human beings. Norms of reciprocity, however, can be only shared effectively among a small subset of a groups' members. While groups Putnam terms "membership groups," such as the American Association of Retired People (AARP), often have huge memberships, there is no reason to think that any two given members of such a group will trust one another or engage in coordinated action just because they pay annual dues to the same organization. The fact that, of all groups in the United States, the AARP has a membership second in size only to the Catholic Church, should therefore not be weighed heavily in evaluating its contribution to the nation's civil society. The exclusion of such "membership groups" strengthens Putnam's case but does not explain why voluntary activities seem to be increasing in some sectors of American society. The United States thus presents a rather confusing picture. Empirical data does not clearly suggest that civil society is in decline, but there is a strong popular perception that it is, evidenced, among other things, by the responsive chord struck by Putnam's original article. As anyone who experiences contemporary American society knows, expressions of cynicism and distrust have dramatically displaced respect for authority in American popular culture, suggesting some sort of erosion of civil society.

INTERNATIONAL COMPARISONS

How does the United States compare to other societies in terms of the health of its civil society and the prevalence of social values such as trust and willingness to cooperate? One source of very relevant data is the long-running World Values Sur-

Table 2:

Illegitimacy Rate—% of children born to unmarried mothers

	France	UK	Canada	Ger.	Neth.	Italy	Japan
1960	6	5	4	6	1	2	1
1970	7	8	10	6	2	2	1
1980	11	12	13	8	4	4	1
1991	32	30	26	15	12	7	1

(US Census Bureau,, Statistical Abstract of the United States, 1997)

Overall Crime Rate—Crimes per 100,000 population

	France	UK	Canada	Ger.	Neth.	Italy	Japan
1965	1561	2379	3206	n/a	n/a	878	1636
1970	2237	3183	5794	3924	2751	1021	1852
1980	4890	5419	8510	6603	7157	2019	1552
1990	6169	8958	9863	7108	11376	4339	1795

(Various national statistical offices)

vey conducted by the University of Michigan. This survey asked respondents in 43 countries a long series of value-related questions in both 1981 and 1991.

The results of the University of Michigan study confirm that the United States remains a trusting place relative to other countries, as the accompanying chart shows, despite the fact that trust may have declined in the United States. The data also confirms a common observation that Latin Catholic countries tend to be more atomized and less trusting than Protestant ones: of the eleven countries with a Christian cultural heritage, the five most trusting are majority Protestant and five of the six least trusting are majority Catholic.

The World Values Survey also addressed levels of civic engagement by asking respondents whether they were active members of a variety of organizations, including social welfare, religious, cultural, and political groups, as table 1 shows. International data on organizations and memberships is more or less consistent with what was said above about the Putnam data on the United States: while some types of organizations, including religious groups and trade unions, have seen their membership decline during the 1980s, other groups, such as environmental organizations, have seen increases. Japan alone shows a trend of decreasing group membership across the board, while South Korea shows a striking pattern of increasing membership. But for the most part, developed countries do not exhibit a clear trend toward either declining or increasing group activity.

In addition to the general question about the trustworthiness of others noted above, the survey asked respondents whether they would engage in certain unethical behaviors such as tax fraud, accepting stolen goods, lying, and adultery, as the accompanying table shows. In contrast to the group membership data, this ethical data reveals a much clearer pattern: paradoxically, expressed levels of generalized trust increased in most countries, while the ethical attitudes that presumably produce trust apparently declined. This seems to contradict Putnam's findings. The United States, Britain, Canada, Italy, and Germany all exhibit significant declines in self-reported ethical attitudes. Japan, on the other hand, showed a small increase in the ethical variables, while Spain and particularly South Korea showed extremely large increases. Latin American countries were split: Argentina showed large increases in most ethical variables, while Mexico showed equally dramatic declines.

America seems to have witnessed a substantial decline in expressed levels of trust, while showing ambiguous trends with regard to group membership, a pattern characteristic of other developed countries such as Germany, Italy, Sweden, and Canada. This suggests that Putnam is wrong in claiming that group membership and trust are positively correlated across societies. It is possible to have stable or increasing group activity

and steadily declining levels of trust and ethical behavior. One possible explanation of this apparent paradox is that many of the groups that are increasing in membership are the so-called "membership groups" which produce little by way of social capital.

OTHER MEASURES OF SOCIAL CAPITAL

An alternative to counting groups and group memberships exists which may be a more effective metric of the health of American civil society. If it is difficult to measure social capital as a positive quantity for the reasons suggested above, it is perhaps possible to measure the *absence* of social capital through what sociologists have traditionally labeled "social deviance" statistics—measures of crime, suicide rates, family breakdown and illegitimacy, tax evasion, and the like. Deviance data is subject to its own measurement problems, but it is far more abundant on a comparative basis than data on group memberships.

The incidence of social deviance has grown rapidly in virtually all OECD countries since the mid-1960s, with the exception of Japan.

The problem with using deviance data as a proxy for either social capital or civil society more broadly is that it ignores questions of distribution, a problem shared by the Putnam data as well. Social capital and the propensity to work cooperatively in the groups that constitute civil society are not evenly distributed among different social classes, ethnic groups, or other strata within a given society. This problem is especially significant for a large and diverse society such as the United States. It has long been recognized, for example, that low-income African American communities tend to be far more atomized and less prone to self-organization

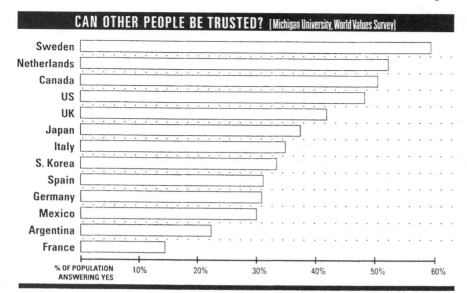

CAN OTHER PEOPLE BE TRUSTED? [Michigan University, World Values Survey]

Sweden
Netherlands
Canada
US
UK
Japan
Italy
S. Korea
Spain
Germany
Mexico
Argentina
France

% OF POPULATION ANSWERING YES   10%   20%   30%   40%   50%   60%

A more difficult question has to do with the causes of those differences. It is not clear that democracy per se is related to social disorganization: Japan, after all, is an Asian country with low levels of deviance and workable democratic institutions. Western countries, which are all democratic, vary considerably among themselves in levels of deviance. It is quite likely that social indicators such as family breakdown and (more weakly) crime are related to narrower variables such as female labor-force participation. For reasons that cannot be fully elaborated here, the single most important value difference between Asia and the West has to do with the role of women. As demographic pressures in Japan and other industrially mature Asian societies increase the demand for female labor over the next generation, those societies will likely begin to see increases in their deviance indicators.

than various Asian-American communities. Deviance data runs the risk of measuring the absence of social capital within those sectors of society that tend to be atomized, while revealing little about other parts of the same society. It is perfectly possible that social capital can decline in some sectors while increasing in others, a scenario that is quite likely in the case of the United States.

With this caveat in mind, behavioral data confirms the trends evident in the World Values Survey data on ethical values, as table 2 shows. The incidence of social deviance has grown rapidly in virtually all Organization of Economic Cooperation and Development (OECD) countries since approximately the mid-1960s, with the exception of Japan. This may resolve the paradox noted above: stable or ambiguous levels of group memberships exist across different societies but are accompanied by increasing levels of expressed distrust and cynicism in those same countries.

Like the United States, many developed countries have experienced sharply increasing levels of crime and family breakdown. These two types of deviance may not have much of an impact on that part of civil society most relevant to the democratic political process—often the province of national elites—but they are related to the broader social functions of civil society—the socialization and education of children, the maintenance of safe and stable neighborhoods, and the like. In the case of the United States, it would seem that much of the decline in

expressed levels of trust noted by Putnam can be tied directly to social trends of crime and family breakdown, and it is at least plausible that a similar process is unfolding in other countries as well.

A NOTE ON ASIAN VALUES

One interesting sidelight of the data presented above is the fact that Asian societies seem to defy the trends detailed above. Japan and South Korea exhibited large increases in self-described levels of ethical behavior in the World Values Survey data between 1981 and 1991, and relatively unchanged levels of social deviance. Findings such as these have prompted many to conclude that perhaps Asian societies are fundamentally different from other OECD societies.

Asian spokesmen, notably former Prime Minister Lee Kuan Yew of Singapore and Mahathir bin Muhammed of Malaysia, have been quick to note the difference in deviance levels between their societies and those of the West. They have argued that by accepting the economic but not the political principles (individualism and democracy) of modernity, countries such as Singapore and Malaysia have achieved high standards of living while avoiding many of the social problems that plague the United States. The empirical data does suggest that there are important differences between Asia and the West in both self-expressed values and actual social behavior.

THE GLOBAL DECLINE

Academic debate about the state of American civil society has up to now been rather parochial, concentrating on trends in US society alone. It is clear, however, that many of the phenomena suggested by the Putnam debate characterize other industrialized societies as well. In searching for explanations for the shifts in trust levels and social capital, it is critical to avoid excessively insular explanations that relate only to the particular history and experiences of the United States. The Vietnam War, Watergate, Iran-Contra, and other US political developments are not sufficient to give an account of increasing levels of cynicism and distrust in Italy and Australia. While we might be tempted to give country-by-country accounts of why levels of trust and ethical behavior began to deteriorate—distrust in Italy, one might be tempted to argue, increased because of the revelations of public corruption arising from the ongoing Tangentopoli investigations—it is striking that these indicators began to move more or less in tandem for a wide range of countries over the past two decades. This suggests that a larger socioeconomic process has been at work, disrupting civil society in all of these countries, one that has nonetheless been avoided by Asia's culturally distinct societies.

Whither Western Civilization?

Achievements and Prospects

Thomas Sowell

Mr. Sowell is a Senior Fellow at the Hoover Institution.

There are many reasons to enumerate and reflect upon the achievements of Western civilization, other than a parochial vanity. For several centuries now Western civilization has been the dominant civilization on this planet, so that its fate is intertwined with the fate of human beings around the world, whether they live in Western or non-Western societies. The products of Western civilization, from the sophisticated technology of air travel to various flavors of carbonated drinks, can be found in the most remote and non-Western regions of the world. More important, the ideas and ideals of Western civilization are in the minds and hearts of people of non-Western races with non-Western traditions. Perhaps the most dramatic examples were the throngs of Chinese people who risked their lives in Tiananmen Square for Western concepts of freedom and democracy.

Unfortunately, even to speak of the achievements of Western civilization goes against the grain of the intellectual fashions of our time. Both Western and non-Western intellectuals tend to judge and condemn the West, not by comparison with the achievements and shortcomings of alternative cultures and traditions, but by comparison with standards of perfec-

tion which all things human must inevitably fail. Such attitudes of sweeping, corrosive, and incessant condemnation from within are among the principal dangers to the survival of Western civilization.

WESTERN CIVILIZATION AS GLOBAL CIVILIZATION

Western civilization today no longer means simply the civilization of Europe, where it originated. Transplants of this civilization in the Western Hemisphere, Australia, and New Zealand are among its most vigorous elements, and its leadership and survival in a nuclear age depend crucially on the United States of America. The cultural penumbra of Western civilization reaches even farther. Its science and technology are today also the science and technology of Japan. Its languages span the globe and provide a common medium of communication among peoples whose respective mother tongues are incomprehensible to one another. Pilots speak to control towers in English around the world, even if they are Japanese pilots speaking to an Egyptian control tower. English is spoken by a billion people of all races—more people than speak any other language.

Much of the global sweep of Western civilization today, as its critics are quick to point out, is a product of conquest over

the past five centuries and of the enslavement of millions of human beings torn from their homelands. Magically the horrors of war, subjugation, enslavement, plunder, and devastation are the common heritage of all mankind, on every continent, and in every civilization—Western and non-Western. Conquerors and tyrants whose very names struck fear into every heart have come from every region of the globe and have come in every color and countenance found among the human species. What has been peculiar to the West has not been its participation in the common sins and agonies of the human race but its special ways of trying to cope with those sins and agonies—the philosophy, religion, and government of Western civilization, which provided the intellectual and moral foundation on which rise the benefits of freedom, of science, and the material well-being of hundreds of millions of humans around the world.

Western civilization has not always been in the forefront of world civilizations, though it clearly has been for the past two or three centuries. A thousand years ago, China was far more advanced than Europe. As late as the sixteenth century, China had the highest standard of living in the world. There were Chinese dynasties before there was a Roman Empire—indeed, before Rome itself was founded. Confucius had died before Plato and Socrates were born. The Chinese empire had cities of more than a million in-

From *Current*, September 1991, pp. 18-25. Adapted from "Western Civilization: Achievements and Prospects" by Thomas Sowell, from *The World & I*, May 1991, pp. 585-603.

habitants each, at a time when the largest city in Europe contained only fifty thousand people. Even after the emergence of classical Greek and Roman civilization, the evolution of Christianity from its Judaic background, and the rise and fall of the Roman Empire over a period of several centuries, Western civilization was still just one of the great civilizations of the world—not yet preeminent. As late as the Middle Ages, Russian rulers were vassals of the Mongol conquerors, to whom they paid tribute. The Ottoman Empire also penetrated deep into Europe, conquering the Balkans and holding them in subjugation for centuries. As late as the sixteenth century, Ottoman armies were at the gates of Vienna. The organization, science, technology, and scholarship of the Ottoman Empire were comparable to those of Europe, and its military forces won victory after victory against European nations. But, from the seventeenth century on, the tide turned decisively in favor of Western civilization—technologically, militarily, economically, and politically. More than anything else, Western civilization became the free world.

Historically, freedom was a very long time developing in the West, though it developed here earlier and more fully than in any other mass civilization. It has been less than a thousand years since the Magna Charta, yet that document exemplified a crucially distinctive idea with deep roots in the Western tradition—the idea that the *law* is supreme and not the ruler. Whatever controversies may rage among scholars and polemicists as to the immediate effect or social bias of the Magna Charta, what has made it a landmark in the development of human freedom is that it established the supremacy of law—what has also been called "the rule of law" or "a government of laws and not of men."

THE RULE OF LAW

Like so many of the blessings of Western civilization that we so easily take for granted, the idea of the rule of law is radically different from the principles on which other great civilizations were founded. Even late in the twentieth century many people in other cultures around the world found it incomprehensible that a president of the United States could be forced out of office on charges that he violated the law. Within Western civilization itself, it is little

more than 300 years (not long as history is measured) since Louis XIV said, "I am the state." Yet, even then, the idea so conflicted with Western notions as to be worth remembering. Neither Genghis Khan nor Sultan Süleyman of the Ottoman Empire would have found it necessary to remind anyone that his word was the supreme law—and if anyone did need reminding, that reminder would be in blood and not in words. The West itself has of course also had rulers who were above any law—Hitler and Stalin being the most notorious examples, though unfortunately not the only examples. The West itself has not always lived up to Western ideals. The point here is that those ideals were distinct from the ideals of other great civilizations and, ultimately, they have made the West different in reality.

The rule of law—the principle that the law is supreme and that rulers are subject to it—goes far back into Roman times. The Emperor Julian once fined himself ten pounds of gold for a minor transgression and, in the words of Edward Gibbon, "embraced this public occasion of declaring to the world that he was subject, like the rest of his fellow-citizens, to the laws." Roman emperors in general were among the most flagrant violators of this principle, but the principle outlived the emperors and the empire—and ultimately the principle triumphed. The Magna Charta was only one landmark on the road to that triumph. The Constitution of the United States was another.

Other great civilizations might have traditions or religions to which the ruler was at least nominally subject, but no human being was authorized to disobey, oppose, or nullify the edicts of the ruler, as appellate courts under the U.S. Constitution can nullify the edicts of presidents or Congress. In the great Chinese dynasties, for example, as a scholar has noted:

> Chinese law was always merely an instrument of government; it was not thought to have divine sanction, nor was it considered an inviolable constitution. It was part of, and inseparable from, routine administration. There were no provisions limiting state authority, and there was no church or independent judiciary before which the state could legally be called to account.

In the Ottoman Empire, the supremacy of the ruler was likewise subject to no constraint. According to Lord Kin-

ross, classic study of the Ottoman Empire, a fifteenth-century sultan "who was known to have ambivalent sexual tastes sent a Eunuch to the house of Notaras, demanding that he supply his good-looking fourteen-year-old son for the Sultan's pleasure." Notaras, a Christian, chose instead that he and his son would be beheaded—but that was the only alternative. There was no law higher than the sultan's command. The rule of law seems like such a mundane phrase, but without it, freedom and human dignity are in deadly peril. It is, perhaps, Western civilization's greatest gift to the world.

The rule of law, the supremacy of law, a government of laws and not of men—different ways of saying the same thing—is not a result of words written on pieces of paper. The Magna Charta was not accepted because King John thought it was a good idea but because the amount of military power lined up against him by his barons left him no choice. *Power offset by power* has remained the key to freedom through the rule of law. When the Constitution of the United States was crafted, the separation of powers was the heart and soul of it. The ability of each branch of government to impede or nullify the powers of the other branches means that there is no individual with supreme power.

What is to prevent whoever controls the military—the ultimate power of brute force—from imposing his will on the other branches of government and on the people at large? This has in fact happened in a number of Third World countries that received their independence after the Second World War, even though many of these countries copied the institutions of Western democracy—in some cases, right down to the powdered wigs of lawyers and judges in the British legal tradition. What they could not copy, however, were the centuries of history, distilled into the traditions that make free institutions viable. In a society where such traditions are deeply imbedded in the moral fiber of its people, no ruler can issue orders to violate the Constitution with any assurance that his officers or troops will obey—and if they do not obey, he may be facing not only the end of his power but imprisonment and disgrace as well. Behind the institutions of freedom are the traditions of freedom that give those institutions strength. Both are among the highest achievements of Western civilization.

SLAVERY AS AN INSTITUTION

Freedom has many dimensions and we so often take them all for granted that we find it almost inconceivable that other places and other times could have seen things so much differently. To virtually anyone raised in modern Western civilization, it is painful to realize that the evil and inhuman institution of slavery has existed in civilizations on every continent inhabited by human beings. Slavery existed for untold thousands of years in China. It existed in the Western Hemisphere long before Columbus' ships ever appeared on the horizon. Africa, Europe, the Middle East—it was virtually everywhere. The eastern European peoples known as Slavs were for centuries slaves—and their name provided the basis for the word. Ten million Africans were shipped as slaves to the Western Hemisphere but fourteen million were sent as slaves to the Islamic countries of the Middle East and North Africa. The sweeping scope and long history of slavery make it entirely possible that most of the peoples on this planet today are descendants of slaves, from one time or place or another.

What is even more incomprehensible to us today than the magnitude and endurance of slavery is that it aroused little, if any, moral concern in most parts of the world. A few offered moral apologies for it but in many places the institution was so widely accepted that no apologies were considered necessary. Only very late in the history of the world's great civilizations did a major moral revulsion against slavery begin. It began in the West.

Those who spearheaded the organized effort to abolish the slave trade were British evangelical Christians. The worldwide abolition of slavery was a long, arduous, and costly struggle—partly because of opposition within Western civilization but much more so because the non-Western world (Asia, Africa, and especially the Arab world) bitterly resisted abolition of this institution, around which their own economies were often built. For more than a half a century, British warships patrolled the waters off the coast of West Africa, capturing slave ships and setting the slaves free in Sierra Leone. It would be difficult, if not impossible, to find in history another example of a great nation committing such resources, for so many decades, for a cause which would gain it neither money nor territory.

The next phase of the struggle was to abolish slavery itself. This abolition first took place in the British Empire in 1834. Within sixty years, slavery was abolished in country after country throughout the Western Hemisphere. A worldwide institution, untold thousands of years old, was gone from three of the five inhabited continents (North America, South America, and Europe)—all in less than a century. What doomed slavery was that all of Western civilization had finally turned against it.

Other civilizations still retained slavery for generations after it was abolished in Europe and in European offshoot societies around the world. In African societies where the enslavement of other Africans had been going on for centuries before the white man came, there was bitter resistance to the increasing pressures from European nations for an end to the slave trade and an end to slavery itself. Among the Arabs, opposition was the most determined. Even czarist Russia, a despotic government by Western standards, forced the abolition of slavery in Central Asia over the opposition of its Central Asian subjects, who evaded the prohibition, when they dared not defy it.

With slavery, as in other areas, the West has not been immune to the sins that have disgraced the human species around the world for centuries. But what was different about Western civilization was the way it attempted to cope with the sins that have plagued mankind. It is only the fact that the peoples of Western nations share all the shortcomings and evils of other peoples that makes their experience relevant to the rest of humanity and their example an encouragement to others. This is especially true of the United States, which has very few indigenous people and is populated by the peoples of other lands. It is the American traditions and American institutions that keep us free, not our individual virtues or our individual wisdom.

MATERIAL PROSPERITY

While freedom has been the highest achievement of Western civilization, material prosperity has been its most visible achievement. Stark as the contrast is today between an affluent, Western way of life and the grim poverty of many Third World countries, it has been just a few centuries since the masses of people in Europe lived on a level not very different from that found today among the masses in many parts of the Third World. In Scotland, at the beginning of the seventeenth century, people were still using farming implements as primitive as those in ancient Mesopotamia and it was common for ordinary people to live in unventilated, shantylike homes, homes shared with their animals and abounding with vermin. There were somewhat higher standards of living in England and on parts of the European continent but Ireland, southern Italy and parts of eastern Europe were not better off. As late as the eighteenth century, visitors to Edinburgh found it worth mentioning that the inhabitants of that city no longer disposed of their sewage by throwing it out the windows—which had been a source of considerable unhappiness to passersby, even when warnings were shouted.

What changed all this? No great invention or discovery remade the economies of Europe or of European offshoot societies overseas. Instead, a gradual but persistent economic improvement continued over the years, with occasional setbacks, but building incrementally a new economic world of greater abundance. Here and there the wonders of science and technology gave Western civilization railroads, steamboats, electric lights, radio, and eventually the ability to fly. But the world did not stagnate between great inventions. Progress was virtually continuous and only cumulatively did it become dramatic. It was the wide diffusion of skills rather than the occasional outbursts of genius that was crucial. It was the spread of those skills from one Western nation to another that marked the rise of Western civilization to preeminence in the world, and the diffusion of its products that spread the benefits to non-Western regions of the globe as well.

England, for centuries lagging behind the economic and cultural progress of continental Europe, became in the eighteenth century the spearhead of economic development in Europe and the world. Englishmen introduced railroads to the world, not only by the example of railroad building in their own country, but also by themselves building and manning the first railroads in Germany, Argentina, India, Russia, Kenya, and Malaya—among other places. The steam engine was of course crucial to the railroad, and revolutionized industry and transport in general. For the first time in human history, man could *manufacture his own power* and was no longer dependent on his own muscles, or the muscles of animals, or on the spontaneous forces of nature (such as wind or water power) to get massive amounts of work done.

The modern technology of iron and steel making, on which a whole spectrum of industrial activities depends, also originated in the British Isles. Britain likewise spearheaded the development of the modern textile industry, supplying not only the major inventions but also initially the managers and skilled workers needed to train foreign workmen to operate British-made machinery in Russia, China, India, Mexico, and Brazil. In short, British know-how and British capital were transplanted and took root around the world—in Asia, Africa, and Latin America, as well as in such offshoots of British civilization as the United States, Canada, and Australia.

Once set loose in the world, the skills and technology acquired a life of their own, traveling unfettered, and flourishing wherever the social climate was favorable. While Englishmen had to install industrial equipment in Germany and teach the Germans how to use it, this knowledge was not merely absorbed but improved. By the last decade of the nineteenth century, Germany overtook Great Britain in the production of steel—and by 1913 German steel output was double that of Britain. Across the Atlantic, the United States took the industrial technology in which the British had pioneered and developed it to become the leading industrial nation in the world. In 1870, Britain produced 32 percent of all the manufactured goods in the world, followed by the United States at 23 percent and Germany at 13 percent. By 1913, however, Britain's relative share of the world's growing supply of manufactured goods was down to 14 percent—exceeded by Germany at 16 percent and by the United States at 36 percent. Far away in Asia, Japan was already busy acquiring Western science and technology, though its own rise to prominence in the international economy was still decades away.

Why some countries and cultures seized upon the leading development in Western civilization and others did not is a question that may never be fully answered. It was certainly not due to "objective, material conditions" as some Marxist or other predestination theorists would have us believe. The industrial revolution did begin in a country (Britain) rich in coal and iron ore, among other natural resources used in industry. But one of the most spectacular current examples of high-technology industrialization is Japan, which is almost totally lacking in natural resources, while countries with rich natural resources (such as Mexico) are often lagging in economic and technological developments.

THE THIRD WORLD AND WESTERN CIVILIZATION

Different responses to the leading scientific, technological, political, and moral developments in the West have not been confined to those nations or cultures within Western civilization itself. Much of the ethnic strife within newly independent Third World countries is between groups who seized the benefits of Western civilization to differing degrees during the colonial era and achieved differing levels of progress and prosperity as a result. In Nigeria, for example, the Muslim northern region did not want Christian missionary schools established in their area. Therefore the majority of Nigerians, who lived in the northern region, did not receive the exposure to Western education received by the Yoruba and Ibo peoples of southern Nigeria. The Ibos, a weaker, poorer tribe in a less productive part of the country, were especially avid for Western education and Western ways. The net results, after two or three generations of British rule in Nigeria, were dramatic inequalities, now favoring southern Nigerians.

As of 1926, there were more than 138,000 Nigerian children in primary school, of whom only about five thousand were in northern Nigeria, where most Nigerians lived. In the middle of the twentieth century, as Nigeria was moving toward independence, there were a total of 160 physicians in the country—only one of whom was from the north. In the army, three-quarters of the riflemen were from the north but fourfifths of the commissioned officers were from the south. As late as 1965, half of the officer corps were from the Ibo minority. Within northern Nigeria itself, at one time most of the factory workers, merchants, and civil servants were from

the south. The envy and resentments this generated—especially when inflamed by ambitious political leaders—led eventually to blood-baths in the streets, in which thirty thousand Ibos were slaughtered by raging mobs in northern Nigeria. Surviving Ibos struggled back to their region of origin in southeastern Nigeria, which tried to secede from Nigeria to form the independent nation of Biafra. A million more lives were lost in the civil war that followed.

American missionary schools were established on the northern tip of the island of Ceylon, off the eastern coast of India, during the era of British colonial rule. This happened to be a region inhabited by the Tamil minority who, like the Ibos of Nigeria, lived in an agriculturally less productive part of the country and who were also eager to seize upon Western education as a way to improve their otherwise limited prospects in life.

By contrast, the Sinhalese majority, who had rich, fertile land, had no such sense of urgency about Western education and their Buddhist leaders were not anxious to see them attend schools run by Western Christian missionaries. With the passing years, the Tamil minority—about 15 percent of the population—became over-represented among those in the educated professions. By 1921, 44 percent of all doctors in Ceylon were Tamils, compared with 34 percent who were from the Sinhalese majority (the rest being members of other minority groups). Even in later years, after education became more widespread, the historical head start of the Tamils was evident in their continued over-representation in high-level professions. As of 1948, on the eve of Ceylon's becoming the independent nation of Sri Lanka, the Tamils were still 40 percent of all engineers and 46 percent of all accountants.

Until this time, Ceylon or Sri Lanka was widely known for having some of the most harmonious relations anywhere among its various ethnic, linguistic, and religious groups. Inequality alone was not enough to cause polarization—but all it needed was one skilled demagogue to whip up group against group. This happened in the 1956 election campaign and Sri Lanka has never been the same. Mob violence of Sinhalese against Tamils erupted again and again over the years, as a country once held up as a model of harmonious intergroup relations saw Sinhalese mobs capture Tamils at random and burn them alive in the streets.

Fortunately, not all intergroup inequalities among groups with differing exposure to Western culture have led to such dramatic and ghastly consequences. But such inequalities have been widespread, from India to Sierra Leone to Latin America. Those indigenous peoples who happened to be located where Western imperial powers established schools, colonial capitals, industry, or port facilities have tended to acquire decisive advantages over those in the hinterlands, and these advantages have persisted long after the Western powers have withdrawn and the former colony has become independent. There is a special irony to this pattern, for many intellectuals—both Western and non-Western—depict the Third World as exploited by the West, its poverty caused by the West, and Western prosperity as being extracted from the colonized nations. In reality, the poorest people in the Third World have typically been those with the least contact with Western civilization, while those who have achieved prosperity and leadership have been those most able and willing to absorb what Western civilization has had to offer.

Much has been said about the prospects of a decline of Western civilization, its eclipse by other, rising civilizations or its institutions and values succumbing to forces within the West with radically different ideas and goals. If there were some better world likely to be created by some new civilization replacing that of the West on the world stage, our fondness for what is familiar to us might have to compete for our loyalties with a broader concern for the happiness and progress of the whole human race. But no such conflict exists. There is no higher and nobler civilization standing in the wings. The alternative political and economic systems contending with Western democracy have little attractive power for the peoples of the world and in some cases have difficulty preventing their own citizens from fleeing to the West.

THE SURVIVAL OF WESTERN CIVILIZATION

With all its achievements, what are the prospects of survival for Western civilization? The external military danger is only one of the threats to the survival of Western civilization. Signs of internal degeneration are both numerous and dangerous: declining educational standards, the disintegration of families, drug addiction, and violent crimes are just some of the more obvious signs. Will such things alone destroy a society and a civilization? Perhaps not. But the internal and external threats are not wholly separate today, any more than they were in the days of the decline and fall of the Roman Empire. Internal demoralization of a free people cannot help affecting the confidence and zeal with which they are prepared to defend themselves—or the resignation with which some are willing to accept other systems that seem only marginally different from what they have.

In the Roman Empire, as in much of Western civilization today, there was a growing class of people who would not work but instead lived off the government. Today, healthy-looking young beggars are as common in Paris as they are in the streets of New York or San Francisco. The economic drain of such people may be overshadowed by the social demoralization they represent and which they contribute to in others.

THE TREASON OF INTELLECTUALS

Much more active agents of demoralization are the intelligentsia, including the media, schoolteachers, and academics. Despite some welcome exceptions, these classes tend generally to take an adversary stance toward Western civilization. Sins and tragedies common to the human race around the world are discussed as if they were peculiarities of "our society." Slavery is only one of these indictments of Western civilization. *Colonialism* or *imperialism* to the intelligentsia mean, almost exclusively, Western colonialism or Western imperialism, even though non-Western countries had empires long before the West and even though the West has been abandoning most of its former empires since World War II. The only empire that has expanded overseas in the postwar era is the Soviet empire, often using Cuban troops to suppress any uprising against unpopular communist regimes in Africa.

Double standards have become almost too common to notice. No matter how many billions of dollars Americans or other Westerners donate to humanitarian causes, at home or overseas, they are still called selfish and materialistic, while other countries are called spiritual and high-principled, on the strength of their words, unsupported by deeds. Representatives of foreign countries, where racial or ethnic clashes have killed more people in a week than such clashes have killed in the United States over the past half-century, nevertheless, lecture Americans on the subject.

Why intellectuals have so often repudiated their own country and civilization in the West is a large question on which there are many theories. Perhaps it is precisely the freedom of the common man—including his ability to ignore intellectuals and live as he chooses—that has made intellectuals look so favorably on so many foreign despotisms that impose a master blueprint from the top down. These despotisms to which many leading Western intellectuals gave praise have included both imperial Russia and China and communist Russia and China. Intellectuals have romanticized despots from Robespierre to Stalin and Castro. But they have not favored *all* despots; the principal difference between those despots who have been praised by intellectuals and those that have not been is that despots with a master plan to remake the common man in a predetermined image have had the intellectuals' support. Ordinary, garden-variety despots seeking power and money, but leaving the common man alone to live as he pleases, have not had the support of the intelligentsia. Intellectuals supported Castro but not Batista, though Castro was more of a despot. Similarly, they supported Mao Tse-tung but not Chiang Kaishek, Lenin but not Czar Nicholas. It is hard to deny Edmund Burke's observation, two hundred years ago, that intellectuals like theories more than people. And they support those who promote social theories. . . .

FREE MARKETS

The success of free market policies in the 1980s in the United States has spread the idea of free markets, not only to countries like Britain under Margaret Thatcher but also to left-wing and socialist governments in France, Australia, and New Zealand. Behind these practical political results have been a growing number of free market intellectuals. Friedrich Hayek once said that he was optimistic for the future because he was virtually alone when he wrote *The Road to Serfdom* in 1944. Now there are such intellectual giants as Milton Friedman and organizations—think tanks—springing up across the United States, in Britain, Jamaica, Hong Kong, Peru, Australia, and New Zealand. The political Left remains still dominant among intellectuals but today, at least, there is a struggle going on to save the basic values and institutions of Western civilization. Moreover, it is a struggle that can be won.

While millions of refugees from all parts of the world have flooded into Western democratic nations over the past half-century or more, some have come from totalitarian countries within Europe—first from Nazi Germany and its satellites and subjugated nations during the 1930s and 1940s, and now from the Soviet bloc. Russia has always been only partly a Western nation, whether under the czars or under the communists. It is not primarily a question of geography, though more of that country lies in Asia than in Europe. Nor is it a matter of racial composition, for people of European origin are about as high a proportion of the Soviet population as of the population of the United States. Russia has always been a fringe member of Western civilization in the deeper sense that the West's greatest achievements—freedom, democracy, and material prosperity—have come to the Russian empire (for that is what it still is) slowly, incompletely, and with a lag, if at all.

Nazi Germany likewise illustrates the fact that some of the greatest dangers to the survival of Western civilization can come from within Europe itself. Had Hitler triumphed, nothing that we would recognize as Western civilization would have survived—not freedom, certainly not democracy, nor any of the other humane or spiritual achievements we call Western civilization. It is doubtful how long even material progress could have continued under suffocating economic controls by the Nazi state.

Western civilization today is endangered primarily from within the West—ideologically by Marxism, militarily by the Soviet bloc, morally and socially by degeneration within Western democratic nations. Let us look first at the external dangers and then at the internal dangers. Finally, let us console ourselves with a few hopeful signs that all may not be lost, though the hour is late and the outcome still uncertain.

Shortly after the end of the Second World War, Winston Churchill said: "There was never a war in all history easier to prevent than the war which has just desolated such great areas of the globe." How could the leaders of the Western democracies have failed to prevent a war that was preventable—a war in which forty million human beings lost their lives? They failed by operating on assumptions very much like our assumptions today and following policies very much like the policies of Western democracies in our time.

THE ILLUSION OF PACIFISM

One of the fundamental assumptions of the Western democracies throughout the period between the two world wars was that military weapons were the problem and that international treaties to reduce weapons were the answer. Strong pacifist movements and pacifist sentiments existed throughout the West, in the wake of the terrible carnage and devastation of the First World War. The shadow of that war hung over a whole generation, much as the grim shadow of Vietnam has hung over a generation of Americans. The determination to avoid another war is not only understandable but highly laudable. What was tragic was that the policies chosen led directly into another—and even worse—World War. At the heart of those policies was the assumption that disarmament treaties meant peace and that building a military deterrent meant war. Then, as now, maintaining and modernizing military forces sufficient to deter potential aggressors was called an "arms race"—something to be avoided at almost any cost.

If the theory that disarmament and international treaties mean peace were correct, there would never have been a Second World War. The two decades leading up to that war were filled with disarmament agreements and international peace treaties—perhaps more so than any other two decades in the history of the world. This long string of ineffective treaties began with the Treaty of Versailles that ended the First World War. That treaty severely limited the military forces Germany would be permitted to have, did not allow those forces to be stationed in Germany's Rhineland, and forbade the Germans from having military conscription. Those

were the peace terms imposed by the victors on the vanquished.

Almost immediately after the war, new international disarmament agreements and treaties were signed among all the leading powers of the world, including not only large and small nations in Europe but also the United States and Japan. The 1920s saw the Washington Naval Agreement of 1922, the Kellog-Briand Pact, and the Locarno Pact, among others. The 1930s saw the Lausanne Conference of 1932, later an agreement between Britain and Germany limiting each side's naval forces, the Munich agreement of 1938, and the nonaggression pact of 1939 between Nazi Germany and the Soviet Union. Added to all this, and often part of the process, were repeated visits of heads of states, to establish "personal contacts" as British Prime Minister Neville Chamberlain repeatedly called them. Heads of state had met before to work out international agreements, as at Versailles in 1919 or at the Congress of Vienna in 1815. But now there were repeated, almost incessant meetings, supplemented by public exchanges of letters between heads of state. . . .

Why did all these efforts for peace end so tragically in war? Fundamentally, it was because international peace, like domestic freedom, depends on a *balance* between opposing forces. Both pacifist movements and disarmament treaties had completely asymmetrical effects on democratic nations and totalitarian powers. Pacifist movements operate freely and pacifist sentiments influence foreign policy only in democratic nations. They weaken the ability of democratic nations to maintain sufficient military forces to balance those of totalitarian nations. Disarmament treaties are likewise asymmetrical. It is much easier for a totalitarian government to maintain secrecy when it cheats on a disarmament treaty, even when the treaty itself is evenhanded. In addition, the political pressures are on democratic leaders to sign an agreement, which will be regarded as a "success," while returning home empty-handed from an international meeting will be considered a "failure." The actual specific terms of an agreement are likely to be known and their implications understood by far fewer people than those who measured "success" or "failure" by whether or not a treaty was signed. A totalitarian government, which does not have to meet the same pressures and potential public criticism at home, is in a much better position to hold out for favorable terms before signing.

History need not inevitably repeat itself. Recent changes within the Soviet bloc may be matched by changes in their foreign policy as well. It is much too early to know how real or how lasting any of these changes are. But it is worth looking back at what preceded these changes. It was Ronald Reagan's insistence on matching the Soviet nuclear buildup in Europe with new American missiles in Europe, pointed at the Soviet Union. While many in the media decried the futility of a new "arms race," declaring that the Soviet Union would match everything we did, round after round, the Soviets themselves understood that they did not have the unlimited resources implied by that argument. In fact, the stresses of maintaining their existing military forces were being felt economically and politically.

Now that a show of strength and resolve has brought some pullbacks by the Soviets and some hope of better future relations, the cry is already heard, in Congress and elsewhere, that we should cut back our military forces, as they are no longer so necessary. This attitude is painfully similar to the attitude that developed after the discovery of a polio vaccine, which led to sharp reductions in the incidence of that disease. When there was less polio, fewer people felt a need to get vaccinated—with the result that more people were needlessly afflicted by polio. Now that military deterrence has produced beneficial results, unilateral cutbacks seem dangerously similar to the polio fallacy. Reductions in military forces on both sides can be mutually beneficial if they mean a balance of power—but *not* if they mean simply maintenance of Soviet military superiority at a price the Soviet bloc economies can afford.

Military superiority matters, even if a shot is never fired. "Power wins, not by being used but by being there," someone once said. The implicit threat of military power provides the framework within which all sorts of political and economic decisions are made, all over the world. The Soviets have not invested such huge resources in military weaponry for no reason—and certainly not for defensive reasons. Whether the current pause in their overseas expansionism will last probably depends on how long the resistance of the West will last.

Powers, Francis Gary, 165
Prempe, Asante king, 120
Priestly, Joseph, 51
"Project Sapphire," 158
"proteinaceous infectious particle," 193
Prussia, 8–13, 69
Putnam, Robert, 214–215

Test Your Knowledge Form

We encourage you to photocopy and use this page as a tool to assess how the articles in **Annual Editions** expand on the information in your textbook. By reflecting on the articles you will gain enhanced text information. You can also access this useful form on a product's book support Web site at **http://www.dushkin.com/online/**.

NAME:

DATE:

TITLE AND NUMBER OF ARTICLE:

BRIEFLY STATE THE MAIN IDEA OF THIS ARTICLE:

LIST THREE IMPORTANT FACTS THAT THE AUTHOR USES TO SUPPORT THE MAIN IDEA:

WHAT INFORMATION OR IDEAS DISCUSSED IN THIS ARTICLE ARE ALSO DISCUSSED IN YOUR TEXTBOOK OR OTHER READINGS THAT YOU HAVE DONE? LIST THE TEXTBOOK CHAPTERS AND PAGE NUMBERS:

LIST ANY EXAMPLES OF BIAS OR FAULTY REASONING THAT YOU FOUND IN THE ARTICLE:

LIST ANY NEW TERMS/CONCEPTS THAT WERE DISCUSSED IN THE ARTICLE, AND WRITE A SHORT DEFINITION:

ANNUAL EDITIONS revisions depend on two major opinion sources: one is our Advisory Board, listed in the front of this volume, which works with us in scanning the thousands of articles published in the public press each year; the other is you—the person actually using the book. Please help us and the users of the next edition by completing the prepaid article rating form on this page and returning it to us. Thank you for your help!

ANNUAL EDITIONS: Western Civilization, Volume II, Eleventh Edition

ARTICLE RATING FORM

Here is an opportunity for you to have direct input into the next revision of this volume. We would like you to rate each of the 41 articles listed below, using the following scale:

1. Excellent: should definitely be retained
2. Above average: should probably be retained
3. Below average: should probably be deleted
4. Poor: should definitely be deleted

Your ratings will play a vital part in the next revision. So please mail this prepaid form to us just as soon as you complete it. Thanks for your help!

We Want Your Advice

RATING

ARTICLE

1. The Emergence of the Great Powers
2. London and the Modern Monarchy
3. A Golden Age: Innovation in Dutch Cities, 1648–1720
4. A Taste of Empire, 1600–1800
5. "Thus in the Beginning All the World Was America"
6. Brazil's African Legacy
7. Descartes the Dreamer
8. A New Light on Alchemy
9. Declaring an Open Season on the Wisdom of the Ages
10. Witchcraft: The Spell That Didn't Break
11. Blacks in the Gordon Riots
12. The Passion of Antoine Lavoisier
13. The First Feminist
14. Napoleon the Kingmaker
15. Napoleon in Egypt
16. Arkwright: Cotton King or Spin Doctor?
17. Samuel Smiles: The Gospel of Self-Help
18. Giuseppe Garibaldi
19. Conversations with Malthus
20. The Age of Philanthropy
21. Women Murderers in Victorian Britain

RATING

ARTICLE

22. 'The White Man's Burden'? Imperial Wars in the 1890s
23. Albert Robida's Imperfect Future
24. When Cubism Met the Decorative Arts in France
25. Two Cheers for Versailles
26. How the Modern Middle East Map Came to Be Drawn
27. Nazism in the Classroom
28. Six Days to Reinvent Japan
29. The Future That Never Came
30. Face-Off
31. Mutable Destiny: The End of the American Century?
32. Exhibiting the Nation
33. The Way the World Ends
34. A Brief History of Relativity
35. The Viral Superhighway
36. Belonging in the West
37. Folly & Failure in the Balkans
38. The Poor and the Rich
39. Who's Top?
40. Falling Tide: Global Trends and U.S. Civil Society
41. Whither Western Civilization?

(Continued on next page)

ANNUAL EDITIONS: WESTERN CIVILIZATION, VOLUME II,
11th Edition

NO POSTAGE
NECESSARY
IF MAILED
IN THE
UNITED STATES

BUSINESS REPLY MAIL
FIRST-CLASS MAIL PERMIT NO. 84 GUILFORD CT

POSTAGE WILL BE PAID BY ADDRESSEE

McGraw-Hill/Dushkin
530 Old Whitfield Street
Guilford, CT 06437-9989

ABOUT YOU

Name   Date

Are you a teacher? ☐   A student? ☐
Your school's name

Department

Address   City   State   Zip

School telephone #

YOUR COMMENTS ARE IMPORTANT TO US !

Please fill in the following information:
For which course did you use this book?

Did you use a text with this *ANNUAL EDITION*? ☐ yes ☐ no
What was the title of the text?

What are your general reactions to the *Annual Editions* concept?

Have you read any particular articles recently that you think should be included in the next edition?

Are there any articles you feel should be replaced in the next edition? Why?

Are there any World Wide Web sites you feel should be included in the next edition? Please annotate.

May we contact you for editorial input? ☐ yes ☐ no
May we quote your comments? ☐ yes ☐ no